WEST POINTS

Perspectives on Officership

SELECTED READINGS

Department of Military Instruction
United States Military Academy

Course Director
Captain Christopher J. Cox USA

Deputy Course Director
Major Gregory Bendewald USA

Course NCOIC
Sergeant First Class Rickey Naylon USA

Alliance Press
A Thomson Company

Editor: Timothy Spurlock
Production Manager: Staci Powers
Production Coordinator: Spring Greer
Marketing Coordinator: Sara L. Hinckley

Copyright © 2001 by United States Military Academy at West Point

All rights reserved. No portion of this manuscript may be reproduced or utilized in any form or by any means, electronic or mechanical, including photocopying, recording, or by any information storage and retrieval system, without permission in writing from the author: United States Military Academy at West Point.

ISBN 0-7593-0646-X

The Adaptable Courseware Program consists of products and additions to existing Custom Publishing products that are produced from camera-ready copy. Peer review, class testing, and accuracy are primarily the responsibility of the author(s).

WEST POINT'S
Perspectives on Officership

SELECTED READINGS

Department of Military Instruction
United States Military Academy

Course Director
Captain Christopher J. Cox USA

Deputy Course Director
Major Gregory Bendewald USA

Course NCOIC
Sergeant First Class Rickey Naylon USA

January 2002

TO: The Class of 2004
SUBJECT: Perspectives on Officership

Perspectives on Officership was created to encourage reflection and discussion about the military profession. The chapters correspond to important roles of the officer in today's Armed Forces, specifically the officer as a Servant of the Nation, a Member of a Time-Honored Profession, a Leader of Character and a Warfighter.

Chapter One focuses on the commitments inherent in accepting a commission in the Armed Forces and the societal and governmental expectations of military officers. The selected readings in this section address the officer's moral obligation to the Constitution, the civilian leadership and the citizenry.

Chapter Two examines the uniqueness of the military profession, its differences and similarities with other professional fields, and the importance of its traditions. It also examines the processes and institutions by which a democratic society selects and trains its military leaders.

The readings in Chapter Three address the philosophical and ethical dimensions of the military profession. They illustrate leaders whose valiant actions exemplify the highest standards of soldierly virtue.

Chapter Four explains the role of the Warfighter. In addition to technical and tactical competence, society expects its military officers to possess a warrior ethos, courage and the will to lead.

It is paramount that members of the officer corps understand the enormous responsibility placed into their hands. America's sons and daughters deserve the best leaders possible. This anthology frames the crucial issues of officership and the military profession for those preparing to accept a military commission, and serves as an informative guide for leaders at the highest levels.

Eric T. Olson
Brigadier General, US Army
Commandant of Cadets

Acknowledgements

This is the third year that the United States Military Academy will teach "Perspectives on Officership," as a core military science course for second year cadets at West Point. Its purpose is to develop the 3rd class cadet's knowledge and understanding of what it means to be a professional military officer.

This course differs from most at the academy because it focuses on affective learning. Cadets participate in a wide range of activities including seminar discussions, interviews with combat veterans, a visit to the West Point Cemetery, a film study. Instructors function primarily as "mentors" who, through personal interviews, small group activities, and e-mail, maintain continuous thought-provoking communication with students.

Inspired and directed by the Commandant of Cadets, the continuing development and implementation of this course is an Academy-wide effort. Numerous individuals eagerly contributed to this and the previous edition. We are truly indebted to those who lent their time, creativity, experience, and effort to this endeavor.

In closing, we want to recognize all of the men and women of our Armed Forces. Their deeds of valor, whether written or unwritten, are never forgotten. All of those who have gone before us continue to provide shining examples on the importance and necessity of "Duty, Honor, Country".

Christopher J. Cox
CPT, CM
MS 202 Course Director

Rickey L. Naylon
Sergeant First Class, USA
MS 202 Course NCO

Table of Contents

CHAPTER III: THE OFFICER AS A LEADER OF CHARACTER

CHAPTER IV: THE OFFICER AS A WARFIGHTER

The Professional Officer

Societies look to professional organizations to provide functions that are essential for their well being and survival. The military is one such institution, serving society as a whole, providing that which fellow citizens cannot provide for themselves—national security. Officers, based on their professional competence, provide the intellectual and ethical leadership of the Army and determine the professional standards.

Any fundamental approach to officership must start with the commissioning Oath. The Oath of Office formalizes the moral obligation for officers, acting as agents of society, to "support and defend the Constitution of the United States against all enemies, foreign and domestic," and to "bear true faith and allegiance to the same." This obligation serves two purposes: the establishment of the officer's individual accountability to the Nation and the strengthening of the claim of the military profession on the affections and support of the American people.

Society invests responsibility in the military profession through the officer's Commission, which charges the officer to "carefully and diligently discharge the duties of the office" and "to observe and follow" the orders and directions of the President and other superior officers "acting in accordance with the laws of the United States." In meeting these responsibilities, commissioned officers are guided by the following principles:

Duty. Professional officers always do their duty, subordinating personal interests to the requirements of the professional function. They are prepared, if necessary, to lay down their own lives and the lives of their soldiers in the Nation's interest. When assigned a mission or task, its successful execution is first priority, above all else, with officers accepting full responsibility for their actions and orders in accomplishing it—and accomplishing it in the right way. The officer's duty is not confined, however, to explicit orders or tasks; it extends to any circumstance involving allegiance to the commissioning oath.

Honor. An officer's honor is of paramount importance, derived historically from demonstrated courage in combat. It includes the virtues of integrity and honesty. Integrity is the personal honor of the individual officer, manifested in all roles. In peace, an officer's honor is reflected in consistent acts of moral courage. An officer's word is an officer's bond.

Loyalty. Military officers serve in a public vocation; their loyalty extends upward through the chain of command to the President as Commander in Chief and downward to all subordinates. Officers take care of their soldiers and families. This loyalty is central to the trust that binds together the military profession for its public servant role.

Service. An officer's motivations are noble and intrinsic: a love for the technical and human aspects of providing the Nation's security and an awareness of the moral obligation to use that expertise self-sacrificially for the benefit of society. The officer has no legacy except for the quality of his or her years of service.

Competence. The serious obligations of officership—and the enormous consequences of professional failure—establish professional competence as a moral imperative. More than knowing one's job or proficiency in the skills and abilities of the military art, professional competence in this sense includes attributes of worldliness, creativity and confidence. Called to their profession and motivated by their pursuit of its expertise, officers are committed to a career of continuous study and learning.

Teamwork. Officers model civility and respect for others. They understand that soldiers of a democracy value the worth and abilities of the individual, both at home and abroad. But because of the moral obligation accepted and the mortal means employed to carry out an officer's duty, the officer also emphasizes the importance of the group as against the individual. Success in war requires the subordination of the will of the individual to the task of the group. The military ethic is cooperative and cohesive in spirit, meritocratic, and fundamentally anti-individualistic and anti-careerist.

Subordination. Officers strictly observe the principle that the military is subject to civilian authority and do not involve themselves or their subordinates in domestic politics or policy beyond the exercise of the basic rights of citizenship. Military officers render candid and forthright professional judgments and advice and eschew the public advocate's role.

Leadership. Officers lead by example always, maintaining the personal attributes of spiritual, physical, and intellectual fitness that are requisite to the demands of their profession and which serve as examples to be emulated.

CHAPTER

The Officer as a Servant of Society

"Do your duty in all things. You cannot do more. You should never wish to do less."

General Robert E. Lee

What is Now Worth Dying For?

by Dr. Don M. Snider

Intro

- We celebrate today Veteran's Day, instead of Armistice Day as it was celebrated in 1918.
- The celebration then was for the signing of the Armistice that ended the First World War, the "war to end all wars" as it was known at the time, the war that was to "make the world safe for democracy."
- But today it is a holiday to remember and honor all American Veterans, all who have died in our several national wars that America might be as she is today, free and independent, her citizens at liberty to travel about the world both in leisure and in commerce and able to enjoy—as we here gathered enjoy—the benefits of "life, liberty, and the pursuit of happiness."
- But I must remind you, starkly, that those Veteran's who we remember today, died ... they are dead and gone, their hopes and dreams, and those of their loved ones, extinguished and lost forever... they died in the tens of thousands in that first Great War, and in the millions in the wars since. These are numbers, sacrifice on such a scale, that it overwhelms our feeble responses of compassion and empathy for them and their families and, as well, often our abiding gratitude for what they did. Many died in the worst kind of fear, misery, and pain. Most were, and remain, known only to their families, friends, and comrades-in-arms.

The Question

- **So I ask you, "What can we say, or do, here today that is worthy of their abnegation and self-sacrifice?**
- I suggest to you one answer for your consideration.
- It is, in the words of Lincoln, **that we rededicate our lives now and for the future to be lived is such manner that "these honored dead shall not have died in vain."** By that I mean that we as citizens conduct our nation's business such that we ensure that our soldiers enter harms way only for caus-

Source: Speech by Dr. Don M. Snider at Culver Military Institute, 8 minutes. (November, 1999) Reprinted by permission.

es that are "worth dying for." And to do this, we must today have a clear consensus on what that cause is, what it is that is "worth dying for."

- I suggest to you as a soldier who was lucky enough to have survived, that I could hold no deeper remorse than for soldiers who died to have done so in vain, that the cause for which they gave their very existence was subsequently determined to be unworthy by the society who sent them to their deaths.

- **What is it that today is "worth dying for?"**

One Answer

- Now I do not suppose there is a common answer, a consensus answer, to the question I have posed, either from you older folk or from the next generation here assembled, the students of the Academies of Culver.

- The faith traditions, and in my case the Judeo-Christian Scripture in particular, give us one insight . . . (Romans 5:7 "We can understand someone dying for a person worth dying for, and we can understand how someone good and noble could inspire us to self-less sacrifice." [*The Message*]. . .)

- **So one answer is "men will die for a good man," we will die for each other... and truly, Americans have given their lives on battlefields around the world for two centuries so that other good Americans, a good society and way of life, may live . . . a way of life, I remind you, embodied in less than 50 words:**

  - "We hold these truths to be self-evident, that all men are created by their Creator with certain unalienable rights, that among these are life, liberty and the pursuit of happiness. That to secure these rights, governments are instituted among men, deriving their powers from the consent of the governed."

- **Yes, we have died "for each other." Since its Founding, the American nation, its unique form of self-governance and its civil society have been "worth dying for."**

- It has been a society founded on the rights of individuals and fully aware that rights entail obligations that must be fulfilled by each citizen (or there are no rights at all); a society that understands the necessity of a well-informed conscience that gives rise to individual duties and thus to civility among our people.

- But, we will continue to die "for each other" only so long as we determine that "each other" are good people, and that together we constitute a good society. And in our Republic, two groups of people must independently arrive at that determination at the same time. First, are the soldiers, sailors and airmen who have responded to the call for service and accepted the moral obligation to defend a defenseless society. Second is the society who sends them into harm's way and, under the doctrine of civilian control of the military, determines the manner in which our nation's wars will be fought.

- This means that American soldiers, sailors and airmen, regardless of race, sex or culture, must be like-minded with the American society as to what is "worth dying for." **And my caution for you today is that we, as a nation, may be in a period when that common view no longer prevails. I remind you that we just fought a war in Kosovo without a ground campaign because our political leaders did not think the cause was worth American "soldiers dying for it." Unfortunately, as our European allies now remind us, we have shown them "what we will kill for," but they wonder yet in this new era "what we will die for."**

- Are we losing our like-mindedness as a people? Are we so enamored with diversity and multiculturalism that we no longer believe in "E Pluribus Unum?" Can we no longer create a political consensus on the worth of our cause? After three decades without a draft, and with no other form of national service, it is the case that the responsibilities of American citizens have changed. Instead of the citizen-soldier, our conflicts are now fought by volunteers who do not represent the influential elites of America. There are today no children of any member of Congress serving in Bosnia nor in Kosovo.

- Further, scholarly research over the past two years has shown that there is a gap growing between some segments of American society and the military who serve the nation, a gap in attitudes and perceptions that could destroy the necessary like-mindedness among the polity as to what is "worth dying for."

Conclusion

- **So my question to you all today, especially you students who will run this country in just a few years, my question is, "what is now worth dying for?"** What is it that will cause some of you to volunteer to serve in the armed forces, accepting the noble task of defending your peer generations?

- **And the answer I suggest, somewhat paradoxically, is that you, yourselves, are the answer**—good fellow-citizens who take their citizenship seriously, well combined with civility, and who together make a society worth serving and "worth dying for." That is the enduring answer to my rhetorical question. You, together, have the potential to be "worth dying for."

- **And were that ever not to be so, then I tell you that the fears of the previous generations would be realized in the most terrible way, for those we honor here today would then surely have "died in vain."**

American Ideals

In a pragmatic sense, an officer's career will span that of at least four presidential administrations. Budgets will change, national priorities will run a spectrum, and those politicians who represent the nation will come and go as a reflection of that will. The economy will fluctuate, universities will open and close, and even religions will grow and shrink in emphasis and influence. Nations will come into being and disappear. In short, the business of the planet will continue its checkered progress.

The constant in this warp and weave will be the service officer, whose commitment to the Constitution, morals, ethics and the nation is the real shining light of liberty. It is the bedrock that will guarantee the freedom of the American people and the continuance of our nation.

The nation can accept nothing less. Armed Forces officers have no right to determine national policy. They must not, as has happened in our nation's history, distort information to serve the ends of anything other than the Constitution. Any such temptation must be ruthlessly controlled and stopped in its tracks.

The American military plays a special role in our nation. In one limited sense, it can be viewed as an instrument of national policy, that last bastion of diplomacy to be employed when the talking stops, the club that the politician wields to ensure that his point of view is the one that dominates the table of discussion, just as the legions of Rome or the hordes of Genghis Khan or the troops of Imperial Japan served the point of view of the leader.

The American military establishment will have a number of roles within any officer's lifetime. The officer may well be called upon to give life, fortune and sacred honor in defense of the nation. He or she will have to go through training that will teach the art of destruction of life and property and will be given chances to win the right to wear badges and ribbons that attest to prowess in these arts or in positions of

Source: *The Armed Forces Officer* (1998). 66-68. Reprinted by permission of the Armed Forces Information Service, Department of Defense, U.S. Government Printing Office.

great responsibility. The officer literally may be given the power to determine who will live and who will die. He or she will be given great responsibility and authority in the name of your nation.

At the same time, the officer will be given the mandate to ensure that every action directly contributes to the defense of the Constitution and is legal and morally correct. That is the dichotomy that some can never understand. They see the destruction, but never the moral imperative. They can see only the similarities in the development of standards, training and armed forces. They cannot see, or choose not to see, that the fundamental purpose of the Armed Forces is totally different in free societies. They appear to be using Machiavelli as the principal philosopher for the control of people without reading all of the story and finding out that Machiavelli was perhaps the most unsuccessful military leader in history.

If people are to risk their lives, there must be a good, accepted reason, or they simply will not do it. People who are urged to sacrifice themselves and the future of their children for the notion that one end of an egg is better than the other will soon use on their leaders the business end of some instrument that terminates stupidity.

The problem with freedom is that once given, it becomes almost impossible to take away. Ours is a free society, and generation after generation of Americans has participated in the struggle to keep that freedom. It will always be in danger and must always be defended. Even today, in at least one city in America it is illegal to fly the national flag from city-owned buildings. In the very recent past, Americans have sold vital national secrets for the proverbial 30 pieces of silver. It would be all too easy to seek harsh and repressive "solutions" to these kinds of problems. That is not our way.

What other roles does the American military play in the defense of the Constitution? In one literal sense, the military is the very foundation for the continuance of the nation. In the military, the concept of civilian control of all aspects of national life is taught and upheld as a cornerstone of democracy. In the military, one out of every six members of the nation learns a trade or skill. In the military, the concepts of duty and discipline are taught and sustained.

The American military provides the nation with a repository for national honor, ethics and a way for young people to learn fundamental skills that will get them started as productive members of the nation. Remnants of racism, sexism and religious prejudice surface in the military from time to time. Sadly, these "anti-somethings" are reflections of society in general. Because the biases are so counterproductive and disruptive, the military has spent vast quantities of time and effort to counter and eliminate overt signs of bias.

One military role is to provide the nation with a single salad bowl, where young men and women from all parts of the nation, with all kinds of backgrounds and goals and motivations, can be taught common standards of language, ethics and behavior. Learning that there are things bigger than self is important for the nation. It is the exposure to the person who is "different" and the subsequent understanding that the "differences" are superficial that has helped the nation reduce prejudice. Each officer has a moral imperative to meet the standards of non-biased conduct and treatment of people.

When people are put in harm's way, there is no time to remember that Charlie is an "X" or Sally a "Y." It is important to know that Charlie and Sally are the best "Z's" available, the best "Z's" that can be molded. It is interesting to note that when people are treated as people, they display similar aspirations, fears and needs. We no longer conscript people into the military. Everyone wearing the uniform is doing so by choice. They are where they are because of a belief that what they are doing is going to be good for the nation and for themselves.

The 1922 Manual for Cadets at West Point devoted more space to the need to beat Navy in sports than it gave to the honor code. Cadets in all service academies have a time-honored tradition of seeing the other academies as the enemy. Nothing is inherently wrong with students being interested in student things. It is easier to identify with a specific unit or branch or service than with a nation. However correct and necessary it is to create a feeling of "us" and pride in unit or service, it is also correct and necessary always to keep in mind that the Armed Forces officer serves the nation, first, last and always.

The concept of unit or service is useful, but national goals, ideals and the totality of the Armed Forces are more important. The debate over roles and missions is just a debate whose end-purpose is the defense of the nation, not the size of the service budget or the right to be the sole possessor of information or equipment. It is as important as the debate over the structure of the Joint Chiefs of Staff.

The nation that places its future in the hands of a group of Armed Forces officers must also provide that group with both the tools and safeguards to make sure it can function as the nations civilian leadership intended. The Armed Forces must be able to respond to the national demands for adequate defense in a balanced manner. They must serve the nation well, even if that means accepting personally unpalatable service mission changes.

Every Armed Forces officer must understand the national defense system and how it works. When an officer understands the national imperatives and his or her role in the defense of these imperatives, the nation can be secure in the knowledge that the trust given to its military officers is warranted. Only then can the nation be sure that legal exercise of authority and the determination of national policy will remain in lawful hands. Anything less is unacceptable.

American Society: Where Are We Headed?

by Everett C. Ladd

My colleagues and I are partial to surveys that look broadly at a society, examine the social and political values of its people, help us understand where important change is occurring—and, conversely, where the persistence of long-standing norms and behavior is the story.

Like many researchers, we have admired and made extensive use of the National Opinion Research Center's General Social Surveys (GSS)—comprehensive social trackings that were begun 25 years ago and are conducted annually (with only a few years skipped since 1972). GSS director **Tom Smith** describes the origins, development, and use of this important social science resource on pages 28-30 of this issue. In the following article, **James A. Davis,** who fathered the GSS in 1971, discusses the extent and direction of the shifts in social outlook this series has charted.

Societies are, obviously, complex things, and no single survey examination, however well-designed, can cover all or even most important aspects of them. We were especially pleased, then, to see a few months ago the first reports of a major new survey of American political culture, conducted in the winter and spring of 1996, under the direction of James Davison Hunter and Carl Bowman, as part of the Post-Modernity Project at the University of Virginia. The field work was done by the Gallup Organization. This intellectually innovative exploration of Americans' sociopolitical experience and beliefs deserves the attention of all students of the society. **James Davison Hunter and Daniel C. Johnson** report on some of the study's prinicipal findings on pages 35-38. Along with these three articles, my colleagues and I have compiled, and publish here, 26 pages of what we consider some of the most important findings of the GSS and the 1996 Survey of American Political Culture.

What have we learned? The answer is, happily, "Quite a lot." Analysts will inevitably differ as to how some of the findings should be understood. For example, Jim Davis stresses in his essay the extent of the shifts that the GSS has uncovered in

Source: *The Public Perspective* (March, 1997): 1-30. Reprinted by permission of The Roper Center: Hall and Bill Printing Company.

its 25 years. While recognizing that some important changes have indeed occurred, notably in thinking about gender roles and norms of sexual conduct. I'm more impressed by the extent of the continuities. And, when it comes to deeper national values, the picture that Hunter and his colleagues develop so ably from their 1996 survey looks very much like the one American social historians of the late 18th and 19th centuries developed from other types of materials.

Hunter and Johnson ask whether "the American political system [is] facing a legitimation crisis," and conclude that the answer is both yes and no. "No" because we aren't seriously questioning the ideals of the system, are committed to our political institutions, share important beliefs about our common history, and express "civic mindedness" in high degrees. "Yes" because the public's "assessments of current trends in America are highly pessimistic," because there is a continuing loss of confidence in the performance of national government, and because in evaluating the country's governing elite "people's opinion turns toward cynicism."

Rarely enthusiastic about the state historically, Americans *are* now highly critical of important aspects of government performance. We *do* believe that current leadership leaves much to be desired. And we *are* troubled by deficiencies in the moral life of the nation, evident in family break-up, crime, and a degraded television culture. But there *are* real problems in these areas: If the public were unable to see them—*that* would be cause for deep concern. If we believe, as most Americans do, that our institutions are well defined and the country's constituent values worthy of continued respect, but that current performance with respect to these institutions and values falls short, the call must be for reform *within* the established framework. It is not a call for the sorts of actions that would be appropriate if, indeed, the US faced a "legitimation crisis."

The NORC Series on Confidence in Leaders of National Institutions

Question: I am going to name some institutions in this country. As far as the people running these institutions are concerned, would you say you have a great deal of confidence, only some confidence, or hardly any confidence at all in them? . . .

	Congress			Executive Branch of Government			Military		
	Great Deal	Some	Hardly Any	Great Deal	Some	Hardly Any	Great Deal	Some	Hardly Any
1996	8%	47%	43%	10%	45%	42%	37%	49%	11%
1994	8	50	40	11	52	35	37	49	12
1993	7	50	41	12	53	32	42	45	11
1991	18	53	26	26	51	21	60	33	6
1990	15	59	23	23	50	23	33	51	14
1989	17	58	22	20	54	22	32	50	13
1988	15	62	19	16	53	27	34	49	13
1987	16	63	17	19	52	27	34	50	12
1986	16	61	20	21	53	24	31	52	14
1984	13	64	22	19	51	29	36	48	13
1983	10	64	23	13	54	30	29	55	13
1982	13	62	22	19	54	24	31	52	15
1980	9	53	64	12	50	34	28	52	16
1978	13	63	21	13	59	25	30	54	13
1977	19	61	17	28	54	14	36	50	10
1976	14	58	26	13	59	25	39	41	13
1975	13	59	25	13	55	30	35	46	14
1974	17	59	21	14	43	42	40	44	13
1973	24	59	15	29	50	18	32	49	16

For the Most Part We are Less Confident in Them Now Than in the Early Seventies

Banks and Financial Institutions			Major Companies			Organized Labor			
Great Deal	Some	Hardly Any	Great Deal	Some	Hardly Any	Great Deal	Some	Hardly Any	
25%	56%	17%	23%	59%	14%	11%	51%	30%	1996
18	61	20	25	61	10	10	52	32	1994
15	57	26	21	63	12	8	53	32	1993
12	52	34	20	62	13	11	48	34	1991
18	58	22	25	61	11	11	53	31	1990
19	59	19	24	60	10	9	51	33	1989
27	58	13	25	60	11	10	50	35	1988
27	57	14	30	58	8	10	51	33	1987
21	60	18	24	62	10	8	47	39	1986
32	55	11	31	57	9	9	53	36	1984
24	58	16	24	59	13	8	49	39	1983
27	55	16	23	58	14	12	53	30	1982
32	50	16	27	53	14	15	50	30	1980
33	54	12	22	58	16	11	46	38	1978
42	47	9	27	56	12	15	50	32	1977
40	48	10	22	51	22	12	48	33	1976
32	54	11	19	54	21	10	54	29	1975
*	*	*	31	51	14	18	54	25	1974
40	48	10	29	53	11	16	55	26	1973

Political Institutions, the Press, and Education Show Big Declines

Question: I am going to name some institutions in this country. As far as the people running these institutions are concerned, would you say you have a great deal of confidence, only some confidence, or hardly any confidence at all in them? . . .

	Press			Television			Education		
	Great Deal	Some	Hardly Any	Great Deal	Some	Hardly Any	Great Deal	Some	Hardly Any
1996	11%	48%	39%	10%	46%	42%	23%	58%	18%
1994	10	50	39	10	50	40	25	57	17
1993	11	49	39	12	51	37	22	58	18
1991	16	54	28	14	54	30	30	55	13
1990	15	58	24	14	58	27	27	59	12
1989	17	54	27	14	55	29	30	58	10
1988	18	53	25	14	58	26	29	60	9
1987	18	56	24	12	58	29	35	55	9
1986	18	54	26	15	56	28	28	60	11
1984	17	59	22	13	57	28	28	59	11
1983	14	61	24	12	58	28	29	57	13
1982	18	59	21	14	57	27	33	52	13
1980	22	58	17	16	55	28	30	56	12
1978	20	58	20	14	53	31	28	55	15
1977	25	57	15	17	56	25	41	50	9
1976	28	52	18	19	52	27	37	45	15
1975	24	55	18	18	57	22	31	55	13
1974	26	55	17	23	58	17	49	41	8
1973	23	61	15	19	58	22	37	53	8

Medicine and Science Get High Marks

Organized Religion			Medicine			Scientific Community			
Great Deal	Some	Hardly Any	Great Deal	Some	Hardly Any	Great Deal	Some	Hardly Any	
25%	51%	19%	45%	45%	9%	39%	45%	8%	1996
24	52	22	42	48	10	38	49	7	1994
23	50	25	39	51	9	38	47	7	1993
25	51	21	47	44	8	40	46	6	1991
23	49	24	46	47	7	37	47	7	1990
22	45	30	46	45	7	40	45	6	1989
20	46	31	51	42	6	39	48	6	1988
29	49	19	52	42	5	45	42	6	1987
25	50	21	46	45	8	39	48	8	1986
31	47	19	51	42	6	45	44	6	1984
28	51	17	52	41	6	42	47	5	1983
32	50	15	45	46	7	39	46	6	1982
35	43	18	52	39	7	42	43	6	1980
31	47	18	46	44	9	36	48	7	1978
40	45	12	52	41	6	41	46	5	1977
31	45	18	54	35	9	43	38	8	1976
24	48	21	51	40	8	38	45	6	1975
44	43	11	60	34	4	45	38	7	1974
35	46	16	54	39	6	37	47	6	1973

While the Current Performance is Faulted, Regard for the Nation is Undiminished

Question: Do you think the United States is (1) **the greatest country in the world, better than all others;** (2) **is a great country but so are certain other countries;** or (3) **that there are some other countries better than the US?**

	(1)	(2)	(3)
Everyone	55%	41%	4%
By Ethnicity			
African American	60	35	5
Hispanic	48	45	7
White	55	41	4
By Gender			
Female	55	41	5
Male	55	41	4
By Marital Status			
Single	43	51	6
Married (1st marriage)	58	38	4
Married (2nd+ marriage)	60	37	3
Divorced or Separated	51	43	6
By Age			
18–34	45	48	6
35–49	53	42	5
50–64	62	36	2
65 or Older	69	29	2
By Region			
East	54	42	4
Midwest	50	45	5
South	63	34	3
West	48	45	7

	(1)	(2)	(3)
By Religion			
Evangelical Protestant	68	31	2
Mainline Protestant	52	44	3
Orthodox Catholic	58	39	3
Progressive Catholic	52	43	5
Secularist	46	48	7
By Education			
Less than H.S.	61	37	2
H.S. Graduate	59	38	4
Some College	52	42	6
College Graduate	49	45	6
Post-Graduate	48	48	4
By Social Class			
Poor Laborers	51	43	6
Low-Mid Income Laborers	54	41	5
Managers & Entrepreneurs	54	42	4
Professionals	56	40	4
Social Elite	35	64	2
By Political Party			
Democrat	58	38	4
Republican	61	37	2
Independent	45	49	6
By Political Interest Level			
High	58	37	5
Moderate	53	44	3
Low	54	41	6

And It Extends Evenly Across Social Group Lines

Question: . . . [W]here would you place yourself [using a scale in which "1" means none at all, and "7" means a great deal]…for [the following statement]…**To what extent are you proud to live under our political system?** [Responses of 5, 6, or 7 = Proud and 1, 2, or 3 = Not proud.]

	Proud	Not proud		Proud	Not proud
Everyone	76%	13%	**By Religion**		
By Ethnicity			Evangelical Protestant	78%	12%
African American	73	15	Mainline Protestant	74	14
Hispanic	71	16	Orthodox Catholic	75	9
White	76	13	Progressive Catholic	79	10
By Gender			Secularist	68	19
Female	76	13	**By Education**		
Male	75	13	Less than H.S.	76	11
By Marital Status			H.S. Graduate	73	16
Single	72	17	Some College	75	15
Married (1st marriage)	76	11	College Graduate	77	9
Married (2nd+ marriage)	77	15	Post-Graduate	80	9
Divorced or Separated	72	16	**By Social Class**		
By Age			Poor Laborers	69	19
18–34	69	17	Low-Mid Income Laborers	75	13
35–49	79	11	Managers & Entrepreneurs	79	10
50–64	77	11	Professionals	75	14
65 or Older	78	9	Social Elite	84	6
By Region			**By Political Party**		
East	76	14	Democrat	78	11
Midwest	76	11	Republican	79	10
South	75	12	Independent	72	16
West	74	15	**By Political Interest Level**		
			High	79	11
			Moderate	75	12
			Low	70	18

What's More, We See the Best Ahead for the US

Question: . . . [W]here would you place yourself [using a scale in which "1" means none at all, and "7" means a great deal] for [the following statement]…To what extent do you think the best years for America are in the future? [Responses of 5, 6, or 7 = Best years ahead and 1, 2, or 3 = No, not ahead.]

	Best years ahead	No, not ahead		Best years ahead	No, not ahead
Everyone	55%	27%	**By religion**		
By Ethnicity			Evangelical Protestant	50%	30%
African American	56	28	Mainline Protestant	54	27
Hispanic	57	20	Orthodox Catholic	56	26
White	55	28	Progressive Catholic	66	16
By Gender			Secularist	50	37
Female	55	28	**By Education**		
Male	55	25	Less than H.S.	54	24
By Marital Status			H.S. Graduate	52	31
Single	49	32	Some College	58	28
Married (1st marriage)	59	24	College Graduate	57	24
Married (2nd+ marriage)	56	27	Post-Graduate	57	26
Divorced or Separated	50	33	**By Social Class**		
By Age			Poor Laborers	50	36
18-34	51	32	Low-Mid Income Laborers	53	28
35-49	56	27	Managers & Entrepreneurs	58	21
50-64	60	21	Professionals	56	25
65 or Older	58	23	Social Elite	59	23
By Region			**By Political Party**		
East	61	23	Democrat	58	24
Midwest	58	25	Republican	54	28
South	51	28	Independent	55	28
West	49	32	**By Political Interest Level**		
			High	59	27
			Moderate	58	24
			Low	47	32

Old Verities Are Endorsed

Questions: In teaching the American story to children, how important is the following theme...?

	Essential/Very important	Somewhat important	Somewhat Unimportant/Very Unimportant/Leave it out of the story
With hard work and perseverence, anyone can succeed in America.	83%	14%	4%
American democracy is only as strong as the virtue of its citizens.	83	14	4
Our founders limited the power of government, so government would not intrude too much into the lives of its citizens.	74	19	8
America is the world's greatest melting pot in which people from different countries are united into one nation.	73	21	5
America's contribution is one of expanding freedom for more and more people.	71	22	6
From its start, America had a destiny to set an example for other nations.	65	22	13
Our nation betrayed its founding principles by cruel mistreatment of blacks and American Indians.	59	24	17
Our Nation was founded upon Biblical principles.	58	26	15
Ours has been a history of war and aggression—our expansion occurred at the cost of much suffering.	58	26	16
America has a special place in God's plan for history	50	22	29
Our founders were part of a male-dominated culture that gave important roles to men while keeping women in the background.	38	28	35

1996 Survey of American Political Culture

The Work Ethic and Job Satisfaction Look Strong and Stable

Questions: If you were to get enough money to live as comfortably as you would like for the rest of your life, would you continue to work or would you stop working?; Some people say that people get ahead by their own hard work, others say that lucky breaks or help from other people are more important. Which do you think is most important?; On the whole, how satisfied are you with the work you do?

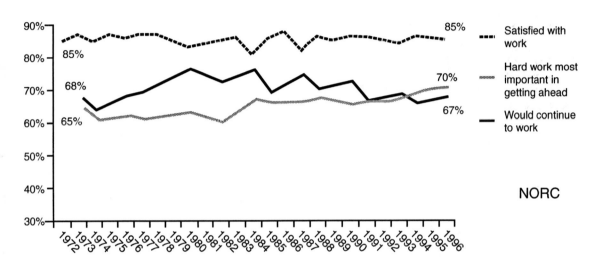

Our Country's Main Challenges Are in the Moral Dimension, Not in Economics or Power

Questions: How strong would you say the US decline or improvement is in [each of the following areas] . . .?

Area of Decline/Improvement	Strong/Moderate Decline	Holding Steady	Moderate/Strong Improvement
The area of crime and public safety	74%	17%	9%
The quality of television and entertainment	71	19	11
Its moral and ethical standards	70	24	6
The area of our criminal justice system	67	26	8
The area of family life	64	26	9
Our education and schools	61	26	14
The quality of our national leaders	57	34	8
The area of our health care system	56	32	12
The American work ethic	56	34	10
Our standard of living	54	33	14
The honesty and integrity of the average American	50	42	8
The area of business and the economy	48	37	16
The area of racial and ethnic relations	45	39	16
The area of religious and spiritual life	43	43	14
Its global influence	34	49	18
The area of churches and religious institutions	29	54	27
Its military power	27	51	23

1996 Survey of American Political Culture, pp.10-11, and through p.18

Again, Americans Across Group Lines See the Problems in Much the Same Terms

percent responding "strong/moderate decline"

	Moral and ethical standards	Family life	Honesty and integrity of the "average American"	Business and economy	US global influence	Churches and religious institutions
Everyone	70%	64%	50%	48%	34%	29%
By Ethnicity						
African American	63	50	50	57	32	27
Hispanic	68	56	52	48	34	23
White	71	66	50	46	33	30
By Gender						
Female	72	67	50	50	34	28
Male	69	61	50	46	32	30
By Marital Status						
Single	63	57	48	43	26	27
Married (1st marriage)	72	63	49	45	35	30
Married (2nd+ marriage)	73	66	59	52	39	33
Divorced or Separated	68	70	52	56	35	30
By Age						
18-34	69	60	53	46	29	24
35-49	68	62	50	48	33	32
50-64	69	69	47	50	35	28
65 or Older	78	69	48	48	39	31
By Region						
East	70	61	45	51	33	26
Midwest	71	62	50	44	35	30
South	68	62	50	43	32	27
West	74	73	56	55	32	31
By Religion						
Evangelical Protestant	78	72	56	53	38	36
Mainline Protestant	67	62	47	45	29	25
Orthodox Catholic	69	58	49	49	40	22
Progressive Catholic	71	61	48	40	28	26
Secularist	62	62	50	45	34	27
By Education						
Less than H.S.	64	59	51	49	33	23
H.S. Graduate	73	61	51	53	34	27
Some College	73	67	53	50	36	31
College Graduate	71	70	46	37	26	29
Post Graduate	66	68	41	37	34	35
By Social Class						
Poor Laborers	66	61	52	54	35	25
Low-Mid Income Laborers	71	62	52	51	32	31
Managers & Entrepreneurs	75	61	58	45	32	30
Professionals	71	72	44	36	27	29
Social Elite	55	55	30	41	25	27
By Political Party						
Democrat	66	58	44	47	26	23
Republican	79	72	57	45	39	30
Independent	72	67	52	49	35	33
By Political Interest Level						
High	76	72	49	45	34	30
Moderate	69	61	49	46	33	27
Low	65	59	52	53	34	29

1996 Survey of American Political Culture

The Solutions We Identify Match Our Definition of the Problems

Questions: How much do you think the following would help to improve this country . . .?

	Help a lot	Somewhat Not at all	Only a little/ Not at all
If there were tougher laws and penalties to deter crime	59%	28%	13%
If fathers would focus more on their families and less upon other things	52	40	8
If traditional values were taught in public schools	51	36	14
If people were more involved in voting and politics	44	39	17
If society put less emphasis on money and material things	44	40	16
If more people regularly went to church or religious services	40	37	24
If there were more government programs to fight poverty, drug abuse, and other social problems	39	34	28
If organized religion were allowed in public schools	33	30	38
If more parents used spanking to discipline their children	31	30	39
If more women gave up their jobs and stayed home to care for their children	26	32	43
If people would just lighten up about the things that happen	19	36	46

1996 Survey of American Political Culture

Most Groups of Americans See Solutions Much the Same Way

percent responding "help a lot"

	Tougher laws and penalties to deter crime	Parents used spanking to discipline their children	Traditional values were taught in public schools	Fathers would focus on their families and less upon other things
Everyone	59%	31%	51%	52%
By Ethnicity				
African American	57	46	56	57
Hispanic	51	26	35	56
White	60	30	52	51
By Gender				
Female	61	30	52	52
Male	56	32	50	52
By Marital Status				
Single	51	27	39	49
Married (1st marriage)	61	28	50	51
Married (2nd+ marriage)	60	37	59	58
Divorce or Separated	57	37	52	52
By Age				
18-34	58	23	40	51
35-49	57	33	52	54
50-64	58	37	54	48
65 or Older	65	38	63	54
By Region				
East	56	23	43	39
Midwest	63	31	54	54
South	63	38	54	56
West	50	31	50	58
By Religion				
Evangelical Protestant	66	44	67	62
Mainline Protestant	59	30	49	50
Orthodox Catholic	66	30	56	51
Progressive Catholic	57	23	39	49
Secularist	45	25	36	40
By Education				
Less than H.S.	63	40	55	51
H.S. Graduate	61	35	54	52
Some College	62	31	52	55
College Graduate	50	21	39	52
Post-Graduate	48	17	42	45
By Social Class				
Poor Laborers	56	44	57	54
Low-Mid Income Laborers	60	28	47	52
Managers & Entrepreneurs	62	28	47	51
Professionals	50	22	44	54
Social Elite	43	9	37	32
By Political Party				
Democrat	59	32	50	51
Republican	61	34	60	54
Independent	55	28	43	53
By Political Interest Level				
High	56	30	51	54
Moderate	58	28	48	48
Low	64	35	53	55

1996 Survey of American Political Culture

What Are Some Essential Obligations of American Citizenship?

Questions: Is…[statement] an absolutely essential obligation of Americans, a very important obligation, a somewhat important obligation, or is it a matter of personal preference?

Preference	Essential Obligation	Very Important Obligation	Somewhat Important	Personal
Treating all people equally regardless of race or ethnic background	57%	33%	6%	4%
Reporting a crime that one has witnessed	54	36	7	4
Taking action to help if you hear someone screaming or see them being attacked	54	34	7	6
Being able to speak and understand English	53	33	11	4
Voting in elections	53	29	9	9
Working to reduce inequality and injustice	41	42	12	6
Being civil to others with whom we may disagree	35	45	14	6
Keeping fully informed about the news and other public issues	30	42	19	10
Donating blood or organs to help with medical needs	20	37	18	26
Volunteering time to community service	16	42	26	16

1996 Survey of American Political Culture

Young Adults Answer This Question Exactly Like Their Elders

Responses of 18-34 Year Olds

Preference	Essential Obligation	Very Important Obligation	Somewhat Important	Personal
Treating all people equally regardless of race or ethnic background	57%	33%	6%	4%
Reporting a crime that one has witnessed	55	34	7	5
Taking action to help if you hear someone screaming or see them being attacked	54	33	7	6
Being able to speak and understand English	49	35	12	4
Voting in elections	47	33	10	10
Working to reduce inequality and injustice	44	39	11	7
Being civil to others with whom we may disagree	31	47	13	9
Keeping fully informed about the news and other public issues	27	42	20	11
Donating blood or organs to help with medical needs	20	36	18	27
Volunteering time to community service	16	40	27	17

1996 Survey of American Political Culture

What's Right and Wrong? What Should Be Legal or Illegal?

Questions: How wrong do you personally think it is when people engage in the following behavior. . . ?

	Wrong for all/ and should not be legally tolerated	Wrong for all/but should be tolerated	Right for some, but not for me personally	Right for me, but not necessarily for others	Right for all	Not a moral issue
Cheating on taxes	68%	11%	10%	3%	2%	7%
Smoking marijuana	51	13	19	4	3	10
Marriages between two persons of the same sex	41	19	24	3	4	10
Sexual relations between two adults of the same sex	33	23	27	3	5	10
Watching porno-graphic movies	39	17	26	6	3	8
Failing to follow through on commitment	23	33	21	4	3	15
Making negative remarks about someone who is not present	22	33	21	4	3	18
Swearing or using offensive language	22	33	22	6	4	14
Mistreating someone who first mistreated you	26	27	26	5	5	12
Abortion during the first three months of pregnancy	34	16	24	6	11	8
Medically assisted suicide for someone terminally ill	32	13	26	9	13	7
Sex before marriage	16	27	22	15	9	11
Smoking cigarettes	13	19	30	13	8	18
Withdrawing life support from someone who requests it	16	12	23	14	28	8
Marriages between blacks and whites	13	13	39	5	15	17
Drinking alcohol	11	14	29	17	10	18
Divorce	5	18	42	10	13	12
Spanking a child	10	11	24	19	20	16
Suing someone who has wronged you	8	12	27	10	28	15
Accepting a welfare payment from the government	7	12	45	6	14	16

1996 Survey of American Political Culture

A Referendum on Political Issues

Questions: . . . Please select the number that best expresses how much you favor or oppose [the proposal being discussed] . . . [Responses of 5, 6, or 7 = Favor; 4 = Neutral; and 1, 2, 3 = Oppose.]

	Favor	Neutral	Oppose
Guaranteeing every American adequate medical care, whether or not they can pay for it	81%	8%	11%
Balancing the federal budget	73	16	8
Making English the official language of the US	73	12	10
The death penalty for persons convicted of murder	67	14	18
Setting term limits for members of Congress	66	18	11
Allowing Voluntary prayer in public schools	65	18	14
Reducing the size of federal government	64	21	11
Passing stronger restrictions on the sale and use of handguns	63	12	23
Reducing the size of state governments	57	25	15
Shifting many government functions from the federal level to the states	57	21	18
Increasing government spending on prisons and law enforcement	52	20	27
Passing stronger restrictions against smoking in public areas	50	20	25
Allowing gays to serve in the military	38	22	35
Increasing defense spending	36	27	36
Ending affirmative action programs for women and minorities	35	23	39
Reducing federal regulations aimed at protecting the environment	34	19	45
Using American soldiers to keep peace in Bosnia	32	21	46
Reducing welfare payments to persons living in poverty	31	20	48
Increasing foreign aid to impoverished nations	29	27	44

Norms of Sexual Conduct Have Changed Greatly With Generational Replacement

Question: Did you live with your husband/wife before you got married?"

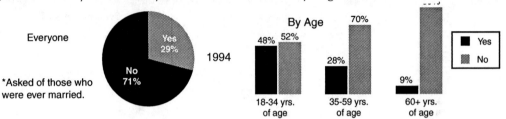

Everyone

*Asked of those who were ever married.

Question: Do you agree or disagree…[I]t's a good idea for a couple who intend to get married to live together first?

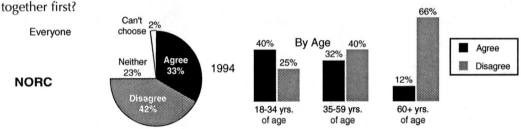

Everyone

NORC

Question: If a man and a woman have sex relations before marriage, do you think it is always wrong, almost always wrong, wrong only sometimes, or not wrong at all?

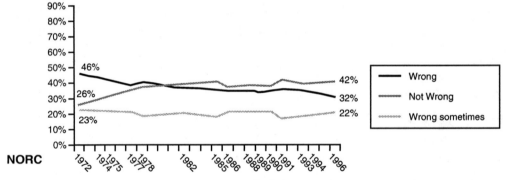

NORC

Marital Status

Question: Are you currently married, widowed, divorced, separated, or have you never been married?

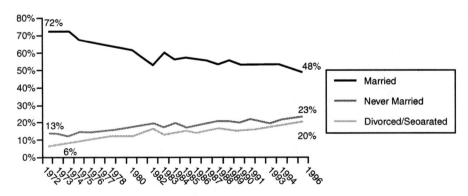

Since *Roe*, Opinion on Abortion Issues Has Changed Little

Questions: Please tell me whether or not you think it should be possible for a pregnant woman to obtain a legal abortion if . . . She is married and does not want any more children; The family has a low income and cannot afford any more children; The woman wants it for any reason?

percent responding "yes" in each instance

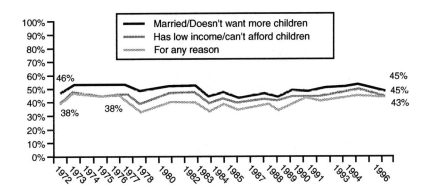

NORC

Questions: Please tell me whether or not you think it should be possible for a pregnant woman to obtain a legal abortion if . . . The woman's own health is seriously endangered by the pregnancy; She became pregnant as a result of rape; There is a strong chance of serious defect in the baby?

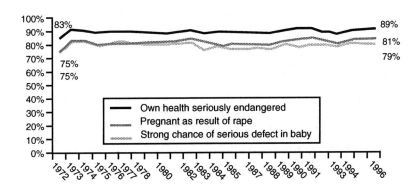

percent responding "yes" in each instance

NORC

Sharp Differences on Abortion as a Moral Issue by Religious Tradition and Education; Small by Age and Gender

Question: Which of these statements best describes your feelings about abortion: (1) **Abortion is just as bad as killing a person who has already been born—it is murder;** (2) **Abortion is murder, but it is not as bad as killing someone who has already been born;** (3) **Abortion is not murder, but it does involve the taking of a human life;** (4) **Abortion is not murder—it is a surgical procedure for removing human tissue.**

	(1)	(2)	(3)	(4)		(1)	(2)	(3)	(4)
Everyone	38%	10%	26%	16%	**By Religion**				
By Ethnicity					Evangelical Protestant	58	10	16	7
African American	40	9	15	17	Mainline Protestant	28	8	31	19
Hispanic	49	13	22	9	Orthodox Catholic	54	9	23	6
White	36	9	28	17	Progressive Catholic	33	15	31	11
By Gender					Secularist	6	5	28	45
Female	39	8	27	16	**By Education**				
Male	37	12	24	15	Less than H.S.	49	10	18	11
By Marital Status					H.S. Graduate	40	12	24	13
Single	33	10	25	18	Some College	36	8	29	15
Married (1st marriage)	42	10	25	13	College Graduate	30	9	28	27
Married (2nd+ marriage)	35	9	33	18	Post-Graduate	26	10	35	19
Divorced or Separated	28	9	30	19	**By Social Class**				
By Age					Poor Laborers	47	8	18	12
18-34	34	10	31	14	Low-Mid Income Laborers	34	11	30	15
35-49	36	10	28	16	Managers & Entrepreneurs	43	9	28	13
50-64	46	10	16	16	Professionals	36	12	26	18
65 or Older	41	10	21	16	Social Elite	26	4	27	35
By Region					**By Political Party**				
East	37	13	25	16	Democrat	36	9	25	19
Midwest	39	7	30	14	Republican	46	10	27	11
South	43	12	22	11	Independent	33	11	27	17
West	30	7	28	24	**By Political Interest Level**				
					High	34	10	29	19
					Moderate	37	10	25	17
					Low	44	10	21	10

The 1996 Survey of American Political Culture was conducted by the Gallup Organization between January 27 and April 14, 1996. Face to face interviews were conducted with 2,047 adults, with a questionnaire that included over 200 discrete items.

Americans' Religiosity Strong and Unchanging

Question: . . . [T]ell me which statement comes closest to expressing what you believe about God . . . I don't believe in God. I don't know whether there is a God, and I don't believe there is any way to find out. I don't believe in a personal God, but I do believe in a Higher Power of some kind. I find myself believing in God some of the time, but not at others. While I have doubts, I feel that I do believe in God. I know God really exists and I have no doubts about it.

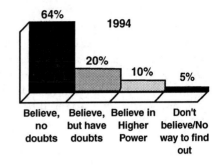

Question: Which of these statements comes closest to describing your feelings about the Bible? (A) **The Bible is the actual word of God and is to be taken literally, word for word:** (B) **The Bible is the inspired word of God, but not everything in it should be taken literally, word for word;** (C) **The Bible is an ancient book of fables, legends, history, and moral precepts recorded by men.**

	Statement A	Statement B	Statement C
1996	30%	50%	17%
1994	31	52	15
1993	33	49	15
1991	35	48	15
1990	33	49	15
1989	31	50	16
1988	34	47	16
1987	37	46	15
1985	36	49	13

Question: How often do you attend religious services?

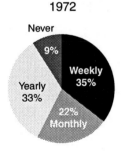

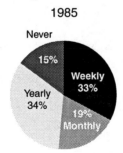

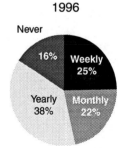

Question: About how often do you pray?. . . Several times a day, once a day, several times a week, once a week, less than once a week, never.

NORC

	Daily	Weekly	Less Than Weekly
1996	58%	22%	21%
1994	56	21	24
1993	57	22	23
1990	52	23	25
1989	53	22	25
1988	54	24	22
1987	56	23	21
1985	58	20	22
1984	57	21	21
1983	55	21	25

One Third of All Americans, and 3 in 10 Among the Young, Describe the *Bible* as the Actual Word of God, Inerrant, to be Taken Word for Word

Question: Which of these statements comes closest to describing your feelings about the Bible: (1) **The Bible is the actual word of God, not mistaken in its statements and teaching, and is to be taken literally, word for word;** (2) **The Bible is the inspired word of God, not mistaken in its teachings, but is not always to be taken literally, word for word;** (3) **The Bible becomes the word of God for a person who reads it in faith;** (4) **The Bible is an ancient book of legends, history, and moral precepts recorded by men.**

	(1)	(2)	(3)	(4)
Everyone	34%	32%	20%	13%
By Ethnicity				
African American	50	22	21	5
Hispanic	37	30	22	10
White	32	34	20	14
By Gender				
Female	37	30	20	12
Male	32	34	20	14
By Marital Status				
Single	30	34	19	16
Married (1st marriage)	34	34	20	12
Married (2nd+ marriage)	38	26	24	11
Divorced or Separated	31	26	24	18
By Age				
18–34	31	32	21	14
35–49	31	34	21	13
50–64	36	33	18	11
65 or older	43	27	19	11
By Region				
East	20	43	20	15
Midwest	27	37	24	12
South	55	23	16	4
West	28	27	21	24

	(1)	(2)	(3)	(4)
By Religion				
Evangelical Protestant	66	21	13	1
Mainline Protestant	25	37	25	13
Orthodox Catholic	45	33	17	4
Progressive Catholic	9	50	27	13
Secularist	9	14	11	59
By Education				
Less than H.S.	53	18	19	9
High School Graduate	37	30	22	9
Some College or Tech.	32	35	20	12
College Graduate	17	39	21	22
Post-Graduate Study	18	44	14	23
By Social Class				
Poor Laborers	45	18	21	13
Low-Mid Income Laborers	32	35	19	13
Managers & Entrepreneurs	30	34	25	10
Professionals	26	40	16	18
Social Elite	9	43	10	35
By Political Party				
Democrat	39	29	18	13
Republican	35	36	22	7
Independent	26	32	22	18
By Political Interest Level				
High	28	35	20	17
Moderate	34	34	20	12
Low	42	27	21	8

1996 Survey of American Political Culture

Nearly 6 in 10 Said "Four or More" Children is the Ideal in 1959; 1 in 10 Say That Today

Question: What do you think is the ideal number of children for a family to have?

	Ideal Number of Children						**Ideal Number of Children**			
	0–1	**2**	**3**	**4 or more**			**0–1**	**2**	**3**	**4 or more**
1996	4%	57%	22%	11%		1974	3	44	23	19
1994	4	53	22	11		1972	3	40	23	25
1993	3	55	20	9		1970	2	37	23	34
1991	4	52	22	12		1967	*	23	30	40
1990	3	54	23	12		1966	1	18	27	35
1989	4	53	21	14		1965	1	18	28	37
1988	4	50	26	14		1962	1	16	24	46
1986	3	51	25	16		1959	1	2	35	58
1985	4	55	22	15		1957	2	18	34	39
1983	3	51	23	14		1953	2	27	28	39
1982	4	55	20	17		1952	2	27	28	38
1978	3	51	24	17		1947	1	26	26	41
1977	3	49	23	19		1945	1	22	28	49
1975	3	48	23	16		1941	1	31	27	41

Data on this page through p. 27 are NORC, except where time line is carried back before 1972, where Gallup askings of the same questions were used.

Question: If you had to choose, which thing on this list would you pick as the most important for a child to learn to prepare him or her for life?

	To think for him/herself	**To work hard**	**To help others when they need help**	**To obey**	**To be well-liked or popular**
1996	51%	17%	13%	18%	1%
1994	54	15	13	18	1
1993	53	14	13	19	1
1991	52	15	13	20	*
1990	51	16	14	19	1
1989	53	14	12	20	1
1988	49	14	13	23	1
1987	55	12	12	21	1
1986	52	11	14	23	1

*less than 0.5%

Men and Women Don't Disagree on "Women in Politics," But They Divide When Maternal Responsibility is Invoked.

Question 1: Do you agree or disagree with this statement? A working mother can establish just as warm and secure a relationship with her children as a mother who does not work.

Question 2: Do you agree or disagree with this statement? A preschool child is likely to suffer if his or her mother works.

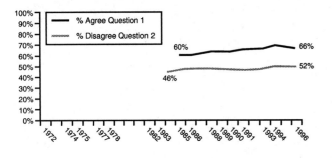

	Agree Question 1		Disagree Question 2	
Responses by Gender				
	Men	Women	Men	Women
1996	56%	73%	44%	58%
1994	60%	75%	48%	62%
1993	58%	72%	49%	60%
1991	58%	69%	42%	57%
1990	56%	68%	43%	54%
1989	58%	67%	43%	55%
1988	55%	69%	43%	57%
1986	55%	67%	41%	53%
1985	52%	67%	36%	52%

Question 1: If your party nominated a woman for president, would you vote for her if she were qualified for the job?

Question 2: Do you agree or disagree with this statement? Most men are better suited emotionally for politics than most women.

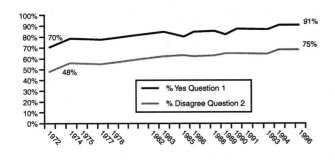

	Yes Question 1		Disagree Question 2	
Responses by Gender				
	Men	Women	Men	Women
1996	88%	92%	73%	76%
1994	88%	90%	72%	76%
1993	87%	87%	73%	75%
1991	85%	87%	71%	69%
1990	87%	85%	66%	70%
1989	79%	84%	61%	68%
1988	87%	83%	59%	68%
1986	86%	82%	62%	59%
1985	82%	78%	59%	58%
1983	83%	84%	58%	64%
1982	83%	83%	57%	61%
1978	81%	78%	55%	53%
1977	80%	74%	46%	50%
1975	80%	76%	50%	47%
1974	78%	77%	47%	51%
1972	70%	70%	—	—

Taking One's Own Life: We're Changing Our Minds when the Person Has an Incurable Disease

Question: Do you think a person has the right to end his or her own life if this person has an incurable disease?

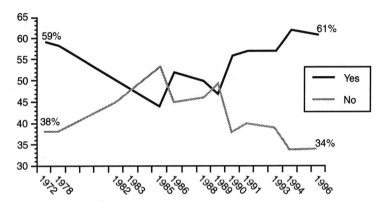

Questions: When a person has a disease that cannot be cured, do you think doctors should be allowed by law to end the patient's life by some painless means if the patient and his family request it?; Do you think a person has the right to end his or her own life if this person is tired of living and ready to die?

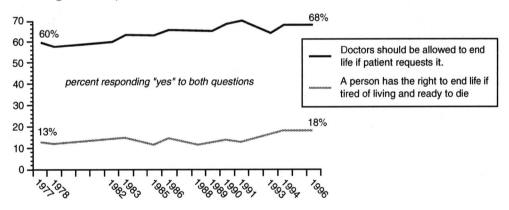

Use of Marijuana Should Not be Made Legal

Question: Do you think the use of marijuana should be made legal or not?

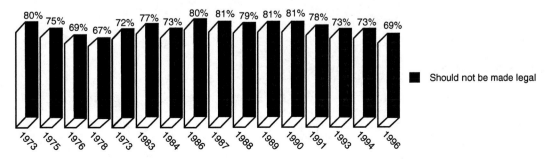

Crime: Four in Ten Are Afraid to Walk Alone at Night Near Their Homes

Question: Is there any area right around here—that is, within a mile—where you would be afraid to walk alone at night?

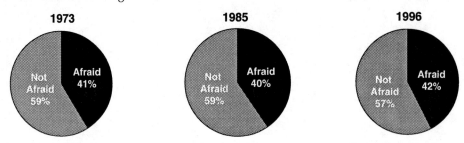

Require a Police Permit When Buying a Gun? A Strong "Yes"

Question: Would you favor or oppose a law which would require a person to obtain a police permit before he or she could buy a gun?

Three-Fifths of Americans Own No Guns

Question: Do you happen to have in your home (or garage) any guns or revolvers?

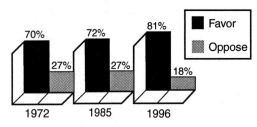

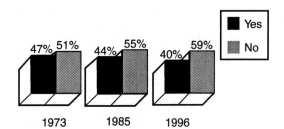

Support for Death Penalty Has Climbed Sharply Since the Sixties

Question: Do you favor or oppose the death penalty for persons convicted of murder?

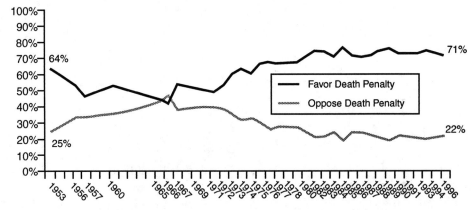

Data on this page are NORC, except where time line is carried back before 1972, where Gallup askings of the same questions were used.

TALL OAKS FROM LITTLE ACORNS GROW: THE GENERAL SOCIAL SURVEYS, 1971-1996

By Tom W. Smith

The National Data Program for the Social Sciences of the National Opinion Research Center (NORC) at the University of Chicago is a social indicators and data diffusion program. This program has two basic purposes. The first is to gather and disseminate data on contemporary American society. Through use of these data, researchers may monitor and explain social trends and constants in attitudes, behaviors, and attributes and examine the structure and functioning of society in general, as well as the role played by various subgroups.

Second, the program aims to compare the United States to other societies in order to place American society in comparative perspective, develop cross-national models of human society, and make high quality data easily and quickly available to scholars, students, policy makers, and others.

Both these purposes are accomplished by the regular collection and distribution of the NORC General Social Survey (GSS) and its allied surveys in the International Social Survey Program (ISSP).

Origins

In 1971, James A. Davis, then at Dartmouth College, drew on two intellectual currents of the 1960s to conceive the GSS. During this period, the social indicators movement was stressing the importance of measuring trends and of adding non-economic measures to a large repertoire of national accounts indices. At the same time, scholarly egalitarianism was advocating that data be made available to scientists at all universities and not restricted to an elite group of senior investigators at large research centers and laboratories. In 1971 Davis put these ideas together in a modest proposal to the National Science Foundation (NSF). The proposal called for the periodic asking of "twenty-some questions" to develop social indicators on national samples, with these data immediately distributed to the social science community for analysis and teaching. Approval from NSF, plus supplemental funding from the Russell Sage Foundation, spawned the first GSS in 1972.

Growth

Since 1972 the GSS has conducted 21 independent, cross-sectional, in-person surveys of adults living in households in the United States. By the 1996 GSS a total of 34,577 respondents had been interviewed in the cross-sections, along with 707 black respondents included in the oversamples carried out in 1982 and 1987. During most years there have been annual surveys of about 1,500 respondents. Currently, 3,000 cases are collected in a biennial, double-sample GSS.

Besides accumulating this long time series, individual GSSs have also greatly expanded in length. The 1972 GSS had only 151 variables, but since 1988 there have been over 700 variables in each GSS. At 90-95 minutes in length each GSS is about seven times longer than a typical public opinion poll.

In addition, since 1982, the GSS has expanded internationally. A growing number of countries have established GSS-like programs, and we have formed ties to these counterparts. Like the GSS, the cross-national research started modestly with a bilateral collaboration between the GSS and the ALLBUS of the Zentrum fuer Umfragen, Methoden. und Analysen in Germany (ZUMA) in 1982 and 1984. Then, in 1984, the GSS and the ALLBUS joined with the British Social Attitudes Survey of Social and Community Planning Research in London and the National Social Science Survey of the Research School of the Social Sciences at Australian National University to form the ISSP. Along with Eurisko in Italy and the University of Graz in Austria, the founding four fielded the first ISSP in 1985. An ISSP survey has collected data annually since then. and there are now 26 member countries (Australia, Austria, Britain, Bulgaria, Canada, Cyprus, the Czech Republic, France. Germany, Hungary, Ireland, Israel, Italy, Japan, the Netherlands, New Zealand, Norway, the Philippines, Poland, Portugal, Russia, Slovakia, Slovenia, Spain, Sweden, and the United States) collecting upwards of 30,000 cases a year.

Content

The General Social Survey lives up to its title. It is indeed *general*. The 2,999 variables in the 1972-1996 cumulative file run from ABANY (legal abortion if a woman wants one for any reason) to ZODIAC (astrological birth sign) and include major batteries on such topics as civil liberties, confidence in institutions, crime and violence, feminism, governmental spending priorities, psychological well-being, race relations, and work.

While the balance of components has changed over the years, currently half of the GSS consists of replicating core questions, one-sixth is cross-national (i.e., the ISSP questions), one-sixth forms an in-depth topical module, and one-sixth is a combination of experiments, extensions of existing batteries, and new items. Recent ISSP modules include the environment, gender and work, national identity, and the role of government (social welfare, economic regulation, civil liberties). Topical modules in the 1990s cover work organizations, culture, family mobility, multiculturalism, emotions, gender, mental health, and market exchanges. Other recent additions include experiments in measuring church attendance, race and ethnicity, and supplements on sexual behavior, giving and volunteering, religious identity, and genetics.

Research Opportunities

The design of the GSS greatly facilitates several important types of research. First, the replication of items from survey to survey allows the study of social change. Since all surveys and all variables are organized into one cumulative file, one does not have to patch together time series from numerous different and often incompatible data sets. One merely asks for cross-tabulations or correlations by *year*, and over 1,000 trends can be tracked. Moreover, since the GSS draws heavily from baseline surveys by NORC, Gallup, the Survey Research Center at the University of Michigan, and others, it is possible to follow hundreds of trends back as early as the 1930s. (In this case you do have to access these separate data sets from the Roper Center or elsewhere.)

Replication also means that subgroups can be pooled across surveys to aggregate an adequate sample for analysis. For example, African Americans, at about 12% of the population, account for about 175 respondents in a 1,500-case GSS—too few for detailed analysis. But in the combined 1972-1996 GSSs there are 4,783 black respondents—more than enough for analysis. Other numerically small subgroups that can be studied in the cumulative GSS file include the self-employed (3,755), the currently divorced (3,659), those with graduate degrees (1,916), Jews (757), and nurses (578).

With many of these sub-groups, one can both track trends and pool cases. For example, blacks from the 1970s, 1980s, and 1990s can be combined to have three time points and still have over a thousand black respondents in each sample.

Comparative research is facilitated by the 11 ISSP studies (1985-1996), which offer the largest and most readily accessible body of cross-national social science data available. In keeping with the GSS's core interest in social trends, the ISSP research also has an across-time component. The first module on the role of government in 1985 was repeated in 1990 and 1996: the 1987 social inequality module was refielded in 1992 and will appear again in 1999: the women and work module was asked in 1988 and 1994: and the 1990 religion module will appear again in 1998.

The large number of variables in a GSS means that one can examine relationships across dozens or even hundreds of variables. For example, Peter Rossi examined the differences between homeowners and non-homeowners in over 300 variables, and Andrew Greeley compared Protestants and Catholics in 117 questions. The extensive variable list gives a more comprehensive view of patterns, and associations can typically be ascertained.

Finally, because the GSS employs a detailed and extensive set of demographics, in-depth analysis of background influences is possible. For example, the GSS doesn't just have a single measure of education, but eight standard measures, including the exact number of years of schooling completed and the highest degree obtained for respondents, their mothers, their fathers, and their spouses. In terms of occupation the GSS has three-digit Census codes. International Standard of Occupation Codes, NORC-GSS prestige scores, and Duncan SEI values for respondents, parents, and spouses.

Impact on the Social Sciences

As the largest and longest-running project funded by the Sociology Program of NSF, the GSS has had a tremendous impact on social science research in the United States. The 1996 Annotated Bibliography documents 3,771 uses of the GSS, and new usages are accumulating at over 300 per year. Among the top sociology journals (*American Journal of Sociology. American Sociological Review*, and *Social Forces*) the GSS is second only to the Census/Current Population Survey in frequency of use and is utilized as often as the next eight most frequently used surveys combined. Moreover, on average the GSS articles in the top sociology journals have been cited 60% more often than non-GSS articles from the same journals.

The GSS has also had a large influence on college teaching. Hundreds of thousands of students have learned about American society and research methodology in courses built around the GSS. MicroCase Corporation has developed more than a dozen textbooks in sociology, criminology, political science, and statistics around the GSS, and the CHIPendale statistical analysis system developed by Davis has GSS-based workbooks covering such topics as inequality, marriage and the family, social problems, working women and the family, and research methods. Texts by Earl Babbie (*Adventures in Social Research* and *The Practice of Social Research*) include diskettes with GSS sub-sets. These GSS-centric courses have allowed students to learn about society through hands-on analysis of fresh, high-quality, relevant data.

Conclusion

The GSS has aptly been described as a "national resource,"[1] as a "public utility for the community at large."[2] and as "a unique source for comparative," historical, methodological, and cross-sectional research."[3]

And its value grows with time. As the GSS extends into the future, the time series lengthens. So far the GSS is only halfway towards following a cohort from entering adulthood to entering retirement (the 2020 GSS will capture them becoming seniors). By measuring the entire life cycle of cohorts we will be better able to understand the complex interaction of age, period, and cohort. In addition, econometric time series analysis is becoming increasingly possible with the GSS series.

At the same time, the ISSP continues to add more countries. In particular, several developing countries will join within the next few years. Thus, the ISSP is increasingly becoming representative of the world as a whole.

Finally, the GSS continues to explore cutting-edge research questions that will expand our general knowledge of human society. The GSS has preliminary plans for a study of inter-group relations and pluralism (including an Hispanic oversample and possibly related investigations of recent immigrants) and a module on social capital which will examine changes in institutional trust and social cohesion.

The GSS is grounded in the past, but growing toward the future. It joins together replication and innovation, incorporates both the social-change and comparative perspectives, and combines patrician quality standards with plebeian applications. Through these synergies it has served and will continue to serve the social science communities.

Endnotes

1   Duncan R. Luce, Neil J. Smelser, and Dean R. Gerstein (eds.). *Leading Edges on the Social and Behavioral Sciences* (New York: Russell Sage, 1989).

2   Office of Inspector General. "National Opinion Research Center. Chicago, Illinois: Inspection Report." National Science Foundation, 1994.

3   Thomas A. DiPrete. "Review of The NORC General Social Survey: A User's Guide." *Contemporary Sociology*. (July 1992). pp. 549-550.

The U.S. Military
Sovereign or Subordinate?

by James H. Toner

In its proper manifestation the jealousy between civil and military
spirits is a healthy symptom.

—Alfred Thayer Mahan (1903)

In Robert Heinlein's remarkable novel *Starship Troopers*, a student is asked to explain
the difference between a soldier and a civilian. Drawing upon his course text, the student responds: "The difference . . . lies in the field of civic virtue. A soldier accepts
personal responsibility for the safety of the body politic of which he is a member,
defending it, if need be, with his life. The civilian does not."[1]

Aristotle argued that in order to understand something, one had to inquire into its
functions: What, after all, was it supposed to do? To understand the United States military, one has to ask the same question. What is the United States military supposed to do?

Military Tasks

The preeminent military task, and what separates it from all other occupations, is that
soldiers are routinely prepared *to kill*. Even policemen, who must also often deal with
violence, do not routinely train to kill. One can argue, of course, using the Army as
an example, that there are combat support and combat service support branches in
addition to the combat arms (such as infantry and artillery). But every soldier under-
goes initial entry training known as BCT (basic combat training), and every soldier
has to be qualified in BRM (basic rifle marksmanship). Every soldier, in short, is an
infantryman. If U.S. Army positions are overrun in the heat of combat, enemy forces
do not pause to investigate a soldier's MOS (military occupational specialty).

Source: *True Faith and Allegiance: The Burden of Military Ethics* (1995): 22-38. Reprinted by permission of The University of Kentucky Press.

Contending that every soldier is a "trained killer" brings on self-conscious chuckles among, young soldiers and invites scorn from critics. For many years the U.S. military itself has downplayed this most basic fact of its existence: its purpose is to kill national enemies of the United States. Soldiers are, or are supposed to be, masters of the arts of violence. That is why they are paid. But the thought of killing is unsettling, as it should be, to decent and rational people. Military ethics is a burden precisely because the profession of arms is centrally concerned with killing but must also be a paragon of virtue, able always to distinguish the honorable from the shameful—one of the reasons military ethics must study examples both of integrity and of corruption.

An army or a navy or an air force is thus not primarily about job training—or building roads, or delivering mail, or milking cows. There are many other organizations and agencies to do those things. But only the military is called upon, in time of war, to risk life and limb to protect the nation's safety. When soldiers are not actually killing, they should be training to kill. The president of Boston University, John Silber, explains this concept succinctly:

> I was once asked by a friend to recommend his son for the U.S. Naval Academy. I asked in response, "Does your son want to be a professional killer?" And he said, "Well, no, of course not. He wants to be a peacemaker." I replied, "Well, then, tell him to enter a seminary."
>
> A person not prepared to use his skill, knowledge, techniques, and all the weapons at his disposal for the purpose of killing on behalf of the United States of America when ordered to do so has no business in the military. That is the military's ultimate business.[2]

In addition to killing and preparing to kill, the soldier has two other principal duties, rarely discussed—and probably never discussed by recruiters. Some soldiers die; when they are not dying, they must be preparing to die. From time immemorial, young men (and now young women) have joined armies the world over in time of national peril. Only very occasionally are these youths forced to consider their mortality. (As we grow older, we attend funerals more frequently, an all too constant reminder of our own approaching end.) It is difficult enough—and a good thing too,—to convert decent young people into soldiers prepared to kill; it is practically impossible for them to think of themselves as the objects of other's military actions.

Everyone who has been a soldier in time of war has witnessed friends go off to battle questioning, in most cases, only their enemies' mortality rather than their own. Few American soldiers who went to Vietnam were persuaded of their own imminent deaths, although 58,000 Americans perished in that war. A reading of the "Code of Conduct for Members of the Armed Forces of the United States" puts the matter squarely, however: "I am an American, fighting in the forces which guard my country and our way of life. I am prepared to give my life in their defense" (Article I). Still, a corollary of that article might be (there is, of course, no such language): "I am an American, fighting in the forces which guard my country and our way of life. I am prepared to kill in their defense."

During the Korean War (1950-53) the U.S. Army, fighting under the banner of the United Nations, kept North Korean and Chinese Communist prisoners of war

(POWs) in a camp on Koje Island off the southern coast of the Korean peninsula. In order to gain a propaganda triumph, the POWs planned to capture the commanding general of the compound and then to trade him back to U.S. forces after extorting a statement to the effect that Americans routinely tortured North Korean and Chinese prisoners. Such a statement, however false, could be used to advantage by the Communists in the negotiations then under way at Panmunjom. Brig. Gen. Francis Dodd, the hapless Koje commander, was taken hostage by the POWs. His successor, Brig. Gen. Charles Colson, afraid for the life of his friend and fellow officer, delivered a note to the Communists essentially admitting to torture practices on the island. Dodd was released.

The general officer then in charge of the United Nations Command in Korea, Gen. Matthew B. Ridgway, U.S.A., later observed:

> While I could sympathize with the desire . . . to save a friend's life, I felt that Dodd, like every other professional soldier, had accepted the risk of violent death when he chose his profession. A great many men had already given their lives to back up our government's refusal to confess uncommitted offenses to the Communists or to compromise our stand on repatriation. In wartime a general's life is no more precious than the life of a common soldier. Each is asked to risk his life every day to protect the safety, the freedom, and the honor of his country. If, in order to save an officer's life, we abandoned the cause for which enlisted men had died, we would be guilty of betraying the men whose lives had been placed in our care.[3]

In early 1968 the US.S. *Pueblo*, in international waters off the coast of Korea, was ordered by North Korean vessels to "heave to." The *Pueblo* was a floating listening post with highly sensitive electronic eavesdropping devices on board. When its skipper, Commander Lloyd "Pete" Bucher, U.S.N., became convinced that the North Koreans intended to seize his vessel and its highly classified cargo, he stalled as best he could to allow his sailors time to smash equipment and shred documents. But before they had finished, the North Koreans became impatient and fired on the *Pueblo*, killing one crewman. Bucher surrendered his ship, as one of his officers read the Code of Conduct to crew members over the loudspeaker system.[4]

Once the North Koreans had ordered Bucher to surrender, however, his mission had changed, from one of listening to Korean broadcasts to protecting the classified data and machinery on board. For Commander Bucher and the crew of the *Pueblo*, the time had come to risk life and limb to buy more time to protect those materials. "Buying more time," in this case, would have meant heading for the open seas, no doubt taking enemy fire, and preparing to repel boarders—a drill routinely practiced by Navy crews on ships of such size. It would have meant more American deaths. Confronted with the terrible choice between saving the lives of his crew and accomplishing his new mission of document destruction, Bucher chose the former. He proved to be a heroic leader in captivity. About a year after being taken prisoner (and having suffered a terrible ordeal in North Korea), Bucher and his crew were released after the United States signed another false propaganda statement.[5] The *Pueblo* is still in Korea today.

If your friend were going to be killed by his captors, would you sign an obviously phony statement to effect his release? If your crew were going to pay with their lives while you stalled for the time essential to your mission, would you decide to surrender? I believe that any decent *civilian* would have chosen as Colson and Bucher did. I also believe, with Ridgway, that Colson was wrong. By the same token a U.S. Navy board of inquiry considered punishing Bucher but chose not to in recognition of his exemplary leadership and courage while a prisoner.[6]

Note that questions of military ethics—honorable and shameful conduct—are rarely crystal clear. The second article of the Code of Conduct says, "I will never surrender of my own free will. If in command, I will never surrender the members of my command while they still have the means to resist." Did the *Pueblo* have the means, such as flight or fight?[7] Frequently, the problems of military ethics are far easier to resolve in the comfort of a classroom than on the battlefield or high seas.

Military commanders are supposed to accomplish their mission *and* look out for their people. This is a vital concept requiring more analysis, but at this point it is enough to ask: in times of peril, when getting the mission done means getting members of your command killed, which comes first, mission or people? (By the way, beware the fallacy of the false dichotomy! Usually, when something is X *or* Y, with no other possibility offered, you are dealing with a "stacked deck.") We will return to this quandary.

The Loyalty Dilemma

Aside from the "mission vs. people" problem, there is a perhaps equally burdensome problem that professional soldiers must face. What I call the "loyalty dilemma" can be so perplexing that it is rarely examined. Simply put, the loyalty dilemma poses two difficulties. Soldiers pledge obedience to constitutional precepts—but whose interpretation of them? And soldiers are responsible to superior authority—but not always.

The officer's oath is a short, solemn statement: "I [full name], having been appointed a [rank] in the United States [military service], do solemnly swear that I will support and defend the Constitution of the United States against all enemies, foreign and domestic, that I will bear true faith and allegiance to the same; that I take this obligation freely, without purpose of evasion, and that I will well and faithfully discharge the duties of the office upon which I am about to enter, so help me God."[8]

In 1951, General of the Army Douglas MacArthur was relieved of command in the Far East after a series of disagreements with President Harry Truman (making clear, in my view, Truman's plain responsibility to take action). The immediate cause was a letter MacArthur had written to Massachusetts Congressman Joe Martin, clearly indicating that the general disagreed, in significant ways, with the president's policies for prosecuting the war in Korea.

MacArthur never questioned Truman's *right* to relieve him, only Truman's judgment (or lack of it) in firing him. After his return to the United States, the general said (among many other things): "I find in existence a new and heretofore unknown and dangerous concept that the members of our armed forces owe primary allegiance or loyalty to those who temporarily exercise the authority of the Executive Branch of the Government rather than to the country and its Constitution which they swore to defend. No proposition could be more dangerous."[9] MacArthur was arguing that allegiance to the person of the president and to temporary political policies should not command primary military loyalty. German officers during the Hitler era, for example, were required to swear an oath of personal fealty to Hitler. Should American officers swear an oath of loyalty to President Clinton? Though Truman, of course, was arguing for no such thing,[10] is there not a strong case to be made in behalf of the generals position?

Sir John Hackett, however, contends that "MacArthur's insistence upon his right as an individual to determine for himself the legitimacy of the executive's position, no less than his claim of the right of a military commander to modify national policies, can never be seen in any way other than completely out of order."[11] Wasn't MacArthur, then, contending that his chief loyalty should be to *his own version* of the Constitution? Having concluded that Truman's policies were mistaken or defective, MacArthur had the responsibility—or so he claimed—of correcting or at least refusing to follow those policies.

Therein lies the dilemma. Of course, no commander's loyalty to the temporary occupant of the White House should be supreme; presidents can be wrong. But MacArthur was not thus empowered to choose for himself what to do and whom to obey. Quietly and discreetly, through the chain of command, to make known his reservations; manfully to insist that his position be heard; finally, to resign in protest if he could not, in true faith and allegiance, carry out his orders—these were his options, of Constitution and of conscience. But MacArthur had no right to challenge frontally the authority of his commander in chief.

At the same time, *total* obedience is not owed by any soldier to any politician (or even to a commanding officer). Though soldiers are not free to substitute their own version of the Constitution for the political decisions made by democratically elected officials, neither are soldiers free, in good conscience, merely to accept unthinkingly the military and geopolitical decisions of their superiors. The doctrine of *respondeat superior* ("Let my boss answer because I was just following orders, so I'm 'off the hook'"), which we will explore later, was struck down by the war crimes trials after World War II. Even generals are not free simply to say, "I was just following orders."

Obedience to personal constitutional interpretation will not do. Total obedience to political leaders will not do, either. "True faith and allegiance," then, depend upon well-formed conscience. The danger in the notion, heard even during the Gulf War of 1991, that once wars start the politicians should get out of the way was once realistically assessed this way, *by a soldier*, General Ridgway: "The persistent contention by some of our own private citizens as well as military men that wars, once started, should be shaped and conducted solely by the military indicates that, improbable as it now may seem, and incompatible as it is with our whole way of life, military dominance over our affairs 'could happen here.'"[12] MacArthur was certainly not planning a coup d'état. But the late Samuel Eliot Morison, a distinguished American historian, said of MacArthur: "He never crossed the Rubicon, to be sure, but his horse's front hoofs were in the water."[13] Forty years after MacArthur's insistence that it was up to him to read the Constitution his way, another officer—this time a Marine lieutenant colonel—would make a very similar claim.

Twenty years after MacArthur was relieved, there was a spectacular (in the sense of "spectacle") military trial involving Lt. William L. Calley, Jr., accused (and subsequently convicted) of the murders of unarmed and unresisting inhabitants of the Vietnamese village of My Lai. Calley argued that he was merely following the orders of his chain of command in slaughtering the men, women, and children of that rural hamlet; he was simply doing his duty. An improbable mix of Americans on the left of the political spectrum (arguing that Calley was just a scapegoat for a rotten capitalist system) and on the right (insisting that Calley was just a clean-cut American hero with a silver bar on his shoulder) seemed to agree that Calley should be released. After Calley's conviction, President Nixon personally intervened to lessen his sentence. An anguished Capt. Aubrey Daniel III, Calley's prosecutor, protested Nixon's action, saying that he was "shocked and dismayed at the reaction of many people across the nation . . . [who] undoubtedly viewed . . . Calley's conviction simply as the conviction of an American officer for killing the enemy. Others . . . have seized upon the conviction as a means of protesting the war in Vietnam." He added, "For this nation to condone the acts of Lieutenant Calley is to make us no better than our enemies and make any pleas by this nation for the humane treatment of our own prisoners meaningless."[14]

In response to Calley's argument that he was merely following orders and killing enemies, one of the members of the jury said that there has to be a "higher law" to which soldiers must be responsible: "There are some things that a man of common understanding and common sense would know are wrong."[15] We return once more to the bedrock notion of military ethics that there are some things so shame that we can understand them without much effort and that there are also certain "rules" that have come down from the centuries which help us distinguish between honor and shame. Mass murders committed against unarmed and unresisting men, women, and children cannot be explained away by invoking the defense of *respondeat superior* or by claiming that those slaughtered were enemies. There is a higher loyalty, available to reasonable human beings.

The "Semper Fidelis" Corollary

Forty years after MacArthur's arguments that his first loyalty would be to his reading of the Constitution and of the national interest and not to the temporary occupant of the White House, another military officer, Marine Lt. Col. Oliver North, wrote, "I never saw myself as being above the law, nor did I ever intend to do anything illegal."[16] But Congress had passed laws in 1982 and 1984, the Boland Amendments, which had forbidden American aid to the Contras, who were fighting to topple the Sandinista regime in Nicaragua. A number of people in the Reagan administration—apparently including CIA Director William Casey—believed that continued aid should be given to the Contras. North conducted covert operations from the National Security Council with the approval of Vice Admiral John Poindexter, U.S.N., the assistant to the president for national security affairs. American arms were shipped to Iran, funds from which were diverted to the Contras. As one group of analysts explained, "Although this involvement of North and Poindexter was an isolated incident, their influence on U.S. policy toward Iran and the contras was so extensive that at least one senator argued that 'in effect there was a junta within the government of the United States.'"[17]

North later admitted that, in testimony before the Congress, he had lied under oath. "Congress is to blame," he said, "because of fickle, vacillating, unpredictable, on-again, off-again policy" toward the Contras.[18] North claimed, "Until Congress resumed its funding for the Contras, we fulfilled the mission assigned by the President: to keep the [Contra] resistance alive." He argued that the Boland amendments were not meant to abandon the Contras. North was eventually acquitted of nine counts but found guilty of three, including helping to obstruct Congress and tampering with documents.[19] His loyalty had been to his conception of the national interest. Forty years before North's book *Under Fire* appeared in 1991, General MacArthur had determined that the government's policies were mistaken. In the American system of government, national policies are not dictated by generals—or by lieutenant colonels. Yet after MacArthur's relief from command in 1951, during Calley's trial in 1971, and again during North's trial, there was public outpouring of sympathy for these military men—*for very different reasons and for three very different officers and human beings.* But the lesson is that the American public, viewing the military as a model of patriotism (and often for good and substantial reason), is sometimes unable to sort out quickly the emotional facts bearing upon seemingly difficult cases. The American public—with the exception of a radical leftist fringe—retains strong loyalty to its soldiers, sailors, airmen and women, and marines (if not always to the U.S. Army, Navy, Air Force, and Marine Corps).

The military's task is always to return that loyalty to the American public by being "always faithful" to the legitimate orders it receives. The difficult case of Marine guards at the U.S. embassy in Moscow from 1985 to 1986, who allegedly were recruited as spies after sexual encounters with Soviet women, illustrates the problem. The charges were that these Marines—as well as numerous other spies (such as Jonathan Jay Pollard and the Walker family)—had lost their ethical compasses. How could that happen? Former CIA analyst George Carver, Jr., had it exactly right: "The real problem is that we're feeling, as a country, the corrosive effects of 20 years and more of situational ethics. We've lost the sense of 'off-limits'—that there are things you simply don't do, principles that aren't subject to analysis by deconstructionists at the Harvard Law School. One of them is that you don't betray your country."[20]

If loyalty is to "me first," the timeless notion of obligation appears. As military sociologist Charles Moskos said about the Marine spy scandal, "There's no real institutional center, either in the military, or in the country, telling people what's right and wrong, and enforcing it."[21] If there is no sense of obligation, there is no sense of honor and shame; without a sense of honor and shame, the idea of treason disappears. All that matters then is loyalty to self.

By naming this problem the "Semper Fidelis corollary" to the loyalty dilemma, I do not mean for a moment to malign the Marine Corps, whose well-known and highly honored motto that is. The question is, who receives the highest loyalty? An old Marine saying is that a Marine on guard duty has no friends—or lovers. The wisdom of that adage was apparently forgotten in Moscow a few years ago.

The "Boss Is Always Right" Corollary

If the President of the United States is not always right, then we can safely assume that your boss—even your professor—is not always right. Loyalty to one's boss is a prized and worthy thing. But it can become an evil and a danger, as Kermit Johnson put it, "when a genuine, wholesome loyalty to the boss degenerates into covering up for him, hiding things from him, or not differing from him when he is wrong."[22] Johnson paraphrases Gen. David M. Shoup, a former Marine Corps commandant (1960-63) who said that he didn't want a "yes man" on his staff because all he could give back to the general was what he already knew.[23]

We use unpleasant words such as *obsequious, servile, sycophantic, fawning, groveling* to describe this attitude of subordinates toward superiors. Granted, no person of sense wants to court problems with a boss. If loyalty means anything, however, it is something well beyond self-serving behavior or craven cowering. The boss deserves better, and a mature and upright boss will not only want honesty but demand it. On the other hand, there may be times when a subordinate's attitude can be spiteful and malicious. As an obsequious demeanor cannot be tolerated, neither can a rancorous one. For example, at a banquet in the Netherlands on 24 May 1993, Air Force Maj. Gen. Harold N. Campbell referred to President Clinton as "dope smoking," "skirt chasing," and "draft dodging." He was soon fined $7,000, reprimanded, and retired. Air Force Chief of Staff Gen. M.A. McPeak said of the Campbell incident, "This is not a trivial matter," because the chain of command "has to be almost pollution free. It runs from the President all the way down to the corporal who pulls the trigger."[24] Campbell had violated Article 88 of the Uniform Code of Military Justice, which forbids "contemptuous words against the President" and other governmental officers. For his public denunciations of the commander in chief, Campbell could have faced a court-martial.

"Loyalty" was defined early in the twentieth century as "the willing and practical and thoroughgoing devotion of a person to a cause."[25] The cause to which one is devoted clearly should be one beyond the limits of one's own skin—and a certain amount of reason is always called for. Loyalty is one manifestation of integrity, and integrity involves neither timidity nor stupidity. Sidney Axinn, for example, tells the story of Hachiko, the loyal dog, who used to walk with his master to the train station every day and came back to meet him in the evening. In 1925 the master died while away from home, and Hachiko, subsisting on handouts, waited at the station for ten years for his master. After the loyal dog died, a statue was erected to him.[26] Such extreme "faith and allegiance," given by a human, would be regarded as a symptom of mental illness, not as loyalty.

Loyalty to constitutional principles, loyalty to a government, loyalty to a service, loyalty to a boss—all these depend for their beginning and their end upon a well-formed conscience. With out that conscience, "true faith and allegiance"—that is, genuine loyalty—is not possible. But there will always be great anxiety—*anguish* may not be too strong a word—in forming, or dissolving, the bonds of loyalty.

"I Pledge Allegiance . . ."

The bonding of men and women in a loyal confraternity of commissioned violence leads to a sense of fellowship that, in the words of philosopher Manuel Davenport, "is almost inherently anti-civilian" and that "has an addictive effect upon the normally intoxicating influences of possessing the ultimate powers of destruction."[27] MacArthur and North, for very different reasons, objected to allowing the president or the Congress to make policy. Yet, as Professor Davenport points out, "duty to client [that is, our country] must take priority over duty to the profession, and in this nation we recognize this by the principle of civilian control of the military."[28] No stronger principle of American civil-military relations exists than this: In the United States, the professional military is wholly subsidiary to the civilians elected to high office in our republic.[29] Despite fiction and fantasy, there is no real prospect of a military takeover in this country.[30] (If anything, the greater danger for the past thirty years is the civilianization of the military arm.)

To understand civil-military relations in the United States, one has to develop a clear picture of the basic organizational concept behind the US. government. Dissenting in the case of *Myers v. United States* (1926), Justice Louis Brandeis wrote that "the doctrine of the *separation of powers* [emphasis added] was adopted by the Convention of 1787, not to promote efficiency but to preclude the exercise of arbitrary power. The purpose was, not to avoid friction, but, by means of the inevitable friction incident to the distribution of the governmental powers among three departments, to save the people from autocracy."[31] The division of political power—*horizontally* among the executive, legislative, and judicial branches; *vertically* between the national government and the individual states— deliberately complicated the processes of decision-making in the United States in order to thwart tyranny. Since 1787, the system has worked.

A basic question for soldiers has always been, which branch receives my first loyalty? According to the Constitution, Congress (legislative branch) has the responsibility of declaring war,[32] of raising armies (that is, imposing a draft or conscription), of maintaining a navy, and of establishing rules for military regulation (Article I section 8). But the president is commander in chief of all armed forces (Article II, section 2). As Army Gen. J. Lawton Collins once said, "As a military man my Commander in Chief is the President of the United States. My loyalty is therefore to him."[33] But General Ridgway, a brave soldier who rarely complained about the enemy, did complain that, when he was Army chief of staff, the executive branch pushed him hard to tell Congress its position: "The pressure brought upon me to make my military judgment conform to the views of higher authority was sometimes subtly, sometimes crudely, applied."[34] And during the Gulf War of 1991, Air Force Chief of Staff Gen. Michael Dugan was summarily fired by Secretary of Defense Dick Cheney after Dugan made some observations clearly out of step with Bush administration policies.[35] In fact, Dugan was the first chief of staff to be fired since Admiral Louis Denfield was fired by the Truman administration in 1949, and the highest-ranking officer to be fired since MacArthur. So the relationships between the highest ranking officers of the US. military and the executive branch are not—nor should they be—entirely settled and secure.

The president of the United States as the chief executive is constitutionally responsible for "tak[ing] care that the laws be faithfully executed" (Article II, section 3) and is sworn to "preserve, protect, and defend the Constitution of the United States" (Article II, section 1). That means that the president is not free to devise policy wholly independent of congressional wishes. As long ago as 1956, one scholar said that "if Congress is to have the information from which debate flows and policy is resolved, the military must be allowed, and indeed encouraged, to speak freely."[36]

Civilian control of the military does not mean that there will be no tension between a fundamentally liberal American society and a basically conservative American military.[37] Samuel Huntington, for instance, has discussed two general approaches to the civilian control of the military in the United States. The first is "subjective control," by which he means an increase of civilian control to the point even of virtually civilianizing the military. "Objective control," by contrast, recognizes the particular expertise and professionalism of the military.[38] In essence, civilian control of the military is built upon two pillars. First, civilians determine the ends of the government, particularly in the area of national security policy; the military is limited to discussions about the *means* to achieve those ends. Second, the civilian leadership decides where the lines are drawn between ends and means, between civilian and military responsibilities.[39]

In the United States, the president, the secretary of defense, the secretaries of the army, navy, air force, and transportation (in the case of the Coast Guard) are civilians, whereas the chiefs of the uniformed services are professional military officers. This can lead to confrontation and controversy of course.[40] But there is not a single episode in twentieth-century American history of any American soldier challenging the *principle* of civilian control.[41] (There are, however, plenty of examples of soldiers challenging particular applications of that principle.) In an effort not only to reduce interservice rivalry,[42] but to strengthen the Joint Chiefs of Staff, Congress in 1986 passed the Defense Reorganization (Goldwater-Nichols) Act of 1986. The new law substantially increased the power of the chairman of the Joint Chiefs, who was established as the "principal military advisor to the President, the National Security Council, and the Secretary of Defense." There have been few challenges to the wisdom of that law.[43]

The American military thus works for our elected and appointed civilian leaders. The principle of civilian control is sacrosanct, whatever the occasional bewilderment owing to the concept of separation of powers. Constitutionally, the Supreme Court in the United States (the judicial branch) has the responsibility of judging the meaning of the Constitution. Although the courts generally play a small role in civil-military affairs, one thought runs like a red thread through the fabric of American civil-military relations: the subordinate sovereignty of the U.S. military.

If there is anxiety about ethics in the military, there is a similar kind of tension about politics in the military. The courts have generally supported "objective control of the military," contending, in essence, that the U.S. military, though of course subordinate to the civil authority, nonetheless, retains its own character and its own unique tasks. Two examples from 1974 will do. The Supreme Court, speaking through Justice Lewis Powell and citing precedents, contended:

> The military is "a specialized society separate from civilian society" with "laws and traditions of its own [developed] during its long history." *Parker v. Levy*, 417 US., at 743. Moreover, "it is the primary business of armies and navies to fight or be ready to fight wars should the occasion arise." *Toth v. Quarles*, 350 US. 11, 17 (1955). To prepare for and perform its vital role, the military must insist upon a respect for duty and a discipline without counterpart in civilian life. The laws and

traditions governing that discipline have a long history; but they are founded on unique military exigencies as powerful now as in the past. Their contemporary vitality repeatedly has been recognized by Congress.[44]

And Justice William Rehnquist, now Chief Justice, put it this way:

This [Supreme] Court has long recognized that the military is, by necessity, a specialized society separate from civilian society . . .

While the members of the military are not excluded from the protection granted by the First Amendment, the different character of the military community and of the military mission requires a different application of those protections. The fundamental necessity for obedience, and the consequent necessity for imposition of discipline, may render permissible within the military that which would be constitutionally impermissible outside it.[45]

The military's unique duties thus endow it with distinctive obligations and with a kind of "sovereign subordination" to the civilian government of which it is a distinctive part. Almost forty years ago, Huntington asked, "Is it possible to deny that the military values—loyalty, duty, restraint, dedication—are the ones America needs most today?"[46] A thesis of this book is that it is *not* possible to deny the need in our society today for those values, that we might resurrect the eagle.

Conclusions

The principal task of the military is to maintain true faith and allegiance to the republic by preparing to kill or die in its defense. While that statement appears to be severe, the central purpose of the military is to be an *armed force*.

This special purpose can lead to the "Loyalty Dilemma": soldiers' responsibility to be true to friends but not to the point of betraying professional duty; to be devoted to their chain of command and immediate superiors but not to the point of behaving obsequiously or illegally; to be faithful to the Constitution but not to the point of confusing their own political goals with those of elected leaders. Military recognition of the supremacy of constituted civilian authority is a chief principle of U.S. civil-military relations; civilian control of the military should always be coupled with a respect for the unique character of the armed services.

Army Values and American Values

by Peter Maslowski

The author, Professor Peter Maslowski, spent the 1986-1987 academic year as the Morrison Professor on the faculty of the US Army Command and General Staff College. In this article, Maslowski discusses a disparity, found during his many seminars and numerous exchanges with the Army majors who made up the student body, between those values held by the military and those that have evolved as America's societal values.

Values are the bedrock of our profession. (Former) Secretary of the Army John O. Marsh Jr.

Following the practice established in 1981 of annually choosing an important theme for the Army, in 1985 Secretary of the Army John O. Marsh Jr., and Chief of Staff John A Wickham Jr., announced that "Values" would be the theme for 1986. In "White Paper 1986: Values," Marsh set forth a two-tier concept of values, the first encompassing "universal values that are common to all soldiers in any era, in any army, and in any country," and the second dealing with broader national values that explain "why the American soldier is unique."[1]

Among the first-tier values were discipline, stamina, skill, loyalty, duty, courage, selfless service, integrity and commitment. Some of these might be considered *traits* rather than *values*, but whether trait or value, each received explicit definition and discussion. By contrast, the second-tier values received scant attention. Only one paragraph *mentioned*, but did not discuss, the sources of these values (Judeo-

Source: *Military Review* (April, 1990): 10-23. Reprinted by permission of Military Review.

Christian religious base, Magna Carta, Declaration of Independence and Constitution). Nor did it discuss several other of these values (trial by jury, free expertise of religion, civilian control of the military and procedural safeguards of law).

Since Marsh designated the Constitution as the Army's theme for 1987, the late 1980s became a propitious time to focus more fully on these broader national values. Indeed, because of some of the Army values enunciated in the "White Paper: 1986" collide with the ideology that prevails among the overwhelming majority of American citizens who are not professional soldiers, this task takes on a special significance as we embark on a new decade.

> *Even where there is a necessity of the military power, within the land, which by the way but rarely happens, a wise and prudent people will always have a watchful and a jealous eye over it: for the maxims and rules of the army, are essentially different from the genius of a free people, and the laws of a free government.*
> Samuel Adams[2]

Professional soldiers acquire their unique traits and values only through years of specialized education and training. Once acquired, they become the foundation for the distinctive patterns of thought and behavior that are at the heart of the professional military ethic. For good reasons, the Army emphasizes loyalty, discipline, obedience and the good of the group over that of any particular individual. Concerning this last value, Marsh emphasized that a professional soldier must put "the welfare of the Nation and the accomplishment of the assigned mission before individual welfare. All who serve the Nation must resist the temptation to pursue self-gain, personal advantage, and self-interest ahead of the collective good."[3] From the perspective of the military professional's internal logic, these attributes are impeccably correct. Working closely for many years with other professional soldiers who share these values, many officers assume, perhaps unconsciously, that these are the *only* worthy values.

No more profound misconception could pervade the officer corps. Within the nation as a whole, the traits that officers consider the highest virtues are often at variance with broader social values, which are embodied in the Declaration of Independence and the Constitution. During the colonial era, the colonists had developed a new identity as Americans. Founded and settled by peoples of differing ethnicity, religion, economic status and traditions, the emergence of *any* cohesiveness among the British North American colonies was rather astonishing. Despite the absence of those factors that normally serve as the basis for a national identity, as the crisis with the mother country worsened after 1765, it became evident that a common ideology bound most colonists together.[4] Two closely related elements in this ideology were an emphasis on the "natural rights" of mankind, rather than simply on the rights of Englishmen, and a desire to expand individual freedom by restraining the arbitrary power of government.

The emphasis on natural rights found consummate expression in the Declaration of Independence with its dramatic assertion that "all men" enjoyed "certain unalienable Rights, that among these are Life, Liberty and the pursuit of Happiness." The phrase "pursuit of Happiness" sounds nebulous, but in the late 18th century, it had a concrete connotation. John Locke's *Second Treatise on Government*, which profoundly influenced the Founding Fathers, listed three inherent rights: life, liberty and property. Why Thomas Jefferson, who drafted the declaration, substituted "pursuit of Happiness" for property remains unclear, but the phrase and the word meant the same thing. To people of Jefferson's era, the pursuit and security of property was a basic right, essential to individual liberty.[5]

The Constitution wrestled with the difficult problem of providing maximum national cohesion consistent with minimal coercion of the individual (and the states). The Founding Fathers believed that power was a corrupting influence, that rulers always sought to aggrandize their power at the expense of the people's liberty. On the other hand, they knew that liberty could degenerate into licentiousness. Could a government be created that would have sufficient power to prevent anarchy, yet would not invest so much power in one person, or a relatively small group of people, that it would become tyrannical? The framers of the Constitution believed they could. Their solution to the puzzle of preserving liberty while avoiding anarchy was to devise a governmental structure that diffused power widely: between the states and the federal government; among the latter's three branches; and within two houses of the legislative branch. Thus, although the Constitution contained only a few explicit provisions (such as those prohibiting ex post facto laws and bills of attainder) that protected individuals from despotic government actions, the Founding Fathers believed that liberty was secure because the "atomization of authority" resulting from the system of checks and balances and the separation of powers would always frustrate a ruler's natural and insatiable lust for power.[6]

Despite the Founding Father's arguments in behalf of their handiwork crafted at Philadelphia in the summer of 1787, many citizens (collectively known as the Antifederalists) believed the document did not adequately safeguard personal liberty. They demanded that the Constitution contain a Bill of Rights—an explicit statement of individual liberties— to shield individuals from potential government oppression. So widespread was this sentiment that in a few crucial states, ratification of the Constitution occurred only after the Federalists promised to add a Bill of Rights as amendments.

To fulfill the pledge, Congressman (and future president) James Madison considered 210 amendments that had been submitted to Congress and reduced the number to 19. Congress pared the number still further to 12 and submitted them to the states for ratification. The states approved 10, which became part of the

Constitution in 1791. Although each amendment hedged the federal government's power, the one that has been most vital in preserving individual liberty is the First Amendment, which protects freedom of religion, speech, press and assembly.[7]

Within the First Amendment guarantees, the freedom of the press warrants particular attention. Believing that speaking and writing, privately and publicly, without fear were prerequisites for all other liberties, the Founding Fathers included in the supreme law of the land the principle that "Congress shall make no law" abridging freedom of speech or of the press.

By the mid-18th century, most Americans recognized the virtues of an unfettered press. As the Continental Congress declared in 1774, the significance of a free press lay not just in its "advancement of truth, science, morality, and arts in general," but also "in its diffusion of liberal sentiments on the administration of Government, its ready communication of thoughts between subjects, and its consequential promotion of union among them, whereby oppressive officials are shamed or intimidated, into more honourable and just modes of conducting affairs."[8] In essence, the Revolutionary generation viewed the press as an unofficial fourth branch of the government, one that was especially well suited to expose misdeeds by the other three branches. As such, the press was as vital as the executive, legislature and judiciary in the system of checks and balances. Thus, although the British common-law practice regarding freedom of the press prevailed in theory during the colonial era, Americans rarely enforced it. British practice prohibited prior restraint, but permitted punishment after the fact for seditious libel, which was malicious, scurrilous or false condemnation of the government.[9]

As rival political parties formed during the1790s, the highly partisan newspapers of the Federalists and Jeffersonians bristled with ill-tempered, intemperate denunciations of their respective political opposition. The scathing invective hurled at opponents by the early republic's obstreperous newspapers reached a new level of raging fury during the quasi-war with France in 1798. Driven by a mixture of fear and hate, the pro-British Federalists enacted a sedition act the embodied the seditious libel concept and determined to enforce it. In response, the pro-French Jeffersonians specifically repudiated the concept. They argued that a law inflicting punishment after publication had the same deadening affect on free political discussion as prior restraint and that *all* political discussion should be exempt from any legal restrictions.

In the long run, the Jeffersonian argument in behalf of a free press prevailed. After 1800, the idea became increasingly entrenched that dissent—even if seemingly pernicious, impertinent and vile—did not equate with disloyalty. No matter how severe the provocation, suppression ws a worse evil than toleration. As Jefferson declared in his first inaugural address, "If there be any among us who would wish to dissolve this Union or to change its republican form, let them stand undisturbed as monuments of the safety with which error of opinion may be tolerated where reason is left free to combat it." Or, in the words of Alexis de Tocqueville, that astute Frenchman who visited the United States in 1831–1832, in a country "where doctrine of the sovereignty of the people ostensibly prevails, the censorship of the press is not only dangerous, but absurd."[10]

But freedom of the press has never been as unfettered in fact as civil libertarians have advocated from Jefferson's day to the present. The Constitution stated a comprehensive principle—the First Amendment contains no ifs, ands or buts to dilute its injunction that Congress shall make "*no* law" abridging freedom of the press. But, in practice, the amendment has been subject to varying interpretations. Generally, it has been construed to mean that the freedoms of speech and press must be exercised responsibly. No one has the right to falsely shout "Fire!" in a crowded theater and thereby cause a panic that might result in death or injury. Moreover, Congress and the courts have tried to balance community concerns, such as public safety and pornography, against individual rights. And in some wars, criminal prosecution to curtail free speech and press has been implemented. For the government to feel secure in suspending constitutional liberties, the war must be judged absolutely necessary by a large majority of citizens, which means the threat must be perceived as direct, immediate and unambiguous. Such a situation occurred noticeably during the Civil War and the world wars, but only in World War II was the policy accepted virtually without dissent.[11]

While acknowledging the necessity for occasional wartime infringements when national survival is at stake, most citizens would, in the abstract, agree with the ideal state by the Supreme Court in the late 1860s. "The Constitution of the United States is a law for rulers and people, equally in war and peace, and covers with the shield of protection all classes of men, at all times and under all circumstances," the Court decreed in a case involving one of the Lincoln administration's many wartime abuses of civil liberty. "No doctrine involving more pernicious consequences was ever invented by the wit of man than that any of its great provisions can be suspended during any of the great exigencies of Government."[12] Even in national emergencies people have good reason to regard suspension of any civil liberties with suspicion. In other countries, at other times, liberties "temporarily" suspended during an emergency have had a disconcerting habit of becoming permanently lost.

By the early 19th century, then, the lineaments of the characteristic values of American society were well established. Three words that best encapsulate society's closely interrelated values are capitalistic, unrestrained, individualistic. Contrast these with military values! Instead of the selfless sacrifice and denial of "self-gain, personal advantage, and self-interest" called for by Marsh, civilians appear selfish as they pursue happiness through the accumulation of private wealth. From the military perspective, this seemingly greedy materialism (or as one general phrased it, this "sordid commercialism"), with its emphasis on personal aggrandizement even at the expense of the responsibilities of good citizenship, threatens to leave the nation wealthy but weak.[13]

During the colonial era, the traditional restraints on individual behavior, such as the state, established religion and hereditary class hierarchy, either disappeared or diminished greatly.[14] And government established under the Constitution ensured that these constraints would never be reimposed. Thus, instead of the hierarchical orderliness of military life, civilian society is decidedly unregimented. General George Washington recognized this gulf between civil and military life. "Men accustomed to unbounded freedom, and no controul," he wrote, "cannot brook the Restraint which is indispensably necessary to the good order and Government of an Army; without which, licentiousness, and every kind of disorder triumphantly reign. To bring Men to a proper degree of Subordination, is not the work of a day, a Month or even a year..."[15]

In an essay titled, "Self-Reliance," the mid-19th century transcendentalist Ralph Waldo Emerson wrote that he hoped "in these days we have heard the last of conformity and consistency. Let the words be gazetted and ridiculous henceforward."[16] Conformity and consistency, obedience and loyalty, represent the heart of military discipline; within military organizations they can never be ridiculous. But in the civilian realm, they represent the abnegation of conscience and reason, of the individual dignity and self-determination that is central to democracy. The Army's chain-of-command system has a structure and symmetry altogether lacking in civil society, which, by comparison, is hyperactive and in constant disarray. Yet, despite the rampant individualism—the lack of conformity and consistency—by and large the society functions so successfully that it remains the envy of most of the world. The genius of the American people is that they have created a cacophonous harmony in their national affairs.

How important are these social values that comprise "the American way of life?" NSC-68, one of the seminal state papers of the post-World War II era, considered them essential and discussed them at length.[17] It recognized that military power served not only to deter an attack, but also to fight, if necessary, to preserve American lives and property *and* "to defend the integrity and vitality of our free society"—that is, to protect "the system of values which animates our society—the principles of freedom, tolerance, the importance of the individual and the supremacy of reason over will."

NSC-68 argued that American values were a tremendous strength. They gave the United States "a unique degree of unity. Our society is fundamentally more cohesive than the Soviet system, the solidarity of which is artificially created through force, fear and favor." The document warned against those who "would seek to defend the United States by creating a regimented system" since this would corrupt national morale and subvert "the integrity and vitality of our system." Indeed, said NSC-68, "It is only by a practical affirmation, abroad as well as at home, of our essential values, that we can preserve our own integrity, in which lies the real frustration of the Kremlin design."

Professional officers thus have the intimidating task of internalizing two sets of values that, in their fundamental aspects, can be contradictory. Can they be good soldiers and still be good Americans? Can they be good Americans and still be good soldiers? The nation's safety from external foes, and from domestic militarization that would undermine the American way of life, depends on the answer.

Unfortunately, many mid-career officers have apparently mastered military values, but have little appreciation of broader societal values. For example, the majors who attended the US Army Command and General Staff College (CGSC) in 1986-1987 exhibited an almost unanimous collective contempt toward civilians who, of course, exemplify national values but do not, in the ordinary course of events, typify military values. With distressing regularity, the majors denigrated ordinary civilians as "stupid," displayed a genuine viciousness toward the press and heaped opprobrium upon Congress in particular and "politicians" in general.[18] Would men and women who understood American values and the workings of a democracy hold such beliefs?

> *Since war is not an act of senseless passion but is controlled by its political object, the value of this object must determine the sacrifices to be made for it in magnitude and also in duration. Once the expenditure of effort exceeds the value of the political object, the object must be renounced and peace must follow.*
>
> Carl von Clausewitz [19]

Compounding the majors' inadequate understanding of national values was their insufficient knowledge of military history. These two deficiencies merged and became evident whenever the subject of the Vietnam War arose.

Michael Howard, an eminent British military historian, insisted that officers must study military history in width, depth and context to minimize the risks that arise when using history for didactic purposes. By width, he meant the study of military history throughout the ages; by depth, the thorough investigation of a single campaign to try to understand "what war is really like"; and by context, the necessity to understand not just the armed forces of societies at war, but also the societies themselves. "The roots of victory and defeat often have to be sought far from the battlefield," he wrote, "in political, social and economic factors which explain why armies are constituted as they are, and why their leaders conduct them in the way they do."[20]

Many of the students at the CGSGC violated all of Howard's maxims. Few of them had even a rudimentary understanding of American much less of European, Asian or African, military history. Fewer still had an in-depth knowledge of any campaigns, beyond the simple (and simplistic) creed that in Vietnam "we won all the battles," a questionable assertation that depends on the definition of "won" and battles." And virtually none demonstrated any insights into the war's societal context except to note, with a disdainful glare, that Vietnam generated opposition on the home front.

Perhaps the students' ignorance of military history is not surprising. Howard's insights, after all, come from a lifetime devoted to the subject. But professional officers rising to the rank of major have little time for reading and reflection, because mastering their craft's technical intricacies is a full-time job. Recognizing the students' weakness in military history, the CGSC offered a superb course on 20th century US military. The CGSC's Combat Studies Institute taught the course and assigned, among other books, General Bruce Palmer Jr.'s *The 25-Year War: America's Military Role in Vietnam*, one of the most important books written about Vietnam.[21]

I participated in four iterations of this course and had the same experience each time. During the discussions from World War I through the Korean War, most students demonstrated a willingness to probe to question, to understand what had happened with an open, inquiring attitude that was exemplary. With a critical (yet empathetic) eye, students identified errors in training, tactics, logistics and even strategy. The students' examination of the armed services' mistakes in World War I, World War II and Korea, and their efforts to draw lessons from those mistakes, repeatedly elicited classroom exchanges worthy of the country's best history graduate student seminars.

But when the classes got to Vietnam, it became obvious that discovering military errors in past victorious wars (Korea looks more and more like a victory since the United States now knows what a genuine defeat is), was entirely different from admitting errors in a recent, clear-cut defeat.

If the students read Palmer's book, the vast majority of them surely did not *understand* it. When classes discussed Vietnam, an iron curtain of preconceived notions slammed down. The students believed they already *knew* what caused defeat: yellow-streaked politicians, irresponsible journalism and the collapse of home front morale. A twinge of truth adheres to each of these causes. Historians will never confuse Lyndon B. Johnson with Franklin D. Roosevelt; at times the press did not perform as responsibly as it should have, if we lived in either a perfect world or a totalitarian regime; by early 1968, home front dissent against the war had escalated to epidemic proportions. But as Palmer points out in painful detail that the students invariably ignored, along with the politicians, press and people, two other elements share responsibility for American defeat: the Armed Forces of the United States and the enemy. As usual in an unsuccessful war, there is plenty of blame to spread around.

A careful reading of Palmer's book reveals a large number of mistakes made by the Armed Forces that had little to do with political constraints, critical press clippings or citizens exercising First Amendment rights. For instance, the Joint Chiefs of Staff (JCS) failed to inform the president or secretary of defense that the strategy being pursued would probably fail, and the JCS gave the president "unanimous" advice even when they were, in fact, divided on key issues. Since the military failed to understand the war's true nature. General William C. Westmoreland employed a faulty strategy emphasizing the "big unit" war instead of Vietnamization, which Palmer believes should have always been the military's top priority. Excessive reliance on firepower and helicopters had many adverse ramifications; intelligence and counter-intelligence efforts were dismally inefficient; the logistics system was a shambles; and the command system was unnecessarily cumbersome. The Army conceded the night to the enemy, used an unwise one-year rotation system for career officers and noncommissioned officers, and fought with a fatal arrogance, embodied in the "can-do" attitude. Self-confidence had become self-worship, and as a result, the United States underestimated both the Vietcong and the North Vietnamese army.

Despite his candor in analyzing the *military's* mistakes (most of them egregious), Palmer cannot bring himself to pronounce the judgment that logically follows from his analysis. After specifically referring to a number of these problems, he asks "whether any significant improvements in US performance would have made any difference in the outcome," and concludes that the answer is "probably 'no.' The war was lost primarily at the strategic, diplomatic, and domestic political levels…" The difficulties with this conclusion are threefold. First, he hedges by using the word "probably"; the answer might just as reasonably be "probably 'yes.'" Second, his statement assumes that ineffective military performance had no impact on the strategic, diplomatic and domestic political levels, which is illogical. Third, he undermines his conclusion by admitting that "American military professionals have much to learn from the tragic experience of Vietnam, because heeding those lessons *could mean the difference between winning and losing in a future conflict.*"[22]

Aside from their unwillingness to confront Palmer's candor—to *think* about the war rather than rely on tired clichés—the students made three unwarranted assumptions when discussing Vietnam. First, they assumed that if only the restraints had been taken off, the United States would have won. This is one possible outcome, but two other effects were possible. It might have made no difference in the outcome, but only created a stalemate at a higher level of violence, because North Vietnam's "will to persist was inextinguishable," according to Palmer. Or it might have made the situation *much worse* by involving new belligerents, particularly China. "One cannot quarrel with the decision not to invade North Vietnam," writes Palmer, "because it was too close to China; our experience in misjudging the Chinese intervention in Korea was still fresh in our memory."[23] But because the Chinese did not intervene, the students argued that they never would have no matter what the United States did. Neither the JCS nor the political leadership could afford to make such a leap of faith.[24]

From the assumption that fighting an unlimited war could have yielded victory came the second assumption: winning was worth any price. But this assertion contradicts the Clausewitzian concept that *"war is only a branch of political activity; that it is in no sense autonomous."* Therefore, "wars must vary with the nature of their motives and of the situations which gave rise to them."[25] Wars vital to national survival demand extreme exertion. Like World War II, they will be large and long. Since these wars are, in many ways, simpler to fight than limited wars, the Armed Forces seem to prefer them.[26] But what about a war like Vietnam, which, as Palmer admits, was "not vital"?[27] Were limited, nonvital goals in Southeast Asia worth an unlimited commitment that would possibly impair the economy and endanger more vital international obligations such as those in Europe or Korea?

Finally, the failure to prevail in Vietnam, students declared, was further proof that a democracy cannot fight a long war. What does "long" mean? The United States fought from 1775–1783 in the Revolution; from 1861–1865 in the Civil War; and from 1964–1973 in Vietnam. These seem reasonably long. Should the United States have fought on against Britain in 1815; Mexico in 1848; Spain in 1898; the Philippines in 1902; and China in 1953, when it had already achieved its war aims? Should it have battled on against Germany after November 1918 even though an armistice had been declared? Whose fault was it that all US enemies had surrendered by September 1945? In other words, the democratic United States like other systems of government, has fought long wars or short wars, all-out wars or limited wars, depending on the political motives animating them and the correlation between the importance of the policy objectives and the sacrifices necessary to obtain them.

> *It is true that you may fool all the people some of the time; you can even fool some of the people all the time; but you can't fool all of the people all the time.*
> Abraham Lincoln[28]

What is the nature of "the people"? No definitive response is possible since the answer is a matter of perceptions, not literal truth. Jefferson's view of mankind was optimistic. He believed humans had an innate sense of right and wrong, much like the sense of hearing or sight. With their instinctive wisdom and good sense, the people could be trusted to govern themselves with minimum coercion.[29] Many Federalists were more pessimistic, believing that instinctive public virtue was a scarce commodity compared to greed, ambition and immorality. Good government depended upon an elite composed of the well-born and well-educated who could make correct decisions for the people.[30]

The majors who attend CGSC in 1986–1987, with their widespread disdain for civilians, adhered more closely to the Federalist than the Jeffersonian perspective. Undoubtedly, some civilians are, as so many majors said, stupid—perhaps even a few Army officers fall into that category. But does the blanket assertion that "civilians are stupid" make sense? Civilians include doctors, lawyers, corporate managers, teachers, ministers and so on, all of whom are as well educated as the the majors.

When they denounce everyone else in the country but themselves, professional soldiers may mean that most civilians have little understanding of the military profession's specialized technical knowledge, rituals, insignia and language. To that charge, most civilians would plead guilty. Few of the men and women in the Congress today have been professional soldiers, and thus do not have much expertise in technical military matters that take years of study and experience to master. On the other hand, few professional soldiers have experience as politicians and, apparently, have little appreciation for the political process in a democratic society.

What, exactly, do the majors so despise about the people's elected representatives?

First, Congress never seems to attach sufficient importance to military affairs. With their specialized perspective on the world, Army officers suffer from monomania when it comes to defense. With a single-mindedness akin to Captain Ahab pursuing Moby Dick, they insist on bigger defense budgets and more weaponry, convinced that military strength is the sole source of national security. Congressmen know better, and consequently make decisions that, considered in a vacuum from a *solely military* perspective, seem illogical. They understand that in assessing national security, other elements must be factored into the equation: economic strength, the vitality of scientific research and technological development in academia and the private sector, the strength of the US alliances, national morale and the appeal of our way of life.[31] Regarding the last point, a State Department official emphasized "the importance of articulating our values strongly, continuously, and persuasively. Western ideals of individualism, personal dignity, and representative government strike responsive chords everywhere.[32] The United States has to set immigration quotas primarily because of the attractions of its way of life, not because it has an abundance of high-tech weaponry!"

A second objection to Congress is that it does not quite fit in the chain of command, which runs downward from the president. Yet Congress constantly intrudes in military matters, primarily by controlling the purse strings and by various investigations. From the military view, Congress holds the purse strings too tight and investigates the Armed Forces too frequently and thoroughly.

Finally, while the military wants swift, precise policy guidance, the democratic process seems murky, ambiguous, indecisive. Slowly, awkwardly, representative government muddles along, infuriating officers who thrive on energy and action, on having a specific mission and getting it done—now! Yet, in a republic, with its widespread distribution of power that protects the people from despotism, a variety of different interests (of which the Armed Forces are only one of many specialized lobbies) have access to the government. Reconciling these competing interests requires lengthy deliberations through governmental mechanisms that can seem cumbersome. The "messy" decision-making process is *inherent* in the democratic system established by the Constitution.

Almost any professional soldier accepts Clausewitz's concept of the "fog" or "friction" of war—that constellation of factors that renders warfare so difficult, inefficient and wasteful. Those who have read Howard's essay on "Military Science in an Age of Peace" will also be familiar with the "fog of peace," which obscures the shape, size and character of the next war and hence instills uncertainty in peacetime preparations.[33] Yet the majors at CGSC were unwilling to accept a third concept, the "fog of politics," that makes precise, swift decision making difficult.

Perhaps attitudes developed by mid-career, when many officers (and many academics) are so cocksure of their judgments that they run the risk of being intellectual without being intelligent, represent only a passing phase. "Older people *can* be wiser," wrote a historian (and former navy officer) who had many profound insights into human nature.[34] Some individuals become ossified in their thinking at an early age, but in other cases new experiences and increasing maturity foster more profound perspectives.

Washington serves as an instructive example. From the beginning of his military career, he displayed many of Marsh's first-tier values. But as a young officer commanding the Virginia Regiment during the French and Indian War, he was also a hot-tempered, petulant, arrogant critic of his political superiors. Especially exasperating to him was the Virginia government's inability to give explicit guidance. "My orders," he complained, "are dark, doubtful, and uncertain; *to-day approved, to-morrow condemned.*" His anomalous position meant that he was "left to act and proceed at hazard, accountable for the consequence, and blamed without the benefit of defence!"[35]

By the time of the Revolution, however, Washington had developed an inexhaustible patience with the democratic process based on a great respect for American values. The transformation occurred, in part, because of natural maturity. Equally important, Washington had become immersed in civilian life as the manager of his plantation and as a legislator, first in the Virginia House of Burgesses and then as a delegate to the Constitutional Congress. Absorbing and studying civilian concerns, he came to understand the deliberative, slow nature of representative government and the many concerns other than military matters that demanded its attention, even in wartime.[36]

Certainly, Washington continued to exercise a soldier's inalienable right to complain. During the Revolution, he complained often to and about Congress regarding inadequate manpower and logistic support. But his criticisms were tempered by the realization that national values were paramount, that it did no good to fight the war in a manner that undermined those ideals. Despite his complaints, he remained unswervingly loyal to civil supremacy, even when, in desperation, Congress attempted to invest him with dictatorial power, even when congressional inefficiency threatened his army's survival. On matters large and small, immense and trivial, Washington consulted with and obeyed Congress. He know that congressmen were doing their best to hurdle insurmountable obstacles, that they had no more desire than he did to suffer a traitor's fate. "We should all be considered Congress, Army…as one people," he wrote, "embarked in one Cause, in one interest; acting on the same principle and to the same End."[37]

Revolutions often spawn permanent presidents, emperors and kings, but because Washington never forgot that he was a citizen first and only secondarily a soldier, the American Revolution did not end that way. Contrary to many historical examples, Washington rejected personal power. He had no desire to become an American Caesar or Cromwell. Liberty, he said, was the basis for American independence and the national character, "and whoever would dare to sap the foundation, or overturn the Structure, under whatever specious pretexts he may attempt it, will merit the bitterest execration, and the severest punishment which can be inflicted by his injured Country…"[38]

Perhaps the 1986–1987 CGSC class will eventually yield a George Washington—or a Ulysses S. Grant, George C. Marshall or Dwight D. Eisenhower. Each of these men displayed the intellectual capacity and common sense (an altogether too scarce commodity) to reconcile being a good soldier with being a good American.

NOTES

1. Secretary of the Army John O. Marsh Jr., *White Paper 1986: Values*, 9. The following two paragraphs are also based on this document. The quotes are on pages 5 and 6.
2. *The Writings of Samuel Adams*, ed. Harry Alonzo Cushing, 4 vols., (G.P. Putnam's Sons, 1904–1908), 1:264–65.
3. Marsh, 7. For discussion of the professional military ethic, see Samuel P. Huntington, *The Soldier and the State: The Theory and Politics of Civil-Military Relations* (Harvard University Press, 1957).
4. This discussion of ideology relies heavily on Yehoshua Arieli, *Individualism and Nationalism in American Ideology* (Harvard University Press, 1964).
5. Page Smith, *A New Age Now Begins: A People's History of the American Revolution*, vol. 1, (McGraw-Hill Book Company, 1976), 696–97; Arieli, 137 and 145.
6. For a detailed discussion of these complex matters, see Gordon S. Wood, *The Creation of the American Republic, 1776–1787* (Chapel Hill: The University of North Carolina Press, 1969).
7. This discussion of the Bill and Rights, especially the First Amendment, relies heavily on Leonard W. Levy, *Emergence of a Free Press* (Oxford University Press, 1985) and "The Bill of Rights," in his *Constitutional Opinions: Aspects of the Bill of Rights* (Oxford University Press, 1986). See also Irving Brant, *The Bill of Rights: Its Origin and Meaning* (Bobbs-Merrill Company, 1965).
8. *Journals of the Continental Congress, 1774–1789*, ed. Washington C. Ford et al., 34 vols., (Washington, DC: US Government Printing Office [GPO], 1904–37), 1:108.
9. Levy, *Emergence*, makes these points.
10. *Compilation of the Messages and Papers of the Presidents, 1789–1897*. ed. James D. Richardson, 10 vols., (Washington, DC:GPO, 1907), 1:322; Alexis de Tocqueville, *Democracy in America*, 2 vols., (Vintage Books, paperback reprint of 1945 edition), 1:190.
11. John Braeman, *Before the Civil Rights Revolution: The Old Court and Individual Rights* (Westport, CT: Greenwood Press, 1988) shows some of the restrictions that have been imposed on freedom of expression and the difficulty "of balancing—of deciding how far the rights of the individual may be limited for the larger community good." As Braeman also demonstrates, one great expansion of First Amendment rights occurred as a result of the Supreme Court extending "to the states via the due process clause of the Fourteenth Amendment the First Amendment rights of free speech, free press, and assembly." The quotes are from pages 120 and 117.
12. The case was *Ex parte* Milligan, which dealt with the constitutionality of using military courts in areas where civil courts were functioning.
13. Huntington, 267–68. Civilians, especially those closely connected to military affairs, sometimes share the same concern. For example, in 1817 a House of Representatives committee that had studied the question of militia reorganization urged "the diffusion of military discipline and a military spirit through the whole body of the people" to counteract "that inordinate desire of wealth which seems to have pervaded the whole nation." See *The New*

American States Papers: Military Affairs. 19 vols., (Wilmington: Scholarly Resources, Inc., 1979), 14:204.
14. The breakdown in traditional restraints is a main theme in a history of the United States written by Benjamin G. Rader and John M. Dobson, forthcoming by West Publishing Company.
15. *The Writings of George Washington*, ed. John C. Fitzpatrick, 39 vols., (Washington, DC: GPO, 1931–44), 6:111.
16. *Selections from Ralph Waldo Emerson: An Organic Anthology*, ed. Stephen E.Whicher. (Houghton Mifflin Company, 1957), 154.
17. NSC-68 is reprinted in the *Naval War College Review* (May/June 1975):51-108.
18. These comments are based on my experience as the John F. Morrison Professor of Military History at the US Army Command and General Staff College during 1986–87. Fortunately, despite their fervent and frequent criticism of *civilians*, particularly the men and women in Congress and in the journalism profession, the majors remained respectful of *civilian* control, especially as exercised by the president. As long as the paradox of contempt for civilians yet respect for civilian control remains intact, then democratic government is secure. But might not this disdain for civilians lead to a severe challenge to civilian control sometime in the future? I should add three other points. First, numerous students and I debated these issues in a forthright manner that I found intellectually stimulating: few disagreed when I used the words "contempt" and "disdain" to describe the major's attitudes toward civilians. Second, and somewhat paradoxically, the students and faculty treated me as "one of their own"—that is, with the utmost friendliness and courtesy—not as a civilian who had never worn a uniform. I consider some of the officers I met there to be among my best friends—despite our differences on many substantive issues! Third, I was in college during the height of the anti-Vietnam War movement, with which I sympathized: so I may be hypersensitive about issues involving civil-military relations.
19. Carl von Clausewitz, *On War*, ed. and trans. by Michael Howard and Peter Paret. (Princeton University Press, 1976), 92.
20. Michael Howard, "The Use and Abuse of Military History," in his *The Causes of Wars and Other Essays* (Harvard University Press, 1983). 195–97.
21. General Bruce Palmer Jr., *The 25-Year War: America's Military Role in Vietnam* (The University Press of Kentucky, 1984).
22. Ibid., 171 (italics added).
23. Ibid., 176–77.
24. For a brilliant exposition of the fallacy that loosening the restraints imposed on air power early in the war would have led to victory, see Marx Clodfelter, *The Limits of Air Power: The American Bombing of North Vietnam* (The Free Press, 1989).
25. Clausewitz, 605 and 88.
26. Palmer, 192, makes the point about total war being easier to fight than limited war, as did Douglas Pike during two lectures in the Combat Studies Institute's S.L.A. Marshall

Lecture Series during the 1986–1987 academic year.

27. Palmer, 8 and 189.

28. Alexander k. McClure, *Lincoln's Yarns and Stories*…(J.C. Winston Company, 1904), 124.

29. As an example, see Jefferson to Peter Carr, 10 August 1787, in *The Papers of Thomas Jefferson*, ed. Julian P. Boyd at al., 22 vols. to date. (Princeton University Press, 1950–), 12:15.

30. See for example, John Adam's *Discourses on Davila: A Series of Papers on Political History by an American Citizen* in *The Works of John Adams, Second President of the United States*, ed. Charles Francis Adams, 10 vols. (Little, Brown and Company, 1856), 224–399.

31. Historically, of course, some soldiers have understood that defense matters do not exist independently from the rest of society. For example, in 1750, Secretary of War Henry Knox wrote that "The Strength of the Government, like the strength of any other vast and complicated machine, will depend on a due adjustment of its several parts: its agriculture, its commerce, its laws, its finance, its system of defence, and its manners and habits, all require consideration, and the highest exercise of political wisdom." *New American State Papers Military Affairs*, 14:167.

32. *"National Security and U.S.-USSR Relations,"* an address by Matthew Nimetz, Counselor for the Department of State at Duke University on 17 November 1979, and distributed by the Department of State's Bureau of Public Affairs as "Current Policy No. 113."

33. Michael Howard, "Military Science in an Age of Peace," *RUSI: Journal of the Royal United Services Institute for Defence Studies*, vol. 119, no. 1, (March 1974):3–11.

34. Michael T. Isenberg, *Puzzles of the Past: An Introduction to Thinking About History* (Texas A&M University Press, 1985), 73.

35. *The Writings of George Washington*, 1:528.

36. Don Higginbotham, *George Washington and the American Military Tradition* (University of Georgia Press, 1985) describes this transformation.

37. *The Writings of George Washington*, 11:291. When Washington resigned to the Continental Congress in December 1783, the president, Elias Boudinot commended Washington for having "conducted the great military contest with wisdom and fortitude, invariably regarding the rights of civil power through all disasters and changes." Ford, 25:838.

38. *The Writings of George Washington*, 26:487.

Peter Maslowski is professor of history, University of Nebraska-Lincoln. He received a B.A. from Miami University, and an M.A. and Ph.D. from Ohio State University. He has written and taught extensively in the field of military history and was the 1986–1987 John F. Morrison Professor of Military History, US Army Command and General Staff College, Fort Leavenwoth, Kansas.

The Commander's Concept of Duty

by Roger Nye

Duty, Honor, Country. These three hallowed words reverently dictate what you ought to be, what you can be, what you will be.

—General of the Army Douglas MacArthur
Thayer Award Address, May, 1962.

Shortly before the 1942 American invasion of North Africa, the Task Force commander, George S. Patton, wrote in his diary, "I hope that, whatever comes up, I shall be able to do my full duty. If I can do that, I have nothing more to ask. Fate will deliver what success I shall attain . . ." Three centuries earlier, the Frenchman Pierre Corneille advised in *El Cid*, "Do your duty, and leave the rest to heaven." Since the Age of Pericles, philosophers, playwrights, and generals have never doubted that duty was the central virtue of the professional military man. But this was not so in 1984, when two Washington study groups wrote 500-word statements of philosophy for Army systems that governed officer personnel management and professional development—never using the word Duty. Moreover, they did not mention Honor or Country. Instead, they wrote of commitment, selfless service, loyalty, and candor.

Was this a mere substitution of modern words for antique ones? Or was there a new message, a departure from a long tradition?

Subordinating "duty" to newer Army values seems to have evolved from the American experience in Vietnam. In 1980, the Chief of Staff of the Army, General Edward C. Meyer, spoke and wrote of Army values, emphasizing not duty but, rather, loyalty to institution, loyalty to unit, personal responsibility, and selfless service. A year later, General Donn A. Starry also omitted duty from his assessment of important military values; he expanded the Chief's list to include competence, commitment,

Source: *The Challenge of Command* (1986): 115-130. New Jersey: Avery Publishing Group.Reprinted by permission of Mrs. Mary Ann Nye.

candor, and courage. ("In Pursuit of an Ethic," *Army*, Sep., 1981, 11) The goal of this new language was to correct an evil that had come upon the Army—too many officers misbehaving and thinking it necessary to lie, cheat, and steal in order to get ahead.

The new language might well achieve this goal, for it underscored those values that would assure obedience to authority, be it to regulations, superior commanders or institutions. The new words said little about mutual trust and obligations, about the professional growth of officers and NCO's, or about the importance of the strong individual in creativity, leadership, and command. The new language was the answer to a special problem in the Officer Corps. It was apparently necessary, because the old traditional concepts were too difficult to be taught and grasped by young people from contemporary American society.

The substantive difference between old and new was in the concept of self, the worth of the person, and the place of the individual in a shared human enterprise. While the new word "commitment," for example, implied giving over one's will to the cause (be it institution, ideal, or group), the old word "duty" implied that the individual should determine the nature and extent of his obligation, and then give the obedience and allegiance that reason dictated.

While the new "candor" called for truthfulness and frankness, it did so as an institutional requirement, for automatic conformance by the individual involved. The old word "honor" called for truthfulness and honesty to sustain, not only the institution, but the honor or reputation of the individual, whose most valuable asset was his good name for integrity and trustworthiness.

In the new language, loyalty to institution and unit became a requirement of conduct boldly demanded by superiors. In the old language, loyalty was subordinated to other values, a commodity to be earned by authority, and then offered as a duty by the individual because the object of his loyalty merited it.

Finally, the introduction of the new concept of "selfless service" seemed to advocate that the strong, self-centered personalities like Patton and MacArthur be avoided, as subversive to loyalty and good morals. In contrast, the old language did not necessarily probe into the motivations of the individual, but assumed that selfishness was ever-present and ineradicable, and that the self, while inviolable, was always in need of discipline, restraint, and temperance. The old philosophy wisely coped with "weakness of character," rather than foolishly trying to order evil into oblivion. In so doing, it nurtured the strong-willed and often self-centered personalities that breathed creativity, leadership, and discipline into Army life. The strength and meaning of these "old school" military values were delineated by Edgar F. Puryear in Nineteen Stars, a comparison of the ideals and careers of Marshall, MacArthur, Patton, and Eisenhower.

The future commander, looking for a settled philosophy about military conduct, might well ask whether he would prefer the old or new language in counseling subordinates. If he accuses a wayward lieutenant of not giving "selfless service" in the performance of his tasks, the junior officer may well assume that he has been insulted, ask for proof, and effectively terminate the conversation. If, on the other hand, the commander suggests that he and the lieutenant talk about the latter's conception of what his duty is and how it might be performed, no insult about motives need be inferred and some progress might be made. In the traditional language of duty, personalities could be left out, and an impartial discussion of a third entity entertained.

In the early chapters of these commentaries on military command, the lieutenant who thought his commanders too self-centered might have had a different view if he had been trained to think in terms of duty rather than of selfless service. If asked, "Does your commander carry out his duty in a worthy manner?," the lieutenant would have had to assess the nature of the senior's duty and whether he handled it well. The old language provided for distance between ranks, more suitable for cool assessment and dispassionate appraisal.

For the commander who would organize his thoughts and actions around the concept of duty, military memoirs and biographies offer a wide array of mentors. *The Eisenhower Diaries*, for example, reveal a five-star general's arguing within himself as to whether he should be a candidate for the Presidency. In August, 1951, as Supreme Allied Commander in Europe, Ike wrote that Republican leaders had come to persuade him to run for the job.

> They recognize that I have an important duty in this post. They believe that I have (rather, will have) a more important duty, to accept the Republican nomination. . . . I've told them, as I tell all, that I'll certainly always try to do my duty to the country, when I know what that duty is. As of now I have a duty; I cannot yet even describe the circumstances that would be conclusive in convincing me that my duty had changed to that of assuming a role in a political field. (198-199)

Two months later he wrote:

> I entered upon this post only from a sense of duty—I certainly had to sacrifice much in the way of personal convenience, advantage, and congenial constructive work when I left New York [as president of Columbia University]. I will never leave this post for any other governmental task except in response to a clear call to duty. I will not be a participant in any movement that attempts to secure for me a nomination because I believe that the presidency is something that should never be sought, just as I believe, of course, that it could never be refused. . . . I would consider the nomination of which they speak, if accomplished without any direct or indirect assistance or connivance on my part, to place upon me a transcendent duty. . . . As of now I see nothing to do but keep my mouth shut. (204)

In the early part of 1952, Ike agreed that a nomination by the Republican Party constituted a valid call to a more important duty. His diary entries reflected three characteristics of the person who has guided his life toward a star of duty. First was his ingrained desire to do the right thing—to obey the law, to meet obligations, to await a mandate from others. Second was his determination to uphold principles that he had adopted for himself—to serve is country, and keep out of politics when in uniform.

Third was his awareness that one has many duties, which may often be in conflict. One must make choices about which duty is transcendent at any given time.

THE NATURE OF SOLDIERLY DUTY

While few men have the burden of deciding if it is their duty to become President of the United States, all Army officers face challenges to their sense of duty every day. At the working levels of the Army, the questions are quite mundane: Is it my duty to see that this Hispanic soldier learns to read English? Is it my duty to volunteer for a combat assignment? Is it my duty to stay in the company overnight, to see that we are ready for tomorrow's inspection? Is it my duty to stand in for a fellow officer when he is unaccountably absent?

Each of these questions arises from the demands of duty which, for military people, has at least eight faces. or varieties that must be honored. Chart 5 is a quick summary of the scope of the soldier's duty.

The first four varieties of duty stem from the officer's commissioning warrant, the oath of office, and acceptance into a profession with a special responsibility. The remainder are the responsibilities of any human being, although they take on greater meaning because of the public nature of the officer's work; it is the duty of military leaders to set an example. They do not have the freedom of civilians to ignore these charges. Only the eighth duty is self-selected, since it is for those officers whose God and religion are a fundamental allegiance in their lives; they adhere to Ecclesiastes XII, 13: "Fear God and keep His Commandments, for this is the whole duty of man."

The Chart's listing of the varieties of a soldier's duty includes both professional and personal obligations. This is considerably at variance with those who would speak only of professional matters, leaving the officer's private life to "his own time." Human beings are not divided into such neat categories; they each have one mind and one character, and weigh their decisions and actions as a total person. To some degree, officers are "on duty" twenty-four hours a day, and are never entirely professional or entirely personal. Rather, military people must consider all facets of their duty concurrently, as though holding a cut diamond to the light and looking at each of its facets as an expression of the whole.

Chart 5

The Varieties of the Soldier's Duty

1. The duty to obey orders and carry out assigned missions.
2. The duty to care for subordinates and build strong units.
3. The duty to defend the nation, its people, and its values.
4. The duty to uphold the profession and its ethical code.
5. The duty of self-development to one's highest potential.
6. The duty of fidelity to family, friends, and colleagues.
7. The duty to uphold the moral principles of civilized man.
8. The duty to one's God and religion.

It is normal for these varieties of duty to be in conflict with each other. For those concerned with doing their duty, life is a succession of choices that relegate the myriad of obligations and duties to their proper time, place, and importance. Often, choices result in compromise. The combat commander, for example, may estimate that his mission will produce excessive casualties if conducted according to the operations order; he may seek to resolve this conflict between duty to mission and duty to the troops by requesting an alternative timing or route of advance, which can complete the same mission with fewer casualties.

In 1951, General Douglas MacArthur, who spoke more about duty than any other soldier, felt that he had to choose between obeying the orders of President Truman and defending the nation's interest by waging war more aggressively against the Chinese. He found no compromise, persisted in his dogma, and was relieved of his command. In succeeding years, he argued that the soldier's first duty is to the Constitution rather than to the men temporarily in power. The same "higher duty" argument was used by officers dissenting from service in Vietnam. This pressing problem of disobedience in the sixties is analyzed in Michael Walzer's *Obligations: Essays on Disobedience, War, and Citizenship*.

When claims of duty are used to govern decisions and actions, the soldier becomes aware of the limits and terminal points of one's duty. Like MacArthur, some take their dissent to the point of giving up their commissions and leaving active service. More customary is the decision to limit one's dissent at the point where argument over policy has ceased, a decision is made, and unity is needed to carry out the policy.

Another important limitation of the duty to obey is the code clearly stating that an officer should not obey an unlawful order. Whether one can prove that the order is or could be illegal may be very difficult. Unless the issue involves murder or some other equally heinous crime, the refusal to obey is usually worked out between contending parties before a court must decide whether or not an order is legal. The important effect of the code is to deter commanders from issuing illegal orders, rather than to safeguard those who disobey.

The most significant limitations of the soldier's duty are those that must be self-imposed by the soldier himself. Duty to the family cannot be met fully if one's duty to subordinates and units is to be fulfilled effectively. Each professional finds his own individual compromises between these claims. Soldiers often feel that they must limit the duty owed to friends and colleagues, particularly when such friends misuse a friendship to ask for favors bordering on unethical, illegal, or immoral activities. In these cases, one "discharges" the duty with which one has previously "charged" oneself.

How do commanders judge between the demands of conflicting duties? Some do it well; others, poorly. Many barely recognize that the problem exists, and are continually surprised to find their decisions ill-advised and not carried out. These commanders are usually out of touch with their people, although they may talk with them every day. They appear to be without strong moral convictions, are easily swayed by the last person they talked to, and are pliable in the hands of their seniors. They react to fear for their popularity and to opportunities for immediate gain. They are at the beginning stages of moral growth, as suggested in Lawrence Kohlberg's *Essays on Moral Development: Moral Stages and the Idea of Justice*.

The majority of American military commanders fit into Kohlberg's intermediate moral stages much better; they adhere to the set of moral principles brought to the Army from their early years of family and religious training. They make their judgments heavily in favor of the values of the institutions that they serve—the Army, the nation, and the units to which they are assigned. Obedience, patriotism, loyalty to the mission and the unit: these are the duties weighing the most in their judgments. For some, however, the results are often crude and misguided—decisions that reflect the jargon of the trade, such as "I go by the book," and "We accept only zero defects." This narrow orientation produces old responses to new challenges, a failure to serve the real needs of the Army, and a cookie-cutter standard reaction to problems rather than the creative solutions that are needed.

In contrast, the best commanders tend to put strong emphasis on their duty "to uphold the moral principles of civilized man," using it to make judgments about the many varieties of duty they face. They are aware of the moral principles that have been passed down through the ages. They believe in the efficacy of these principles in sustaining worthy communities and institutions, and act in accordance with them. Through this knowing, believing, and doing, they are identified with Kohlberg's higher levels of moral development. Chart 6 presents a listing of these moral principles, derived from Dr. Arthur Dyke's *On Human Care*, a textbook that has been used in courses in military ethics at the U.S. Army War college.

Chart 6
Moral Principles of Primary Concern to Military Commanders

Beneficence towards others, as reflected in:
- not inflicting evil or harm on others, killing, stealing, bearing false witness
- preventing evil or harm from coming to others
- removing evil from institutions and society

Fidelity towards others, as reflected in:
- truth-telling
- promise-keeping.
- reparation for previous wrongful acts
- gratitude for previous beneficial acts, such as giving and preserving life.

Justice towards others, as in assuring a proper distribution of rights, benefits, and injuries

It is evident from this Chart that moral principles have to do with one's actions towards other human beings, whether beneficence, fidelity, or justice. These "rules" govern the actions of men and women in dealing with each other as human beings—as part of a society of mankind. Commanders who adhere to these principles see themselves as leaders of a community over which they have the authority to act. Here there is little room for the ego-gratification or self-aggrandizement that afflicts commanders who see themselves standing in splendid isolation above the masses.

PERFORMING DUTY FOR REASONS OF JUSTICE

Cadets who came into the Army in the fifties often listened to the following story told by a chaplain. There was once a traveler on the road to Jericho who had been beaten, robbed, and left to die. Two noble citizens passed him by as if they did not see him. Then a Samaritan, a stranger in the land, came by. He stopped, dressed the traveler's wounds, and took him to an inn to recover. The chaplain finished his story of The Good Samaritan with an observation. Had there been a soldier stationed on the road to Jericho, whose duty was to protect travelers from evil, the victim would have never been assaulted, the passersby would not have been mocked for their hypocrisy, and the Samaritan would not have been tested for his compassion, nor delayed on his journey. The cadets left the sermon convinced that the life of the soldier was worthy, made so by his duty to safeguard the citizenry of a nation.

But the chaplain did not go quite far enough. How do we know that the soldier posted on the road to protect travelers would actually carry out his duty? Might not the soldier ignore the robbers if they were better armed than he? Was there any guarantee that he would not join them in their plundering? Or suppose that a group of citizens came to the soldier one day, saying, "The government is corrupt and exploits the people. You have more important things to do than to protect this road. It is your higher duty to join us and employ your weapons to pull down this evil government." What, if anything, will cause the soldier to resist such temptations?

Obedience and discipline, if properly understood and enforced, can keep the soldier aware of his duty in ordinary times. But the commitment to duty that is necessary under exceptional circumstances must be reinforced by values that tie the soldier to the service of other human beings. Chief among these soldierly values is a sense of justice.

In 1939, General Sir Archibald Wavell foretold an audience. at Cambridge University:

> In a future war . . . discipline should be a different matter from the old traditional military discipline. It has changed greatly since I joined, and is changing still. But, whatever the system, it is the general's business to see *justice* done. The soldier does not mind a severe code, provided it is administered fairly and reasonably.
> —Wavell, *Soldiers and Soldiering, 28.*

Like Wavell, most soldiers equate justice with fairness, the fairness of one's dealing with other human beings. This is *distributive justice*, wherein equal individuals merit equal shares of social goods and evils. The commander, however, is also concerned with two other kinds of justice. One is *contributive justice*, wherein each person must contribute equally to the sustaining of institutions that benefit him, such as his government or his infantry company. The other is the justice of *human rights*, wherein every human being is entitled to certain inalienable rights, such as freedom from murder, bondage, theft, and libel. The legal justice that must be provided by the military commander is largely in the justice of human rights. The inquiring commander finds further analysis of these three concepts of justice in Mortimer J. Adler's *Six Great Ideas* and John Rawls' *A Theory of Justice.*

Aristotle argued that man is governed by love in his dealings with his family and very close friends. But beyond this tight inner circle, in the absence of love, man must be governed by justice, as promulgated by a tribal, institutional, or state government. Through justice, each receives according to what is due him; the determination of "just dues" within the organization may be based on law, merit, or fairness.

Not everyone agrees with Aristotle that rewards should be based on merit, and that those who are unequal should receive unequal shares of the rewards or punishments. By the test of fairness, however, each man is entitled to equal treatment with others, and if some are given disproportionate shares of material wealth, power, or freedom, this inequality must be justified on the grounds that it benefits everyone in the organization. Hence, a commander acquires more power or physical comforts than that of his subordinates only if the least advantaged man in the organization benefits from this unequal distribution.

Justice is said to be the first virtue of social institutions, just as truth is of systems of thought. Wise commanders of military "social institutions" know that justice demands fairness as well as lawfulness, and that they must insist that every soldier willingly contributes his fair share of the work to the cooperative enterprise of the unit. But they also know that every obligation of the soldier has an earned right attached to it. These are obverse sides of the same coin, and for every sacrifice of freedom of movement and speech that a soldier makes, he can rightfully expect commanders to use restraint in curbing the soldier's fundamental liberty.

Understanding the citizen-soldier's right to basic freedoms has been most difficult for American commanders of the past two generations. All citizens are guaranteed freedom of thought and conscience; freedom of speech, assembly, and personal movement; freedom to participate equally in political affairs; and a variety of basic civil liberties. But if men are to act as one in a fighting organization, obedient to civilian and military command and able to live together in close quarters without harming each other, they are required to forego some of their inherent freedoms.

The wise commander, however, knows that subordinates need sufficient freedom to develop their capacities and to avoid losing their identities as men and women. He also knows that the protection of this freedom is the fundamental reason for America's wars with Naziism, Japanese militarism, and communism in Korea and Vietnam. Such commanders recognize that to curb the soldier's liberty beyond what is demanded by real military necessity is to perpetrate injustice and unfairness among the troops. Commanders who substitute personal whim and craving for power for military necessity in determining the liberties of their subordinates suffer the consequences—a decline in unit morale and effectiveness.

The respect for an individual's dignity that causes the commander to give a subordinate extensive freedom also causes him to resist the temptation to manipulate the soldier into shameful or wrongful deeds. To lead, we are told, is to cause others to do willingly what one wants them to do. Commanders who are unused to power find security in manipulating men through fear, intimidation, or false promises, thereby manipulating them into "willing" performances. Such commanders may misunderstand the writings of psychologists (such as B. F. Skinner in *About Behaviorism*) that describe how researchers can manipulate their human objects into certain behavioral patterns. Commanders who seek "the good" of their troops, however, are more prone to look upon manipulation of subordinates as the philosophers do; that is, as unethical and an assault upon the integrity and worth of other human beings. The trick is, of course, to distinguish between proper demands on subordinates and the unethical manipulation of them. A concern for justice and fairness makes this discernment easier.

In 1804 Napoleon wrote, "There is no strength without justice." Today, the strength of the American Army is sapped by the injustice that arises from neglect or miscalculation—errors in pay, promotion, rotation of assignments. Correcting injustice here is a matter of sensing the problem and pursuing it with skill through the labrynthine system. Much of the injustice is also due to bad policy decisions, ordering conflicting requirements without providing the time and resources for accomplishment, until men are senselessly overworked, deprived of deserved liberty, or wrongly rated on their performances. These injustices call for a quick policy change; only commanders who are aware of the real price paid for injustice can avoid or correct such wrongdoing.

When neither miscalculations nor erroneous policy are to blame, we look for the villain who forces injustice on subordinates for a variety of ego-gratifying reasons—the desire to see lackeys jump, the urge to keep other races or ethnic groups in servility, the hankering to savor anachronistic rules long after they have become unjust, only because they are symbolic of a more comfortable past. Nevertheless, the villains argue that they are only acting in the organization's best interest, in which they crave a more generous share of power and privilege. It is most difficult to avoid or correct injustice coming from this source. But the process of eradicating these miscreants goes on. In the words of the Naval Board investigating the mutiny on H.M.S. Bounty: "If justice be not in the mind of the Captain, it be not aboard."

THE DUTY OF SELF-DEVELOPMENT

On 7 July, 1970, Captain John Alexander Hottell was strapped in a helicopter that was caught up in a tropical storm and slammed into a hillside in a remote mountain area of Vietnam. Shortly before, while commanding a company of the 1st Cavalry Division, he had written a sealed letter to his wife, Linda, which began:

> I am writing my own obituary . . . [because] I am quite simply the last authority on my own death.

> I loved the Army: it reared me, it nurtured me, and it gave me the most satisfying years of my life. Thanks to it I have lived an entire lifetime in 26 years. It is only fitting that I should die in its service. We all have but one death to spend, and insofar as it can have any meaning it finds it in the service of comrades in arms.

> And yet, I deny that I died FOR anything—not my Country, not my Army, not my fellow man, none of these things. I LIVED for these things, and the manner in which I chose to do it involved the very real chance that

I would die in the execution of my duties. I knew this and accepted it, but my love for West Point and the Army was great enough—and the promise that I would someday be able to serve all the ideals that meant anything to me through it was great enough—for me to accept this possibility as a part of a price which must be paid for all things of great value. If there is nothing worth dying for—in this sense—there is nothing worth living for.

The Army let me live in Japan, Germany, and England, with experiences in all of these places that others only dream about. . . . I have climbed Mount Fuji, visited the ruins of Athens, Ephesus, and Rome . . . and earned a master's degree in a foreign university. I have known what it is like to be married to a fine and wonderful woman and to love her beyond bearing with the sure knowledge that she loves me: I have commanded a company and been a father, priest, income-tax advisor, confessor, and judge for 200 men at a time; I have played college football and rugby, won the British national Diving Championship two years in a row, boxed for Oxford against Cambridge only to be knocked out in the first round. . . . I have been an exchange student at the German Military Academy, and gone to the German Jumpmaster school. I have made thirty parachute jumps from everything from a balloon in England to a jet at Fort Bragg. I have written an article for *Army* magazine, and I have studied philosophy.

I have experienced all these things because I was in the Army and because I was an Army brat. The Army is my life, it is such a part of what I was that what happened is the logical outcome of the life I lived. I never knew what it was to fail, I never knew what it is to be too old or too tired to do anything. I lived a full life in the Army, and it has exacted the price. It is only just.

Just, yes, in the personal philosophy of Alex Hottell. When the obituary eventually appeared in the press, it was admired for its expression of gratitude for being permitted such opportunities to learn, and for the sense of justice in the tradeoff of a life well lived for a cause well merited. Some felt that it expressed well the sixties' absorption with self. They could not, however, attribute selfishness to his willingness to give up life in fulfillment of that self. This was not "selfless service," but "self-in-service."

Hottell had been an excellent commander at the company level. He had earned two Silver Stars, and some said that he had been "rescued from himself" by sudden orders to division headquarters. If there was an explanation for his nascent capacity to command, it lay in his incessant desire to learn—to read, to experience new phenomena, to question, to experiment. The duty of "self-development to one's highest potential," although stated crudely in Chart 5, symbolized Hottell's personal philosophy of daily living. His enforcement of it, however, was more in keeping with Theodore Ropp's reason for reading military history—"because it is fun."

Learning about the role of a military commander must start early enough for a person to acquire a vision of himself in command roles at several levels higher than then held.

Hottell saw a model in Major General George W. Casey, who died in the crash with him: "He is imaginative, aggressive, charming, and has a more complete grasp of the complex missions that confront the American division commander than I would have thought possible. It will be almost a religious experience for me to serve with the Cav when this man commands it." Such visions of what a commander should be came not only from Hottell's reading of military biography, but also from his study of philosophy and literature; he had read not only Plato's description of the "man of virtue," but also the modern expressions of same theme, such as John F. Kennedy's *Profiles in Courage.*

The duty of self-development for commanders seems to call for three study objectives. First is the acquisition of knowledge and skills associated with the several roles of the commander—leader, manager, tactician, warrior, strategist, and moral standard bearer. Second is the acquisition of knowledge, insights, and values associated with the virtuous human being, perhaps best stated in Plato's ideal of the man of wisdom, courage, temperance, and justice. Third is the acquisition of insights gained from thought about oneself the personal style that is suited best to a commander's role in the twentieth century Army environment.

For pursuing the first of these objectives, the early chapters of these commentaries cite books useful in developing one's vision as a tactician, warrior, professional, leader, and manager. In addition to these, future commanders will want to read the recent mind-expanding popular works that widen the vision of the management expert, such as John Naisbit's *Megatrends: Ten New Directions Transforming Our Lives*; Scott and Hart's *Organizational America*; and Peters and Austin's *A Passion for Excellence*. In the field of leadership, some of the best works deal with political leaders, such as James McGregor Burns' *Leadership*, Field Marshal Bernard Montgomery's *The Path to Leadership*, and Dankwart A. Rustow's *Philosophers and Kings: Studies in Leadership*.

In order to develop a more complete understanding of Plato's "virtuous leader," commanders must turn to some of the classic and popular works of philosophy, religion, literature, and history. Mortimer J. Adler has made some of the best ideas on justice and duty readable in *Six Great Ideas* and *Aristotle For Everybody: Difficult Thought Made Easy*. For a remarkably penetrating analysis of the relationship between justice and man's ability to cope with modern society, there is Alasdair MacIntyre's *After Virtue: A Study of Moral Theory*. Recent popular works exploring the problem of self and its place in the philosophy of public leaders include Erich Fromm's *Man For Himself* and C. S. Lewis' *The Abolition of Man*. The problems of holding power, with its dangers of corruption by hubris and arrogance, are explored by Thucydides, Macchiavelli, Hobbes, Lord Acton, and the fathers of the American Revolution; David Kipnis attempts to pull these ideas into some understandable pattern in *The Powerholders*.

The most dramatic portrayals of military commanders who have lost track of their sense of justice and the reality of their duty are Cecil Woodham-Smith's *The Reason Why* and C.S. Forester's *The General*. In contrast, Forester's story of *Rifleman Dodd* portrays the trials of a private soldier trapped behind the lines in the Napoleonic Wars, and driven to heroic feats by his sense of duty.

The third objective for commander self-development is the most difficult. It requires the creative generation of insights about one's strengths and limitations, and the finding of a person style of command that best matches one's personality with the demands of the job in the reality of modern times. Not all are to be Pattons, some might be Marshalls, none should be Custers. All should assume that command may be thrust on them in time of need; many should step aside, so that commanders of greater potential can get experience.

Assessing self, present and potential, requires the intake of ideas generated by first-hand experience, and by the vicarious experience of reading. But the gestation and analysis of this intake often requires writing. "I do not know what I think until I try to write it down," is the byword of men and women intent on probing into their beliefs and competencies. Nearly all the inquiring soldiers discussed in these commentaries in military command have been writers as well as readers; Clark and Hottell started personal journals before entering cadet training. Writing articles for professional periodicals seems to be standard fare for future commanders. Senior commanders finish their careers by publishing books. All reflect a lifetime of note-taking, research, experimental speeches, records of conversations, summaries of reading, diaries of current thoughts, file-drawers of trial paragraphs and short talks, and "commonplace books" of poems, quotations, and speeches. These are the tools of inquiring minds, who look upon books as fuel for the mind, as gasoline is to the internal combustion engine. Reading is a means, not an end; expressing one's thoughts is the end. Xenophon's *Anabasis*, Caesar's *Commentaries*, and Napoleon's *Maxims* are summary statements of thinker-doers who were writers. Modern military men and women who are writers customarily have a reference shelf of best books alongside their dictionaries; there is distillation of these military writers' reference collections at the end of this chapter.

Alexander Pope wrote that the proper study of mankind is man. It then follows that the proper study of military command is military commanders. The biographies and memoirs described in Chapter 2 provide such a study. There is, however, a special way of thinking about other men's battle experiences if one asks "How am I suited for this and what is my best style?" Questions form in the reader's mind, and he asks them of the biographies and memoirs, which then become a goldmine of research, as well as a task undertaken "because it is fun." Each researcher has his own questions, based on his own particular inventory of hopes, fears, biases, and ambitions. In the final analysis, it remains true that there is no stereotypical commander around whom all must model their lives. Command is so unique a blend of personality and task that no two commanders should mirror each other. To the extent that they share common qualities, it is in their common search for courage, truth, duty, and justice.

USMA Class of 2000, One-Hundredth Night Banquet
Washington Hall, US Military Academy
26 February 2000

comments by Don M. Snider, Ph.D.

I. Introduction:

- Thank you for the honor you bestow by inviting Caroline and me to join you tonight, a special night in the rites of passage of this institution.

- In your minds, there are now just 90 days until the culminating events of your four years here. In my view that will be the Commissioning Ceremony and your personal acceptance of the moral obligation to defend, even at the risk of death, a defenseless American society.

- As members of the Long Grey Line (LGL) you will take your honored place as #56576 to #57516 among the graduates of this venerated institution. Then, one in every fifty graduates will be one of you! And we older grads know that when you join us, as we "grip hands together," the LGL will be "stiffened and strengthened" as our hymn says. And we all look forward to that.
  - I remember, in 1962 in the mural wing of this historic mess, my own first awareness of what it meant to be a part of the LGL. General MacArthur told us then that *"The LGL has never failed us. Were you to do so, a million ghosts in olive drab, in brown khaki, in blue and gray, would rise from their white crosses thundering those hallowed words, Duty, Honor, Country."*
  - Needless to say, I did not fully comprehend then what I know now about the importance of understanding and fulfilling one's Duty.

Source: Comments by Don M. Snider, Ph.D. (February, 1999). Reprinted by permission.

- Thus, Graduation will represent the end of one short preparatory journey of four years, and the beginning of another journey vastly more important for both you and the society you serve. It will be a journey of at least five years in uniform; and then for the majority of you, a lifetime of service to the nation, whether in uniform or not. And, it is that second journey I seek to address with you tonight in my brief time, using the opportunity to pass on to you some "received wisdom" from my own experiences and from those who went before and mentored me from their experiences in WWII and Korea.

II. First, to the Class of 2000, two items of advice.

- The first I can relate most easily with a story. Early in 1964 as a Lieutenant advising the Vietnamese Special Forces, I was about to make my first jump into the border region between Laos and Vietnam. We were in a very old C-46, so old I wondered as we taxied down the dirt strip if it would ever get off the ground. It was "sanitized" in order that our government had "plausible deniability" if we went down outside the country we were supporting. This also meant that without modern electronics we often didn't know where we were flying or where we would be inserted, thus the trail intersections we were to recon we often missed by many miles when we jumped. It was night, we were to jump from roughly 700' so we wore no reserve chute over our smoke-jumpers gear. The idea, seldom achieved, was for the chute just to have time to open and stabilize our decent so we would hit the double canopy straight on. The jumpmaster standing in the dim red light was a sturdy Sergeant, ethnically a Nung (Vietnamese of Chinese descent). Such soldiers had little to do with the ethnic Vietnamese but they were, themselves, excellent fighters.

- And I noticed from the other end of the plane where I was to "push the stick" that he first pulled a 9mm. revolver from a shoulder holster and chambered a round and then lowered it to his side, while giving the jump commands with his free hand. I thought that was odd, since I had been taught as a jumpmaster that to overcome the noise one had to give the visual signals with both hands. Even though I had "come from the farm" just a few years earlier, it didn't take me long to figure out that he was going to shoot any soldier that did not exit ... including me and SFC Johnston!

- I learned that night that I was privileged not to serve in a mercenary army that threatened its soldiers into obedience, but in a professional Army where mutual trust "lubricates" the necessary obedience between leaders and soldiers.

- So my advice for you is that, as an officer, such trust is absolutely necessary and it must be earned, as the advertisement says, "the old fashioned way." It is not freely given by soldiers, it does not come automatically with the rank you will pin on at your Commissioning. To that rank your soldiers will be obedient and respectful, but as you well know, trust is another thing, particularly the trust necessary for them to follow you into the face of death in a firefight.

- Your challenge is how to earn that trust, and I suggest there are two keys. First, be tactically competent. You are leading soldiers; they want a very competent officer as "their Lieutenant," one of whom they can boast to their comrades. It matters to them whether you shoot expert with your weapon and whether you earn the APFT badge. They expect more from you than they expect from themselves — and, in my view, they deserve it.

- But it takes more than competence. It takes, secondly, humbleness and the right attitude as a leader, an attitude your soldiers will discern in a flash. The best way to illustrate this attitude is with another story.

- As a Lieutenant, I was selected to be an aide to our new Brigade Commander, who was also a new Brigadier General just arriving on Okinawa. At one of our first meetings I asked him what my duties were. Mind you he was a WWII and Korean War veteran, six Silver Stars and five Purple Hearts; he had fought from Omaha Beach to the Ruhr and later for two years in Korea. Needless to say I was a bit apprehensive, but his answer was profound. He said, "First, let me tell you first what my duty is. It is always to conduct myself so that every officer in this Brigade wants to be like me and, ultimately, to be in my position." "And your responsibility, Lieutenant, is to tell me whenever any Lieutenant or Captain sees that I am not doing that."

- You see, this remarkable officer knew what it takes for a leader to earn the trust of subordinates, whether the relationship be officer to officer or officer to enlisted. The key is to model, "24/7" as you cadets say, individual competence and professionalism, and to accept fully that responsibility as your daily duty.

- Of course, your soldiers will listen politely to what you have to say. But my advice is to save your breath. They will take their real cue as to your trustworthiness from your actions.

- Thus the keys to creating the necessary trust for your soldiers willingly to follow you are: *competence* and *humbleness* modeled through absolutely *consistent leadership by example*.

III. And now, let me speak for a moment to you "very significant others" those here tonight not in uniform. I offer to you the question, "How should we think about these young men and women and their future, and as well in many cases your own future with them?

- First, we must respect them for what they are about to accomplish the successful completion of the leadership program here at West Point. And I use that term, leadership, advisedly. We here at West Point are much more in the business of developing future leaders than we are in undergraduate education. Better education can be had elsewhere, many places in fact; but better leader development cannot be found. And in giving them due recognition, I believe President Teddy Roosevelt's insight to describe quite aptly those we honor here tonight. He said:

The credit belongs to those people who are actually in the arena... who know the great enthusiasms, the great devotions to a worthy cause; who at best know the triumph of high achievement; and who, at worst, fail while daring greatly, so that their places shall never be with those cold and timid souls who know neither victory nor defeat.

- These cadets will soon be in the arena, they will know both victories and defeats. And they will need your help to shoulder both.
- But secondly, we must note that their development has only just begun, they are still in the process of "becoming." And in this case what they are "becoming" is a member of a noble profession — officers within the profession of arms.
- Professions are, at least in America, the very few vocations accorded an unusually high status by the American people. They perform functions necessary for our society's existence but which the society cannot do for itself. These functions require expertise drawn from a specialized body of knowledge. In this case the specific expertise is keeping the peace and warfighting, as drawn from the profession's deep knowledge of the political and social nature of warfare at each level of combat. Members of such professions consider their vocation a life-long calling, one necessary to develop and maintain the profession's body of knowledge and their own expertise.
- And in return for this dedicated service, professions are granted by the American society a limited autonomy within which they create their own ethos and professional standards to maintain the effectiveness of their service. Over time, they also establish their own culture supportive of their unique function and which distinguishes their members from the society they serve. (I am sure you have noticed how "distinguished," how different these young folks already are! Just look at their hair, the code-language with which they speak, the odd things with which they are interested!)
- "Officers" of the state are commissioned by American society to be both their *servant* and their *agent*, two words of immense importance to the fully formed self-concept these remarkable young folks will eventually hold, (and I must add that to their immense credit, a few of them already do hold!!)
- Because their future learning will be largely on-the-job it will take time to develop fully this self-concept of an officer, perhaps most of the five years of their mandatory service. And you will be an important, and in many cases, vital, part of that continued developmental process. Let me explain how.
- These years of learning will be done in a profession that is now struggling to change its identity from that of "Cold War victor," to whatever it is that America wants its servant-soldiers to be and to do in the future. The options currently range from warfighter (as in the Gulf War) to constable or policeman (as now in the Balkans) to nationbuilders (as recently in Haiti, and a role the Army fulfilled superbly earlier in its history).
- Further, as the Army Chief of Staff told the Congress last week, we do not now have a "C-1 (meaning fully combat ready) Army. Readiness has declined because of many

more missions and a much higher tempo of deployments during the past decade. Recently completed research in which I participated has documented clearly a "stressed" institution, and a growing gap between it and the society it serves.

- Suffice it to say, this not an easy time for new members to enter the profession. But all of that said, I know that they are better equipped to enter it in June than they think they are. The healthy trepidation that they hold will serve them well, even if you and I know it is a bit unfounded.

- Unfounded, that is, except in one area and this is where you, the guests here tonight, come in. There is a key element of their self-concepts that for most of them is not yet in place. It is that very personal sense of Duty that will allow them successfully to be servants to our society at this trying time. They are going to have to, each one, justify to themselves the self-sacrifices that they and their families are required to make to serve the State on its demanding terms.

- That personal sense of Duty, as different for the members of this class as their personalities and circumstances, is what they will have to search for and find within themselves if they are to enjoy, as Caroline and I have, a lifetime of service to their nation. The officers here tonight in Army Blue have found it, as have so many others from the Long Grey Line. But, as Colin Powell reminded this class just last year, it is not to be found in the coldness of the stone that has been for the past four years their "Granite Palace." Nor is it to be found in the stillness of the many monuments and plaques they pass by every day.

- It will be found, individually, only in their own hearts. So I encourage each one of you to assist them in their search during the coming years. Help them to their own understanding that, "as courage is the mastery of fear, so for the solider Duty is the mastery of life."

IV. Now, in closing, a final bit of advice for all of you, advice on understanding personal success. I believe that truly professional officers never, *but never*, allow the Army to define personal success for them. That is your individual responsibility, and if you ever fail in it, the institution will tend to conform you into the role of the careerist, those who serve for personal gain and glory.

- Careerists look for success in the mirror, noting the rank, the ribbons, the skill badges on their uniform, and their concerns will be where they have been and where they might be going to enhance their career.

- But for the truly professional officer I suggest there is a different place to look, in fact three places. And in each of these places you will find reliable measures of real success, measures of your personal contribution and legacy to this noble profession. You should look at the eyes of your soldiers, at the smile of your spouse, and into the hearts of your children.

- Why these places? If your soldiers trust you and follow you, the unit you lead will be successful with the missions it is given. If your spouse is smiling along side you then you will have correctly balanced the roles of spouse, parent and professional.

And if you know what is in the hearts of your children (as opposed to just what where they are and they are doing) then you will have built at the right time the relationships that cannot be put off and built later.

- With this personal approach to success, I submit that you will become a true professional who knows what success in life really is. And in my own experience, and that of Caroline and our daughters, the intrinsic satisfaction of these three successes has been more than sufficient to offset the self-sacrifices of an Army career.

- My advice is that it can be the same for you. And that is why as a representative of the Class of '62, the "Can Do" class; I am proud to "grip hands" tonight with you, members of the Class of 2000.

- And now, let's move on into the evening and let the Show begin!

Summary

These readings have been selected to help you understand the role of the military officer as a Servant of Society. The readings for this chapter were intended to:

- inspire you in your future role as an officer serving the American Nation
- help you understand the positive and negative aspects of society
- assist you in arriving at a personal answer to the question, "What is now worth dying for?"
- enable you to describe the moral obligation created between one who accepts a commission and the society he or she serves
- aid you in developing a personal concept of duty for future service as an officer.

How well these readings support these objectives you will have to determine for yourself in the course of your studies and personal reflection.

This chapter consisted of nine readings, ranging from scholarly articles to opinion surveys and speeches. You should not start your personal search through the material available here by thinking about either the number of readings or the time it took to read them. Rather, your concern should be the focus of the readings and how they fit together to facilitate your personal search for meaning about the role of "officer as servant."

To facilitate your search, consider the readings as insights from three different perspectives, each with something of importance to say to you about the role of "officer as servant." The first perspective is that of the American society. The second perspective is that of the military institution – the Army – as represented by the officer corps, those responsible to the American people for the professional status of the institution. Third is the perspective of the individual officer, each of whom must correlate his or her own beliefs and values with those of the professional institution.

By definition, a servant is one who is employed to perform services. Thus, for the officer/servant, service and duties are inextricably related. That relationship is at the core of this chapter. You are encouraged to reflect on the proposition that officers, like all soldiers, serve with unlimited liability when they serve the American society. If need be, they are prepared to sacrifice their lives for the moral obligation of the mission.

In your first reading, a 1999 Veteran's Day speech, Dr. Don M. Snider asked a question each of you must reflect on and answer for yourself: "Is American society, its values and way of life in the year 2001 and thereafter, worthy of your personal sacrifice. The next reading, a brief chapter of the current Armed Forces Officer (1988), entitled "American Ideals" reminds us, officially, that officers ultimately serve the higher ideals of the nation as embodied in the Constitution, irrespective of the norms of current citizens. Rounding out the social perspective is a 1977 opinion survey compiled by Everett C. Ladd, "American Society: Where Are We Headed?" In reviewing this survey, you are encouraged to focus on those beliefs and norms that interest you personally, noting where you agree or disagree with the perspective of the society you have chosen to serve and defend. Note the societal values which have changed over time, how slowly (or rapidly) they have changed, as well as the degree of continuity that exists in the values, beliefs, and norms of American society.

The second perspective, that of the institutional Army, is revealed in the next two readings. These selections addressed the moral obligations as well as the burdens and responsibilities you will bear as an officer committed to an absolutist ethic. "The U.S. Military: Sovereign or Subordinate?" (1995) is a chapter from Professor James H. Toner's remarkable book True Faith and Allegiance: The Burden of Military Ethics. Toner identifies and describes the four tasks of the soldier in a stark yet accurate manner. He also clearly articulates his rationale for a "subordinate" military. In "Army Values and American Values" (1990), the military historian Peter Maslowski gives insights into the contemporary issue of how Army Values fit with those of American society and how officers should deal with the inevitable incongruities.

The third perspective is that of the individual officer. Specifically, how are you to reconcile your own personal beliefs and values with those of the institution, the Army? Put another way, how does an officer-apprentice "fit" his or her developing self-concept as an officer with the institutional identity of the Army? This is a critical perspective, one that many of us have probably not considered introspectively. One of the keys to making that "fit" is your personal concept of duty, a concept that allows you to accept the rigors and sacrifices inherent in a military career for the intrinsic satisfaction of having "done your duty." Colonel Roger Nye, former head of the History Department at West Point addresses the importance of the individual perspective in his book The Challenge of Command. Chapter One, "Visions of Our Military Selves," and Chapter Seven, "The Commander's Concept of Duty," should facilitate your personal search both for a self-concept and a concept of duty. In similar fashion,

Dr. Don Snider's remarks to the USMA Class of 2000 on their One-Hundredth Night underscore the core role of the duty concept in an officer's developmental journey through and after the cadet experience at West Point.

If officership as a profession, and within it the officer's role as a servant of American society, entails such vital but subtle understandings as "moral obligation of the mission" and "personal duty concept," you are probably thinking it is a difficult set of concepts to "get your arms around." You are correct, to a degree. But like all complex developmental tasks, it can be better understood if presented to you in a "principled" fashion. There are some well-tested and proven principles to be followed when developing as an American military officer. To assist you in your personal search, the ninth and final reading in this chapter has been extracted from a recent monograph on Army Professionalism. It provides you with one set of "principles of officership." These are not offered as the only, or even the best, principles for you to follow. These principles have, however, been under consideration and review since the end of the Cold War when we began to realize that this generation of Army officers will serve in an environment quite different from that experienced by previous generations. Thus, these principles offer you a starting point for your generation's use in developing a personal duty concept in service to the Republic.

CHAPTER 2

The Officer as a Member of a Time-Honored Profession

"The direction, operation, and control of a human organization whose primary function is the management of violence is the peculiar skill of the officer."

Samuel Huntington

Officership as a Profession

by Samuel P. Huntington

PROFESSIONALISM AND THE MILITARY

The modern officer corps is a professional body and the modern military officer a professional man. This is, perhaps, the most fundamental thesis of this book. A profession is a peculiar type of functional group with highly specialized characteristics. Sculptors, stenographers, entrepreneurs, and advertising copywriters all have distinct functions but no one of these functions is professional in nature. Professionalism, however, is characteristic of the modern officer in the same sense in which it is characteristic of the physician or lawyer. Professionalism distinguishes the military officer of today from the warriors of previous ages. The existence of the officer corps as a professional body gives a unique cast to the modern problem of civil-military relations.

The nature and history of other professions as professions have been thoroughly discussed. Yet the professional character of the modern officer corps has been neglected. In our society, the businessman may command more income; the politician may command more power; but the professional man commands more respect. Yet the public, as well as the scholar, hardly conceives of the officer in the same way that it does the lawyer or doctor, and it certainly does not accord to the officer the deference which it gives to the civilian professionals. Even the military themselves are influenced by their image in the public mind and at times have refused to accept the implications of their own professional status. When the term "professional" has been used in connection with the military, it normally has been in the sense of "professional" as contrasted with "amateur" rather than in the sense of "profession" as contrasted with "trade" or "craft." The phrases "professional army" and "professional soldier" have obscured the difference between the career enlisted man who is professional in the sense of one who works for monetary gain and the career officer who is

Source: *The Soldier and the State* (1957): 7-18. Reprinted by permission of Vintage Books.

professional in the very different sense of one who pursues a "higher calling" in the service of society.

THE CONCEPT OF PROFESSION

The first step in analyzing the professional character of the modern officer corps is to define professionalism. The distinguishing characteristics of a profession as a special type of vocation are its expertise, responsibility, and corporateness.[1]

expertise. The professional man is an expert with specialized knowledge and skill in a significant field of human endeavor. His expertise is acquired only by prolonged education and experience. It is the basis of objective standards of professional competence for separating the profession from laymen and measuring the relative competence of members of the profession. Such standards are universal. They inhere in the knowledge and skill and are capable of general application irrespective of time and place. The ordinary skill or craft exists only in the present and is mastered by learning an existing technique without reference to what has gone before. Professional knowledge, however, is intellectual in nature and capable of preservation in writing. Professional knowledge has a history, and some knowledge of that history is essential to professional competence. Institutions of research and education are required for the extension and transmission of professional knowledge and skill. Contact is maintained between the academic and practical sides of a profession through journals, conferences, and the circulation of personnel between practice and teaching.

Professional expertise also has a dimension in breadth which is lacking in the normal trade. It is a segment of the total cultural tradition of society. The professional man can successfully apply his skill only when he is aware of this broader tradition of which he is a part. Learned professions are "learned" simply because they are an integral part of the total body of learning of society. Consequently professional education consists of two phases: the first imparting a broad, liberal, cultural background, and the second imparting the specialized skills and knowledge of the profession. The liberal education of the professional man is normally handled by the general educational institutions of society devoted to this purpose. The second or technical phase of professional education, on the other hand, is given in special institutions operated by or affiliated with the profession itself.

RESPONSIBILITY. The professional man is a practicing expert, working in a social context, and performing a service, such as the promotion of health, education, or justice, which is essential to the functioning of society. The client of every profession is society, individually or collectively. A research chemist, for instance, is not a professional man because the service he renders, while beneficial to society, is not essential to its immediate existence and functioning: only Du Pont and the Bureau of Standards have a direct and immediate interest in what he has to offer. The essential and general character of his service and his monopoly of his skill impose upon the professional man the responsibility to perform the service when required by society. This social responsibility distinguishes the professional man from other experts with only intellectual skills. The research chemist, for instance, is still a research chemist if he uses his skills in a manner harmful to society. But the professional man can no longer practice if he refuses to accept his social responsibility: a physician ceases to be a physician if he uses his skills for antisocial purposes. The responsibility to serve and devotion to his skill furnish the professional motive. Financial remuneration cannot be the primary aim of the professional man *qua* professional man. Consequently, professional compensation normally is only partly determined by bargaining on the open market and is regulated by professional custom and law.

The performance of an essential service not regulated by the normal expectation of financial rewards requires some statement governing the relations of the profession to the rest of society. Conflicts between the professional man and his clients, or among members of the profession, normally furnish the immediate impetus to the formulation of such a statement. The profession thus becomes a moral unit positing certain values and ideals which guide its members in their dealings with laymen. This guide may be a set of unwritten norms transmitted through the professional educational system or it may be codified into written canons of professional ethics.

CORPORATENESS. The members of a profession share a sense of organic unity and consciousness of themselves as a group apart from laymen. This collective sense has its origins in the lengthy discipline and training necessary for professional competence, the common bond of work, and the sharing of a unique social responsibility. The sense of unity manifests itself in a professional organization which formalizes and applies the standards of professional competence and establishes and enforces the standards of professional responsibility. Membership in the professional organization, along with the possession of special expertise and the acceptance of special responsibility, thus becomes a criterion of professional status, publicly distinguishing the professional man from the layman. The interest of the profession requires it to bar its members from capitalizing upon professional competence in areas where that competence has no relevance and likewise to protect itself against outsiders who would claim professional competence because of achievements or attributes in other fields. Professional organizations are generally either associations or bureaucracies. In the associational professions such as medicine and law, the practitioner typically functions independently and has a direct personal relationship with his client. The bureaucratic professions, such as the diplomatic service, possess a high degree of specialization of labor and responsibilities within the profession, and the profession as a whole renders a collective service to society as a whole. These two categories are not mutually exclusive: bureaucratic elements exist in most associational professions, and associations frequently supplement the formal structure of bureaucratic professions. The associational professions usually possess written codes of ethics since each practitioner is individually confronted with the problem of proper conduct toward clients and colleagues. The bureaucratic professions, on the other hand, tend to develop a more general sense of collective professional responsibility and the proper role of the profession in society.

THE MILITARY PROFESSION

The vocation of officership meets the principal criteria of professionalism. In practice, no vocation, not even medicine or law, has all the characteristics of the ideal professional type. Officership probably falls somewhat further short of the ideal than either of these. Yet its fundamental character as a profession is undeniable. In practice, officership is strongest and most effective when it most closely approaches the professional ideal; it is weakest and most defective when it falls short of that ideal.

THE EXPERTISE OF OFFICERSHIP. What is the specialized expertise of the military officer? Is there any skill common to all military officers and yet not shared with any civilian groups? At first glance this hardly seems to be the case. The officer corps appears to contain many varieties of specialists, including large numbers which have their counterparts in civilian life. Engineers, doctors, pilots, ordnance experts, personnel experts, intelligence experts, communications experts—all these are found both within and without the modern officer corps. Even ignoring these technical specialists, each absorbed in his own branch of knowledge, just the broad division of the corps into land, sea, and air officers appears to create vast differences in the functions performed and the skills required. The captain of a cruiser and the commander of an infantry division appear to be faced with highly different problems requiring highly different abilities.

Yet a distinct sphere of military competence does exist which is common to all, or almost all, officers and which distinguishes them from all, or almost all, civilians. This central skill is perhaps best summed up in Harold Lasswell's phrase "the management of violence." The function of a military force is successful armed combat. The duties of the military officer include: (1) the organizing, equipping, and training of this force; (2) the planning of its activities; and (3) the direction of its operation in and out of combat. The direction, operation, and control of a human organization whose primary function is the application of violence is the peculiar skill of the officer. It is common to the activities of the air, land, and sea officers. It distinguishes the military officer *qua* military officer from the other specialists which exist in the modern armed services. The skills of these experts may be necessary to the achievement of the objectives of the military force. But they are basically auxiliary vocations, having the same relation to the expertise of the officer as the skills of the nurse, chemist, laboratory technician, dietician, pharmacist, and X-ray technician have to the expertise of the doctor. None of the auxiliary specialists contained within or serving the military profession is capable of the "management of violence," just as none of the specialists aiding the medical profession is capable of the diagnosis and treatment of illness. The essence of officership is embodied in the traditional admonition to Annapolis men that their duty will be to "fight the fleet." Individuals, such as doctors, who are not competent to manage violence but who are members of the officer corps are normally distinguished by special titles and insignia and are excluded from positions of military command. They belong to the officer corps in its capacity as an administrative organization of the state, but not in its capacity as a professional body.

Within the profession itself there are specialists in the management of violence on sea, on land, and in the air, just as there are heart, stomach, and eye specialists within medicine. A military specialist is an officer who is peculiarly expert at directing the application of violence under certain prescribed conditions. The variety of conditions under which violence may be employed and the different forms in which it may be applied form the basis for subprofessional specialization. They also form the basis for evaluating relative technical competence. The larger and more complex the organizations of violence which an officer is capable of directing, and the greater the number of situations and conditions under which he can be employed, the higher is his professional competence. A man who is capable of directing only the activities of an infantry squad has such a low level of professional ability as to be almost on the border line. A man who can manage the operations of an airborne division or a carrier task force is a highly competent professional. The officer who can direct the complex activities of a combined operation involving large-scale sea, air, and land forces is at the top of his vocation.

It is readily apparent that the military function requires a high order of expertise. No individual, whatever his inherent intellectual ability and qualities of character and leadership, could perform these functions efficiently without considerable training and experience. In emergencies an untrained civilian may be capable of acting as a military officer at a low level for a brief period of time, just as in emergencies the intelligent layman may fill in until the doctor arrives. Before the management of violence became the extremely complex task that it is in modern civilization, it was possible for someone without specialized training to practice officership. Now, however, only the person who completely devotes his working hours to this task can hope to develop a reasonable level of professional competence. The skill of the officer is neither a craft (which is primarily mechanical) nor an art (which requires unique and nontransferable talent). It is instead an extraordinarily complex intellectual skill requiring comprehensive study and training. It must be remembered that the peculiar skill of the officer is the management of violence not the act of violence itself. Firing a rifle, for instance, is basically a mechanical craft; directing the operations of a rifle company requires an entirely different type of ability which may in part be learned from books and in part from practice and experience. The intellectual content of the military profession requires the modern officer to devote about one-third of his professional life to formal schooling, probably a higher ratio of educational time to practice time than in any other profession. In part this reflects the limited opportunities of the officer to acquire practical experience at the most important elements of his vocation. But to a large degree it also reflects the extreme complexity of the military expertise.

The peculiar skill of the military officer is universal in the sense that its essence is not affected by changes in time or location. Just as the qualifications of a good surgeon are the same in Zurich as they are in New York, the same standards of professional military competence apply in Russia as in America and in the nineteenth century as in the twentieth. The possession of a common professional skill is a bond among military officers cutting across other differences. The vocation of the officer also possesses a history. The management of violence is not a skill which can be mastered simply by learning existing techniques. It is in a continuous process of development, and it is necessary for the officer to understand this development and to be aware of its main tendencies and trends. Only if he is aware of the historical development of the techniques of organizing and directing military forces can the officer expect to stay on top of his profession. The importance of the history of war and military affairs receives sustained emphasis throughout military writings and military education.

The military skill requires a broad background of general culture for its mastery. The methods of organizing and applying violence at any one stage in history are intimately related to the entire cultural pattern of society. Just as law at its borders merges into history, politics, economics, sociology, and psychology, so also does the military skill. Even more, military knowledge also has frontiers on the natural sciences of chemistry, physics, and biology. To understand his trade properly, the officer must have some idea of its relation to these other fields and the ways in which these other areas of knowledge may contribute to his own purposes. In addition, he cannot really develop his analytical skill, insight, imagination, and judgment if he is trained simply in vocational duties. The abilities and habits of mind which he requires within his professional field can in large part be acquired only through the broader avenues of learning outside his profession. The fact that, like the lawyer and the physician, he is continuously dealing with human beings requires him to have the deeper understanding of human attitudes, motivations, and behavior which a liberal education stimulates. Just as a general education has become the prerequisite for entry into the professions of law and medicine, it is now also almost universally recognized as a desirable qualification for the professional officer.

THE RESPONSIBILITY OF OFFICERSHIP. The expertise of the officer imposes upon him a special social responsibility. The employment of his expertise promiscuously for his own advantage would wreck the fabric of society. As with the practice of medicine, society insists that the management of violence be utilized only for socially approved purposes. Society has a direct, continuing, and general interest in the employment of this skill for the enhancement of its own military security. While all professions are to some extent regulated by the state, the military profession is monopolized by the state. The skill of the physician is diagnosis and treatment; his responsibility is the health of his clients. The skill of the officer is the management of violence; his responsibility is the military security of his client, society. The discharge of the responsibility requires mastery of the skill; mastery of the skill entails acceptance of the responsibility. Both responsibility and skill distinguish the officer from other social types. All members of society have an interest in its security; the state has a direct concern for the achievement of this along with other social values; but the officer corps alone is responsible for military security to the exclusion of all other ends.

Does the officer have a professional motivation? Clearly he does not act primarily from economic incentives. In western society the vocation of officership is not well rewarded monetarily. Nor is his behavior within his profession governed by economic rewards and punishments. The officer is not a mercenary who transfers his services wherever they are best rewarded, nor is he the temporary citizen-soldier inspired by intense momentary patriotism and duty but with no steadying and permanent desire to perfect himself in the management of violence. The motivations of the officer are a technical love for his craft and the sense of social obligation to utilize this craft for the benefit of society. The combination of these drives constitutes professional motivation. Society, on the other hand, can only assure this motivation if it offers its officers continuing and sufficient pay both while on active duty and when retired.

The officer possesses intellectualized skill, mastery of which requires intense study. But like the lawyer and doctor he is not primarily a man of the closet; he deals continuously with people. The test of his professional ability is the application of technical knowledge in a human context. Since this application is not regulated by economic means, however, the officer requires positive guides spelling out his responsibilities to his fellow officers, his subordinates, his superiors, and the state which he serves. His behavior within the military structure is governed by a complex mass of regulations, customs, and traditions. His behavior in relation to society is guided by an awareness that his skill can only be utilized for purposes approved by society through its political agent, the state. While the primary responsibility of the physician is to his patient, and the lawyer to his client, the principal responsibility of the military officer is to the state. His responsibility to the state is the responsibility of the expert adviser. Like the lawyer and physician, he is concerned with only one segment of the activities of his client. Consequently, he cannot impose decisions upon his client which have implications beyond his field of special competence. He can only explain to his client his needs in this area, advise him as to how to meet these needs, and then, when the client has made his decisions, aid him in implementing them. To some extent the officer's behavior towards the state is guided by an explicit code expressed in law and comparable to the canons of professional ethics of the physician and lawyer. To a larger extent, the officer's code is expressed in custom, tradition, and the continuing spirit of the profession.

THE CORPORATE CHARACTER OF OFFICERSHIP. Officership is a public bureaucratized profession. The legal right to practice the profession is limited to members of a carefully defined body. His commission is to the officer what his license is to a doctor. Organically, however, the officer corps is much more than simply a creature of the state. The functional imperatives of security give rise to complex vocational institutions which mold the officer corps into an autonomous social unit. Entrance into this unit is restricted to those with the requisite education and training and is usually permitted only at the lowest level of professional competence. The corporate structure of the officer corps includes not just the official bureaucracy but also societies, associations, schools, journals, customs, and traditions. The professional world of the officer tends to encompass an unusually high proportion of his activities. He normally lives and works apart from the rest of society; physically and socially he probably has fewer nonprofessional contacts than most other professional men. The line between him and the layman or civilian is publicly symbolized by uniforms and insignia of rank.

The officer corps is both a bureaucratic profession and a bureaucratic organization. Within the profession, levels of competence are distinguished by a hierarchy of ranks; within the organization, duties are distinguished by a hierarchy of office. Rank inheres in the individual and reflects his professional achievement measured in terms of experience, seniority, education, and ability. Appointments to rank are normally made by the officer corps itself applying general principles established by the state. Assignments to office are normally somewhat more subject to outside influence. In all bureaucracies authority derives from office; in a professional bureaucracy eligibility for office derives from rank. An officer is permitted to perform certain types of duties and functions by virtue of his rank; he does not receive rank because he has been assigned to an office. Although in practice there are exceptions to this principle, the professional character of the officer corps rests upon the priority of the hierarchy of rank over the hierarchy of office.

The officer corps normally includes a number of nonprofessional "reservists." This is due to the fluctuating need for officers and the impossibility of the state maintaining continuously an officer corps of the size required in emergencies. The reservists are a temporary supplement to the officer corps and qualify for military rank by education and training. While members of the corps, they normally possess all the prerogatives and responsibilities of the professional in the same rank. The legal distinction between them and the professional is preserved, however, and entrance into the permanent corps of officers is much more restricted than entrance into the reserve corps. The reservists seldom achieve the level of professional skill open to the career officers; consequently, the bulk of the reservists are in the lower ranks of the professional bureaucracy while the higher ranks are monopolized by the career professionals. The latter, as the continuing element in the military structure and because of their superior professional competence as a body, are normally charged with the education and indoctrination of the reservists in the skills and the traditions of the vocation. The reservist only temporarily assumes professional responsibility. His principal functions in society lie elsewhere. As a result, his motivations, values, and behavior frequently differ greatly from those of the career professional.

The enlisted men subordinate to the officer corps are a part of the organizational bureaucracy but not of the professional bureaucracy. The enlisted personnel have neither the intellectual skills nor the professional responsibility of the officer. They are specialists in the application of violence not the management of violence. Their vocation is a trade not a profession. This fundamental difference between the officer corps and the enlisted corps is reflected in the sharp line which is universally drawn between the two in all the military forces of the world. If there were not this cleavage, there could be a single military hierarchy extending from the lowest enlisted man to the highest officer. But the differing character of the two vocations makes the organizational hierarchy discontinuous. The ranks which exist in the enlisted corps do not constitute a professional hierarchy. They reflect varying aptitudes, abilities, and offices within the trade of soldier, and movement up and down them is much more fluid than in the officer corps. The difference between the officer and enlisted vocations precludes any general progression from one to the other. Individual enlisted men do become officers but this is the exception rather than the rule. The education and training necessary for officership are normally incompatible with prolonged service as an enlisted man.

The Military Mind: Conservative Realism of the Professional Military Ethic

by Samual P. Huntington

THE MEANING OF THE MILITARY MIND

The unique or functional aspect of the military has often been discussed in terms of the "military mind." This chapter attempts to define this concept precisely enough so that it may serve as a useful tool of analysis. The military mind may be approached from three viewpoints: (1) its ability or quality; (2) its attributes or characteristics; and (3) its attitudes or substance.[1]

Writers employing the first approach have normally emphasized the low caliber of the "military mind." The intelligence, scope, and imagination of the professional soldier have been compared unfavorably to the intelligence, scope, and imagination of the lawyer, the businessman, the politician. This presumed inferiority has been variously attributed to the inherently inferior talents and abilities of the persons who become officers, the organization of the military profession which discourages intellectual initiative, and the infrequent opportunities which an officer has actively to apply his skill. This general approach deals with one feature of the military mind, but it does not help to define the peculiarly "military" aspects of that mind. The mere fact that the military mind occupies a particular point on the intelligence scale says nothing about its distinctive characteristics. The point might well be the same one occupied by the engineering or dental minds.

The second approach holds that the uniqueness of the military mind lies in certain mental attributes or qualities which constitute a military personality. Military and civilian writers generally seem to agree that the military mind is disciplined, rigid, logical, scientific; it is not flexible, tolerant, intuitive, emotional. The continuous performance of

Source: *The Soldier and the State* (1957): 59-79. Reprinted by permission of Vintage Books.

the military function may well give rise to these qualities. Intuitively one feels that these descriptions, also intuitive, come close to the mark. But until more knowledge is accumulated about the personality traits of military men and other politically significant groups and also about the relation between personality, values, and behavior in social situations, this approach will not be very useful in analyzing civil-military relations.

A third and more fruitful approach is to analyze the substance of the military mind—the attitudes, values, views of the military man. This has customarily been done through one of two techniques: to define the military mind in terms of content, or to define it in terms of source. The former method describes certain values and attitudes as military in content, and then asserts that these values and attitudes are widely prevalent among military men. Emphasis has generally focused upon two sets of attitudes assumed to be characteristically military: bellicosity and authoritarianism. The military man is held to believe that peace is stultifying and that conflict and war develop man's highest moral and intellectual qualities; he favors aggressive and bellicose national policies. He is also thought to be opposed to democracy and to desire the organization of society on the basis of the chain of command. Irrespective of whether these conclusions are accurate, the method used in arriving at them is both subjective and arbitrary. The *a priori* assumption that certain values are military and that military men therefore hold those values may or may not be true, but there is nothing in the procedure which requires it to be so.

An alternative approach is to define military values by source. This is to assume that any expression of attitude or value coming from a military source reflects the military mind. But the difficulty here is that everything which comes from a military source does not necessarily derive from its character as a military source. Military men are also Frenchmen and Americans, Methodists and Catholics, liberals and reactionaries, Jews and antisemites. Any given statement by a military man may not reflect his attitudes *qua* military man but may instead stem from social, economic, political, or religious affiliations irrelevant to his military role. This difficulty could be overcome if it were possible to cancel out these accidental characteristics of military men by surveying a broad, representative sample of communications from military men from all walks of life, all countries, and all times. The magnitude of such an undertaking, however, makes it desirable to find an alternative path to the military mind: to arrive at the substance of *l'idée militaire* by defining it as a professional ethic.

People who act the same way over a long period of time tend to develop distinctive and persistent habits of thought. Their unique relation to the world gives them a unique perspective on the world and leads them to rationalize their behavior and role. This is particularly true where the role is a professional one. A profession is more narrowly defined, more intensely and exclusively pursued, and more clearly isolated from other human activity than are most occupations. The continuing objective performance of the professional function gives rise to a continuing professional *weltanschauung* or professional "mind." The military mind, in this sense, consists of the values, attitudes, and perspectives which inhere in the performance of the professional military function and which are deducible from the nature of that function. The military function is performed by a public bureaucratized profession expert in the management of violence and responsible for the military security of the state. A value or attitude is part of the professional military ethic if it is implied by or derived from the peculiar expertise, responsibility, and organization of the military profession. The professional ethic is broader than professional ethics in the narrow sense of the code governing the behavior of the professional man toward nonprofessionals. It includes any preferences and expectations which may be inferred from the continuing performance of the military occupational role.

The military mind is thus defined abstractly as a Weberian ideal type in terms of which the beliefs of actual men and groups can be analyzed. Obviously, no one individual or group will adhere to all the constituent elements of the military ethic, since no individual or group is ever motivated exclusively by military considerations. Any given officer corps will adhere to the ethic only to the extent that it is professional, that is, to the extent that it is shaped by functional rather than societal imperatives. Few expressions of the ethic by an officer corps indicate a low level of professionalism, widespread articulation of the ethic a high degree of professionalism. The professional military ethic, moreover, is "non-dated and non-localized" just like the profession of which it is the intellectual expression. So long as there is no basic alteration in the inherent nature of the military function there will be no change in the content of the professional ethic. Simple changes in military technique, such as developments in weapons technology or the increased importance of economics in military affairs, do not alter the character of the military ethic any more than the discovery of penicillin altered medical ethics. The military ethic consequently is a constant standard by which it is possible to judge the professionalism of any officer corps anywhere anytime. For the sake of clarity, this ideal model may be referred to as the "professional military ethic." The views actually held by a concrete group of officers at some specific point in history may be termed the "nineteenth-century German military ethic" or the "post-World War I American ethic."

In the sections that follow an attempt will be made to elaborate the professional military ethic with respect to (1) basic values and perspectives, (2) national military policy, and (3) the relation of the military to the state. The accuracy of this definition of the ethic depends upon the extent to which the views stated are necessarily implied by the performance of the military function. These deductions as to the nature of the ethic will be illustrated by occasional references to typical expressions drawn from military literature. Since the historical evolution of the military ethic in the United States will be described in some detail in later chapters, the citations from American sources will purposely be limited. These references, moreover, are just examples; they do not prove that the views expressed are part of the professional military ethic any more than a completely contradictory statement from a military man would invalidate their inclusion in the ethic. The sole criterion is relevance to the performance of the military function.

THE PROFESSIONAL MILITARY ETHIC

MAN, SOCIETY, AND HISTORY. The existence of the military profession presupposes conflicting human interests and the use of violence to further those interests. Consequently, the military ethic views conflict as a universal pattern throughout nature and sees violence rooted in the permanent biological and psychological nature of men.

As between the good and evil in man, the military ethic emphasizes the evil. Man is self-ish. He is motivated by drives for power, wealth, and security. "The human mind is by nature one-sided and limited."[2] As between the strength and weakness in man, the military ethic emphasizes the weakness. Man's selfishness leads to struggle but man's weakness makes successful conflict dependent upon organization, discipline, and leadership. As Clausewitz said, "All war presupposes human weakness, and against that it is direct-ed." No one is more aware than the professional soldier that the normal man is no hero. The military profession organizes men so as to overcome their inherent fears and fail-ings.[3] The uncertainty and chance involved in the conduct of war and the difficulty of anticipating the actions of an opponent make the military man skeptical of the range of human foresight and control. As between reason and irrationality in man, the military ethic emphasizes the limits of reason. The best schemes of men are frustrated by the "friction" existing in reality. "War is the province of uncertainty," Clausewitz said; "three-fourths of the things on which action in war is based lie hidden in the fog of greater or less uncertainty." Human nature, moreover, is universal and unchanging. Men in all places and at all times are basically the same.[4] The military view of man is thus decided-ly pessimistic. Man has elements of goodness, strength, and reason, but he is also evil, weak, and irrational. The man of the military ethic is essentially the man of Hobbes.

The existence of the military profession depends upon the existence of competing nation states. The responsibility of the profession is to enhance the military security of the state. The discharge of this responsibility requires cooperation, organization, disci-pline. Both because it is his duty to serve society as a whole and because of the nature of the means which he employs to carry out this duty, the military man emphasizes the importance of the group as against the individual. Success in any activity requires the sub-ordination of the will of the individual to the will of the group. Tradition, *esprit*, unity, community—these rate high in the military value system. The officer submerges his per-sonal interests and desires to what is necessary for the good of the service. As a nine-teenth-century German officer put it, the military man must "forego personal advantage, lucre, and prosperity... Egotism is beyond all doubt the most bitter enemy of the quali-ties essential to the officer-corps."[5] Man is preëminently a social animal. He exists only in groups. He defends himself only in groups. Most importantly, he realizes himself only in groups. The "weak, mediocre, transient individual" can only achieve emotional satis-faction and moral fulfillment by participating in "the power, the greatness, the perma-nence and the splendour" of a continuing organic body.[6] The military ethic is basically corporative in spirit. It is fundamentally anti-individualistic.

The military vocation is a profession because it has accumulated experiences which make up a body of professional knowledge. In the military view, man learns only from experience. If he has little opportunity to learn from his own experience, he must learn from the experience of others. Hence, the military officer studies history. For history is, in Liddell Hart's phrase, "universal experience," and military history, as Moltke said, is the "most effective means of teaching war during peace." The military ethic thus places unusual value upon the ordered, purposive study of history.[7] History is valuable to the military man only when it is used to develop principles which may be capable of future application. The military student of history constantly tries to draw generalizations from his study. Yet the military ethic is not bound to any specific theory of history. While it rejects monistic interpretations, it also emphasizes the importance of force as contrasted with ideological and economic factors. The permanence of human nature makes impossible any theory of progress. "Change is inevitable. Progress is not inevitable."[8] Insofar as there is a pattern in history, it is cyclical in nature. Civilizations rise and fall. War and peace alternate, and so also does the supremacy of offensive and defensive warfare.[9]

NATIONAL MILITARY POLICY. The military view toward national policy reflects the professional responsibility for the military security of the state. This responsibility leads the military: (1) to view the state as the basic unit of political organization; (2) to stress the continuing nature of the threats to the military security of the state and the continuing likelihood of war; (3) to emphasize the magnitude and immediacy of the security threats; (4) to favor the maintenance of strong, diverse, and ready military forces; (5) to oppose the extension of state commitments and the involvement of the state in war except when victory is certain.

The Primacy of the Nation State. The existence of the military profession depends upon the existence of nation states capable of maintaining a military establishment and desiring to maintain such an establishment because of threats to their security. There is no necessary reason why nation states should be the only socio-political groups maintaining professional forces. But with a few peripheral exceptions, this has been true. The military man consequently tends to assume that the nation state is the ultimate form of political organization. The justification for the maintenance and employment of military force is in the political ends of the state. The causes of war are always political. State policy aimed at continuing political objectives precedes war, determines the resort to war, dictates the nature of the war, concludes the war, and continues on after the war. War must be the instrument of political purpose. The purpose of the state cannot be its own destruction. Consequently "total war" or "absolute war" is to be avoided if it is likely to produce the mutual devastation of the combatants.[10]

The Permanency of Insecurity and the Inevitability of War. In a world of independent nation states, the problem of military security is never finally solved. Competition among the states is continuous, and war is only an intensification of this competition which brings to a crisis the ever present issue of military security. War is always likely and is ultimately inevitable. Its immediate causes spring from conflicting state policies, but its fundamental causes lie deep in human nature where exist the sources of all human conflict. "To abolish war we must remove its cause, which lies in the imperfection of human nature."[11]

If the causes of war are in human nature, the complete abolition of war is impossible. Consequently, the military mind is skeptical of institutional devices designed to prevent war. Treaties, international law, international arbitration, the Hague Court, the League of Nations, the United Nations are of little help to peace. The decisive factor is always the power relation existing among the states. "In the last analysis the action of States is regulated by nothing but power and expediency."[12] Diplomacy itself only provides a superficial covering for the existence and uses of power. Treaties and other international agreements have meaning only insofar as they reflect the realities of international power. A state can achieve little by diplomacy unless it has the strength and the will to back up its demands with force. As Nelson once said: "A fleet of British ships of war is the best negotiator in Europe."

The Magnitude and Immediacy of the Security Threats. The military man normally views with alarm the potency and immediacy of the security threats to the state. As Lord Salisbury once remarked: "If you believe the doctors, nothing is wholesome: if you believe the theologians, nothing is innocent: if you believe the soldiers, nothing is safe." The military man recognizes the continuing character of threats to the state, but he also stresses the urgency of the current danger. The goal of professional competence requires the military man to estimate the threat as accurately as possible. But the military man also has a professional interest and a professional duty to stress the dangers to military security. Consequently the objective realities of international politics only partially determine the military estimate of the situation. The military man's views also reflect a subjective professional bias, the strength of which depends upon his general level of professionalism. This professional bias, or sense of professional responsibility, leads him to feel that if he errs in his estimate, it should be on the side of overstating the threat. Consequently, at times he will see threats to the security of the state where actually no threats exist.

In estimating the security threats the military man looks at the capabilities of other states rather than at their intentions. Intentions are political in nature, inherently fickle and changeable, and virtually impossible to evaluate and predict.[13] The military man is professionally capable of estimating the fighting strength of another state. But judging its policies is a matter of politics outside his competence. Human nature being what it is, a stronger state should never be trusted even if it proclaims the friendliest intentions. If a state has the power to injure one's own security, it is necessary to assume that it will do so. Safety requires attributing to other powers the worst intentions and the shrewdest abilities. It is a military responsibility to be prepared for any eventuality. The military "opinion must never be coloured by wishful thinking. . . The military man will be dealing with military fact, hard figures, grim realities of time and space and resources."[14] Military planners of one country may prepare elaborate plans for a war with another country without necessarily indicating that it is the purpose of the first country to attack the second.

The Level and Sources of Military Strength. The concern of military men with the dangers to national security leads them to urge the enlarging and strengthening of the military forces available to protect the security of the state. The most common manifestation of this is the demand for a larger share of the national budget. The same concern also leads the military to desire the conversion of military resources (the economic and human potential of the state) into actual military strength. The military man typically prefers regular troops to reserve forces and stockpiles of weapons to factories capable of building weapons. He wants force in being, not latent force. He also desires forces capable of meeting virtually every possible contingency. The limitations of human foresight make it dangerous to assume that security threats will necessarily take one particular form. Consequently the military man favors maintaining the broadest possible variety of weapons and forces provided that each weapons system is kept sufficiently strong so that it is capable of dealing with the threat it is designed to meet. Since the state normally is incapable of maintaining forces to meet all or most possible threats, the military man is usually required to establish a ladder of military priorities. Theoretically he should do this in terms of the objective requirements of military security. In reality, of course, he tends to stress those military needs and forces with which he is particularly familiar. To the extent that he acts in this manner he becomes a spokesman for a particular service or branch interest rather than for the military viewpoint as a whole. No matter what hierarchy of priorities he establishes, however, his military instincts lead him to urge the state to go as far down the ladder as possible.

The military man also favors protecting the state through guarantees and alliances, provided that these arrangements increase the strength of the state more than they increase its commitments. Weak, unstable, and adventurous allies are a liability rather than an asset. Allies should be selected purely on the basis of mutuality of national security interests regardless of ideological and political concerns. "Alliances between States should be regarded entirely from the point of view of might [power] policy."[15] The author of this dictum was a German monarchist but he had no more compunctions about military cooperation with communist Russia in the 1920's than American military leaders had about cooperating with fascist Spain in the 1950's. National strength may also be increased by the expansion of national territory and the acquisition of foreign bases. Here too, however, it is essential that the expansion of territory result in a real increase in power and not simply an overextension of commitments. The military man has no desire to acquire isolated, overseas territories which are vulnerable to attack and difficult to defend.

The Restriction of Commitments and the Avoidance of War. The military man has no concern with the desirability or undesirability of political goals as such. He is, however, concerned with the relation between political goals and military means since this directly affects the military security of the state. The politician must beware of overcommitting the nation beyond the strength of its military capabilities. Grand political designs and sweeping political goals are to be avoided, not because they are undesirable but because they are impractical.* The military security of the state must come first. Moral aims and ideological ends should not be pursued at the expense of that security. The political object is the goal, but in Clausewitz's words, it "is not on that account a despotic lawgiver; it must adapt itself to the nature of the means at its disposal . . ." The statesman furnishes the dynamic, purposive element to state policy. The military man represents the passive, instrumental means. It is his function to warn the statesman when his purposes are beyond his means.

The military man normally opposes reckless, aggressive, belligerent action. If war with a particular power is inevitable at a later date with decreased chances of success, the military man may favor "preventive war" in order to safeguard national security. Normally, however, he recognizes the impossibility of predicting the future with certainty. War at any time is an intensification of the threats to the military security of the state, and generally war should not be resorted to except as a final recourse, and only when the outcome is a virtual certainty.[16] This latter condition is seldom met except in

---

*"The duty of a professional military man obliges him to be a pessimist. He must be the 'no' man for idealism and wishful thinking. Unpopular as it makes him during periods of peace and prosperity he must assume that such conditions are transient, and that the pendulum of history will eventually swing back to the point where the country must risk its well-being and possibly its survival on the final arbitration of armed force." R. A. Hall (Capt., US), "The Peacetime Duties of the Armed Services," U.S. Naval Institute *Proceedings*, LXXX (June 1946), 781.

the case of a powerful state fighting an isolated minor or backward nation. Thus, the military man rarely favors war. He will always argue that the danger of war requires increased armaments; he will seldom argue that increased armaments make war practical or desirable. He always favors preparedness, but he never feels prepared. Accordingly, the professional military man contributes a cautious, conservative, restraining voice to the formulation of state policy. This has been his typical role in most modern states including fascist Germany, communist Russia, and democratic America. He is afraid of war. He wants to prepared for war. But he is never ready to fight a war.

This pacifist attitude may well have its roots in institutional conservatism as well as concern for state security. The military leader is at the top of one of the great power structures of society. He risks everything if that society becomes engaged in war. Whether victorious or not, war is more unsettling to military institutions than to any others. A Tsarist officer once said that he hated war because "it spoils the armies," and American naval officers complained that the Civil War "ruined the navy."[17] This attitude reflects an orientation about means to the point where means become ends, to where, in Merton's terms, the latent function supersedes the manifest function. The military man in his concern with power may come to consider the accumulation of power as an end in itself irrespective of the uses to which it may be put. He may become most reluctant to dissipate that power in any manner.

The military man tends to see himself as the perennial victim of civilian warmongering. It is the people and the politicians, public opinion and governments, who start wars. It is the military who have to fight them. Civilian philosophers, publicists, academicians, not soldiers, have been the romanticizers and glorifiers of war. Military force as such does not cause wars. The state which desires peace must be well armed to enforce its desire. Weak states invite attack. The tendency of the civilian politician is to court popular favor by curbing the arms budget and simultaneously pursuing an adventurous foreign policy. The military man opposes both tendencies. The military ethic thus draws a sharp distinction between armed strength and bellicosity, the military state and the warlike state.[18] The former embodies the military virtues of ordered power: discipline, hierarchy, restraint, steadfastness. The latter is characterized by wild, irresponsible excitement and enthusiasm, and by the love of violence, glory, and adventure. For the professional military man, familiar with war, this type of mentality has little appeal. Believing in the ultimate inevitability of war, he raises the strongest voice against immediate involvement in war.

THE MILITARY AND THE STATE. The military profession is expert and limited. Its members have specialized competence within their field and lack that competence outside their field. The relation of the profession to the state is based upon this natural division of labor. The essence of this relationship concerns the relative scope of competence of the military expert and political expert or statesman. Before the professionalization of military science in the nineteenth century, the same person could be simultaneously qualified in both fields. Now this is impossible. Napoleon embodied the old unity of military science and politics. He was replaced by Bismarck and Moltke who symbolized the new dichotomy.* The exact character of the relationship which should exist between statesman and military officer cannot be defined precisely. But it is possible to state some of the principles which should govern that relationship.

Military science is an area in which specialized competence acquired by professional training and experience is necessary for decision and action. This field, which concerns the implementation of state policy by armed force, is divided into constant and variable components. This division was recognized only after the emergence of the military profession. The constant element reflects the permanency of human nature and physical geography. This may be called strategy, and so distinguished from the variable elements, tactics and logistics, or it may be formulated into a set of "fundamental," "immutable," "eternal," "unchanging and unchangeable" principles of war. Military historians differ as to the number and content of these principles but they do not question their existence as the fundamental core of military science. Their application, however, is constantly changing with changes in technology and social organization. The ideal military man is thus conservative in strategy, but open-minded and progressive with respect to new weapons and new tactical forms. He is equally expert in both the constant and variable aspects of military science. The essence of his art may indeed be defined as the relation between the two: "the unchangeable fundamental conditions of good generalship in their relation to changeable tactical forms . . ."[19] It is this area within which the statesman must accept the judgments of the military professional.

Politics deals with the goals of state policy. Competence in this field consists in having a broad awareness of the elements and interests entering into a decision and in possessing the legitimate authority to make such a decision. Politics is beyond the scope of military competence, and the participation of military officers in politics undermines their professionalism, curtailing their professional competence, dividing the profession against itself, and substituting extraneous values for professional values. The military officer must remain neutral politically. "The military commander must never allow his military judgment to be warped by political expediency."[20] The area of military science is subordinate to, and yet independent of, the area of politics. Just as war serves the ends of politics, the military profession serves the ends of the state. Yet the statesman must recognize the integrity of the profession and its subject matter. The military man has the right to expect political guidance from the statesman. Civilian control exists when there is this proper subordination of an autonomous profession to the ends of policy.

The responsibilities of the military man to the state are threefold. He has, first, a representative function, to represent the claims of military security within the state machinery. He must keep the authorities of the state informed as to what he considers necessary for the minimum military security of the state in the light of the capabilities of other powers. The extent to which he may carry the presentation of his views is difficult to define but he must recognize and accept the fact that there are limits. In general, he has the right and the duty to present his views to the public bodies, whether executive or legislative, which are charged with the apportionment of resources between the military and other claims. Secondly, the military officer has an advisory function, to analyze and to report

---

*"Interchangeability between the statesman and the soldier passed forever, I fear, in the last century. The Germans professionalized the trade of war; and modern inventions, by increasing its technicalities, have specialized it. It is much the same with politics, professionalized by democracy. No longer can one man hope to exercise both callings, though both are branches of the same craft, the governance of men and the ordering of human affairs." Field Marshal Earl Wavell, *The Good Soldier* (London, 1948), pp. 27-28.

on the implications of alternative courses of state action from the military point of view. If the state leaders are weighing three possible policies, the military man, of course, cannot judge which is the most desirable. He may, however, say that the first policy could easily be carried out with the military strength currently available, that the second policy would involve serious risks unless there is a considerable augmentation of military forces, and that the third policy is simply beyond the military capability of the state to implement effectively. Finally, the military officer has an executive function, to implement state decisions with respect to military security even if it is a decision which runs violently counter to his military judgment. The statesmen set the goal and allocate to him the resources to be used in attaining that goal. It is then up to him to do the best he can. This is indeed the meaning of military strategy in relation to policy: "the practical adaptation of the means placed at a general's disposal to the attainment of the object in view." [21]

Obviously a considerable area exists where strategy and policy overlap. In this realm the supreme military commander may make a decision on purely military grounds only to discover that it has political implications unknown to him. When this turns out to be the case, considerations of strategy must then give way to considerations of policy. The military man must recognize that a wide number of conceivably purely military decisions, such as the selection of a theater of war, also involve politics, and he must be guided accordingly. As Clausewitz said, "the art of war in its highest point of view becomes policy, but, of course, a policy which fights battles instead of writing notes." The top military leaders of the state inevitably operate in this intermingled world of strategy and policy. They must always be alert to the political implications of their military attitudes and be willing to accept the final decisions of the statesmen. When required in his executive capacity to make decisions involving both military and political elements, the military man ideally should formulate his military solution first and then alter it as needs be on the advice of his political advisers.

The military profession exists to serve the state. To render the highest possible service the entire profession and the military force which it leads must be constituted as an effective instrument of state policy. Since political direction comes only from the top, this means that the profession has to be organized into a hierarchy of obedience. For the profession to perform its function, each level within it must be able to command the instantaneous and loyal obedience of subordinate levels. Without these relationships military professionalism is impossible. Consequently, loyalty and obedience are the highest military virtues: "the rule of obedience is simply the expression of that one among the military virtues upon which all the others depend . . ."[22] When the military man receives a legal order from an authorized superior, he does not argue, he does not hesitate, he does not substitute his own views; he obeys instantly. He is judged not by the policies he implements, but rather by the promptness and efficiency with which he carries them out. His goal is to perfect an instrument of obedience; the uses to which that instrument is put are beyond his responsibility. His highest virtue is instrumental not ultimate. Like Shakespeare's soldier in *Henry V*, he believes that the justice of the cause is more than he should "know" or "seek after." For if the king's "cause be wrong, our obedience to the King wipes the crime of it out of us."

An officer corps is professional only to the extent to which its loyalty is to the military ideal. Other loyalties are transient and divisive. What appeals politically one day will be forgotten the next. What appeals politically to one man will inspire the hatred of another. Within the military forces only military loyalty to the ideal of professional competence is constant and unifying: loyalty of the individual to the ideal of the Good Soldier, loyalty of the unit to the traditions and spirit of the Best Regiment. The most effective forces and the most competent officer corps are those which are motivated by these ideals rather than by political or ideological aims. Only if they are motivated by military ideals will the armed forces be the obedient servants of the state and will civilian control be assured. In the modern army the professional motivation of the officers contrasts with that of the temporary citizen-soldiers who are conscripted or who enlist because of economic or political appeals. The professional officer corps is the instrument of the state in insuring the obedience of the enlisted personnel. The latter, of course, can never develop professional motivation and the sense of professional responsibility characteristic of the West Point or St. Cyr graduate. Nonetheless, the difference between the professional officers and the enlisted personnel is minimized to the extent that the enlisted personnel become indifferent to outside motivations and influences. The professional army which fights well because it is its job to fight well is far more reliable than the political army which fights well only while sustained by a higher purpose. The United States Marine Corps and the French Foreign Legion serve their governments with unvarying and impartial competence whatever the campaign. The military quality of the professional is independent of the cause for which he fights.

The supreme military virtue is obedience. But what are the limits of obedience? This question arises in two separate connections. The first concerns the relation between military obedience and professional competence, the moral and intellectual virtues of the officer. The second concerns the conflict between the military value of obedience and nonmilitary values.

Military Obedience versus Professional Competence. The conflict between military obedience and professional competence usually involves the relation of a military subordinate to a military superior. It arises in two broad senses: operational and doctrinal. The former concerns the execution by a subordinate of a military order which in his judgment will result in military disaster. Assuming he has made his views known to his superior and the superior persists in his order, or assuming he does not have the opportunity to present his views, does the subordinate nonetheless obey? The purpose of obedience is to further the objective of the superior. If the subordinate is thoroughly acquainted with this object, and circumstances unknown to the superior make it possible to achieve the object only through a disobedience of orders, the subordinate may then be justified in disobeying. Only rarely, however, will this be the case. Normally the disruption of the military organization caused by disobedience to operational orders will outweigh the benefits gained by such obedience. The greater competence and knowledge of the superior officer must be assumed. In operations, and even more particularly in combat, ready obedience cannot conflict with military competence: it is the essence of military competence.*

---

*The classic instances of the disobedience of operational orders involve Lord Nelson, who justified his behavior in one case on the grounds that: "I find few think as I do but, to obey orders is all perfection. What would my superiors direct, did they know what is passing under my nose? To serve my King and to destroy the French I consider as the great order of all, from which little ones spring, and if one of these little ones militate against it, I go back to obey the great order." See A. T. Mahan, *The Life of Nelson* (Boston, 2 vols., 2d ed. rev., 1900), I, 56–63, 189–191, 445–451, II, 89–92, and *Retrospect and Prospect* (Boston, 1902), pp. 255–283.

The second possible manifestation of the conflict of military obedience with professional competence involves nonoperational doctrinal issues. Rigid and inflexible obedience may well stifle new ideas and become slave to an unprogressive routine. It is not infrequent that a high command has had its thinking frozen in the past and has utilized its control of the military hierarchy to suppress uncomfortable new developments in tactics and technology. In a situation of this sort, to what extent may a junior officer be justified in disobeying his superiors to advance professional knowledge? There are no easy answers to this question. The authority of superior officers is presumed to reflect superior professional ability. When this is not the case, the hierarchy of command is being prostituted to nonprofessional purposes. Yet the subordinate officer must tread judiciously in pushing doctrines which seem to him to be manifestly superior to those embodied in the manuals. In particular, the subordinate must consider whether the introduction of the new technique, assuming he is successful in his struggle, will so increase military efficiency as to offset the impairment of that efficiency caused by the disruption of the chain of command. If it does, his disobedience is justified. Ultimately, professional competence must be the final criterion.[23]

Military Obedience versus Nonmilitary Values. The second set of problems concerns the relation of military obedience to nonmilitary values. What is the responsibility of the officer when he is ordered by the statesman to follow a course which he knows will lead to national disaster? Or when he is ordered to do something which manifestly violates the law of the land? Or when he is ordered to do something which is an equally clear transgression of commonly accepted standards of morality? It appears possible to divide these issues into four groups.

First, there is the conflict between military obedience and political wisdom. We have already said that a military subordinate may be justified in forcing upon military leaders new developments which will increase professional efficiency. Should not the same relationship exist between the higher commander and the statesman? If the statesman is pursuing a course which seems to be sheer political folly, is not the military commander justified in resisting it by appeal to the standards of political wisdom? The subordinate officer "bucking" his superiors defends himself by appealing to professional wisdom. There is, however, a vast difference between these two cases. The criteria of military efficiency are limited, concrete, and relatively objective; the criteria of political wisdom are indefinite, ambiguous, and highly subjective. Politics is an art, military science a profession. No commonly accepted political values exist by which the military officer can prove to reasonable men that his political judgment is preferable to that of the statesmen. The superior political wisdom of the statesman must be accepted as a fact. If the statesman decides upon war which the soldier knows can only lead to national catastrophe, then the soldier, after presenting his opinion, must fall to and make the best of a bad situation. The commanding generals of the German army in the late 1930's, for instance, almost unanimously believed that Hitler's foreign policies would lead to national ruin. Military duty, however, required them to carry out his orders: some followed this course, others forsook the professional code to push their political goals. General MacArthur's opposition to the manner in which the government was conducting the Korean War was essentially similar. Both the German officers who joined the resistance to Hitler and General MacArthur forgot that it is not the function of military officers to decide questions of war and peace.

Second, and at the other extreme, there is the conflict between military obedience and military competence when that competence is threatened by a political superior. What does the military officer do when he is ordered by a statesman to take a measure which is militarily absurd when judged by professional standards and which is strictly within the military realm without any political implications? This situation, provided that the last qualification holds and that it is completely removed from politics, represents a clear invasion of the professional realm by extraneous considerations. The presumption of superior professional competence which existed in the case of a military superior giving a questionable order does not exist when the statesman enters military affairs. Here the existence of professional standards justifies military disobedience. The statesman has no business deciding, as Hitler did in the later phases of World War II, whether battalions in combat should advance or retreat.

Third, and between these two extreme cases, there is the conflict between military obedience and legality. What does the military officer do when he receives an order which his civilian superior does not have the legal authority to issue? Presumably, the military officer as the servant of the state is the servant only of the legitimately constituted authorities of the state. If the statesman in ordering his action recognizes himself that he is acting illegally, then the military officer is justified in disobeying. If the statesman claims to be acting legally, but the action seems illegal to the officer, then the issue is one of the relative competence of the officer and the statesman to judge what is legal and illegal. Most modern states which have military professions also have a group of specialized experts, the judiciary, whose function it is to decide such issues. If their judgment can be obtained, the military officer is bound to accept it. If this is not possible, either because of the urgency of the situation or because the legality of the judiciary itself is in doubt, the military officer can only study the law applicable to the situation and arrive at his own decision. The standards of law are generally far more precise than those of politics but less definite than those of military science. In any event, the officer is bound to give a considerable presumption of validity to the opinion of the statesman. If there are two governments in the state, each claiming to be duly constituted and to be deserving of military obedience, the military officer cannot escape the political choice between them.

Finally, there is the conflict between military obedience and basic morality. What does the military officer do if he is ordered by the statesman to commit genocide, to exterminate the people of an occupied territory? So far as ability to judge and apply ethical standards are concerned, the statesman and the soldier are equal. Both are free individuals morally responsible for their actions. The soldier cannot surrender to the civilian his right to make ultimate moral judgments. He cannot deny himself as a moral individual. Yet the problem is not as simple as this. For politics as well as basic morality may be involved here. The statesman may well feel compelled to violate commonly accepted morality in order to further the political interests of the state. That this is frequently the case, there is no denying. If the statesman rejects the private claims of conscience in favor of the *raison d'état*, is he also justified in implicating the military man too, in subordinating, in effect, the military man's conscience as well as his own? For the officer this comes down to a choice between his own conscience on the one hand, and the good of the state, plus the professional virtue of obedience, upon the other. As a soldier, he owes obedience; as a man, he owes disobedience. Except in the most extreme instances it is reasonable to expect that he will adhere to the professional ethic and obey. Only rarely will the military man be justified in following the dictates of private conscience against the dual demand of military obedience and state welfare.

SUMMARY CONSERVATIVE REALISM. The military ethic emphasizes the permanence, irrationality, weakness, and evil in human nature. It stresses the supremacy of society over the individual and the importance of order, hierarchy, division of function. It stresses the continuity and value of history. It accepts the nation state as the highest form of political organization and recognizes the continuing likelihood of wars among nation states. It emphasizes the importance of power in international relations and warns of the dangers to state security. It holds at the security of the state depends upon the creation and maintenance of strong military forces. It urges the limitation of state action to the direct interests of the state, the restriction of extensive commitments, and the undesirability of bellicose or adventurous policies. It holds that war is the instrument of politics, that the military are the servants of the statesman, and that civilian control is essential to military professionalism. It exalts obedience as the highest virtue of military men. The military ethic is thus pessimistic, collectivist, historically inclined, power-oriented, nationalistic, militaristic, pacifist, and instrumentalist in its view of the military profession. It is, in brief, realistic and conservative.

On Entering
The Military Profession

by Martin Blumenson

When Bucknell University's cadets graduated and were commissioned this year, ARMY's Contributing Editor Martin Blumenson spoke to them on the origin and significance of the military profession. Excerpts of his speech follow:

Today is a day of celebration and congratulations. Young men and women of the university have completed their preliminary work. They have proved their merit. They have been admitted to and are entering into the military profession.

The origins of the modern military profession are to be found, like the other early professions, in the guilds and brotherhoods of medieval times. I speak of medicine, the law, theology and the military. As professions, they all display the same characteristics.

Each exists to render beneficial service to the society, the community. Each requires special education, medical or law school, Id theological seminary and, for the military, an academy, officers candidate school or ROTC. The special education imparts not only practical knowledge but also theoretical understanding of the profession's activities, methods and endeavors. Each profession engages in full-time employment for pay. It is not only the pay that distinguishes professionals from amateurs; each profession provides its members with standard responses to given situations.

Each profession regulates its own procedures, code of behavior, style of dress. Each selects certain members for promotion and honor. Finally, each member of these professions requires a license to practice—the commission in your case. This is what we celebrate today, the commissioning of our ROTC graduates.

It used to be that military service was prerogative of class. Only members of the upper class, the nobility, the aristocracy, could be warriors. To be armed, to carry weapons was a special privilege limited to the elite. That idea, or traces of it, persisted until at least the 19 century.

Source: *Army Magazine* (September, 1996) 13-15. Reprinted by permission of the U.S. Army Magazine.

Gradually, as the medieval structure gave way to the emergence of states, a higher level of education became necessary for the military. As technology developed and as new weapons came into being, one needed to know some mathematics in order to fire artillery with some degree of accuracy. Aristocrats who lived in isolated castles were less likely to be learned than certain non-nobles or member of the bourgeoisie, that is, wealthy commoners who lived in towns. Educated commoners were better equipped to handle technical matters of increasing complexity. And over the years, they were allowed to enter the military profession. Today, our democratic society imposes no test of class on those who can be commissioned. Anyone adequately qualified in the modern sense can be an officer. But the tradition of the aristocrat continues.

How are you who are new officers likely to function in your profession. Historically, the task of the military is to defend its society against threats, both internal and external. The military thus has a twin mission. Against internal threats, in domestic disturbances, the military aids in the police power. Troops also aid the civil power and protect lives and property in time of natural disaster or special crisis.

Allied to the police power in another distinct mission. Because the military is an organized force trained and ready to act immediately in any capacity, the federal and state governments may call upon it for a particular task such as responding to natural disasters. In earlier times, stringing telegraph wires in Alaska, flying the mail in the 1920s or building dams were jobs the military was asked to perform. These were special jobs—at a particular time and place—that only the military could undertake and carry through.

Of course, the main purpose of the military is to wage warfare against external enen-des. This is what the military is trained to do. This is the area where the honors, the decorations, the recognitions of greatness and fame are won. War is, of course, a political act determined and shaped by the political authorities. This remains a constant, but the nature of warfare has changed over the years.

The history of modern warfare may be said to begin with the Thirty Years' War in the 17th century. This war was so brutal—there were so many deaths—that it threatened to destroy the aristocracy in Europe. The war was simply killing off members of the nobility. To save them from extinction, the Peace of Westphalia, which ended the war in 1648, set up new rules to regulate warfare. The main features of what has come to be termed the Westphalian system are these:

First, each state then in existence was sovereign. It was independent and free to govern itself within its borders.

Second, the state had a monopoly to wage war. Only the state could make war, and it did so by means of a regular, uniformed army. Since the state was responsible for all legitimate violence, all other groups resorting to war or violence were, per se, criminal.

Third, regular forces fought against enemy regular forces. Everyone else was a noncombatant. Fourth, at the time of the Peace of Westphalia, because making war was expensive, regular forces or armies tended to be small and wars to be short. The objectives of a war were small—a piece of the enemy's territory or a seaport or a mine. We call this "limited" in the number of people involved and limited in objectives.

This is the essence of the Westphalian system, and it makes a great deal of sense. But since its inception, the principles have been eroding. For example, sovereignty has declined. The freedom of a state to govern itself within its borders is no longer regarded as quite so sacred as before. Whatever Nazi Germany did within its borders before World War II, even its campaign of genocide, was perfectly all right according to Westphalian doctrine. Thus, no outside state interfered. After World War II, human rights acquired great importance. Concern for human rights now transcends national borders. We are interested in human rights everywhere, and thus sovereignty no longer has the exclusivity it once had. In addition, the United Nations has assumed some of the powers of the state. Regular military forces are now operating under U.N. command throughout the world.

Another change in the Westphalian system has been the nature of the state and the war it wages. The American and French Revolutions, particularly the latter, changed states into nations. The inhabitants, instead of being subjects of the state, became citizens of the nation. The nation belonged to them, not to the royalty. All the owners of a nation wanted to participate in war, and warfare became democratized. Regular armies swelled to unheard-of size in wartime.

In France, *la patrie*, the country or the nation, became an emotional entity, and patriotism emerged, a special kind of love and respect and regard for one's country. Military campaigns were supported by public opinion and turned into emotional drives motivated by hatred for the enemy. Passions rather than statecraft drove hostilities. Not only regular soldiers but also civilians became potential casualties. Weapons were no longer selective; they could no longer distinguish between combatants and combatants. War became total, total in the means employed to win, that is, total exertion to destroy the enemy. What was wanted was a total victory over the adversary.

During our Civil War, the North destroyed the South, politically as well as economically. In World Wars I and II the Allies destroyed the German government both times. This kind of warfare, total war, lasted from about 1800 to 1945, the end of World War II. By then, technology had made that kind of war obsolete. The weapons of war, not only the atomic bombs, were simply too lethal, too destructive, for this kind of war to continue. For war is, as I have said, a political act, fought for political aims, and total destruction, potentially of our planet, is hardly a political objective except for the insane.

Still another Westphalian tenet has eroded. During the French expansion late in the 18th and early in the 19th century, French armies occupied much of Western Europe, including Spain. Spanish patriots objected to the occupying forces and instituted guerrilla warfare against them, small wars by irregular forces. When these irregular soldiers were captured, they were executed, shot or hanged because they were not the regular forces recognized by the Westphalian system. According to the doctrine, they were criminals.

During the Franco-Prussian War of 1870-71, Prussian regular troops occupied much of France. French patriots, irregular forces, attacked the occupiers. Once again, those who were captured were executed, for they were not regulars, and they had no rights as belligerents; they were criminals.

By the time of World War II, guerrilla warfare was legitimate. Under important Geneva Conventions, so long as partisan forces were organized into units with recognized leaders, so long as the members wore a distinctive identifying badge, armband, hat, shirt or bandanna, they were regarded, at least theoretically, as having the same rights as regular soldiers.

Today, states or nations no longer have the sole right to wage war. So long as organized troops, usually representing ethnic groups, fight for political aims and not purely for violence or for criminal ends, they have gained the right to be recognized as legitimate warriors.

The newest form of warfare is the use of terror to gain a political objective. Like the modern weapons of regular forces, terror is nonselective. It harms noncombatant civilians as well as legitimate targets.

For quite some time now, military forces have engaged in peacekeeping. Instead of using their weapons in a quest for force and violence, the military has been called upon to maintain peace. It is a new and nontraditional mission, and the military so engaged has been splendid in its performance.

During your active duty, however, you may participate in waging war. You have to be prepared to. In that pursuit, you can do no better than to emulate the great officers who have gone before you. What the future holds, no one knows. I believe that we have entered a new historical age and are not yet aware of its parameters, it regulations, its meaning.

Despite the fundamental alterations evident in our particular society, we still rely on the military to protect us, to defend us against the threat of violence and intimidation.

So we count on you. Serving in the military has always been and continues to be challenging work. You who are entering the profession will have problems and difficulties. You will also enjoy finding solutions to crises of one sort or another. You will have great satisfaction in discharging enormous responsibilities, including responsibility for the lives of those who are placed in your charge. I urge you to read about your profession, to learn its history and traditions. And I wish you the best.

In conclusion, I should like to read an excerpt from a talk given by George S. Patton Jr., one of our greatest and most professional soldiers, to his officers in 1919. This is what he said.

"We as soldiers . . . are not only members of the oldest of honorable professions, but we are also the modern representatives of the den-d-gods and heroes of antiquity. Back of us stretches a line of men whose acts of valor, of self-sacrifice, and of service have been the theme of song and story since long before recorded history began . . . In the days of chivalry, knights-officers were noted as well for courtesy and gentleness of behavior, as for death defying courage. From their acts of courtesy and benevolence were derived the words, now pronounced as one, Gentle Man. Let us be gentle, that is, courteous and considerate of the rights of others. Let us be men, that is, fearless and untiring in doing our duty. Our calling is most ancient and like all other old things it has amassed through the ages certain customs and traditions which decorate and ennoble it, which render beautiful the otherwise prosaic occupation of being professional men at arms."

MARTIN BLUMENSON, contributing editor of ARMY and the editor of the two-volume Patton Papers, *is a graduate of Bucknell University, and the author of* Patton: The Man Behind the Legend, *1885-1945 and* The Battle of the Generals: The Untold Story of the Falaise Pocket-The Campaign That Should Have Won World War II.

Is the Military Profession Legitimate?

by Lloyd J. Matthews

Of course it is, but once we step outside 'our own informed circle and its associated community of military historians and sociologists, we are likely to encounter an entirely different view.'

By Col. Lloyd J. Matthews
U.S. Army retired

The question asked in the title of this article will seem impertinent to the career soldier. Certainly we take ourselves to be professionals in the fullest sense of the term; we take our vocation to be bona fide calling, ranking shoulder to shoulder with the long-venerated fields of medicine, law, divinity and pedagogy. Our periodicals and publications, more than those of any other vocational group, are pervaded by self-congratulatory allusions to our status as professionals.

Field Manual 100-1, The Army, our capstone document on principles and values, devotes an entire chapter to "the profession of arms." The first sentence of this chapter captures perfectly the tone we regularly use to characterize our standing: "The men and women serving in today's army are members of a proud profession long in history and rich in heritage and tradition."

Further, our status as professionals is sanctified by such distinguished military sociologists as Samuel Huntington, Morris Janowitz and Charles Moskos. These good gentlemen, with their hypotheses, models and paradigms, have lent a scientific gloss to our own subjective claims to professional standing. And if all this weren't enough, General Sir John Hackett, perhaps the foremost soldier-scholar of our time, has provided a magisterial historical tracing of the man-of-arms' rise to ranking among the elite professional groups.

Source: *Army Magazine* (September, 1994) 14-23. Reprinted by permission of the U.S. Army Magazine.

All this being so, what's the problem? The problem is that once we step outside the comfortable ambit of our own uniformed circle and its associated community of military historians and sociologists, we are likely to encounter an entirely different view.

Take, for example, A. M. Carr-Saunders and P. A. Wilson's seminal study *The Professions*, which has long served as the starting point for all serious discussion of vocational status in the English-speaking world. These scholars exclude the military from the professional domain "because the service which soldiers are trained to render is one which it is hoped they will never be called upon to perform."

> '*What difference does it make whether what we do is perceived as a profession or a mere occupation? Most military professionals will instinctively arrive at the one valid short answer: the defense of this country is too important to be left in the hands of occupational timeservers.*'

Then we have Eliot Freidson, who in his definitive treatment of medical professionalism cannot resist a typically snide side-thrust at the mere pretenders:

The military, we are told by Janowitz, is a profession. But we can only thank the stars for the fact that, by my usage, it is not. If the military were a profession by my usage, it would be free to set its own ends and do to us what it felt was appropriate from its point of view. (*Profession of Medicine: A Study of Sociology of Applied Knowledge*)

Ernest Greenwood, in an oft-noticed piece titled "Attributes of a Profession," lists 19 professional occupations from accountant to teacher, but nowhere does he mention the soldier. Similarly, the U.S. Bureau of the Census omits the military from its exhaustive listing of managerial and professional specialties, which are deemed to be exclusively civilian. Statistics on the military are reported separately. Less formal but no less damning to the soldier's professional credibility are the calculated put-downs by antimilitary writers whose views have been widely circulated in the lay press. Obvious examples are Anthony Lewis of *The New York Times*, Lewis Lapham Jr. of *Harper's* magazine, Norman Cousins, former long-time editor of *Saturday Review*, and Colman McCarthy of *The Washington Post*.

McCarthy wrote a piece called "The Cowards' Air War" in the 17 February 1991 issue of the *Post* that in terms of sheer malevolent invective against a professional class is remarkable even by his debased standards.

One brief excerpt will illustrate: "The sadistic ritual of daily bombing [against Iraq] by the U.S. military is in keeping with its picking fights—in Grenada, Libya and Panama—with enemies expected to be done in quickly."

This is quite a revelation. Until reading McCarthy on the warmongering connivances of U.S. military leaders, most of us would have assumed was civilian political authorities who chose for us to fight in those places.

But even otherwise responsible commentators have been seduced to the view that because the soldier's business is war his professional standing is suspect. Bernard Brodie, who should have known better, could scarcely conceal his disdain:

[The soldier] is far from perceiving himself as a monster. Much of the ceremony and punctilio that go with the profession, for example, the peculiarly frequent use of the word *gentlemen* in addressing or referring to brother officers, appear designed to ward off the disturbing thought that one belongs to a trade devoted to slaughter. (*War and Politics*)

The hypocrisy involved in making this odious insinuation must somehow have escaped Brodie, who spent virtually the entirety of his long professional career devising U.S. nuclear strategy at Rand, where he was a charter member of an elite inner circle dubbed by Fred Kaplan "the wizards of Armageddon."

Laurence Martin, though not sharing Brodie's view himself, provides a good summation of the ambivalence felt by significant numbers of people toward the professional soldier:

For many Western taxpayers, the military are on the way to becoming latter-day remittance men, given a small slice of the family income on condition they go off and pursue their unsavory activities quietly where they will not embarrass decent folk. ("The Utility of Military Force" in *Force Modern Societies: Its Place in International Politics*)

Perhaps the unkindest cuts of all have come from within. Zeb Bradford and James Murphy, while serving officers, wrote that "the military is not a profession in the way that certain other groups are, such as law or medicine."

They claim that the military lacks a defining expertise or skill, the traditional sine qua non for professional status. In their view, the career soldier is simply a paid jack-of-all-trades, a professional servant of the state, broadly prepared to move from one portfolio to the next.

Sharing the notion that the military vocation lacks a unique skill is the proposal—apparently made with a straight face—by then newly resigned Maj. Josiah Bunting. As an antidote to the Army's imperviousness to enlightened outside influence, Bunting would infuse the leadership ranks with nonsoldiers:

Appoint general officers from the civilian professions for…four- or five-year terms, such appointments to be made by the President on the advice of Congressional committees…Large numbers of general officer billets can be filled with intelligent amateurs from the other professions. Of this there is no question. ("The Conscience of a Solder," *Worldview*)

Even our patron saints Janowitz, Huntington and Moskos, though they would dispute allegations that the military vocation lacks specific content and a unique defining essence, seem to agree with the proposition that the profession doesn't quite measure up.

Huntington, in *The Soldier and the State: The Theory and Politics of Civil-Military Relations*, says that "the public, as well as the scholar, hardly conceives of the officer in the same way that it does the lawyer or doctor, and it certainly does not accord to the officer the deference which it gives to the civilian professionals."

In a similar vein, Janowitz (in *The Professional Soldier: A Social and Political Portrait*) tells us that "officership remains a relatively low-status profession." Moskos has decried the military's creeping "occupationalism," which he sees as the antithesis of professionalism.

Finally, what of today's incumbent president, who sets the ideological tone for the Administration and is a powerful opinion maker throughout the land? What does President Clinton as commander in chief of all U.S. forces think of the military professional? Alas, apparently not much.

Col. Harry Summers, U.S. Army retired, wrote that President Clinton is "the only commander in chief in history who is on the public record as loathing the institution he now commands." I issued a good-natured challenge to Col. Summers, an old friend of mine, to document this charge. Accepting the challenge, he sent me a copy of a letter that Bill Clinton once wrote to Col. Eugene Homes—himself a survivor of the Bataan Death March—who was director of the ROTC program at the University of Arkansas.

Clinton's letter, dated 3 December 1969, reads in part as follows:

> I am writing…in the hope that my telling this one story [about enrolling in ROTC to get a draft deferment and then not reporting for ROTC] will help you to understand more clearly how so many fine people have come to find themselves still loving their country but *loathing* the military.

Evidently Rhodes scholar Bill Clinton in 1969, like Colman McCarthy today, failed to pick up on the minor detail that the military did not order itself to Vietnam to fight a war, but rather that it was ordered there by competent civilian authority.

I believe, however, that we should not be too harsh on the 23-year-old Bill Clinton for his invidious characterization of the military. How many of us would suffer cherry-red faces to have publicly recalled the assorted indiscretions, gaucheries and plain jackass lunacies of our early twenties?

Rather, it is the Bill Clinton of today, now a quarter of a century older, that we look to for cues as to how the military will be perceived within the Administration.

Sadly, the news is little better than it was in 1969. We can safely pass over the more celebrated issues broached by the Administration such as the proposed induction of avowed gays in the military and the draconian defense budget cuts, and focus instead on a single microcosmic episode involving a distinguished Army general and a Clinton staffer.

> *U.S. News & World Report* describes the event as follows:
> Not long after Clinton took office, [this officer] was visiting the White House and tried to exchange pleasantries with a woman in the West Wing. She angrily replied that she didn't speak to people in uniform. (15 March 1993)

This officer is a veteran of three American wars and is among our most heavily decorated soldiers, having been wounded in combat three times. Ironically, several of his decorations—the Distinguished Service Cross, two Silver Stars, Bronze Star Medal, Air Medal and Purple Heart—were earned in Vietnam in 1968–69, precisely the period when Bill Clinton was enjoying his Rhodes scholarship at Oxford University in England. For an American officer to suffer such an indignity at the hands of an insect *apparatchik* in the presidential White House is unconscionable on the part of those who allowed it to happen.

The larger truth is that the nameless staffer was not speaking solely in her own right. Minor political bureaucrats soak up the institutional ethos like Pampers, and we can be certain that her reflexive slur against soldiers had been nourished by deep immersion in a work environment where antimilitary values were not only condoned but encouraged. The White House claims that if the woman is identified she will be fired, but no one familiar with the Washington scene expects this ritual assurance ever to be realized.

Our survey thus far reveals and that through career soldiers loudly and proudly proclaim their professional status, there is in fact a powerful countervailing sentiment outside the fraternity that calls such status into doubt.

One can of course ask "So what?" What difference does it make whether what we do is perceived as a profession or a mere occupation? A lot could be said in answer to this question, but I believe most military professionals will instinctively arrive at the one valid short answer: the defense of this country is too important to be left in the hands of occupational timeservers.

If the nation's defenders are not members of a true higher calling and if that calling is not accorded the reverence of taxpayers and political leaders alike, then as surely as night follows day, the soldier's advice will come to be depreciated, the fighting forces and their leadership will be depleted of numbers and quality, and the security of this nation will fall into jeopardy.

I claim here nothing less than that the military profession is the most vital, the most worthy of exaltation—and, yes, the most legitimate—of all professions; and the balance of this article will be devoted to demonstrating the truth of that proposition.

Before proceeding to an analysis of the military vocation in terms of whether it conforms to the traditional professional criteria, I want to address three nagging impediments to professional respectability that seem to dog virtually all published discussion of the matter.

First is the charge that the military, as subsumed within a vast government bureaucracy, lacks the autonomy and interaction with a bona fide clientele enjoyed by the traditional professions. Those who worry about the adverse effects of bureaucracy are chiefly concerned with its authoritarian nature, which presumably threatens the free exercise of professional discretion.

They are also concerned with the problematic nature of a bureaucracy's clientele, which may well be collective and distant, thus undermining the traditional concept of the personalized one-on-one relationship between the professional and those he serves.

Second is the allegation that the military is automatically disqualified from professional status because it celebrates death rather than life.

How, our gainsayers ask, could the soldier even remotely contemplate high professional standing when his trade is devoted singlemindedly to unleashing death, destruction, and ruination upon fellow members of the human race?

Don't these iniquitous aims contrast diametrically with the benevolence of true professions like medicine, which seeks to heal rather than to kill?

Martina Edmonds sums up this view as follows:

> There are some who would contest that the armed services of the state
> are properly professional on the grounds that...military values are the

antithesis of liberalism, the political philosophy upon which Western concepts of professionalism are based. (*Armed Services and Society*)

Third, there is the persistent theme that true professional activity ministers to the enduring needs of mankind, whereas war, being a feature of man's primitive early phase, will no longer require professional practitioners once the stage of permanent peace (which now lies just around the corner) finally arrives.

Even in the face of the Iraqi war, the Bosnian outrage, the intractable violence on the Horn of Africa and the civil war in Georgia, there continues among many well-intentioned observers a strong undercurrent of belief that the end of the Cold War has rendered war obsolete, and that the United Nations surgical operations and police actions are the model for the future.

Let us address in turn each of these three objections to the military as profession. With respect to the alleged incompatibility of bureaucracy and professionalism, Professor Allan R. Millett frames the questions squarely: "Can a profession really exist within a hierarchically-structured, bureaucratized organization?" (The most focused discussion of the American military as profession is Professor Millett's *Military Professionalism and Officership in America*, Mershon Center Briefing Paper No. 2, Mershon Center of The Ohio State University, May 1977)

Roscoe Pound, a legal scholar writing in 1953, had already answered the question just as squarely: "The idea of a profession is incompatible with performance of its functions, or the exercise of its art, by or under the immediate supervision of a government bureau."

Under Pound's dictum, the military would obviously be disqualified for professional status. Pound, writing 40 years ago, could not have foreseen the extent to which all aspects of modern life would come to be dominated by huge institutional octopuses—not just departments of the federal and state governments, but sprawling corporate, educational, medical, charitable and other such entities.

Like it or not, bureaucracy is now a fact of life. It would be silly today, to deny and group professional standing on the grounds of bureaucratic affiliation, because to do so would delegitimate huge blocs of bona fide professional activity. It is far more sensible simply to acknowledge that times have changed and that professional endeavor is adapting to the evolving organizational structures characteristic of the 21st century.

Physicians, for example, are moving in ever greater numbers from private practice into large institutional settings.

Law school enrollments increased to such an extent during the 1970s that by the following decade the American bar was unable to accommodate all the lawyers who wished to practice.

Accordingly, law school graduates are turning increasingly to highly specialized fields of law or to other fields—business, politics, accounting, taxation, insurance, law enforcement and so on—where their legal training is effectively capitalized upon within the context of complex organizations. Though schooled as lawyers, they are not practicing law before the bar in the traditional sense.

Take a lawyer who works for a large casualty insurance company, analyzing claims and advising the company officers on the trial prospects of claims cases. Is he any less a professional than the small-town lawyer who hangs his shingle outside his office door and tries traffic cases before the local judge?

And is a career soldier, given scope to ply his trade and prove his mettle, any less a professional because he serves Uncle Sam as part of an Army of 550,000 men and women? Clearly the answer is no in both cases.

As to the comparative benevolence of the professions, let us return to Carr-Saunders and Wilson's argument that the military must be disqualified because soldiers render a service "which it is hoped they will never be called upon to perform." This is analytical claptrap. The soldier's most valuable service—deterring war and maintaining a secure peace—is in fact one that we devoutly hope he will perform. Beyond this elemental point, and this is fundamental to understanding, we must recognize that all professions—*without exception*—ultimately traffic in human misery, misfortune and privation.

The physician deals with sick bodies, the attorney with transgressions of the law, the minister with diseases of the spirit, the teacher with uninformed or misinformed minds—and the soldier with human conflict. All at times deliver services "which it is hoped they will never be called upon to perform."

Is medicine any less a profession because one "hopes" that bodily illnesses will never occur?

Is law any less a profession because one "hopes" that crime, torts and contract breaches will never occur?

Is divinity to be demeaned because one "hopes" that sin is a thing of the past?

And is the military any less a profession because one "hopes" that war among nations will never occur?

In heaven, where perfection in all things presumably reigns, there is no need for doctors, lawyers, preachers, teachers and soldiers to ply their trades. But in this world below, imperfection is the rule.

Our only recourse is to prepare professional specialists to mitigate the lapses from the ideal that are inevitable in the human condition. All the professions are blood brothers in this one elemental respect, whether their practitioners and apologists will admit it or not.

The military, far from aiming to visit death, destruction and ruination upon fellow members of the human race, aims to do precisely the opposite: it strives to maintain a state of tranquility between our nation and its global neighbors.

Paradoxically, however, it can do this only by keeping serviceable the gun it in fact hopes it will never have to fire.

The military need make no apology for this paradox. The psychology of deterrence is lodged deeply in human nature, and if one is going to pick a quarrel over it, he'd best go to his Maker, not to his Soldier.

Gen. Douglas MacArthur, addressing the U.S. Corps of Cadets at West Point on 12 May 1962, said it best:

> [Being prepared for war] does not mean that you are warmongers. On the contrary, the soldier above all other people prays for peace, for he must suffer and bear the deepest wounds and scars of war.

The U.S. Army War College, where the Army's top professionals receive the final phase of their formal military education, institutionalizes MacArthur's sentiment in a motto that pervades the thinking of faculty and students alike: Not To Promote War, But To Preserve Peace. No profession could have a higher aim.

The third impediment to professional acceptance is the alleged transient nature of the utility of arms. Certainly we can concede, along with General Sir John Hackett, that "the military life…would disappear if violence vanished among men. Ah, but have nations and men now become so peace loving that the United States can dispense with a large professional force and hazard its security instead on UN gendarmes?

True, the prophets come and go, trumpeting the end of war. But each in turn, before the last shrill trumpet note dies, is belied by the next despot who takes a yen for his neighbor's land and resorts to arms to get it.

Edward Gibbon, having surveyed 13 centuries of unremitting war in his masterwork *The History of the Decline and Fall of the Roman Empire*, nonetheless included a famous paean to the peace and security that in his reading of the future lay before the citizens of Europe as the 18th century drew to a close:

> Cannon and fortifications now form an impregnable barrier against the Tartar horse, and Europe is secure from any future irruption of barbarians; since, before they can conquer, they must cease to be barbarous.

In an arresting irony, even as Gibbon was girding himself to write his great history that would prophesy the end of barbarism and war, Europe's own Tartar—the infant Napoleon—lay gestating in his mother's womb. During the Napoleonic wars soon to be unleashed, Europe was laid waste for some 15 years.

Writing in the context to the Anglo-German rivalry, Norman Angell "proved scientifically" in 1910 that it was "an economic impossibility for one nation to seize or destroy the wealth of another, or for one nation to enrich itself by subjecting another."

He also found positive news on the psychological front:

> Human nature is changing out of all recognition. Not only is man fighting less, but he is using all forms of physical compulsion less, and as a very natural result is losing those psychological attributes that go with the employment of physical force. (*The Great Illusion: A Study of the Relations of Military Power in Nations to their Economic and Social Advantage*)

Apparently Angell neglected to inform Kaiser Wilhelm and the German generals of the economic futility of empire, because four years after Angell's heartwarming revelation, the German armies engaged those of France, England and Russia in a clash of arms of such magnitude as to demand a new coinage in the glossary of conflict: "The Great War."

America then joined the fight, and the world rejoiced at Woodrow Wilson's solemn pledge that this was the war by which the world finally would "be made safe for democracy."

A score of years after the world had been made safe for democracy, Britain's Prime Minister Neville Chamberlain emerged from his infamous meeting with Adolph

Hitler and Benito Mussolini in Munich, where, with the promise of "peace in our time" to a vastly relieved world, Czechoslovakia was shamelessly dismembered.

Chamberlain's optimism, incidentally, was abetted by the strategic sagacities of Liddell Hart, who was proclaiming to receptive ears—including those of Chamberlain and his defense minister—the "futility of aggression" and the "superiority" of the defensive over the offensive, meaning that France would be able to stand up to Hitler nicely without the necessity of a British commitment on the continent.

Within 11 months Chamberlain's fatuous foreglimpse of peace. Hitler took what was left of Czechoslovakia and attacked Poland, thus precipitating World War II, a seismic collision of armed powers such that the Great War blushed at the comparison.

As with that earlier war, the United States rode to the rescue of its allies, and as with Woodrow Wilson, American President Franklin D. Roosevelt banished fears of renewed conflict with another stirring prophecy of peace: "More than an end to war, we want an end to the beginnings of all wars."

Yet, the end of that mighty conflagration in 1945 saw the immediate inception of the Cold War, which spawned two sizable hot wars in their own right—Korea and Vietnam. The Cold war continued to make the world unsafe for democracy for the next 45 years.

Those who professed to descry the end of state conflict, however, refused to be discouraged.

The latest is Professor John Mueller, whose much-ballyhooed book *Retreat from Doomsday: The Obsolescence of Major War* doubtless evoked great sighs of relief from those who naively believed that war would be round for awhile. Mueller is worth quoting at some length:

> The long peace since World War II is less a product of recent weaponry than the culmination of a substantial historical process. For the last two or three centuries major war—war among developed countries—has gradually moved toward terminal disrepute…In fact, within the first and second worlds warfare of *all* sorts seems generally to have lost its appeal. Not only have there been virtually no international wars among the major and not-so-major countries, but the developed world has experienced virtually no civil war either….Actually, *third* world countries apparently *have* gotten the message…There have been virtually no wars among the 44 wealthiest countries—a total that includes quite a few countries outside the first and second worlds. War has taken place almost entirely within the *fourth* world.

Although Mueller takes care to interlard his text with fuzzy qualifiers like "generally," "virtually," and apparently," and although our heads swim at his analysis of the presence or absence of war in terms of four worlds, what he has given us at bottom is the self-congratulatory message that we civilized folk don't do wars anymore. It is a practice now carried on solely by ruffians from the outback.

Mueller's book was published in 1989 and reviewed widely, with one review, in *Journal of American History*, appearing in June the next year.

On 2 August 1990, only a few months after that review appeared, Iraq invaded

Kuwait. A coalition of 35 nations rose to defeat that invasion, a coalition, I daresay, involving states from all four of Mueller's worlds, a combination of states deploying 737,000 soldiers on the ground, 190 vessels on the seas, and 1,800 aircraft in the skies.

Then, in a second quick cruel mockery of Professor Mueller's encomium in behalf of this now-pacified planet, the war in Bosnia-Herzegovina erupted in March 1992.

The refugees from that obscene conflict number in the millions; the dead, wounded and mutilated are uncounted; the horrors, atrocities and cruelties are spoken only in the imagination. Where that war will eventually lead the world's community of nations I leave to the prophets to say.

The deep-seated impulse among men of good will to prophesy the end of war, and their prospects for eventually proving correct, could perhaps be better understood were we able to resolve the related question of whether humans are genetically predisposed to aggression.

This question was evoked by Charles Darwin's *Origin of Species*, which propounded the law of survival of the fittest among all species, including man.

The issue continues into the present day, with writers like Robert Ardrey (*African Genesis* and *the Territorial Imperative*), Desmond Morris (*The Naked Ape*), Konrad Lorenz (*On Aggression*), and, most recently, Edward O. Wilson (*Sociobiology: The New Synthesis*) all taking the position that human behavior—which would include fighting—is determined to some extent by the genes or instincts inherited from our animal forbears.

Arrayed against this group are such men as anthropologist Ashley Montague (*Man and Aggression*) and opponents of sociobiology like Harvard biologist Richard Lewontin, who would emphasize individual free will and the ameliorative possibilities of environmental forces.

Ideologically, their concern is that if human behavior comes to be popularly accepted as wired into our genes, then the prospects for reform—banishment of war, in the present case—are diminished.

Unfortunately, the state of scientific knowledge and research today is not such that we can proclaim with certainty the degree to which, or even whether, Homo sapiens are endowed with a warring instinct or are genetically predisposed to violence or aggression. What we are left with, then, are our extrapolations from history as reinforced by the evidence of our eyes and by plain common sense.

No objective reading of the historical record will provide persuasive grounds for optimism. We have already seen this in our survey of the failed prophets of peace in the latter 18th, 19th and 20th centuries, when humankind was presumably emerging from its primitive darkness. But no century has cornered the market on bellicosity.

Martin Luther during the Protestant Reformation assured the faithful that "it is both Christian and an act of love to kill the enemy without hesitation, to plunder and burn and injure him by any method until he is conquered, except that"—and here a tenderly solicitous caveat—"one must be aware of sin and not violate wives and virgins!"

An English bishop told his flock prior to World War I that "watered by war's red rain, virtue grows: cannonade is an oratorio, almost a form of worship."

And then, from our own age, Iran's Ayatollah Khomeini revealed to his followers that "war is a blessing for the world and for all nations. It is God who incites men to fight and kill."

Indeed, the clash of religions has often paved the way for the clash of arms. Examples abound. The Moorish Emir Yusuf ibn Teshufin, after defeating King Alfonso's Christian force at Sagrajas in 1086, showed his Islamic fervor by ordering the heads of his Christian foes cut off and piled into mounds. Standing atop one such mound, a muezzin called the faithful to prayer.

But the Christians had their moments in the sun. In 1189, Richard Lionhart, the "Crusader King," ordered the execution of 2,500 Saracen prisoners captured when the Moslem garrison of Acre fell to the beseiging Christian force: "Richard himself looked on as his soldiers...fell upon the bound prisoners and literally hacked them to pieces."

The chroniclers of war, however, don't generally cavil over whether it is religious or secular, and if the Ayatollah is right in claiming that war is a blessing, then surely such blessings have rained upon the human race in wondrous profusion.

Will and Ariel Durant, writing in 1968, recounted that "in the last 3421 years of recorded history, only 268 have seen no war."

In the compilation *Dictionary of Wars* by George Kohn, covering "major wars, revolutions, revolts, and rebellions...throughout the world from 2000 B.C. to the present," 1,700 such conflicts are noted.

John Laffin in *Brassey's Battles: 3,500 Years of Conflict, Campaigns, and Wars from A-Z,* treats over 7,000 instances.

Wars have become so ubiquitous that we need yearly updates to keep track. John Laffin's *War Annual 1*, reporting on wars in 1985–86, counted 32. His *War Annual 2*, reporting on wars in 1986–87, counted 34. In 1988, a Washington research institute called World Priorities reported on 25 wars in progress.

In Laffin's *War Annual 3*, covering 1989, the figure rested at 32. Laffin is now up to *War Annual 5*, and the wars are still going strong.

There is no need for us to dance on the head of Professor Mueller's pin, boggling our brains with scholastic distinctions as to whether wars are major or minor and which of the four worlds they inhabit.

To the professional soldier getting shot at in the front lines, all wars are major, and all require a professional response.

We recite this sad litany of war not to exult in it but to learn from it. Its moral may be summed up in a parable I once heard during a sermon by an Army Chaplain at West Point: Three pacifists, all friends, were in a bar talking. On the stool next to them was an old Army sergeant, a veteran of three wars and wearer of many decorations for bravery under fire.

All of a sudden, the first pacifist struck the second flush in the face with his fist, knocking him to the floor. Bloodied, the second arose and replied with a roundhouse right to the chin of the first, whereupon the third began pummeling both his friends, and a wild melee ensued.

The old sergeant, who had been observing the action with interest, grabbed all three by the scruff of the neck, set them back on their stools and calmed them down. After a while, he asked why three pacifists would be fighting in such unseemly fashion.

The first said he struck his friend because the latter had insulted his wife's virtue, which he held to be more previous than his pacifism.

> '*A fully legitimated military profession–skilled in the art of war so that our nation's citizens may practice the art of peace–is a necessary precondition for the flowering of all other professions.*'

The second said he fought because he was attacked first, self-defense taking precedence over his pacifism.

The third said he knocked the hell out of the other two because they were making pacifists look like hypocrites.

The chaplain's point to his uniformed congregation was that no matter how principled our opposition to violence as professed in the ordered calm of church and study, the hurly-burly of daily living sometimes leads us into situations where a higher principle compels us to employ force. So it is with civilized nations, whose peace-loving impulses must sometimes give way before the harsh imperatives of a higher interest.

It should be apparent to any reader of history, regardless of where he stands on the issue of innate human aggression, that men, and the aggregations of men we call nations, will fight whenever their vital interests are seriously threatened and there is no other satisfactory recourse.

Further, men and nations are generally disposed to take a capacious view of what constitutes their interests. These things we know to be true from our reading of the past and from peering deeply into our own hearts. Whenever our nation's interests are threatened sufficiently that we become disposed to fight, we will require a professional force in being in the hope that merely having it will induce the nation that threatens those interests to desist.

As Michael Howard said in his demur to John Mueller's *Retreat from Doomsday*: "A credible and evident capacity to fight remains necessary if war is to be seen as counterproductive...[Mueller] will be proved right only if we continue to act on the assumption that he is wrong." (*The New York Times Book Review*, 30 April 1989)

If the threatening state decides to move against our interests despite our professional force in being, then we shall require that force to act accordingly.

It may be that in some hazy utopian future the world's powers will come to cede responsibility for maintaining their individual security to a fully integrated world political structure such as a strengthened United Nations. But even if that should happen, we as a nation shall have to maintain a standing force of our own, if only to meet levies by the world organization for its campaigns to pacify renegade states and to serve as a hedge against abusive aggrandizement by the world organization itself. On this reading, the military profession will have an essential and honorable role for as long as man continues to occupy the planet.

With so much as prologue, we may move to an examination of whether the military meets the formal definition of a profession. In seeking out the traditional standards for professional status, we must honestly concede that no universally agreed-upon criteria exist. William Goode finds two core criteria. Huntington cites three. Greenwood finds five. Professor Millett finds six. We shall use his more inclusive scheme because it is informed by plenty of nonlegalistic common sense, and it takes account of the earlier studies. According to Millett's six criteria, a bona fide profession—

(1) **Is a full-time and stable job, serving continuing societal needs.** The day when the nation could be adequately defended by a part-time force, if such a day ever existed, has long since dissolved. The complexity of modern war demands a full-time corps of practitioners, and that is exactly what we are. As to the "continuing" nature of the "need" satisfied by the military profession, we have earlier remarked at length upon the enduring threat of state violence and the elemental necessity of maintaining professional military forces to counter it.

(2) **Is a lifelong calling by the practitioners, who identify themselves personally with their job subculture.** The key word here is "calling." On entering the Army, true professionals don't simply "take a job." Instead, they "profess to a sacred calling," one that totally immerses them, along with their band of professional brethren, in a career dedicated to a single transcendant cause.

If this characterization strikes some readers as a trifle exalted, I would invite them to read, or reread, the telling set of contrasts Charles Moskos has developed to distinguish the professional soldier from the eight-to-five time-server (*The Military: More than Just a Job*, Pergamon, p. 16). Reading Moskos on this subject can be a good tonic, leading to professional reaffirmation. Or it can be an embarrassing exercise in self-discovery.

(3) **Is organized to control performance standards and recruitment.** The salient point here is that professionals, who possess unique expertise not shared by laymen, are alone qualified to judge whether applicants to the profession have met the standards, and whether practitioners of the profession are performing up to snuff. Members are thus expected to police their own profession.

Through such devices as commissioning boards, promotion boards, school selection boards, assignment decisions, awards and decoration boards, officer efficiency reports and court-martial panels—all executed overwhelmingly by uniformed professionals—the military exercises a degree of self-regulation over its members found in no other calling.

(4) **Requires formal, theoretical education.** The crux here is whether, in addition to the liberal arts prerequisite symbolized by the baccalaureate degree, the military possesses a required disciplinary field uniquely its own, that is, a coherent body of military theory, knowledge, doctrine, art, science, and history transmissible with academic rigor through its school system.

For those familiar with the military's progressive emphasis at the command and staff colleges and the senior service colleges on the philosophy of national defense, the theory of war, the concepts of warfighting, and the principles of leading large organizations of men in the ordered application of violence—it may seem self-evident that the military profession meets Millett's fourth criterion.

Still, as we have seen, there are those such as Bradford and Murphy who deny that the career soldier today possesses a unique defining specialty: additional to his sometime role as warfighter, in their view, he is diplomat, peacemaker, nation builder, bureaucrat, adviser, teacher, manager, rescuer of the hurricane-beset, feeder of the starving and so on. I believe this claim is dangerously misleading.

No one can deny the versatility and adaptability of the soldier in performing a broad spectrum of nonmartial functions useful to the nation. But we must continue to insist that the professional soldier always have one supreme, critical role that defines his essence and commands priority over all other functions—to lead the nation's arms in the nation's defense. To forget or blur this bedrock function is to court disaster. Those who imply that the roles of the military professional break cleanly between combat and humanitarianism should glance at Somalia, where to feed the starving we must fight the starvers. Unless we do the latter well, we cannot do the former at all.

Further, the extraordinary skills required for successful operational command on today's battlefield should never be discounted. Asking one of Bunting's "intelligent amateurs" to conduct a military operation like Desert Storm would be about as sensible as asking Albert Einstein to conduct a kidney transplant.

A second challenge to the military profession's claim to defining body of disciplinary theory and knowledge comes from a group of training pragmatists who Maj. Gen. Edward B. Atkeson, U.S. Army retired, has well-described in his book *The Final Argument of Kings*.

The pragmatists dismiss the notion of an overarching body of military theory, insisting instead that it is the business of the Army's schools to train students in a narrowly utilitarian way by focusing on their next assignments. The emphasis should be upon practical "how to" techniques as opposed to the more abstract concerns normally associated with individual growth and education for the long haul. It should be the role of the schools simply to adapt the latest technological wizardry produced by scientists and engineers to the demands of this year's battlefield.

In this view, the theoretical constants of war would have no place. If granted unbridled sway, the effect of the pragmatist philosophy would be to make of West Point a Ft. Benning on the Hudson, or of the Army War College a Pentagon Preparatory School on the Letort.

The proper analytical reply to the pragmatists is to acknowledge that all professional schooling—military or otherwise—contains a creative tension between theoretical and practical demands. No physician will be worth a tinker's damn if he knows only the theory of medicine.

He has to know how to diagnose and treat patients as well—thus his periods of internship and residency. No trial lawyer, regardless of how well he has mastered his Blackstone and common law, will prosper if he can't function before the judge and jury—thus his exercise in moot court as supplemented by various apprentice courses. Such dichotomies are well reconciled in our military school system, where a substructure of theory and educational development provides the necessary foundation for the superstructure of practice.

(5) **Has a service orientation in which loyalty to standards of competence and loyalty to clients' needs are paramount.** The essential word here is "client," to be understood in contradistinction to "customer." In Greenwood's words, "A nonprofessional occupation has customers; a professional occupation has clients." A customer shops around until he finds the thing or service he wants, the premise being that he is

competent to decide what he needs. But in the case of the client seeking to meet his professional needs, no such competency is presumed. It is the professional who tells the client what he needs.

If his physician says the client needs a heart bypass graft, the client cannot on competent grounds decide that balloon antioplasty will do the trick just as well. Because of the special dependency and vulnerability of the client in a client-professional relationship, society has imposed a severe burden of obligation on the professional—to act unswervingly in the client's behalf and never in the professional's own selfish interests.

Obviously, such is only the ideal, not a uniform actuality, but it does provide a clear standard for professional conduct.

The military professional's clientele must be construed broadly. His clients ultimately are the American people. Lacking military expertise themselves, they have collectively placed their solemn trust in his professional judgment, he being the guarantor of their freedom and security and the sworn upholder of the Constitution. Since his relation to his clients is mediated by intervening layers of civilian government and a military chain of command, he serves his clients by serving his superiors.

Thus they, too, in a very real sense, become part of his clientele. It is by following their legal orders—to include the application of expert soldierly technique and the invariable rendering of honest advice—that he defends the nation and its citizenry and vindicates his claim to professionalism.

And finally, the most professional among military professionals regards even his subordinates as clients, for it is these same lowly subordinates after all who translate orders from above into concrete battlefield effects. He holds their live and welfare in his hands, and he risks them to the minimum degree consistent with mission accomplishment.

The concept of altruistic service to clients is nowhere stronger and more in evidence than in the military, where the incentive of a day's hardtack and the chance to be of use stand in stark contrast to the opportunities for enrichment offered by some of the other professions.

(6) **Is granted a great deal of collective autonomy by the society it serves, because the practitioners have proven their high ethical standards and trustworthiness.** Obviously, civilian control of the military is a deeply embedded principle in democratic governance, and it is effectively exercised through the civilian bureaucracy of the Pentagon and the Administration and through the appropriations authority of Congress. But within the military chain of command itself, the uniformed professional reigns supreme. During the business of war, whose coin are soldiers and stupifyingly expensive weapon systems, the military professional is accorded near absolute authority to spend the nation's treasure and the lives of its youth. No other professional can lay claim to such sweeping and sobering responsibility.

Our society will continue to place such high trust in the military profession only so long as it remains convinced tha tthe career soldier is animated by impregnable ethical principle and a purely disinterested regard for the nation's security.

It is in this context that the need for an officer's code of professional ethics is often broached. Codes of ethics are characteristic of professional groups—the American Medical Association's Principles of Medical Ethics, the American Bar Association's

> '...the military vocation
> is indeed the most vital,
> the most worthy of
> exaltation–and, yes,
> the most legitimate–of
> all the professions.'

Model Rules of Professional Conduct and the American Institute of Certified Public Accountant's Code of Ethics being examples.

Of course, no one claims there is a shortage of ethical guidance for the military professional. From the Army's total ethical canon, we might mention such elements as the oath of office; the injunction on the commission itself (the officer's commissioning is analogous to licensure to practice a civilian profession); the motto Duty, Honor, Country; the Uniform Code of Military Justice; *Field Manual 100-1, The Army*; the Laws of War; the Code of Conduct; and the Constitution itself.

Collectively, the American professional military ethic covers the necessary ground. But, one can properly question the diffuseness of such ethical guidance and the lack of a single, comprehensive, authoritative declaration of ethical principle. Ideally, such a declaration should encapsulate with dignity, clarity, and compelling style the essential precepts that govern the actions of the military professional in peace and war.

Though its case would be even stronger with the adoption of a fitting code of professional ethics, certainly the military more than meets the sixth criterion for professional status.

By way of summation, what we have so far seen is that none of the oft-cited pretexts for disqualifying the military from full professional standing will stand scrutiny. We have also seen that when judged against the most rigorous definitional criteria yet adduced, the military profession more than measures up. Field Marshal Lord Carver, who rose to be Britain's highest soldier not long back, reflected on his vocation as follows:

> The sad fact of life is that, if evil is not resisted, it will prevail. That is the justification for . . . maintaining in the service of the community and the state forces who are trained, skilled, and well-equipped to meet that challenge when and wherever it arises. Their profession is an honorable one. (Quoted by Henry Fairlie in "What the Falklands Teaches Us." *New Republic*, 2 July 1982)

Buy I think we can go further yet. Adam Smith, that most unsentimental of economists and author of the epochal tract, *Wealth of Nations* (1776), opined that "the art of war . . . is certainly the noblest of arts." He was right on the money.

A fully legitimated military profession—skilled in the art of war so that our nation's citizens may practice that art of peace—is a necessary precondition for the flowering of all other professions. For without the national freedom underwritten by our military, the remaining professions would be subject to unprincipled exploitation by a repressive state—witness the debasement of law, history, art and psychiatry, for example, under the Soviet system or the unspeakable atrocities committed in the name of medical search in Nazi Germany.

Thus, to repeat a claim made earlier, the military vocation is indeed the most vital, the most worthy of exaltation—and, yes, the most legitimate—of all the professions.

Despite the detractors that still remain, the career solder of the 1990s, is consulted in the highest councils of state; he testifies before the key committees of the House and Senate; he briefs his televised military campaigns, on which the fate of nations depend, to an awestruck world.

At such times, he rubs elbows with the high and mightly from all the other professional groups. He stands among them not as a rude petitioner, hoping for a place, but as the man of the moment, secure in the knowledge of his publicly esteemed professional competence. For he has come to pronounce on the sublimest of all earthly goals—the maintenance of peace and security for our free land.

Earlier in this article, we had occasion to remark that the principle of altruistic service to clients is far stronger in the military than in all other professions. But even this superlative fails to suggest adequately the courage and sacrifice uniquely associated with the military vocation.

John Ruskin, the great Victorian art historian and certainly no warmonger, captures the essence of the soldier's true nobility as well as can be done:

> The consent of mankind has always, in spite of the philosophers, given precedence to the soldier. And this is right. For the soldier's trade, verily and essentially, is not slaying, but being slain. This, without well knowing its own meaning, the world honors it for. . . . Our estimate of him is based on this ultimate fact—of which we are well assured—that, put him in a fortress breach, with all the pleasures of the world behind him, and only death and his duty in front of him, he will keep his face to the front; and he knows that this choice may be put to him at any moment.

All of us recall the drill sergeant who, eyeing a drooping recruit at parade, barks out, "Look proud, solder!" And that is the message I would leave with the military professional today—"Pop up that chest, take heart, and look proud, soldier, for verily you are a member of the proudest calling of them all!"

The Future of Army Professionalism: The Need for Renewal and Redefinition

by Don Snider, PhD and LTC Gayle Watkins, PhD

Introduction

The Army that won the battles of Gulf War in 1991 was one of the most professional ever fielded by America. As General Schwarzkopf commented, "We could have traded equipment with the Iraqis and still won."[1] And when that Army returned home, it was welcomed by a supportive, even adoring, public. Now, almost one decade later, the situation has changed dramatically. During the past eight years, the US Army has undergone radical changes—major force and budget reductions, revised modernization programs, and successive base realignments and closures. All were intended by design to adapt the institution to the post-Cold War geo-political situation.

But, there are many indications that the result is an Army quite unlike the victors of the Gulf War battles. It is instead an Army of decreasing effectiveness, one which suffers from a weakening relationship with the American public and, more of concern, with its own members.

The last decade has been one of massive change to which the Army profession has yet to adapt fully. Simply stated, the end of the Cold War, which roughly coincided with the culmination of other shifts in the organization of western, post industrial societies, has drastically altered the expectations of where and how the profession of arms will apply its expertise. Today, in this new interwar period,[2] the Army is expected to operate effectively across the entire spectrum of violence, from major theater wars to domestic disaster relief. Further, it must be prepared to conduct these varied operations worldwide in any physical and political environment, and to do so in very

Source: *Parameters* (Autumn, 2000) 5-20. Reprinted by permission of *Parameters*.

rapid order. With these shifts in society's expectations came the need for a huge expansion in the profession's knowledge base and in the application of that expert knowledge to new situations. Such growth in expertise should have generated changes throughout the Army's leadership and management systems—from organizational structure to applied technology, from measures of readiness to measures of effectiveness, and from military training systems to professional military education.

The Army is, however, faltering in its attempts to adapt to these stark changes; this inability to adapt is itself a significant manifestation of a decline in effectiveness. Unfortunately, this potentially dangerous situation remains, at the systemic level, largely unrecognized by the institution. Even worse, it is not clear that there is currently within the officer corps of the Army a consensus on just what "Army Professionalism" is nor a common language with which to analyze and discuss it. Absent such analysis and dialogue, the Army is currently looking elsewhere for solutions to the decline in effectiveness by studying individually the recurring symptoms as they reach crisis proportions, such as recruiting shortfalls, an exodus of captains, unfunded adaptations in structure and technology, leadership failures, etc.

There are two ways to look at the Army. The first is as a large, bureaucratic organization. The second is as a profession. The Army has, over past decades, increasingly moved toward using organizational concepts for decision-making to lead, design, and structure the institution's systems, and away from using professional concepts to do so. Such is also the case today; operations research, efficiency goals, outsourcing, reengineering, and bonuses dominate the institution's analyses and solutions. As such, efficiency is a dominant goal, surpassing military effectiveness. Due to an excessively organizational perspective, the Army has borrowed aspects of human resource systems from corporations and wonders why the members of the profession are acting like employees. The Army is missing (and thereby losing) competitions with other professions and organizations at the boundaries of its expertise. And, it is resisting change because that threatens present force structure, rather than viewing the needed change in the context of how it affects the Army's expertise and jurisdiction, and thus its professionalism.

This approach denies the Army's professional nature and accentuates its bureaucratic elements. Although professions and organizational bureaucracy often coexist in modern society, they differ in their approach to their work and to their members—their emphasis on effectiveness versus efficiency, their commitment to knowledge development rather than knowledge application, and their view of members as professionals versus employees.

It appears that today's Army sees professionalism as a property of individuals—its officers, noncommissioned officers, Army civilians and soldiers—rather than of the institution.[3] To our knowledge, there are no ongoing Army studies of professionalism *per se*, nor have there been any since early in the 1970s.

One might argue that the Army should be allowed simply to deprofessionalize, becoming an obedient, but non-professional, military bureaucracy. One need look no further than Europe to see western democratic societies readily accepting this outcome. But if this happened here, American society would lose two key benefits of military professionalism—the development and adaptation of military expertise and social control over and within an institution capable of terrible destruction. Professions are by nature more adept than bureaucracies at evolving expert knowledge and controlling human behavior in complex and chaotic environments (e.g., threatening or using coercive force to maintain the peace and/or fight wars). Since the continual development of military expertise and control of a military engaged on behalf of American society are both essential to the Republic's future security, a non-professional Army is certainly not in America's best interest. Perhaps equally important to the readers of this essay, neither do we believe it in the Army's best interest. We doubt whether citizens of the necessary character and capabilities will ever voluntarily serve in large numbers in a nonprofessional, bureaucratized military.

In this essay, we propose an alternative perspective, one that emphasizes the Army as a profession over the Army as a bureaucracy. If the Army is to overcome its current problems, we believe it must make institutional professionalism the predominate criteria in decision making while opening a dialogue with its own professionals about the state of the institution. Based on recent advances in the understanding of professions, our suggested perspective transcends the Army's historic emphasis on the ethical component of professionalism—military values and ethics—to use a broader definition of the Army profession. Using this perspective, we view the Army's present situation as the result of dramatic changes in the objective and subjective nature of the Army's professional work and in the number and diversity of professional and organizational competitors vying for jurisdiction over this work. Focusing first on the Army's professional nature offers an alternative to organizational criteria by which policy and structural changes can be assessed; an alternative that emphasizes task effectiveness, the Army's relationship with the client (society), and the institution's implicit contract with its own professionals.

The task of this essay, then, is to: (1) assess the Army's task effectiveness, which suggests to us a problem with the institution's professionalism,[4] (2) review how the Army has traditionally understood its professionalism; and (3) provide an alternative explanation of the Army's decline based on a more recent understanding of professions, suggesting new ways in which to think about the issue. We do these tasks in sequence, including a suggested framework within which to facilitate an informing dialogue among the officer corps.

Indications of a Decline in Military Effectiveness

Indicators of a decline in Army effectiveness are numerous. First, there is a gross mismatch between institutional capabilities and national needs for strategic projection of land power. Army forces—units and equipment—are neither rapidly deployable nor well suited for operations at the lower end of the spectrum of conflict. Acknowledged by the Army's current leadership when announcing the institution's transformation initiative,[5] this mismatch was even more apparent during the unsuccessful deployment of Task Force Hawk to Albania in the fall of 1999. Unable to move combat equipment and retrain soldiers quickly, Americans concluded that the Task Force's combat capabilities never played a useful role in the conflict.[6]

In addition to a lack of strategic agility, there are recurring indicators that current operational readiness has markedly declined since the Gulf War. A respected independent study coordinated by the Center for Strategic and International Studies (CSIS) recently concluded that, "Morale and readiness are suffering from force reductions, high operations tempo, and resource constraints; military culture may suffer in the longer term".[7] In fact, Army leaders have recently testified to the excessive operations tempo, now averaging "on any given day" over 141,000 soldiers engaged or deployed world wide (outside CONUS).[8] These concerns were more recently validated when the new commander of the 1st Infantry Division in Germany and the Balkans rated his unit "not combat ready" in the first quarter of this year. COL John Rosenberger, commander of the National Training Center's opposing forces, told a similar story when testifying to Congress (fall 99) that the combat battalion task forces he opposed were less well prepared, learned less while training there, and departed at lower levels of combat preparedness than in previous years.[9] And, the Army's own think tank, the Arroyo Center, recently documented the existence of a "tactical gap" (knowledge/proficiency based on experience) in junior grade combat arms officers, a gap they consider only the top of the iceberg when these same officers assume company/troop command in the future.[10]

A third indicator of declining effectiveness is reflected in a recent *New York Times* article that cited a young officer saying, "Senior leaders will throw subordinates under the bus in a heartbeat to protect or advance their own career (sic)." As noted in the CSIS Study, the degree of distrust within the Army officer corps, particularly between younger officers in the field and their senior leaders in Washington DC, is at historically high levels. Captains are voting with their feet, with annual losses now exceeding ten percent, four percent more than pre-Gulf War rates. The Army is now sufficiently short of Captains that, to fill the ranks, it has reduced the time-in-grade for Lieutenants to be promoted (thus exacerbating the "tactical gap") and established a general-officer led task force to assess leadership and training issues throughout the Army.

Fourth, the Army's future effectiveness is declining because the persistent mismatch between multiple missions and fiscal resources has left Army modernization plans in shambles. Three Army Chiefs of Staff have proposed within the past eight years evolutionary concepts for the post-Cold-War modernization of the Army. However, the only modernization that has been effected, even partially, has centered on using advances in informational technologies to improve the capabilities of the heavy armored formations that have dominated the service's combat power for decades. Yet these forces lack the strategic agility to project such power. The current Chief of Staff, General Eric Shinseki, has proposed the creation of medium-weight forces for exactly this reason,[11] but already his plans for eight such brigades have been cut because of the same resource shortfalls.[12] Thus, the absence of consistent and credible (resourced) institutional vision has blurred the institution's identity, particularly for younger officers, and continues to suggest a decline in future effectiveness within the Army.[13]

Fifth, and lastly, it is not just the scope and pace of current missions nor the lack of resources that is diminishing the Army's effectiveness. There is also the issue of how the Army is executing the operations other than war (OOTW) missions it is assigned today, specifically the manner in which it is responding to political guidance to suffer "no casualties." Simply stated, the Army has not recognized the ethical implications of supporting a national policy that considers force protection a higher priority for deployed units than mission accomplishment. This has eroded the professional ethic and ruptured officers' traditional concept of duty. It has seriously reduced junior officer discretion and fostered risk-averse behavior among junior leaders and their units. Without doubt, the exodus of captains mentioned earlier has been exacerbated by this institutional implementation of what is, admittedly, very difficult political guidance.[14]

If expert knowledge is the heart of a profession, then effectiveness, the profession's ability to apply that knowledge, is its pulse. These five indicators of declining operational effectiveness signal to us that the Army's professionalism is in jeopardy; the Army is increasingly unable to accomplish professional tasks, meet its own professional standards, and acquire adequate resources to accomplish the tasks expected of it now while simultaneously preparing for the future. In terms of professionalism, the Army is struggling to adapt its expert knowledge to its new circumstances.

In general, as an increasingly ineffective profession is devalued by its clients, it exposes itself to meddling by non-professionals (e.g., society's representatives dictating to the Army how to conduct its basic training) and to competition within its jurisdiction from the expertise of other organizations and professions. To highlight other indicators of the state of professionalism, we now turn to social factors and the Army's bond with American society.

Indications of Changing Relations with American Society

Another key set of indicators is the state of the profession's relations with its client, American society. Although not yet as serious as the deterioration in operational effectiveness, these issues are interrelated; as effectiveness declines, we would expect increased dissatisfaction on the part of an attentive client. Several things indicate that this is occurring. First, the Army will likely miss its recruiting goal for the second consecutive year in FY2000, even after slightly lowering standards and significantly restructuring pay and bonuses to increase accessions.[15] There could scarcely be a clearer indicator of the willingness of American society to support its Army than the degree to which its sons and daughters decide to join for a period of personal, volunteer service.

Second is the documented "gap" between the attitudes of the military and American society, particularly its elected leadership. There is a widening gap in values and perspectives between Americans serving in our armed forces, including the Army, and the society they serve.[16] Part of the gap is both expected and beneficial for the institution's functional effectiveness; however, several aspects of it are of relevance to professionalism. For example, the officers surveyed in the study (including Army War College students, future senior Army leaders) believed that the values of the military institution were not just different from, but also in several respects better than, those of the society they are protecting. This is a pernicious perspective for an officer corps serving under precepts of civil-military relations that posit selfless service as motivating the soldier, and the supremacy of civilian values over those of the subordinate profession. Triumphalism within the officer corps with respect to martial values simply does not support the professional military ethic; what thinking soldier will sacrifice his life on a lonely battlefield for a society he does not love and respect?[17]

The relationship between the profession and society has been further ruptured by repeated and well-publicized ethical violations by Army leaders. The high degree of expertise found in professions requires relative autonomy in the application and adaptation of their expert knowledge. This limited autonomy from society also allows the profession to establish and maintain at the core of its unique culture a professional ethic, a critical trust-building bond between the society and its professional "experts." However, in return for this limited autonomy, the American society expects the profession to police itself, exhibiting a high degree of behavioral control through social structures such as education, selection processes, character inculcation and ethical codes. Yet, repeated cases of misconduct at the highest levels reflect ineffective policing of the senior ranks.[18] This inability to control unprofessional behavior at the top levels is, undoubtedly, also fueling the current high level of distrust between the higher and lower echelons of the Army officer corps.

Finally, the Army's client, the American public, appears increasingly unsure how to distinguish the Army's jurisdiction from those of other organizations and professions. American corporations, international governmental and non-governmental organizations (IGOs and INGOs) are now so deeply involved in military operations that American Army units work with and even, in some cases, for them.[19] Within the United States, the Army is involved in monitoring our southern border with the US Border Patrol, conducting anti-drug operations with the Drug Enforcement Agency (DEA) and disaster relief with the Federal Emergency Management Agency (FEMA). Further, the "efficiency movement" toward privatization has resulted in the contracting out of many traditionally Army activities such as information technology management, maintenance of family housing, overseas operational logistics, and even the conduct of military-to-military assistance programs, as in Columbia.[20]

With this jurisdictional blurring of the Army's expertise, and thus its roles and missions, the Army has entered competition for human and fiscal resources from these new organizations and professions to a degree that it has not faced in the memory of serving leaders. Traditionally, the three services have competed among themselves for recruits and budget shares. As such, there are processes in place to ameliorate this quasihealthy competition so that the nation normally benefits. However, the more recent incursions by non-military, non-governmental and non-American organizations into this system of professions has, we believe, wide-ranging repercussions for the Army. As such, these incursions into the Army's traditional jurisdiction must be consciously and carefully considered by the institution's strategic leaders.

Situation Complicated By International Factors

Although the Army historically has survived similar inter-war crises following the resolution of major wars (albeit often at terrible costs in American blood, e.g., TF Smith, Korea), today's situation is complicated by the "new times" in the international security structure. Globalization, economic interdependence and coincident societal changes are influencing the legitimacy and capabilities of the American Army as well as those of militaries in allied, western democratic countries.

For example, the present generations that are governing western democracies have expectations and goals quite different from those of past generations; the concept of citizenship and one's responsibilities to the State has been redefined .[21] For these reasons, youth are less and less inclined to serve in the military. It is also the case that professions in general in western democracies are being devalued by the societies they serve owing to influences quite independent of the end of the Cold War—professional competition and new client power exceeding the producer power of professions.[22]

Among professions, the military faces even further pressure because its two historic relationships established with the rise of the nation-state—with the Nation and with the State—are undergoing significant change. For example, the profession's relationship with the Nation has changed because the lack of a recognized major threat has devalued society's need for the military's function, blurring it with the role of a national police more appropriate for service in conflicts which do not threaten significant national interests. Thus, militaries now lack a shared interpretative framework with their publics. As a result, post-modernist and anti-institutionalist cultural shifts in public attitudes and opinion further devalue the military institution and its absolutist ethos.[23]

The profession's relationship with the State has also changed, owing to (1) declining State sovereignty (e.g., the use of military force, including that of the United States, is more and more influenced by coalitions and inter-governmental organizations); and, (2) the State's increased focus on non-military aspects of security such as economic competition, both externally via globalization and internally by expecting increased efficiency of public institutions, including the military. Thus, in addressing its own situation the Army must contend both with its own internal manifestations of declining effectiveness and internal relationships, and as well, with these significantly and perhaps permanently altered external relationships.

Responses to Date

Given the importance of professionalism, it might be thought that the Army regularly analyzes it. In fact, it has done so only episodically and then only when confronted with a crisis such as during the Vietnam War in the early 1970s.[24] At that time the Army was confronted by a similar crisis in professional identity, but one caused by quite different factors than are influencing the situation today: the divisive Vietnam War and the end of conscription. However, a key factor in the rebuilding of the Army post-Vietnam was a revalidation of the importance of its status as a profession in two critical ways. First, it re-intellectualized its professional expertise through the collective training revolution and an internal dialogue among the officer corps that resulted in a strategic and doctrinal focus on Europe.[25] Within a decade, middle level officers understood and identified with their revised role of "collective skill trainers" creating a "trained and ready Army." This self-concept was congruent with the new institutional identity of the European-focused Army. Second, the Army examined and then revamped many of its management systems, particularly those for human resources, to reinforce professionalism rather than diminish it. One important example was the revision of officer assignmnent priorities and policies, including the lengthening of command tours.

Through this systemic emphasis on being a profession, the Army renewed its professional identity, which in turn enabled its members to align their personal and professional self-concepts. *This is a critical connection, one increasingly missing today.* The alignment between individual officers and the profession's identity is critical for long-term viability since professionalism ultimately resides in the expert knowledge, character and personal motivation of its leaders.[26]

Traditional Understandings of Military Professionalism

The traditional conception of Army professionalism paralleled the broader investigation of professions taking place in the United States and Europe. Early in the 1930s, professions were identified as a unique means of organizing and controlling work, different from the more common formal organizations and labor unions. Research into professions began as descriptive case studies of professions, progressed through the identification of professions' differentiating characteristics, and, by 1960, modeled the professionalization process by which occupations were converted into professions.[27] The two foundation characteristics that separated professions from occupations were the application of *abstract knowledge to specific situations*. Other essential characteristics included organization of the occupation, extensive education of members, service to society, and shared ethics.[28] Professionalization was seen as a one-way street; an occupation's status as a profession was relatively static, something to be maintained over time through its unique characteristics.

Classical writings on the military profession, including Vagts, Huntington, Janowitz, and Abrahamsson,[29] drew on this more general study of professions. Most important were the characteristics that identified the military as a profession. As succinctly summarized in the late 1970s by military historian Allan Millet, the attributes and character of the military occupation which caused society to give it "professional" status included that:

> the occupation was full-time and stable, serving society's continuing needs; it was regarded a life-long calling by the practitioners, who identified themselves personally with their vocational sub-culture; it was organized to control performance standards and recruitment; it required formal, theoretical education; it had a service orientation in which loyalty to standards of competence and loyalty to client's needs were paramount; [it] was granted a great deal of autonomy by the society it served, presumably because the practitioners had proven their high ethical standards and trustworthiness; and, overall, the profession's work was the systemic exploitation of specialized knowledge applied to specialized problems.[30]

From this traditional conception of the military profession came the self-concept of the individual professional:

> [The officer's] identity is partly inherited, partly self-developed. He inherits the broadly defined characteristics of his career and the special institutional setting within which he finds himself. He must develop stable and lasting concepts of self that are compatible with his profession. This transformation or "professional socialization" is not taken lightly by the other practitioners with whom he begins his career.[31]

This conception also fit the military's understanding of war as a subordinate instrument of policy to be exercised by a democratic government, the Clauswitizian duality of war. As explicated by Huntington and widely accepted by generations of American officers, objective control of the military meant that in return for limited autonomy in which to develop their expert knowledge and conduct their professional duties, the military's natural and self-interested role would be one of self-policing, nonpolitical, internal focus on its expertise and moral responsibilities.

The Vietnam War, however, shattered the illusions of the Crowe-Powell generation of officers (the mentors and developers of today's senior military leaders) about that role of the military professional and created an officer corps that was, contrary to Huntingtonian logic, both more professional and more political.[32] This created significant tensions in American civil-military relations, tensions that were bound to surface as society turned, in a trend not without historic precedent, to more subjective forms of civilian control for this new interwar period.[33]

Given these tensions, there has been a very large amount of scholarly analysis and debate about the military's role at the senior level in post-Cold War civil-military relations. Much of this has focused on criticism of the Weinberger-Powell doctrine on the use of military force and General Colin Powell's role as Chairman of the Joint Chiefs of Staff, 1990-1994.[34]

During the same period, however, military professionalism as such has been a subject little studied within academe.[35] One exception is the work of Professor Samuel C. Sarkesian, who has consistently argued for a broad interpretation of military professionalism with multiple levels of analyses, as displayed in the first four columns of the Figure below.[36] We have filled in the framework with those symptoms of declining professionalism discussed in the first section of this essay.

This three-by-three matrix framework, which incorporates well the traditional views of military professionalism, allows visualization of several things that we believe vital to the officer corps' successful introspection and dialogue. First, it is clear that each aspect of professionalism should be analyzed and understood from three perspectives: the client's (society); the professional institution's (Army); and the professional member's (officer, non-commissioned officer, Army civilian, soldier). Second, the two horizontal boundaries dividing these three perspectives are areas of current tensions (civil-military relations and Army-soldier relations) owing to the different perspectives held within each level. And third, in contrast to the relative clarity of these horizontal boundaries, the vertical divisions between components are much less precise. Is the task of force protection a military-technical issue (doctrinal), or a moral-ethical issue (a matter of institutional values), or even a political-social issue (a matter of adapting to unhelpful political guidance)? We would say it involves all three, but primarily lies within the political component. But more important, such mapping facilitates, even necessitates, dialogue if different officers, or agencies, see the issue as residing in different locations and contexts.

While still very useful, this traditional conception of "Army Professionalism" must, we believe, be rethought and renewed, particularly at the institutional level of analysis. It is abundantly clear that at the individual level, both young Americans (who are not join-ing the Army) and Army captains (who are leaving the institution) have given the insti-tution's state of professionalism some serious thought, enough to guide their individual actions. It is now past time for the keepers of Army Professionalism—the officer corps—to do the same, but from a renewed understanding of professions and their behavior.

A New Understanding—Systems of Professions, Jurisdictions of Expert Knowledge

Today's understanding of professions builds on these earlier efforts, specifically the distinction of professions from other occupations based on the application of abstract knowledge to specific circumstances, the equivalent of Millet's "specialized knowledge applied to specialized problems." However, theorists have moved beyond the static description of individual professions toward a dynamic conception of the profession-al world. Modem professions are competitors—for members, resources, and, most importantly, jurisdiction—within a "system of professions." This system includes other professions, professionalizing occupations, and organizations, each of which vie for jurisdiction, the legitimated claim to apply its expertise to specific situations. It is from this jurisdiction that strategic leaders must develop the detailed require-ments for professional systems—education, ethics, oversight, and credentialing, to name but a few. Professional systems that are decoupled from jurisdiction will hinder the profession's effectiveness and weaken its claim over its tasks.[37] For example, the "tactical knowledge gap" of junior officers weakens the Army's claim over future warfighting jurisdictions.

It is the abstract element of professional knowledge that enables this dynamic, pro-viding flexibility in the circumstances in which knowledge can be applied. Through this process professions attempt to claim new jurisdictions, like the medical profession claimed alcoholism from the ministry by identifying it as a disease rather than a weak-ness in character or will. However, the malleability of a profession's abstract knowl-edge also makes it vulnerable to change in the objective and subjective character of its professional tasks.

Objective changes in a profession's tasks arise from sources outside the system that open new jurisdictional opportunities or do away with old ones, that introduce new com-petitors into the system or cause others to disappear. These external changes are usually caused by technical, organizational, natural or cultural shifts. Subjective changes in tasks originate from the actions of other players within the system and are usually more grad-ual in nature. In this case, subjective characteristics of the profession's work are redefined as others—professions or organizations—grapple for jurisdiction over it.

Professions seek to best their competitors by establishing legitimate control over jurisdictions through a variety of channels. In the US, the most binding, durable and dif-ficult to achieve means of control is legal, where the law establishes who can and cannot do specific work. However, the "court of public opinion" is also an important legitimat-ing mechanism that is more easily attainable; if the public assumes a profession is the appropriate source of a service, then its jurisdiction is strengthened. Finally, the most common form of professional legitimation takes place in the workplace where local mechanisms distribute work across professions and other players—through referral networks, organizational structures and policies.

While professional knowledge is adaptable, professional systems and structures are far less so. Therefore, professions adapt better to some changes than they do to others; rapid jurisdictional expansion is particularly difficult. Sudden expansion in either the amount of traditional work (quantitative) or the circumstances in which the profession must work (qualitative) challenge its education, personnel selection processes, and value systems. A profession whose jurisdiction is rapidly expanding will face an invasion by outsiders seeking to claim legal, cultural or workplace legitimacy over its work.

So, how might we apply this new understanding to the Army? Using the Army's present situation as an example, we can see that it is facing both qualitative and quantitative expansion of and challenges to its jurisdiction (right-side column of figure). Twenty years ago, America focused the system of professions in which the Army competes on major military conflicts. As such, this system consisted of the military services, including the Coast Guard, and the State Department. Competition existed within the system but it was organizationally regulated and each profession's jurisdiction was delimited by law, policy, and culture when the services' roles and missions were negotiated and renegotiated.

Today, the Army's professional situation has become far more complex by every measure. Quantitatively, the amount of work has increased dramatically, as measured by number and duration of deployments. Qualitatively, extensive objective and subjective changes have taken place in the Army's tasks. The fall of the Berlin Wall, the dissolution of the Soviet Union, and subsequent shrinking of the defense budget caused objective changes for the Army. More subtle influences, such as the evolving international security structure and the Army's changing relationships with the Nation and State, have expanded the Army's jurisdiction across the spectrum of conflict. Such significant changes are particularly critical for the Army because, unlike most other professions, military professions do not independently select their jurisdiction. Instead, selection results from negotiation with their clients, the American government and people.

As we enter the 21 st Century, the system of professions providing the nation's security is much broader as America has redefined security to include illegal drugs, illegal immigrants, terrorists, rogue states, international natural disasters, humanitarian assistance, peacekeeping, and most recently, homeland defense. Thus, the system of professions within which the Army competes is crowded with American government agencies such as the other military services, State Department, Border Patrol, DEA, Federal Bureau of Investigations (FBI), Central Intelligence Agency (CIA), and FEMA. Furthermore, other non-traditional entities are invading this system so that it now also includes the United Nations, NATO, corporations involved in logistical support, coalition and allied militaries, and non-governmental organizations. The Army's formerly well-organized system of professions has mushroomed without a commensurate expansion in the legal, cultural or workplace mechanisms that legitimate each profession's jurisdiction.

Throughout these recent changes, the Army has done little to negotiate a redefinition of its jurisdiction; instead, it has passively accepted expansion of its jurisdiction simultaneous with a massive downsizing of its membership and resources. The traditional Army "can-do" attitude has left it poorly positioned to respond to looming jurisdictional battles, both within the traditional military establishment and without.[38] Instead of seeing this as an opportunity to reaffirm its professional status, the Army has embraced business methods to assist with these changes. As we noted in the introduction, these models tend to have efficiency as their primary goal compared to a profession's emphasis on effectiveness. Furthermore, without a renewed understanding of the Army's jurisdiction, any adaptive actions it takes may be completely decoupled from its professional tasks. Ultimately, as a result of this ambiguity in the Army's institutional professional identity and its decoupling from organizational actions, the professional identities of its individual members have become increasingly uncertain, resulting in declines in commitment and retention.

Conclusion: An Alternative for Dialogue and Renewal

How might this new perspective help us think about the Army's present situation of declining effectiveness? Is this a matter of professionalism or is this simply a matter of organizational change? Can the Army continue to separate its organizational decisions from professional considerations? Furthermore, can it simply rely on the traditional conceptions of "expertise, responsibility and corporateness" as the whole of professionalism in this new interwar period? Or should it reconceive itself as existing in a "systems of professions," competing fiercely within such a system on the basis of each profession's jurisdiction of expert knowledge and work?

We believe all three perspectives—the new professionalism, the old professionalism, and organizational—can contribute to an analysis of the troubling aspects of the Army's current decline. However, if the Army is to accomplish the essential tasks of strengthening and revitalizing its professional nature, the *new professionalism* view must predominate the others. This will require that the Army's strategic leaders analyze and assertively renegotiate the boundaries of the institution's expert knowledge and legitimate jurisdiction, first with its own professional members and then with the American people. While this is ongoing, they must redesign the professional and organizational support systems congruent with the evolving jurisdiction. However, in all of these decisions, maintaining the Army's professional status must be paramount; America needs an effective professional Army more than an efficient, budget-conscious bureaucracy.

The new professionalism framework establishes that almost everything the Army does or does not do is part of the institution's expert work—the application of its specialized knowledge to new situations—and therefore, its professionalism. And therein lies the conclusion we seek to emphasize. Who should decide what Army Professionalism is at any point in time, and in what priority issues affecting it should be addressed? We submit that for the past decade the public dialogue has been episodically initiated and carried by elements of American society and from their perspectives. The Army has played a passive and reactive role in such public discourse.

However, if the Army is to remain a profession, we believe that must change; and, it must be changed by the profession itself, through its officer corps—the Army's change agents—by dialogue and analyses within the profession. Then, once understanding and relative consensus have been reached internally, the Army must firmly present its case publicly, well supported by its own professional judgments and analyses, as to what is needed to renew and maintain this absolutely vital aspect of America's Army.

Framework for the
Analysis of American Army Professionalism

Level of Analysis	Components of the Army Profession			New Professionalism Levels of Analysis
	Military-Technical	Moral-Ethical	Political-Social	
Societal *National and global context in which Army exists*	**National and international uses of military forces.** *Issues:* mismatch between national needs for strategic projection and institutional capabilities; TF Hawk	**National and international values and beliefs.** *Issues:* Post-modern or egoist ethic; generational differences; intercultural differences; globalization.	**National and international political and societal systems.** *Issues:* changing definitions of security; globalizaiton; economic growth; casualty-averse politicians; diminished state sovereignty and influence; redefinition of democratic citizenship.	**System of professions in which the Army exists.** *Issues:* other professions, occupations and organizations in system; actions that maintain positions in system; historic and future development of this system.
Institutional *Internal context and systems*	**Internal Army systems supporting military-technical capabilities.** *Issues:* unit readiness; lack of strategic force protection capability; medium-weight division; OOTW scope and duration.	**Internal Army systems that establish, communicate and maintain the profession's norms and values** *Issues:* emphasis on force protection; HR systems; ethical violations by military leaders.	**Internal Army systems focused on political and societal actions.** *Issues:* maintaining limited professional autonomy; civilian control of the military; recruiting; resource acquisition; candid advice-giving.	**State of profession.** *Issues:* Army profession's expert knowledge and jurisdiction; institutional identity; legitimacy of claim on jurisdiction; legal, cultural, policy support for claim.
Individual *People who comprise the Army*	**Individual knowledge and skills required to be successful in the Army.** *Issues:* tactical gap; breadth and depth of skills required across spectrum of conflict.	**Individual moral-ethical values** *Issues:* senior military leaders willingness to be role models; diminished loyalty and commitment; intrinsic motivation.	**Political and societal knowledge and skills held by or necessary for Army members.** *Issues:* Civil-military gap; aversion to professional participation in government systems.	**Individual perceptions of the profession.** *Issues:* primacy of professional identity; congruence in professional identity with institutional identity.

Civil-Military
Tensions

Army-Soldier
Tensions

NOTES

1 Stephen Biddle, "Victory Misunderstood: What the Gulf War Tells Us About the Future of Conflict" (*International Security*, Fall 1996): 139-179.

2 We use this phrase to indicate that, unlike the earlier interwar period which separated eras of global, land warfare concentrated in Europe and the Pacific, this interwar period separates that era of half a century from the next era of great power conflict. Then, we believe, a highly professional Army will be an imperative for America.

3 Since we are recommending an institutional focus on the Army as a profession, then its members are, by definition, professionals to varying degrees. Each strata—commissioned officer, non-commissioned officer, and enlisted solider—is a sub-profession that falls under the larger professional umbrella. Although commissioned officers are very important for a number of reasons (they are individually accountable to society via their commission, they are the institution's change agents, they are the senior leaders, they control strategy, budgets and systems, etc), they are not alone in their import, nor in their status as professionals.

4 We must also make clear to the reader what we are not arguing in this essay. We are not contending that the Army's problems (declining effectiveness, etc.) are either the cause of, or the effect of, declining professionalism. That depends on what definition of professionalism one is using, and as we have noted, we doubt that there is a common definition extant within the Army today. Thus, until more research can be completed, we can only conclude that the two issues are concurrent in their manifestations.

5 Honorable Louis Caldera and General Eric Shinseki, *A Statement on the Posture of the United States Army, Fiscal Year 2001* accessed at the Army Homepage, http://www.army.mil.

6 Whether the Task Force was effective in a non-combat role remains debatable, see Dana Priest, "Army's Apache Helicopter Rendered Impotent in Kosovo (*Washington Post*, December 29, 1999): 1.

7 Joseph Collins and Walter Ulmer, *American Military Culture in the Twenty-First Century* (Washington DC: Center for Strategic and International Studies, 2000): xx. and chapter six, 62-76.

8 Caldera and Shinseki, 2.

9 See testimony by Colonel John D. Rosenberger, Commander Opposing Forces, National Training Center, Ft Irwin CA, before the Military Readiness Subcommitee, Committee on National Security, U.S. House of Representatives, 26 February 1999, (Accessed on-line).

10 See Maren Leed, "Keeping the Warfighting Edge-An Empirical Analysis of the Army Officer's Tactical Expertise Over the 1990s: Summary Briefing (RAND: Arroyo Center, 2000).

11 General Eric Shinseki, *Intent of the Chief of Staff*, Department of the Army, June 23, 1999, accessed at: http://www.hqda.army.mil.csa.html.

12 See, Theodore G. Stroup, Jr., "The Ongoing Army Transformation," *ARMY* (July 2000): 7- 10.

13 Lest Congress be blamed excessively for this situation, we note that within the tradition of western democratic societies, the acquisition of such resources is the responsibility of the leaders of the professional institution, both uniformed and civilian. In past cases of success, senior leaders often had to make undesirable tradeoffs to gain the political support necessary. See Allan R. Millett, Williamson Murray, and Kenneth H. Watman, "The Effectiveness of Military Organizations," (*International Security*, Summer 1986, 37-71.

14 See, Don M. Snider, John A. Nagl and Tony Pfaff, *Army Professionalism, the Military Ethic and Officership in the 21st Century* accessed at <http://carlisle www.army.mil/usassi/ssipubs/pubs99/ethic/ethic.htm>

15 Vince Crawley, "The Services' War on Attrition," accessed at <https://ca.dtic.mil/cgibin/ebird?doc_url=/Jun2000/s20000602services.htm>

16 Peter D. Feaver and Richard H. Kohn, "Project on the Gap between the Military and Civilian Society - Digest of Findings and Studies," accessed on-line at < http://www.poli.duke.edu/civmil>.

17 Don M. Snider, "America's PostModern Military," *World Policy Journal*, (spring 2000): 47-54.

18 The Army's Aberdeen scandal and the more recent cases of MG Smith and BG Hale come to mind.

19 Major John Nagl and Cadet Elizabeth O. Young, "Si Vis Pacem, Para Pacem:Training for Humanitarian Emergencies" (*Military Review*, March-April 2000).

20 See, Deborah D. Avant, "Privatizing Military Training," *Foreign Policy in Focus*, Vol. 5, No. 17 (June 2000):1-3; and, David Schearer, "Outsourcing War," *Foreign Policy* (Fall 1998). For indications of future trends in this area, see the report of the DoD Commission, lead by BG® Peter M. Dawkins, on "Commericializing Activities in the Department of Defense," Washington DC: Department of Defense (Spring 2000).

21 James Burk, "Introduction, 1998: Ten Years of New Times" and "Thinking Through the End of the Cold War" in James Burk (ed), *The Adaptative Military* (New Brunswick: Transaction Publishers, 1998): 1-48.

22 This shift in power to the profession's client is largely due to the emergence of information, vice industrial, economies and the explosion of available information, much of it formerly within control of professions. See Chris Dandeker, "A Farewell to Arms? The Military and the Nation-State in Changing Times" in James Burk (ed), *The Adaptive Military* (New Brunswick: Transaction Publishers, 1998): 139-162.

23 See James Toner, *True Faith and Allegiance: The Burden Of Military Ethics* (Lexington: University Press of Kentucky, 1995), and *Morals Under the Gun: The Cardinal Virtues, Military Ethics, and American Society* (Lexington, University Press of Kentucky, 2000).

24 The seminal study of this period was done at the Army War College, *Study on Military Professionalism* (Carlisle Barracks, June 1970) available through the Defense Technical Information Center, Ft Belvior Virginia.)

25 For official history of this period, see Robert K. Griffith, *Today's Army Wants to Join You: The US Army's Transition from the Draft to an All-volunteer Force* (Washington DC: Center for Military History, 1995) and Anne W. Chapman, *The Army's Training Revolution, 1973-1990* (Ft Monroe, VA: Training and Doctrine Command, 1990). For a very readable current history version of the same events, see James Kitfield, *Prodigal Soldiers*, (New York: Simon and Schuster, 1995).

26 We note that in the past decade, the creation of OPMS XXI is the one example of institutional adaptation that holds potential (it is too early yet to tell) to enhance Army Professionalism.

27 See A.P. Carr-Saunders and P.A. Wilson, *The Professions* (Oxford: Oxford University Press, 1933) for initial case studies on professions. Wilensky's "The Professionalization of Everyone?" in the 1964 American Journal of Sociology (70: 137-158) presents the professionalization sequence for American professions.

28 Millerson, Geoffery, *The Qualifying Associations* (London: Routledge, 1964).

29 The classics include: Alfred Vagts, *A History of Militarism* (revised edition, New York: Free Press, 1959; Samuel P. Huntington, *The Soldier and The State* (Cambridge: Harvard University Press, 1959; Morris Janowitz, *The Professional Soldier: A Social and Political Portrait* (Glencoe: The Free Press, 1960); Bengt Abrahamsson, *Military Professionalism and Political Power* (Beverly Hills: Sage Publishing, 1972).

30 Allan R. Millett, *Military Professionalism and Officership in America*, (Columbus, Ohio, The Ohio State University: Mershon Center Briefing Paper Number Two, May 1977): 2.

31 Millett, 5.

32 For loss of political neutrality of today's officer corps, see Oli R. Holsti, "A Widening Gap Between the US Military and Civilian Society? Some Evidence, 1976-1996," *International Security* 23, no 3 (Winter 1998/9): 8. See also commentary and reply by Joseph J. Collins and Oli Holsti, *International Security* 24, no 2, (Fall 1999): 199-207. For an overview of post-Cold War civil-military tensions, see Deborah D. Avant, "Conflicting Indicators of Crisis in American Civil-Military Relations, *Armed Forces and Society*, vol 24, no 3 (Spring 1998): 375-387.

33 See Charles C. Moskos, "Toward a Post-Modern Military: The United States as Paradigm," in Charles C. Moskos, John Allen Williams and David R. Segal (eds), *The PostModern Military* (Oxford: Oxford University Press, 2000): 14-31.

34 For both sides of this debate, see: Richard Kohn, "Out of Control," *National Interest* 35 (Spring 1994): 3-17, and Richard Weigley, "The American Military and the Principle of Civilian Control from McClellen to Powell," *Journal of Military History* 57 (October 1993): 27-58; and, Deborah D. Avant, "Are the Reluctant Warriors Out of Control?" (*Security Studies*, 6, 2 (Winter 1996/7).

35 To be sure there have been academics who have continued to focus on separate, specific aspects of the military profession, mostly members of the Inter-University Seminar on Armed Forces and Society (IUS); website at http://www.bsos.umd.edu/ius. However, a policy study of a service's policy toward women in combat units, for example, is but a single aspect of a military institution's professionalism.

36 This framework is adapted from, Samuel C. Sarkesian, *Beyond the Battlefield: The New Military Professionalism* (New York: Pergamon Press, 1981). See also, Sarkesian and Robert E. Connor Jr., *The US Military Profession into the Twenty-First Century* (London, Frank Cass Publishers, 2000).

37 This discussion is drawn primarily from Andrew Abbots' *The System of Professions: An Essay on the Division of Expert Labor* (The University of Chicago Press: Chicago, 1988). Additional sources include Elliott Krause, *Death of the Guilds: Professions, States and the Advance of Capitalism, 1930 to Present* (Yale University Press: New London, 1996) and Eliot Freidson, *Professionalism Reborn: Theory, Prophecy and Policy* (The University of Chicago Press: Chicago, 1994). 38 Examples include the Air Force's claim to space which places the Army's role in theater air defense in question; and the Army's acceptance of nation-building roles in long-term, international police actions such as Kosovo legitimizes the US government's expectation of the appropriateness of these roles.

Summary

The readings for this module were selected to facilitate your understanding of the officer and his profession. The readings in this chapter were intended to:

- assist you in grasping how a profession differs from a "job" or a career.
- identify the uniqueness of the military profession; how and why it is different from other American professions.
- gain an awareness of some fo the stresses of the military profession today and how those stresses affect the self-concept of the commissioned officer.

Unlike the previous chapter on the Officer as a Servant of the Nation, this chapter had only a few readings, five to be exact. It is not that this chapter was any less important, rather that these readings were a bit longer and introduced you to more new material and ideas with which you may not have been previously introduced in any depth.

You started your reading on the Officer as a Member of a Time-honored Profession with the clear understanding that the words "profession," "professional," and "professionalism" are the most misunderstood and misused words in the American lexicon. They tend to be use not to describe how and how well an individual does their chose work, as in "Michael Jordan is a real Pro!" In fact, however, the words have precise sociological meanings that are intended to convey something quite different! Webster's defines a profession as "a calling requiring specialized knowledge and long and intensive academic preparation..." this is little understood among today's American citizenry.

To assist you over this cultural divide and to broadly summarize what you read in this chapter, I will make the following assertions and then challenge you to verify them, or not, by the readings offered.

- A profession is a unique vocation that is highly valued by the society it serves (medicine, the law, the clergy, the military....)

- It is highly valued because it serves a socially useful, indeed vital, function that the society cannot do for itself (in case of the Army, defends the society)
- Members of that profession constantly maintain, on behalf of the society, a systematic body of specialized knowledge on their social function (in the case of the Army, how to prevent and, if need be, to successfully fight wars)
- It takes years of study to learn the professional skills and to keep them sharp
- Members of the profession are "called" to the profession, motivated by the intrinsic satisfaction of the act of service itself (re: Chapter I) and committed to a lifetime of learning and adapting their profession and to service
- Societies determine which vocations are professions by how they treat them, their autonomy and self-regulation they grant them
- Members of a profession develop over time a unique culture and ethos; they police it and adapt it to maintain the profession's functional effectiveness well as the trust of the society they serve
- Professions are dynamic institutions, some die, and all must compete to survive as professions adapting their expert work and jurisdiction as necessary

Even though the U.S. Army became a profession during the late 1800s (between the Civil War and the first World War) it was little studied as a profession until after the Second World War. Two of your readings were taken from the classics in the literature of that era; chapters 1 and 3 from Samuel Huntington's Soldier and State provide you with an introductory understanding of officership as a professional vocation.

You also had two readings from more recent times. One is a speech on what it means to join a noble profession, given at an Army commissioning ceremony by the military historian Martin Blumenson. The second is a recent article by Professor Lloyd Matthews defending the assertion that the military is today truly a profession. Together they provided you an "end of the 20th century" view on military professionalism.

Lastly, you had a very recent (Autumn, 2000) article by faculty here at West Point. Dr. Don Snider and LTC Gayle Watkins, which introduced very recent ideas about the dynamic nature of professions in America, including the military. These new theories about professions explain both the character and the necessity of the broad transition the Army is beginning to undergo.

Your challenge is to understand what a profession is in America; what responsibilities you will assume as one of its members, individually and collectively; and how those conceptions are changing, ultimately to be maintained by your generation of officers.

CHAPTER 3

The Officer as a Leader of Character

"I hope I shall always possess firmness and virtue enough to maintain what I consider the most enviable of all titles, the character of an 'honest man.'"

George Washington

The Way to Do Is to Be

by Malham M. Wakin

Loyalty and obedience, integrity and courage, subordination of the self to the good of the military unit and the nation-state—these are among the moral virtues critical to the military function, and they take the form of universal obligations. Seen in this context, the moral tone must be pervasive for both public and private actions of the ideal military leader. These qualities are essential to the effective and appropriate functioning of all military people, but those who lead are most responsible for exemplifying them and inculcating them in others. Only a narrowly faulty view of the moral life could sustain the view that one must be honorable in his public duties but that one's private moral code might operate on some other level. Consider the inconsistency in a leader who might insist on truthful reporting but falsifies his personal income tax return. Consider also the leader who asks for trust and loyalty from his subordinates but is unfaithful to his wife on temporary duty trips. Narrow views of ethics will not do for one who aspires to effective military leadership. Ones character is what counts and evaluations of character are all-encompassing.

Because the military function is so directly related to our highest human values, those charged with the leadership of that function must be sensitive to those values and must exhibit some understanding of them. The values of American society are said by many to be "liberal," yet the military services responsible for defending those liberal values are said themselves to be "conservative," for those who would defend the status quo are so labeled. Concern for the individual dignity of each person suggests a liberal orientation while those who would fight to preserve individual dignity must be asked to sublimate in many ways their own individualism for the sake of the group. It is in this sense that contemporary commentators are wont to point out a paradoxical discrepancy between supposed civilian values and the military virtues. Yet,

Source: *War Morality and the Military Profession.* (196-197). Reprinted by permission of Sage Publications

most acknowledge that without the conservative values of loyalty, obedience, and self-restraint, the military function would disintegrate. Hackett suggests that it is the responsibility of the military leader to bridge this seeming paradox when he reminds us that "the young officer . . . has to be made to remember that only a person of liberal mind is entitled to exercise coercion over others in a society of free men."[30] The authority of military superiors over their subordinates is stronger and more complete than that of almost any other human relationship in our societal structure. With that authority goes the frightening responsibility to respect the dignity of individual subordinates at the same time that military order and discipline are preserved. It is precisely in the person of the military leader that the liberal and the conservative values must be brought together in a daily attempt at fragile balance. It is not an easy thing that we ask of these leaders, but it is necessary.

In this context, how does a military leader inspire loyalty, the loyalty which leads one to accept enlightened obedience in an understanding way as a moral obligation in a military structure? In his excellent treatment of this topic, Captain Michael Wheeler suggests that loyalty is best engendered in subordinates when they can reside their full trust in their leaders and that trust itself is readily given only to those superiors who are perceived to be persons of high moral integrity.[31] How often we are driven back to this critical point! We must ask as much of our leaders as Tennyson attributed to the Duke of Wellington when he referred to him as "The statesman-warrior, moderate, resolute/ Whole in himself, a common good."

Where military leadership has been less than ideal, it has faltered because of a faulty view of the whole man; it has seen the role of morality in military leadership too narrowly or from a relativistic framework. We ask of today's leader that he be neither absolutist nor relativist but retain a balanced perspective that understands the full complexity which characterizes the interweaving of moral value with military function. We ask him to be that good man, that wise man, that the Greek philosopher could advise subordinates to find and imitate. Fully accepting the Aristotelian wisdom that moral character develops out of repeating good actions, that it cannot be ordered but can be exemplified and imitated, our advice to those who aspire to become worthy military leaders can be none other than that of the ancient Chinese sage: "The way to do is to be."

NOTES

1. Alfred Vagts, *A History of Militarism* (New York: Free Press, 1959), p. 13.
2. Dean Acheson, "Ethics in International Relations Today," in M. Raskin and B. Fall, eds., *The Vietnam Reader* (New York: Random House, 1965), p. 13. See R. Wasserstrom's analysis on pp. 391ff., this volume.
3. Sir John Winthrop Hackett (General), "The Military in the Service of the State" (Harmon Memorial Lecture, U.S. Air Force Academy, Colorado, 1970), Chap. 7.
4. Ibid.
5. Ibid.
6. Sir John Winthrop Hackett (General), *The Profession of Arms* (London: Times Publishing, 1962), p. 45.
7. Hackett, "Military in the Service of the State."
8. Samuel P. Huntington, *The Soldier and the State* (New York: Random House, 1957), p. 62. Further delineation of Huntington's view of the professional military ethic is taken essentially from Chapter 3, which is descriptively entitled "The Military Mind: Conservative Realism of the Professional Military Ethic."
9. Huntington, pp. 64-65.
10. Morris Janowitz, *The Professional Soldier* (New York: Free Press, 1960).
11. Vagts, "History of Militarism," p. 42.
12. Janowitz, *Professional Soldier*, p. 217.
13. Huntington, *Soldier and the State*, p. 73.
14. Ibid.
15. Telford Taylor, *Nuremberg and Vietnam: An American Tragedy* (New York: Bantam, 1971).
16. U.S. Army, *The Law of Land Warfare*, U.S. Army Field Manual, Department of the Army, 1956, p. 182.
17. Thomas Hobbes, *The Leviathan*, 1651.
18. Huntington, *Soldier and the State*, pp. 74-78.
19. *Congressional Record—Senate*, 1974, pp. 56257-56262.
20. Ibid., p. 56258.
21. John D. Ryan (General), "Air Force Policy Letter for Commanders," Washington, D.C., 1 November 1972. General Ryan' s view of integrity versus obedience starkly contrasts with that of Murray Kempton, who stated, "The good soldier will lie under orders as bravely as he will die under them." ("Review of Eisenhower's *Mandate for Change, New Republic* [30 November 1963].)
22. M. T. Smith (Lieutenant Colonel), "Reporting Inaccuracies—a Rose by Another Name," *Air University Review*, 1974.
23. Ibid., p. 85.
24. U.S. Army War College, *Study on Military Professionalism* (Carlisle Barracks, Pa.: US. Army War College, 1970), pp. 13-14.
25. Ibid., p. 24.
26. Ibid., pp. 30-31.
27. Ibid., p. 29.
28. Janowitz, *Professional Soldier*, pp. 272ff.
29. Chaplain Kermit D. Johnson (Colonel), "Ethical Issues of Military Leadership," *Parameters* 4 (1974), pp. 35-39. Chaplain Johnson makes an interesting comment on the relationship between "what works" and ethical relativism, suggesting that the pragmatic outlook is in fact a "subtle and disguised form of ethical relativism practiced frequently in the military setting." Johnson identifies ethical relativism as one of four pressing issues concerning military leadership. The other three are the exaggerated loyalty syndrome, the obsession with image, and the drive for success.
30. Hackett, "Military in the Service of the State."
31. Michael O. Wheeler, "Loyalty, Honor, and the Modern Military," *Air University Review* (1973), pp. 50-55.

The Ethics of Leadership

by Malham M. Wakin

The central theme of this chapter is that a person's view of human nature is essentially relevant to the type of leader he or she becomes. Social contract theories such as that of Thomas Hobbes are said to lead to "transactional" leadership, encouraging adversary relationships between the leader and those led. The classical Greek view of humans as societal beings by nature is held, by contrast, to foster a "transformational" view of leadership stressing the role of education, persuasion, and cooperation in mission accomplishment. The contractual view is seen as generating amoral attitudes toward the military function while the transformational view holds more promise for concern with the development of the moral character of leaders and those led. A case is made that professional competence is legitimately viewed as a moral obligation, most especially in the military profession. It is suggested that advancing technology and specialization have made it more difficult to identify moral concerns with the military function, thus placing more burden on the leader to emphasize the moral dimensions of the profession of arms.

—M.M.W.

A leader is best
When people barely know that he exists,
Not so good when people obey and acclaim him,
Worst when they despise him.
"Fail to honor people, They fail to honor you;"
But of a good leader, who talks little,
When his work is done, his aim fulfilled,
They will all say, "We did this ourselves."
                    —Lao Tzu, Sixth Century B.C.;
                    Verse 17 of the *Tao Teh Ching*

Source: *War Morality and the Military Profession*. (1981). Reprinted by permission of Sage Publications

It is possible to infer much more from this verse in the *Tao Teh Ching* concerning ethics and leadership than its author could have intended so many centuries ago. Lao Tzu saw human leadership at its best when it imitated the most harmonious ways of nature, flowing smoothly like a natural stream, without harshness or aggressive struggle, and marked always by a gentleness that naturally pulled subordinates to their tasks. This is a view totally inimical to that of the leader as an egoistic order-giver who forces compliance from subordinates by threats, and claims sole credit for any positive results of their efforts. With some trepidation, I would like to reflect on these two extreme characterizations of superior-subordinate relationships, pursuing a fundamental notion first suggested to me in a paper delivered by William May,[1] and developing the ethical implications of adopting one mode of leadership rather than another. Following these reflections, I hope to be able to establish the critical, importance of ethical considerations to military leadership in the light of the unique function of the military profession.

Social Contract or Polity[2]

In the many criticisms of military leadership which have been published in recent years, much attention has been given to the image of a ruthless, ambitious careerist, intent upon furthering his own interests in his climb up the hierarchical ladder in spite of or even because of the high personal cost he may extract from contemporaries, subordinates, or the actual military mission itself. This is one of the anecdotal statements made by an Army major who was interviewed during the Army War College's research for their *Study on Military Professionalism*: "My superior was a competent, professional, knowledgeable military officer who led by fear, would doublecross anyone to obtain a star, drank too much and lived openly by no moral code. He is now a Brigadier General!"[3] But the "careerists" are not a peculiar military phenomena; they are to be found in many of our professions. And it is not as though ethical considerations are irrelevant for these professional climbers—they have an ethic, but as Max Lerner puts it, "It is the wrong one." Lerner refers to this ethic in contemporary business parlance as the "bottom line' ethic.

> For a politician, the ethic is to get power and hold on to it; for a lawyer, it is to win his case and get his fee ... for a corporate executive, the ethic is to win out in the lethally competitive struggle for profits, markets, stock values. The bottom line is what counts, whatever the means used. It is the cancer of the professions.[4]

How does one find oneself caught up in this bottom line ethic, not only without sensitivity for the means employed but often with the seeming conviction that promotion (the symbol of success) is evidence of virtue? The means employed "worked"; can there still be ethical questions to ask? Promotion itself provides vindication for the means employed. One possible explanation of the "ethic" is that it is an understandable extended outcome of a certain position on the nature of man, advocated in its most primitive form by Thomas Hobbes.

Hobbes is used as one of the classic representatives of egoism in most textbooks of moral philosophy. His view of man in the *Leviathan* begins with the assumption that all men are equal in the state of nature; that is, as they appear in the world considered apart from any formal social or political structure. In the primal condition, every man has an equal right to everything and moral terms have no meaning. There can be no right or wrong if every person has a right to everything; the fundamental rule of behavior involves personal survival by the use of one's own devices. This natural condition of man is chaotic, savage, and marked by violence. Indeed Hobbes tells us that "during the time men live without a common power to keep them all in awe, they are in that condition which is called war; and such a war, as is of every man, against every man. " Life for man in such conditions is "solitary, poor, nasty, brutish, and short" (*Leviathan*: Ch. 13). But man is also endowed with reason which ultimately leads him to conclude that if he is to survive, he must seek peace with other men. He must give up his right to harm other men if he can persuade them to do likewise and enter into an agreement, a social contract with them. However, the mere fact of the existence of an agreement does not change human nature. It is still the case that "of the voluntary acts of every man, the object is some *good to himself*" (*Leviathan*: Ch. 14). So to guarantee that men will abide by their agreements, tremendous powers must be granted to government (the real leviathan) so that men win live up to their social contract out of fear of punishment. For the first time, moral terms have meaning once the agreement is made: Living up to the contract is "justice"; breaking it is injustice. All laws passed by the agreed-upon government become moral obligations; morality itself rests on the agreement—it is man-made and not found either in nature or in accordance with nature. Moral rules are legislated.

This brief elaboration of Hobbes's account of the nature of man and the origins of government through a social contract is relevant to any analysis of military leadership. The Hobbesian view of man is held by several commentators on the military profession to be essential to the military ethic.[5] This view might also be at the root of the moral comfortableness of the careerist mentioned previously. If self-interest is the primary focus of human action, or if, more to the point, it *ought* to be, then one may feel morally justified if hierarchical ambitions are realized even at high cost to others. Here, we may reflect on William May's suggestion that social contract theories "tracing the origin of the state to a supreme evil" (namely man's predatory nature) give rise to adversary relationships on every side. May made specific reference to John Locke's version of the social contract theory rather than to that of Hobbes, perhaps because Locke is viewed as having more direct influence on the framers of the American Constitution. Locke, of course, did not share Hobbes's extreme egoistic view of man although he placed great stress on innate human rights, especially the right to private property. For both Hobbes and Locke, however, it seems accurate to conclude that governments are essentially founded in negative fashion to provide security to the individual from the threat posed by other men.

If one stops for a moment to place the Hobbesian contractual view into the context of the military profession, it is easy to develop the least attractive picture of military leadership. Orders can be seen as justified *because* the military leader gives them (he is authorized by contract to do so), not because they make sense or are appropriate to the task addressed. A legitimate answer to the query "Why?" on this analysis would always be, "Because the general said so." Further if Hobbes's version of psychological egoism were correct, one could hardly expect to find any examples of self-sacrifice or subordination of the good of the self to the good of the unit, service, or nation. And yet, if we analyze the critical and essential functions that are uniquely military (more on this later), we see immediately that self-sacrifice rather than self-interest is an essential ingredient both of military leadership and of military service in general. Self-interest theories of ethics and the view of human nature in which they are grounded are simply not appropriate for the military profession (nor indeed for any of the professions focused on service to the greater society).

In one sense at least the military profession is more akin to the classical Greek notion of polity than to the communities of the social contract theorists. The fundamental mission of the military under a constitutional government must be associated with the common good, the good of the community it serves. When the military or any branch of the military places its own interests ahead of the nation's overall interest, we soon see elements of the militarism that Alfred Vagts,[6] General Hackett,[7] and others have adequately described. Militarism is, as it were, careerism writ large, and both are grounded in the ethics of self-interest. In reflecting on Aristotle's position that man's natural habitat is the society of other men and that human development seems intended by nature to take place in the social context, Hackett suggests that a properly functioning military may be an ideal societal form.

> Living in a group demands some subordination of the self to the interests of the group. The military contract demands the total and almost unconditional subordination of the interests of the individual if the interests of the group should require it. This can lead to the surrender of life itself. It not infrequently does. Thus in an important respect the military would appear to be one of the more advanced forms of social institution.[8]

The Aristotelian notion of man as *zoon politicus* is worth some attention if only to contrast with the view of Hobbes mentioned earlier. Aristotle, and the classical Greeks generally, would not grant Hobbes's view that man's nature is totally egoistic, requiring political arrangements and constraining moral rules to be artificially imposed. The family and the state are in fact viewed as natural to the man who works out his development in the context of these organizations: They are not essentially contrived to hold back man's selfish egoism but rather provide the context and education for each person's growth and contribution to the polis. In this view, political structures are intended to educate individuals for their contributive roles in human societies. Based on the fundamental and unique role of reason in the life of man, the Greek view seeks rational harmony within the individual and in the state; peace and not war would better describe the "natural" state of man. Balance, moderation, development of the intellect—these are the ethical aims appropriate to man and required to be fostered by the state. An ethic based on self-interest, cost-benefit, or the "bottom line" must be totally uncongenial to this perspective of the role of man in society.

It may be necessary to distinguish between self-interest viewed as "selfishness" and self-interest viewed as "self-development." We attribute selfishness to those who seek their own advantage without regard to the consequences of their actions for others or in spite of causing harm to others. To develop one's talents can be viewed as self-interested action, but it need not be selfish. Certainly, some self-interested actions can be morally right and justifiably encouraged (developing one's mind or skills which will be employed for the benefit of all). It is the extreme egoistic sense of self-interested action (selfishness) which gives rise to Hobbesian views of the need for a governmental leviathan. It is also selfishness which characterizes the careerist and his organizational counterpart, militarism.

The root notion of service to the polity seems more accurate and appropriate for understanding the military profession than does the root notion of social contract. William May suggested the possibility that social contract theories remove individuals from active participation in the governing process. "Government is not what one does but what one purchases with taxes." Citizens may, in this view, be active at the founding and dissolution of the state but passive in between. One can easily venture a parallel suggestion when the military function is also viewed as a contractual relationship with the society: "Defense is not what one does but what one purchases with taxes." Thus the average citizen, especially when not under immediate threat of attack, may not feel any obligation to provide anything other than financial support to the military profession; his role is passive. Even when the nation is under immediate attack, if the military function is viewed as contractual only, the nonmilitary citizen remains passive and expects the military professional to protect his client (society) against external enemies.

May had suggested that the extended application of the social contract thesis to the profession in general produces "adversarial" relationships; society as the client of the professions and faced with the threat of the negative (pain, lawsuits, crime, aggression, and the like) is involved only in the formation and dissolution of the relationship which has the professional protecting the client against threats. Analogies in medicine and law are obvious, but perhaps the critical notion to be learned from May is that when governments or professions are dominated by negative motives (formed to suppress evil) rather than positive motives (formed to promote the general good), adversarial relationships are almost certain to be promoted. It is easy to agree with his concern that when professional authority is invoked by fear, it will be difficult to limit and will ultimately generate resentment against the professionals.

Jacques Barzun observed that for the past decade, the professions have been under fire because the competence and ethical standards displayed by many practitioners in medicine, law, education, and other professions have been exposed and found wanting.

> The message for the professions today is that their one hope of survival with anything like their present freedom is the recovery of mental and moral force. No profession can live and flourish on just one of the two. For its "practical purpose" it requires the best knowledge and its effective use. But since that purpose is to transfer the good of that knowledge from the possessor to another person, the moral element necessarily comes into play. *Moral* here does not mean merely honest; it refers to the nature of any encounter between two human beings.[9]

Like the professions for which Barzun has expressed concern, the military profession has also been "under siege" and needs to reexamine, if not to recover, its "mental and moral force." These reflections contrasting the egoistic foundations of social contract theories with classical Greek notions of man may lead us to fruitful judgments concerning the ethical dimensions of military leadership.

Ethical Implications

The military leader who views his oath of office as merely a contractual arrangement with his government sets the stage for a style of leadership critically different from the leader who views that oath as his pledge to contribute to the common good of his society. For the former, "duty, honor, country" is a slogan adopted temporarily until the contract is completed; for the latter, "duty, honor, country" is a way of life adopted for the good of all and accepted as a moral commitment not subject to contractual negotiations.

If one adopts the contractual view, it is relatively easy to attempt to divorce the military function from moral considerations. War is a dirty business, and the task facing this military leader is to develop armies and weapons systems which can efficiently destroy potential enemies; the body count is the bottom line. This conception is analogous to the adoption of the contractual view in the teaching profession, which envisions the role of the teacher as transmitter of value-free objective knowledge, packaged and distributed; grade-point average is the bottom line. Neither approach accepts responsibility for forming the character of the people being led (to war or to knowledge), and hence there is no predicting the uses to which their weapons or knowledge may be directed. But leadership is not a valuefree enterprise; approaches which ignore the critical ethical dimensions of leadership must always be viewed as unsatisfactory. This latter assertion assumes, of course, that the role of the professions, and especially the military profession, is best viewed as more nearly approximating the Aristotelian than the Hobbesian idea.

In the American context, a leadership committed to the development of character can be on precarious ground. In our pluralistic society, there will always be the question, what kind of character, what virtues can be legitimately taught and inculcated? It seems clear, however, that an ethic for any of the public professions based on a total laissezfaire, egoistic, and self-interested view of man will not do. Professions which do not exercise constraints over their members' standards of competence and over the costs of professional services invite governmental controls. Professions whose members lose sight of their service function in society and allow the values of the marketplace to become dominant invite unionization. Precarious ground or not, concern for virtue among professionals is critical if the professions are going to survive with anything at all like their past and current status. The medical, legal, and military functions continue to be critical to society, but that is not to be confused with continuing preeminence of the associated professionals.

> What every professional should bear in mind is the distinction between a profession and a function. The function may well be eternal; but the profession, which is the cluster of practices and relationships arising from the function at a given time and place, can be destroyed—or can destroy itself—very rapidly.[10]

The function of the military profession (its mission) is relatively well fixed; and it is a noble one whether it is characterized as the management of violence (Huntington), the containment of violence (Hackett), or as constabulary (Janowitz). The latter two characterizations are similar and seem most accurate for the U.S. military profession currently. They do not presume so wide a gulf between war and peace as has been the American predilection prior to the end of World War II, nor do they avoid the essential moral concern that total war, with its potential for the destruction of all humanity, has become an irrational option. Already one sees that the military leader cannot afford the luxury, if luxury is what it is, of viewing his function in some sort of "scientific" or objective value-free way. The uses of military force always involve moral considerations; the decision to go to war is a moral decision; and the judgments on the employment of means are always more than merely military judgments. At least since President Lincoln's acceptance of Lieber's "Instructions for the Government of Armies of the United States in the Field" in 1863, the public position of the United States has been that all is *not* fair in war. This position has been reaffirmed many times through the Hague and Geneva Conventions, in the Army pamphlet, *The Law of Land Warfare*, and through our participation in war crimes tribunals at Nuremberg and Tokyo after World War II. Military leaders are charged with the responsibility of observing the moral positions developed through this tradition, and with educating all members of the profession with regard to the provisions of these "laws of war."

The "military" virtues are virtues in any human society, pluralistic or not; but they are called military virtues because of their essential connection to the specific military function. The end (military mission) is essentially fixed—the choice of means to bring about that end often involves moral considerations and always requires a display of certain virtues in effecting those means. In some professions the most obvious specific virtues are easy to identify; in medicine and law, for example, client confidentiality receives unanimous, clear, dominant, and obvious emphasis. The military virtues are no less obvious: *subordination of the good of the self to the good of the nation and military unit, courage, obedience, loyalty, integrity.* I have argued elsewhere[11] that integrity is the foundation virtue for military leaders if they wish to successfully develop loyalty and obedience in their subordinates. But the critical thing to notice here is that these virtues are obvious because of their functional necessity; success in battle is impossible without them; preparation for battle requires their inculcation. Please note that these moral virtues are not merely "nice to have," they are functional imperatives in the military profession. Notice also that if the list is a correct one and self-subordination is as crucial as I believe it to be to the military function, then a contractual view of one's role in the profession generated from the Hobbesian view of man cannot adequately serve as the ethical foundation for military leadership.

Superior-Subordinate Relationships

Given the enormous authority over the lives of subordinates that the hierarchical military structure provides to its leaders, what are the moral demands on those to whom subordinates are required to be loyal and obedient? Again the fundamental position on the nature of human relationships is extremely relevant. If the relationship between superior and subordinate is viewed as merely contractual, then each association takes on the dimensions of a transaction.[12] The subordinate expects that the superior will respond to his needs; the superior expects that subordinates will "do their job" in response to his commands. Each has contracted to act in specified fashion. The more Aristotelian view of leadership would have the leader accept responsibility for transforming subordinates with an eye to inculcating the virtues mentioned earlier. The transactional leader places emphasis on objective performance; the transformational leader adds to performance an emphasis on education. The transactional leader is less likely to accept responsibility when his mission fails; in those cases he can easily place the blame on subordinates who did not "fulfill their contract." The transformational leader resembles more the "good leader" depicted by Lao Tzu in the quotation appearing at the beginning of this chapter. The contrast between these two approaches seems authentic when placed in practical context as in the following comments made by officers participating in the Army War College's study of professionalism:

> [There is] fear in the subordinate of relief and a bad Officer Effectiveness Report if he admits that his unit is less than perfect or he is presenting a point his superior doesn't want to hear... The subordinate must have the integrity to "tell it like it is" in spite of fear for his career, etc., while the superior owes it to his subordinate to help him as much as possible as opposed to the attitude of "you get it squared away or I'll get someone who will" over a one-time deficiency.
>
> Across the board the Officer Corps is lacking in their responsibilities of looking out for the welfare of subordinates. Everyone is afraid to make a mistake with someone always looking over his shoulder.
>
> They are afraid that if they delegate authority to subordinates . . . they themselves will suffer. . . . Subordinates are not being properly developed and there is a general feeling among junior officers that seniors are untouchable, unapproachable, unreasonable, and constantly looking for mistakes. . . . A commander who takes a genuine interest in the welfare and training of his subordinates is getting rarer.[13]

It is easy to see from these comments made by officers of different ranks that their perceptions of actual leadership practice in 1970 was that it was transactional (in our terms) when it ought to have been transformational. Is it going too far to attribute many of the moral lapses in the military profession in the United States in recent years to the contractual (transactional) relationship? One of the ethical scandals accompanying the all-volunteer army conception in the middle and late 1970s was the occurrence of recruiting irregularities. Several newspaper articles reported on congressional investigations which revealed that fictitious names were placed on computers to meet recruiting quotas;. police records were altered so that those possessing them could be fraudulently enlisted; test scores were altered so that others could be qualified for enlistment. The enlistment quota was viewed by many as a contract, a "bottom line"; and the resulting pressures were seen by some recruiters as reason enough to cheat and lie. Similar pressures, sometimes generated by unrealistic goals or demands for perfection, are frequently adduced as reasons for false reporting of AWOL rates, false readiness reports, cheating on training examinations, false aircraft incommission reports, and falsification of a host of other quantitative indicators which we have institutionalized and used to evaluate the effectiveness of our leaders at all levels.

Common sense suggests that the "bottom line" ethic most easily accompanies institutionalized overemphasis on *quantitative* measurements of leadership. "When we can't measure the things that are important, we ascribe importance to the things we can measure" (attributed, perhaps erroneously, to Milton). Along with the emphasis on quantitative measurements comes often the requirement to report 100 percent of the quantity measured. Misinterpretation of a "zero-defects" program can lead and has led subordinates to believe that a single mistake or any performance that produces a "bottom line" that is less than 100 percent can lead to career disaster. Professor Flammer suggested that the institutional pressures generated by exaggerated emphasis on "zero-defects" led to bad superior-subordinate relationships, even to the point of compromised integrity.

> [The Zero Defects System], interpreted literally, as some image-conscious and ambitious commanders were inclined to do, automatically moved from the realm of the plausible and desirable to the impossible and impractical. In many instances, the program evolved into a "Zero Error Mentality," that is, the commander felt that his command had to be error free. . . . Yet outlawing risk precludes initiative, which is a basic requisite for modern combat effectiveness. In the end, many errors were made and consequently covered up, for the zero error mentality is automatically wedded to the grotesque philosophy that it is worse to report a mistake than it is to make one.[14]

The transformational leader sets the moral tone for his subordinates by the example of integrity he provides in both his official duties and in his private life. Honesty cannot be instilled by contract—but it may be enhanced by education about its importance to mission accomplishment and by example. Courage cannot be instilled by contractual arrangement, nor should it be expected if the basic mission orientation is merely contractual. It seems clear that selfishness is more generated than sublimated by any contractual/transactional grounding of the military ethic. Army Chief of Staff General Edward C. Meyer seemed to be summarizing this point of view when he commented recently: "The obligation of service and commitment inherent in the military ethic imposes burdens not customary in the larger society where obligations are normally contractual in nature and limited in degree of personal sacrifice expected. For the soldier, the obligation is complete: to death if necessary."[15]

Is Professional Competence a Moral Obligation?

It is not immoral under normal circumstances to fail a course in school. If a military person is incapable of learning to deal appropriately with a sophisticated weapons system, that is not immoral. But the leader who knowingly assigns the incapable to equipment they cannot operate is not merely foolish; where the stakes are so high in terms of the survival of his society, loss of human life, and use of national treasure, it seems clear he has entered the moral realm. With respect to the development of tactics, weaponry, long-range strategy, and the conditions for employing those weapons systems which pose serious threats to noncombatants, the military leader's competence is a crucial issue. Literally, he has a moral obligation to be competent in these areas. There are analogies in other professions. Judges are morally obliged to research and understand legal precedent relevant to cases over which they have jurisdiction. Incompetence on the judge's part can lead to injustice; and, of course, justice is a very important moral value. Surgeons are morally obliged to develop an understanding of the human organs on which they operate, and they are obliged to study and understand surgical techniques before deciding to employ them. In these areas it seems clear that the obligation to be competent is not merely prudent; where justice and human life are at stake, and where authority to act has been bestowed, the obligation to be competent must be viewed as a moral one. Often in the military context, the authority of the military leader to act is nearly absolute and the stakes at issue are crucial to society. The strength of the moral obligation must be commensurate with that responsibility.

Within the context of the professional ethic, it appears the line between incompetence and immorality is a very thin line, perhaps most obviously so in the military profession. It is obvious that an incompetent physician may, in a lifetime of practicing bad medicine, harm many of his patients, perhaps even cause some deaths. It is also disheartening to contemplate the damage that an incompetent junior high school teacher may do to developing young minds. But the incompetent military leader may bring about needless loss of life and indeed, at the extreme, may have at his fingertips, the ability to destroy humanity as we know it. Given this critical uniqueness of the role of military leaders, no nation can afford to have them be intellectually incompetent or morally insensitive. Further, it seems clear that military leaders must extend this concern for competence to all levels of the military hierarchy. It is also quite clear that neither competence nor moral sensitivity are acquired by mere contract; military leadership in these areas must proceed by example and by education. Transformational leadership holds far more promise than transactional leadership where competence and character are at issue.

Perhaps we may lay at the door of advancing technology some of the explanation for our need to connect moral concerns with military leadership in a fashion that was unnecessary for professionals of the past. When there was some possibility that the majority of persons wearing uniforms were likely to confront an enemy in direct combat, the primacy of courage was so obvious as not to require commentary. When unit survival in battle depended on each soldier's fulfilling his assigned task, the need of subordination of self to the common good, conceptions of loyalty and obedience were all so clearly seen as fundamental and functionally imperative that example and encouragement were adequate to guarantee their inculcation. But in the modern U.S. military services, there is great need to call attention to the ultimate purpose of the military profession because technological specialization has brought about a state of affairs that places the majority of uniform wearers in specialized roles remote from anything resembling battle engagements in past wars. Even those in direct control of our most devastating weapons systems will never confront their enemies face-to-face; indeed, their knowledge of the target of their weapons is frequently restricted to location and numbers.

As early as 1960, Professor Janowitz was pointing out that the tasks of military leadership had become segmented into at least three identifiable characterizations: the direct combat roles of the heroic leader, the organizational and administrative functions of the military manager, and the specialized skills of the military technologist.[16] The traditional military virtues and moral considerations are most easily associated with the heroic leader because he most directly employs the instruments of violence and places himself and his men at risk. The moral consequences of incompetence in that role are easiest to discern. Not so with the leader whose essential contribution to the profession is the management of large contracts, or developmental programs, or large numbers of people engaged in support functions. He may see himself in a role analogous to that of a manager in a large business firm or industrial complex and may use analogous measures of successful operation: productivity, cost effectiveness, "bottom line" numbers. In this environment it is remarkably easy to lose sight of the ultimate function of the military profession. What kinds of measurements are the relevant ones to determine if the profession is best prepared to defend our way of life? Productivity is important only if the "product" is contributing to the success of the military function. In a psychological warfare campaign, for example, does the number of sorties flown and the number of leaflets dropped (easily measured and easily increased) provide a measure of the success of the psychological operation?

The military technologist may be the farthest removed from the direct military function. He may spend an entire career in military laboratories, contributing to basic research in optical physics, laser development, analysis of radiation effects, development of computer software, and so on. He may be outnumbered by the civilian researchers participating in the same projects, working the same hours, and differing only in the circumstances of pay and work uniform. How much more like the civilian specialist his daily life appears to be than like the traditional military leader whose principal concerns might have been the inculcation in his subordinates of unity, loyalty, obedience, and the other military virtues. The officer researcher's status in the military profession seems more to resemble that of the military doctor than that of the traditional heroic leader. The military doctor may identify more closely with the medical profession than with the military profession. But both the military technologist and the military doctor may be called upon to place themselves at risk by carrying out their specialized functions in combat zones, while their civilian colleagues are not bound by the same unlimited liability. The danger of diminishing effectiveness of the military profession seems directly proportional to the growing identification of military specialists (technologists or managers) with their specialty at the cost of less identification with the profession of arms.

It is important to notice that often the rewards of daily effort are connected immediately with one's specialized activity and only mediately with the ultimate military function. This is not often true in other professions. The medical doctor who saves a life by timely surgery or relieves pain by curing an illness sees himself fulfilling his function directly and daily. The Air Force major who solves a critical data systems problem leading to more efficient usage of the comptroller's computers gets the immediate fulfillment of the data systems analyst, but may have to extrapolate remarkably well to perceive herself as contributing to the ultimate military mission. The moral dimensions of competence in this environment are easily overlooked, perhaps replaced entirely by prudential considerations. Duty, honor, country; responsibility for the lives of one's subordinates; victory on the battlefield—all seem remote from the many specialized tasks performed in the extremely complex, technologically oriented, modern military structure.

As the distinction between certain military and civilian "jobs" becomes narrower, the relationship between leader and led may have a tendency to become even more contractual and less transformational. It is not sheer coincidence that the standard terminology for civilian assistance to the military has included the phrase "defense contractor." With the word "contract" comes the emphasis on the values of the marketplace, concern for working hours, pay scales, and perhaps even collective bargaining. Charles Moskos has highlighted perceivable dangers to military effectiveness and legitimacy should the military institution see its traditional professional values replaced by the self-interested values of the contractors who work so closely with the military.[17]

Conclusions

The nature of modern defense policy and the composition of the U.S. defense organization have placed strains on the professional military ethic. Complexity, however much it may conceal the functional importance of the ethical-military virtues, is not an excuse for failure to understand the crucial role these virtues must play. With complicated command, control, and communications networks comes an even more critical need for integrity in reporting. Command decisions are more centralized but depend entirely on honest inputs. There is still need for the heroic leader, but his role must be complemented by the military manager and the military technologist. It is not inconceivable that our most able military professionals will have to demonstrate characteristics of all these roles, sometimes all at the same time.

In an era when miscalculation can lead to tragic consequences for humanity, technological competence takes on an added and crucial moral dimension. If, under the umbrella of a nuclear deterrent posture, future military engagements must be carried out with the intention of containing violence at the lowest possible level, military leaders will have to be totally aware of the political uses of the military instrument. In the context of limited engagements for specific political aims, courageous action and the subordination of self to mission accomplishment become more difficult for the military professional (especially for those immersed in the ethos of "total victory"), but even more important than ever before. Integrity, obedience, loyalty—these qualities take on even more significance in the modern military as it becomes more difficult for military leaders to inculcate them in their people. The military function retains its noble and necessary role of protection of a way of life; the military profession in the United States will be equal to the task of carrying out that function only in proportion to its ability to attract and retain leaders who understand the ethical dimensions of professional competence and who themselves exemplify the highest intellectual and moral qualities.

NOTES

1. In July 1980, William May (currently at the Kennedy Center for the Study of Ethics, Georgetown University) read a paper on "Adversarialism in America" at Vassar College as part of a workshop on professional ethics sponsored by The Hastings Center. His paper has caused me to reevaluate formerly held views of social-contract theories, but Professor May should not be held responsible for any distortions of his insights at my hands.

2. These two views are not proposed as the *only* approaches to citizenstate relationships or to leadership-follower relationships. I deal only with these two in this chapter because (1) it seems likely that social-contract theory approaches are most common, and (2) I think they easily lead to harmful practices and should be supplanted by an approach based on the classical conception of the polity.

3. U.S. Army War College, *Study on Military Professionalism*, Carlisle Barracks, PA: Author, 1970, p. B-1-2.

4. Max Lerner, "The Shame of the Professions," *Saturday Review* 3:3, 1975, p. 11.

5. Samuel P. Huntington, *The Soldier and the State*, New York: Random House, 1957, Ch. 3.

6. Alfred Vagts, *A History of Militarism*, New York: Macmillan, 1959.

7. Lieutenant General Sir John W. Hackett, *The Profession of Arms*, London: Times Publishing, 1962.

8. Ibid, p. 45.

9. Jacques Barzun, "The Professions Under Siege," *Harper's* 257 (1541), 1978, p. 68.

10. Ibid., p. 63.

11. In Chapter 14 of this text.

12. The terms "transactional leadership" and "transformational leadership" are borrowed from William May (Note 1), who in turn credits their usage to James McGregor Burns.

13. See Note 3, pp. 14-16.

14. Philip M. Flammer, "Conflicting Loyalties and the American Military Ethic," *American Behavioral Scientist*, (May/June), 1976, p. 597.

15. General Edward C. Meyer, "Professional Ethics Is Key to Well-led, Trained Army," *Army* 30:10, 1980, p. 14.

16. Morris Janowitz, *The Professional Soldier*, New York: Macmillan, 1960, Ch. 2.

17. Charles C. Moskos, Jr., "From Institution to Occupation," *Armed Forces and Society* 4:1, 1977, pp. 41-50.

The Military Character

by Edgar F. Puryear, Jr.

There is absolutely nothing which can take the place of the qualities in a man which are referred to as character. Generals such as George Washington, Robert E. Lee, John J. Pershing, Stonewall Jackson, to mention a few, are remembered not only as great field leaders, but as generals whose character transcended the wars in which they fought.

To some, success is the only common denominator applicable to eminent commanders because success signified leadership and created conscience. But General Washington lost many battles before the final victory, and the majority of his men did not lose confidence in him. General Robert E. Lee was the commander of the losing side, but his name is synonymous with leadership. Why? Because both were men of character.

Of all the components of leadership discussed thus far the most important is the quality of character. Leadership is really the unconscious expression of the character and personality of the leader. But what is character, and what is its role in leadership? General Eisenhower, in a discussion of military leadership, stated that "character in many ways is everything in leadership. It is made up of many things, but I would say character is really integrity. When you delegate something to a subordinate, for example, it is absolutely your responsibility, and he must understand this. You as a leader must take complete responsibility for what that subordinate does. I once said, as a sort of wisecrack, that leadership consists of nothing but taking responsibility for everything that goes wrong and giving your subordinates credit for everything that goes well."[1]

To General Omar N. Bradley character means "dependability, integrity, and the characteristic of never knowingly doing anything wrong, that you would never cheat anyone, that you would give everybody a fair deal. Character is sort of an all inclusive thing. If a man has character everyone has confidence in him. Soldiers must have confidence in their leader."[2]

General Mark Clark remarked about the qualities necessary for successful leadership, "I would put character way up on the list. If you want to select an officer for your command you want one who is confident of his abilities, who is loyal and who has got good

Source: *19 Stars* (1994) 287-289 and 336-349. Reprinted by permission of Presidio Press.

character. It is the man of good character that I am going to seek out. There are a lot of people who know the 'smart' way of getting things done, but they also ride roughshod over people that they are supposed to be working with. I don't want that."[3]

"Character," said Lucian K. Truscott, "as we used to say when I was in elementary school, is what you are." Reputation is what others think you are. The reason that some fail to climb the ladder of success, or of leadership if you want to call it that, is that there is a difference between reputation and character. The two do not always coincide. A man may be considered to have sterling character. Opportunity might come to that man; but if he has the reputation for something he is not, he may fail that opportunity. I think character is the foundation of successful leadership."[4]

To General Carl Spaatz, first Chief of Staff of the Air Force and air commander in Europe during World War II, character is a strong will. "You can't be wishy-washy as a military leader," he commented. "You must be able to size up the situation and make a decision. Indecisiveness is weakness of character. You must be able to have confidence in what a leader tells you."[5]

General J. Lawton Collins stated, "I would place character as the absolutely number one requirement in leadership. By character, I mean primarily integrity. A man whose superiors and, even more important, whose subordinates can depend upon that leader taking action based on honesty and judgement. If he does not base his actions on honor, he is worthless as a leader."[6]

General Williams H. Simpson believes that "there are many qualities that go into a man of sterling character. I don't know how to break it down. A man of high character has integrity, he is honest, he is reliable, he is straightforward in dealing with people. He is loyal to his family, his friends, his superiors."[7]

"I get accused all the time," General Jacob Devers answered when asked what character meant to him, "of using the word integrity when I mean character and character when I mean integrity. I think character is everything in leadership. It is what we try to build in all our young officers. It means the truth to me. That's the only way I can put it. To stand up and tell the truth and not be in the gray area."[8]

The personal meaning of character to General Albert Wedemeyer is, "an officer who stands up under fire, who has the courage to defend his convictions, not arrogantly, not stubbornly, but intelligently. Someone who does not believe he knows all the answers, who will listen to others with different experiences and different knowledge. It means a deep sense of loyalty. Unless an officer has character nothing he can do can cause his men to love and respect him."[9]

"Character plays a tremendous role in military leadership," said General Anthony "Nuts" McAuliffe; "It's a combination of many things—personality, clean living, presence. I just don't know; it's a very difficult word to describe because, as everyone knows, leaders come in all shapes and sizes and all sorts of personalities. I don't suppose I ever knew two men whom I knew well who differed as much as General MacArthur and General Patton, yet both were tremendous leaders of mass armies, both were men of great character."[10]

Seldom, in any group larger than two, can one find unanimous agreement on a point. As reflected in the above comments from military officers who achieved the highest pinnacle of leadership distinction—as Army commanders in time of war and as Chiefs of Staff—there is unanimous concurrence that character is the foundation of military leadership. The belief in the importance of character in leadership was also unanimous among over five hundred other general officers with whom the author has talked and corresponded. But agreement on what the word means is not unanimous. Actually, character defies definition; it must be described.

Perhaps the need for character was greater during the years of peace than in time of war. The four generals in this comparative study were dedicated men, but they were also human. There were times when they were tempted—because of slow promotions, poor pay, frequent moves, inadequate equipment for training their men, and other hardships—to leave the service.

General Marshall, after he had served as Chief of Staff of the Army, Secretary of State, and Secretary of Defense, was once asked what the most exciting moment of his life had been. "Being promoted to first lieutenant," he replied. He had spent five years as a second lieutenant. In spite of his outstanding success in various assignments and schools, Marshall at 35 years of age was still a first lieutenant in 1915, fourteen years after his graduation from VMI. In a mood of despondency, that year, he wrote to the Superintendent at VMI, General Edward W. Nichols:

> The absolute stagnation in promotion in the infantry has caused me to make tentative plans for resigning as soon as business conditions improve. Even in the event of an increase as a result of legislation next winter, the prospects for advancement in the Army are so restricted by law and by the accumulation of large numbers of men nearly the same age all in a single grade, that I do not feel it right to waste all my best years in the vain struggle against insurmountable difficulties.[11]

Marshall did not leave the service in 1915 and, upon his return from the Philippines in 1916, he was pleased to be assigned, a second time, as aide-de-camp to a man for whom he had tremendous respect and admiration, General J. Franklin Bell. This challenge and World War I undoubtedly were factors in his decision to remain in the Army.

Because of his brilliant performance as a staff planner and operations officer in World War I, Marshall came to the attention of several prominent and wealthy businessmen who were patriotically serving in responsible positions on Pershing's staff. One of these men offered Marshall, in 1919, a starting salary of $20,000 to leave the service and go with the J.P. Morgan financial firm. He turned it down, even though he knew he would soon lose his wartime rank of colonel. In 1920, he was reduced to the rank of major, and a salary of $3,000 a year. Still, he remained in the service.

In 1947, after General Eisenhower had retired as Chief of Staff of the Army to become President of Columbia University, the Eisenhowers bought their first new car. It was delivered to their home; and, after he inspected it, the former Chief of Staff wrote a check for the full cost of the automobile, almost wiping out their savings. Getting up from the table where he wrote the check, he took Mamie by the hand and walked with her to the door, saying "Darling, there's the entire result of thirty-seven years' work since I caught the train out of Abilene."[12]

A man certainly did not stay in the Army for money.

"There were three times," General Eisenhower said, "when I was offered what you might say were attractive opportunities to leave the service. The first was right after World War I. I was right here in this town (Gettysburg). There was a man whose name, strangely enough, was Patton, who was a manufacturer in Ohio or Indiana—someplace in the Midwest—who wanted me to go with him at double the salary I was getting then as a lieutenant colonel. For a while our Army pay looked pretty low. Mamie had quite an influence upon me. I was very disheartened that I hadn't gotten over into the battle; and I thought my army career was ruined. I was fed up. After all the studying and hard work, I wouldn't get into the war. Mamie kidded me a little bit, and we decided to go in the Army."[13]

The next offer for then Major Eisenhower came in 1927; a group of people were forming a new oil company. The man who was putting up a large part of the money was someone Eisenhower had met only a few times; but the investor said he wouldn't contribute unless Eisenhower agreed to enter the new firm, not as the top man, but as one of the executives. The backer wanted Eisenhower because he considered him honest and believed he would watch his money for him. Again, Eisenhower turned down the temptation of more money.

In the Philippines, several men who wanted Eisenhower to enter business with them offered to put $300,000 in escrow in the bank if he would join them, the money to be used by Eisenhower if things didn't work out.

As the offers came forth he always discussed them with Mrs. Eisenhower; "We always said we got this far in the Army and we're going to stay with it. The only offer I really considered was the first one because of my disappointment over not getting into the war."[14]

There was probably only one occasion when General MacArthur ever gave thought to leaving the service. He did not get married until he was a brigadier general, at the age of forty-two. His wife was a rich divorcee with two children, and right after their marriage he was assigned to the Philippines. Mrs. MacArthur, who was used the gay, exciting social life of New York and Washington, became bored. She believed her husband to be too brilliant, so the story goes, to waste himself by making a career of the Army; she wanted him to leave the Army to enter the business world. It finally reached the point where MacArthur had to decide between the Army and his wife. He decided to remain in the Army, and the marriage ended in divorce.

George Patton was never really tempted to leave the service. He had independent means which provided all the money he could want, and his wife also had considerable wealth. It was truly remarkable for a man of such opulence to make the service—a life so filled with hardship and frustration—his career. But a soldier's life was what Patton wanted, and that was the life he led.

Service life before World War II involved constant sacrifice; nevertheless, fortunately for the United States, we had a group of outstanding military leaders who were ready when Pearl Harbor was bombed on December 7, 1941. Why did these men remain in the service?

When General of the Army Omar N. Bradley was asked that question he replied, "Well, just the fact that I liked military work. I like working with men. I like to teach; and, you know, most of your service involves teaching your own men or instructing at some service school. I liked the outdoors—and you spend a great deal of time outdoors in the Army. There is another angle to it, which was more true then than now. In the old days, you had a rather small Army; and you knew practically every officer in the Army, either personally or by reputation. You usually lived on the post, you were one big family, the atmosphere was pleasant, and you had a nice group to work with. Your contemporaries spoke the same language. There was the feeling that in serving your country you were accomplishing something. There was always something to be done, something to learn."[15]

General Mark W. Clark, who spent sixteen years as captain, felt much the same way. "I like," he said, "working with men, training young people. That is why I took it up [he was then President of the Citadel, a state military school in South Carolina] after I retired from the Army. I like the outdoors. I was fond of hiking, riding and all kinds of outdoor activity. I had been raised on an Army post and I liked the life an Army officer lead—the fine families you met, the children you associated with, because they were invariably raised in Christian families and they were always well disciplined."[16]

General J. Lawton Collins was a lieutenant for seventeen years! He almost left the Army in 1919 to study law. He wrote to a friend who advised him that he would be "crazy" to leave the service for law, since good lawyers could be hired for $250 a month. "Your natural bent," that friend said, "is military service. You would be crazy to give it up." General Collins decided, since he was stationed in Europe, to postpone resigning for a year. "I evaluated the situation very carefully," he said of his position at the end of that year; "I finally decided that there were three things that appealed to me about military service which I could never get anywhere else. The first was that I was not competing with my fellow officers for money. I was actually holding down jobs that normally went to more senior people. Even though I was drawing just a captain's pay, I was given the opportunity to do things irrespective of my age and rank; and that appealed to me. The second thing that I liked was the people I was associated with. They were men of high caliber, men of integrity; and at no time in my then two or three years of service did anybody ask me to do anything that didn't meet my own standard of conduct."

"At the same time," he continued, "I met the girl I later married, and that had considerable influence. I decided then I would stick it out in the service for better or worse, and I gave up any thought of resigning from the Army."[17]

During the thirties General Spaatz almost left the Army Air Corps along with General of the Army H. H. Arnold, to join the embryonic Pan American Airways. But they both stayed. General Spaatz remained because he liked the life, his friends, and the flying. "There really wasn't any incentive to stay in the service between World War I and World War II as there is now. There was no apparent threat of war in those days. There was, however, a feeling among most of us who came into the old aviation section, the Signal Corps, that there was going to be a growth in military aviation. We had confidence that it was going to get its due position, and we decided to stay with it."[18]

The answers given by the other outstanding world War II generals were the same: they like the life, working with men in the outdoors, teaching, the association with people of integrity, the reward of giving service in a dedicated manner to something that counted. There were surely men who remained in the service during time of peace because it was a soft life, but Army life was not a leisurely, lazy life for those men who reached the top. While others played, they were working, studying, and preparing. The real explanation of why they stayed is that these men had character; they possessed the feeling of belonging to something greater than themselves; they believed in the code, "Duty, Honor, Country."

One aspect of character is the answer to the question, "Was he there?" Had it not been for the duty of country concept of Marshall, MacArthur, Eisenhower, and Patton, they would not have been around to accept the top positions of responsibility in World War II. How fortunate our country has been that these men were sufficiently patient with the slow promotions, poor pay, inadequate housing, inadequate money for training, the hardship of many moves, the unhappiness of children uprooted from friends, and the many other difficulties. Only a dedicated and selfless man would make such a sacrifice.

Selflessness

On June 12, 1944, a week after the D-Day invasion, General Marshall, along with General H. H. Arnold and Admiral King, made an inspection trip to Europe. With General Eisenhower as their escort, the officers went over and up and down the beachheads in jeeps. They stopped at noon at a field lunch mess; and as they sat on ammunition boxes, General Marshall turned very suddenly to the Supreme Commander and said, "Eisenhower, you've chosen all these commanders or accepted the ones I suggested. What's the principal quality you look for?" General Eisenhower reports that "without thinking, I said selflessness."

Selflessness was certainly part of Marshall's character, and the epitome of this was never illustrated more sharply than by his actions during the discussions of who would lead the Allied invasion force—the most overwhelming aggregate of arms and men in the history of warfare.

It was agreed upon by President Roosevelt and Prime Minister Churchill early in 1942 that the Supreme Commander of the Allied invasion would be a British officer. As the war developed, however, it became obvious that there would be a preponderance of American troops and material in the invasion force. This presented an awkward political position for both Roosevelt and Churchill. The former would have to inform the

American people, should the commander be British, that a foreigner would command an invasion force composed largely of American soldiers. On the other hand, Winston Churchill would find it politically difficult to explain to the British people that an American would be commanding a European invasion to end a British war. Churchill relieved Roosevelt from this embarrassing situation by voluntarily saying to him that the commander should be an American.

The selection of the Supreme Commander, a matter of vital interest to everyone, required a long and indecisive two years. After it was agreed that it would be an American, Roosevelt deferred naming him for eighteen months, during which time Churchill pressed frequently for a decision. At Teheran in 1943, Stalin asked peremptorily, "Who will command OVERLORD?" (the code name replacing ROUNDUP for the Allied invasion of Europe). The President replied he had not yet decided. Stalin declared his preference for General Marshall as supreme commander and tried to pressure Roosevelt into a decision by saying it was clear to him that until a supreme commander was named he could not consider the Allies were sincere about invading Europe. Stalin was desperate, but Roosevelt would not be pressured.

General Marshall was indeed the primary American contender for the role. On July 31, 1942, Winston Churchill sent a wire to President Roosevelt stating, "It would be agreeable to us if General Marshall were designated for Supreme Command of ROUNDUP." On August 10, 1943, in a letter to President Roosevelt, Secretary of War Stimson gave his position on the selection of the D-Day Commander:

Finally, I believe that the time has come when we must put our most commanding soldier in charge of this critical operation at this critical time. You are far more fortunate than was Mr. Lincoln or Mr. Wilson in the ease with which that selection can be made. Mr. Lincoln had to fumble through a process of trial and error with dreadful losses until he was able to discover the right choice. Mr. Wilson had to choose a man who was virtually unknown to the American people and to the foreign armies which he was to serve. General Marshall already has a towering eminence of reputation as a tried solder and as a broad-minded and skillful administrator. This was shown by the suggestion of him on the part of the British for this very post a year and one-half ago. I believe that he is the man who most surely can now by his character and skill, furnish the military leadership which is necessary to bring our two nations together in confident joint action in this great operation. No one knows better than I the loss and the problems of organization and world-wide strategy centered in Washington which such a solution would cause. I see no other alternative to which we can turn in the great effort which confronts us.

> Faithfully yours,
> HENRY L. STIMSON
> Secretary of War

Almost two weeks later, on Sunday, August 22, 1943, Stimson and Roosevelt discussed the matter at lunch. Stimson said of the lunch, "He told me that Churchill had voluntarily come to him and offered to accept Marshall for the Overlord operation. This, the President said, relieved him of the embarrassment of being obliged to ask for it. He also discussed with me Marshall's successor [as Chief of Staff], mentioning Eisenhower."[79]

General Marshall was clearly Roosevelt's number one choice for the Supreme Command position. In November 1943, Roosevelt visited North Africa. While there he had a long talk with General Eisenhower. "Ike," the President said, "you and I know who was the Chief of Staff during the last years of the Civil War but practically no one else knows, although the names of the field generals—Grant, of course, and Lee, and Jackson, Sherman, Sheridan, and the others—every schoolboy knows them. I hate to think that 50 years from now practically nobody will know who George Marshall was. That is one of the reasons why I want George to have the big Command—he is entitled to establish his place in history as a great General."[80]

As it became clear that the Allies would soon have to name the D-Day commander, rumors began to spread in Washington, most of them naming General Marshall. Since his appointment had been more or less decided at Quebec in August 1943, it was true at the time. But when the news leaked out that General Marshall was going to leave to take command of the invasion, it created a furor of discussion in Washington. Three senior members of the Military Affairs Committee, Senators Warren R. Austin, Styles Bridges, and John Gurney protested that General Marshall was too important to Congress to leave Washington. "They told me," Stimson said, "how much they relied on him not only individually, but how they were able to carry controversial matters through with their colleagues if they could say that the measure in question had the approval of Marshall."[81] The Senators were concerned that there was an ouster movement, aided and abetted by enemies who wanted to remove Marshall from the position of Chief of Staff because his influence was great with the President and the Joint and Combined Chiefs of Staff.

The Washington *Times Herald* even carried an article on the "rumor", maintaining that General Marshall was going to be taken away from Washington and sent abroad because he had attacked the President. On September 28, 1943, another story accused the President of a plot to get Marshall out by "kicking him upstairs" and putting General Somervell in as Chief of Staff. Roosevelt was doing this, so the story went, to enable General Somervell to use the patronage of his position for Roosevelt's 1944 Presidential campaign.

General Pershing too was opposed to General Marshall's leaving the position of Chief of Staff. In a letter to President Roosevelt, Pershing expressed his conviction that it "would be a fundamental and very grave error in our military policy" for Marshall to be transferred. President Roosevelt replied to the AEF commander of World War I that he wanted General Marshall to be the Pershing of World War II.

Admiral Leahy, General Arnold, and Admiral King had all gone to President Roosevelt, individually and privately, to urge the President to keep General Marshall in Washington. All three believed Marshall to be too important to the harmony of the Joint and Combined Chiefs organizations to be spared. He was recognized by all the service chiefs as the dominant figure, particularly in deciding upon and implementing joint strategic decisions. He was vital to service unity in these decisions. He was, according to General Arnold and Admiral King, the acknowledged leader in the Joint Chiefs of Staff.

Admiral King informed President Roosevelt, "We have the winning combination here in Washington, why break it up?" General Arnold stated that no one else could have General Marshall's "extraordinary sense of the requirements of global war, his knowledge of land, sea and air logistics, his balanced judgment as to the importance of one theater or one ally or one arm of the service as opposed to another."[82]

An editorial in the unofficial organ of the services, the *Army and Navy Journal*, said that to remove General Marshall as Chief of Staff "would shock the Army, the Congress, and the nation at large."

Finally Secretary Stimson took a strong position on the stories about General Marshall. "I can make a statement," he said at his press conference on September 30, 1943, "about some of the reports that have come out...I am in a position to say with absolute confidence that whatever duties General Marshall may hereafter be called upon to perform will be decided by the President in a spirit of entire confidence in General Marshall and with the sole purpose of placing this superbly able officer in the United States Army in the position where he can render the best service towards a successful conclusion of this war."

Often a man performs a responsible job in such a brilliant manner that he makes it look easy. This was the way General Marshall performed as Army Chief of Staff. The result was sometimes that his outstanding job was taken for granted. Certainly the rumors about his transfer gave emphasis and public recognition to the brilliant work General Marshall was accomplishing.

At the Cairo Conference in December 1943, President Roosevelt announced his decision. General Dwight D. Eisenhower was going to be Supreme Commander. He made the decision in favor of General Eisenhower over General Marshall in spite of the "impassioned" advice of two of his closest advisors, Harry Hopkins and Secretary Stimson, both of whom wanted General Marshall in the job. Stalin and Churchill also had made known their preference for Marshall.

When then was Eisenhower selected and not Marshall? Part of the answer lies in the character of General George P. Marshall. Had General Marshall indicated at any time his preference for the job as Supreme Commander he would have had the position. At Cairo in December 1943, before the decision had been finally made, President Roosevelt called him to his villa. General Marshall wrote of this meeting at which the President asked him about the Supreme Commander position: "I recalled saying that I would not attempt to estimate my capabilities; the President would have to do that; I merely wished to make clear that whatever the decision, I would go along with it wholeheartedly; that the issue was too great for any personal feeling to be considered. I did not discuss that pros and cons of the matter. If I recall, the President stated in completing our conversation, 'I feel I could not sleep at night with you out of the country.'"[83]

Secretary Stimson recorded Roosevelt's account of this conversation. "The President," during lunch with General Marshall at Cairo, "brought the subject [of Supreme Commander] up in a rather noncommittal way and asked Marshall what he wanted, or what he thought ought to be done. Marshall, as usual, dug his feet in and said it was not for him to say what should be done. But then, he added, on one subject he would give his opinion and that was that if he, Marshall, went to Overlord, the President should not leave the position of Chief of Staff open but they should put Eisenhower there as full Chief of Staff [they were considering putting Eisenhower in as "acting" Chief of Staff], that any other course would not be fair to Eisenhower or to the Staff."[84]

Then the President announced his decision. He told General Marshal, "I've been thinking this matter over and have decided that I will keep you as Chief of Staff and put Eisenhower in as head of Overlord."[85] Marshall accepted the President's decision without displaying any emotion. He discussed the meeting with McCloy, right after it had taken place, and McCloy observed that Marshall did not "seem as if he were a very greatly disappointed man." But Stimson averred that "I think I know better. I know his deepest ambition to his heart is and it was to command the invasion into France. It was simply his matchless power of self-sacrifice and self-control that gave the other impression."[86]

On December 18, 1943, President Roosevelt told Stimson in detail about his conversation with Marshall in Cairo. Secretary Stimson reported his lunch with President Roosevelt in detail:

> The President described how he reopened this matter [of the Supreme Commander] with Marshall at their solitary luncheon together and tried to get Marshall to tell him whether he preferred to hold the command of Overlord or whether he preferred to remain as Chief of Staff. He [the President] was very explicit in telling me that he urged Marshall to tell him which one of the two he personally preferred, intimating that he would be very glad to give him the one he preferred. He said that Marshall stubbornly refused, saying that it was for the President to decide and he, Marshall, would do with equal cheerfulness whichever one he was selected for. The President said that he got the impression that Marshall was not only impartial between the two but perhaps really preferred to remain as Chief of Staff. Finally, after having been unable to tell him his preference, the President said that he decided on a mathematical basis that if Marshall took Overlord it would mean that Eisenhower would become Chief of Staff but, while Eisenhower was a very good soldier and familiar with the European theater, he was unfamiliar with what had been going on in the Pacific and he also would be far less able than Marshall to handle Congress; that, therefore, he, the President, decided that he would be more comfortable if he had Marshall at his elbow in Washington and turned over Overlord to Eisenhower.

Stimson himself was disappointed. "I was staggered," he told President Roosevelt, "when I heard of the change..." Stimson had thought Marshall to be the best man for the job. He would be able to overcome the obstacles and delays of launching the invasion which "I felt certain he would meet in Great Britain on account of the attitude of the Prime Minister and the British Staff." A second reason for Stimson's desire to see Marshall as D-Day Commander was based upon his understanding of Marshall's true feeling. "I knew," he said to the President, "That at the bottom of his heart it was Marshall's secret desire above all things to command this invasion force into Europe; and I had had very hard work to wring it out of Marshall..." He then laughingly said to Roosevelt, "I wish I had been along with you in Cairo. I could have made the point clear."

Stimson then went on to say of his conversation with President Roosevelt, "I had had great difficulty in getting Marshall to speak on such a subject as his personal preference, but that I had finally accomplished it [he got General Marshall to say, 'Any soldier would prefer a field command']"; and that "when he was on the point of leaving for the Teheran Conference I had begged him not to sacrifice what I considered the interest of the country to the undue sensitiveness of his own conscience in seeming to seek a post."[87]

Stimson recorded his continuing efforts over several months to get General Marshall to express his preference: "I called in Marshall who has been very reluctant to talk about the matter at all and has not helped me a bit in my decisions and efforts, and told him that he had to help me..." The next day there were further discussions between the two. Stimson said of that day's talk, "Marshall himself is very reticent on the matter because he is personally and directly involved, and I have therefore to make a good deal of effort to be in a position to help him..."[88]

As the rumors grew about General Marshall as D-Day Commander, he became even more reluctant to discuss it. He was "so upset and shy about it that the President," Stimson remarked, "complained to me rather wistfully at our last talks that he couldn't get any advice out of him on the subject."[89]

The rumors of late 1943, prior to Roosevelt's announcement of the Supreme Commander, were very harmful to British-American relations. They had, among other things, alleged that the Supreme Commander role was going to be more than a European position; it was to be a global command of all Allied forces in the world. It was difficult enough for Churchill to explain an American general in the key role in the European theater. The global command was too much.

General Marshall had a solution calculated to soothe British wounded pride. He suggested to Stimson that he would be willing to serve under Field Marshal Sir John Dill as Supreme Commander. This, Marshall thought, would ease the opposition facing Churchill at home. Stimson said no to this proposal because he thought it would have the opposite effect in the United States; as he remarked, "Our peoples' faith in Marshall is one of the things that will carry us through the tragedies that may go with Overlord."[90]

After the decision was made that General Eisenhower would be Supreme Commander, by mutual consent, further discussion of Marshall's commandership of Overlord was dropped in conversation between Stimson and Marshall. Stimson's comment on Marshall's reaction to the decision was that he showed "his usual bigness about the whole darn thing."[91] In all probability, Marshall had decided that, regardless of his personal desire, his duty was in Washington.

Marshall had made his reputation as staff officer. Would he have been successful as D-Day Commander? There seems no doubt that he would have. As Supreme Commander his primary responsibilities would have been dealing with statesmen, generals, and other high-ranking officers. He was not a flamboyant character; the job did not call for flamboyancy. He had proved as Army Chief of Staff that he had the respect of American generals, of political figures, and of Allied officers. He had proved his competency to deal with the press. And, as attested by the fact that both British and Russians had advocated his selection for the supreme command post, he had proved his ability to get along with the Allies.

Apparently the most important factor in the decision was President Roosevelt's conviction that General Marshall could not be spared, as evidenced by his comment, "I could not sleep soundly at night with General Marshall out of Washington." Marshall was needed in Washington by the President, by Congress, by the Joint Service Staffs, and by the American people who had so much confidence in him. To them the job of the Chief of Staff was more important than that of the invasion commander. For them, at that time, Marshall was the indispensable man.

This example, of Marshall refusing to express his strongest desire, was the epitome and the high point of a life of selfessness. The same life of selflessness was led by MacArthur, Eisenhower, and Patton.

The Role of Character

There is a high purpose for the American military man. He does not want war. He only desires the opportunity to live in a democracy, free from tyranny and secure from those nations who seek to destroy our way of life. Their high purpose was based not only on patriotism; as observed, it was also founded on deep religious faith and self-lessness.

In writing this manuscript the author discussed the quality character with over five hundred officers who achieved the rank of brigadier general through five-star general. Each was asked, "How do you define character?" There were many, many definitions given for this word. There are men of "no" or "bad" character; but when there is no qualifying adjective used with the word character, it was agreed that it implies a favorable connotation. Character is a personal attribute that encompasses all of the admirable qualities of human nature. Character is the ennobling attribute of man. But really, as it has already been stated, character is a word that should not be defined; it should be described.

These generals were also asked, "What role does character play in American military leadership?" In reply there were statements such as, "Without character there is no true leadership;" "Character and leadership are like the popular 'Horse and Carriage.' Both go to make marriage. You can't have one without the other." "Character is the base on which leadership is built;" "Character is the number one attribute of leadership;" "I cannot separate leadership from character except that you can have character without leadership, but not leadership without character;" and that "Character is leadership."

More briefly others said that the role of character in leadership is 'all important," "vital," "the keystone," "the basis," "the most important factor," "the basic element," "the major role," "the whole work," "decisive," "dominant," indispensable," "a must," and, as General Eisenhower summed it up, "everything."

Although these answers give emphasis to the importance of character, they do not specifically come to grips with just what role character plays.

Lincoln once said that you can fool some of the people some of the time, but never can you fool all of the people all of the time. In the military, you can't fool a soldier *any time*. You might fool the people above you as to what you are, but never the men under you. Character is a state of mind that reflects the inner qualities of an individual. With the close association most men have in a military unit it doesn't take long for a soldier to size up his leader. Men do not want to trust their lives or reputations to leaders whom they consider to be unqualified. A person with a low, weak, immoral or vacillating type of character may have a brilliant mind; but this intellect won't make them leaders. Men instinctively rally to the leadership of strong, bold, and inspiring leaders who demonstrate their qualification for leadership by adopting sensible courses of action and who have the will to follow through and overcome all difficulties until victory is obtained.

A man of strong character will honorably follow his conscience under all conditions, regardless of public opinion, if he is convinced he is right. The weak man will be swayed by public or private opinion because he fears what effect his actions may have on his reputation. It is not necessary to be right all the time, as long as the followers know that the leader did *what he thought was right* for the situation. Men must believe that their leader knows what he wants, means what he says, that he'll do what he says to the best of his ability, that he can be depended upon to be consistent.

But there must be a proper balance. As one general put it, "The individual who, in the face of adversity, makes the least compromise with what he believes to be right has the finest character. The individual who makes no compromise doesn't exist." There must be give and take in life as long as no one is perfect. If a leader is too positive he can lose his effectiveness—unless he is always right, a quality that only one man has been known to have in the history of the world.

Good character is necessary to gain respect, and respect is a requirement for leadership, particularly for the long run. When a commander has the respect of his subordinates they will emulate his actions, habits, mannerisms, and dress. It can almost be said that personnel will react in direct ratio to the character of its commander, whether good or bad.

Men have confidence in leaders they respect and trust, knowing that the leader will always have their well being in mind under all conditions.

The leader will succeed or fail by the example he sets. If he is disciplined, his followers will be. If he dsciplines in such a fashion that the recipient believes he has been treated fairly and without bias, there will still be respect even though there will not be any popularity. Unless there is a sense of fair play, men will not follow long.

Any organization reflects the character of its leader. Character is reflected directly in the morale of an organization, and without high morale an organization will be unable to accomplish its mission in an above average manner. Morale is a state of mind that causes men to give their all to the leader and to the mission, regardless of the cost. With the leader who has character the men do it because "the old man wants it." It could be done by driving fear into the men, but then a subordinate will do no more than is necessary to get by. You can buy a man's time; you can, within the military, "order" a man's time, but not his loyalty and enthusiasm. These latter two qualities are part of the difference between mediocrity and above average results.

When the statement is made that character is the foundation of leadership, it might come to the reader's mind, "Well, how about Napoleon or Hitler or Stalin or the gangland dictator, Al Capone? Were they not leaders?" In the first place, it must be emphasized that the statement is made that character is everything in *American military leadership*. This study is concerned with why Marshall, MacArthur, Eisenhower and Patton were successful; it is not about dictators. It should be emphasized, however, that Napoleon, Hitler, Stalin, and Capone *failed*; they did not accomplish their ultimate objective in their lifetime. The character of the leader must be compatible with the desired goals and in harmony with the dominant motivating forces of those whom he seeks to lead. France and Germany under Napoleon and Hitler collapsed.

Capone went to jail and died there, a broken man. The Soviet Union under Communist rule has fallen terribly short of its evil goals and is presently losing the gains it has made, rather than gaining. These dictators failed to understand men, and their purpose was not to really noble one that people would willingly give their all for or die for. "When Napoleon started to fight for Napoleon, and not France," General Eisenhower remarked, "France fell."[92]

Character produces enduring leadership. Someone might attain limited success despite obvious character deficiencies; but generally, only the men with sound character attain the top positions. If a man of low moral character reaches high rank, there is always the possibility that his subordinates will be influence by his bad characteristics to the detriment of the mission. If the leader kills, lies, steals, or cheats, why should the followers do otherwise?

The leader is someone who is set apart from his followers. Character implies traits that set a man apart from the crowd. No strong man is without weaknesses (and no weak man is without strengths!); but a man of high character can be depended upon at all times. If a follower can say of his leader, "I can depend on him, not necessarily always to be right, but to do his best and what he considers to be right. I know his word is good. I can depend upon him to be honorable in his dealings with me. I can depend upon his moderation, his temperance, his fairness, his judgment. I trust him. I admire him," that is the type of leader men have confidence in and whom men die for. Decisions are not easy in time of war, and the follower must believe in a decision that means life and death.

In summary, character shapes the actions of the individual leader, it offers an example to follow for those he leads, it commands respect, it promotes confidence in those whom he commands, it sustains him in moments of great crisis, it causes him to do instinctively the honorable and right thing when he is confronted with great decisions, and it instills in those he commands the desire to obey because they know that the orders they receive are just, sound, and necessary.

While the word character is difficult to define, if one were forced to decide on a definition, or a description, there is no better way to express either than to cite the historic motto of West Point—Duty, Honor, Country.

The Death of Captain Waskow

by Ernie Pyle

In this war I have known a lot of officers who were loved and respected by the soldiers under them. But never have I crossed the trail of any man as beloved as **Captain Henry T. Waskow** of Belton, Texas.

Captain Waskow was a company commander in the Thirty-sixth Division. He had led his company since long before it left the States. He was very young, only in his middle twenties, but he carried in him a sincerity and a gentleness that made people want to be guided by him.

"After my father, he came next," a sergeant told me. "He always looked after us," a soldier said. "He'd go to bat for us every time."

"I've never known him to do anything unfair," another said.

I was at the foot of the mule trail the night they brought Captain Waskow down. The moon was nearly full, and you could see far up the trail, and even partway across the valley below.

Dead men had been coming down the mountain all evening, lashed onto the backs of mules. They came lying belly-down across the wooden packsaddles, their heads hanging down on one side, their stiffened legs sticking out awkwardly from the other, bobbing up and down as the mules walked.

The Italian mule skinners were afraid to walk beside dead men, so Americans had to lead the mules down that night. Even the Americans were reluctant to unlash and lift off the bodies when they got to the bottom, so an officer had to do it himself and ask others to help.

I don't know who that first one was. You feel small in the presence of dead men, and you don't ask silly questions.

Source: http://www.ghgcorp.com/burtond/36th/36infpyle.html (August, 2000). Reprinted by permission.

They slid him down from the mule, and stood him on his feet for a moment. In the half-light he might have been merely a sick man standing there leaning on the others. Then they laid him on the ground in the shadow of the stone wall alongside the road. We left him there beside the road, that first one, and we all went back into the cowshed and sat on water cans or lay on the straw, waiting for the next batch of mules.

Somebody said the dead soldier had been dead for four days, and then nobody said anything more about it. We talked soldier talk for an hour or more; the dead man lay all alone, outside in the shadow of the wall.

Then a soldier came into the cowshed and said there were some more bodies outside. We went out into the road. Four mules stood there in the moonlight, in the road where the trail came down off the mountain. The soldiers who led them stood there waiting.

"This one is Captain Waskow," one of them said quietly.

Two men unlashed his body from the mule and lifted it off and laid it in the shadow beside the stone wall. Other men took the other bodies off. Finally, there were five lying end to end in a long row. You don't cover up dead men in the combat zones. They just lie there in the shadows until somebody comes after them.

The unburdened mules moved off to their olive grove. The men in the road seemed reluctant to leave. They stood around, and gradually I could sense them moving, one by one, close to Captain Waskow's body. Not so much to look, I think, as to say something in finality to him and to themselves. I stood close by and I could hear.

One soldier came and looked down, and he said out loud, "God damn it!"

That's all he said, and then he walked away.

Another one came, and he said, "God damn it to hell anyway!" He looked down for a few moments and then turned and left.

Another man came. I think he was an officer. It was hard to tell officers from men in the dim light, for everybody was bearded and grimy. The man looked down into the dead captain's face and then spoke directly to him, as though he were alive, "I'm sorry, old man."

Then a soldier came and stood beside the officer and bent over, and he too spoke to his dead captain, not in a whisper but awfully tenderly, and he said, "I sure am sorry, sir."

Then the first man squatted down, and he reached down and took the captain's hand, and he sat there for a full five minutes holding the dead hand in his own and looking intently into the dead face. And he never uttered a sound all the time he sat there.

Finally he put the hand down. He reached over and gently straightened the points of the captain's shirt collar, and then he sort of rearranged the tattered edges of the uniform around the wound, and then he got up and walked away down the road in the moonlight, all alone.

The rest of us went back into the cowshed, leaving the five dead men lying in a line end to end in the shadow of the low stone wall. We lay down on the straw in the cowshed, and pretty soon we were all asleep.

Vietnam Letters

by Daniel P. Garcia and Gen. Barry R. McCaffrey, USA Ret.

Barry McCaffrey recently received a letter from one of his platoon sergeants in Vietnam. He shared that letter and his response with me and others who had survived Vietnam. These letters are powerful descriptions of the Vietnam experience, and I told him that I thought they deserved a wider audience. Eventually, he and Dan Garcia agreed to publication of these extensive excerpts in ARMY. Their experiences in Vietnam clearly had a profound impact on them and shaped their lives forever afterwards. The descriptions here are a consummate distillation of close combat. The drama and candor of these intensely personal letters portray a young NCO who accepted responsibility and served his country admirably under the command of a competent and compassionate young officer.

The lessons of leadership and trust have rarely been so clearly articulated. I hope that every sergeant in the Army, and every officer as well, will read these letters not only for what they tell us about Vietnam but also—and especially—for what they tell us about the meaning of leadership.

They also serve as excellent examples of the substantial contributions many Vietnam veterans continue to make every day.

—GEN. JACK N. MERRITT, USA RET.
President, AUSA

Dear Gen. McCaffrey,

For many years I labored under the delusion that you had been killed in Vietnam after I returned. The one letter I received to this effect was obviously exaggerated and the discovery of your survival, let alone your achievements, induced a nearly metaphysical reaction within the darkest corners of my soul. When Joe Galloway finally pieced together the fact that we had known each other and as I fully grasped that after all these years I might actually speak to you again, I suddenly realized that to do so I

Source: *Army Magazine* (November, 1977) 24-37. Reprinted by permission of the U.S. Army Magazine.

would need to walk amid the wreckage in my own memory to clarify my thoughts and tell you what it meant to know that you are alive and well. Upon reflection, I further realized that to effectively communicate my thoughts to you, without being overcome or distracted by the rush of excitement or reawakened pain and confusion, I would need to write to you first. This then is my meager effort to relate back to you some of what we lived through together, what it meant to me—all told to you in a way that I would never have told you as a mere enlisted man in your company.

Speak Memory.

(Thank you, Mr. Nabakov.)

I remember that the 2-7th Cavalry left I Corps at the end of October and took up residence at a base camp 300 miles south in the flat, forested area on the Cambodian border. As President Johnson stopped the bombing of Cambodia on November 1, 1968, we were there to await the anticipated movement of NVA [North Vietnamese Army] troops from their now safe havens across the border. And they did come. I remember clearly the pitched battles and firefights the first week of November. I remember your predecessor, shot through the head and hauled by us back to our base camp. On the gray day as I was returning from the hospital to rejoin the outfit, we had lost 30 men without having encountered a single enemy soldier.

It was in this state that you came to us, our new "Amber Outlaw 6." I do not remember the exact date, but I can see the place and feel the silent mixture of apprehension and resentment masked by an outward apathy borne of fear and hardship upon our first meeting with you. You told us that at the first signs of danger you would call in artillery fire or gunships and that we would proceed with caution, not with recklessness. You made a point of coordinating our movements with support fire. We heard, we listened, but along with the rest of our innocence, faith in the words and promises of another commander had long since perished. But even among those of us in whom the beasts of death and survival were most ferocious, a spark of a single human frailty called hope was rekindled by your words.

As fate would have it, within a day or two you had a chance to prove that you were true to your word. And you were. Not long after you joined us, I remember talking to one of the platoon leaders. Those of us responsible for our platoons acknowledged that you were different from our previous leaders, that you seemed genuine. After we left the border, we had a few skirmishes, or so it seems to me now, but after the intense fighting in early November we were okay until that day in December—the 16th or so. I remember very clearly that one or two platoons were scouting on recon. My platoon was in the lead and you were not far behind. I recall one of my machine gunners saw movement and blasted away, managing to scare away two chickens! We found a bunker; no one would go in. I went down and found the rotting corpses of two NVA soldiers, whom I shot, because I caught a flicker of rat movement from the corner of my eye. My shots burst the corrupt flesh. I recall that I was sick and disgusted and that I was in such a hurry to blow the bunker up that I barely gave anyone, including myself, time to scatter as I dropped the fragmentation grenade onto the bunker floor and fled. It was as though I could seal away the memory and disgust of that putrid bunker by burying its physical evidence.

One of my squad leaders rushed up and told me in the gravest tone that I needed to go ASAP to headquarters as something was up. I scrambled back and found you on two handsets talking to battalion command and someone else. You were dead serious. My RTO was in the cluster around you and he motioned to me. Over his frequency I heard the screams of the dying in Delta Company, and I knew at once you were ordering choppers for us to fly to their relief. They came shortly thereafter. I could see in their jerky, erratic flight movements that the pilots were scared, and it told me that we were headed to a place of death.

Alpha Company had gotten there first and, as I recall, the firing was sparse, but by the time we got there most of us knew that Delta Company had ceased to exist as a unit, that many had died and most of the others were wounded. As we moved to broaden their perimeter, we passed their remains: broken, bullet-hole-riddled equipment, a smashed helmet here, body parts there. We saw where the NVA had burned the tall grass and shot the men at close range. It was very hard. Some of my own men recognized a handkerchief or some other belonging from one of their friends and knew that he was alive no more. But we did not speak a single word to one another. I remember the fighting that followed over the next five days as we tried time and again to break out of the more or less surrounded position we were in. I remember an NVA charge at Alpha Company as I and others from Bravo came to their relief. I remember the bomb strikes sailing directly over our heads, exploding in front of our perimeter. Maybe I'm dreaming, but I recall your anger at the battalion commander who had failed to coordinate the artillery prep with the air assault so that the NVA had hours to set up their .50-caliber machine guns and mow down doomed and unsuspecting Delta Company. At least that is what I thought all these years.

I remember how on the third day or so of this engagement, the battalion commander showed up for an award ceremony in the middle of the perimeter. In fact, I think I received one—only to have it broken up by enemy rockets and mortars. It was folly and so we finally withdrew. I was the last one to leave the perimeter that last day near Christmas 1968, and as I left, for the only time during my combat experience, I fired from the chopper as it left the ground a sort of signal of defiance mingled with respect for a grim, determined enemy who had taken much and given little.

During those five or six days, our casualties were comparatively light. Other units with us were not so lucky. I recall several wounded and a few men (ours or Alpha's?) lying on ponchos in a row while the snipers fired at them. I recall my rage at seeing them exposed and so I returned the fire above the heads of our own mortar crews, who were angry at me. But the sniper stopped and a chopper came.

That chopper pilot was scared out of his wits. He left so hastily he whacked a tree branch while taking off. We watched as the chopper lurched downward, but his main rotor held and he was able to limp away noisily back to base. We heard he made it and we were relieved, for nothing seemed worse to us than dying on a medevac chopper after being hit. In the main, however, as danger lurked behind every tree, every rock, you protected us. By the end of that week, those of us who had any powers of observation left believed in you.

We fled to mud and elephant country and some place I recall with the bizarre name of LZ Odessa. Somehow an R&R allocation came down for me and I left for six or seven days in Manila. But no matter what I drank or what woman I was with, the sounds of gunfire and the screams of the wounded and dying were, by now, as with all of us, permanently locked inside my mind and heart.

When I came back, I remember a few slow days. Then we encountered "the complex." January 18, 1969. This day was the turning point in my life, and you played a key role in it. I have played out these events through the lens of my mind's eye many times. As I write this, I can feel the celluloid strip of memory project each image on the screen of my consciousness.

It was late morning. It was hot, and the humidity was its normal low 90s. The second platoon was on point; my third platoon was next in line. The gunfire between Delta Company (again cursed with ill fortune) and the NVA, who apparently surrounded them, rumbled somewhere in the distance, vaguely in front of us. Our advance to relieve Delta had been slowed because of the growing sounds of machine gun and automatic weapons fire. We could hear the flutter of gunships running sorties somewhere above the jungle's triple canopy.

Suddenly, machine gun fire erupted in front of me. As I was third man in my column, I could see a few flashes and soldiers scrambling for cover. The second platoon leader had pulled his men up on a crude line, and I brought my platoon up alongside. Firing was heavy. Some of my men disappeared, hiding at the first sound of contact. The 2nd platoon's men were firing weakly, as were mine. A period of perhaps 10 minutes ensued, although it seemed like hours, while both sides exchanged intense fire to little effect. I could not find all of my platoon as I tried vainly to direct fire toward several bunkers ahead of us which were pouring hundreds of rounds into our ranks.

After much arduous screaming, one grunt pointed to a bunker we had passed perhaps 25 yards behind, saying that some of my men were hiding there. I realized that without my missing soldiers, I was immobile and unable to direct any movement or fire. The 2nd platoon had three or four men shot already, and they seemed desperate as they were receiving the sharpest fire and were closely pinned down. I took a chance and stood up, running to the rear, hoping to find my troops. As I ran, I could see bullets felling vines and perforating jungle leaves immediately next to and ahead of me. One bullet passed directly under my arm, slightly ripping my loose fatigue shirt.

The ground sloped slightly from the area where the main action was taking place. I reached the bunker and could see one figure in the half shadow below. I called twice but received no answer. Finally, I went down the steps and threatened to kill anyone who didn't come out. I didn't know if I meant it, for anger, adrenaline and desperation had driven me to the brink. Either way, I must have been convincing because five of my men quickly emerged, their faces filled with shame and fear. My own deep anger and contempt raged inside of me until I saw my best friend, whom I loved as a brother, come out. When I saw him, I thought my heart would break.

Our eyes met, but only for a moment as he hung his head. As he ran back to the line I could see his tears, and the anger that had built up inside me, its own separate force, suddenly burst. I ran back to the center of the line. Once again the firing was thick and my body was tiring. Machine gun bullets were now close on me and I threw myself behind a large anthill. I can still see the brass-colored machine gun slugs slamming into the anthill I lay behind, spinning over my head, their lead sparkling in the pockets of deep azure shining through the gaps in the layered trees. These slugs began to form a pile between my feet as I lay on my back.

Eventually, the bunker in front of me and I exchanged many rounds until I think I killed the gunner and his ammo bearer. After that, I was able to find my RTO. Thus, you, I and the others were able to communicate. At your direction, the 2nd platoon leader popped smoke on the far right of his side of the line, my men on the far let of ours. We were so close in contact we did not throw the smoke to mark our positions in front, but rather a bit behind our positions. The gunships you had called were near and they streaked in quickly. Their first burst of cannons and rockets crossed into our lines and two of my men were hit, including a private who lay next to me, his cheeks and face riddled with shrapnel. I hollered to you over the net and you helped redirect the fire almost at once, saving our lives. Some time passed and under the cover of gunships and bunker support, you rallied us to an immense old bomb crater to the left rear of our ragged line.

By this time, I had seven casualties, none fatal. One of my squad leaders had been shot in the thigh, so I had made a corporal temporary squad leader. As we all scrambled under what was now irregular NVA gunfire, we reached the perimeter of the bomb crater. I was amazed that we all fit in one bomb crater, as if it were a company-sized foxhole. You had told us that napalm was coming soon—to be dropped on our vacated positions. When it came, we were to flank the contact area and circle around to link up with Delta Company. As I had the squad leaders report to me the presence of each of their men, we suddenly realized that two were missing.

From my vantage point I could see two men alone and 50 yards away—a machine gunner and his ammo bearer. I knew that if they stayed there, they were doomed. Time was fleeting and I wasn't sure what to do, so I resigned myself to retrieving them. I remember crossing myself as I got up to go back. One of my squad leaders saw me leaving and pulled at me, begging me not to. But I was cold inside now. In a detached way, I figured I wouldn't make it, but I was so determined not to leave two of my men abandoned that I shrugged him off and ran back to the contact area.

As I got within 10 yards of their position, I stopped, screaming for them to move out while I gave them covering fire. I stood up and began shooting at the trees and bunkers in front of us. As they began to scramble out of their frozen supine positions, I could see a flicker of enemy movement. It was an RPG crew, and we shot at each other simultaneously. I'm certain I got them, and their rocket exploded into the soft earth almost directly between my legs. The explosion blew me straight up, twisted my rifle like a pretzel and lacerated my pistol belt with shrapnel. When I landed I knew I was hurt, but I didn't know how badly as, I suppose, I was in shock.

I reached out and begged for help from the machine gun crew as they were running right at me. But I could see they were terrified. One soldier brushed my hand aside. They both glanced at me but continued running to the rally point in the bomb crater. I was now alone with no weapon. I pulled a piece of the rocket's tail fin out of my thigh with my fingers. I remember it was still hot, but it had not penetrated deep. Forty yards or so away I could see men from my own platoon watching me. I called out for help, but no one budged. By now the NVA had seen me move, so they began to open fire on me. Because the ground sloped a little where I was, their bullets seemed high. I was afraid, and felt more alone than I had ever felt in my whole life; more alone than I would ever feel again. I began to crawl back to the bomb crater.

I could see and feel the enemy's bullets whizzing over me and chewing up earth and foliage all around me. I could hear men screaming, but I did not know what or who they were screaming at. I have no idea how long it took me to crawl back; it could have been three minutes, maybe 10. It was a dark, pitiless eternity to me.

When I was a few yards away from the crater, I could hear our own machine guns firing to cover me. Finally my medic, the same one I had evicted from his hiding place in the bunker earlier, risked his life as he ran upright and dragged me in the rest of the way. As he quickly examined me, he shoved some ammonia up my nose and told me that I had shrapnel in my legs and hip and some superficial facial wounds but nothing serious. This woke me from my stupor and I found I could walk. Within the crater you were clearly in charge, your grim determination steadied me and gave me faith. Events moved quickly. We got set to move out. I distributed the remainder of my gear to my other men. Since I was walking fine and had no equipment other than bandoleers of M16 ammo, I agreed to be a human crutch for a sergeant, whose thigh was severely wounded by a machine gun bullet.

Our exodus then started. Two lieutenants from other platoons (and maybe you, too) stood firing machine guns as we began to stream out, single file, on the far side of the crater. Small arms fire rattled everywhere. The din was incredible. As we exited the crater on our way to Delta Company, I could hear the jets overhead waiting to drop their deadly bombs. I was near the end of the column and could see and hear the "woosh-woosh" of the first napalm canisters as they began to fall toward the initial contact area. At the first explosion, we could feel the heat from the burst and the air seemed to be sucked out of us for a moment. We could see panic-stricken NVA soldiers vacate bunkers and start to parallel our movements maybe 15 to 20 feet away from us. We began a steady exchange of gunfire, but now we seemed to have the upper hand. We shot down several NVA soldiers during this retreat.

The march seemed to take forever. After a while, the level of gunfire gradually slackened, although I don't remember it ever stopping completely. Toward dusk we found Delta's position, such as it was. They seemed pathetic, shell shocked, disorganized. Their position on the return slope had few foxholes. I remember most of them were lying under or behind felled trees in little groups. They seemed exhausted and frightened to the point of near paralysis. They clearly did not have the same disciplined organizational structure that you had ingrained in us.

Finally, as dusk was settling in, you agreed to let me come in on the last chopper with some of the other ambulatory wounded. Only one chopper could land in the tiny LZ we had hacked out of the forest and it was a near vertical descent and ascent for the choppers, making them a great target. I was unsure of whether I should leave, but I was very tired. As my chopper lifted upward, I saw another sight still seared in my mind. There, on a scarred sloping hillside littered with fallen timber, debris and a few enemy corpses, 150 or so American infantrymen had set up a perimeter awaiting the next contact. The smell of cordite and gunpowder choked the humid air, and a cloud of white and black gunpowder smoke seemed to linger over the whole area. The earth, denuded now of foliage from the intense combat, was a pocket of brown surrounded by a forest wall of green. No animal or insect noises were apparent. Every minute a tracer round or two was shot aimlessly at our perimeter by hidden NVA snipers. As the chopper I boarded moved higher, the small circle of men, their dirty faces and sweat-matted fatigues became less visible, then smaller and smaller while the impenetrable jungle and forest around them grew. The scene reminded me of something…one of Bosch's visions of hell. That picture in the An Loc forest became the embodiment of hell to me.

What happened next in this endless day, you do not know. We finally reached our base camp and went to the MASH ward, I and six others from B Company, 2-7th. We waited a long time while the doctors were feverishly operating on what looked like an NVA soldier. I became restless and felt a surge of anger that my men were being ignored. I rose to do something about it when a male nurse glided up next to me and put his hand on my arm, which I found to be holding a weapon. He must have been watching. He said something to me and I finally looked at his kind eyes. He told me, "Sarge, there are only sick and wounded human beings here and we'll get to you and your men in a few minutes." His words deflated my senseless rage and I sat down, ashamed of what I had been thinking.

Later we were treated, released and sent, all seven of us, to a tent with a wood floor and canvas cots—luxury! It was apparently next to the officers' tent. Even in my enervated state, my sleep was racked with tormented images. I could hear conspiratorial whispering somewhere in my dream. Some animal instinct shook me awake. I bellowed with all my might for the men in my tent to get out, and pushed the last two down the steps and into the dirt outside just as the grenade exploded inside, ripping the tent apart. I found I had landed near the open urine pits and I vomited hard. It was as if by vomiting, I could purge my body and soul from the nightmare this had become.

By morning I had resolved to return to the unit even though my wounds were not healed. I figured I'd rather die fighting the NVA than stay behind and be fragged.

I came back to our company sometime that afternoon. By then our unit had discovered that the NVA had been protecting the evacuation of a huge underground hospital complex that we had inadvertently stumbled upon. The enemy had withdrawn; the crises had quietly evaporated. You and I spoke that evening. You told me that I was being put in for a Silver Star. It was then or perhaps a little later—but I think then—that you asked me to stay, offering me a battlefield commission. Could you possibly remember this conversation? I do because it created an immense conflict within me. I had long since ceased caring about my physical safety. In my own rough way I was dedicated to my men, and I was, for the first time in my life, being told by an adult male whom I admired that I was needed. Someone needed me.

But the events of the day before had taken away from me the last vestiges of strength. I feared what I would become if I stayed. I assumed I would die if I stayed. But it was not fear of anything that caused me to say no to you. Rather, it was that for the first time in months I suddenly found a will to live. The physical and emotional pain from my gunshot wounds in July 1968 no longer obscured my desire to live. And so I declined, and in doing so I did not tell you "no." I said, "I can't." You said you understood. During that conversation I remember looking at you closely and seeing your pain, your isolation, the humanity in your eyes and in the expression on your face. It was a powerful turning point in my life. I realized suddenly that our leader, a man we all respected, had simply become a human being to me, with all the strength and weaknesses of other human beings. It was there, in this moment, and through our other experiences, that great truths were revealed to me about the nature of leadership.

After this my memory becomes confused. I was wounded one more time in a small firefight and left shortly thereafter in early March 1969. Between the January 18th action and my departure, however, I remember that the other young platoon sergeants and I became increasingly worried about you. You seemed to be taking more personal risks. You were pushing yourself and, sometimes, us harder. It seemed to all of us that something had happened inside of you. We noticed because, you see, we cared very much about what happened to you.

One episode stands out—maybe it's distorted, maybe by now it's confused. About the last time I was hit, we found ourselves, once again, with 2nd platoon. We were in a dry creek bed. A small, flat clearing lay in front of us. On its far side, up near the treeline 25 yards away or so, was an enemy bunker, a high one that was clearly visible.

The memory is jumbled now. The 2nd platoon leader is hit in the neck. We pour fire into the bunker; it falls silent. You begin to order some of us to move on the bunker. You change your mind. All of a sudden, you get up and charge the bunker holding only a pistol. We are all dumbfounded. I crawl out of the creek bed and stand ready to kill anything if you are shot. You reach the bunker. No one has fired. You throw a smoke grenade in the bunker. You go inside! Four or five others and I start running toward the bunker. We are all afraid for you. You emerge from the smoke. Your face is red. You are coughing. There is a baby in your arms. In a few seconds, an old woman also emerges. We are all silent. We have never seen a child on a battlefield.

Later a chopper comes to pick up the wounded sergeant and maybe me (why?). The sergeant has sort of gone loony. He is crying out—but for what? His neck is hurt badly, but it looks like he'll make it. The chopper lands. They put him in first on a stretcher. I hop in the other side. I have a pistol on me (why?). Someone gives the infant to the wounded sergeant. The door gunner nudges me and waves his head toward the sergeant, who is holding the child in his hands, arms outstretched. Is he mad? The medic outside the chopper is shouting something at the sergeant, and I start to panic, afraid that something terrible may occur. I reach for the pistol, realizing I may have to shoot. I pull it out of my holster. My heart is sinking. The sergeant then lowers the child to his chest, embracing it. He is crying softly. The crisis passes. We begin to rev up for takeoff. Someone plops a nine-year-old girl in my lap. I'm sitting in the doorway, as usual, my legs dangling out, and now so is she. She is scared. I can feel her tiny frame shaking. We begin to take off. She bites me, not hard, but firm. All I can think is that she is scared and believes that I'll throw her out of the chopper. Finally I stroke her and find a voice in me I've never had before, and it says, "I won't hurt you." We leave. I know not any longer if all of this happened. I think it did, at least most of it. Maybe the little girl wasn't real. Maybe she's a symbol of my guilt, our collective guilt. Either way, for years she visited my dreams. She is with me still.

This ends my story. The windup is tortured and long because these memories are so. But I tell you this in detail so that despite the differences of time and space and rank, and all of the later experiences of our lives, you will know what happened there, at least in my eyes. One of us has lived to tell you now directly, on paper, how important you were to us. You were the first company commander who cared about us. I think we would have done anything for you. It was not lost on any of us that despite the combat in these months and the awesome losses in our sister companies, our own losses were light. But more than that, we came to trust you and believe in who you were. In that way you allowed us to believe in ourselves, and in doing so you saved some part of each of us. This may have been your greatest achievement in that theater.

When I saw you last, I had great fear because I thought I saw death in your eyes. It seemed to me that your concern for yourself had ceased, and that you would continue to take risks and that someday you would be obliged. Thus, when I left Vietnam and was later written to and led to believe that you and others had been killed, I felt a great loss and believed that I had betrayed you all by not staying.

And now the essence of my message. From you I learned that leadership, particularly in times of great crisis, is a demanding and isolating experience. I learned that understanding and compassion must be combined with technical competence and strength to lead, and that selflessness, not selfishness, is required. I learned that through one leader the lives of many can be changed, and thus every human being has the ability to influence the behavior of the world in some small way. I learned that calm in the center of a storm is crucial, and that whatever the distractions, one must focus on the big picture. You taught me all this from your example.

War had caused me to watch everything in life with discernment. You removed much of the mystery of the human experience. In many ways, you taught me more about the world than anyone, including my own father. Yet we were not close. You were Amber Outlaw 6 and I, a simple platoon sergeant, was Amber Outlaw 3-5. Nonetheless, you were, and always have been, a powerful force in my life.

My experience in the military shaped the rest of my life. Having survived, I felt a special sense of obligation to live, in effect, for many who did not return. I dedicated and drove myself and my career in a way that I hoped would make some small contribution to the world beyond my own petty existence. While my personal life has been uneven and filled with mistakes in relationships, I've certainly wandered an eventful and diverse professional trail. If I have contributed anything to this world, much of it is attributable to your influence on a hardened, watchful 21-year-old platoon sergeant who once served, proudly, under your command.

I thought long about writing you this letter for fear that it could revive memories that you'd rather not have. But I chose otherwise and, once started, it assumed its own course. I hope that someday not too distant I will see you again. Until then, I hope that you and those closest to you are safe and well.

—Dan Garcia
Once "Amber Outlaw 3-5"

DANIEL P. GARCIA is senior vice president of real estate planning and public affairs for Warner Bros. in Burbank, Calif. He has served on the boards of directors of the Kaiser Foundation, the Los Angeles Chamber of Commerce and the Rockefeller Foundation. He served with distinction in Vietnam where he earned three Purple Hearts, the Silver Star, two Bronze Stars and an Air Medal. A graduate of Loyola University, he holds an MBA from the University of Southern California and a Juris Doctorate from UCLA School of Law.

Dear Dan,

Your letter of Vietnam memories was a treasure—a capsule of time that reappeared from 29 years past. The power and clarity of your letter make it one of the most profound pieces of writing on our war I have ever read. Dan—it seems like just yesterday to me, even now. I can see your face with film clarity—such a young man of integrity, courage and leadership under such enormous pressure, responsible for the lives of other even younger soldiers who were barely beyond being boys. You and the others were my family, my brothers, and my constant burden of worry during the eight months I commanded B Company, 2-7th Cavalry.

All that you have achieved with your life is a source of great pride to me. The discipline, sheer talent and energy you showed as a 21-year-old rifle platoon sergeant in combat has followed you. You did all that was asked of you and more. You were wounded three times. You took care of your soldiers. You were an example to all of us.

Your letter awakened some terrible sleeping memories. I have shared your letter with my family and some close friends—particularly the Vietnam vets who have stayed close throughout the years. I can see your memories as an out of body experience from your stark images. My recollections capture the same pictures from different angles and with other hazy, distorted and bloody perspectives.

A handful of soldiers—and particularly you—have stayed in my thoughts and prayers throughout the decades. I really loved all of you and desperately wanted you to live and go home intact in spirit. Our country did not treat any of you with the respect, support and compassion you deserved. It was a shameful blot on our history to send the country's young men off to this terrible conflict and then use our soldiers as objects of blame for the divisive political struggle that ripped the nation apart for a decade.

Dan, you are a superb example of a Vietnam veteran with life-long dedication to America when you returned to civilian life.

When I met you as I took command of B Company, 2-7th Cavalry, in November 1968, I was *five years older than you*. I was also on my third combat tour; had been wounded twice; had a wife, son and a baby daughter whom I adored; was a West Point and Ranger School graduate; and was *an old man*. All my youthful spirit for adventure, for war, for glory was gone—ground out of me in the mud and artillery fire of the DMZ fighting as part of the Vietnamese Airborne Division.

Fresh out of West Point, I had volunteered for the 82nd Airborne Division as a new 2nd lieutenant in 1964 because I believed the division would go to Vietnam. We ended up instead in the Organization of American States intervention in the Dominican Republic. Our combat experience was minimal, but I got the shock of seeing American soldiers lying dead on canvas stretchers. Now I knew.

From the Dominican Republic, I immediately volunteered for Vietnam. After extensive language and advisor training, I ended up based in Saigon with the Vietnamese 2nd Parachute Infantry Battalion. Those were the days of wine and roses: air conditioned BOQs, jeeps, nightclubs, older airborne NCOs, and the cool beauty of the surf on the beaches at Vung Tau. The other reality was midnight alerts: the roar of C-47s and C-130s lifting us from Tan Son Nhut Air Base and heading out to some savage firefight on the frontier or a besieged provincial capital. Within days of leaving city lights, milk shakes and PXs, we might be involved in a massive battle with hundreds killed or wounded. In many cases the NVA would outnumber us and have overmatching rocket, mortar and artillery firepower.

After coming home, I went directly from Vietnam to Panama to be a general's aide. My poor West Point Spanish got me a wonderful year-long interlude of peace. My beautiful young wife and children shut the door on Vietnam. I worked for a wonderful old general who was a Bataan death march survivor. He treated me like his son. He wanted me to follow in his footsteps as an instructor in political science at West Point. I was to go to graduate school at Harvard and then join the faculty. In your letter you mentioned your feelings of abandonment as you left your friends upon departing Vietnam after your *third* Purple Heart. It is a common feeling among American soldiers who have survived combat.

In my case, I was still in Panama when the Tet Offensive started on Christmas 1968. The graphic news media coverage was on our Armed Forces Network television each night—ferocious scenes of combat. Our soldiers, *our soldiers*, were dying in great numbers. I was one of three infantry captains with a Combat Infantryman Badge serving among the 15,000 troops in Panama. My sense of guilt at seeing our Army fighting for its life while I prepared to head off to graduate school broke me within a few days. Without telling the general, I called the infantry assignment officer in Washington and volunteered for immediate return. I told my wife Jill, who understood. She was scared, but she always understood. The general was scared, sad and regretful. He wanted me to be a general; he wanted my friendship. He let go reluctantly.

When I left Jill with her parents in Corona Del Mar, Calif., I had a powerful sense of letting go. This was what I was supposed to do. My friends were dying and being maimed in massive numbers. There was simply no option but duty.

When you saw me take command of B Company at LZ Billie on the Cambodian border in III Corps, I had been the 2-7th Cavalry assistant battalion operations officer (S-3) for two months. The 1st Cavalry Division conducted an emergency deployment from I Corps to Quan Loi in III Corps in response to intelligence of a planned 100,000-soldier NVA offensive. The enemy's intention was to sweep out of Cambodia down the Surgess Jungle Highway to capture the huge American logistics complex at Long Binh. Long Binh was the biggest military installation in the world—destruction of its millions of tons of supplies, ammunition and fuel was to be a war-winning knockout blow. The garrison of 40,000 REMFs would be easy pickings. The emergency mission of our 1st Cavalry Division was to put a reconnaissance-in-force on the Cambodian border and then fall back in a fighting covering force to bring about the attrition of the enemy offensive. In the largest sense we succeeded admirably—Tet '69 was eventually stillborn. Only *one* NVA battalion ultimately survived the 100-kilometer meat grinder campaign offensive and stumbled out of the jungle a few kilometers from Long Binh. This one NVA battalion was then killed almost to the last man by the 11th Armored Cavalry Regiment.

We had done our job. But what a trail of tears the 1st Cavalry Division left behind during our bloody full-court press with the attacking NVA divisions and logistics troops. So many *Garry Owen* soldiers in green bags, so much suffering, so much blood, confusion, despair, courage, sacrifice and love. So many memories brought back by your powerful letter: Dan Garcia—handsome, poised, serious, intelligent. Your fellow platoon leader—one of the most gifted natural leaders I have ever met.

The lieutenant who loved his soldiers and controlled his fear with enormous combat courage. The endless memories of the faces of teenage soldiers with their energy, respect, affection for each other and enduring courage. Our 1st sergeant was a rock to me. He helped shoulder the moral burden. He was also on his third combat tour and would earn his third Purple Heart with B Company. He had first served in 2nd Battalion, 7th Cavalry, in the Korean War and had been badly wounded as a young private. For most of my command tenure, the 1st sergeant was the only other soldier in our company who was both Regular Army and more than 25 years old.

Our company ranged in strength from 73 to 125 men. We were essentially all draftees, ages 18 to 22—the officers, the NCOs, the soldiers. The 1st sergeant and I absolutely loved and respected all of you young men. We knew in our hearts that many of you would be wounded or killed while serving in the company. We also believed that if we could do our job properly—coordinate air and artillery; maintain tactical coordination with other battalion elements; ruthlessly enforce security, digging-in, helmets, noise/light discipline and use helicopter reconnaissance—most of you would go home alive. That was our abiding passion and purpose month after month.

I took command of B Company from a captain who was killed in action on LZ Billie after the company had been badly chewed up in our first III Corps firefight. One of the rifle platoon leaders had gotten aggressive, stupid and lost. (He survived to die of a tragic self-inflicted accidental gunshot wound 18 months later.) All of our brigade fire bases came under heavy NVA attack. An ARVN [Army of the Republic of Vietnam] firebase off to our east was overrun. Delta Company from our battalion attacked out from the firebase toward the frontier to try to push back the 107-mm rocket, 122-mm artillery and mortars that were pounding us. They promptly got stuck in close combat. The company commander (an old friend) and the company head medic were both killed and their bodies left. Alpha Company, which was commanded by another friend, then attacked out to link up with D Company and was also promptly caught in a buzz saw. Charlie Company was then in turn committed to the attack and barely got in to the jungle line before the NVA machine guns opened up. Their company commander was also killed.

All day, as your brand-new B Company commander, I listened with growing dread on the radio to the sounds of D Company disintegrating and the mounting tragedy of casualties in A and C Companies. The battalion commander was a wonderful and brave man (later to be replaced by an honorable but incompetent lieutenant colonel who did indeed play a role in the later destruction of the same D Company during the Christmas fighting). In the very late afternoon, I heard the battalion commander give the orders to launch our B Company at dusk by helicopter to land directly on the remnants of Delta. When I received the order, the 18 helicopters were already inbound and were to land within 45 minutes. *Dan—I did not know any of you.* I assembled the B Company command group and platoon leaders and gave a simple five paragraph combat order. My hands were shaking but my head was clear. I then explained the attack order in Vietnamese to the "Kit Carson" NVA scout (turncoat) and the two Viet interpreters who served with us. (All three promptly deserted on an outgoing medevac chopper.)

The company XO was a shaken young man. He listened in anguish to my attack order and then said quite clearly to the entire command group, "Captain, these soldiers aren't going to go. They're scared and won't get on the choppers." I told him to get out of the company and report to the battalion headquarters. We also left behind one more of the platoon leaders—a young, frightened, stupid officer who should not have survived OCS. Finally, I told the 1st sergeant, "I'll go out on the first aircraft. You come in on the last helicopter and give me a closing report." Looking around the circle of officers and NCOs, I laid it on the line. "Our friends are dying—we need to help."

There was an immense choking swirl of dry season dirt from 18 landing helicopters. I jumped aboard the lead "Huey" with my CP element (whose names I barely knew). My RTO was holding on to my web gear as I hung out the side of the Huey, desperately trying to visualize the terrain as we roared across the jungle treetops. The sun plunged below the horizon as the choppers turned short on final approach. Heavy enemy gunfire erupted from the ground. A gigantic blow hit our Huey as a round tore through the floor behind the RTO; his eyes widened and he laughed and gave me a thumbs up. Then the LZ came into sight. Thirty or so D Company survivors lay flattened as enemy mortar rounds smacked into the ground. They were wraiths in the gathering dusk as they clawed their way onto our departing choppers and left. (They had been told to stay with us, but were leaderless, disorganized and scared.)

My CP group and I headed in the 12 o'clock direction on the LZ and set up our CP on a large recognizable mound in the deepening darkness. (It turned out to be an occupied NVA bunker.) The last of our B Company helicopters could be heard as they lifted off in a burst of suppressive gunfire. Then the 1st sergeant emerged from the darkness. "Captain," he said, "they all came. We have 123 soldiers on the ground." Dan, I had spent all of my 25 years getting ready for that night. I had buried my brother-in-law, who had been in killed in action in August of 1964. I knew my dad, an Army lieutenant general, would honor me in death. I dearly wanted to live to see my wife and children. But, Dan, that night three kilometers north of LZ Billie—with automatic weapons gunfire whipcracking across the LZ, with the ferocious roar of bamboo burning and exploding from the artillery strikes, with the stench and fear of death around us—I said a prayer that I could live up to the demands of commanding a company of brave young soldiers like you—soldiers who would fly into a savage night firefight because other unknown teenage soldiers from 2-7th Cavalry were dying and needed help. That night I was home in B Company.

The following months of combat are distorted now. I was so very proud to command such a group of soldiers. The memories of unending vigilance; ripped hands from constant digging; the shock of making contact as firing built up quickly in a crescendo; the acrid smell of grenades, cordite, C4 explosives, trip flares; the incredible stench of filthy soldiers, the sight of torn uniforms, the constant pain from bites, destroyed feet, pulled muscles from carrying 80 pounds of water, ammunition, weapons, packs; and the agony of seeing screaming, wounded soldiers and dragging the dead to helicopters. Thank God for our extremely low B Company casualties. Much of it was due to the incredible diligence of young NCOs like you. Much of it was due to the experience and cunning that the 1st sergeant and I had gained from surviving many years of combat between us. Some of it was luck and the hand of God.

I can remember all the images drawn so vividly in your letter. The terrible battle at Christmas which went on for a week and nearly destroyed D Company, A Company and C Company in sequence. We were fortunate to have no one killed despite our many wounded. I recall shooting two NVA soldiers at close range with a .45-caliber pistol and throwing dozens of grenades. I also remember calling in thousands of rounds of artillery and mortars—and bringing in dozens of armed choppers and tactical air strikes. The superb division commanding general—Maj. Gen. George Forsythe, who was a courageous and experienced World War II Normandy invasion vet—finally pulled us. He understood we were being ground up piecemeal by larger NVA forces.

I do remember offering to nominate you for a combat field direct commission. You were such a superb leader. I did understand that you could not do it. You were way beyond the limit and had to go. Death was waiting to harvest you.

Your other memories are also a common reel of film in my mind: The B Company fight in the complex—the huge bomb crater; your single-handed attack to recover your soldiers; my CP group and me pinned down behind an NVA bunker while two heavy machine guns chopped down bamboo inches over our heads; the shock when we first made contact, walking into a surprised group of 30 or more NVA soldiers; our brave point man with a stutter and a .38-caliber pistol yelling "*dung-lai*" (surrender) as the rest of us opened up on automatic fire.

After you were medevac'd from that fight, the battalion commander ordered us to attack at dusk to get an enemy body count to justify the enormous number of friendly air strikes. I argued with him to no avail. We had heavy leader casualties and little ammunition. Night was falling, and we were outnumbered and trying to get organized. New replacements and boxes of unopened ammunition were scattered throughout the company. The adjourning D Company commander reported an attack his company never made. In our B Company, my brave RTO, our huge company medic who was known for his courage, and one volunteer platoon leader and his RTO moved out with me, crawling forward into the enemy contact zone. I reported over the radio that B Company minus was across the line in attack. We moved about 150 meters into the contact zone and then encountered bunches of moving NVA trying to withdraw. We froze—then the medic shot an M79 40-mm round at an NVA soldier on top of a bunker 20 feet away. The 40-mm didn't detonate, but it did kill him. The place then came alive with enemy fire. We were able to back out throwing hand grenades to cover our withdrawal. The battalion commander, miles away, could then report that his battalion had continued the attack but had been repulsed.

I also remember the day both you and another one of our platoon leaders were wounded in an attack on what turned out to be an armed field support complex. That was a disgusting day. I shot an NVA soldier dead in the face while clearing a bunker. I also remember the company saving the children and their mother in the bunker, and our enormous relief that they had not been killed. I remember giving the children cartons of field ration milk when we put them on the chopper that medevac'd you and the other wounded platoon leader. The children were so terrified their faces were numb with fear. I cried—thinking of my own children and also because I was terrified that the other platoon leader might die from his throat wound.

After you "DEROS'd" home, B Company kept fighting nearly nonstop as the 1st Cavalry Division fell back on the final defensive rocket belt 12 kilometers out from the Long Binh Field Logistics Base—a series of violent skirmishes and meeting engagements—a constant drain of casualties. The lieutenants and sergeants were going out faster as casualties in other companies than in B Company because of our ferocious concentration on security, camouflage and digging. I was starting to feel the pressure. I desperately didn't want our soldiers to die. You are correct that I did become more uncompromising and demanding and started to take greater personal risks. My face had a giant twitch under the left eye. I was having combat nightmares that required my CP group to cover my mouth and slap me awake during sleeping breaks.

It couldn't go on—too much fighting, too many exposures. On my last day in B Company, we encountered a huge NVA assembly area and bunker complex. Our three platoons fanned out in a cloverleaf. The third platoon immediately made heavy contact with the enemy and was pinned down. The 1st sergeant, as usual, was with them and was reported wounded and in unknown condition. My heart was again frozen with fear for our soldiers. We got two rifle platoons on line and attacked under heavy fire through moderately open jungle and successfully linked up with the isolated third platoon. Then things turned nasty with heavy enemy fire. We managed to knock out all the NVA bunkers in close proximity. I called in a 105-mm artillery battery 6 × 6 shoot. The rounds shrieked in to smash the complex. Our one B Company mortar opened up. The armed choppers rolled in and then we attacked. Our company bugler blew the attack. (I still have the bugle.) One bunker in particular held us up. I snapped, and assaulted it twice with grenades and finally got it. Dan, to this day I can't understand how I lived through the attack. There was an enormous amount of fire directed at me during the two assaults. The NVA kept throwing their potato masher grenades. We'd scramble and roll in terror a yard or so away and then be blown sideways with splinters in our exposed skin.

Finally, we had the upper hand, I thought—heavy friendly fire outgoing, sporadic NVA fire incoming. The B Company assault line lurched forward screaming, firing M16s on automatic and throwing grenades. Then it happened. An enemy RPD machine gun opened up on our right flank almost under the feet of our assault line and knocked us down like bowling pins. One of our men went down as if a sledgehammer had hit his helmet. I had a pistol shot out of my hand and my canteen off my hip. My face kept grinding the dirt—couldn't sort it out—sat up with the enemy machine gun hammering by my ears and saw two broken bones sticking out past my elbow—no apparent arm and my blood pumping a foot out with the frantic beating of my heart. A brave young sergeant charged forward to get the machine gun and was cut down dead. One of our platoon leaders finally stopped the slaughter by jumping on the enemy bunker and shooting the NVA machine gunner in the face with his shotgun. The incredibly brave and unarmed company medic then jerked me into defilade. The rest is a haze of me trying to organize and extract B Company while swimming through the shock waves of increasing pain.

The wounded 1st sergeant and wounded lieutenant finally got us out. I was medevac'd out on a helicopter jungle penetrator with our other 15 wounded and 3 killed in action. I left in physical agony but with an even more terrible pain in my heart that I was going to the safety of an Army MASH hospital. I would have gladly died there that day if I could have protected B Company from harm.

So, Dan Garcia, here we sit after all these years—alive with our memories and grateful that we both survived to write these letters on Vietnam. We have bridged this chasm of time and opened a door on the courage and pain we shared in combat. I'm proud of your enormous accomplishments: the law degree, the partnership in a famous firm, the high corporate office in an international company and your splendid record of public service in city government.

Mostly, though, I'm proud of the vivid image I have of the courage in ferocious combat of a 21-year-old rifle platoon sergeant in B Company, 2nd Battalion, 7th Cavalry. You were a superb soldier. You took care of your men. You led by example. I'm glad my prayers have been answered, with one more *Garry Owen* soldier home at last.

—*Barry McCaffrey*
Captain, Infantry, 1968–69
Once "Outlaw 6"

GEN. BARRY R. McCAFFREY, USA Ret., served as commander in chief, U.S. Southern Command, before being appointed by President Clinton in 1996 as director of the White House Office of National Drug Control Policy. In addition to his combat tours in the Dominican Republic and Vietnam, he commanded the 24th Infantry Division (Mechanized) in Iraq during Operation Desert Storm. He now serves on the National Security Council and the President's Drug Policy Council. A graduate of the U.S. Military Academy, he holds a master's degree from American University.

Selected Readings from "She Went to War"

Rhonda Cornum as told to Peter Copeland

We were flying fast and low, so low that the pilot of our helicopter had to pull up to fly over the convoy of American trucks streaming through Iraq. I was sitting on the floor in the back of the Black Hawk, leaning against my medical gear and a stretcher we had cut down so it would fit inside the helicopter. I could see endless columns of American tanks and trucks full of water, ammo and fuel driving across the hard-packed, rocky sand. We were flying close enough to the ground that I could clearly see the faces of the soldiers below as they waved back at us. It was another chilly gray afternoon, February 27, 1991, the fourth day of ground war against Iraq.

I had wakened that morning at about 6 a.m. in a tent so small that our cots overlapped. Rucksacks, medical bags, food, weapons and supplies were crammed into every inch of space and were covered with a fine dust of sand that made everything look frosted. We were fortunate to have a tent, though, since some of our soldiers were sleeping on the ground with nothing to protect them except a tarp thrown over the tail boom of their helicopter. The air was cold outside my sleeping bag, and I could see my breath in the faint light. We were moving north again, and I didn't know when I'd have another chance to take a bath, so I kicked my three medics out of the tent. As it turned out, it would be my last bath for some time. I grabbed two metal buckets and filled them with cold water from a tanker truck that followed our battalion. We carried the buckets to wash soldiers in case they were sprayed with deadly chemical agents, but they also were handy for heating water for baths. I walked carefully back into our tent, trying to keep the water from sloshing over the top of the buckets and onto the floor and set one of the buckets on top of the kerosene stove.

When steam finally rose off the water into the chilly morning air, I set the bucket on the ground and got out of my clothes. When we first arrived in Saudi Arabia in August we scurried for shade to escape the broiling sun, but now the days were

Source: *She Went to War: The Rhonda Cornum Story.* p. 43-59. (1992). Reprinted by permission of Presidio Press.

cold, damp and steel gray. Naked and shivering in the middle of the tent, I curled up my toes and stepped inside the bucket. I'm only five feet, five inches tall and weigh 110 pounds, so I'm probably one of the few people in the entire U.S. Army who can actually bathe in a bucket. I even shaved my legs. It wasn't like I was going out to dinner that night, but I felt refreshed and cleaner. I guess it was the same for some of the guys who shaved every day of the war; it just made us feel better.

After I had sponged off my body as best I could, I set the other bucket at the foot of the cot and stretched out on my back to lower my head into the water. I used the kind of shampoo with conditioner in it because we never had enough water to rinse twice. There really was never enough water for anything, and the desert easily overwhelmed our attempts to keep clean. When I was more or less clean, or had at least moved the dirt around, I dried my light brown hair with a towel and brushed it straight. At home I prefer to wear my hair down on my shoulders, but for work I braid it into a ponytail, twisted it around my finger, and pinned it up under my helmet.

I dressed in clean underwear and a flight suit, which is a green jumpsuit that zips up the front. The uniform makes my eyes look even more green. I pulled on thick green knee socks and combat boots, scuffed and dusty after six months in the desert. The layered look was popular during those bone-chilling desert mornings: first I put on my flight jacket, then the bullet-proof flak jacket. Next I fastened my gas mask around my left hip, with one strap around the left thigh. I carried a semi-automatic 9mm Beretta pistol in a shoulder holster under my left arm so I could draw the weapon with my right hand. Last came the survival vest, which had an emergency radio in case we were shot down.

I hadn't worn my wedding ring since we arrived in Saudi Arabia, because I'd seen too many soldiers lose their fingers when their rings became caught in heavy machinery. Instead, I kept the ring with my dog tag on a chain around my neck. My husband, Kory, and I had designed and ordered matching rings when we were married eight years before. The ring was a diamond-shaped cluster of gold strands, sort of a bird's nest, with a diamond in the center.

Like me, Kory is a flight surgeon, but he's in the Air Force. As flight surgeons, we're doctors who have pilots for patients. The biggest difference between us is that I fly helicopters and was attached to an army Apache helicopter battalion for the war, and Kory is in a squadron of Air Force F-15 fighter jets. He'd told me years before that if he ever crashed at sea and they couldn't find his wedding ring, that I should have the doctors X-ray his stomach. He was going to try to swallow the ring before he went down so it wouldn't come off when his finger shrank in the cold water.

Clean and dressed, I left the tent for TOC (Tactical Operations Center) to find out exactly what we were doing that morning and when we would be leaving. As always, there was hot coffee in the TOC, which made the whole day seem better. For breakfast I ate peanut butter on crackers. The coffee tasted good. When we were married, I had stopped drinking it because Kory hates coffee breath and coffee-flavored kisses. But when I went to Saudi Arabia, he said he understood what it's like in the field, and how coffee is a key ingredient in army life, so he wouldn't mind if I started drinking it again. He was sent to the Middle East about a week after I was, but he was living at an Air Force base seven hundred miles away, so I kept drinking my coffee.

We were moving north and east again, deeper into Iraq, and I packed a rucksack with my essential gear to carry on the helicopter. Everything else would come later, in the massive convoy of trucks that followed us to war. My rucksack held three days' worth of MREs, which stands for Meals, Ready-to Eat. Those are the individual field rations that come packed in heavy brown plastic pouches. By that time I'd learned to like them all. Well, most of them, anyway. I'll never eat the sticky cherry nut cakes – they're disgusting – and the oatmeal cookies come in little, sharp-edged blocks that could be used to hone a knife. The soldiers joke that "Meals, Ready-to-Eat" is really three lies in one, and that MRE actually stands for Meals Rejected by Ethiopia.

We took down the tent and packed it with the other equipment. I helped the medics get organized and launched two of them in our 2 1/2-ton truck, known in the army as a deuce-and-half. Another medic would ride in a second truck. By this time in the war, traveling was the most dangerous thing that we did, and we had lost more soldiers to motor vehicle accidents than to enemy fire. I was riding in a helicopter, and we would meet later at a new position in Iraq that was closer to Kuwaiti border.

The medics drove off, and I trudged across the sand to another tent where the coffee always was hot. The ground was grayish sand peppered with small stones as far as I could see, which was not that far. There was no horizon: the light was so flat that in the distance I could barely tell where the ground ended and the sky began. This desolate, barren place couldn't have been more different from our sunny farm in Florida with its rich green fields and little creek – but I couldn't think about home now. The weather was getting colder as we went farther north into Iraq. At least it wasn't raining again.

There was a ridge in front of our helicopter battalion, and when I climbed to the high ground there, I could see some of the other battalions. There was movement and activity everywhere, people packing and preparing to leave. The Allied planes had been pounding the Iraqis for forty days and nights before we invaded Iraq, and when we flew in, many of the Iraqi soldiers were ready to surrender. So far, the war was going better than we had expected, and our intelligence estimated the fighting would end some time during the next twenty-four to forty-eight hours. We were part to the largest helicopter assault in history, but the fighting might be over before we even got into a major battle.

Everyone was anxious to move out quickly that morning and do something significant before the fighting ended. No one I knew wanted to go home without seeing action. We had been moving north quickly, however, and had seen little opposition. None of us wanted to kill Iraqis, and we were just as happy to blow up tanks and trucks with no people in them, but that was why most of us were in the military: to go to war. During the past two weeks, I had logged a lot of combat hours flying search–and–rescue helicopters and had helped capture a group of Iraqi prisoners, but real war – as compared to the way I had imagined it- seemed relatively easy for us. I hadn't slept much since the ground war began, but a steady flow of adrenaline – and strong army coffee – kept me going. All of my energy was focused on one thing: keep the pilots healthy enough to fly and destroy the enemy. No more forms to fill out, no more paper to push. Fly and fight. I loved it.

After my last cup of coffee, I walked out of the tent and bumped into CW3 Robert Gary Godfrey, a stocky thirty-two-year-old helicopter pilot. He would be the pilot in my helicopter later that day. We had gotten to know each other pretty well by that time. We always joked around and punched each other in the arm, but on this particular morning he grabbed me and gave me a big hug. I thought that was kind of odd. We were friends, but it had always been an "I-can-be-more-obnoxious-than-you" kind of friendship. Now, however, emotions were raw and close to the surface. This was no time to take friends for granted. I hugged Godfrey back, but I didn't really think about that hug until later.

It was probably 10 A.M. by the time all the trucks in the convoy were on their way. The next step was to make sure the Apaches and scout helicopters could get off the ground and move toward our next destination. Finally I climbed aboard our UH-60 Black Hawk helicopter, which is the utility and assault helicopter designed to replace the old "Huey" of Vietnam fame, and took off for our next destination: a very small abandoned airfield from which we would launch our next attacks. There we hovered in a line of helicopters for about an hour waiting for gas at division's Forward Arming and Refueling Point (FARP). When we had a full load of fuel, we were ordered to pick up some soldiers we had just dropped off at another location. Now they wanted us to drop them somewhere else.

Our helicopter was part of the shuttle service for the rest of our 2-229th Attack Helicopter Battalion, which was attached to the 101st Airborne Divisions (Air Assault). During attack missions my normal job as battalion flight surgeon was to fly behind the Apache attack helicopters. If an Apache was shot down, we'd be close enough to rescue the two pilots before they were captured, and I'd provide emergency medical care until we could evacuate them. At that point some of the aircraft had been hit but none shot down. There were no missions that morning, however, so we became a taxi service. There were eight people to be shuttled this time, and they had maps and gear and weapons. We had taken the back seats out of our helicopter and left them in Saudi to make more room, but it still was a tight fit with seven of us in the crew and eight new passengers.

We were sitting on ammo boxes and rucksacks, and someone was sitting on my lap. Godfrey was at the controls with another pilot, CW4 Philip H. Garvey. Before volunteering for Desert Shield, Garvey and Godfrey were instructor pilots at Fort Rucker, Alabama, where I worked in the Aeromedical Research Laboratory and cared for pilots. I knew them to be two of the best Black Hawk pilots around. I tend to be a backseat driver – in a car or a helicopter – but with those two I could relax and admire their skill. I've flown hundreds of times, but I still feel a delicious thrill in the pit of my stomach every time all that metal and power lifts into the sky. I watched the pilots go through the preflight checks and run up the engine.

Sitting in the back of the helicopter, I was wearing a flight helmet with a headset to listen to the radio. Just before takeoff I heard a call for "Bengal one-five," which was Garvey's call sign. Mine was "Bengal zero-zero," commonly know in the battalion as "Bengal Balls." I recognized the voice on the radio: it was Capt. Dave Maxwell, the assistant S-3, one of the officers in charge of operation for the battalion.

"Bengal one-five, do you have Doc Cornum on board?" I thought maybe somebody had been hurt.

"Bengal one-five, roger," one of pilots answered.

"Do you have her stuff on board?"

"Yeah," the pilot said. Then I knew somebody had been hurt.

"Do you have gas?"

"We just left the FARP."

Maxwell explained that an Air Force F-16 pilot, Capt. Bill Andrews, had been shot down in Iraq. We were the closest helicopter unit that had a chance of rescuing him. The Air Force has Special Operations units that were assigned to rescuing downed pilots during Operation Desert Storm, and they must have known about Andrews, but apparently they weren't in the area. It was clear that if we didn't reach him soon he'd be captured. Andrews was in radio contact with one of our airborne command posts and said he had a broken leg and might have other injuries; that's why they wanted a doctor.

Our pilots asked if we should first deliver the eight passengers to their destination, but Maxwell said this was an emergency. Dump the passengers and go. Now. The soldiers scrambled to grab their gear and jump to ground. The wind was picking up, and it whipped sand across our faces. The pilots were talking with Maxwell about the exact coordinates where Andrews was located and how to get there. Those were things I didn't need to know, so I tuned out the radio transmissions and began the mental checklist of exactly what we needed and how we'd do this mission.

A lean young soldier from our unit, Sgt. Troy Dunlap, was watching the frantic effort to unload the helicopter and prepare to fly. He was shouting above the rotors, aching to get on board. Dunlap found out we were going on a combat search-and-rescue mission, and he didn't want to miss it. Like the rest of us, he'd flown on many missions since the war began, but he seemed to miss the ones where we captured prisoners or cleared bunkers or did the things that soldiers like Sergeant Dunlap are trained to do. He's a Pathfinder, a tough infantryman specially trained for helicopter missions.

A fellow Pathfinder already on board waved for Dunlap to join us, but one of the pilots said leave him- the rotors were already turning for takeoff. The other pilot said let him come, so we leaned over and pulled Dunlap into the aircraft. I understood how Dunlap felt: This was the real thing, combat search and rescue. There was no mission that we trained for that was more important, more exciting, or more dangerous. My heart beat faster, and my stomach tightened. This was it. We were doing it for real.

The crew included two pilots, two crew chiefs who worked the door guns, the three Pathfinders, and me. The senior Pathfinder on board was Sgt. Patbouvier Ortiz, 27, who was monitoring the radio. Dunlap and the third Pathfinder wore regular Kevlar helmets without radio headsets. Unless we had something to say to the pilots, we stayed off the radio to keep the channel clear. Sergeant Ortiz and I were yelling over the noise of the rotors to plan the rescue. We knew the Iraqis would be scouring the desert for Andrews, and with a broken leg he couldn't go far. Some of us had to get off the helicopter, the Pathfinders had to secure the area from attack, and the other crew members would carry Andrews back to the helicopter. Someone had to carry the stretcher and the medical bag. We had plenty of IV fluid and Hare Traction Splint for his leg. I was concerned that if he had internal injuries, such as a fractured pelvis, he'd be bleeding heavily. So I was prepared for everything from a minor fracture that I could splint when we got him on the helicopter, to having to resuscitate him pretty heavily on the ground.

I planned to jump off with one of the Pathfinders to see if Andrews' leg was so bad that we'd need to splint it on the ground before we put him on a stretcher, or whether I could wait to work on him in the aircraft. I knew he was conscious because he was in radio contact, but we still had to move fast to get him on board. We couldn't leave him in the desert long, and the entire crew was vulnerable while we were on the ground. If we started taking fire on the ground, our Black Hawk would leave us three, while the Apaches – the heavily armed attack helicopters – suppressed the enemy fire. The Pathfinders, who took their job very seriously and always went armed to the teeth with grenades and machine guns, would try to hold off any attack. I'd work on Andrews until the Black Hawk could return.

I hoped that Andrews had parachuted away from his F-16, and landed in an empty part of the desert (Kory and his Air Force buddies who fly the bigger F-15s call the deadly little F-16s "lawn darts," partly because of how they look but also because of how they crash.) The Iraqis probably were heading for the wreckage, and we were liable to land right in the middle of a nest of enemy soldiers who had just proven their skill at shooting down American aircraft.

Listening on the radio, I could tell we had two AH-64 Apache attack helicopters flying with us for protection. They were armed with Hellfire missiles, Hydra 70 rockets, and 30mm chain guns in the nose. In the Black Hawk, we just had two small machine guns mounted in the side doors. The Apache, the most sophisticated helicopter in the world, looks like a big metal dragonfly bristling with sensors and antennae and hung with missiles and rockets. They can be flown with special optical equipment that allows the pilots to see at night while looking through a monocle connected to an infrared camera outside the aircraft. It can be terribly disorienting to fly, and back home at Fort Rucker I was doing research on how to improve the pilots' ability to operate the optical systems.

I recognized the voices of the Apache drivers – they all were my patients back home and most of them were my friends. I was glad to hear that one of them was Lance McElhinery arguable the best Apache pilot in the army and certainly my best friend in the world. He could be wild and crazy at times, but when he flew, all that energy and wildness was channeled into manipulating the helicopter, turning a very complicated piece of machinery into a lethal weapons system. His confidence, at the controls and everything, was contagious. When my fourteen-year-old daughter, Regan, had worried about me going to war, my husband told her, "Don't worry, Lance will be there and he won't let anything happen to Mother." That was good enough for Regan.

Overhead an Air Force Airborne Warning and Control System (AWACS) radar plane, call sign "Bulldog," was going to direct us toward the downed pilot. The AWACS, one of the unarmed jets packed with radar and radio equipment that had been orchestrating the air war for six weeks, would fly orbits high above Saudi Arabia, staying in contact with Andrews on the ground and us in the air. We needed directions because the weather was getting worse, and blowing sand made it hard to see. Thick black smoke and choking soot form burning oil wells in nearby Kuwait had darkened the sky early. The pilots debated whether to use their night vision goggles, even though it wasn't yet four in the afternoon.

I heard the Black Hawk's turbine engine whine and rotor picked up speed. The helicopter vibrated and jumped off the ground, creating a dust bowl of sand beneath us. We slipped effortlessly across the desert, just above the ground. We always flew very low because it made us a smaller target. Some of our helicopters had already taken fire, and the pilots were cautious. Now we were heading deeper into enemy territory. For the first fifteen minutes both Apaches, loaded with fuel and "Hellfire heavy," were behind us. Then Lance moved out in front, and the other attack helicopter stayed behind. We were protected in the middle between the two gunships, hurtling over the desert at close to 130 knots.

I remember crossing over a convoy and seeing American vehicles with inverted Vs painted on the sides and tops. Some of the vehicles were flying pieces of orange and yellow cloth to indicate they were friendly forces. We waved to troops bundled up in their bulky chemical gear, and they waved back at us. The air was filled with smoke and soot from oil fires. The door gunners were keeping close watch on the ground below, their hands firmly on the two 7.62mm machine guns that pointed out the side doors.

About forty-five seconds after we passed over the last American vehicle, and without any warning, green tracers began streaking up at us from the ground, while I heard the crack-crack of weapons firing. The empty desert below us erupted with fire and white flashes of light. It was if we were a lawn mower that had run over a beehive, and the bees were coming up to sting. Sergeant Ortiz, the lead Pathfinder, took my head and slammed it to the floor, and in a second all three Pathfinders instinctively were half laying on me with their weapons ready. I almost laughed at their reaction: it would have been a good way to cover me in a foxhole, but we were in a helicopter. I'm sure their hearts were in the right place, but the rounds were coming up at us from the ground, so I was actually shielding them. The Pathfinders were very protective of me because that was their mission: protect the doctor and the patient. We didn't have the patient yet, so they worried about protecting me.

The two door gunners – SSgt. Daniel Stamaris and Sfc. William T. Butts – were fighting back and spraying machine –gun fire at the ground. I heard the sharp pop-

pop-pop and clank of metal, and smelled acrid burning gunpowder inside the helicopter. The shell casings were jumping out of our smoking black door guns like brass popcorn, and one hit me in the face. It felt hot against my skin. One of the pilots shouted over the radio, "We're taking fire." Looking back, I'm sure he was informing the AWACS plane about what was happening, but at that moment, pressed to the floor under the weight of the Pathfinders, all I could think was, No kidding.

We heard the rattling Iraqi antiaircraft guns following us across the sky, and the rounds began tearing through the metal tail boom and the fuselage and rocking the aircraft. I clutched the floor in front of me, not knowing if a bullet would come ripping up through the helicopter and into my body. It would only take one round, and we were flying through a wall of lead, as if we had been caught in a sudden cloudburst of bullets. The pilots tried to get away by breaking sharply to the left. The army would call it an "evasive maneuver," but we call it "yanking and banking." The helicopter was still just a few feet off the ground, but I never saw any Iraqis, only their tracers and the muzzle flashes.

I felt something big hit the aircraft and I knew it wasn't doing well. The engine strained and the fuselage shook and shimmied. Then Garvey yelled, "We're going in!" I was trying to make myself smaller on the floor during the shooting. The firefight probably lasted only twelve seconds, but there was a big adrenaline rush that made my brain work faster so time seemed slower. I remember having time to hold on, knowing we were going to crash. I was thinking, I wonder if this is it, is this the end? What will it be like? I don't even remember being scared; it was more like curiosity. I took hold of something on the door frame and felt the aircraft shuddering. We were still banked to the left when the left nose hit the sand, flattening, and then twenty thousand pounds of aircraft went end over end in a ball of flying metal and gear and spinning rotors. Everything went black.

I was lying on my back with a big piece of the wreck on my chest pinning me to the ground. It seemed like it was completely dark already, but it couldn't have been because it was afternoon. The air was chilly, but I didn't feel cold. My head was lying to the left, my arms were at my sides and I was very conformable, very peaceful. I had no desire to move. Nothing hurt as I lay motionless. The gray sky above me was empty and quiet. In fact it was absolutely still. There was no more shooting, no rotor sounds, no yelling or scratchy radio traffic; there was nothing. It was just still, and my first thought was that maybe I was dead and this was an out-of-body experience. I could see, or rather I could feel, this scene on the desert floor: a big piece of the fuselage and me pinned under it.

I was relaxed, calm, nestled in the sand, until I glanced farther to the left toward an embankment and say a yellow flame. The fear was like a spark beneath me: Fire. Fuel lines. Explosion coming. I wasn't totally convinced that I was alive, but if I was, there was no way I was going to die in a post-crash fire. That was the only thing that motivated me to try to move; otherwise I could have stayed there forever. I didn't think to call out for help. I was on my own, alone. The pile of broken metal was so quiet that I was sure I was the only survivor. And if the enemy was nearby, I didn't want to call out and alert him that I was alive.

I had to get out by myself, but I couldn't move my arms, presumably because they were pinned. I took stock of what I could use to escape from under the fuselage. The only part of my body that still worked reasonably well was my left leg. I pulled the good leg toward me and straightened it again to push the sand away. I pushed and pushed to clear the sand from underneath my right leg. Luckily we had crashed on sand and not on rocks, so the ground was soft. I dug and scraped at the sand until there was a shallow hole underneath me that freed my legs from the fuselage. With my body in the slight hole, I could move my right leg a little, but my knee hurt badly. I didn't mind, though, because if it hurt, I figured it was still connected, and it was another sign that I was alive.

The flame flicked in the corner of my eyes. Keep digging, All I could think about was, I have to get out from under the helicopter. I dug the heel of my left boot deeper into the ground and pushed away more sand. When I was clear enough to move, I tried to turn over and crawl out, but I couldn't turn or crawl. My arms were no longer stuck under the fuselage, but they wouldn't respond. I couldn't move them at all. I'm hurt worse than I thought, I realized. Things are broken. Still, there was no pain, just numbness as the shock of the crash froze the nerves.

I was wiggling around on my left side trying to get out and away from the helicopter when I looked up and saw four or five Iraqi soldiers standing over me. They were wearing good uniforms and helmets and carrying AK-47s, the Soviet-made assault rifle. They had a professional way about them, and I recognized them as members of the Republican Guard. One of them, without saying anything, reached down and grabbed my right arm. He pulled hard to get me up, and the pain shot through me and came out my mouth in a piercing scream. It wasn't even the pain that got to me as much as the sound: a crunching noise or the sound of grinding teeth, a sound not so much that I heard but felt. My arm was broken between the shoulder and the elbow, but it wasn't a displace fracture. At least not until the Iraqi pulled apart the pieces of bone.

The men were talking among themselves in Arabic. I couldn't understand the words, but it seemed they were trying to decide what to do with me. A couple of them swarmed over me like ants, taking off my pistol, my survival vest with the radio, my flak jacket, and my helmet. I stood still, looking at the ground. When they took off my helmet, my hair came tumbling down. That's when they realized I was female. There was a flurry of comment about it, and they talked louder and faster for a minute, but I couldn't understand them. I stared straight ahead, standing with my weight on my left leg since my right leg hurt when I tried to stand on it. I was just a few feet from the wreckage. The helicopter had disintegrated and pieces were thrown everywhere, but I didn't see any fire. The flames I'd seen must have been from a nearby campfire or from oil wells burning in the distance. Or maybe I just imagined them.

One of the Iraqis grabbed my arm again and tried to drag me forward. I yelled sharply in pain, and he dropped my arm. The arm flopped in front of me like a piece of meat, completely out of my control. Then he grabbed a bunch of my hair, and pulled me along with him across the sand. I had no choice but to follow, trying to keep my balance. It sounds like caveman behavior, but actually it was far better than trying to take me by the arm. I realized that not one arm, but both of them, were broken between the elbows and shoulders, and they were swinging uselessly beside me like sticks tied to my shoulders with string. They reminded me of horses I had seen with their legs broken so badly that only the skin was holding on the hooves, like rocks in a sock. I stumbled along in the sand, trying not to fall but unsure of my right knee. It felt like a busted hinge on a broken door, and I thought it might collapse under me. If I fell, I couldn't protect myself, and I'd hurt my arms even more.

What if my arms weren't just broken? Oh, God, what if they're severed? What if they're being held on by my flight suit? No, they hurt too much. They must be attached. Thank goodness for the pain. I imagined there were open fractures beneath the thick sleeves of the flight suit and I was losing blood. I felt weak and nauseous, which must have been caused by a lack of blood, but I couldn't see any serious open wounds. There was blood on one hand from a cut and I knew there was blood above my eye, but not enough to make me feel so dizzy. I still wasn't sure how badly I was injured.

The sky was growing darker. The Iraqis didn't have flashlights, but they obviously knew where we were going. I wasn't going fast enough, and one of them kicked me in the butt, making me lurch forward and almost most knocking me down. I stumbled but didn't cry out or yell. Keep control. Don't succumb. I recovered my balance and kept walking, my eyes straight ahead. The soldiers were excited about having a prisoner, and they were saying things to me in guttural Arabic, a language I'd always considered pretty. But now their shouted words and harsh invectives didn't sound pretty at all.

I wasn't afraid at that point. There had been times in the past when I'd thought about being captured and tried to imagine what it would be like, but there wasn't really any way to prepare for the experience. Actually, I'd always thought it more likely that I'd be killed rather than captured. I'm not overly pessimistic; it's just that usually Air Force or Navy pilots eject from their high-flying jets, parachute to the ground, and are captured. In the Army we don't even wear parachutes in a helicopter because we fly so low. If you managed to somehow eject, you'd be decapitated by the rotor, so in the army we "ride in" the wrecks. If you crash in a fast-moving helicopter, there is little chance of surviving to be captured by the enemy.

Crew members frequently survive in slower-moving accidents, however, and I remember talking to my Army pilots about this before the war. They weren't afraid of death; they were afraid of landing behind enemy lines or having engine trouble that led to being captured. All the pilots had heard stories about what the Iraqis would do to the "infidels" if they caught us, stories of torture and abuse. Back where we lived in Saudi before the start of the ground war, we'd seen the Iraqi pictures of captured American pilots. They'd been forced to make videos denouncing the war. We'd also heard about the special abuse reserved for the woman of Kuwait. Some Iraqi soldiers had behaved like animals, raping and sexually torturing Arab and foreign woman living there.

Back home before the war, Kory and I had talked about something bad happening to one of us, but we always thought he was in more danger because he flew jets. From his base in Florida, he often flew F-15s far out over the ocean, and he could have been lost at sea in a mid-air collision or if something happened to the aircraft. The likelihood of me being captured or killed doing research at the Aeromedical Laboratory at Fort Rucker was pretty low. I had thought occasionally about dying, especially when we deployed to Saudi Arabia and were preparing for war. I did that on purpose, though; it was part of my psychological survival plan. In any dangerous situation, I always try to imagine the worst thing that could happen to me. Then whatever does happen has to be better, or at least no worse.

I'd talked about dying in my final letters to my family, just before February 24, when we launched the air assault north and west of Kuwait to cut off the Republican Guard. We only half-jokingly called the mission the "Air Assault to Hell," and we knew it would be dangerous. I wanted my family to know that I went to war because the battalion wanted me to go, and I wanted to be with them. I wrote my grandparents that I was proud of what I was doing, and that if anything happened to me, they should remember that I chose to be here. I told my sister that if something bad happened, she should make sure my parents didn't do anything embarrassing. My worst fear was that they would shame me or the army, that they would be hysterical, try to sue the government, or say I shouldn't have been in combat because I was a doctor or a woman or just because I was their daughter. All I hoped was that my parents would take their folded American flag gracefully after the funeral, say "Thank you," and quietly hang it on the wall somewhere. As things turned out, they didn't exactly follow my plan.

I'd been writing to my daughter, Regan, every day since the air war began on January 17, but once the ground campaign began, I wanted to send her a special letter. She was only fourteen, but I wanted her to understand what I was doing and why. During all those months in Saudi Arabia, not having her with me was the only hole in my life. Regan was born when I was still in college, and we had grown up together. She already was bigger than I am, and was a pretty good fullback on her soccer team at school. She was at that stage in life where she felt she had to choose between wearing makeup and playing sports with boys, and for now, she was leaning toward sports. I was so proud of her, and my love for her was beyond any words I could find to put on paper.

The Iraqis led me toward a hole that opened in the earth like the shadowed entrance to a coal mine. In the fading light of the darkening evening I could see sandbag stairs leading down into an underground bunker. This network of bunkers was the reason we had not seen any Iraqi soldiers form the helicopter. They had been completely protected when firing at us as we flew overhead. The passageway was fairly wide, but there were soldiers lining both sides of the stairs. Two guards went ahead of me and two followed behind, pushing me step by step through the gauntlet of soldiers. They jeered and shouted at me, but no one tried to touch me as I slowly negotiated the stairs with a bad leg and two broken arms. I didn't know what the men were saying, but it was clear they weren't happy to see me. I had the feeling they were gloating because they had just shot us down, and we had crashed right on top of their bunkers.

The bunker was very well made, about fourteen steps underground. If they had wanted to the Iraqis could have stayed there defending it forever. There was a kerosene lantern below, and as my eyes adjusted to the faint light, I could see that the walls had been scraped out of the earth with a backhoe. It smelled of dirt and men and sweat. I didn't see any other members of my crew, and I assumed I was the only survivor. At the bottom of the stairs, there was a junior Iraqi officer, probably a lieutenant, sitting at a wooden table, staring at me and processing of jeering soldiers. He questioned one of my guards and then said to me in heavily accented English, "Who are you?"

"Major Rhonda Cornum."

I was not going to keep my name secret, since it was printed on the name tag on my flight suit. I noticed that my dog tag chain was partially out of my flight suit, and I remember my wedding ring threaded on the chain. I thought about trying to swallow the ring, remembering what Kory and I had talked about, but I couldn't move my arms at all.

The lieutenant ignored me, and talked to his men. One of them loosely tied my hands in front of me with a thin piece of rope. They searched me again and took my journal and the little camera I kept in the right leg pocket of my flight suit. I felt bad because the camera actually belonged to my daughter, who had let me borrow it to take to Saudi Arabia. I had some good pictures of our unit taking Iraqi prisoners on that roll, so it was probably a good thing they didn't have anywhere to process the prints.

The lieutenant barked an order at his men. I didn't understand, but they started to move me toward the stairs. The guards pushed me up the sandbag stairs again, past the same group of soldiers who had nothing better to do than jeer at me. I had to walk slowly because my knee wasn't working well as I left the warmth and yellow lantern light of the bunker and stepped back into the cold air and flat gray light above ground.

It was then that I saw Sergeant Dunlap, the young Pathfinder who had desperately wanted to get on the helicopter. He was in the center of a circle of ten Iraqi soldiers, kneeling down in the sand, looking at the ground in front of him. His hands were tied behind his back. My hands were tied in front, which was a good thing, really, because it kept my hands from flopping. I didn't know Dunlap well at all; we had spoken maybe fifty words since coming over to Saudi, mostly of the "Good Morning" or "Yes, ma'am" variety. He'd never been one of my patients; he must never have gotten sick.

I'd known some of the other crew members on board well, such as Sergeant Ortiz. We had gone on many missions together, and just before we deployed Iraq, I'd done a physical on him so he could apply to flight school. Godfrey had given me that big hug just this morning. There were no jokes between us then, none of the usual wisecracks, just a genuine hug. Godfrey, Ortiz, and the others must be dead.

I'd never even seen Dunlap without his helmet. Now I saw his close-cropped haircut, scraggly blond mustache, and big eyes wide with fear. He looked strange without his helmet, vulnerable. I was relieved to find another American, and it didn't matter if I knew him well. Right then he felt like a friend. I felt responsible for him, even though I was in no condition to be responsible for anybody.

Dunlap and I didn't try to say anything, but the Iraqis kept yelling, "No talking!" One of the guards led me into the circle of men and pushed me alongside Dunlap. The guard put his hand heavily on my shoulder and tried to shove me to the ground. I resisted for a moment because I was afraid I would fall on my bad knee, but then I carefully went down on my left knee and balanced precariously. Dunlap glanced over at me and gave me a little smile. I nudged him, as much as I could nudge him with my arms broken, and I said something stupid, something motherly: "It's going to be okay." He smiled weakly. Dunlap was almost young enough to be my son. He was twenty; I was thirty-six. I was a doctor and an officer; he was an enlisted man. I couldn't really do much for him, but I felt responsible and I wanted to make him feel better. "No talking!" one of the Iraqis yelled in English.

There were two soldiers standing behind us, both with rifles pointed at our uncovered heads. I could feel the cold metal barrel poking me in the back of the neck. The Iraqis were having an animated discussion, and it seemed they were trying to decide what to do with us. This was the first time I was truly afraid. It was then that I realized we would be killed.

The war had been going badly for them, and many of their comrades had died. Some had been buried in bunkers just like these when American B-52 strikes turned the underground shelters into sandy tombs. The American enemy had been elusive, distant, airborne. The Americans dropped their bombs from high above, never within range of Iraqi small arms, and flew back to the safety of Saudi Arabia. Now these men had a chance for revenge. The soldiers who had found us could have saved themselves the trouble and killed us at the crash site, but they'd waited for instructions from their commander. The lieutenant must have ordered them to kill us.

My head was lowered, and my hair had fallen in my face. I couldn't see out of my left eye; it was smashed shut and my hair was stuck to it with matted blood. My right eye swept back and forth across the ground in front of me, and I saw pebbles on the ground, small rocks with jagged edges. The air was cool around us. One of the guards spoke a few words of English and he seemed to say, "Kill them! Kill them!" I waited for the click of metal and the explosion. The moment seemed to last forever. My pain had vanished with fear. My last thought was, At least it won't hurt.

Without warning, a strong hand grabbed me by the hair and jerked me to my feet. Another soldier roughly pulled up Dunlap. The ring of shouting Iraqis parted, and they marched Dunlap across the sand to a small civilian pickup truck, with me following. What are they doing? Maybe we're not going to be killed. At least for now. It seemed the Iraqis couldn't decide what to do with us, and the discussion continued. I followed quietly; there was nothing else to do. We were prisoners, but maybe we were being allowed to live.

I was badly injured, but I knew I'd heal eventually. The crash had been so devastating that I should have died then, and I regarded every minute I was alive as a gift. The Iraqis could have killed us easily when they found us at the crash site, but they chose not to. Then in the circle of men, a slight pressure on a single trigger would have been enough to kill us, but we had been spared. It was just enough good luck for me to grab on to and hold. I vowed to survive.

The soldiers pushed Dunlap into the truck first. I walked to the back and put my left leg up on the bumper, trying to ease myself into the truck. But someone pushed me up from behind and hurled me into the truck. I couldn't catch myself, and I rattled down on my shoulder and let out a raw scream of pain. Dunlap tried to catch me and strained against the bonds that held his arms; I could see the anguish in his dirt-streaked face. Two guards got in and sat down next to us. I managed to sit up in the bed of the truck and straighten my bad leg. It was horribly frustrating to not be able to control my own body. Everything I had done in my life until then had been active. I didn't make a living sitting around; I made a living doing things. Now I was helpless.

As the truck lurched along, I concentrated on keeping my arms forward and slowly walking my fingers together until I could hook them in my lap. If I could do that, then my arms were still attached, and I had some control. It meant I had circulation to the arms and that the nerves had not been severed. Well, maybe this problem is fixable after all, I thought. With every bump on the pitted road, I was tossed around in the bed of the truck, banging my knee and arms and wincing in pain. It was excruciating if my arms swung lose, so I kept my fingers locked together in front of me. I bit my tongue and vowed not to scream. Dunlap was watching me, and without saying anything because the two guards in back didn't allow us to talk, he put his strong legs on top of mine so I wouldn't bounce. I smiled a thank you.

As long as I didn't move anything, my arms didn't hurt. The brain is very good at knocking out pain when it's not useful. I was withdrawn, pulled inside of myself, concentrating on staying conscious because it would have been so easy to have just given up and relaxed, drifting off into sleep. Stay awake. Remain an active participant. Stay with Dunlap. Mostly, I didn't want to be unconscious with the Iraqis. I felt them staring at me, their dark eyes raking over my body. I didn't know if I was afraid of what they might do to me, or if I wanted to present an image of strength, but it was very important to concentrate on being conscious. I didn't have much energy left to expand on anything else.

The bouncing pickup truck finally stopped, and this time one of the guards lowered the tailgate so I could get out more easily. They led Dunlap and me about twenty-five yards across the sand toward the entrance to another bunker. I was having trouble seeing because it was dark, and my eye was pasted shut with dried blood and mud and hair. I couldn't control my arms at all, and although they didn't hurt too much if I was still, every time they did move it was as if I'd been stuck with a hot knife. One of the soldiers took what appeared to be a shoelace and tied my hands loosely in front of me again. Since I was clearly unable to use my arms, and obviously couldn't threaten him, perhaps he did it just so my arms wouldn't flop as I walked. We walked down into another bunker. The single room was about twelve feet long and six feet wide and had two feet of dirt overhead held up by timbers for protection from bombs. It smelled dank and musty. At the bottom of the steps there was a young officer, maybe thirty years old and probably a captain. When I entered this second bunker, the officer stood up from his wooden chair.

"Who are you?" he asked.

"Major Rhonda Cornum."

There were six Iraqis in the bunker with Dunlap and me, and we could stand easily. I was clearly the senior officer of the two Americans, even though I was a woman, and the Iraqis directed their questions to me. One of the Iraqis was taking notes on a clipboard. They wore uniforms with green sweaters and had their pants tucked into their boots. They were neat, well shaven, and well groomed.

"What is your unit?" the young officer asked.

I looked out at them, all a head taller than me. I knew I should tell them as little as possible, and I didn't want to give them the name of my unit. But I was wearing a green patch on my flight suit that had tiny black swords and little winged tigers (because of the "Flying Tigers" nickname). The patch read "2-229th Atk-Hel-Regt," which even the Iraqis çould have figured out meant a battalion of the 229th Attack Helicopter Regiment.

"The 229th," I said.

"What are you?" the officer asked.

"I'm a doctor."

"A doctor in the army?"

"Yes," I said, figuring it was better to appear reasonable than to refuse to speak. I wasn't going to tell them anything important, but I didn't want them to beat me just to find out the obvious, like the name of my unit or my job.

"What are you doing here?"

"We were shot down on a search-and-rescue mission, sir."

"Who were you going to rescue?"

I looked him in the eye and told my first lie. "I don't know."

"What kind of airplane were you looking for?"

"I don't know that either, sir."

"What shot you down?"

"I have no idea."

I noticed again that my dog tags had spilled out of my flight suit and were lying across my chest. I could see my wedding ring. I looked back into the face of the Iraqi officer, but he had noticed the ring, too. He said something in Arabic to the soldiers and gestured at me. One of the soldiers took hold of my dog tags and tried to lift the chain up over my head. I leaned back so he wouldn't take it, but he yanked the chain off anyway. The officer didn't say anything, he just looked at my name and Social Security number on the tags. He held the ring, but made no comment.

While he was pondering what to do, his soldiers peeled off my name tag and the "Flying Tigers" patch, and cut off the XVIII Aviation Brigade patch, which was sewn onto the left shoulder of the flight suit. I don't know why they removed the markings from my uniform, except perhaps to strip me of my rank and drive home the fact that I was their prisoner. Maybe they wanted souvenirs.

Going through my pockets again, the soldiers found two little rocks. They handed them to the captain.

'What are these?" the officer wanted to know. "What are they for?" asked, apparently expecting them to be some secret weapon.

"Well, as a matter of fact," I admitted, "they were going to be souvenirs from Iraq."

"What?"

"Never mind."

"You can leave now," the officer told me, and gave an order in Arabic to my guards.

"May I have my chain back? May I have my ring?" I asked.

He didn't respond, and the guards pushed me back up the stairs to the desert floor. They were less rough with me now; I think they realized that I was badly hurt. There was no advantage to yelling at me and kicking me, because I simply could not move any faster. I wasn't resisting; I was injured.

We walked over to the pickup, and luckily for me, they had left down a tailgate. I sat on it and swung my legs up onto the bed. Then I back along the gritty metal floor to the rear. Dunlap, whose hands were tied behind his back, climbed in after me and draped his legs across mine. We bounced down another track, a dirt road, but there was no way to know where we were going. It looked like a bulldozer had been through and carved roads out of the hard sand. Apparently, we had crashed in the middle of a Republican Guard bunker complex. I knew our AWACS radar plane had been in radio contact with us until the crash so they must have known where we were captured. Outside the second bunker, I could hear what sounded like the crump of artillery in the background. They might have been bombs, but whatever they were, I figured they were ours. In a way it was comforting to know were pounding the Iraqis; but at that point I was afraid we would hit by one of our own munitions.

After about fifteen minutes, we arrived at the third bunker. This was turning out to be a House and Garden, tour of the desert bunker complex, but I don't think that was the Iraqis' intention. More likely they were trying to figure out what to do with us, and were sending us up the chain of command. Rather than make a decision about our fate, each officer we saw was passing us along to the next level of command. I understood that behavior very well.

The third bunker was a larger, two-room chamber that had walls lined with sand bags and was lit with a kerosene lantern. There was a burlap divider in the middle, with wooden supports holding it taut. My guess was that this bunker belonged to a battalion-level commander. It was obvious that someone lived there and also used it as an officc. There was a Persian rug on the floor, books on the shelves, and a pallet made up as a cot on the ground.

A good-looking, neatly dressed officer, about thirty-five or forty years old, was waiting for us. Some of the Iraqi prisoners we had taken early in the war did not look very soldierly, but these men were all squared away and disciplined. One of the soldiers who had escorted me into the bunker led me to the pallet and tried to push me down to sit. I think he was trying to make me more comfortable, but I was rocked by a powerful wave of nausea. I was no longer as afraid as I had been in the first bunker, and I was trying to be very professional and polite, but now I thought I was going to be sick, from both pain and blood loss. I didn't want to vomit on my host's rug, I walked toward the entrance, expecting them to yell at me or push me down, but I was not going to stop. The Iraqis said nothing, and no one offered to help me.

The nausea came in waves, more like ripples, that pulsed through my entire body. I made it to the bottom of the stairs and leaned against the sandbag wall. Sweating and shivering, I tried to pull the cool air from outside down into my lungs. Slowly, the dizziness eased and I recovered. I realized that I must have lost a substantial amount of blood, but I still couldn't figure out where I was bleeding. I felt blood on my face, and I saw a little on my hand, but not enough to make me so weak.

When I could walk again, the guard pointed me back to the pallet to sit. I couldn't bend my leg, though, and wasn't sure how I could sit. Even worse, I was sure I wouldn't be able to get back up by myself, and I desperately wanted to avoid being raised by my arms again. The Iraqi guard thought I didn't understand what he was saying, so he pushed me harder. I fell with my back against the wall, trying to slide down as slowly as possible onto the pallet. This was the officer's bed, and it had a colorful quilt spread on top of the thin foam mattress. The officer stood in front of me and looked down into my face.

"What are you doing here?"

"A search-and-rescue mission, sir," I said coldly.

At that point, I didn't hate my captors or snarl at them, but I was not feeling very sociable. I was very mad at the one who had taken wedding ring. I was obsessed with just how unfair it was, and I was afraid that Kory would be disappointed that I hadn't swallowed it. By that time in the war, we had taken hundreds of Iraqi prisoners our in unit, and we had not stolen anything from anyone. These guys stole my ring. There was no nice way to say it; they just flat stole it.

I didn't have a wallet with me, and I had purposely left my Geneva Conventions card and identification cards packed on our truck with the medics. I figured that if I was going on these kinds of missions, I had given up my protected status as a doctor. Technically, medical personnel are not supposed to be made prisoners of war. The Geneva Conventions state that doctors are to be returned to their side unless they are caring for soldiers from their units who also are prisoners. I didn't want to make a big deal of being a doctor, however, partly because I didn't want to be treated differently than other officers, but also because we all had heard the Iraqis didn't like doctors.

The story was that Iraqi soldiers had been interrogated and tortured by doctors when captured during their bloody, eight-year war with Iran.

I couldn't lie about being a doctor, though, and like my name, it is printed on the badge I wear on my uniform. On the leather name tag, where a pilot has wings and a shield, I have wings and a caduceus. The insignia has the winged staff of Mercury, with two serpents coiled around it, and symbolizes the medical profession. The badge identifies me as a flight surgeon.

This officer appeared very professional to me, but he was tired, battle-weary. It seemed that they were still fighting, but he was not gloating at all about having two American prisoners. He gave the impression of being genuinely concerned about me, and if he resented Dunlap and me, it probably was only because we meant more paperwork for him. Most of the time during those first few hours in captivity was spent on logistical problems, trying to decide what to do with us and where to send us. No one seemed to care that I was a woman The Iraqis apparently accepted the fact that there are women physicians, and that I was one of them.

They did not seem very interested in interrogating either of us. They asked Dunlap the same kind of questions: his name and what he was doing. That's all. I was relieved because I didn't want to tell them anything that could hurt the war effort or endanger people in my unit. Pilots in air force, navy, and marines, as well as special operations, are given entire courses on what to do if they are shot down, what they can say and what they should not say. Kory had taken the course—known as Survival, Escape, Resistance and Evasion (SERE)—and told me about it, but to tell the truth, most of what I knew about being a prisoner of war came from old war movies: give only your name, rank, and serial number. No one ever asked me my serial number. I'm sure I had taken training on the military Code of Conduct at some point during my career, but I think it was thirteen years earlier at the Officer Basic Course, and all I could remember was that I shouldn't accept favors from the enemy and shouldn't do anything to hurt my fellow prisoners or the mission. I knew in my heart that I would refuse to make a video for Iraqi television denouncing the United States, but I also knew my captors could eventually make me do anything, just as they had the other prisoners of war.

I was thinking more clearly now, When the Iraqi patrol first pulled me out of the wreck, I was in a foggy daze and was easily led around by my captors. My focus was on survival. The longer I was conscious, the stronger I felt. They could have killed me at any time, but apparently they wanted me alive. What really sharpened my thinking was the theft of my wedding ring. It was the anger that finally snapped me out of my daze. Before then I had been responding, following their orders, but not really thinking for myself. Now my mind was working again.

The officer quickly tired of talking with me. I realize now that his world was collapsing around him, and the last thing he needed was two American prisoners. He said something to the guard, who reached down and pulled me up by the front of my uniform. Fortunately he didn't try to grab me by the arm. Another guard pushed Dunlap forward, and we went back up the stairs, outside and into the darkness.

They led us across the sand to a different truck. I think we were at an airfield or

some base not far from Basra, but there were no lights or markings to help me identify the location. The guards loaded us onto a pickup truck that had benches and rails
on the sides. They put Dunlap on the bench across from me, and a guard sat alongside each of us. It was dark and cold—it must have been around 9 P.M.—and they put
army blankets over us. I was wet, and I wondered if I had crashed in a puddle or a
patch of mud. I shivered in the cold, even with the blanket over me. I sat leaning forward, hunched over, because if I leaned back against the side of the truck I felt a stinging pain in my right shoulder. In the cab of the truck, there were a driver and another soldier riding shotgun.

They drove out onto a paved road, and the cool air going by made me shake with
cold. We passed thick sand berms and protected positions that formed a network of
bunkers shaped like giant mole hills. We had to slow down to climb up and over some
of these berms, and for the first time in months, I noticed bushes and trees growing
in the sand. I thought we must be near the fertile Euphrates River valley. We had
been doing missions there, but I didn't recognize anything.

The guard was sitting so close to me that our shoulders touched, and I tried to lean
away from him. My arms hurt so much that I could not lean very far either way and,
giving up, I tried to just stare ahead and ignore him. Dunlap, whose arms were tied
behind his back, had one of his legs stretched across the bed of the truck, and I could
feel his boot on the bench beside me. The guard next to me quietly reached my blanket, and I could feel him untie my hands. What is this guy doing? I thought.

Suddenly he started pawing my head and face and trying to push the muddy,
blood-caked strands of hair out of my face. He kissed me on the mouth and face. I
could feel his clean-shaven face rubbing mine, and I could smell him against me. He
actually smelled good. I thought, Why does he want to do this? I couldn't believe it.
Normally I don't consider myself ugly, or even unattractive, but all I felt then was beat
up and dirty. I certainly wasn't feeling amorous. I remember thinking, Hey, you could
do better than this. I was not only repulsed by his advances, but amazed. But he
wouldn't stop, and I moved my head and shook it away from him. Then he tried kissing my neck and my ears. "No, no, no," I insisted. He pulled the blanket over our
heads so we would not be seen and to muffle the sound. He reached of me, grabbed
the zipper on my flight suit and clumsily pulled it down. I squirmed but there was no
place to go. I had promised myself I wouldn't scream unless I was in life-threatening
danger or something so painful I couldn't stand it, but when he tried to yank the flight
suit down over my shoulder, it was like a jolt of electricity had shocked mo to the
bone. My scream made him stop for a second, but then he fondling my breasts and
kissing me. When I leaned away again, he tried to push me off the seat and onto the
bed of the truck, but the blast of pain made me scream again. He stopped. Every time
I yelled, he stopped.

I realized then that he stopped not because of my pain, but because he was doing
something he was not supposed to do, and he was afraid his comrades in the cab would
hcar mc scream. Sergeant Dunlap could hear me and helplessly watched the battle
under the blanket. It drove him wild with rage. My bigger fear was not so much being
raped, but that Dunlap might try to do something stupid to defend me and get him-

self shot. I could feel Dunlap's boot against my side, and I reached down as beat I could until I managed to lightly wrap my hand around his boot. I focused my energy into my hand and firmly squeezed the young sergeant's ankle. Even though the action sent bursts of pain through my arm, I desperately wanted Dunlap to know that I was conscious and that I appreciated him being there. "It's okay, sergeant," I tried to say with every painful squeeze of my hand, "I'll be okay."

We had heard the stories of what the Iraqi soldiers had done to women in Kuwait, so I had thought about the probability that I would be sexually abused if I were captured. I had never considered that I would be so badly injured, though. When I really was shot down, I was thinking of myself as a soldier, and a POW, and a very severely injured person. I was not thinking of myself as a woman. I was amazed that this Iraqi soldier could only see me as a woman.

My screams, and the fortunate impossibility of getting me out of my flight suit with two broken arms, kept the molester at bay until finally, after driving for what seemed like forever but in fact was probably only thirty minutes, we stopped in front of a squat, single-story building. In the darkness, it appeared to be a small prison. There were no lights on anywhere, but I'm not sure whether that was because the electrical grids had been destroyed by American and allied bombs or because the Iraqis practiced good light discipline, which means they switched off the lights to avoid attracting enemy bombs.

Someone from inside the darkened building came out to greet the soldiers driving the truck. They got out and pulled Dunlap and me down from the back. The molester said nothing, and he stayed with the truck while we were led through a door and down about seven steps. They marched us along a cinder-block hallway past two closed metal doors. At the third door, we stopped and they pushed Dunlap into a cell. I was led a few more steps on the damp, concrete floor. The thick, cool air made me think we were underground again. The guards opened a wide metal door and led me into my cell. It had a single, roughly eight inch-square window above my head, There was a bar across the window but even as small as I am, I could not have squeezed through the tiny hole. There was a small opening in the door covered with a curtain on the outside, so the guards could look in, but I couldn't see into the hallway. The metal door, as thick as the door on a bank vault, was secured outside with a deadbolt.

The entire room was about six feet by eight feet, and a wooden bench ran the length of one wall. The bench had been worn smooth and shiny by prisoners perched there. I managed to sit on the edge of the bench, but I couldn't lean back because my arms, left untied by the molester, would swing and I couldn't bear the pain. Also, there was something wrong with my back. I had a sharp, stinging pain, especially when I leaned against my right side. A faint light, probably from a lantern, came under the door from the hall. I could barely see, but when I looked carefully, I could make out the smeared remains of tiny bugs and mosquitoes that had been smashed on the walls by the previous occupants of the cell.

It was in that cell that I first realized I had not lost everything. For a few moments, I even found my sense of humor intact. That was when my concerns over the big issues of torture, captivity, the military Code of Conduct, and even death, evaporated in the face of a more immediate problem: I bad to go to the bathroom.

I looked around the cell and didn't see a toilet, a bucket, or even a hole in the floor. I had last been to the bathroom about 1 P.M., and now it had to be about 10:30 that night. I couldn't be sure of the time, because the Iraqis had taken my watch, too. It was only an eighteen-dollar watch, but it had an alarm, and I remember hoping the alarm would go off and drive them crazy trying to stop it.

The guards had closed the door and left me alone. I sat on the bench for maybe fifteen minutes pondering what to do about my bladder, until I stiffly struggled to my feet and hobbled over to the door. I heard the guards talking in the hall, and I didn't want to interrupt. I'm naturally polite, really, and I was afraid of making them mad. When it finally was quiet, I called out for the guard. No answer. I yelled, "Guard!" and kicked the door, and the noise boomed down the hallway. A man wearing a white robe and leather sandals shuffled slowly to the door and pulled back the curtain on the outside to peer into the cell. He was forty-five or fifty years old and looked like he had been in bed when I called. I stepped away from the door, and he pushed it open.

"I need to go to the bathroom," I explained.

He looked at me quizzically.

"Bathroom. I need the bathroom."

"W.C.?"

"Yes, yes. W.C. Water closet. That's it. I need to go to the water closet."

He motioned for me to follow, but I said, "No. My flight suit."

He waved at me again and said to follow him to the water closet. I sighed in frustration. "I can't go to the water closet with my flight suit on." I couldn't move my arms, so there was no way I could get the suit off by myself. I couldn't even raise my hands to lower the zipper, and the pain had been unbearable when the soldier on the truck had tried, to yank it down past my shoulders. I tried to point to the zipper with my chin, but I looked like a pigeon with my head bobbing up and down.

"Water closet," he insisted.

"Flight suit," I responded. I was afraid I would get to the bathroom, and he would leave without helping with the flight suit. I had to go so badly that I didn't think I could walk down the hall and then have a long discussion with him about how I was going to do it. I didn't want to talk with my captors at all, and I even considered going in my pants, but I didn't know how long this flight suit would be my only set of clothes. On the bright side, and this was the optimistic doctor in me, I thought that if I had to urinate so badly, it meant that my kidneys were still working. That meant I had not lost a truly dangerous amount of blood.

The gray-haired guard looked at me with a baffled expression on his acne-scarred face. Then he turned around, walked out the door, and closed it behind him.

He came back a few moments later with another guard, this one so skinny that his military uniform was hanging from his body. "Water closet," the first guard said.

'Take off my flight suit," I repeated, trying to point with my head to the suit, I had my fingers locked together in front of me to keep my arms from swinging, and I tried to knock my hands against the flight suit.

"Water closet," he repeated.

"You can say it as loudly and as slowly as you want to," I said, "but I can't do anything until you take off my clothes.'

They spoke to each other in Arabic, walked out of the cell, and closed the door behind them. Two minutes later, I heard the dead bolt slide back and the door was pushed open. In walked the first guard in the robe, the second skinny guard, and now a third guard, also dressed in a military uniform but stout and strong. The new guard was carrying a dark blue robe with black stripes, the type of robe worn by the Arab men and made of a heavy wool. It had three buttons down the front and a little collar.

The third guard, apparently the brains of the operation, rolled up the blue robe the way a woman would roll up a stocking before stepping into it. He placed the rolled robe over my head and let it rest on my shoulders like a tire. The guards were very serious about this operation and were quiet except for a few traded words of instruction in Arabic. I stood quietly, hoping they knew what they were doing but mostly hoping they would hurry.

The front zipper on the flight suit was not damaged, and one of the guards pulled it all the way open. My arms were so sore and swollen, however, that the suit could not be pulled down over them. Every time my arms moved, the pain was excruciating. I gritted my teeth and vowed not to scream. I could feel the bones grinding together, and I had to force myself to relax the muscles to ease the bones back into place. The guards quickly understood the problem, and after more discussion in Arabic, the two uniformed guards reached into their pockets and pulled out folding knives.

I wasn't scared, even when I saw the knives. I could tell these men wanted to help me. They saw the situation as a problem to be solved, not an opportunity to be taken. Luckily, the molester was gone. The man in the white robe took hold of the blue robe resting on my shoulders, while each uniformed guard gently took one of my arms. They opened their knives and began to pick at the fabric of the sleeves, cutting slits up to the collar. I could not stand any movement of my arms, and each time they jerked, I felt a deep, sharp pain like being stabbed. Only the pain lasted longer than a stabbing. I made more noise than I wanted, and I felt bad, because they were trying to do the right thing.

The guards were careful with the knives, but I could feel the cold blares on my skin and little pricks when the sharpened points popped through the sturdy fabric. The men pinched the cloth between their fingers, pushed the knives through, and then pulled the blades back towards their chests, slicing open little gashes. I didn't know if they were cutting my skin along with the suit, but by then, with the goal in sight, I had to go to the bathroom so badly that I really didn't care.

When they reached the shoulders and started up the collar, the sleeves fell off. With that, the flight suit started to peel itself down my body like a banana. The robed man guided the blue robe over my shoulders, over the bra, and down my body. All three of them averted their eyes, or looked me straight in the eye, so I would know they weren't leering. The flight suit came down a bit, then down went the robe. A little flight suit, a little more robe, so I was covered every step of the way. These men were much more sensitive about my modesty than I expected them to be. In fact, they were more sensitive than some of my American colleagues, who had been known to catch a peek at the women soldiers going to the shower.

The guards were unable to maneuver my arms into the sleeves of the robe, so I kept my hands joined at the thumbs underneath the fabric. The robe itself fit me like a tent and touched the floor. Next they had me sit down, and one of them unlaced my combat boots. He pulled them both off, leaving me in my big green knee socks and finally able to step out of the rags of my flight suit. They pulled my boots back on, and the two soldiers walked out the door, triumphant.

I was left alone with the guard in the white robe. "Come with me," he ordered.

"No." I shook my head, smiling at him.

He looked at me with that quizzical face again and motioned toward the open door. "Water closet," he said hopefully, using his one expression in English.

"Not quite," I grimaced, flapping my arms underneath my robe, trying to gesture. But he couldn't see my hands. "Un-der-wear," I said. "I can't go with my underwear still on."

Finally, reluctantly, he got the message, and leaned over in front of me. He looked behind me at the wall, put both hands under the robe, hooked his fingers on either side of my orange bikinis, and pulled them down. Gentle is not the word I would use to describe the effort—I'm not sure if "gentle" was in his vocabulary—but he didn't try to knock me to the ground. He got the panties down, and I stepped out of them, one booted foot at a time. The guard tossed them on the bench and motioned to the door. This time I followed.

The wooden door was open to the small water closet and the guard pointed me inside. It smelled sharply of urine, excrement, and bad drainage, and I was glad they had put on my boots because the floor was wet and filthy. Apparently the aim of Iraqi soldiers in the bathroom is about as good as that of our own men. Instead of a toilet, there was an oblong hole in the floor with little foot pads on either side. The idea was to stand on the foot pads and squat over the hole. There was no toilet paper, but there was a black hose coming out of the wall at knee height.. There was no way I would be able to clean myself anyway. Nor could I squat over the hole, because my knee wouldn't bend. I couldn't even lift up the robe because my arms didn't work at all. I had to keep from soiling the robe; it might be my only piece of clothing for some time. I looked down at the hole. After all those months in Saudi Arabia, I never had figured out which way to face when using those things.

I placed my feet on the foot pads with my back toward the closest wall. I stood straight, measured the distance, and started leaning backward, teetering actually, since my body was stiff. My head went back and clunked against the cement wall, and I was jammed there like a plank leaning against a barn. That position caused the robe to swing out away from me, clearing my trajectory to the target. My neck was stiff and my legs were trembling, but I managed to relieve myself without hitting the robe or my boots.

After congratulating myself on a mission accomplished, I realized I could not move. My head was mashed against the wall, and I was looking up at the ceiling, thinking I could not balance there much longer. My legs were tired and my arms hurt. One, two, three; I jerked forward and yelped from the pain in my leg. I thought my knee was going to collapse like a broken table log as my body went forward. The pain shot my right leg, and I shifted my weight to the left one. I caught my balance and stood there for a minute, breathing deeply so the pain would dissipate. My inability to perform that simple movement made the diagnosis of my knee for me: I had blown out at least the anterior cruciate ligament. Unfortunately, having the right diagnosis was of absolutely no value at that point.

Once I recovered and the pain had stopped surging through my leg, I pushed the door open with my shoulder. The step down was only about four inches, but I navigated it carefully because I was afraid of falling. I knew there were bone splinters or fragments in my arms, and I was afraid of causing more damage. The white-robed guard was waiting for me and led me back to my cell. We walked inside and he picked up my orange underwear from the bench. He waved them at me and said something in Arabic that I didn't understand. I took his message to be that no green-eyed infidel woman in any of his cells was going to be naked under a blue wool robe.

"If you put them back on," I said, "you'll just have to take them off again when I need to go to the bathroom."

But he insisted, and one foot at a time, he slipped the panties up my legs and over my hips.

The guard closed and bolted the door on the way out, and I was alone. I sat perched on the smooth wood bench. I had only two available positions: standing, or sitting on the edge of the bench. It was too painful to lean back against the wall or lie down, which is what I really wanted to do. I hadn't slept much the night before our rescue mission, and this day had been fairly traumatic. At least I was not alone. Dunlap was in a nearby cell, although we couldn't communicate. I wondered if they would interrogate him separately. Would he be tortured? Too tired to think. My eyes burned and felt heavy; my brain was fuzzy. I was exhausted, frazzled. Sleep seemed like an escape. If I could just sleep until morning, life would have to get better.

Sleep was elusive, though, as the heavy door scraped open again in a few minutes. The skinny guard with a baggy uniform entered carrying a glass of water and a thick china plate holding a tomato and a fist-sized, brown roll. The guard set the glass and the plate on the bench beside me. This guard, maybe twenty-five years old, did not like me and was quick to make his feelings known. He never said anything, but I could feel the meanness in him. It was contempt, hate. He banged the plate next to me and waited for me to pick up the food and eat.

"I can't," I said. Broken arms."

With a horrible, sour look on his face, he picked up the water glass and clinked it against my teeth He resented me, probably as an American and as a woman. I imagine he didn't want to be there waiting on me, and I think by then the Iraqis knew how badly the war was going for them. I drank deeply. The cool water tasted so good and refreshing because I was dehydrated. He set the glass down and tore off pieces of the roll, dropping them into my mouth until the roll was gone. I watched his hands and noticed the dirt under his nails. Then he fed me the tomato the same way. I knew I should eat to keep up my strength, and the food actually tasted good. I had not eaten fresh, moist bread during those months living in Saudi Arabia, nor had we seen many fresh vegetables.

When I finished, the guard picked up the plate and glass and started out the door without a word.

"Thank you," I called after him, but he kept silent.

I appreciated what these men had done for me so far. They could have just left me alone in the cell, but they helped me. I didn't feel that way about all the Iraqis I had met up to that point. I did not appreciate the guy kissing me and touching me—I would've loved to let Kory spend a few minutes with him. And for the soldier who had taken my ring, I wished only the worst. I imagined our guys going in there and blowing up everything. I resented that they had taken my nag. I didn't have any problem with them capturing me; we would have done the same thing if we had shot down an Iraqi helicopter. Obviously, the military exists to break things and kill people, but stealing was not acceptable.

My blue robe was heavy wool, and I was grateful to have it, but I was shivering with cold. It was cold in the cell, probably just above freezing, and I had lost a lot of blood. I was happy to have my socks and boots. The skinny guard opened the door again and put a wool blanket on the bench next to me. I looked longingly at the brown blanket, but I couldn't grab it. The guard looked at me. He picked the blanket shook it out and draped it across my chest. A normal person would have put the blanket over my shoulders and across my back, but Mr. helpful was not cooperating. I did not complain.

The guard left, and I sat as still as I could, perched on the edge of the bench and terrified the blanket would slide down onto the floor and leave me uncovered all night. I bent my head forward as slowly as possible and snatched the edge of the blanket in my teeth. I sat that way all night, half asleep and sucking on the edge of the blanket, fearing that if I drifted off too soundly, I would lose my toothy grip and die of exposure.

Perched in the darkness, the blanket in my teeth and my body shivering under the blue robe, I wondered if anyone else had survived the crash. There had been eight of us on board, and I had seen only one other survivor, Sergeant Dunlap. I didn't remember seeing any bodies in the wreckage. I felt lucky to be alive, and I didn't think anyone else could have survived the crash. The wreckage was in little pieces, thrown across the desert. Dunlap was in a cell two doors away, but I was afraid to call out to him.

I wondered if the two Apaches that were escorting us had made it back. My friend Lance was flying one of them, and I hoped he was safe. I knew he would be sick about what had happened to me. I knew he would feel responsible, especially after we had told Regan that Lance was going to watch out for me.

I met Lance in December, 1987, at Fort Rucker. At that time, and up until he volunteered to go with the 2-229th to Saudi Arabia, he was the standardization instructor pilot for D Company, which means he set the standard for the company that trains all the Apache pilots in the army. Lance was one of the first twenty people trained to fly the Apache when it was initially fielded, and he could make that helicopter do whatever he asked it to. When we had flown together, he told me, "You have to treat it gently, like a lover." Lance looks young for his age, 43, and in truth, he looks just like an Apache pilot—so much so that McDonnell Douglas, the company that makes the Apache, has a full-page picture of Lance in the company's book about the aircraft.

A twenty-two-year veteran, Lance had 283 confirmed kills in Vietnam. In the air force, when the pilots talk about "kills," they mean the airplanes they've shot down. We don't live under such illusions in the Army, because in a helicopter you see the people fall when you shoot them. Early in the war with Iraq, Lance was the pilot who took the first group of prisoners. It was unheard of for an attack helicopter to take prisoners, and the capture had added to Lance's stature in the battalion. Lance told me he was glad the Iraqi soldiers had surrendered instead of trying to fight. He didn't want to kill them if it wasn't necessary.

In some ways, Lance is a typical attack-fighter pilot: desperately trying to grow up, but not quite there, seeking out every thrill from skydiving to scuba diving to hang gliding. In other ways he is very wise; he's seen a lot in a few years, and many of the younger pilots want to be just like him. Despite the constant, and sometimes serious, competition between the attack pilots like Lance and the utility pilots, Lance was well liked and respected by our Black Hawk crews. On an earlier mission, Garvey had commented that it was a good thing we had Lance. "At least," Garvey said, "there is one gun pilot with brains."

Sitting in the darkness, thinking about Lance and the fate of the other aircraft on our mission, I hadn't yet grasped the seriousness of my own situation. I was shivering with cold in a prison cell deep inside Iraq. I was badly injured, perhaps permanently disabled. More interrogation, and maybe torture, lay ahead. I knew we were winning the war, but I didn't know how long it would last. I did know that long after the war in Vietnam had ended, Americans were still being held prisoner. In Lebanon, Western hostages had been held for years, chained to walls in dark cells, and used as bargaining chips. Still, I felt lucky to have survived the helicopter wreck. I felt lucky just to be alive, and I was confident I would get out of this mess.

Doing What's Right: Shaping the Army's Professional Environment

By Lewis Sorley

Professional studies often include exposure to the ideas of the classical philosophers, and that is all to the good. It is important to know the ethical touchstones that have guided the great civilizations, the great societies, of the past. It is important to know that men have agreed upon standards of conduct, have established mores and sanctions to encourage observances of those standards and to punish transgressions against them, and have thus sought to determine the ethical character of their lives.

It is perhaps more important, with hose studies as background, to think hard and seriously about the ethical standards that soldiers choose to guide their live, both personal and professional. This is because there cannot be a lack of congruence between personal and professional standards, between private man and the public man in value terms, without devastating harm to one's ability to perform professionally.

This essay concentrates on one further essential step-beyond understanding the great value systems that have guided men over the generations, and beyond establishing a commitment to a value system that will guide one's actions. It deals with the final, difficult, and all-important tasks of translating those values into guidelines for day-to-day activities and then, after adapting them and manifesting them in our own lives, teaching them to those who are entrusted to our leadership, and gaining their will acceptance and ultimately their own whole hearted commitment to those same values.

This last step is at the heart of professional leadership. Such leadership is in essence, the task of establishing and transmitting values. Certainly there are many other desirable attributes of leadership. Technical competence, energy, physical brav-

Source: *U.S. Army War College Quarterly* Volume XIX, p. 11-15 Reprinted with permission.

ery and moral courage, intellectual capacity, commitment-all these and more are undoubtedly desirable attributes of the successful leader. None of the great leaders, of course, has manifested all these in equal parts. Men are, after all, both fallible, and infinitely diverse.

But these attributes, however important, are secondary to set and impart values. Professionalism is, after all, the hewing to a set of values as postulated as the ideal of performance in the profession at hand. It is important to remember, in thinking about these matters, that they all take place within a given cultural and societal context. Thus what constitutes the canons for ideal professional behavior for the leaders of American soldiers in the 20th century may vary substantially, even radically, from the imperatives to which other leaders, at other times were expected to respond.

Thus I argue that the essence of professionalism is character. Character may be defined as the commitment to an admirable set of values, and the courage to manifest those values in one's life, not matter the cost in terms of personal success or popularity. One writer referred to "those hard outcroppings of character that determine a life." It is no accident that one of the key phrases in prayer taught to cadets at West Point concerns the need to "choose the harder right instead of the easier wrong."

Now "those hard outcroppings of character," as I understand them, refer in those key situations-ethical crises, we might say-in which we have the opportunity to stand up and be counted, to weigh in on the side we believe to be right, regardless of the consequences. Such crises, fortunately for us all, only seldom confront us. But that does not mean that we are only rarely faced with the necessity to manifest values in our daily actions. Quite the contrary, as I see it. Virtually everything we do has a value component to it, and-whether we like it or not, whether we realize it or not-we are revealing our values, and teaching our values to others, in an almost constant stream of words and deeds throughout each day.

This realization is both daunting and encouraging. It means that we carry enormous responsibility as leaders, perhaps greater than we ordinarily realize (and here I am not speaking of the self-evident heavy burden of those who lead troops in combat). It means that we are constantly being observed, and our actions are constantly being assessed, by those we leader (and, of course, by our seniors and our peers as well). The dean of George Washington University's business school once observed, tellingly, that "management is one of the performing arts." He was quite right, and the corollary is that the leaders, or manager, is never off stage. But while that is a heavy responsibility, it is also a magnificent opportunity. It means that literally hundreds of times a day the leaders has an opportunity to touch the people he comes into contact with and to shape their approach to duty and responsibility.

One of our finest soldiers, Lieutenant General Arthur S. Collins, Jr., wrote a superb book called Common Sense Training. In it he pointed out how virtually everything a unit does in the course of a day may be used for training by a wise commander. And it was not just training in specific techniques or tasks he had in mind, but indoctrination in such fundamental attributes as discipline, patriotism, responsiveness to command, initiative, and unit cohesion. General Collins held that training is all-encompassing, with the result that "individual training is designed to improve the whole person." "Improve the whole person"—think of it, and what that say about the trainer (the leader) and his responsibility to set and impart values.

A shared commitment to professional values, and to service, transcends the individual and constitutes the basis for our Army's corporate persona, it central values. We teach these values to our young leaders, who in turn inherit a responsibility to see that they are preserved and passed on. In this way we maintain the continuity and solidarity of our profession.

When new officers leave their basic schools and training centers and enter the Army at large, they have a major adjustment to make. Things are different and radically so, in this larger world, where practice takes over from theory. They must be prepared to go out and deal with the problems which those differences can cause, differences which have the capacity to undermine the very essence of the Army— it's ability to carry out it's mission. An important part of being prepared to deal with such differences is understanding just how much influence a leader can have.

Most men, it seems to me, are inherently neither good nor evil. Each has within himself the capacity for actions that are admirable or reprehensible. What brings out the best or worst in us is often the organizational climate in which we find ourselves. In the Army there are units and posts that, at particular times and under particular commanders, come close to living up to the ideal standards to which we aspire. There are others which fall lamentably short.

It is not that the one post or unit happened to have assigned to it a high proportion of principled soldiers, while another had many of lesser quality. Rather it is that in one case the leaders were able to build an environment supportive of the kind of behavior (in ethical terms) they professed to want, while others elsewhere failed to do so (and perhaps even failed to understand their responsibility for doing so). The late General Bruce C. Clarke, a renowned Army commander in Europe in the early days of the Cold War, told his commanders that "the outstanding officer is the one who get superior results from average soldiers." There is much wisdom in that. There are units in the Army which, because of the high priority of their missions or other factors, get more than a fair share of the talent and assets the Army has to pass around. But most units get a representative cross-section of talent, and do a better or worse job of making use of it.

What this brings us down to is building an environment in which people (soldiers) are encouraged and enabled to live up to the highest standards of professionalism. The Army's declaratory policy on ethical standards has always been of the highest order. Its operational policy, unfortunately, has not always matched those high declaratory standards. Perhaps the best example is the distortions of the body count as a measure of operational success in Viet Nam, a measure widely acknowledged even by senior commanders to be both corrupt and corrupting. In that case our operational standards failed to come up to our declaratory ones, and the integrity of the whole enterprise suffered as a result.

Many similar problems come up in the course of professional service. But there are many practical things that the individual leader can do to enhance the climate for professionalism. Some of the most important are these:

First, and by all odds the most important, is to set the example in terms of personal and professional conduct by demonstrating commitment to the highest standards of professionalism and diligent efforts to live up to those standards.

Second is communicating to all subordinates what your standards are, and that you expect them to live up to those standards as well. Be sure that they understand what you mean, and what you expect; then help them appreciate how that translates into day-to-day behavior.

Third is ensuring that the professional environment (to the extent you have any control over it) is supportive of ethical behavior, and not supportive of behavior that is ethically flawed. This entails ensuring that in all aspects of your leadership (evaluations of subordinates, etc.) you operate in a way that encourages and rewards ethical behavior on the part of your subordinates, and discourages unethical behavior (by not rewarding and, where necessary, punishing it).

Fourth is recognizing that you have more control over the professional environment than you may realize. If you communicate your commitment of high standards to your fellow officers, they will be more likely to respect those standards in their dealings with you. If you form alliances with like-minded peers, the solidarity of your joint commitment to high standards can improve the organization's professionalism. If you detect unethical practices, and devise other—more acceptable—ways to get the mission accomplished, you can change undesirable patterns of behavior. If you are generous in recognizing highly professional performance, even (or especially) on the part of those with whom you are in professional competition, you can build new bonds of shared commitment to high standards. And if, when it may become necessary, you set an example that seniors, peers, and subordinates alike can take counsel from.

Undeniably, there are risks in such a course of action, especially if the command of which you are a part is not at the moment distinguishing itself in terms of professional behavior. No one could possible argue that adherence to ethical standards, and the responsibility to leaven the officer corps in terms of its ethical norms, is free of risk, or even easy. It is just essential.

It is as simple as that. Doing what is right yourself, teaching what is right to your troops, and encouraging all with whom you come in contact (including peers and seniors) to do what is right—that is what we are training officers to do, what the Army needs them to do, and what the nation relies on them to do. On this all else depends.

The Commander as Moral Arbiter

by Roger Nye

A few honest men are better than numbers. If you choose godly, honest men to be captains of horse, honest men will follow them.

—Oliver Cromwell. *Reorganization of the Army,* 1645.

Every military organization has its moral arbiters—those people who, by their words and deeds, set the standard for moral conduct. One would hope that the senior commander is the chief moral arbiter in a unit, although this is not always the case.

Not long ago, during a hot summer month in South Korea, an infantry company commander was required to put 120 armed patrols into the demilitarized zone facing North Korea. They carried live ammunition and were expected to intercept infiltrators from the North. One morning, the S-3 (the battalion operations officer, a major) told the company commander that higher headquarters had ordered an additional patrol that afternoon; they were to make repairs on an engineer installation in the zone. The company commander pointed out the reasons why this would violate policies about mandatory briefings for the men, equipment checks, soldier rest requirements, and so forth. The argument became heated and was taken to the battalion commander. After extensive huddling with the S-3, he announced that the company would not have to send out the additional patrol. Instead, higher headquarters would simply be told that it had been done. Faced with the prospect of a conspiracy to lie, the company commander suggested an alternative: to cancel one of the scheduled patrols, and substitute this special one—same manpower, different mission. Everyone like this solution, and the plot to lie to higher headquarters was aborted.

This incident raises the question of why some commanders reach their positions so ill-prepared to be moral arbiters for their people. While the issue could be dis-

Source: *The Challenge of Command* (1986) 99-13. New Jersey, Avery Publishing Group. Reprinted *by* permission of Mrs. Mary Ann Nye.

missed as being of minor importance, the impact on the organization's moral climate could be major if repeated in the commander's other decisions. In contrast is the commander who establishes a climate that encourages junior officers to make the right moral decisions.

This was the case in a stateside unit, where Lieutenant Jim Riffe was given command of an anti-tank platoon of TOW missiles (Tube-launched, Optically-sighted, Wire-guided). This platoon had been known for having every member qualified as an expert gunner on the TOW. But when Lieutenant Riffe took them to the range and had them evaluated by three sergeants from other units, he found that he had only a handful of experts, the rest having difficulty even in bringing the weapon's simulator under control.

Lieut. Riffe brought all the falsified readiness reports to the battalion commander, who had them destroyed. A new firing program eventually produced an accurate record—it again met the required standards for readiness reports. The moral arbiters had done the right thing. The only question remaining was why the previous platoon leader had felt impelled to falsify the records in the first place.

This story raises some familiar questions. How can commanders be sure that their people are telling them the truth? What accounts for two lieutenants, faced with the same responsibilities, pursuing honest and dishonest means to reach the same results? What consequences do false readiness reports have on the combat effectiveness of a unit? How does a commander prepare to cope with the problems of dishonesty in his command?

In the days of a small Regular Army, a senior commander might assume that the bulk of his officers had been prepared at home and in college to live by some code of honor. This assumption withered in the large standing Army that came with World War II and the Cold War. Those years of change were also marked by increasing deception and fraud in the Officer Corps, as standards more closely resembled those of society in general, rather than those of an elite, professional corps. As a result, frustrated senior commanders often felt impelled to march their lieutenants to the post theater and lecture them on the evils of lying, cheating, stealing, and other moral lapses. Afterwards, the seniors usually felt better, but the lieutenants muttered about having heard it all before.

The lieutenants usually had a point. The often-repeated lectures argued that military people should be honest with each other, since lying caused casualties and failed missions. They heard Story One, where the lieutenant reported that he was at position A when he was really at Position B; the battalion commander called fire on B and obliterated the platoon. In Story Two, the lieutenant reported taking his patrol to Hill X and finding no enemy, while in actuality he had stopped short and came home without checking it; the battalion commander launched an advance that was snuffed out by an enemy attack from Hill X. Story Three described the lieutenant who reported that his weapons had all been checked; yet in the combat showdown they failed to fire and the unit was lost. As such stories were repeated, they became less and less connected with the wartime experiences that might have produced them. Therefore, they became less believable, since history does not often record military action in such detail.

Additional theoretical arguments for soldier honesty began to appear as the post-World War II generation wrote new texts for classes on modern military morality, politics, and professionalism. Story Four: Congress and the press discover that an air force general sent false reports about bombing in Cambodia; they conclude that the necessary public trust in the military's words and deeds has been damaged. This results in fewer funds and manpower for the military.

Story Five: A Colonel makes it known, as he moves from assignment to assignment, that he expects a silver tray or a set of golf clubs as a farewell gift to his wife from the officers of his command; this violates the code of ethics of the profession he espouses. Story Six: A company commander promises his troops weekend passes in return for their extra efforts in preparing for a command inspection; afterwards, he denies having made such promises, thereby forfeiting his ability to lead them in the future. As mandatory classes in Ethics and Professionalism increased in the seventies, arguments for building trust with the public and with subordinates joined arguments for combat efficiency in lectures to military novices.

Outside the classroom, and in quiet conversations, one hears soldiers give different reasons why they should be honest. Some will say, "I want my kids to think of me as an honest man." Or, "I want my friends and colleagues to feel that I am trustworthy and won't let them down." Occasionally, one will say, "I took an oath," or, "God says that I should not bear false witness," or simply, "It is wrong to lie." These are reflections of the inner being. They are expressions of the moral character that the soldier brings to his work from his earliest days. They are manifestations of the "bag of virtues" which, according to Plato, constitutes the worthy man—virtues such as truthfulness, benevolence, and trustworthiness. When soldiers choose to act in accordance with these virtues, they are doing so to uphold their reputations in the eyes of family, friends, colleagues, their "public," their religion, and their own esteem.

To some degree, military lying and cheating comes from people who have never developed the character traits that will engender good conduct. Such men and women fail to develop a trust for institutions, a high regard for the dignity of others, a sense of justice, or any of the other foundations of good character. It is such people about whom Viscount Morley wrote, "No man can climb beyond the limitations of his own character."

More often, however, the military problem is one of coaxing people of good character to act in accordance with their beliefs when operating in situations of great pressure and very little moral support. Behavioral researchers attest that everyone lies or cheats at one time or another, sometimes because they disagree over what constitutes lying or deception, sometimes because they are caught in dilemmas of conflicting loyalties, sometimes because they are trapped into no alternative. This is an environmental or situational viewpoint, which suggests not only that men and women have good character training in their youths, but also that they need favorable conditions in order to exercise those characters. Does the reality of military life meet these expectations?

THE POWERS EXPERIENCE

Few soldiers have had to cope with Army lying more than Robert D. Powers, who chaired a cadet honor committee, was commissioned in infantry in 1972, and then commanded platoons and a company in a stateside airborne organization. Later, during his command of a company in the Alabama National Guard, I asked him whether he thought that liars and cheaters were people of bad character, or merely average people caught up in bad environments.

"In my five years on active duty," he said, "I learned that most new officers have good enough character, but some must learn how to translate that into real world terms. We had an excellent lieutenant who took pride in a set of stereo headphones that he had liberated from an air force C-130 used in jumping. I suggested that this misappropriation of government property set a bad example for the company; he replied that he had paid for the headset with a case of C-rations taken from the Army. I told him that the company commander should decide the issue, but the CO vacillated until I asked to take the matter to the battalion commander. A few days later, the lieutenant told me that he had returned the headphones, and knew that I was right when I had first brought it up. Until then, he had known that he would never steal, but had never been required to admit that his borrowing and misappropriation was, in fact, stealing."

"Most soldiers," said Powers, "are honest by nature and want to do the right thing. This is especially true of young noncoms who like to tell it like it is, and to hell with the consequences. When good noncoms and junior officers begin shading the truth, it is rarely for their own benefit but, rather, for the good of their troops or unit. Unfortunately, they are often misguided about what is 'good.'"

"Keeping honest men honest is only one part of coping with lying in the military. Apparently, every major organization has a handful of officers and NCO's who, with malice aforethought, put themselves on a course of lying, false reporting, and other deceptions. My first experience with them was when I was assigned to a special weapons platoon in a headquarters company. This was a notorious collection of AWOL's, drug abusers, brawlers, and a few men with armed robbery on their records. When the next one went absent without leave, I sought a heavy punishment as a multiple offender. But then I found out that his previous offenses had not been recorded; falsified morning reports of 'All Present' had been sent forward. Later, the culprit had been punished illegally through the platoon sergeant's work details."

"These false reports were widely used, and gave the company a favorable statistical record on discipline. The company commander had a variety of excuses for this deception; sometimes he blamed the first sergeant's bad paperwork, and other times he said he had found out about it too late to do anything. After I made enough noise, I was able to get my AWOL's reported as they happened, but I don't think the policy changed much for the rest of the company.

"Once I became company executive officer, the scope of the deception became more apparent. When we changed company commanders, I had to review the readiness reports in personnel, training, and maintenance. Weapons firing records had been falsified to inflate statistics on qualifications; in some cases, men we credited with range firing on days when they were not even present for duty. The new company commander and I took the evidence to the battalion S-3 and worked out a plan for range time, ammunition, and schedules that allowed for new qualification. The battalion commander directed that accurate readiness reports replace the old ones as new statistics were developed. Much the same situation appeared in the maintenance and personnel reporting; we even discovered a man being listed present-for-duty when he had been in the Indiana state penitentiary for the past two years."

"You cannot blame this deception on the education and training of that company commander, because he had a Regular Army commission from one of the best colleges with a working honor system. But he lacked competence—he was very nervous, talking and chain-smoking all the time. He was afraid of the men and terrified of the battalion commander. He had a wife and children, and was a candidate for the post-Vietnam forced reduction in the Officer Corps. He was generally disorganized and did not control the events that always engulfed him. To him, lying and cheating was a matter of survival."

"He might have done better under a different battalion commander; ours used intimidation and fear to get what he wanted. He was the kind who refused to let the troops go on pass until a quota of fund-raising tickets for the Youth Activities Center had been bought: our captain would finally pay for the tickets out of his own pocket rather than face up to the men or the commander. The other three company commanders were more successful than my boss. They ran better companies, stood up to the battalion commander, and probably did not feel a need to falsify records. They had the competence and energy to keep up with the game without a lot of deception."

"To some degree, Army policies forced all of us into deception. Company commanders were required to verify all sorts of things with their signatures, things they could not possibly know about. I had to verify that every soldier who left my command had turned in his post library card. Was I supposed to walk each departing soldier to the library? When I had my company on summer training assignments at other Army posts, I signed statements saying my equipment stored at home base was ready for combat. There was really no way for me to inspect it; I was forced to believe the word of my XO who was back there."

"We were all co-opted into writing inflated efficiency reports. We knew that a bad report could be used in Washington to kill the career of a mediocre officer who did an average job; a less than perfect report could permanently put the career of a superb officer to rest. I have had no qualms about rating people higher than the system told me to; for good men, it was a matter of survival. Some of us were enraged when we learned that this captain was given a maximum efficiency report for his command of that company—*after* higher authorities were made aware of his falsification of reports. He was placed on an advanced promotion list to major not long afterwards."

Powers was not surprised to find that this falsification of records went unpunished. "I learned over time that you get little support from above as you expose wrongdoing. They either see a threat to the image of the organization, or perhaps they have been swept into similar practices in the past. In many situations, the wrongdoing cannot be substantiated legally, to the degree that punishment will be carried out. In the case of my company commander, however, we have to wonder if we face a career of working for and competing with men who will do such things and never be held accountable."

"One cannot cope with deception, however, unless he has the courage to investigate it when he encounters it. It is easy to jump to the conclusion that the deception is deliberate and the product of a malicious mind. Very often, however, the problem is one of monumental ignorance rather than deception. We had a company commander who turned in 400 blankets, and a week later blindly signed a statement saying that he still had them; it took us months to straighten out that case of 'reverse deception.' Although in this case, carelessness acted against the individual, there are many situations in which the government is being bilked through the sheer stupidity of its personnel. In such instances, it is foolish to go on a crusade to stamp out deception and evil-mindedness."

"Deliberate deception, however, must be exposed if it is to be corrected. The culprits are usually experienced and know how to protect themselves. If it comes to a showdown between you and them, you will need a pretty good reputation at the higher levels for military competence and good judgment. You will also need to have done your homework on the administrative and legal details. The experienced liar and cheater will back away from a power base equal to his, and will perhaps desist in the practices. Again, higher authority may either press the issue against him or let him off the hook."

"In coping with lying and other forms deception, you should always ask, 'What are the alternatives?' It often appears that soldiers think they are trapped in a box that can only be broken open by a little deception when, in fact, they are just too lazy or to uninformed to discover honest ways of moving forward that would redound to their credit. Once, when I was in charge of a battalion social fund, I was told to write a check for an obviously unauthorized expenditure. When I refused, the battalion commander signed the check himself. Later, the Inspector General's annual audit of the fund censored the commander and ordered him to restore the money from his own pocket. All the while, there were alternative ways of getting the money, but the CO had no intention of pursuing them."

Powers said that, when asked to sign something that he was unsure about, he frequently used the alternative of attaching a letter that explained the conditions under which he signed it, or why he did not. Occasionally, he would get a telephone call asking for further clarification, but he was never ordered to reverse his position. "The higher headquarters realize that they are vulnerable to a charge of setting up requirements that cannot be met without some deception, and they are not going to go to the mat to defend their directives. Most people will tell you privately that they are glad someone raised the issue."

"Anyone who wants to cope with lying in the Army should listen carefully to the kinds of excuses used by liars to justify their misdeeds. Of course, their first line of defense is that they are doing it for 'the good of the men,' or 'the welfare of the unit.' Sometimes, this is merely a cover-up for their own laziness or incompetence, and the men and unit would be better off if they simply improved things so lying would not be 'necessary.' On the other hand, a deceptive act, some good may bring to the unit and troops, but the perpetrator fails to calculate the long-range impact on the trust of the troops, who are quick to observe, 'If he lies to them, when will he start lying to me?'"

I asked Powers if we could explore the difference between lies that were not justified by the excuses and alibis given for them, and the lies and deceptions that might be validly justified, such as those forced on the soldier by the efficiency report and verification systems. We agreed that lying to the enemy in order to deceive him into making mistakes and misjudgments had long been accepted among soldiers and statesmen. Then we dwelt on lesser versions of that same rationale when, as in poker or sports, one played out little deceptions to "fool the competition." Somewhat akin to these acts of deception are the little "white lies" that are employed on a regular basis to remove awkwardness from social situations, such as praising the hostess for her "marvelous" dinner. Finally, I questioned Powers as to the impact of his continuing search for honesty on his career—would he recommend that others take the risk of getting low efficiency reports from seniors who preferred less rocking of the boat? "The risks," he said, "are not that great if you also have a reputation for competence in military duties. I was docked a couple of points but was not moved out of my outstanding ratings. All but one of the reports were maximums. In fact, the system of reports had become so scandalous that my last one declared 'This Report is *Not* Inflated.'"

"The more important point is that a good OER is not the goal of the exercise. I learned at home in Illinois that a man's most precious possession is his reputation. I prefer my friends, colleagues, and particularly my family, to know and remember me for my honesty and straightforwardness."

"It was—and still is—great fun, not a burden, to build a reputation for competence and honesty. When I took over this National Guard company, I was required to sign for property that included clips of ammunition and 2643 loose rounds. I asked to see those loose rounds. Later, the warrant officer said that I was the first officer in 28 years to count those rounds. I told him that it was just an old habit of mine. I imagine the word got around about that."

THE COMMANDER AS MORAL TRAINER

If we accept the Powers philosophy that both character and environment influence the commander's search for honesty in his command, then it follows that the commander will pursue certain tasks on a continuing basis. He becomes a constant trainer and teacher, especially in reaffirming the importance of character and interpreting moral principle into the concrete conditions of the command. He might even march the lieutenants to the theater and talk about air force headsets.

The commander also demonstrates his feelings toward honesty by taking actions that are visible to his people. It is not enough for a commander to be quietly honest. His beliefs must be overt, so that others can follow his example. He must announce policies that will help to establish a moral climate, such as clear guidelines on what constitutes right and wrong actions. His people will know him by the kinds of rewards and punishments he uses for proper and improper conduct. They will also judge him on his ability to keep competition and stress at levels that are short of generating cheating and lying among his subordinates.

The effective commander cannot be too far removed from the moral actions of his people, under the argument that "all of them are presumed honest until proven otherwise." In some units, this distant attitude will allow the least qualified to set the moral standard of the organization. Commanders need to create cross-checks on reports, and to establish periodic, impersonal audits and inspections, all of which occur automatically and do not imply that individuals or groups are being singled out for special investigation.

Even this short list of tasks presents some problems. How does one know if competition and stress are at the right level? Powers' battalion commander had one company cheating, but three not; is that too much, too little, or the right amount of pressure? We can also consider the commander who is told to support a program he does not believe in. Is he wrong in standing before the troops and praising it, even though he thinks he is misleading them?

What about the commander who is faced with a media reporter known for misrepresenting the facts in a manner hostile to the military; should the commander protect himself and the Army by his own evasions and misrepresentations? Concerning the commander in combat who is faced with low morale and probable defeat: is it wrong to tell the troops that they are invincible and near victory, if it means that they will make that one last supreme effort?

These questions, being typical moral dilemmas, have no fixed answers, nor even best answers. They have least-worst answers every time they are asked. They require pre-thinking. That is, they require reading, discussion, and reflection before being encountered. They require a settled philosophy concerning one's own moral make-up, and the moral capabilities of those with whom one is dealing.

For example, it is useful to have pre-thought the question of how humankind generally confronts moral dilemmas in their daily lives. A reading of Lawrence Kohlberg's *Essays on Moral Development* suggests that a commander who is making an appeal for more honest reporting may get different reactions from his troops, according to their different stages of moral development. He will have some soldiers at the most primitive stages of moral growth, where moral conduct is ruled by considerations of "What's in it for me?"—that is, by fear of punishment or hopes of immediate reward, or by some favorable exchange of favors.

On the other hand, he may have some subordinates who, because of their education and experience, are at the highest stages of moral development. They act to uphold values and principles, whether stated in law or a social contract like the Constitution, or as broad abstract principles, such as justice, equality, and respect for the dignity of the individual.

Between these extremes, most subordinates fall into the middle categories of moral development, where moral conduct is undertaken in order to maintain the expectations of the group, the family, or the nation. By acting morally, one conforms to the social order, demonstrates loyalty to authority, and "does one's duty."

Kohlberg's analysis indicates the need for a commander to present several levels of appeal, with strong emphasis on restating and supporting the core policies of the Army and the profession. This had not been done sufficiently by the commanders of the unit that perpetrated the massacre of Vietnam citizens at My Lai. Kohlberg interviewed all participants and found that the one enlisted man who clearly refused to fire his weapon tested out at the highest stages of moral development. He said he acted on principles that he had acquired in soldier basic training.

LEARNING ABOUT LYING

One does not explore lying and deception without finding that there are few valid authorities on the subject. Lieutenant Powers formulated his ideas and practices through his own experience and what others had told him. He did not read a single book, nor consult any analyst of military life or critic of American contemporary society who could lend sanction to his thoughts. He knew of regulations, laws, sermons, and essays that declared in absolutist fashion that deception and lying were evil and punishable. But he knew of no authority that defined these terms, addressed the extent of their practice, or described the processes through which humans cope with their effects.

In 1978, however, Sissela Bok undertook the publication of *Lying: Moral Choice in Public and Private Life*, a book that can provide guidance to future commanders in search of honesty in the military. In her work as Professor of Philosophy at Harvard University, she explored the writings of Aristotle, Augustine, Aquinas, Bacon, Kant and the modern philosophers. She applied their thinking to contemporary American society, both in those face-to-face relationships of everyday life and in the matters of grand statecraft. She explored military lying about U2 spyplanes, Cambodian incursions, and U.S. Army body-count symbols of victory.

Bok finds that lying is one of many forms of deception, which also includes evasion, exaggeration, disguise, silence, and inaction when these are designed to mislead. Lying requires the making of a statement in words, hand signals, or body gestures, with the intent of misleading or deceiving. Lying cannot be accidental. A person may become uninformed in many other ways, such as by a mirage. Some lies can be justified; most cannot.

Bok supports Powers' view that lying is prevalent throughout our society, and the military is no exception. "We lead our lives amidst all forms of duplicity," she says, "and from childhood we develop ways of coping with them. We all know what it is to lie, to be told lies, to be falsely suspected of having lied." (28 and 242)

This is rather strong medicine for senior officers who were schooled that "the truth, the whole truth, and nothing but the truth" is the Army standard for all, at all times, in all situations. For them, lying is a rare disease that must be cut out like a cancer; liars are to be discovered and purged. Powers and many of his cohorts see this reaching for the ideal world as quite noble. It becomes however, a rationale for calling lying by some other name, and an excuse for marching lieutenants to the lecture hall rather than correcting the conditions that spawn deception.

Bok leaves no doubt that lying is evil, branded a sin by theologians, and a violation of the fundamental moral principles that sustain civilized society. She believes that deceiving another is as evil as doing violence to another—both are assaults on human beings. But, being evil, lying has its appeal to all. She sees life as a continuing process of making moral choices between the apparent benefits of using deception and the liabilities of knowingly committing evil and having to pay a price. She describes how this price is so high that it is self-defeating of one's own goals, such as one's reputation for excellence or one's being able to live in a society of trust and mutual respect. "Trust and integrity are precious resources," she says, "easily squandered, hard to regain." (18 and 249)

What is necessary to justify a lie when one is about to undertake it? Bok doubts that one's own conscience is sufficient; it is best to get the opinion of other, hopefully disinterested people. But what if it is in time of crisis, with no time to consult? She answers that the competent public servant will rarely come across situations that have not occurred before; his previous reading and study should tell him and his close associates the losses and gains he can expect from a public lie at that time. Bok presumes, however, that there should be much more extensive pre-thinking of crisis lying situations than we do now. Examples might be lying to prevent panic in a nuclear accident, lying to the enemy about the extent of damage he has caused in a bombing raid, or well-known situations where lying has done more harm than good, as in the Watergate fraud of the mid-seventies.

Bok is very sure of the culpability of institutions. "The social incentives to deceit are at present very powerful; the controls very weak. Many individuals feel caught up in practices they cannot change. It would be wishful thinking, therefore, to expect individuals to bring about major changes in the collective practices of deceit by themselves. Public and private institutions, with their enormous power to affect personal choice, must help alter the existing pressures and incentives." (244)

This gesture of sympathy for the individual caught up in modern institutions should not be interpreted as absolving them from any guilt for lying when under institutional pressures. Throughout the book, Professor Bok outlines why and how men and women should be constantly struggling to identify deceptive practices, to understand how and why they came about and, if they are leaders in institutions such as the Army, to take action to provide a new direction for all concerned.

After ten years of coping aggressively with dishonesty in the military, Captain Powers read Sissela Bok's *Lying*. He wished it had been available to him a decade earlier. "It is strong on the dilemmas one should consider in one's personal conduct, weaker on what organizational leaders need to do to reduce pressures for lying. If I had had this analysis in the beginning, I would have felt more comfortable in what I was doing, been a little braver about it, and known better how to answer my opposition."

The commander's search for honesty is more than a campaign to root out lying. The search starts with gaining an understanding of the nature of truth itself. Why is truth so valuable? How are men and organizations better off if truth prevails? Who says that truth is good? In addition to her book *Lying*, Sissela Bok provides answers in her 1984 *Secrets: On the Ethics of Concealment and Revelation*. More answers from philosophy are found in the first eight chapters of Mortimer J. Adler's *Six Great Ideas* and in the essay on truth in *The Great Ideas, A Syntopicon of The Great Books of the Western World*.

In recent years, many polemic tracts have been written about deception in public life, including journalist David Wise's *The Politics of Lying: Government Deception, Secrecy, and Power*. In *All The President's Men*, Carl Bernstein and Robert Woodward produced a bestseller about their investigation into the Watergate deception of President Nixon and his aides.

Lying by military people in wartime is not particularly well recorded y in history and biography. The novelists of war, however, make it a central theme. Colonel Peter Stromberg, U.S.M.A. Professor of English, analyzed some fifty novels written about the Vietnam War while it was in progress. He found that the authors tested their soldiers in a variety of ways, especially in their capacities to exhibit honesty and integrity under the pressures of fighting an unpopular war against an implacable enemy in a distant tropical land. These fictitious commanders were required to stand up to four kinds of tests of character: honesty and integrity, skill in their work, compassion, and courage (with a willingness to sacrifice their lives). Many failed the test of honesty. Stromberg quotes Aeschylus, "In war, truth is the first casualty," and notes that, for the novelists of the Vietnam War, truth is a foremost target.

In Anton Myrer's *Once an Eagle*, Sam Damon passes the test of character, but Courtney Massengale fails. In Josiah Bunting's *The Lionheads*, General Lemming establishes the conditions that assure deception in the reporting of enemy body counts. Stromberg cites Daniel Ford's *Incident at Muc Wa*, whose Captain Olivetti is portrayed as a professional officer who "is never conscious of any ideal of decency; he lacks integrity, courage, and compassion." (Stromberg, *A Long War's Writing*, 280.) Ultimately, he abandons his colleague and leaves him to die. Unfortunately, some of the best novels on Vietnam portray an Army that seems leaderless or led by corrupt men. The heroic commanders are yet to be discovered.

It is this last point that underscores the difficulty facing aspiring commanders who would prepare for their roles as moral arbiters. Except for the written materials prepared for service school classes in military ethics and professionalism, the literature is sparse and often negative. They must turn to the biographies of commanders who felt strongly about their moral responsibilities, particularly "Stonewall" Jackson and Robert E. Lee.

But their best school is a living one—the men and women around them who have the integrity of character to speak and act in a moral manner. Observing and listening to these moral arbiters reveals the roots of their beliefs, the sources of their values, and the rationales for their actions. Observing and listening also reveals the high value placed on their personal reputations—or, as soldiers have said for centuries, on their personal Honor.

Reading for
Moral Arbiters

Mortimer J. Adler, *Six Great Ideas*.
Carl Bernstein and Robert Woodward, *All The President's Men*.
Sissela Bok, *Lying: Moral Choice in Public and Private Life*.
  Secrets: On the Ethics of Concealment, and Revelation.
Josiah Bunting, *The Lionheads*.
Daniel Ford, *Incident at Muc Wa*.
The Great Ideas: A Syntopicon of the Great Books of the Western World.
Lawrence Kohlberg, *The Philosophy of Moral Development: Moral Stages and
  the Idea of Justice*.
Anton Myrer, *Once an Eagle*.
Peter L. Stromberg, *A Long War's Writing: American Novels About the
  Fighting in Vietnam Written While Americans Fought*.
Malham H. Wakin, *War, Morality, and the Military Profession*.
Daniel Wise, *The Politics of Lying: Government Deception, Secrecy, and Power*.

Leadership in Combat: An Historical Appraisal

by the USMA History Department

"A Study for the Offficer Personnel Management System Study Group, Department of the Army, Conducted by the Department of History USMA."

COL *Kenneth Hamburger, 1984.*

Study Goals

The ultimate functional role of any armed force is to engage in combat. For this reason, successful leadership in combat should be the aim of the system used to manage officers' careers in any Army, and the production of combat leaders must be one of the most important goals of that system. Nonetheless, there is no unanimity of opinion as to what characterizes good combat leadership (other than the obvious criterion of success), and there is no accepted and verified method of producing leaders who will be successful in combat. The purpose of this study is to gain insights into what has historically characterized successful combat actions and combat leaders, and to try to determine what factors in the individuals' backgrounds caused them to develop into successful combat leaders.

At the request of the Officer Personnel Management Study Group, a committee of seven instructors of military history at the U.S. Military Academy was formed to conduct the study. All members of the committee were combat arms officers with advanced degrees in history and with multiple assignments in tactical units in their branch; including company command. The study was headed by an ex-battalion commander.

In the course of the study, the committee searched for and analyzed examples of successful and unsuccessful combat actions, seeking answers to two specific questions:

— What have been the characteristics of leadership in successful combat actions and how have they differed from those traits observed in unsuccessful actions?

— What personal, experiential, and institutional factors appear to have contributed to developing individuals into successful or unsuccessful leaders in combat?

Source: *Leadership in Combat: An Historical Appraisal.* Reprinted *by* permission of The United States Military Academy.

Study Methodology

Initially, the committee gathered examples of successful and unsuccessful instances of combat leadership. The only restrictive criteria initially imposed was that citations must be actions in actual combat and that the incident must involve leadership, not management. Thus, such events as successful fire support or resupply operations not involving enemy contact were eliminated at the outset, as were examples of successful staff work in support of combat operations. It should be stressed at this point that the sole focus of the study was on combat leadership. For this reason, many exemplary officers were not selected for study; as their records of combat leadership did not match those of the individuals selected.

Once the examples were gathered and reproduced, at least five members of the committee intensively analyzed each of them, attempting to discern whether the leader's actions were critical factors in determining the success of the engagement. In addition to such basis data as the time and place of the event, forces engaged, and commanders' names, committee members recorded the characteristics of the action. The characteristics of the leaders and his "leadership style" were particular items of interest at this point of the study.

Upon completion of the analysis for leadership characteristics, the leaders themselves were studied. This research concentrated on the leader's background, looking for a variety of factors which were thought to be possible discriminators in causing a given individual to have become a successful or unsuccessful leader in combat. Some of the factors searched for included the leader's pre-service background and upbringing, his service record and education, combat experience, physical condition and health, personal characteristics, ethical and moral courage, and where appropriate, his career following the incident.

Study Population

Over two hundred examples of combat leadership were initially gathered and screened. These included incidents in warfare throughout recorded history, from all areas of the world. Examples were gathered from all wars the United States has engaged in from the American Revolution through Vietnam. Initial screening involved several criteria: estimated worth of the event to the overall study; availability of detailed and reliable information on the event; availability of similar background information on the leader; and, in the case of foreign examples, an additional criterion of the estimate applicability of the incident to the leadership of American soldiers.

The final population, which was more intensively researched, consisted primarily of officers of the United States, in the twentieth century. Except for a few examples from Great Britain, Israel, and Germany, foreign examples were rejected either because there was not enough information readily available on the background of the leader or because the committee felt that the cultural milieu of the example was so different from that of the U.S. Army today that "lessons" derived from the incident would not have applicability of OPMS.

Although the committee considered the question of females in combat, no historical examples available appeared to be relevant to current or projected OPMS policy. For this reason, no female combat leaders were included in the final study population.

The Nature of Successful and Unsuccessful Combat Leadership

Although no two combat actions are identical, salient characteristics of successful combat leadership tend to be generally identifiable and, in virtually every example of leadership studied, the successful leaders possessed certain common qualities to one degree or another.

Successful leaders were firmly in control of their units and were recognized as such by all concerned. They were almost always physically fit, in the sense of being conditioned for strenuous exertion. This fitness enhanced their image of being "the man in charge." The successful leader somehow had the ability always to be at the decisive point on the ground at the time he was most needed to influence the action. This was probably a function of his knowledge of terrain, as an appreciation for the ground on which he engaged in combat was a strong point in almost every success story, and a failure to appreciate terrain was the ingredient which led to disaster on more than one occasion. The successful leader made a fetish of properly conducted personal reconnaissances, to the extent of more than once moving into enemy-held territory to view his own lines as the enemy would see them.

The successful leader had a particular facility for planning in detail, assessing a changing situation, and continually assimilating large quantities of often conflicting data. Facility in this regard appears to be a function of intelligence, experience, and moral courage. As Clausewitz expressed this attribute:

> . . . the commander . . . finds himself in a constant whirlpool of false and true information, of mistakes committed through fear, through negligence, through haste; of disregard of his authority, either from mistaken or correct motives, . . . of accidents, which no mortal could have foreseen. In short, he is the victim of a hundred thousand impressions, most of which are intimidating, few of which are encouraging. By long experience in war, one acquires the sensitive perception (necessary) for quickly determining the (true) value of these incidents; high courage and stability of character stand proof against them. . . . only an immense force of will . . . can conduct us to our goal.

Successful leaders required aggressiveness, audacity, and vigorous execution from their subordinates, and both they and their soldiers refused to accept defeat. They were ingenious in overcoming obstacles, and in desperate situations, they often took irrational, even foolhardy action to forestall failure. They and their units continued with their mission in spite of casualties, wounds, lost equipment, and shortage of supplies.

The units commanded by successful leaders keyed on the leader and took on the leader's confidence and spirit. This point deserves emphasis, for it is one of the most commonly commented-on features of the study. It is no exaggeration to say that the leader was the most decisive factor in building unit cohesion. Although this process of building unit cohesion took various lengths of time, depending on variables such as individual experience, whether combat was imminent, and how long the members of the unit had been together before the new leader arrived, the leader was the key to the process. Some units in wartime or undergoing intensive and extended field training achieved such a state in a few months, while some peacetime units who did not train rigorously never achieved it. If the unit were engaged before it had developed the cohesion necessary to function effectively, even the best and most positive leadership could not overcome the lack of cohesion. In more than one instance, a leader who had previously been successful first met failure when he was ordered to lead a unit without cohesion in combat. Conversely, a unit which had attained the cohesion brought by good leadership over a period of time could survive and succeed for a limited time without their leader. A successful leader was able to establish full efficiency in a unit which was already cohesive in a remarkably short period of time.

The characteristics of unsuccessful leaders were, in many respects, the opposite of those of their more successful counterparts. An indecisive leader, particularly one who was "prisoner of his fears," infected his unit and his soldiers and was often mentally defeated before being engaged by the enemy. Here, any deficiencies in the will and fortitude of the leader were vividly evident and assumed particular importance; his unit quickly adopted the mental attitude of its leader as well as his confidence or lack thereof.

An unsuccessful leader was often one who waited for orders and did nothing until higher headquarters ordered him to; inaction was the partner of his indecisiveness. Ironically, the leader's indecisiveness had the same effect as if he had made an important and fateful decision: indecisiveness was, in effect, a decision to do nothing. Instead of constantly preparing for the unexpected, he allowed events to take him by surprise. He showed a marked inability to react to changing circumstances, in dramatic contrast to his successful counterpart. Sometimes this shortcoming appeared to be from a lack of intelligence or training, but occasionally the commander appeared to magnify every threat until he was finally paralyzed by the fear produced by an overactive imagination.

It appears that the Army maxim that "the commander is responsible for everything his unit does or fails to do" has usually been quite literally correct in historical terms: the unit has depended on the commander for its spirit, its drive, and its direction. When the commander was decisive, vigorous, and in control, the unit usually succeeded; when he was unsure, inactive, and inept, the unit often faltered.

Character Traits of Successful and Unsuccessful Combat Leaders

Character traits of combat leaders have varied widely, as might be expected, and there was probably no single individual who ever possessed all the "positive" or "negative" traits discussed below. Nonetheless, there has often been a remarkable similarity in characteristics shared by leaders who have been successful in combat. Similarly, unsuccessful combat leaders also shared their own group of character traits.

The *sine qua non* of almost every successful commander was unquestioned integrity concerning his duties, coupled with a solid ethical foundation in matters dealing with combat or warfare. His self-image was unfailingly positive and he refused to take counsel of his fears. The good self-image may or may not have translated into an inflated ego; successful leaders can be found with egos of every size. The positive self-image was probably a product of, or at least enhanced by, the individual's physical fitness and good health. Additionally, physical fitness enabled them to overcome fatigue and minor infections which often seemed to plague the unsuccessful commander. There have been successful commanders who were out of shape and there have been ones who were gravely ill, but they have never been the norm.

Successful leaders invariably commanded the unqualified respect of their subordinates and peers. Paradoxically, they did not always command equal respect from their superiors. More than once, an ultimately successful commander was overlooked within an organization because he did not have the reputation with his superiors that he enjoyed with his peers and subordinates.

"Leading by example" almost invariably characterized the "leadership style" of the successful combat commander. He was usually cool under fire, often to a fault—many good commanders have been killed in the line of duty, as dozens of Medal of Honor citations attest. The successful commander seldom showed any indication of inner fears or doubts; often his own memoirs or autobiography make it clear in retrospect that he had second thoughts or worries, but during the action he suppressed them, often consciously. This imperturbability had a substantial steadying effect on the units led by successful commanders, for many of the accounts of the participants in combat actions mention how the soldiers of the unit watched the "old man" for indications that everything was going according to plan—if he showed signs of breaking, the unit often disintegrated quickly. More than once commanders commented on their awareness of this responsibility to maintain a facade of calm through inner doubts, and the force of will required to accomplish it.

As mentioned previously, a successful commander usually refused to admit defeat, and his men followed his lead. Instead of conceding victory to his opponent, he marshaled every skill and resource, often in desperate and unprecedented action to accomplish the unit's mission. Sometimes such action was taken because "there was nothing else I could do," out of desperation. The fact remains that surrender was almost never an option for these commanders; if such a course was taken, it was only in an attempt to save their men after all hope was lost—more often, it was never considered. The tenacious doggedness with which many successful leaders pursued their goals is remarkable; their single-mindedness of purpose is overwhelming.

By contrast, the commander who was unsuccessful in combat appears to have been less intense than his successful counterpart. In a West Point annual, one cadet was described as "indifferent, easy going, happy-go-lucky"; he later lost half his regiment and surrendered the rest without seriously engaging the enemy. Such a leader may have been out of condition or ill (as this example may have been) or he may have been merely moody and indecisive. He may have lacked the intelligence or "common sense" of his more capable counterpart. Whatever the cause, these unsuccessful leaders imprinted themselves on their units with disastrous results. No case was found where a unit overcame a leader with these characteristics and prevailed; this is not to say that such a case does not exist, but it is not the norm.

Important Conclusions

— Some individuals appear to be "born leaders" while other individuals can be developed into leaders, but a solid foundation of "character" is essential in any successful leader. That is, there appears to be an aggregate of qualities in an individual's makeup, particularly those concerning his integrity and ethical foundation which are absolutely essential in the potential leader, and which cannot be added through schooling or experience.

— The qualities of an individual's personality which set him apart from other men and make him a leader whom soldiers will follow are probably present, to one degree or another, at every point in a successful combat leader's career, with only an evolutionary change over time. Those essential qualities of personality which make a General Officer a successful leader in combat are discernible, if less developed, early in his career.

— A variety of assignments in areas unrelated to troop leadership had little effect on the abilities of a combat leader. Successful performance on high level staffs and in "high visibility" assignments were not effective gauges of successful leaders. Officers can be extremely successful at a variety of demanding assignments unrelated to leading soldiers in combat and be abject failures as combat leaders.

— Native good judgment, or "common sense," is an absolute requirement for successful combat leadership. The ability to perform well in formal schooling, while not a negative characteristic, is a less important factor for a combat leader. In particular, the leader must have a well-developed and practiced ability in making decisions under pressure.

— Successful combat leadership at one level of command is not a solid guarantee of success at higher levels. If, however, failure at a lower level is attributable to the individual's failings as a leader, it may be an indicator of likely failure at higher levels.

— Physical fitness and good health are prerequisites for successful command at every level.

— Solid grounding in leadership early in service is required for later success.

— Technical competence is important for any combat leader; however, technical skills *per se* are not as important for a combat leader as is an appreciation of the capabilities of all the technological devices at his command.

— Short assignments in succession were negative factors.

— Officers who had avoided service with troops were generally not successful as combat leaders.

— The most salient predictor of a successful combat leader was successful leadership in peacetime, particularly of a tactical unit. Longer service before combat with the unit he would lead in combat appeared to improve his performance, probably by increasing unit cohesion and improving mutual trust between the leader and the unit.

A Vietnam Experience, Duty

by James B. Stockdale

The subject tonight is *duty* and I'm going to begin with a Naval reference. Don't be alarmed at the navy film, and now a naval story. Duty for us all is the same; moreover, half the philosophy students you saw in my class at the War College are Army officers. I was in prison with Marine, air force and army officers and I am not parochial.

So I would like to begin this discussion of duty with a well-known British admiral's flag hoist signal to his fleet as they closed on the enemy to commence the Royal Navy's most famous battle. It was, of course, Lord Horatio Nelson's signal before the Battle of Trafalgar, a signal that history has shown to be the beginning of the end of Napoleon's hope to dominate Europe by force. The ultimately victorious Admiral Nelson had ordered the hoisting of flags which said simply this:

England expects that every man will do his duty.
England expects that every man will do his duty.

That signal is a short but complete lesson in the fundamental and necessary concept of *duty*, a lesson I hope you cadets will long remember. One important thing to remember is that it was given by a man in uniform.

Take note of the important word "expects" in Nelson's signal. The idea of expectation is very much a part of the concept of duty.

The old Greeks understood this notion of expectation. They had a word for what we call virtue or moral excellence: *arete*. To the Greeks a good man was a man who did what was *expected* of him depending upon his particular station in the world.

A good cobbler was one who was expected to produce well-made shoes. And this was reiterated by Plato and Aristotle.

Source: Address to the Class of 1983 (July 13, 1979) United States Military Academy.

One should expect a good navigator, then and now, to guide his ship safely over the sea and into harbor.

A good soldier, as Aristotle in particular emphasized, was one who could be expected to display certain characteristics on the battlefield: courage, obedience, loyalty, steadfastness, resourcefulness. Courage (or the Greek word *andreia*, a synonym for manliness) was the first virtue of a man as well as of a soldier. Plato defines courage as endurance of the soul. The Greeks stressed endurance; they admired a man who could give the quick thrust, the audacious dash, but they reserved their highest praise for the man who "hung in there" battling against the terrible odds, the nearly certain defeat. A more modern military leader, Frederick the Great, took as his personal watchword the command "Stand fast!"

Finally, a good man to the old Greeks was a man who could be expected to display those virtues of character proper to a human as a human, not just his occupational standards as a cobbler, or as a navigator, or as a soldier.

The stoic philosophers, most of whom lived right after the heyday of the Greeks, illustrated this idea of expectation in the moral life by the metaphor of the actor, of the stage, of the drama. Men and women are called on in life to play a part. The part may be a big one or a small one, but once the part is given to us on life's stage, it is expected of us to play it well. In Hanoi's prisons at times when I was so depressed that military virtue seemed almost at the point of irrelevance, I was comforted and strengthened by remembering Epictetus' admonition (and I *did* remember it—as I've written, Epictetus' *Enchiridion* was one of my prize memories) "Remember that you are an actor in a drama of such sort as the Author chooses—if short, then in a short one; if long, then in a long one. If it be his pleasure that you should enact a poor man, or a cripple, or a ruler, or a private citizen, see that you act it well. For this is your business—to act well the given part, but to choose it belongs to another." You young men and women of this West Point Class of 1983 have been given a part and your part is that of a military officer. Your duty is doing what is expected of you. You are *expected* to play your part well.

So was it for Lord Nelson, and he played his part well. Courage? He lost an eye in one action and his right arm in another and still fought his greatest battles in the seven years that followed. Nelson's first thought was for his men. Wounded in action as a young officer, he refused to let the surgeons tend to him first. He was famous for saying that he would take his turn with, as he said, "his brave fellows."

Robert Southey published his *Life of Nelson* just eight years after Nelson had been mortally wounded and died in his flagship *HMS Victory* as he turned the tide at that Battle of Trafalgar, the same day he hoisted that signal about expecting Englishmen to do their duty. Southey tell us:

> Never was any commander more beloved. He governed his men by their reason and their affections; they knew that he was incapable of caprice or tyranny; and they obeyed him with alacrity and joy, because he possessed their confidence as well as their love. "Our Nel" they used to say, "is as brave as a lion, and as gentle as a lamb." Severe discipline he detested, although he had been bred in a severe school (he went to sea when he was 12); he never inflicted corporal punishment if it were possible to avoid it.

And when compelled to enforce it, he, who was familiar with wounds and death, suffered like a woman. In his whole life, Nelson was never known to act unkindly towards an officer. In Nelson there was more than easiness and humanity of a happy nature: he did not merely abstain from injury; his was an active and watchful benevolence, ever desirous not only to render justice, but to do good.

Such was the character of the officer who expected every man under his command to do his duty, as he himself surely always did.

The concept of duty is not popular today in some circles. We live in a world of social turmoil and shifting values, a world where people insist on their rights but often ignore their duties. So great is the concern for rights today that people will invoke the total machinery and full power of the law to secure those rights. As a result, our nation in my view is choked with legalism, a situation that even a distinguished persecuted foreigner thought dangerous enough to bring to our attention. Of course I'm talking about Solzhenitsyn in his Harvard commencement address a year ago, when he warned that our nation had shifted the focus from the substance of the good to the rule book of rights. In this he saw the beginning of the decline of our nation's strength and national will. And I agree with him. Unless we are willing to balance each of the rights we claim with a correlative duty, we'll be as a nation like the man who wants a dollar's pay but is not willing to do a dollar's worth of work to get it. Rights incur obligations.

You of the military profession, although just initiated, will soon feel the weight of this responsibility and must lead the way in awareness of the crucial importance of duty. You must be not only leaders to your men but examples to the nation of the truth that for any position of responsibility in society, whether it be in the family, government, business, or military, there is a corresponding obligation to carry out the assigned task.

Where did this idea of duty come from? What are its historical roots? In his book *Essay on Human Understanding*, the 17th-century philosopher John Locke discussed the simple question, "Why a man must keep his word." He found three different answers to this question; answers that I believe are as applicable today as they were then.

First, said Locke, a Christian man will say, "Because God who has the power of eternal life and death requires it of me that I keep my word."

Secondly, said Locke, if one takes the Hobbesian view of life, he will say, "Because society requires it and the state will punish you if you don't." (Hobbes was a very practical kind of hardnosed guy.)

And thirdly, John Locke observed that had one of the old Greek philosophers been asked why a man should keep his word, the latter would say, "Because not to keep your word is dishonest, below the dignity of man, the opposite to virtue (*arete*)."

Two of the answers Locke cites, the Christian and the Hobbesist, seem to derive duty from the command of law, external law, the law of God in one case, the law of the state in the other. But the third answer, the Greek answer, shows that duty can be understood without reference to external law or to compulsion, divine or human. We share this understanding whenever, having made a promise, taken an oath, contracted a debt of duty—as you cadets have recently done—we feel an obligation to discharge it, even if no superior commands the act. Duty in this perspective has an absolute character. Duty is its own justification. It does not have to be propped up by anything outside itself, particularly in the line of reward or punishment. This was the teaching of Socrates who urged that men should obey the law, pay their debts, discharge their obligations, not to avoid the pain of censure or punishment, but simply because they ought to.

Closer to our own time, the great German philosopher Immanuel Kant said much the same thing. Kant was a very bright man. Known generally as a moral philosopher, he gave us much more. He really explained the function of the human mind. Moral obligation in his view rests on an internal conviction of duty, the law we give to ourselves from the outside government. To Kant carrying out our moral obligation is obeying the law we set each for ourselves. He happened to be a religious man but he was very careful in his instruction never to rely on religion as a justification for any of his ideas; he relied only on what he called pure reason. The law we set for ourselves is *free* in contrast with the external law which is *compelling*, said Kant. The argument echoes the age-old irony of the necessity of discipline for freedom. That internal law we may call the voice of conscience. It is the inner awareness of what our duty is, and it rests on no foundation but itself. The obligation to do our duty is *unconditional*. That is, we must do it for the sake of duty, because it is the right thing to do, not because it will profit us psychologically or socially or economically, not because if we don't do it and get caught we'll be punished. The categorical imperative was Kant's name for this inbred, self-imposed restraint, for the command of conscience within that tells us that the only true moral act is done from a pure sense of duty. So you can't ask what benefits will accrue from performing your duty. You must do your duty because it *is* your duty. Period. Simply put, that is the concept I want to leave with you and there's plenty of intellectual background to support it.

I hope this posits the concept of duty in historical perspective. But Locke and Kant may seem a long way from the officer (very likely many of you), soon perhaps to be standing in front of a platoon or leading a group of men in harm's way, into this very peculiar enterprise we call war. On the battlefield, you very well may find yourselves in new decision-making territory where all previous bets are off, where the rational, managerial approach of many of our fathers is no longer valid. I am describing that duty of arms that Clausewitz described as "a special profession . . . However general its relation may be and even if all the male population of the country capable of bearing arms were able to practice it, war would still continue to be different and separate from any other activity which occupies the life of man." Another old warrior, William Tecumseh Sherman (just 143 classes ahead of you plebes here tonight), said "War is cruelty and you can't refine it."

The duty of uniformed men has a long, colorful, and frequently bloody history, and it will be no different in the future. Those who think that we've seen our last war are, in my opinion, dead wrong. I make a Pascal wager that a general war will blight this planet, probably before the end of the century. Pascal, of course, advised us all to wager on that outcome by which one would stand to lose the least in case we were wrong. The trends as I read them make war the safer wager.

A lot needs to be said about the kind of education most appropriate for the professional soldiers you have chosen to be in these times of impending peril. You must aspire to a strength, a compassion, and a conviction several octaves above that of the man of the street. You can never settle for the lifestyle that Joseph Conrad characterized as ". . .skimming over the years of existence to sink gently into a placid grave, ignorant of life to the last, without ever having been made to see all it may contain of perfidy, of violence, and of terror . . ."

How to avoid ignorance of perfidy, of violence, of terror? Your education must include those intense emotional experiences of the sort common here. You will leave this place with more than a diploma. You will likely leave it with a highly developed conscience. It's almost impossible to graduate from an institution like this without it. You will have undergone an irreversible process which will never again allow you the comfort of self-satisfaction while being glib or shallow. You will likely forever carry the burdens, and they are burdens, of loyalty, commitment, passion and idealism. You will have undergone an education of the sort people refer to when they say that education is what's left over after you've forgotten all the facts you learned. And that which is left over, that conscience, that sentiment, is indispensable to that capability for which the graduates of this institution are known. And that capability is leadership.

Here at West Point, you'll learn the range of responsibility that a commitment to duty demands. Some of the things a good leader with a strong sense of duty is expected to do may surprise you. I'd like to examine some of the seldom mentioned obligations of an officer.

I say it's your duty to be a *moralist*. I define the moralist not as one who sententiously exhorts men to be good, but *one who elucidates what the good is*. (Under the press of circumstance this is sometimes unclear—perhaps in a prison camp.) The disciplined life *here* will encourage you to be men and women of integrity committed to a code of conduct and from these good habits a strength of character and resolve will grow. This is the solid foundation from which you elucidate the good, by your example, your actions and your proud tradition. A moralist can make conscious what lies unconscious among his followers, lifting them out of their everyday selves, into their better selves. The German poet Goethe once said that you limit a man's potential by appealing to what he is; rather, you must appeal to what he might be.

Secondly, there are times when you'll have to act as a *jurist*, when the *decisions you'll make will be based solely on your ideas of right and wrong, your knowledge of the people who will be affected, and your strength of conviction*. There won't be a textbook or school solution to go by. I'm talking about hard decisions when you'll be the one with a problem that has seemingly endless complications—when you'll have to think it through on your own. As a jurist, you may be writing the law, or at least regulations, and that's a weighty responsibility. When you're in the hot seat, you'll need the courage to withstand the inclination to duck a problem or hand it off; you've got to take it head on.

One word of caution: Many of your laws will be unpopular. You'll have to learn to live with that. But your laws should never be unjust. Moreover, you must never cross that fatal line of writing a law that cannot be obeyed. You must be positive and clear and not lapse into a bureaucratic welter of relativism that will have others asking what you *really* mean or trying to respond in the most politically acceptable way.

And you'll find it's going to be your duty to be a *teacher*. Every great leader I've known has been a great teacher, *able to give those around him a sense of perspective and to set the moral, social and particularly the motivational climate among them.* You must have the sensitivity to perceive philosophic disarray in your charges and to put things in order. A good starting point is to put some time in on that old injunction, "Know thyself."

Here at West Point you will follow in the footsteps of greatness. During your years here, I challenge you to leave those same clear footprints of greatness. During your years here, I challenge you to leave those same clear footprints for future generations to follow. In John Ruskin's words such a process is "painful, continual and difficult. . .to be done by kindness, by waiting, by warning, by precept, by praise, but above all by example." Teachership (in my view) is indispensable to leadership and an integral part of duty.

Fourth, you must be willing to be a *steward*. By that I mean *you must tend the flock as well as crack the whip;* you have to be compassionate and realize that all men are not products of the same mold. The old Civil War historian Douglas Southall Freeman described his formula for stewardship at my school, the Naval War College, thirty years ago last month. He said you have to know your stuff, to be a man, and to take care of your men. There are flocks outside these walls that will require your attention and test your stewardship. They're not all West Pointers out there.

The final duty is that you must be able to act as *philosophers* in your careers in order *to explain and understand the lack of a moral economy in this universe.* Many people have a great deal of difficulty with the fact that virtue is not always rewarded nor is evil always punished. To handle tragedy may indeed be the mark of an educated man, for one of the principal goals of education is to prepare us for failure. When it happens, you have to stand up and cope with it, not lash out at scapegoats or go into your shell. *The test of character is not "hanging in there" when you expect a light at the end of the tunnel, but performance of duty and persistence of example when you know that no light is coming. Believe me, I've been there.*

Summary

These readings were selected to help you understand the role of the military officer as a Leader of Character. They were intended to help you:

- explain an officer's role in the moral-ethical leadership of soldiers and organizations
- explain an officer's role in moral- ethical decision making
- explain an officer's role in enforcing ethical standards
- articulate the role of the commissioned leader as a moral arbiter

We enter the military profession products of our society with our own unique set of personal values and beliefs. For our entire lives, our personal values have embodied the justification for all of our actions and decisions. Upon entering the armed forces, we quickly assimilate into an organizational culture, an important part of which is accepting institutional values.

In 1984, the West Point History Department conducted a study of leadership characteristics that commonly led to success on the battlefield. Overwhelmingly, the common themes identified were integrity and a solid ethical foundation in matters pertaining to combat. As an officer responsible for the common defense and the lives of young soldiers, a solid foundation in character is essential. These readings will help you address moral dimensions of the military profession, provide some philosophical background on ethics, and identify some examples of leaders of character for you to reflect on and discuss. In several short months you will be personally accountable and responsible to the American people for actions and decisions. Honesty, forthrightness, the ability to use clear judgment and make sound decisions repeatedly is what the nation expects of her officers.

With this in mind, Chapter III, The Officer as a Leader of Character, provides insight into a wide range of moral and ethical issues.

A recognized expert in the field of leadership and military ethics, Malham M. Wakin, Brigadier General USAF (ret.) emphasized Aristotle's theory of character development – that teaching character is best done by modeling character, or as BG Wakin quotes from the Chinese proverb: "the way to do is to be." will provide a discussion of philosophy and modern analysis of the professional military ethic.

The next five selections depict actions and decisions of some selected leaders of character – of which there is no shortage in history. Finally, the last three readings which included excerpts from Roger Nye and ADM James B. Stockdale, offered advice and lessons learned from case studies of actual events in an officer's career.

The intent of this chapter was to help you analyze your own character as it relates to your self concept as an officer.

C H A P T E R

The Officer as a Warfighter

"Officers can never act with confidence until they are the masters of their profession.'"

Henry Knox

The Airborne's Watery Triumph

by T. Michael Booth and Duncan Spencer

It is hard to overestimate the importance of June 6, 1944, D-day, in the history of the West. D-day brought democracy back to the European continent for a good and, backed by American military and economic power, established it in the heart of Europe. What realistic chance did the Nazi army have of repelling the Normandy invasion? Very little, probably, once Eisenhower had recognized his weather advantage - and once Hitler had refused to listen to the pleas of the commander of German forces in the Low Countries and Northern France, Field Marshal Erwin Rommel, for an extra panzer division. A more likely prospect was the one that Rommel aimed for: to keep the Allies penned in a narrow bridgehead, creating an Anzio on the channel, as it were.

But what once might have been the realm of futuristic war fiction did provide a much-needed chance for fluidity early on. That was the airborne landing, which could be as devastatingly disruptive to the enemy as it was risky for the attackers. (In 1941, the slaughter of Nazi paratroops in Crete had led the Germans to suspend airborne operations.) Both British and American parachute and glider drops in the hours after midnight were, as T. Michael Booth and Duncan Spencer write, "part success, part disaster." Target zones were missed. Men fell into marshes or the sea and drowned - or dangled helplessly from trees and were shot. Disorganized groups blundered through a darkened countryside, trying to link up with their fellows. In the area behind Utah Beach where the Americans of the 82nd and 101st Airborne Divisions came down, units were never larger than a company. But these were crack troops and eventually they began to accomplish their mission, seizing key bridges, roads, and towns. For all that we focus on the long-term geopolitical results of the Normandy landings, we should not forget that they were originally the sum of countless isolated melees, many of which became the unexpected hinges of the battle, bit-

Source: *No End Save Victory*, G.P. Putnam's Sons, (2001) 421-441. Reprinted by permission of American Historical Publications.

ter small encounters that could have big consequences. Brigadier General James Gavin and the men of the 82nd proved just that in the confused series of actions that centered on the bridges at La Fière and Chef-du-Pont. Their success would keep the Wehrmacht from concentrating superior forces against the bridgehead at Utah Beach.

T. Michael Booth and *Duncan Spencer* are the authors of Paratrooper, a biography of General James M. Gavin, from which this article was adapted.

Bill Walton watched Brigadier General James Maurice Gavin gripping the door-frame of the C-47 as it flew low over Normandy, buffeting through the cold air. Behind Gavin, Walton stood amidst a "stick" of eighteen paratroopers, straining under the weight of weapons, hooked by a thin static line to a jump cable. For the hundredth time, Walton, a civilian journalist who had begged to get on the plane, cursed this stupid idea. Now he could clearly see his own death in a dozen different versions. The noise was a drug, overwhelming. Numbed by the roar of laboring engines, air sucking and screeching past the metal plane, Walton kept his eyes on the figure in the doorway and tried not to think.

Below, the land looked flat as cardboard, but Walton knew there were thousands of German soldiers down there, ready to kill him. There would be no support or protection. The clumsy transports had flown through the coastline defenses, flak rocking the planes. Preflight briefings had shown the tall poles: "Rommel's asparagus," which the Germans had set up to smash landing gliders. The beaches were bristling with guns and metal obstacles. But the planes droned on, dropping lower. The final stage of the European war, the invasion of occupied France and the destruction of Germany's waning military machine, would begin at the door where Gavin stood.

Walton was glad to be close to Gavin. Before taking off he had hoped for a big story for Time magazine on the man rapidly becoming a legend, but the hopes had dissolved and been replaced by fear. This was Walton's first jump. He vowed then and there never to do such a thing again - if only God would spare him this time, if only the parachute worked! Walton felt himself pushed forward toward the wind-tortured doorframe of the rocking aircraft. At least, he thought, the Germans would not expect them. Then came the buffeting blows and the sound of metal spattering. Flak pinged and pattered, random jagged bits of metal meant to cut, wreck, and kill. There would be no surprise.

That night, all over Normandy, paratroopers jumped in a broad band beyond the beaches, bent on many different errands of war. By the end of the next day, more than 1,000 men of the 82nd Airborne would be dead, wounded, or missing. Many would fall into the marshes and sink, or hit trees, where they would dangle to be murdered later. Some of the missing would be disabled, many with broken bones, and quickly taken prisoner.

Most of the men of the 82nd knew they were jumping into something very big, into history, like Crécy or Waterloo or Cannae. But for days they would fight alone, almost out of touch with the seaborne invaders, not knowing the outcome of the invasion.

The Normandy drop was Gavin's doorway to fame in battle. It captured the attention of the entire world and made him seem larger than life. Looking for heroes,

Americans found them in Gavin and his paratroopers. The unforgettable images of the Normandy beach, by Life magazine photographer Robert Capa, gave Americans the picture of their boys storming ashore past wreckage, past even the corpses of their friends, but irresistible. Gavin's black-faced troopers fulfilled another fantasy: the elite, tough warriors who fought by stealth and surprise, who put their lives at risk behind enemy lines. Gavin was their beau ideal.

Thirty-seven years of age on the night of the Normandy drop, Gavin looked about ten years younger. Throughout his life, until arthritis from a jump injury and, later, Parkinson's disease slowed and finally stopped him, youth was his trademark. But not only youth, a particular brand of it. Lean to an extreme, his strength was of the sinew-and-muscle kind, the strength of endurance. He lived a Spartan regimen, uninterrupted since early childhood, of heavy manual work, long-distance marches, simplicity of diet, and a belief in the virtue of physical toughness.

At the height of his powers the night he hurled himself out of the transport at the German enemy, Gavin had been preparing for this moment for twenty years. He had spent most of his waking moments thinking about his work and ways to improve it. He had read almost continuously about the great soldiers of history, and he had written out favorite aphorisms from their recorded statements for his own reference. Now the hoped-for opportunity had come.

Suddenly the green light came on, the signal to jump, and Gavin, soon to be the youngest major general since George Armstrong Custer, left Walton with a last flashing image - the wind plastering dark cloth against the paratrooper's wiry arms, his form outlined by the naked light, both hands tensed on the alloy doorway. Gavin flung himself forward and disappeared into the prop blast. Like a suicidal caterpillar, the rest of the stick, automatons now, pushed forward, a sharp metallic sound marking each man's exit. "Don't push," Walton heard himself saying, "I'll go quick." Then he, too, reached the door and jumped into the black-and-white photo below. Twisted and tossed by the turbulence of the prop blast, his mind went numb, and then with a wonderful lurch it all stopped. Silently, the canopy blossomed above his head, and he was swaying, masterfully, above the earth. The ground approached fast; then Walton heard gunfire and saw tracers streaming across the ground, and his fear returned.

Jim Gavin landed hard, in an apple orchard about two miles from where he was supposed to be, though he didn't know that until an hour later. At first, he had no idea exactly where he was. Checking that all his parts worked after his collision with the ground, he got out of his harness. About him the tree branches hung low, and among the fallen blossoms cows grazed in the moonlight. Gavin's aide, Captain Hugo V. Olson, had landed nearby. The two men "rolled up" their stick, then moved out toward heavy firing in the distance.

It was a calm, damp, mysterious spring night that Gavin would always remember. The Cotentin Peninsula in Normandy is difficult enough to move about at best; at night and with the danger of ambush, it was treacherous. The land lay in a checkerboard of ancestral fields surrounded by steep fences and walls, some overgrown, some neglected - the characteristic hedgerows of rural Normandy. These walls were fortresses: piled with dirt and brush, often heaped in stout mounds up to twenty feet high, and covered with trees and tangled undergrowth. The Germans had already fortified the hedgerows with rifle and machine-gun pits, and Gavin had found several, unmanned, scattered about the edge of the orchard. He knew that nervous German troops, alerted by antiaircraft fire and the racket of the low-flying transports, were a hazard. Lost paratroopers crackling through the underbrush invited vicious close contact, but Gavin had to risk it. He needed to find the rest of the 508th Regiment.

Right off the orchard was a small, worn, tree-lined road. Gavin and his little group walked along both sides of it, moving in crouched position with M-1s at the ready. Then, about 400 yards down, they encountered a watery marsh where they could see equipment bundles floating. Gavin wanted the bundles retrieved because they contained critical gear - machine guns, bazookas, and radios. While some of the men went after them, a red light began flashing across the marsh, then a blue one. The red was an assembly marker for the 507th Regiment, the blue for the 508th. Gavin sent Olson out to contact those groups. Meanwhile, more paratroopers joined their party, now up to about ninety men.

Olson soon returned with news. He had found a railroad embankment on the far side, which told Gavin where they were. Checking his map, he could see they had overflown their zone and were just west of the Merderet River, about two miles north of La Fière bridge, one of the 82nd's objectives. The Germans had flooded the Merderet, creating the marsh, which had been hidden from aerial reconnaissance because the high grass disguised it as solid ground. What should have been a small river was now a thousand-yard-wide lake. The men of the 508th had told Olson that they were moving out to La Fière. It was the nearest objective they knew of.

Gavin's paratroopers had little success retrieving the equipment bundles. The water was too deep and the bundles too heavy. They were collecting more men every minute, but most of them were of the 507th and green to combat. Furthermore, their commanders had told them to black out all rank insignia, so no one knew who the officers and NCOs were. The men were confused, unsure of themselves, and - exhausted by the shock of the jump - some were falling asleep. As German fire built, they took cover in the hedgerows, where it was impossible to organize them. Gavin was frustrated. With dawn approaching, he still had no idea what had happened to the rest of his command, and he had accomplished virtually nothing. He roused his disoriented men and moved out across the marsh and then south to La Fière.

It was as well Gavin could not see the whole picture of the early hours of invasion. The drop had been part success, part disaster. Paratroopers of the 82nd and 101st Airborne Divisions had landed in Normandy all right, but they were widely dispersed. Individuals and small groups wandered isolated, or fell into skirmishes with the Germans in those early hours; for two or three days, few met their objectives as standard military units.

A small force of pathfinders, whose job it was to help guide the mass of troops following close behind them, had taken off from England about 10:00 P.M. on the night of June 5. Their specially trained pilots took a circular route to the drop, first to avoid the possibility of "friendly fire" from the fleet below, then to approach their targets from an unexpected side, the southwest. Along the way, things went seriously wrong. The planes encountered little antiaircraft fire, but as soon as they reached the Cotentin, they found themselves in thick turbulent clouds. The clouds cleared just as they reached the drop area, but by then the pilots had grown disoriented and only two pathfinder teams hit their drop zones.

About a half hour behind the pathfinders came the 101st Airborne Division with 485 aircraft, 52 gliders for heavy equipment, and nearly 7,000 paratroopers. They, too, hit the clouds, and soon their formations became wildly dispersed. The 82nd, about 6,400 paratroopers in 377 aircraft and 52 gliders, followed at about 11:00 P.M. They formed in the air and headed for the Contentin efficiently enough.

The 82nd's lead C-47s, containing the 505th Regiment and Major General Matthew Ridgway, the division commander, fared best. Their mission was to drop between the Merderet River and Sainte-Mère-Eglise to secure that town and the bridges at the hamlets of La Fière and Chef-du-Pont, while forming blocking forces near the towns of Neuville-au-Plain and Beuzeville-au-Plain. They were ordered to link up with forces of the 101st, which should have been between Sainte-Mère-Eglise and Utah beach itself. Like all the planes before them, the 505th transports ran into the clouds and bucked and twisted their way through blindly. Like the others, they were dispersed, but not so badly. About half of the men landed within one mile of their drop zones. Another 350 landed within two miles of their zones, and the rest of them, around 600, came to earth scattered as much as fourteen miles from their targets.

The 508th, with assistant division commander Gavin's plane, followed the 505th. It was supposed to secure the west side of the Merderet, facing the 505th; however, its drop accuracy was even worse. Men were so scattered that the regiment never formed elements larger than company size - and most units remained platoon size. Some men landed as far as twenty miles from their drop zones. Some went into the sea and drowned. One company landed almost complete - but it hit Utah Beach.

Time and retelling have obscured how random was the emergence of the battle groups. Gavin's own recollections are of organized units and certain actions, and historian after historian has followed his pattern. In fact, it was never that simple. Most groups were at half strength and had in their ranks men of other battalions and regiments.

For the next few days, the little bridges of the Merderet River were the focus of several battles that raged between the outnumbered paratroopers and the defending Germans. Larger numbers of men from both sides gradually moved toward them, intensifying the fighting. Fate gave the fiercest of all these fights - at La Fière - to Gavin.

The bridge at La Fière was critical because it spanned a place in the stream that could make a formidable German defense line. Gavin wanted to make sure it was taken. There were other possible objectives as well, including another bridge near Chef-du-Pont, which was also critical. Squatting in the hedgerows, Gavin made his plan: If he could move his motley force to the opposite side of the river, he could help the imminent bridge action at La Fière and also attack the Chef-du-Pont bridge.

First, he dispatched Lieutenant Colonel Arthur Maloney to see if a better way could be found to cross the flooded river. Then, because Chef-du-Pont was not far, less than two miles, and a Frenchman had told Gavin that there were no Germans there, he took his remaining men, commanded by Lieutenant Colonel Edwin J. Ostberg of the 507th, and moved south to Chef-du-Pont. Perhaps from there they could double back to La Fière. Meanwhile, Moloney's patrols succeeded only in exhausting themselves, finding no boats and no path. The Germans had destroyed them all.

When Gavin's small force reached the small town of Chef-du-Pont, a train was moving from the railway station. Gavin ordered it assaulted. As soon as his troopers opened fire, Germans aboard scattered and sprinted for the bridge. The train contained nothing but empty bottles and Normandy cheese. Disappointed, Gavin ordered his troopers west to the riverbank, where they discovered that rising water had turned the bridge and approaches into a causeway almost a mile wide. An island in the middle bristled with Germans, who immediately fired on them. Gavin ordered Ostberg to take the bridge "whenever it would be feasible," intending the assault to take place that night. Ostberg, a determined man, had other ideas.

While Gavin footed back to La Fière, trying to unlock the tactical situation facing him, an unfortunate incident occurred at Chef-du-Pont. Impatient and bent on seizing the bridge, Ostberg moved troopers closer to the bank. Suddenly a nearby German rose to surrender. A tired trooper shot him. Another German stood up, and he too was shot before anyone could call a cease-fire. Now the Germans who might have surrendered all together found themselves unwilling to retreat down the causeway and unable to surrender. They would fight to the last.

Ostberg organized a charge even though the bridge and the island lay a little over a hundred yards from the closest cover. About fifty brave paratroopers rushed straight into German fire. As soon as they reached the arch of the bridge, the colonel and five of his men were cut down by a stream of machine-gun bullets. (Ostberg survived his wounds, only to be killed later in Holland.) By this time, Maloney, sent by Gavin to take command, had arrived and mounted a second charge. This one stopped at about the same point with roughly the same effect, though Maloney was not wounded. Next, he and his crew crawled onto the bridge approach and fought at close quarters from one foxhole to the next with grenades and rifle fire. This went on inconclusively all afternoon. In the midst of it, Gavin recalled Maloney to La Fière, and command at Chef-du-Pont passed to Captain Roy Creek.

The stalemate then took a bad turn. The stubborn Germans wheeled up a fieldpiece to the western end of the causeway, and now the crouching troopers - numbering just over thirty - endured direct artillery fire. Creek looked to the rear of his position to discover a German platoon deploying for an assault. But help came from an unexpected direction. An American glider carrying a 57mm antitank gun, lumbering in on schedule, landed amidst Creek's position. It seemed miraculous. The troopers quickly turned the 57mm on the field gun across the marsh and scored a direct hit. Next, they turned it on the German infantry to their rear, breaking their ranks with a few shots. As they did, a reinforcing American platoon arrived. The crisis had passed.

Just as the sun set, Creek discovered a position north along the riverbank that offered a perfect field of fire to hammer the remaining Germans on the island. Within ten minutes, the island fell. So instead of being wiped out, Creek now had half a bridge, thirteen dead, and twenty-three wounded. But the western side still loomed a distant 700 yards away, and from all appearances, the Germans held it strongly.

Trouble came elsewhere. Because of the hedgerows, the small crossroads town of La Fière did not fall easily or swiftly, though it was defended by only one German platoon. The Americans assaulted with more than a battalion, but the Germans held all morning. The separate parts of several forces were unaware of their comrades; the hedgerows and the lack of radio communication led many American paratroop elements to assault the town piecemeal. It finally fell in the early afternoon, and A Company of the 1st Battalion of the 505th took up positions on the riverbank, on the north side of the road overlooking a causeway similar to the one at Chef-du-Pont. Captain Robert D. Rae, with a mixed batch of 507th and 101st Airborne men, held the south side of the road. Other 507th men had already crossed to the west side of the river; but they seemed a long way off.

Meanwhile, very little had been happening as it should have on the west bank. The two regiments that should have landed there had not, and only three significant battle groups had formed. The first, commanded by Colonel George V. Millett, had been cut off and battered by the German 91st Division around Amfreville. The second was under the leadership of Lieutenant Colonel Charles J. Timmes, the commander of the 2nd Battalion of the 507th. After extricating himself from the marsh, where he had nearly drowned, Timmes had moved toward thee sound of gunfire near Amfreville. Along his cross-country route, he picked up more men. At Amfreville, large detachments of the 91st Division waited entrenched, and as Timmes and his party got close, the Germans responded with heavy fire. But seeing that they were overmatched, the Americans began a fighting withdrawal, hedgerow to hedgerow, with the Germans in pursuit. Finally, they reached the same orchard Gavin had left the night before. There, with their backs to the marsh, they dug a defensive perimeter. They were soon surrounded by Germans moving into the area.

The third group of American troops had been assembled by Lieutenant Colonel Thomas J. B. Shanley about three miles southwest of the bridge at La Fière, well behind German lines. His battalion was the only one of the 508th that was dropped somewhat intact, though their assembly took time. When, at dawn, he had collected as many men as he could, Shanley found himself facing serious German pressure just holding his own position. Artillery soon found the range of his foxholes, and machine-gun fire raked his force. He and his men prepared for a siege.

On the morning of D day, Colonel Timmes, in the apple orchard, sent a ten-man patrol under the command of Lieutenant Louis Levy to fortify the La Fière bridge. As Levy and the patrol, without radio or further orders, kept anxious watch at the bridge, several other American paratrooper bands passed by, but none of them stayed. They all sought objectives elsewhere. When the 505th began to fortify the east side of the river, they sent up an orange smoke signal, signifying friendly invasion forces. A relieved Levy on the west side, at Cauquigny, responded with orange smoke. The

505th did not know that their signal had been answered by a ten-man platoon and assumed that the 507th or the 508th were across the river in force. Shortly, a German battalion with tank support attacked Levy's little group from the west. The platoon fought bravely - they succeeded in disabling three of the German tanks - but, without relief from the 505th, they were soon forced to retreat to the orchard. At the end of D day, the Americans found themselves blinking with fatigue, but holding only the eastern halves of the two critical bridgeways they had been dropped to capture.

Elsewhere, things were better. The critical town in the 82nd's area of operations was Sainte-Mère-Eglise, the transportation hub for the area, the intersection of all local roads. Holding it meant German reinforcements to the beaches would be severely disrupted. Early on the morning of D day, it fell easily to Lieutenant Colonel Edward ("Cannonball") Krause's 3rd Battalion of the 505th, becoming the first French town liberated in World War II. Krause had learned from a drunken Frenchman, who gaily offered to guide him, that only one enemy platoon remained there; the Germans had thought the fight over. Krause found an ugly sight. Pilots confused by a house fire had dropped their sticks right on Sainte-Mère-Eglise. The Germans had killed most of the unfortunate troopers as they hit the ground. Dead and wounded GIs lay on the streets; many were hanging from telephone poles and buildings. One man dangled from the church steeple for hours saving his life by feigning death. Fortunately, because of Krause's timely arrival, by noon on D day Sainte-Mère-Eglise had become the center of 82nd Airborne operations - and a target of German wrath.

By the time Gavin returned to the La Fière bridge in midafternoon, the situation had deteriorated badly. As he approached, retreating 505th troopers rushed past with news that the Germans had broken through. Aghast, Gavin ordered them to turn back. He found Colonel Roy E. Lindquist, the ranking man, who had a small reserve of about eighty men, and double-timed for the causeway, meanwhile sending a runner for Maloney's men, still at Chef-du-Pont. Gavin arrived at the causeway ready for a fight.

That afternoon, the same German battalion that had scattered Levy's little band launched an armored attack across the causeway. A Company of the 505th, under the command of Captain John J. Dolan, dug in at the eastern end of the causeway and took the attack head-on. The Germans led with a powerful barrage of mortar and artillery fire, then came on with two French Renault tanks, infantry running in their wake. Opposing them, Dolan's men squatted in formerly German rifle pits, supported by two bazooka teams.

The bazookas did their work on the thinly armored French tanks; both stopped after a close-range duel of bazooka rounds and point-blank cannon fire. The foot soldiers, now without their shield, were exposed, cut down, or routed back across the causeway by accurate American fire. Dolan's men still controlled the approach to the causeway, their success bolstering their confidence. The Germans returned several more times, but troopers kept driving them back; however, the artillery barrage never ceased. By morning, it would cost Dolan six more men.

Gavin could do nothing further at either Chef-du-Pont or La Fière, so he moved back toward Sainte-Mère-Eglise and established a command post between the two bridgeheads. His awkward position baffled him. As yet, he had no word from Utah Beach, so he did not know that the landing had gone smoothly and seaborne troops were bearing down on Sainte-Mère-Eglise. In fact, that night the vanguard would reach a point only about a mile east. He had no idea what fate had held for the paratroopers on the west side of the Merderet. He had no jeep or truck to shuttle between his two critical bridgeheads. However, he did have radio contact with division headquarters just outside Sainte-Mère-Eglise, where Ridgway had set up his command post, and he knew that the town was under siege from several points. At evening, headquarters finally sent him a jeep with a radio, and he succeeded in raising the embattled Colonel Shanley, dug in far to the west. Shanley had little good news to share, but at least Gavin knew he was still fighting.

As night fell on D day, Gavin lay down to rest. For a blanket, all he could find was a parachute laid across a dead trooper. He could not bring himself to use the man's shroud for a blanket, so he found a camouflage net, lay down against a hedgerow to give himself shelter from artillery fire, and fell asleep. A runner soon brought a summons from Ridgway's staff. Gavin walked with Olson through the full moonlight back to Sante-Mère-Eglise, only to find that the message had been in error. Ridgeway was asleep himself and annoyed at the visit. Frustrated and weary, Gavin trudged back to his command post and resumed his rest.

The trivial incident rankled in both men for years, even though both were no doubt blameless. Communications are the first thing to be lost in the chaos of combat. It marked the beginning of a coolness between Ridgway and Gavin. Years later, in his own writing, Gavin described the summons by Ridgway as related here. Ridgway, however, in his autobiography, describes the visit from Gavin as if he had been awakened by a panicked messenger bringing news of a counterattack on La Fière. Both of them made a point of mentioning it years after the war. It signaled a break in their friendship, or at least the end of reverence, the start of rivalry. Ridgway would maintain that a distraught Gavin had come to ask for permission to withdraw from La Fière that night, an implication Gavin resented.

Dawn of June 7 found the 82nd in a precarious triangle of French soil. Time was against them, for unless relieved, and unless the overall invasion plan was working, the 82nd had no chance. Ridgway had gathered only about one-quarter of his division. The Germans had tanks, superior numbers, and vastly superior firepower. The 82nd's position was anchored by corners resting on La Fière, Chef-du-Pont, and Sainte-Mère-Eglise. The division's lower echelons still had no assurance of an advance from the beachhead. Soldiers' rumors spread that the invasion had failed. Ridgway and Gavin, however, ignored the rumors. They were determined to hold what they had no matter what - especially Sante-Mère-Eglise.

The Germans had not finished with La Fière. That morning, after a two-hour mortar barrage, they launched a final attack on the bridge with all they had. Four French tanks led the way. Once again the valiant bazooka men fought their duel, this time helped by a lone 57mm gun to their rear. The combination wrecked the first tank, and that stalled the others. But it gave the Germans a steel shield of wrecked tanks just thirty-five yards from Dolan's lead platoon, under the command of Lieutenant William A. Oakley. The Germans zeroed their mortars on the ground and kept up small-arms and tank fire. Oakley fell, badly hit, almost immediately and was dragged to the rear where he died just a few hours later. Sergeant William D. Owens, leader of the first squad, replaced him. Owens found himself in a desperate situation. More than half his men had fallen already, and the survivors had little ammunition. His machine guns fired so fast they quit from the heat. The company first sergeant grabbed the wounded and threw them back into the fight.

Owens, a quiet Detroit punch-drill operator in peacetime, stood his ground and ran from man to man redistributing ammo from the dead and wounded. When his gunners died, he took over their machine guns. Later he said:

> The artillery shells and mortars were coming in like machine-gun fire. I don't know how it was possible to live through it. Then the infantry came again and we gave them everything we had. The machine gun I had was so hot it quit firing. I took Private McClatchy's BAR, he had been wounded earlier, and I fired it until I ran out of ammunition. I then took a machine gun that belonged to a couple of men who took a very near hit. They were killed. The gun had no tripod, so I rested it across a pile of dirt and used it. With this and one other machine gun and a 60mm mortar, we stopped them, but they had gotten to within twenty-five yards of us.

Then, abruptly, the Germans called a halt. Owens was down to fourteen men. He kept firing and yelling for them to hold on. He had no radio because his radio man had taken a direct hit from a German 88mm gun, so he sent a runner to Dolan describing the situation and asking for orders. His answer came back in writing: "I don't know of a better place than this to die." Owens passed along the message, and the survivors hung on. Suddenly, the Germans raised a flag with a red cross. Firing tapered off, then ceased. The Germans indicated they wanted to evacuate their wounded - and their other soldiers went with them. One platoon had broken the back of the last German attempt to secure the bridge at La Fière. The tide had risen to a height, and now Gavin could plan his own attack.

He had a small mobile reserve. As pressure came at the critical points, he kept moving Lindquist and a scratch bunch to the rescue. Both he and Ridgway wondered how long they could hold, for German infantry, armor, and artillery continued to threaten Sainte-Mère-Eglise. Unknown to the airborne commanders, help was coming: The armored task force under Colonel Edson D. Raff had landed on D day as planned, and Raff rushed them toward Sainte-Mère-Eglise with all the speed the armor could make. But two miles east of the town, the Germans had constructed a strongpoint of infantry and 88mm cannon. Not only did it stall Raff's column, it occupied a vantage point overlooking the landing zones designated for gliders. The 88s hit four of Raff's armored vehicles. Then, as the sun set, the gliders came winging in toward a double death trap. The field was too small for proper landings, so most crash-landed heavily. Then, those who survived the crash came under fire from the Germans. Shaken soldiers were unable to defend themselves as they fought to get out of the flimsy planes. In minutes, the landing zone was strewn with crashed gliders and dead and dying glidermen, while Raff could only look on helplessly.

Although at that time the 82nd had no radio link with the outside world, one patrol had gotten out word of the paratroopers' predicament, so the commanders on Utah Beach knew the situation. As soon as General J. Lawton "Lightning Joe" Collins landed on D-plus-one and heard, he ordered a reserve tank battalion, the 746th under Lieutenant Colonel D. G. Hupfer, forward to break through.

On the morning of D-plus-one, German forces launched an assault on Sainte-Mère-Eglise. They opened with an artillery barrage, supported with self-propelled guns. Lieutenant Colonel Ben Vandervoort's 505th troopers resisted with verve. They had been holding well against the Germans, and their confidence ran high. They yielded no ground except to evacuate wounded and to readjust fields of fire. At noon, the 8th Infantry under Colonel James Van Fleet arrived, along with Hupfer's and Raff's tanks, followed by General Collins himself. With the tanks and the help of the 8th Infantry, Vandervoort's paratroopers counterattacked immediately. German troops in the Sainte-Mère-Eglise area were decisively thrown back that afternoon. The liberation of the town was final.

After the 8th and the armor had arrived, the triangle of ground held by the 82nd no longer seemed so tenuous. But the bridges remained blocked, half held by strong German forces, and the Millett, Timmes, and Shanley units, isolated on the west side of the Merderet, remained stranded. Ridgway and Gavin evolved a plan. They would break the deadlock with fresh 325th glider infantry, who had just landed. On the morning of June 8, D-plus-two, the 505th, with elements of the 325th in support and assisted by the 8th Infantry, would attack north toward Montebourg to expand the area the division already held. Meanwhile, the 1st Battalion of the 325th would attack across the river, using a fortuitously discovered ford across the Merderet between the two causeways, to relieve Timmes in the orchard. They then intended to smash the Germans at Cauquigny from the rear. Simultaneously, Lindquist was to assault the Chef-du-Pont causeway with 507th and 508th troopers and relieve Shanley. Millett's force would attack toward the 325th men and in the process break out themselves.

The assault by the 505th proved difficult. The troopers and glidermen advanced rapidly against heavy, determined German resistance, hedgerow to hedgerow; however, the 8th Infantry assisting was not able to make such rapid progress, stalling the overall attack.

Lower-level commanders were allowed to make their own decisions on the assault across the Merderet. Trouble began with Lindquist's group at Chef-du-Pont, where Shanley was ordered by radio to clear out the opposite end of the causeway before an attack was attempted. Shanley sent a twenty-man scratch patrol forward, led by Lieutenant Woodrow W. Millsaps, which proceeded to fight one of the hardest engagements of the invasion. Everyone considered Millsaps an eccentric, but this night he proved pure warrior. As his men approached the head of the causeway, they struck machine gun after machine gun. At first his column buckled, and some of the men tried to run, but Millsaps steadied them. They kept moving forward, methodically destroying the German machine guns with grenades and accurate fire, hedgerow after hedgerow. Then they reached a road junction near the causeway where three machine gunners and riflemen waited. Again Millsaps urged his men forward, and again they destroyed the German positions. Millsaps himself was knocked down three times by German grenades, but neither he nor his men hesitated. They were in a killing frenzy; each man was alone, paying no attention to those who fell. They fought and killed until the Germans broke before their charge. Now Lindquist needed only to charge the causeway.

But Lindquist decided not to mount the attack. He had seen what the fixated Millsaps had not - that artillery was failing near the causeway - and he feared shells would hit the trucks he planned to send over the bridge, blocking it. After all his effort, Millsaps was mortified, and he begged Lindquist to go. But Lindquist would not be moved. Just before dawn, Shanley withdrew the survivors of Millsaps's charge, squandering a military advantage gained through horrible sacrifice. He did not send a relief force across for another full day. Meanwhile, Shanley's men - low on food, water, ammunition, and medical supplies - sweated in their foxholes.

North of La Fière, the 325th men led by 1st Battalion commander Lieutenant Colonel Terry Sanford, made their move across the ford. As they crossed, they drew not a shot, but as soon as they reached the first hedgerow, German machine gunners found their range. The men advanced, but the fight became confused in the hedgerows. Companies lost contact with one another, and the fight grew desperate at close quarters. Ridgway, watching from across the river, remembered it as one of the most intense combat actions he saw in the war. It proved fruitless, and Sanford and his men ended up in retreat, joining Timmes beneath the apple trees.

During the withdrawal of one platoon, Private First Class Charles N. DeGlopper stood defiantly with his Browning automatic rifle, acting as rear guard for his friends until he was killed. He was the largest man then in the 82nd, and those who were there remember the last sight of him, his six-foot-seven-inch, 240-pound frame illuminated by the flickering muzzle flashes of his weapon. When he finally fell dead of multiple wounds, his comrades were on safer ground. DeGlopper was awarded the Congressional Medal of Honor, but his action, too, had been in vain. The Germans still held Cauquigny, the causeway remained useless to the Allies, and a battalion of the 325th now sat bottled up with Shanley. As for Millett's men, they were unable to break through to Shanley or Timmes, and Millett himself was captured.

With the dawn of June 9, D-plus-three, Ridgway faced difficult decisions. His night assaults - which had not been Gavin's responsibility because of their command structure - had been humiliating failures. Now Collins suggested that his newly arrived 90th Division be used to force the La Fière causeway. Ridgway refused to consider it. He was far too proud and determined to let others do what had been assigned to him. He discussed it with Gavin, who agreed, and Ridgway gave the mission to him. Gavin was to force a crossing and drive the Germans back westward toward Amfreville. For the mission, Ridgway augmented his already stretched forces with the 3rd Battalion of the 325th, under the command of Lieutenant Colonel Charles A. Carrell, and one company of 507th paratroopers commanded by Captain Rae. This unit had been defending the La Fière side of the causeway since D day and had been severely punished by the Germans. In support, Gavin also had use of the 90th

Division's artillery, what artillery the 82nd itself could assemble, and twelve Sherman tanks. They scheduled the attack for the morning of June 10, D-plus-four.

Psychologically, the 3rd Battalion was hardly ready for the task it had drawn. The objective looked daunting from the far shore. The Merderet was 500 yards across at that point, and the men would be silhouetted without cover on the causeway as they charged its length. To make matters worse, this battalion had been part of the 101st and was given to the 82nd at a preinvasion reorganization. Carrell thought Ridgway and Gavin were going to sacrifice the transferred battalion. His attitude was infectious, and the troops had little enthusiasm for their mission.

Gavin himself was uneasy with it on the morning of the attack. To get a closer look, he and the commander of 90th Division artillery, Brigadier General John M. Devine, crawled out onto the causeway as close as they dared. Gavin precisely pinpointed targets he wanted the artilleryman to hit. Meanwhile, Olson lined up the tanks to give direct fire support at any targets across the river they could find. By the time Gavin ran, crouching, back from the causeway, it was 9:00 A.M.

A spring-morning calm fell over the placid Merderet waters. It might have been a pretty, deep green landscape, with the hump of the bridge the focus, except for the German fire that raked the American positions. But Gavin saw no scenery; he worried about the glidermen. Their commander had made it clear that he thought the causeway charge stood little chance. To hedge his bets, Gavin called over Colonel Maloney and Captain Rae, both men he trusted. Maloney looked the part that day. He was a huge man, six feet four inches tall and about 240 pounds. The morning of the assault, a close artillery round had sent a large fragment his way, ripping his helmet and gouging a deep wound in the side of his head. Maloney, who could have honorably stood down from the action, had his head bandaged and found a new helmet. When Gavin summoned him that morning, he noticed how tough Maloney looked with his hulking form and blood-streaked stubble of red beard.

Gavin had brief instructions. He told Maloney to have Rae ready to charge instantly if the 325th assault faltered. He wanted them to "yell their heads off" and attack through the 325th in order to carry along the faint-of-heart. Rae and Maloney walked back to brief the anxious troopers, who took the news hard, for a glance showed every man he would be under fire from three sides for 500 yards of hard running. Maloney told them they owed it to Timmes and his men. They would give it a try.

Gavin ordered the 325th gliderman to move into jump-off position using a walled road that afforded a covered approach to the causeway. At 10:30 A.M., artillery, small arms, and tanks cut loose at the Germans' positions on the west bank. It was vicious and accurate. Gavin thought it seemed the whole shoreline caught fire. Stunned Germans with bleeding ears jumped from their positions and dashed across the causeway to surrender. The barrage ceased, and a short lull followed. The Americans had planned to end the barrage with a smoke screen to shield the charging troopers. Everyone waited for its welcome sight, but it never happened - the artillery batteries had no smoke. Then the Germans recovered from the barrage and began firing. The wall shielding the gliderman vibrated with the impact of bullets, and German artillery and mortars pummeled the causeway and the shoreline. Gavin, crouching on a rise to the rear, expected the glidermen to come into view as they charged forward, but they didn't appear. Incensed, he ran to Carrell by the wall and shouted, "Go! Go! Go!"

> Carrell yelled back, "I don't think I can do it!"
> Gavin stopped in his tracks and asked, "Why not?"
> "I'm sick," Carrell responded.

Gavin's voice fell almost to a whisper and he said, "Okay, you're through." In Carrell's place, Colonel Harry Lewis, the 325th's commander, appointed the regiment's S-3, Arthur W. Gardner, to command.

Gardner ordered his new command to move, and they did, but not as they should have. Most of the lead platoon took off, but as the next group moved up, a man fell dead in the gap in the wall, a bullet through his brain. The men behind him froze. As a result, the initial assault consisted of about three squads, thirty men. They charged into the combined weapons of the better part of a German regiment. Captain Al Ireland, Gavin's S-1 with the 505th and a longtime friend, remembered it as a "firestorm of shell and whining bullets." Yet that first bunch of glidermen did not waver. Arms pumping hard, they charged on and reached the other side, miraculously nearly intact. It was not until they had made it across that they realized no one had followed them. Still they pushed on, and they began rolling up German positions in relentlessly sharp actions at close quarters. Soon, other glidermen overcame their shocks and with kicking them, moved forward. Accurate German fire cut down many. Others simply lost nerve and lay in the road ditches. As Gavin watched, the causeway became strewn with the living and the dead. Many men withered into frozen immobility, as if by recoiling they could somehow avoid death. Gavin knew it was the moment between success and failure. He, Ridgway, and Maloney ran out onto the causeway and urged the men on - Maloney bellowing in his deep voice, Ridgway setting a calm example as he tried to move a disabled tank blocking the way. Troopers remember Gavin telling soldiers, "Son, you can do it." All three officers were without cover, yet none of them was hit. The forward observer for the artillery, crouching in his foxhole, was stunned when Ridgway appeared and thanked him for the good barrage that had preceded the first wave.

Gavin turned to Maloney and told him to bring on Rae. Maloney signaled, and Rae led about ninety troopers in a mad rush onto the causeway. Now the wrecked tank proved an obstacle. The dead, the wounded, and those seeking cover filled the space behind and beside it. The wreck offered respite to shocked soldiers who could find nothing to move them on. Rae's men charged the tank like a football line. Kicking, prying, and pushing, they manhandled men out of the way and broke the jam, and their charge rolled on. Troopers ran, fired, reloaded, and ran some more. The wave of olive drab carried forward until it swept into the German embankment. With them went many glidermen who had also been trying to get through, and now the causeway and the bridge - through bodies were already stacked in the gutters - filled with running, shouting Americans sweeping around the wreck and forward. When the wave hit the Germans, they withered and began surrendering in droves. Many who were there, including Gavin, give Rae and his troopers credit for carrying the day, and they did break the attack loose; but they had help. The small contingent of glidermen had gone first and grappled in the teeth of the German defenses, so when Rae's assault came, German fire at the causeway had slackened somewhat. Rae's arrival consolidated a toehold at Cauquigny, but surviving Germans beyond that toehold fought on desperately to contain the breakthrough, and the glidermen and paratroopers trying to push beyond Cauquigny west toward Amfreville ran into stiffer and stiffer resistance.

Once the wreckage was cleared, Gavin returned to the causeway and continued pushing men forward. They needed every man possible to strengthen their assault. When, around noon, all available men and tanks were across, Gavin went to Cauquigny himself, where he found glidermen and paratroopers still routing the last resolute Germans out of firing positions. He learned that his forward troopers had expanded the bridgehead fast, relieving Timme's and Shanley's positions. He headed for Shanley first, because he had to know what shape the men were in after hanging on alone. He needed them now to expand the bridgehead farther.

As he moved gingerly along the riverbank, Gavin found a dead paratrooper, still in harness, hanging from a tree. After the recent vicious action, the sight angered him deeply. The Germans had shot the helpless man, rather than capturing him as the professional code dictated. With his rage came the determination to push punishing offensive operations.

He found Shanley's unit battered but still game. After grouping two battalions of 325th men, Rae's troopers, and Timme's and Shanley's, he set off to find Ridgway in order to make plans. Gavin wanted his troops pushing westward as relentlessly as possible to expand the bridgehead and to beat back the Germans from the counterattack that he knew must come.

Sure enough, even as Gavin conferred with Ridgeway late that afternoon, the Germans hit back, hard. As evening fell, the Americans started to break. A radio message from Colonel Lewis, the 325th commander, told Gavin the new bridgehead was collapsing. He broke off his hurried conference with Ridgeway and ran back across the river to the 325th command post. German guns were sending panicked men streaming rearward, and when Gavin reached the 325th, chaos ruled. Lewis had collapsed from shock. Medics gave him an injection and evacuated him to the rear. (No one knew it then, but he had cancer and died just months later.) In his place Lieutenant Colonel Herbert Sitter, the regimental executive officer, took command. Gavin found Sitter at Cauquigny, recently taken, preparing a withdrawal. Gavin asked what he was doing. Sitter responded, "I can't hold."

Gavin's eyes became icy gray slits, and he told the shaken colonel before him, "We are going to counterattack with every resource we have - including you, regimental clerks, headquarters people, and anyone else we can get our hands on with a weapon." Sitter blanched but did as he had been ordered. Then Gavin located Maloney. The giant, somehow unscathed in the charge, stood calm and ready for instructions. They ran back to the causeway, where, for the second time that day, Maloney stood on the road and forced men back into battle. Gavin remembered it as a magnificent sight - Maloney, this time holding a broken-off tree limb in his hands, bellowing that no one was going to get by him. Gavin's place was now with his forward elements, and he headed for the front lines, farther west of the bridgehead.

That night, the 90th Division arrived and relieved the 82nd. The roads to the beach were now clear of Germans, and American tanks and infantry plowed inland. The Wehrmacht had lost its chance to concentrate superior forces against the beach. Allied air pressure prevented them from reinforcing at the decisive moment, and every day thousands of British and American troops streamed across those beaches into Normandy. The initial crust of enemy behind Utah Beach, caught between strong forces on the beaches and the stubborn resistance of the paratroopers, had been ripped up badly. The Germans had yielded the beaches and the low Merderet country, principally because of the double blow dealt them from behind.

At this point the 82nd's involvement might well have been over, but it continued to play a vital role in cutting off the Cotentin Peninsula. Along the way, it mauled the better parts of four German divisions - including the hated 91st, which had shot defenseless paratroopers caught in trees. While Cherbourg was being taken, a new corps - the VIII, under Major General Troy Middleton - was created. Middleton was given the 82nd to use as needed to punch southward; by the end of June, Middleton had ordered the division to assist with the breakout from the hedgerow county: The 82nd was to provide the main punch in the center.

Ridgway was happy to oblige to please higher command, but Gavin voiced strong misgivings. The division was badly understrength. In many of the combat companies, actual strength totaled around 50 men or less (at least one mustered just 12); there should have been over 150. At least two of his regimental commanders protested the attack order. Gavin concurred, and he took the issue to ridgway.

Ridgeway was unbending, and the division jumped off as planned. Gavin's protests and Ridgeway's insistence that they continue attacking fueled ill feelings between the two men. Gavin felt Ridgeway was wrong, that he did not understand the limits of his own men. There were many other units available for the job, and it was long past time when the paratroopers should have been withdrawn and the division rebuilt.

Yet the breakout attack went off well. The desperately understrengthed companies reached all their assigned objectives. Airborne was beginning to acquire a reputation for performance. Higher command was once again impressed by what those "crazy characters" could do. But Gavin's fears were also confirmed. The final attack, in heavy rain from a bridgehead at Pontl'Abbè, carried them to the outskirts of La Haye-du-Puits with such speed that the other divisions were left lagging, and higher command had to halt the paratroops to protect their exposed flanks. The hedgerow fighting proved costly once again. Understrengthed regiments became more so, several battalion commanders were wounded, including Maloney and Shanley. Other notables, such as Lieutenant Louis Levy, died. When the 82nd Airborne Division finally pulled out of the front lines to return to England, sixteen of its original twenty-one regimental and battalion commanders had been killed, captured, or wounded. In total, the division lost 46 percent in killed, wounded, and missing.

Losses like these have paralyzed most divisions; however, throughout the Normandy campaign, the 82nd never lost combat effectiveness in spite of it. And somewhere, during the desperate night actions and the bloody slog through the hedgerows, legend descended on the division. If their exploits had not been widely reported before, they were after Normandy. Though their dead lay strewn from Sainte-Mère-Eglise to Amfreville to La Haye-du-Puits, their deeds and rakish air captured the American imagination at a time of one of the nation's greatest successes. And above them rose the image of their lean, handsome, and articulate commander, Slim Jim Gavin. He had long been known to higher command. Now the press took him, and he became a public figure. He had achieved more from his war than he had ever planned, but now he wanted sole command of a division. And he was about to get it.

Legacy

by George C. Wilson

The farthest thing from Johnny Libs's mind as he sat on the edge of the jungle clearing in Vietnam on the sunny Easter afternoon of April 10, 1966, was that he would have to shoot someone dead in thirty seconds. His thoughts had instead been pushed away from the Vietnam War and toward home by the chaplain standing before Charlie Company preaching the Easter sermon. The Protestant chaplain had been vaulted by helicopter from the safe world of the rear to the murderous one of the jungle 40 miles east of Saigon near the village of Xa Cam My. His crisp clothes and full face bespoke the fenced safety and hot-meal comfort of one of those fortresses the Americans were building-around Saigon. The man of God was preaching to young men who had been transformed by the war from what-the-hell teenagers to stealthy soldiers living by the jungle commandment: Kill or be killed.

"Think of your loved ones back home," the preacher told the ragged soldiers sitting under the trees in front of him. "They will be going to church on Easter and praying for you."

"I don't think that's going to do us much good this time," Libs told himself. "Not where they're sending us tomorrow."

First Lieutenant John Wells Libs, 23, was leader of 2d Platoon, Charlie Company, Second Battalion, Sixteenth Infantry Regiment within the First Infantry Division, known as The Big Red One. He knew as he sat in the sun vainly trying to keep his mind on the chaplain's words that if the Vietcong struck in force tomorrow, as his commanders predicted, he would not only have to run his own platoon of thirty-five men, but the whole damn Charlie Company. The company going to the field would number 134 men. The rest of Charlie Company's 157 were in the rear or out of action because of injuries, leaves or other reasons that always reduce the number of trigger-pullers available for a fight. He knew the odds were against him surviving Division's new strategy of dangling a small American force in front of a big Vietcong one to entice them to stand and fight. So Johnny Libs this sunny Easter afternoon tried to soak up the warmth and transport himself back to his hometown, Evansville, Indiana.

Source: *Mud Soldiers: Life Inside the New American Army,* George C. Wilson, (1989) 7-42. Reprinted by permission of Charles Scribner's Sons Maxmillan Publishing Co.

He had been warmed in Evansville by a thick blanket of security and happiness: house, family, money, car, friends, prestige. Johnny Libs had been athletic, bright and popular in high school. Even though he was only 5 feet 9 and 160 pounds, he was fast and agile. He captained the Memorial High School football team; ran the 100- and 220-yard dashes on the track team; was vice president of the class; earned high grades; dated lots of pretty girls. He graduated in 1960, went to St. Louis University and then transferred to Loyola University in New Orleans where the males had to join the Army ROTC whether they liked it or not. He was definitely an or-not until he went through infantry training at Fort Sill, Oklahoma, in the summer before his senior year at Loyola.

At Sill he discovered a way to live his boyhood dreams of playing John Wayne in the jungle without looking juvenile. He would join the infantry and lead a platoon in battle. Advancing through the woods to knock out an enemy machine gun without getting gunned down took skill and daring. And it was fun! Energizing. Enlivening. Flirting with death made him feel more alive than ever before. Damn! There is something to this Army after all, he concluded.

Libs vowed to become a blue-corded infantryman, a soldier who often had to go into the mud but got the dirty jobs done whether anybody outside the special fraternity realized it or not. The motto of the infantry platoon leader, "Follow me!" suited Johnny Libs just fine. He related to the mud soldier's bastardization of the 23rd Psalm: "Yea, though I walk through the valley of the shadow of death, I will fear no evil: for I am the meanest son of a bitch in the valley."

But the United States Army had other ideas for Libs, J. W., serial number 054 167 25, when it commissioned him a second lieutenant upon his graduation from Loyola in 1964. Vietnam was just a little skirmish way out there somewhere. President Lyndon B. Johnson had not yet gotten Congress to sign that blank check called the Gulf of Tonkin Resolution. Libs had studied business and finance in college, largely at Army expense, so the Army decided: We need this guy to be a finance officer more than a trigger-puller in a jungle nobody cares about.

"Fuck this," Libs said to himself after a few months of listening to boring lectures at the Army finance school at Fort Benjamin Harrison in Indianapolis, "I'm going infantry." He pulled every string he could reach, including those his family, who owned a big candy business in Evansville, had tied to Senator Vance Hartke of Indiana. "You've got it all wrong, Lieutenant," his superiors at Benjamin Harrison kept telling him. "You go from the infantry to here, not from here to the infantry. You're not going anyplace."

But Libs outmaneuvered them, got transferred to the infantry and took the basic course for junior officers at Fort Benning in Columbus, Georgia, "Home of the Infantry." He went on to earn his Ranger tab. He liked the roughest parts of Ranger training the best. He kept volunteering for Vietnam until the First Division at Fort Riley, Kansas, sent him there in June 1965.

The preacher's Easter sermon about Christ's Resurrection struck Libs as just the opposite of what he had been experiencing in Vietnam for the last ten months. He had been exposed to Death, not Resurrection. Overexposed. He would never get used to holding a dying soldier in his arms, assuring him, "You'll be all right," and then watching him turn gray, white—then die.

"Hey, Chaplain!" Libs asked the crisp man of the cloth in silent questions jumping up in his mind, "do you have any idea how tough it is to live in Vietnam after the kids you've loved and led die? Do you have any idea how hard it is to wash their blood out of your brain?"

Every time the high command flew his 2d Platoon out of the jungle and back to base camp for three days' rest before sending it out for another thirty days of killing and being killed chasing Vietcong, Libs tried to wash the blood out with Budweiser. No amount of beer did it. Nor did trying to bury himself body and soul in a woman he hardly knew. He had tried that on an R & R—rest and recreation—leave in Tokyo. He thought it was working and overstayed his leave by two weeks, asking himself:

"So what are they going to do to me for going AWOL—send me to Vietnam?"

The stolen days of leave failed to wash away either the blood or the war. He returned to his platoon. It was the only place where people understood his disease of hollowness, fear, anger and guilt. His AWOL caused a brief flap at headquarters, but nothing major. It was never put on paper. His superiors needed Libs too much in the jungle to take the time to court-martial him. Johnny Libs had gotten real good at finding and killing VC.

The chaplain finished his Easter sermon at 4:45 P.M., gave the benediction to the weary Army company seated in front of him, looked over their bowed heads and saw a sight so startling that he called out, "What's that?"

Libs snapped his head around. Three Vietcong in black pajamas and web belts were walking across the far end of the clearing about 400 yards away. They appeared to be scouts.

"Come on, you sons of bitches," Libs shouted to his platoon. "Let's get 'em!"

He and the soldiers nearest him jumped up, slammed on their helmets and ran in spread formation toward the Vietcong. Private First Class Phillip Hall was lugging an M-60 machine gun, Sergeant Lawson H. "Ernst" Passmore and Corporal Otis Lee Flake, Libs's radioman, had M-16s. Another trooper tried to rig up his M-79 grenade launcher as he ran. They unloosed this arsenal while sprinting through the knee-high grass outside the Courtenay rubber plantation. Other platoons were firing at the same time. It sounded like the Mad Minute fire demonstration at Benning. One Vietcong went down. A second turned back to grab the downed man's rifle and got hit himself. He fell. The third kept running across the clearing, made it to the woods and disappeared.

"We got two of the bastards!" somebody shouted.

Libs, who had run a ten-flat 100-yard dash in high school back in Evansville another life ago, arrived on the scene first. He saw that one scout was already dead and the other one horribly wounded but conscious. A main artery near the groin of the wounded VC was gushing blood.

"Where's D-800?" Libs demanded.

The dying Vietcong spit on Libs. Libs grabbed the bleeding man's balls and squeezed hard. The Vietcong screamed out a stream of Vietnamese words.

"What's he saying?" Libs asked of the Vietnamese interpreter who, carrying an M-1 carbine, had just reached the scene. He was standing on Libs's left, studying the dying Vietcong.

"He's from an independent unit and was out on patrol," the interpreter said.

Radioman Flake, standing on Libs's right, knew the scout had said more than that. Flake had spent enough time with the Vietnamese tea girls in the Melody Bar and other joints along Saigon's Tu Do Street to understand a fair amount of Vietnamese. Flake had definitely heard the dying scout mention D-800.

"Sir!" Flake said to Libs after the wounded Vietcong had died and the officer and his radioman were walking back toward Charlie Company's encampment, "That interpreter didn't tell you what the guy said."

"Come on now, Flake. This is important."

"I know for sure, sir, that he said he was from D-800 and was sent out to find us."

Division intelligence had expressed suspicions about Charlie Company's Vietnamese interpreter but had no hard proof. Libs resolved to watch him closely from now on, but he had bigger worries at the moment. A bigger Vietcong unit might be snaking through the woods right now to catch the Americans by surprise this Easter afternoon.

"Hall!" Libs shouted to machine-gunner Hall. "Get your ass back in position and set up the 60. Everybody else, back on the perimeter. The bad guys are here."

An officer and sergeant from another platoon ran up to view the bodies of the Vietcong scouts. The sergeant had always talked tough, but also fought tough. He had this weird habit, though, of overdoing it by cutting ears off dead Vietcong. He did his thing to the two dead scouts, to the disgust of other troopers looking on silently.

Libs rushed up to Captain William R. Nolen, commander of Charlie Company, who was back in the woods at the edge of the clearing where the service had just been conducted. The sandy-haired, religious, unassuming Nolen was brand new in Vietnam. He had never been in a big firefight. Lieutenant Colonel William S. Hathaway, battalion commander, had told Nolen to listen to what Libs had to say, to realize that this gung-ho first lieutenant had been in country long enough to know how to kill rather than be killed.

"Sir, we've got to get out of this position," Libs told Nolen. "Flake tells me these guys are attached to D-800. We've got to move over there," Libs said, pointing to the northwest corner of the clearing. "And let's ambush the bodies."

Lieutenant Kenneth M. Alderson, executive officer of Charlie Company, worried about what the Vietcong scout who had escaped into the woods would tell his commanders. The scout obviously had been able to judge the position, size and probably intent of the American rifle company seemingly far from other elements of the First Division.

The company pulled itself together. A few hours later it moved as quietly as it could—which was not very quiet—into the woods at the other end of the clearing. One small ambush team was sent out to a concealed position in killing range of the bodies in case Vietcong came to retrieve them. Another ambush squad lay along the trail the scouts had been following when they were shot.

Just before dusk, the thwacka-thwacka of a Huey helicopter announced the arrival of Major General William E. DePuy, the new, aggressive commander of the First Infantry Division. The helicopter had the white horns of a steer painted on its side to symbolize the helicopter company's nickname, the Long Horns. DePuy's two stars were painted on the helicopter's nose.

"Here comes that old son of a bitch Willy DePuy who loves to fight," Libs said admiringly as the general's chopper settled onto the clearing. He remembered with a smile how, right after taking command of the Big Red One, DePuy had gathered all the First Division officers together and decreed: "I will never, ever hear again over the radio, 'I'm pinned down. I'm breaking contact.' I hear it, that officer is relieved immediately. You're never pinned down. Period." DePuy told them that if they needed it, artillery could be fired extremely close to their perimeter.

DePuy wanted his officers to charge, to break out of any encirclement, to kill even if it meant being killed. He wanted to win this war in a hurry. Period. Libs said "right on" to himself at the time. He cheered the aggressiveness DePuy had triggered since taking over from the cautious Major General Jonathan 0. Seaman in February 1966. Libs, like DePuy, believed in the war and wanted to win it or die trying. He was eager to hear what Old Willy had to say about Charlie Company's part tomorrow in the big push called Operation Abilene.

The plan was for the Second and Third brigades of the First Infantry Division to send small units through Phuoc Tuy and Long Khanh provinces to search out and destroy Vietcong. So far, Abilene had turned out to be mostly search, not much destroy. DePuy hoped Charlie Company would find the big prize, the Vietcong's D-800 Battalion.

"You guys are out here alone," DePuy told the officers of Charlie Company. "By all intelligence, D-800 is nearby. Your chances of getting hit tonight are very good. Our artillery has got you bracketed in."

No win-one-for-the-Gipper talk. Just some cold truth spoken quietly by a general who obviously knew something big was going to happen. Then the big man flew away, leaving Libs to worry as Easter darkened into the ever-dangerous night of Vietnam.

As Libs saw it, DePuy was sending Charlie Company out as bait in hopes of catching the elusive, first-line Vietcong battalion of 400 troops and a backup force of women and children. Simple but perhaps fatal. Charlie Company would be kept far enough away from other companies in the battalion to persuade D-800 commanders they had caught an isolated American unit. The jungle was too thick to reinforce the company by helicopter. DePuy would deny after the battle that he had sent out Charlie Company as bait. He assumed Charlie Company, like every outfit he sent out into the bush, could be reinforced if it suddenly ran into heavy trouble. Another company was supposed to be close enough to come to Charlie's rescue.

What if D-800 struck Charlie Company tonight? Libs fretted. DePuy's helicopter arrival and departure probably had enabled D-800 to know Charlie Company's general location, even though it had moved a short distance since his departure. Were the Vietcong commanders deploying their mortars right now? Would their infantry hit between now and dawn? Libs was nervous, edgy, scared. He dared not lie down, far less sleep. He walked around his platoon hour after hour, checking with his men and staring out into the black clearing, looking for movement. His men had not dug foxholes to sleep in or fire from. Those not on guard were taking mud soldier catnaps on the ground.

"How ya doing?" Libs asked his men at every stop on his ceaseless rounds.

"Hear anything? See anything?"

"Anything going on out there with the bodies? Hear any talk at all? Smell anything?"

"Sir,' it's quiet as hell out here," was the universal response from the men lying at the edge of the jungle.

"Get as many Z's as you can. This is going to be a long night; an even longer tomorrow."

In his rounds, Libs ran into Lieutenant Martin L. Kroah Jr., 30, 3d Platoon's leader, doing the same thing. Libs and Kroah had foxhole adoration for each other, an emotion that no one who has not felt it could understand. They had watched each other under the pressure of battle. Libs saw in Kroah a wild-assed former sergeant who knew how to fight and win. Kroah saw in Libs "a cocky little bastard" who was all soldier in the field and all hell-raiser like himself in the rear.

Kroah's life before joining the Army had been as hard as Libs's had been easy. His parents were divorced. His mother worked as a waitress. Marty bagged groceries for thirty-five cents an hour at Montressor's Market in his home town of Brockway, Pennsylvania. A tall, stringy kid standing 6 feet and weighing 137 pounds, Marty had a job that left no time for after-school sports. He did play the trumpet in the marching band. Montressor's would let him leave the market thirty minutes before the half of football games so he could go home, put on his band uniform and march up and down the field with his trumpet. He could not stay to watch the second half of the game; he had to be back at the market. That was just the way life was in Brockway for Marty Kroah.

After graduating from high school in 1953, Marty saw his options as working at Montressor's or the local glass factory. The Army looked like a way out of Brockway and up in life. He joined; became a paratrooper to get the extra $50 a month jump pay, sending it home to his mother; rose quickly to staff sergeant, was selected for the Non-Commissioned Officer's Academy, the Army's little West Point; and was commissioned a second lieutenant at Fort Benning's Officer Candidate School in 1962 after nine years of enlisted service. Kroah joined Charlie Company as 3d Platoon leader in October 1965.

Libs and Kroah realized this Easter night that they had allowed themselves to grow too close to each other. The loss of one would devastate the other. Marty must have sensed one of them would die in the battle with D-800. He discarded his tough demeanor long enough to put his right arm around Johnny Libs's shoulders and speak about dying in the code of mud soldiers: "Well, we're going to get the shit kicked out of us tomorrow."

"Yeah," Libs replied. "But we found D-800. We're going to kick ass, Marty."

"Yeah. I know- you got Nolen's ear. Watch him."

"Marty, he'll be OK," Libs said of the green company commander. He said Nolen had told him earlier in that evening, "I'll be calling on you for a lot of help." Libs said he had replied: "I'll sure be there, Captain, no problem."

Libs liked Nolen's quiet manner. Bluster often covered weakness and incompetence in combat; quietness usually meant strength. An education at West Point or any other military college did not count for much in a firefight. Libs had learned during his ten months in Vietnam that character, guts, coolness and competence were what counted. But Nolen was so damn green. This Citadel graduate, this cherry-is he going to do something that will get us all killed? Executive Officer Alderson, who would accompany the unit into the field, was less worried about Nolen. He considered his religious commanding officer intelligent and open to advice from more experienced subordinates.

Libs also fretted about how Lieutenant George C. Steinberg, 4th Platoon commander, an intellectual but not a jungle fighter, and Second Lieutenant Smith A. Devoe, 1st Platoon leader, newly arrived in the country, would stand up against the 3-to-1 odds Charlie Company would confront if D-800 struck. "Oh well," Libs consoled himself, "I'll have Marty."

Dawn of April 11, 1966, neared without the Vietcong hitting Charlie Company. The men roused themselves for stand-to at 5:30 A.M. The soldiers took fighting positions during stand-to in case the enemy launched a pre-dawn attack. Nothing happened.

The troops opened C-ration cans of peaches and fruit cake for breakfast, or whatever else they were not sick of eating. They filled canteens, loaded up with ammunition, massaged sore feet, mounted up for another hot walk 10,000 miles from where they wanted to be. One sergeant, in what, fellow troopers regarded as another one of his faked injuries, said he had sprained his ankle and could not go out on the mission. He was flown out of the clearing along with the bodies of the two dead Vietcong that intelligence officers in the rear wanted to examine. Marty," Nolen said, "I want you to be point."

Kroah thought this was unfair. His 3d Platoon seemed to have done more than its share of spearheading the company into one dangerous patch of jungle after another. Kroah did not protest. He figured Nolen wanted one experienced platoon leader out front and the other one, Libs, bringing up the rear. Nolen himself would stay in the middle of the formation. Steinberg's 4th Platoon would follow Kroah's 3d; Devoe's 1st Platoon would be third in the weaving line of four platoons constituting Charlie Company.

"Today is not just another walk in the woods," Kroah told himself as his platoon pushed off due north at 7:30 AM on April 11, 1966. He felt fearful and relieved at the same time. He could not explain the currents and crosscurrents coursing through him. Something was different. He knew it.

An American rifle company pushing through thick jungle is like four tiny, independent armies connected to each other only by radio. Vietnam's triple-canopy jungle, plus tree trunks, vines, brush, all conspired to block vision not only between the four platoons but between the men in one platoon. A trooper pushing through dense undergrowth and thick trees often lost sight of the man nearest him, making his advance toward hidden enemy troops all the more unnerving. Two hours into the march the soldiers discovered ominous trenches, 300 yards long and 4 feet deep. The Vietcong obviously had prepared to defend this patch of jungle.

At 11 A.M., Kroah's platoon swung west. Eleven minutes later it discovered a well-used trail running east to west. Nolen ordered patrols sent out in all four directions of the trail to probe for Vietcong and their encampments. The troopers stayed off the trail itself to avoid ambushes and booby traps. The troopers not out on patrol grabbed more C-rations for lunch, sipped from canteens.

Snap! Snap!

Marty heard one of his troopers he could not see firing off two rounds from his M-16. He rushed to the man, learned he had seen two Vietcong but missed them. It was 12:15 P.M. "Be more alert!," Kroah ordered. "If you see another one, let me know."

No sooner had Kroah turned away from the private than he heard him shout, "Hey! We just saw another one!"

There were no more sightings for a while. Kroah's 3d Platoon stopped for lunch. They kept their eyes on the trail where the first three Vietcong had been sighted. They finished their C-ration lunch and began moving again. A shot rang out; one of Kroah's soldiers fell. Kroah's radioman, Jasper Carpenter, fired off his M-16.

"What are you shooting at?" Kroah asked Carpenter.

"I saw three VC going into the ground!"

Kroah figured the Vietcong had slipped into a bunker on the jungle floor. He grabbed the telephone-shaped hand set off the PRC 25 radio carried by Private First Class Carpenter, a married man with children who talked and looked like the red-necked Alabaman he was. Captain Nolen's radio call sign was Charlie Six and Kroah's November Six."Charlie Six. This is November Six. We had sighting of three VC."

"November Six. This is Charlie Six. Kill your three Charlies?"

"Charlie Six. This is November Six. No, but they saw us."

"November Six. Charlie Six. What do you think we should do?"

"Charlie Six. November Six. Find out where they're going."

"November Six. Charlie Six. That's affirm."

Had the Vietcong sent out a few elusive snipers to draw Charlie Company deeper into the jungle and closer to the base camp of D-800? Should Charlie Company stop right there and call for reinforcements this early afternoon? Or should it try to locate the enemy so it would know what was out there in the jungle? An infantry commander in combat is damned if he is not aggressive enough and damned if he is too aggressive. DePuy had left no doubt he wanted to find and smash D-800. Nolen decided to probe deeper.

Libs, bringing up the rear of Charlie Company, was probing, too. Private First Class Phil Hall was out on the left flank of 2d Platoon feeling very vulnerable. The

21-year-old Hall, of Eagle, Wisconsin, wondered if he had gotten himself into more adventure than he bargained for when he chucked the job of bagging fertilizer in Whitewater, Wisconsin, for this job of infantryman. The husky six-footer was carrying a pump-action 12-gauge shotgun, which the Army used early in the war, and the ammunition for the M-60 machine gun. His buddy, Specialist Four John Noyce, had the 60 itself. Other buddies like John Fulford, Jackie Lancaster, Gil DeLao and Ernst Passmore were out here some place in the dense growth. Their black humor and support was was what made life in the field bearable, sometimes even enjoyable.

Pop! Pop! Pop! Pop! Pop!

Somebody was shooting at Hall. He could not see him. Hall sat down on the jungle floor, shotgun across his knees, and strained to see who was out there in the trees and thick underbrush.

Libs heard the shots in his own area. Kroah had radioed earlier that he was taking sporadic fire from hit-and-run snipers. Libs knew now that the Vietcong had riflemen deployed at the front and rear of the company. The Vietcong could be trying, to surround the company or draw it into a prepared killing zone.

Nolen ordered Steinberg's 4th Platoon to move forward to reinforce the left flank of Kroah's 3d Platoon. The Vietcong opened up on 4th Platoon as it moved up at 12:50 P.M. killing one soldier and wounding a second. This meant the company would have to set up a defensive perimeter around the killed and wounded if and when the medivac helicopters arrived to hoist them out of the jungle, if that was even possible through the triple canopy of treetops. First Platoon radioed that it was receiving fire. Then the firing stopped.

Libs feared the Vietcong were using the time to surround the scattered elements of Charlie Company. This would make it easy for them to annihilate each small group. To save itself from piecemeal destruction, the company would have to form a circle and cover the area outside it with interlocking fire.

"Charlie Six," Libs radioed to Nolen. "This is Mike Six. Roll up the wagons now!"

The long, twisting snake that is an American rifle company searching for an. enemy cannot coil up quickly. Libs ran from man to man, pushing each one into his firing position on the slowly forming circle.

"Now don't fucking move," Libs ordered. "Shoot anything that moves, but watch your ammunition."

The 2d Platoon circled away from Hall, leaving him farther out on the flank. He was still sitting with the shotgun on his knees, scanning the thick weave of jungle. He spotted twelve Vietcong apparently going to their part of the noose forming around Charlie Company. Some wore black pajamas, others khaki uniforms. The khaki was ominous. It indicated first-line officers were directing the farmer-soldiers in black pajamas.

"Lieutenant!" Hall shouted to Libs. "I got people out here with khaki uniforms on!"

The Vietcong blasted at the patch of jungle where the voice had come from. Hall saw bullets hitting the ground all around him. None hit him. He could not see the enemy unless he raised his head above the bushes hiding him. Every time he did that, more fire came at him.

"Withdraw!" Libs yelled to Hall. "Withdraw! Get back here inside the perimeter!"

Hall began to stand up. He saw a Vietcong in black pajamas and a floppy hat walking toward him. He raised the shotgun, pulled the trigger and pumped again and again until the man in front of him fell. Hall sprinted toward the platoon's perimeter. He spotted an ant berm and dove behind it. A small soldier named Owens was already hiding there.

"Are you hit?" Owens asked.

"Fuck no," Hall responded. He tucked up his body, rolled toward the perimeter for several yards, then jumped up to sprint the last 20 yards. The Vietcong fired at him during his dash. Notoriously poor marksmen, they missed. Owens, a green trooper, stayed hidden behind the anthill.

"Hey, now I'm pinned down out here!" Noyce yelled from his hiding place outside the perimeter. He had the M-60 machine gun.

"Come on, Noyce," Hall shouted back. "I made it out of there. You can make it in."

"Get your ass in here, Noyce!" Libs commanded. "We need the 60."

Noyce sprinted for the perimeter and made it in despite the spray of bullets shot at him. Noyce and Hall set up the machine gun on the perimeter and waited for the Vietcong attack.

At the front of the column, Kroah and his 3d Platoon kept getting fire as the battle slowly developed. Kroah and Sergeant Rolf Schoolman moved ahead of their men to determine where most of the firing was coming from. Kroah thought he had located the hot spot and called in ranging rounds.

"Fox Six," Kroah radioed to First Lieutenant Francis Fog, the artillery forward observer traveling with the company, after the ranging rounds hit the right patch of jungle. "This is November Six. That's good enough. Fire for effect." Ten rounds, two from each of the five 105mm artillery pieces in the rear, came whooshing in. Kroah heard screams from his own men behind him. Libs at the same time saw men being cut down in his area in the rear of the company. Nobody would ever know for sure who killed the soldiers with this friendly fire. One report estimated five troopers were killed and another dozen wounded by the errant artillery fire. It was confusing who was killing whom because of the combination of sniper and artillery fire that created sudden chaos around 2 P.M. Kroah blamed himself because he had called in degrees (360 in a circle) instead of mils (6,400 in a circle) in adjusting the incoming artillery rounds. Libs blamed Major M, an artillery officer in the rear. The Army calls such death by friendly fire fratricide. It happens in the close quarters of jungle fighting.

Vietcong snipers opened on Kroah's platoon after the artillery had stopped. Several of his men got wounded. He answered a nervous call from Nolen on the radio.

"November Six, Charlie Six," Nolen began. "We're going to pull back."

"Charlie Six November Six. I can't do that. I've got more wounded than effectives."

"November Six. Charlie Six. Better figure something out. We're pulling out."

Nolen ordered his platoons to pull back from the most intense fire, which seemed to be directed at the front of the company formation. He hoped to avoid encirclement of the whole company, even if he had to lose the point platoon commanded by Kroah that was now in danger of being overrun. It was too late. The company had put itself too far into the closing noose. The other platoons found they could not move, either, without drawing heavy fire. Every time a soldier tried to go into a low crawl, snipers in the trees would spot the movement and shoot at him.

"November Six. Charlie Six. Looks like they've got us encircled. We're not going anyplace."

Two Air Force Huskie helicopters arrived at 3 P.M. to evacuate the men who had been killed or wounded from sniper fire and the misdirected rounds of artillery. Troopers cut a hole in the treetops so the choppers could lower a bullet-shaped jungle penetrator down to the jungle floor. Air Force Captain Harold D. Salem maneuvered his helicopter over the hole in the trees and hovered. Airman First Class William H. Pitsenbarger, 21, of Piqua, Ohio, pulled down one of the jungle penetrator's spring-loaded seats, straddled it and signaled Sergeant Gerald Hammond to release the steel cable that would lower him down to the smoking battleground 200 feet below.

Executive Officer Alderson, radio in hand to coordinate the evacuation, was astonished by the sight of an airman dressed in freshly pressed fatigues and a flak jacket and carrying two .38-caliber pistols on his body voluntarily lowering himself into the mud soldiers' smoking hell. "This Saigon cowboy doesn't know what he's getting into," Alderson said to himself.

Libs, from a farther distance, saw the young man riding down the sky through a hail of enemy bullets. "I'd like to shake that man's hand," Libs marveled.

Once Pitsenbarger was on the ground, Hammond at the side door of the Huskie reeled up the hoist cable, attached a litter basket for the wounded and relowered the cable down to the airman.

"Pits" Pitsenbarger patched up several wounded men and lifted one of them into the litter. Hammond hoisted up this wounded man, lowered the litter again to pick up another one. This first helicopter left the spot over the hole in the trees so it could fly the two wounded to the first aid station at Bien Hoa. The second Huskie found the same hole in the trees, retrieved two more wounded. Each Huskie made three trips to the battleground, rescuing twelve of the fifteen wounded.

The two Huskies returned in hopes of hoisting up the remaining three wounded and two dead. On the ground Pits was trying to get the wounded ready for the painful 200-foot trip up to the side door of the Huskie. He had run out of the splints he had brought down from the chopper and was feverishly fashioning make-do ones out of sticks and vines. But this time the Vietcong opened up on the hovering Huskie, ripping holes in its fuel and hydraulic lines. The Huskie lost power. Hammond motioned Pits to climb into the litter basket so he could be pulled back into the helicopter before it left the battleground. Pits waved off the chopper, electing to stay with Charlie Company. The Huskie struggled out of the hole in the trees under heavy fire. The basket caught on the treetops. Hammond cut the hoist cable, freeing the struggling helicopter. The Huskie made an emergency landing a few miles away.

Left by his own choice with the seemingly doomed men of Charlie Company,

Pitsenbarger joined the fight. He gathered the idle rifles and ammunition off the killed and wounded and distributed them to the men still fighting. He used up all his dressings, picked up an M-16 discarded by a wounded soldier and helped a fire team fight the Vietcong.

An Army UH-1 Huey helicopter hovered over the company to kick cases of ammunition out the side door. The ammo was supposed to land within the company's perimeter. The helicopter pilot radioed down that the fire was so heavy he was going to leave without dropping all the ammunition on board. Kroah radioed back: "If we don't get it, you don't leave." The pilot could not be sure whether the beleaguered lieutenant would make good on his threat to shoot him down. He stayed until all the ammunition was kicked out. It was an accurate drop. The ammunition cases landed only 20 yards from where Nolen and Alderson, were trying to organize their forces.

"We gotta get out of here," Nolen told Alderson. He told him to find a platoon and try to break out of the Vietcong's tightening circle. Nolen got wounded shortly after giving that order. He was already traumatized by his first big battle.

Alderson and Radio Telephone Operator Bash moved toward the perimeter to organize a breakout. Vietcong AK-47s opened up on them as they moved. One round smashed into Bash's helmet, knocking him to the jungle floor, face down. Alderson thought he was dead. He rolled the soldier's body over.

"What's wrong?" Bash asked as he stared back at the astonished Alderson, The bullet had bounced away or through the outer steel of the helmet without hitting Bash's head.

Boom!

Another Vietcong bullet knocked the helmet off Alderson's head. Again, the bullet ricocheted away from its target, Alderson's head.

Bash's radio was attracting so much fire that Alderson ordered him to stash it behind a tree rather than continue to wear it on his body. Alderson could communicate only if he stayed near the radio. This became impossible during the fluid fight. The radio was soon destroyed anyway.

Alderson was trying to reach the center of the perimeter when he encountered a sergeant from the 1st Platoon sitting against a tree with the blank stare of battle shock. The sergeant's rifle was lying unused on the jungle floor. Alderson talked to him, gently.

"The only way we're going to get out of this is to fight our way out," Alderson said. "If we can't do that, let's not make it easy for them. Most of our leadership is already gone. We need you."

The sergeant picked up his rifle and moved toward the perimeter to fight and die.

At 4 P.M., the Vietcong began marching 60mm mortar fire across the company. Most of the men escaped the mortar fragments by hugging the ground. A mortar bursts in a mushroom shape. It will get you if you are standing up. First Battalion of the Seventh Artillery, at a base a few miles behind Charlie Company, zeroed in on the mortars pinpointed by counter-radar, finally silencing the position by firing twenty rounds on top of it.

Lying flat protected the troopers against mortar fragments but not against the

Vietcong snipers high in the trees ringing the company. The troopers kept getting shot in the back as they lay in the prone firing position. Many rolled over on their backs and shot into the trees. The Vietcong would send one of their soldiers running across a clear spot between trees to draw Charlie Company's fire. This would help pinpoint the defenders for the Vietcong snipers blasting away with AK-47 rifles from up in the trees.

Libs concluded the company had been drawn into a carefully prepared kill sack. He knew the company had to break out to survive. Marty could break the Vietcong's choke ring if anybody could. Libs decided to ask him to try. Libs, the most experienced jungle fighter, was out of sight and had no radio contact with his senior officers. He assumed it was up to him to try to save the company and went into action.

"We've got to break it, Marty," he told his buddy.

"Fucking A," Marty responded over the radio.

Kroah and his platoon made a stab at breaking through the enemy lines closing in on the company's spearhead pointing northwest. The Vietcong stopped them with a killing curtain of fire.

"Sorry, John," Marty radioed back. "Couldn't break it."

Libs and a group of riflemen then tried to break the noose in their southeast sector. They ran into another curtain of concentrated fire from the ground and up in the trees.

Vietcong riflemen under covering fire from the trees assaulted the lines of 3d and 4th platoons in a screaming attack. The Americans fought back fiercely. Artillery kept crashing down, preventing the Vietcong' from staying massed against any one position.

At 5:45 P.M., Libs and others heard the heart-sinking chung, chung, chung of two .50-caliber and pat, pat, pat of eight .30-caliber machine guns from outside the company perimeter.

D-800 had moved its heavy weapons out of the nearby base camp and placed them all around Charlie Company's steadily shrinking circle. Machine-gun bullets, especially 50 caliber, are lethal not only because they come in streams but also because they are heavy and cut through brush and branches without losing accuracy or killing power. Two .30 caliber and one .50 caliber were slamming rounds into 3d and 4th platoons on the company's northwest point; a second .50 caliber and a .30 caliber were firing into 2d Platoon holding the northeast quadrant of the perimeter, and two .30 calibers were raking 1st Platoon in the southeast quadrant.

"Damage Five," Libs radioed to Major Bibb Underwood, battalion executive officer, who was 1,000 feet above the raging battle calling in artillery from the back of a Huey helicopter. "Mike Six. Get something more in here. The motherfuckers are all over the place. Up in the trees. The sons of bitches have got .50s. We've lost a lot of people already. Where the fuck is Bravo Company?"

"Mike Six. Damage Five. Hang in here. We'll give you everything we've got. Bravo Company is still 1,000 meters away."

"Damage Five. Mike Six. They'll be too fucking late. We'll be rotting in the jungle by the time Bravo gets here."

Bravo Company was out on Charlie Company's far left flank. The jungle was so thick that Bravo could only move about 100 yards an hour by hacking out a single-file trail. There was no open area anywhere near outnumbered Charlie Company for helicopters with reinforcements to land. Charlie would live or die depending on what it could do all by itself.

At 6:30 PM. soldiers from the 4th Platoon charged the .50 caliber position on the northwest flank while their comrades shot up into the trees to suppress the deadly fire of the Vietcong snipers. The troopers who were not cut down knocked out the .50 with hand grenades.

The wounded, if they had the strength, crawled from the outer edge of the oval-shaped defensive ring to its center. When a man was killed, his buddies left their firing positions long enough to carry him to the center of the oval to lie there with the wounded. Casualties were leaving big holes in Charlie Company's outer perimeter. Libs feared the Vietcong would charge through one of these gaps and wipe out the whole company at any moment.

"Mike Six," Kroah called to his old buddy Libs. "November Six. I'm hit. Think Langston's dead." Fourth Platoon Sergeant Gene Langston, 27, of Leachville, Arkansas, was a company favorite. Everybody called him "The Round Man." He had taken Private First Class Gregory L. Bishop under his wing. The troopers taunted the religious Bishop because he called himself a conscientious objector and would not carry a rifle. He served as Langston's radioman. The beefy sergeant threatened to waste anybody who taunted Bishop. The two became as close as brothers. When Langston died from .50-caliber bullets, which almost cut him in two, Bishop's spirit died with him.

The Vietcong concentrated fire on Kroah and the two soldiers beside him, a medic on his left and Radioman Carpenter on his right. Bullets from snipers in the trees slammed into Kroah's right shoulder, calf and ankle. His medic received a burst in his back and lay helpless and bleeding alongside Kroah. One bullet cut the cord of Carpenter's radio. Another slammed through his helmet and went out the back without hitting his head. A third hit him in the shoulder.

"Help me," Carpenter cried to Kroah. "Help me! I've got a wife and kids. I want to go home and see them. I don't want to die here!"

"Shut the fuck up," Kroah rebuked. "Just lie still and you'll be all right."
A second medic crawled out to Kroah and stuffed a towel into his gushing shoulder. It slowed the bleeding. Another bullet slammed into the already crippled platoon leader.

Kroah heard a shout from First Lieutenant Steinberg, commander of 4th Platoon. "I need some help over here!"

"George, I can't help you," Kroah shouted back. "I've been hit five times."

"I've been hit seven," Steinberg replied.

"Always the bullshitter, huh, George?"

"No bullshit, man.

And it wasn't. Steinberg died with those words.

His 4th Platoon fought on with heroic abandon, even to grappling with the charging Vietcong with bare hands after ammunition ran out. The troopers also hurled their CS gas and smoke canisters at the attackers to stop one of the three waves, halting it long enough for the few troopers with any ammunition left to cut it down.

Sergeant James W. Robinson Jr., 25, of Annandale, Virginia, was fighting with the same abandon in 1st Platoon's southeast sector. A mountain of a man who had chafed during his years of ceremonial duty as a Marine, Robby was now undergoing the test by fire he had always sought. He picked up an M-79 grenade launcher, a thump gun, and fired grenades into the trees where the Vietcong snipers were shooting down on the platoon.

He shifted his attention to the woods just outside the perimeter. He saw a medic and a sergeant pinned down by enemy fire. He ran through bullets, locked one man in each arm, dragged them inside the perimeter, dressed their wounds, gave them shots of morphine and then assessed his fire team's situation. It was desperate. The pile of wounded and dead behind the platoon's defensive line was growing. Robinson collected all the serviceable rifles and ammunition, redistributing the small arsenal among the survivors. He kept the leftover rifles and grenades for his own one-man stand, He hosed through the trees again, killing more snipers.

One of his buddies had been cut down by machine-gun fire. Robinson ran to him. The same machine gun hit Robinson's leg as he ran. He reached his comrade, pushed him behind a tree, tied bandages around the worst wounds and patched himself as best he could under cover of the tree.

"I see the .50!" Robinson shouted to his men. "I'm going for it! Cover me!"

Robinson by this time had no ammunition left for his M-16. He placed the empty rifle beside the private he had just dragged behind the tree. Sitting beside the wounded man where the tree protected him from the machine-gun fire, Robinson pulled two grenades off his web belt. He yanked out the pins so they were ready to go off once he let his fingers off the spoon firing mechanism running down the side of the grenade. Taking a deep breath, Robinson struggled to his feet behind the tree and gathered his strength for the dash to the .50, about 20 yards outside the company perimeter.

With a Marine growl, Robinson ran toward the .50, one grenade in each hand. A tracer round hit him in the leg, setting his trousers on fire. He staggered to within 10 yards of the machine gun despite its withering fire, shifted his two grenades onto his one good arm and lofted them expertly smack into the machine-gun position. The two grenades went off in one giant blast, killing the crew and silencing the .50 for the rest of the battle. Robinson fell dead, his body riddled with the last burst of the machine gun. He would be awarded the Medal of Honor; the nation's highest military award.

Twilight approached. The Vietcong firing stopped except for a few shots here and there. D-800 was holding its fire to give their women employed as a support force time to shoot any wounded outside the perimeter, strip the bodies and report where the biggest gaps seemed to be in the company's ragged perimeter.

With the firing stilled, Libs could hear Vietcong jabbering all around him, both in the trees and on the ground. He noticed his company no longer had enough men in the line to form an unbroken protective ring of fire. He saw only tight pockets of two, three and four riflemen. There were big spaces between these small clusters. Libs knew it was only a matter of time before the Vietcong mounted their final charge and raced through one of the gaps. He also knew he was going to die. He could not think of anything he had not tried except one last do-or-die breakout attempt. He was puzzling out how best to make this suicide drive when he saw a green-yellow cloud of gas rolling toward him. He thought the Vietcong had launched a gas attack before moving in to annihilate Charlie Company. But the gas had been blown southward from the point where 3d and 4th platoons had made their valiant stands and wafted onto 2d Platoon.

"Gas!" Libs shouted, remembering his Fort Benning training.

He instinctively reached into his gas-mask pouch to withdraw his mask. His hands felt catsup, mustard and an onion. "Oh shit, I don't have a mask." He dug a little hole in the ground and put his head in it to escape the CS gas choking him. "They're going to find my head in this hole with a bullet through it," he told himself, "and say, 'Libs was a coward.'" He allowed himself a giggle, saying, "Who gives a shit?"

The wind blew the gas away. The Vietcong had not made their final assault. Breakout was now or never. Libs gathered up the few men still firing and capable of running. They included his big horse with the shotgun, Phil Hall.

"Let's go, you guys! We're going to break through here. Were going to assault! Move! Move! Move! Get your ass out from behind that anthill," he commanded Hall, who was lying behind it firing.

"Jesus Christ!" Hall exclaimed as he stared death in the face again and prepared to charge. They raced forward a few yards before the Vietcong fusillade forced them to drop to the jungle floor. Private First Class Edward W. Reilly, 22, of Upper Darby, Pennsylvania, was killed. The clean-cut, redheaded young man died with his hands clasped together over a cross he wore around his neck. The survivors tried to crawl forward to blast away the enemy. Artillery and heavy firing had stripped much of the jungle away. Libs could see his small force was outmanned and outgunned. Nobody would live long enough to reach the .50-caliber machine gun causing so much havoc. A grenade exploded between Hall and Private First Class Jackie K. Lancaster. The hot fragments missed Hall but hit Lancaster. One fragment went clean through Lancaster's helmet without hitting his head.

"Get back in!" Libs shouted.

"Can you get me back?" the wounded Lancaster asked Hall.

"Yeah, I'll get you back."

Lancaster with painful effort got his arm over Hall's left shoulder as they lay on the ground. Kicking knees and digging with elbows, the two crawled back toward the perimeter together. They stopped inside the perimeter behind a big log that artillery had knocked down. Hall left the wounded Lancaster there and returned to his M-60 machine-gun position on the perimeter. Libs examined Lancaster's wounds. An AK-47 bullet had gone through his helmet and grenade fragments had caught him under his left arm but he did not seem to have broken any bones.

In other sectors Libs could not see, soldiers were still fighting and dying heroically. Private First Class Marion F. Acton, 18, of Huntsville, Alabama, sneaked up on one machine-gun and wiped out the entire crew. He kept firing his M-16 at point-blank range, killing several more Vietcong before a sniper in the trees above him shot him dead.

Libs, having failed at attempts to break out of the ring of fire, knew Charlie Company could not hold the Vietcong at bay much longer with the small amount of firepower it had left. He had to call in artillery, and keep it exploding right next to the few survivors of Charlie Company. He had lost Flake and his radio. Libs called Hall away from the M-60.

"I've got to have a radio to call in artillery or we're dead. Find me one!"

Hall ran and crawled among the dead and wounded lying in the smoke. He found a dying radioman from another platoon and told him: "Sorry. I've got to take this.

"No problem," the soldier rasped. He was lying on his back, bleeding to death. Hall looked into his eyes and saw the hurt and puzzlement of a boy about to die. Hall would see the boy's eyes for the rest of his life. The boy tried to turn his body to make it easier for Hall to take away his radio. Hall had no way to help the dying boy. He left him on the jungle floor to die alone. His radio, set on the same frequency being used by Underwood in the chopper overhead, was soon in Libs's hands.

Libs radioed up to Underwood, who kept over the battle hour after hour, taking time out only to fly back to the field at the headquarters named Bear Cat to jump into a fully fueled helicopter when his own ran low. "I wanted to let them know they had somebody up there in touch with the world," Underwood would say later.

"Damage Five. This is Libs. I've taken command. We've got to have artillery all night long."

Underwood noticed that Libs's voice had gone from frenzy to resignation. Libs sounded through the 1,000 feet of smoky jungle air like a man who knew he was going to die soon. "You've got it," Underwood answered in as reassuring a voice as he could summon up from his sickened soul.

Libs went from one cluster of Charlie Company survivors to another to say goodbye. Night was falling fast. Muzzle flashes showed up against the dark from all around the perimeter. The Vietcong seemed to have riflemen everywhere beyond the little circle that was Charlie Company. Libs heard the Vietcong women and children moving from body to body on the perimeter. He knew what they were doing and grimaced. His message to his men was brief.

"Hey, we ain't gonna make it. So whatever you see, kill it. Whatever moves, kill it."

Libs figured light would help keep the Vietcong jackals away from some of his dead and wounded and also make the attackers better targets. "We've got to have flares," he radioed to Underwood. "It's black down here."

Kroah, his radioman Jasper Carpenter, and a medic who had just joined the platoon-all three of them grievously wounded-lay helpless in that blackness outside the tightened perimeter. Kroah noticed that enemy fire in their forward sector had slackened. He allowed himself to hope the Vietcong were withdrawing and that he might make it out alive after all.

He raised his head to look for Vietcong. He saw bobbing dots of light off in the distant darkness. They were moving toward him. He realized the Vietcong were walking with candles inserted in cans held out in front of them with long poles. The poles were to keep the people holding them from being hit by bullets fired at the lights. Kroah heard the high-pitched sing-song of Vietnamese women. This told him D-800's scavengers were advancing toward 3d and 4th platoons to shoot wounded and strip bodies of rifles, ammunition-anything useful.

"Our only chance is to play dead when they get near us," Kroah told his medic and radioman. The three bleeding men reached for each other's hands, clasped them tight and said the Lord's Prayer in a whisper. Then they lay down as dead as they could manage.

Kroah heard the footsteps of somebody approaching, then heavy breathing. He felt his rifle being pulled away from his body so gently that he thought it must be a woman standing over him. His mind shouted this out while he struggled to lie quiet as a corpse. He felt Carpenter's body being roiled on top of him and could hear the scavengers pulling out the clips of M-16 bullets. The medic lying next to Kroah was stripped next but apparently made a lifelike movement. Kroah heard the deafening explosion of the medic's own .45. A scavenger had shot the medic through the head.

The Vietcong moved on to other bodies. Kroah and Carpenter opened their eyes. Carpenter slowly lifted his head in the inky darkness to look around. It was about 9 P.M.

"See any lights?" Kroah asked.

"No," Carpenter replied.

"Got a cigarette?"

"Christ, man, you're not going to light a cigarette, are you?"

"Give me a cigarette and then go back inside the perimeter and see if you can find me a radio."

Kroah never saw Carpenter again.

Underwood, in his helicopter, passed on Libs's request for Air Force flares, Soon they were drifting down from the sky, taking some of the terror out of the night.

The eerie light enabled Libs to see the South Vietnamese national policeman assigned to Charlie Company standing over his dead German shepherd. The dazed policeman was listening to the high-pitched exhortations of Vietcong commanders outside the perimeter.

"What are they saying?" Libs asked the bilingual policeman.

"They're getting ready for the final attack."

Vietcong commanders shouting through megaphones were ordering their snipers down from the trees. They massed troops for the charge. Libs knew most of his defenders were dead. There were gaps 30 yards wide in his circle. A well-directed Vietcong unit could probe Charlie Company's perimeter until it found one of these big openings and then signal the rest of the force to charge through it. The Charlie Company survivors were so few in their ragged oval that it would take the Vietcong only a few minutes to kill them all.

In the eerie quiet before the final storm, Libs heard the translator who had lied about what the dying Vietcong scout had said the previous afternoon. He was shouting to the Vietcong outside the company perimeter.

"Lieutenant," the national policeman yelled. "He's telling them where we are."

Somebody fired an M-16 burst into the traitor He went down. The Vietcong held back from making their final charge. Libs felt release in the continuing quiet. He called up to Bibb Underwood to bring the artillery in even closer.

'I'm going to lay down this barrage," Underwood radioed back. "Tell me if that's where you want it."

A volley of shells came crashing down about 50 yards outside Charlie Company's perimeter.

"Goddamn it, Bibb! Bring it in closer! It's our only chance!"

Underwood, reading the map full of numbers on his lap in the chopper, radioed back new coordinates to the artillery battery. In less than thirty seconds it sounded to Charlie Company survivors as if freight trains were coming down on them from the sky. The artillery shells hurtling in whizzed, hissed and whooshed before plunging into the ground with explosions so powerful it seemed as if they would split the whole earth in two. Chunks of hot metal, branches and dirt filled the air over the heads of Charlie Company survivors. In the seconds of quiet between artillery bursts, Libs and the rest of the men heard screaming and crying from the Vietcong massing outside the perimeter. Artillery was decimating the massed attackers. Whole minutes went by and still there was no charge.

"Closer! Closer!" Libs yelled up to Underwood.

"You've got it. You're on the ground. You're in control."

Artillery shells soon were exploding even closer to the edge of the Charlie Company perimeter. Soldiers hugged the vibrating ground. They pressed their faces into it, seeking refuge inside Mother Earth. When a shell hit real close, the ground came up and punched them in the gut. The shells kept coming, coming, coming. The ripping explosions turned the Vietcong's ground into a moonscape. The Army would say later that 1,100 artillery shells were fired to help save the company. Libs called in much of the fire. Alderson found a radio and got back in contact with Underwood to help bring other fire to the edge of the perimeter. The Vietcong rifle fire from outside the perimeter slackened. Underwood stayed up there in the chopper calling in the curtain of artillery fire.

"God bless you, Bibb Underwood," Libs said into the earth bouncing into his face. Air Force aircraft kept circling, dropping flares.

Acting Platoon Sergeant Charlie Urconis of 2d Platoon was one of the many who never gave up. He kept crawling from man to man, distributing ammunition. In one crawl to the ammunition crates piled up in the center of the circle, Urconis thought he had been hit. But it turned out to be the impact from a C-ration can exploding under him after a bullet pierced it.

Urconis winced at the cries of wounded he heard as he was crawling around in the dark. The company had run out of bandages, water, morphine-everything that could have eased the pain of the dying.

"Please, somebody shoot me," Urconis heard a bleeding sergeant cry out from the center of the perimeter. "Please, please somebody kill me."

"Somebody help me," begged another soldier.

"Water! Christ, somebody give me some water!"

"Oh! Oh! Oh!"

"Mother, I'm dying out here. Mother!"

"Somebody come and help me."

Groaning. Sobbing. Crying. All the horror of war was concentrated in a small spot nobody had ever heard of or cared about. And the jungle would reclaim it without ceremony.

No further fire came from the Vietcong. Libs and/or Alderson suspended the fire but told Underwood to be ready to resume it in a hurry. Kroah was still lying outside the perimeter. He was covered by branches that had been shot off trees. He heard a soldier call out: "Anybody here?"

Kroah answered and asked him to find a radio. Kroah did not know the trooper. He was from another platoon. But this unknown trooper obliged the bleeding lieutenant and returned with a radio. Kroah still had enough strength to check in with his old buddy, Johnny Libs,

"Mike Six. November Six here. Are you there?"

"Marty?" answered Libs incredulously, having dispensed with call signs long before to save time. It no longer mattered what the enemy heard.

"Yeah."

"I thought you were dead. I've been calling you for two hours."

"I'm out here."

"Hang on, Buddy. I'll send somebody out for you."

"Sergeant," Libs ordered Urconis around 1 A.M., "go out in the 3d Platoon area and get November Six. He's lying outside the perimeter."

Urconis crawled out to that area and started calling softly for Kroah.

"November Six. This is Oscar Five. Where you at?"

"We're over here," replied Kroah's new radioman, whose name was also Carpenter.

Urconis crawled toward the voice. He found Kroah and his radioman lying side by side. Kroah's back seemed to be bleeding the most. When Urconis went through the jungle, he carried two socks tied together around his waist to air them out. He untied this belt to bandage Kroab's wounds with them as best he could, The lieutenant was obviously bad off. His radioman appeared unscathed.

"Crawl back and get a tarp and some sticks so we can carry him out of here," Urconis told the radioman. The radioman would not move. He was frozen with fright.

Urconis could not prod the man to action. The sergeant crawled back to the perimeter by himself, got Specialist Four Noyce to help him, collected sticks and a tarpaulin and crawled back with his helper to Kroah and his radioman. With great difficulty they rigged the tarp and sticks into a stretcher and slid it under Kroah.

"I'm only going to tell you this once, Private," Urconis warned. "You either crawl out of here with us now or we're going to leave you out here to die. Now get your ass moving, soldier, now!"

The wide-eyed radioman got his legs and elbows moving. He was soon performing the infantryman's low crawl and was making his way to the perimeter.

Urconis and Noyce struggled to slide Kroah along the jungle floor as gently as they could. As they bumped Kroah over one of the logs, the earthy lieutenant whose life was pouring out of five bullet holes warmed Urconis's heart and made him smile by saying: "Now look, if you bastards hurt me, I'm going to have your fucking ass!" Then the lieutenant laughed, right there at death's door.

"Pick up the cadence," Kroah ordered his rescuers. "Get in step you! Left, right; left, right; one two, three four."

"Gotta save this guy," Urconis said to himself.

Once in the middle of the company perimeter, Kroah felt comparatively safe.' He managed to open a can of beef stew and suck in its juice with a vengeance. Then he lit a cigarette.

"Put out that cigarette," somebody hissed at him from the dark;

'Fuck off. I've been lying outside 'the perimeter."

Libs walked over to see his old friend. All of Kroah's clothes had been torn off except his undershorts and boots. Blood was all over his tattooed body.

"How ya doing?" Libs asked.

"Great now."

"Marty, you're some looking sight."

"Yeah, well, we're all going to die anyhow."

"I know, Marty. But we'll take 'em one more time because they're' going to bring one more in on us.

"Do your thing, Johnny. Get the job done. Tie me up to a tree." Libs pulled his dying friend over to a tree so he could lean against it while looking out into the dark. He placed Marty's rifle beside him and was about to say some final words to him. But Marty had passed out against the tree.

Libs counted the able-bodied men he had left in his sector to repulse the next Vietcong assault. He counted nine plus Marty, who might or might not regain consciousness and have the strength to fire his rifle or hurl grenades before the Vietcong attackers killed him. The oval-shaped perimeter by now was only 40 yards across, half its original width.

Alderson, whom Libs and Underwood had thought was dead, reunited with Libs. Alderson, Libs, Urconis, Hall and Noyce established a command post for their pathetically small force of survivors behind a big log that artillery had knocked to the jungle floor. They deployed their M-60 machine guns to cover as many avenues of approach as they could when the Vietcong launched the final annihilating attack. Alderson asked for a quick refresher course in firing the M-60 from Hall and Noyce.

"It's awful quiet," Libs told Urconis. "I don't hear them anymore"

"Yeah, even the monkeys aren't making any noise."

Nobody dared think they had won; that they would live; that the Vietcong had broken off the attack. Alderson feared the Vietcong were just waiting for Bravo Company to come to the rescue. Then they would surround that second American company and kill everyone in both of them.

The quiet persisted for more than three hours. Libs, Hall and Noyce agreed to take fifteen-minute catnaps in rotation. Each in turn lay face down behind the log. They were physically exhausted but their minds would not turn off. The desperation that had fueled their movements while under heavy fire gave way to cold fear in the quiet of the pre-dawn hours. The man resting did not want to look over the log because he was afraid he would see the Vietcong coming out of the black shadows for the final attack. But life suddenly looked closer than death. This made the fear of dying more consuming. Not now, God. Not now. The artillery fire had not resumed. Birds started chirping in the distance. The jungle lightened. Dawn of April 12, 1966, was finally breaking over Charlie' Company.

Bang! A shot rang out 40 yards outside the perimeter.

"Aw fuck!" Hall exclaimed to his comrades behind the log. "Here we go again. They're coming again."

Alderson, Libs, Hall and Noyce aimed two M-60s in the direction of' the noise from the single shot. Jungle fatigues marched toward them from the bush. United States Army jungle fatigues! Bravo Company had hacked its way next to Charlie Company during the night and come into the perimeter at 7:15 A.M.

Some Charlie Company survivors would remain embittered for the rest of their lives that Bravo Company did not come to their aid when they were dying from Vietcong assaults. DePuy after the battle blamed himself and other top officers overseeing the deployment for not putting Charlie and Bravo companies closer together, given the thickness of the jungle. He also lamented that Charlie Company commanders pushed so much of their force into the Vietcong kill sack rather than holding back while small squads probed the terrain ahead more thoroughly. Battalion commander Hathaway countered that Bravo Company went into the jungle with the standard separation for such operations. He praised Captain Juris Plakans, Bravo Company commander, for pushing his men through the jungle all night, guiding themselves by the sound of the exploding artillery shells, to reach the edge of Charlie Company's perimeter before dawn. "If there's no fighting," he said he ordered Plakans, "stay outside the perimeter until first light. If the fighting starts up again, get your ass in there regardless." Hathaway said he did not want to risk Charlie Company defenders mistakenly shooting Bravo soldiers In the dark if the Vietcong 'had broken off its attack.

As the day of April 12, 1966, lightened, Charlie Company survivors heard helicopters overhead. Air Force Huskies and Army Chinooks hovered over the battle area. There still was no place big enough to land. Air Force para-rescuemen rode cables down from their choppers to the jungle floor. Rope ladders tumbled out from the rear doors of the Chinooks. Engineers descended down the swinging ladders. Chain saws and other gear were dropped down. Soon trees were falling. A patch of sunlight lit up the inside of Charlie Company's perimeter as the engineers hacked out a big clearing for the Air Force and Army rescue helicopters to land in.

Charlie Company survivors said little. Bravo Company eyed them with awe. Nobody had to tell the relief troopers what the men hanging onto life bad been through in the long afternoon and even longer night. The survivors rummaged for food, bandages and medicines. They looked for buddies. Many of them were dead.

They comforted the wounded as best they could. Medics with fresh supplies were finally on hands Charlie Company troopers drank water by the gallon and peed a thousand nervous pees as the easing of tension loosened up a thousand little muscles that had been clenched like numb fists for more than sixteen hours.

Most of Charlie Company's survivors stood or sat in the now-secure perimeter and cried unashamedly. Urconis told a friend he felt like crying but knew once he started he could never stop. So much pain. So much death. So much being alone. Urconis raged inwardly at the stupidity of leaving Charlie Company out there at the end of such a long string. He was among those who felt Bravo Company should have been kept in much closer to Charlie Company. Urconis went from man to man looking for friends. He found Reilly dead with his hands still clasped in prayer. He found a dead trooper in clean fatigues. He could not figure it out until he noticed the Air Force insignia. It was Pits Pitsenbarger.

Urconis had to get away from so many dead friends. He wandered outside the perimeter where the Vietcong had been. He noticed blood on the bushes and in the trees. They had paid a heavy price, too. He also saw hundreds of little plastic bags. He could not figure out what they were. There were always rumors that the Vietcong were issued dope before making a charge. He doubted this was true. But what were all those empty bags? He never found out.

Phil Hall held off crying until he helped his buddies in Charlie Company put their dead comrades in green, rubberized body bags. Many of his old friends were now bloated bodies turning black. Flies swarmed over the bodies. Hall felt overcome with rage: "All these kids! All these guys! Dead! Dead! What a waste! What was this battle for? Why did everybody die? They're flying us out of here. What did we accomplish? Somebody explain this fucking war to me!"

Libs was also depressed. He did not cry. He sat inside the old perimeter, which Bravo Company was now holding down. He felt bitterness, anger and sadness watching his kids who had fought so hard being zipped into body bags. "They fucked us—fucked us all," Libs lamented to himself. "Bait. Fucking bait. That's all we were. So many great kids. Who will ever know what they did? Nobody. No-fucking-body."

General DePuy's helicopter settled into the freshly cut landing zone. Libs made no attempt to get up and greet him. He was burned out and did not give a damn about anything or anybody-even a general. Fuck it. The United States Arny' is getting no more out of Johnny Libs this day.

DePuy asked Alderson what had happened. "They trapped us. They ambushed us from the trees." Alderson was not bitter. He thought the company should have been sent out after D-800, that DePuy's plan had been sound.

DePuy's officious aide, a captain in the pressed uniform of the safe rear area, strode up to Libs still slumped against a tree. "Lieutenant! The general is here. Get up!"

"Fuck you, Captain."

DePuy took in the scene. He had been in enough battles to know exactly how Lieutenant Libs felt. He knew the exhausted young man at his feet had beaten back D-800, which outnumbered Charlie Company three to one.

"You're excused, Captain!" DePuy snapped to his aide. The captain walked off.

DePuy sat down on the ground next to Libs. "What happened?" the two-star general asked quietly.

"You fucked us, General! You put us out there as bait. And I want that fucking _____fired," he said of the artillery commander whom Libs believed was responsible for the off-target artillery fire that had killed and wounded Libs's men. "He killed our men. I want him fired. It's either that or I'm going to kill him."

DePuy sat silent. Libs knew he had gotten through to the general. He suspected there would be action taken against_____, but DePuy let silence be his answer. Then he said, "I want to know exactly what happened."

Libs wearily went through every phase of the battle as the general sat beside him listening. He ended his debrief by saying, "You walked us into a goddamn holocaust, General."

"Yeah, but there's no other way to get a goddamn fight going," DePuy replied.

"Well you got one going here."

Word had spread through the press corps in Saigon that the Big Red One had been in one hell of a fight. The Army flew a group of reporters and cameramen to the scene. A CBS cameraman spotted DePuy talking to Libs and walked toward them.

"Will you talk to these guys?" DePuy asked Libs;

The television man asked DePuy and Libs a few questions and then took his camera away to record the gore in the clearing. Libs hated the ghouls of the press. He learned later that one good thing came out of the televised interview when it was shown in his hometown of Evansville: Libs's mother learned he was alive at the very time she was reading that everybody in Charlie Company had been killed.

"Here's a good one over here," a cameraman said to one of his buddies. The "good one" was a particularly grotesque body that had been a real live, loved soldier of Charlie Company the previous morning.

"Get the fuck out of here, you assholes!" one of the survivors yelled at the cameramen.

Few of the Charlie Company survivors would say anything to the reporters and cameramen. They stood silently waiting to get on the helicopter that would fly them out of this hell nobody who had not been there could ever feel. Phil Hall was among the survivors who could still stand. He made a count of how many of the 134 members of Charlie Company who fought in the battle could make formation at the base in the rear where the helicopter set them down. He counted twenty-eight enlisted men, including himself. He did not know how many officers besides Libs had made it. Hathaway in his after-action report listed thirty-five killed in the fierce battle, plus Airman Pitsenbarger, and seventy-one wounded. This would leave only twenty-eight unwounded or slightly wounded like Libs. With 106 out of 134 men killed or wounded, Charlie Company's casualty rate for the Easter battle was 80 percent, a rate that top commanders considered unacceptably high even if more Vietcong had been killed. Hathaway estimated in his after-action report that at least 150 of the crack D-800 troops had been killed in the battle. Unwritten in any of the after-action reports were the wounds this battle and others like it in Vietnam would inflict on the men who fought them and on their families.

Libs, Kroah, Urconis, Hall—all of whom I interviewed to reconstruct the Easter battle—were among those who told me the nightmares never stop. Libs could not adjust to civilian life nor talk about the battle to release its demons until we talked it out for hours around the dining room table in his home in Evansville, Indiana. I sat between Libs and Hall as the scenes charged back into their minds. They sweated, shook and fought back the tears as they relived the battle. I sent Libs my reconstruction of the battle after talking to other survivors. He wrote me back a moving letter which said, in part: "I cannot find the words to tell you how much 'Legacy' has affected me and Phil . . . God, George, you must have been there!

"I'll tell you something from my heart that I don't believe I've ever told any man before. Over the years I have agonized over Abilene to the point of damn near insanity.

"I ask the questions: Could I have saved more men? Did I move quick enough? Was I smart? Why, in God's name, am I alive? Am I a coward for being petrified during the battle?

"I know that these are not unique questions, nor particularly earthshaking, but by damn they are brutal and painful.

"I tell you this because, after all these years of sometimes debilitating thoughts comes a stranger who somehow has given Johnny Libs his pride and dignity back..."

Libs would leave Vietnam without knowing that the battle of Xa Cam My would not only shake him and other survivors but also top military commanders all the way up to General Harold K. Johnson, Army Chief of Staff, in 1966.

Johnson flew from the Pentagon to Vietnam shortly after the battle and visited DePuy at his headquarters in Lai Khe, not far from the scene of the battle.

"You know," DePuy told me Johnson warned him, "The American people won't support this war if we keep having the kind of casualties suffered by Charlie Company."

Casualties continued to mount in the rifle companies in Vietnam for no clear purpose. The American people stopped supporting the war. Protesters filled up Washington streets and shouted "Hell no! We won't go!" in regard to the draft. Young men agonized about whether to answer their summons to Army duty or go to jail or flee to Canada. Bearing the burden of this war was no longer a clear-cut obligation for the young men of the nation. A frustrated President Lyndon B. Johnson could not find a way to win the war. The Vietcong and North Vietnamese on January 31, 1968, launched their Tet offensive. They scored a stunning psychological victory, but not a military one, by penetrating all the way to the inside of the U.S. Embassy in Saigon. "From that point on," wrote Colonel Harry G. Summers Jr. in his history of the Vietnam War, "the problem was not how to win, the war but how to disengage."

President Johnson shocked the world by announcing on March 31, 1968, that he would not seek re-election. Richard M. Nixon, seeking to replace Johnson in the White House, promised to end both the Vietnam War and the draft.

On March 27, 1969, shortly after his inauguration, President Nixon appointed a commission chaired by former Defense Secretary Thomas S. Gates Jr. "to develop a comprehensive plan for eliminating conscription and moving toward an all-volunteer armed force."

Less than one year later—on February 20, 1970—Gates, in submitting the commission's report to Nixon, said: "We unanimously believe that the nation's interests will be better served by an all-volunteer force, supported by an effective standby draft, than by a mixed force of volunteers and conscripts; that steps should be taken promptly to move in this direction; and that the first indispensable step is to remove the present inequity in the pay of men serving their first term in the armed forces. We have satisfied ourselves that a volunteer force will not jeopardize national security, and we believe it will have a beneficial effect on the military as well as the rest of our society.

Expounding on those conclusions within its 211-page report, the commission said:

In recent years military service has been scorned and condemned by some Americans. No doubt, the Vietnam War is partly responsible, but the draft has also contributed to the military's unpopularity.

Young men are inevitably skeptical about a career in an organization which has to use compulsion to obtain recruits. Moreover, the low pay implies that society places little value on a soldier. The termination of the draft should immediately enhance the prestige of enlisted service. The knowledge that those in the armed forces have freely chosen to serve their country cannot but improve their image—in their own eyes as well as in the eyes of society...

The return to an all-volunteer armed force should improve the quality of military life. Conscription enables the military to ignore individual dignity and desire, secure in the knowledge that the draft will replace those who do not like the military system. The entire military "atmosphere"—the approach to training, discipline and treatment of individuals—must be re-examined...

Members of both the white and Negro communities have expressed concern that the all-volunteer force might fill its enlisted ranks with the poor and the black. . . We have concluded that the racial composition of the armed forces cannot be fundamentally changed by ending the draft. Even if higher pay appealed only to the poor, twice as many whites as blacks would be attracted... The best estimate of the proportion of blacks in the all-volunteer force is 14.9 percent, compared with 14.1 percent in a mixed force of conscripts and volunteers . . . Even if higher estimates [of blacks] were realized (in an all-volunteer military] we would not consider asking the government— including the military—to cut back on hiring blacks or to set quotas.

Congress at Nixon's urging allowed the authority to draft young men to end on July 1, 1973. The Army struggled to fill its ranks with volunteers. Some Army recruiters in their desperate effort to fill their quotas for volunteers faked credentials and broke other rules to get warm bodies for the ranks. Not until the 1980s did the tide change. Vietnam was ancient history to the new generation. Higher pay and benefits made soldiering look better than working at McDonald's to many young people.

The size of the Army shrunk from its Vietnam high of 1.57 million men and women to 781,000 by 1987, enabling it to be more choosy in accepting volunteers. After years of sending out its message on the wrong wavelength for America's young people, the Army in the 1980s got through with the slogan: "Be all you can be, join the Army."

Today the United States is gambling its safety on this new, small, all-volunteer, post-Vietnam Army. The biggest gamble is whether the Charlie companies of this Army will fight and hold like the old one that fought the Vietcong D-800 Battalion.

Who are these men volunteering to risk dying in terror-filled battles like the one Johnny Libs fought, for a chance at a better life? What are they like? Why do they do it with nobody saluting? Will the new Charlie Company fight and die and win like the old one if the bell tolls?

Thoughts on Small Unit Leadership

by COL John Ripley USMC (Ret)

Colonel John Ripley, USMC (Ret)

Col Ripley, a native of Radford, Virginia, is one of the living legends of the Marine Corps. In Vietnam, on Easter Sunday, 1972, then-Captain Ripley and one other American advisor destroyed a vital bridge at Dong Ha, which halted a major North Vietnamese offensive. His remarkable exploits and courage, for which he received the Navy Cross, are related in the book, "The Bridge at Dong Ha," by Col John G. Miller, USMC (Ret).

First of all, the value of self-confidence is just overwhelmingly important for a Marine. If you don't have self-confidence, you could never be a Marine. I'm not talking about ego, but it borders ego. You have to feel like you're in charge and you have to demonstrate that ... always, always, always. Your unit has to see you as the leader, and they have to gain their confidence from your confidence. They have to see you in a figurehead position, a role model, that takes into account the golden principle that we constantly talk about, "Set the Example." If you have this overwhelming, effusive confidence, you will, without question, give this same level to your unit, and this will enable them to do far more than what they could do otherwise. My style was very simple: I always tried to be as far forward as I could be, within a reasonable distance—not to interfere with the initial action, nor to recklessly endanger myself, as I was no good to my company dead! I would tell my platoon commanders that, too. If you're out picking up casualties, then you're endangering your value to the company; let someone else get the casualties. There are things you have to do that are dangerous enough. Generally, stay with the point platoon, but never with the point squad (when you're moving to contact).

Contact in the jungle was very close; you could tell by sound what you were getting into. My company had the rare distinction of never, ever having been surprised. Not

Source: *From the Horse's Mouth, Selected Thoughts on Small-Unit Leadership.* Reprinted with permission.

once. In all of our engagements, we surprised the enemy. I would not permit "NBCs" (non-battle casualties). I simply wouldn't acknowledge a heat casualty; the term simply went out of our lexicon. When a new Marine felt like he had to stop or he had heat problems, he knew that his compaños had to carry him. That is a wonderful way of solving that kind of problem. If you know that your fellow Marines are going to carry your kit, or carry you, then you get better, or they make you get better (generally, that's what happens).   Not Participative!!

You constantly hear about all of the leadership traits, especially courage, intelligence, fitness, perseverance, and endurance, all of which are important, but I see all of those as given for all Marine leaders (whether it's a corporal squad leader or a general division commander), so I don't even count those. I think the critical element for any combat commander, the one you must have, and you will be an absolute failure without it, is decisiveness in combat. I give a speech on this subject regularly to FBI leaders. My analogy I give to them is, "Indecisiveness equals cowardice." If you can't make a decision without forming a committee, or having a bloody "O-group" (getting all your officers together to talk about it) . . . then that's crazy. You've got to be able to make instantaneous decisions based on the little information at hand, a lot of which you have intuitively. You're moving to contact, you know where you are, where your closest units are, what units are supporting you. All of this information is at your fingertips, so when the situation changes, you don't have to stop and "review" all this, it's all "loaded into your hard drive" so you just smack it out. When you make contact with the enemy, things start happening at warp speed. A phenomenon that a lot of people don't appreciate is that all of your subordinate units start doing things without your telling them. They know what to do, and they do it. You simply orchestrate it. Rarely does a company commander find himself giving commands. They have reacted immediately because they know what you want; it's intuitive. It's "in the ether." That's how it is with a good unit, and how it was with us. If anything, the toughest thing I had to do was put a leash on them and hold them back, to keep them from getting into big trouble from going too far, and to impose the things that I knew, because I was privy to the operations plan, and no one else was (they knew the frag order, but not the whole plan).

Things would happen so fast that it wasn't a jolly-difficult effort to give a five-paragraph order, because most of it had been given. I'd just give a quick frag, a modification, of what we were already doing. As a result of these abilities, in an engagement, we would overpower the enemy in an instant . . . in an instant we were on 'em. We kept casualties very low because of that. Our casualty rate was nearly 10-to-1, and that's very conservative.

Training Marines is not an art; it's something that becomes an extension of a good leader. A good leader know what needs to be done, he has done it himself before, so a corporal who becomes a squad leader has done all of these things, he knows what to do, which is why he's a squad leader. The training aspect of it is not difficult at all; he is doing what it took maybe two years to learn how to do and do well. As a young officer, you don't get the benefit of experience built up over several years that enlisted Marines do. Experience is the best teacher, hands down, but that's not to say that the classroom material is not very critical . . . it is enormously important.

We can teach anyone the "skill to kill." Hell, you could take a primate to the rifle range and teach him how to operate a weapon. The skill to kill is not all we need; we also need the will to kill. We need to teach our Marines the will to kill. But it can never cross that thin line and become the "thrill to kill"; this difference is critical. So, "Skill, will, but never thrill." A leader has to be constantly aware of this. Killing becomes impersonal. That's not to say that you don't have definitive emotions as you do it, but it has to become second nature. You cannot hesitate. Now, people never talk about this. They say, "I never got this kind of training when I was a young officer." When it gets into close combat, as it always does, when you use your weapons, and sometimes your hands, or anything available to you, you are using skill; this is not brute force. If it degenerates into brute force, then something has gone wrong. You have lost much of your advantage. You want as much stand-off distance as you can get, and you need to be out of the beaten zone so that the enemy can't bring his weapons to bear on you. We would teach our Marines in Vietnam how to best employ their weapons in close quarter battle.

There's a lot to say about automatic fire if it's controlled well (which it frequently is not). If it's controlled well, it's by far the most preferable method of engaging a close enemy—by far. Always have your automatic weapons forward . . . always, always, always when you're moving to contact. The idea that you'd protect your automatic weapons by keeping them in the rear means that you're not employing those weapons, and you're going to endanger your Marines. These weapons skills have to become impersonal, rote, functionary actions. Which is to say that you cannot be concerned that you're killing somebody, you have to be concerned with how efficiently you are killing these people. Am I doing it properly? Am I giving him the opportunity to hit one of my people as I move ahead? This level of "skill efficiency" becomes your focus.

There is nothing more efficient on the face of the earth at killing than a Marine rifle company. I have a lot of friends in the FBI. One said to me once, "You know, the most powerful people in the world are U.S. federal judges and U.S. Marine rifle company commanders," and I believe him. I think that's true. You have the means and the clout to stop anything.

I can't tell you how many engagements we had in Vietnam. Every day there was something, every single day in the field there something happened, either direct or indirect fire. There were many opportunities to get hurt. The American public never appreciated how tough a battle Vietnam was and how constant it was. In that level of combat, you become damn good at what you do, or you just don't last long. You know what you're doing, and you're efficient, and you do things well and thoroughly, and you're constantly alert (which raggs you out). People find it very hard to believe that I never slept in Vietnam. Never was I fully unconscious. Anytime the handset on the radio clicked, I was fully awake immediately. I was that attuned to what was going on around me. At night when I was down in my hole, my radio operator was right there with me, we could hear the squelch on the radio; if a handset clicked, we were up in a flash. If there was the tiniest bit of movement out there—bang!—everyone's awake. Even on 50 percent alert, even the guy who's bagged in, he'll snap awake immediately. You feel bum-tired, but you have a reserve of energy that's simply phenomenal. When you go into the attack, and you're required to do things, it's amazing the resources that you can call on that are simply impossible to describe.

That's another thing that's important for young leaders to understand: It's virtually impossible for us to train to that level during peacetime. We can't run our people that hard, because there's a mental block there that tells you, "Oh, I've hit the wall. I can't go any further." In combat, you don't have that mental block. You just keep going until you've accomplished the mission. Leaders appreciate that and know that you've got to push your Marines as hard as you can push them. You've got to push them to the bleeding point. You've got to exhaust them, you got to ignore the endurance factor, pay no attention to creature comfort. If you are pursuing the enemy, and it's a clear mission, never have breaks for chow or water; absolutely none of that counts. The only thing that counts is accomplishment of the mission. Mission accomplishment is on a level so far above everything else that nothing else really matters. You worry about the safety of your men, about their health and comfort, but nothing interferes with your accomplishment of the mission.

The one thing I see today that gives me great concern is how we have had to change our training because people are so concerned about training casualties. Casualties in combat don't matter. You know they're going to happen, but you never, ever, ever, stop the action because of casualties. And that's what many started doing. When people saw a casualty, they'd "turn the war off" and evacuate the casualty. You must never do this in combat. The only person who is concerned about the casualty in combat is the corpsman. Everyone else keeps moving and accomplishes the mission. Now, when you seize the objective and consolidate, yes, then you do worry and you do go back and make every single effort you can to secure and to evacuate your casualties. Generally, it's impossible to deal with on-sight, unless you're surrounded...and I've done that several times. But you never change your operational procedure because you've got casualties. For example, pull a platoon out of the line to go and protect the casualties; that's nonsense. You've got to keep everyone focused on the mission. It's a hard thing to understand, and it's awfully difficult to train people to do that, especially now because we're so fixated on casualties. The press has really made us that way. Every time someone goes down, they go nuts and stick their microphones in your face, that sort of thing. Casualties become a consideration when they get in the way of accomplishing the mission. On a patrol, you become damn near ineffective if you're carrying casualties. It takes four healthy Marines to carry a wounded Marine, and a dead Marine weighs more than a wounded Marine. That's a critical factor that no one appreciates; I don't know why. *Achievement oriented*

A young leader must burn into his brain one phrase, "Accomplish the mission. I will do what I came here to do. I will always, always, always accomplish the mission. I will find a way. If it costs everything I have, I will do it. I will keep my superiors informed." They may say at some point, "It's not worth it, come back," or "Stop your attack and move down the second axis," or "Hold where you are; Second Platoon will move around you." They may alter it, but it is critical that all young leaders understand, believe, that "I will accomplish my mission. I will do exactly what's expected of me." Do what you came here to do.

Our focus in training: Marines are aggressive. If we ever lose that style of fighting, we won't be the Marine Corps. Take the fight to the enemy. Sitting on a piece of ground, preparing good defenses, sometimes we have to do that, but we hate it. When we first got to Vietnam, our Commandant told us, "I don't want anyone caught sitting on their ditty bags. Our job is to defend the Da Nang airbase, and the way to do that is to get the hell out on patrols, well out into the limit of our mortar fan, and when artillery comes ashore, to the limit of our artillery fan, and that's the way we defend. We don't sit around in well-prepared positions." That was the hell of Khe Sanh. Khe Sanh was miserable because they wouldn't let us move off of those damned hills. We are, by nature, aggressive animals. We take advantage of the fact that the male of our species has this in his blood. If you don't have that aggressiveness, you're in the wrong line of work as a Marine. You need to go be a hairdresser, or something like that, but get the hell out of the Marine Corps. If you don't receive a thrill when your superior says, "We're going to attack," if that doesn't give you a rush of adrenaline, then you're in the wrong line of work. By and large, most Marines have the right attitude. I have had to command, "Fix bayonets" on several occasions, and more than once I did it because I knew what effect it would have on my men. I knew what it would do for all of us. It's like giving them an extra bandolier. It motivates the hell out of them. They know they are going into close quarter battle, and they love it. Sometimes we did, sometimes we didn't. Once, I didn't hear one bayonet go on; they were already all fixed.

Again, train the aggressive fighting spirit. If you see a lack of that in any of your subordinate commanders, you're going to have to "re-tool" them, or get rid of them. You simply can't have that in a combat unit. They have to be aggressive. They have to have what I call the "linebacker attitude." Linebackers love to take people, to smash them; that's the thrill of football. Marines must feel that way. If it's not there, you've got a serious flaw to deal with.

Decisiveness. Nothing will ever be perfect anywhere. You will never see a T/O unit. You have to consider what you have, your people, your equipment, your support, and you have to then make a decision and do all of this instantaneously. Generally, your platoons are already doing what you want them to do. It's up to you to continue to form this plan of attack and on the fly. You tell them what to do, because the instantaneous action overwhelms the enemy.

Indirect fire. The purpose of indirect fire is not to destroy the enemy. If you do destroy him with indirect fire, that's great! The purpose to the company commander, the "customer" (I used to tell all my artillery friends that I'm the "customer"), is to force the enemy to go to ground and to change his plan. This is why you always have your FO within choking range. The moment you take fire, the FO is pumping fire in; he's not checking with you. My FO would always know where we were and what to do. He would suppress the enemy's fire and, more importantly, cut off the enemy's avenue of escape. Once you cut him off, you then plan your attack into him. That's the purpose of artillery. Artillery will tell you, on the other hand, that their purpose is to destroy by fire, etc., etc. My answer is, "Yeah, if you can do that, that's great." But your real job is to pin the enemy down, permit me to maneuver, because the moment you take away his initiative, I can get up and maneuver, and I can get him by fire. Same thing with air, but air has a great advantage in that he can see the enemy and tell me what the bastard is doing. And, let's face it, a 500-pound snake is one hell of a piece of ordnance compared to a 45-lb. '05 round. We had a hell of a lot of air; it was always with us. We always had a FAC-A (airborne) who would track our movements and chatter with us constantly, and if we needed help . . . zoom! He was there! In came a damn section of F-4s or A-4s, I mean we had ordnance on target immediately. It was an orchestration of how things should work.

"Street sense" is critical in a leader. You have to have an intuitive awareness of all the things around you. For example, when you're just walking, you have to have a feeling for what the terrain is doing. In the jungle, you can't see more than a few meters, but you must have an intuitive feeling when you're moving whether your ground is going up, or falling away to the left or right, if the canopy is getting thicker, if you're reaching a source of water. All these sensory messages come to you, and you have to read them, and you become good at that. With sense of smell, my rifle company all became "bird dogs." We could detect the enemy by smell long before we saw them. We could pick the son-of-a-bitch out, we knew exactly where he was: whether he was in camp, or had just broken camp, we knew generally how many there were . . . just by our noses. The most recognizable smell was a mixture of wood smoke and camphor. They used camphor for medicinal purposes. We would pick that up. We were also very careful not to generate non-human smells within our rifle company. I had one Marine whose momma sent him about 20 sticks of pepperoni. Well, we wouldn't let him take any of that to the field; he could eat it back at the fire base. Onions were also forbidden.

Any kind of destroyed vegetation is a dead giveaway because animals don't do that. They don't destroy vines and branches and rip leaves off; we were constantly catching the enemy doing these things. We got on their trails, the so-called "Ho Chi Minh trails," very well-established, beautifully done, with handrails, and steps hewn into rock. We could track the bastards, ambush them, literally reach out and snatch them as they went by, I can recall in '72 in a night attack in Dong Ha, the NVA had crossed the river upstream, after about a week of fighting. I told my counterpart, "They're about 500 meters in front of us." He asked, "How do you know?" I said, "I can smell them." Sure as hell, we fired mortars and caught them in the open. They went into the attack, we fired some illumination, and sure as hell, the ones in the attack were trapped, and we got 'em. I could smell 'em before I could hear 'em.

It's easy to become desensitized, or a stronger word I don't like, dehumanized, to things you should be aware of and pay attention to. We would regularly rotate back to our firebase, a little more secure a place. When we were in the firebase, I'd make sure we had our burners brought in so the men could get hot water, hot chow, soup . . . anything like that is wonderful. And always have the chaplain going around, always force people to write letters (if they're not). Ensure that your leaders are going around to their Marines, finding out what they're doing; don't let them just crash and relax. You're constantly on them to behave like Marines and like human beings.

DIRECTIVE LEADERSHIP It's easy to drift off. For example, my men shaved once a day, every day, every single day, even on very limited water (though water was rarely a problem). Shaving marked the day, and it also marked us. It was a clean start to the day. There are many ways to avoid doing what Marines do. You can always compromise; you can always try to justify not doing something. You see it in peacetime. There is never a good enough reason for these compromises, The things we teach our men to do are clearly for the best, and we must uphold this. I've never seen where it didn't make a difference. Make sure that your chaplain spends time with your Marines; ours was very close to us. Men who probably had no faith before they came to Vietnam left there devout in some faith. I didn't give a damn which one it was. Again, all this to avoid the dehumanizing danger of living in the conditions we had.

A word on casualties: You spend time with your men, and invariably, you lose them. I lost 300 percent of my company, three times over (not all killed, mostly wounded). You regret that, obviously. You have to immediately focus on the future and what you are doing at the time. Later, you'd have a memorial service for the dead, or for the evacuated wounded, and you'd stay in touch with letters. That was always a big morale booster. You cannot permit yourself to dwell on the Marines you have lost; it would drive you nuts. Leaders had to be aware of this and had to constantly reinforce, especially to the younger Marines, "Look, he did his duty. You have gained something from this Marine. He will always be a part of you. You now have a job to do to help this other Marine now. You've grown up a lot. You have a new A-gunner now," or "I'm giving you the automatic rifle, and you're going to use it now that Schultz is gone. Now you gotta do it and do as good a job as he did." Stress reinforcement and detachment from emotion. You have to find a way to keep these emotions from getting in the way of a Marine doing his duty. It's hard to do; you really have to experience it, but it is critical. You can't let them dwell on casualties.

They'll see casualties; we saw lots. I would tell replacements (usually 15 once a month, twice if we were lucky) the minute they arrived, "Men, you've left home, gone to boot camp, you've had leave, gone to a staging battalion, flown to Okinawa, spent time there, then to Da Nang, gotten processed, then to Dong Ha, been processed. . . . You have finally arrived to where you are going to work. There is no more training. From this point on, you're going to earn your paycheck. I want you to understand that you've got to rely on all that information you've been learning, so think about all of it, remember it all. Don't think about home; don't think about your girlfriend. You think about what you learned at ITR or staging battalion."

I taught them how to employ a machine gun, even if they weren't a machine-gunner. My entire company got a piece of surgical tubing from the doc, and all of us could apply a tourniquet with our teeth and one hand. Which sometimes they had to do, because if there's only one corpsman with someone else and you're pumpin', you've got to get that tourniquet on before the doc gets to you. That's a critical skill. Every Marine knew how to close a wound with a bandolier pin; every bandolier comes with one (so they don't swing when you're running). We saved those things; they were critical. I taught men how to use these pins to close an open flesh wound. You only have one battle dressing, and if it's a bad enough wound, that may not be enough. We would keep bandolier pins all over us. That's how you could tell a grunt Marine up there—pins "stored" all over his gear and uniform.

We would teach them little tricks of the trade like that . . . how to store your magazines so that you could get to them rapidly, and return them rapidly. The really bad units were the ones that lost magazines. My battalion had to relieve a battalion at Con Thien because they ran out of magazines. We lost Marines doing that. My Marines were lost because another battalion had such poor discipline—losing their magazines. When you

Inspirational appeal

pop a magazine, you don't just throw the son-of-a-bitch away! You've got to reload it! You need that magazine! We teach 'em these little things because, by and large, they haven't been taught them. The M16 was a God-awful weapon. We had to teach men how to operate it, the hasty drills to clear a stoppage, a failure to extract (that was the worst).

Then I would tell them, "Men, listen carefully: Everybody here is going to be wounded, at least once. Some of you are not going to make it. But I want you to understand now that there's not one man here who's not going to get whacked. Everyone is going to get whacked, some of you a couple times, but you're not getting through this without getting hit. Get that in your mind right now." That assurance would have the desired effect; that would eventually put them at ease. They knew it was going to happen when they heard it from me. "If you've gotten all the way here and you still don't have your personal affairs taken care of, it's your fault." I kept my first sergeant back to take care of that, anyone who needed a will or a power of attorney. I tell them to show me their dog tags. So help me, always a couple of 'em wouldn't have their dog tags . . . the damnedest thing you've ever seen! *rational persuasion*

On the firebase, my policy was that you could go around with your shirt off, because in the jungle, the only way you could heal jungle rot was by exposing it to the sun. Some people would go around stark naked to dry out and kill the fungus. So my replacements would see my Marines walking around with these incredible scars on them. They looked like a bunch of pirates with all their scars! That had the right effect for preparing them for what we knew would happen. In those days, the way they would treat a wound, like a flesh wound, was to take this implement—it looked like a grapefruit knife—and scrape all the damaged flesh out, and then just pull the skin over it and do a quick stitch. It looked like a wickery stitch. The scar looked like a stick of licorice, a big purple welt on your body, or a gouge where a grenade had scooped out part of your arm. Every now and then we'd get one who'd go ballistic, just couldn't hack it. We'd keep him for a day or two, gradually introduce him to a patrol. Most of the times it worked, sometimes not.

Business in a rifle company: It's so busy, you don't have time to think about what may be troubling you. You, the individual Marine, are so critical to the success of the unit and have so much to do to make sure that your mates are being looked after, that you can't withdraw into your own shell. You have got to help your fellow Marines survive and make happen what needs to happen. If you're not doing your fair share, it has an immediate impact. There're just too damn few trigger-pullers, especially if you're with a crew-served weapon; you're working constantly. You and your company are always anticipating the next move. Those who are constantly successful don't dwell on the "here and now"; they constantly think a step ahead. Preempt the enemy from whatever the enemy thinks they're going to do. It works. It really works.

I can recall once when we moved up on a hill from a low area, and as we move up, through some elephant grass, we see the open crest of the hill, and there's the enemy sitting in the open, unaware of us! About 25 meters away—pistol range. That's how stealthy we were; that's how good Marines are. We moved our guns forward, got the platoon on line ready to go. I decided to assault immediately because they were so dumbfounded, and I would give my firing command to the artillery as we attacked 'cause I wanted these guys to be in the open when we started.

It was amazing to me—just amazing—that they were so detached and had such poor security that an entire Marine rifle company was in their face before they knew it, and I mean in their face—right there! And hell, we knocked 'em all down, every damned one, the ones that didn't run back over the hill. They were very good at what they did, but they were not stealthy. The Orientals have always been great jungle fighters? Baloney! They couldn't do anything as well as we could! Nothing. We were stealthy. We did all the basic things well: being good navigators, knowing where you are at all times... that's terribly important! That's another thing that gave us enormous confidence. If you want to lose the confidence of your Marines, get them lost! And then stand there, look at a map and argue over where the hell you are. Talk about a "fatal flaw" that's going to give you an immediate "confidence check" with your men.   *Expert power*

In 1967, on the 21st, we had a big ambush. I was with my guys a month ago down in Florida. We had a big battalion reunion, and we talked about this. We were down south of the Rock Pile, a place called Kai Lu, on the road to Khe Sanh. This unit got itself trapped down there, so we went down to help them. On the way down, my company was moving as fast as we could on foot, but they were about seven miles away, so a couple of dusters came by with an ammunition truck, and I flagged them down and put my command group on the dusters so we could get down there to the ambush site and start calling fire while my company closed on me. Knowing full well that the enemy was going to whack us on the way down, I was constantly scanning, and sure-as-hell, while I'm sitting on this duster (a duster's a little antiaircraft tank with an open gun turret), right beside the turret, I look up and see an RPG coming right-smack at us! It was so head-on that all I could see was the cruciform of the fin assembly as it slowly rotated, then I could see the warhead on it. I said, "Oh my God," then grabbed the pintle-mounted machine gun and started firing at this damned rocket, thinking I could hit it (which was ridiculous, but it seemed like a good idea!). Well, I didn't hit it, and this thing went whizzing right by, I don't think anyone on the duster crew ever saw it! And then I could see the enemy firing 12.7-mm. at us, which was a big son-of-a-bitch. It could penetrate the armor on a duster. So I told my command group to bingo off 'cause we're going right into an ambush. It was going about 30 miles per hour, but we just leapt off. I jumped into the jungle, which came right up to the road (and happily, it broke my fall, and I got right back up). Now we're dismounted, out in Indian country, the company is a mile or so away—very far—and we're isolated, and the enemy saw us jump off, so they knew where we were. I assembled everybody, and we started moving along the road in the same direction and set up a hasty defense. I moved to confuse the enemy, who thought that we would stay right where we landed. It worked. In three hours of searching they never found us. We called artillery and air in on them all the while. The guys in the dusters, within 30 seconds of our jump, were hit dead-center in the killing zone of the ambush; the enemy got every one of them. One of the drivers managed to jump out and run, but they chased him down, executed him and stuck propaganda in his mouth, which is what they used to do. We recovered them later when my company came down, and we continued down to clear the first ambush.

The interesting thing about that fight was that everyone in the company knew what to do. They knew that we were cut off and began a concerted effort to get to us. We had one rifle; the rest had pistols and grenades. My company fought their way forward, through ambushes, with amazingly few casualties. It was another example of your knowing that your subordinates know just what to do and will do it and do it perfectly. It was a successful day, whereas these other units were just cut all to hell. We killed 109 of the enemy that day. It was so impressive to Saigon, they sent a couple of people up to learn how an ambushed unit could account so well for themselves.

That was on the 21st of August. On the 7th of September, we had another ambush... same location. My company, now with a reputation for ambush busting, got called out to do the same thing farther down the road. They didn't have a secondary, but they had just eaten one of our companies alive. We had two platoons doing exactly what the hell they were supposed to be doing, exhausted from a long march in dry, hot, hot, hot weather. We go into the attack, and we did manage to clear the ambush, at some expense. It took a lot of effort and a few casualties. When it was all said and done, we had to come back and police the casualties of the initial unit. They didn't get their own casualties out; we had to do that for them. The battalion command group, which tried to get there ahead of us, was so shot up that we had to help them get out, too!

A wonderful SNCO 81 Platoon commander had provided fire for me, knowing where I was moving and knowing what I was doing without any fire commands at all. He could move that 81 fire in front of me by just seeing where I was up the road. He told me he was going to do it as I went by, and I said, "Gunny, just keep it coming!" and he did. Another great example of Marines with intuitive good judgment not following a precise fire command, but it worked beautifully.

Great Marines: Sgt McGowan from Alabama. McGowan was a platoon guide. He had been in Force Recon. He would do exactly what he knew he was supposed to do without any verbal orders at all. He just started to deploy, started to take charge, he was always ahead of his platoon commander. He was a de facto platoon commander. His Marines had enormous confidence in him. He deployed them properly. He would lead them in the attack. On the 2nd of March, in that attack, I'll never forget his yelling. We had two platoons forward, and as we attacked through this base camp, I could hear McGowan on the left, yelling his bloody brains out, getting people to move forward, and it's a good thing he did because we had enemy fire coming up behind us progressively. He led that way the whole time in Vietnam. ᴇxᴘᴇʀᴛ Pᴏᴡᴇʀ ; Sᴜᴘᴘᴏʀᴛɪᴠᴇ Lᴇᴀᴅᴇʀѕʜɪᴘ

Another was Gunny McMillian, a West Virginian; he was so good; he was a platoon commander in India Company. He was beloved by his Marines, and rightly so, because he had not just fighting skills, he had a sense for his Marines that was just amazing. They knew that he cared for them, they knew that he'd push them, they knew that as long as he was in command that they were under the best protection possible. And he did look after them in a very physical way. This guy had more initiative and more common sense in a fight than most Marines I've run across in a lifetime. He simply knew what to do, how to accomplish it.

When I was cut off on the 2nd of March '67, we went into the fight that day with a reinforced company, 215 total, we had attachments, scout dogs, engineer team, a really big unit. We got up there, and after a full day of fighting, there were 15 Marines who were not hit. The company gunny kept the casualty medevac numbers, and he would check them off when we had a casualty, when they left the field. Toward the end of the day, I said to him, "Gunny, what's the casualty situation?" He said, "Sir, we ain't got 15 m—f—here who aren't killed or wounded, and you ain't one of 'em!" I never forgot that. I got hit that day myself, but I was back on my feet. He made it very clear that we were at the end of the rope. Well, this guy McMillian, knowing how bad off we were, fought his way forward and punched his way through my south perimeter. The enemy targeted the medevac helicopters, so our second medevac was our last. That day, I lost all my squad leaders, two platoon commanders KIA, and two platoon sergeants WIA and evacuated. I needed a lot of replacements. McMillian punched a hole and made a corridor for me so we could get our casualties out, and he protected us and led us back to the battalion position. We've been very close friends ever since then.

One of the things that is so common, and it's an anathema, is the tendency of a young leader to disregard what he learns in the classroom and defer to the experience of the Marines around him, especially his platoon sergeant. There is this myth that what comes from the mouth of a platoon sergeant is always, always superior to what came from a classroom or a manual . . . nonsense. I say to all officers, "You've been given the world's best training. Everything we've taught you has competed with a hundred other things to make it on the training schedule. You're getting only the things that we consider damned important. It's there for a reason. Let me tell you, lieutenant, don't ever listen to this crap about 'We don't do it this way in this outfit, we don't follow the book here. . . . ' There are some modifications—some good. But overwhelmingly, the procedures that lieutenants learn in The Basic School and IOC are far, far superior to anything that some well-meaning, experienced Marine is telling him to do. Like, "Don't bring the tripod and the T&E. . . . We don't use that out here." Crap! Or, "Never fire your blooper direct, always make an angled fire . . . " or, "We don't carry our mortars out . . ." Stupid things. "Two bandoliers is always enough." Well, if you get in a firefight and run out, you'll never have to tell your Marines to carry enough ordnance. . . . You run out one time, and you'll never run out again! You can never, never replicate the feeling of running out of ammunition. It is God-awful (and it only happens once)!

Always trust your instincts, your intuitive judgment: You wouldn't be a lieutenant and a platoon commander if you didn't have good judgment. Trust it, trust what your judgment tells you, and be extremely skeptical when someone says to you, "We don't do it that way." Always ask the tough questions: "Why are you doing that'? Explain to me why that is better." Why is it better to put your machine gun on a bipod on the lip of a fighting hole at night, instead of locking on the T&E and tripod? Why not put two SAW-gunners up on point, where each man covers a sector, instead of 180 degrees? That's critical when you're walking a trail. You don't want men trying to move their heads 180 degrees. You want them covering a sector. If you have two automatic weapons, they are far better employed that way.

- Never accept your first "no" or your second "no."
- Ultimately, the winners are those who have perseverance and persistence.
- On the battlefield, endurance is to strength as 10 is to one.
- Endurance is the difference between winning and losing.

Strength is critical and important, but it's not even in the same "grid square" of importance as endurance. Marines are fixated with upper-torso exercises and strength; the "American Way" to get fit is to develop the upper torso. When I served with the Royal Marines, I learned that the Europeans, on the other hand, stress lower-body endurance, not upper-body strength. Let me tell you, on the battlefield, that is to strength as 10 is to one. I can give a million examples of where strength has been a loser and endurance has been a winner. The little flyweights who just keep sloggin' on, while the big tough guys' heads are swimmin' and they can't keep up, and their damned boots are too big, and they come crashin' through the jungle makin' all kinds of noise. The little "sand blowers" just keep goin' and keep goin', and they're just always there and can always be counted on.

These are factors that any young leader doesn't see at the outset, but should, and should pay attention. And again—decisiveness—don't be wishy-washy. If you can't make a decision, you immediately worry your men that this leader isn't quite sure of himself, and they lose some of their confidence in you. On the other hand, if you're decisive, even if you make the wrong decision, rarely will your decision be perfect, rarely will it be black-and-white. There's a little "gray" in every decision, but at least you've made a decision, you have a course of action, and you can begin. Whereas this other idiot is standing there, staring at the map, and his platoon is wandering around. You've made the decision; you're off and running, moving, in the attack. It's far better to make a decision and get going, especially from a confidence standpoint. That is the critical skill of a combat leader. Decisiveness. Stick to it. Do what you're supposed to be doing. Training techniques. I always did the toughest route possible. When I run, I run the outer perimeter, never the shorter, inner perimeter. The inner perimeter is the easy out. I don't think we train tough enough. I don't think we train with endurance in mind. We never train today by pushing Marines to the point of exhaustion, then force them to go into the attack, with a shooting skill at the end of it, or some kind of map problem, or something that forces the Marine to do what he's supposed to be doing when he gets there. That's something we simply must change. I tried to change that. We don't do enough physical work. In training today, they do a 10-mile hump. The first thing they do when they get there is break down, set up bivouac, change socks, instead of going into the attack! It's pervasive, and it's what we do now. In combat, you'll be attacking when you get there, as opposed to some sort of admin bivouac, for God's sake!

I've been enamored all my life of PT and fitness. I don't think I could max the PFT anymore, but it still excites me. I'm the first to admit, as my wife says, I'm a PT nut . . . maybe so. But I think that the way we do business as Marines, even if you're not a nut, you still have to appreciate physical training to a fault. It's one thing to be an athlete. That's wonderful. Most Marines are athletes, skilled in something athletic, and at least have a liking for PT. You couldn't be a Marine if you didn't. So to most people, we are a little nuts in that respect. Some a little more nuts than others! It's one thing to enjoy this in a garrison environment with your running shorts and your new running shoes and have no equipment. It's something altogether different to have equipment banging on your ass, your canteens are slappin' you, your weapon is digging into your shoulder, your mouth is dry, your ruck's not quite right, you're getting hotspots on your feet, and you still have another 10 miles to go! Or a better example is the arctic, where you have a 95-pound load and you're trying to ski uphill, and you're starving and freezing. There it becomes infinitely more difficult, and that's where Marines excel! Marines have an attitude that, "Goddamnit, I'm gonna be the first one on this hill, and nobody's getting me off this hill." It's in our blood. We feel that way, and that's why our fitness is so important to us, because to be physically unable to do what's expected of us (even if it's outrageous), we take as a personally shameful thing. We've got to deliver. We personalize these things to the point where a normal person would say, "He asked you to do too much; we can't possibly do this!" But we don't think like that. The mere fact that the boss asked means that I gotta do it. Maybe we are nuts, but we can perform the things expected of us. It all depends on this attitude of ours. The public expects this of us. If it wasn't difficult, they wouldn't give it to Marines.

We understand that to be asked to do something is an imperative. It's not a "Can you do this?" By the time the question is asked, even if it's in question form, as opposed to a clear order, it's an imperative. "Of course, I can do it."

"Yes, sir, hell yes, I can go do that. Give me another bandolier."

I love this story. It tells you so much of what is good about the Marine Corps:

One of my Recon Marines in Norway, 1980, after a very long day, had this team that had to put a radio relay on this peak. Seven of them were crossing this huge snowfield—almost a glacier—after dark, pulling a gear sled with them. They get halfway across, and the lead man hits a snow bridge and goes through. He's roped-up to the others, but down he goes, and he's now underwater. In the arctic, this is a critical situation, with a set procedure to follow for it. You have three minutes to get him into a warm place, or he dies of hypothermia. Marines are especially vulnerable because they have very low body fat. They were even more vulnerable because they were already exhausted, and with a high heart rate, your pumpin' heat out. Much different than if some fat body fell in, rested, with a regular pulse; he would probably have another two to three minutes. This Recon team goes into immediate action drill: They dragged him out by the rope, not easily. They ripped the covered sled open, got a bag out, got his wet clothes off, got him into the bag (which stabilizes his temperature) and slapped him around to get his pulse active. Generally, that's good enough, but he was too far gone by then. So the squad leader rips his gear off, gets in the bag with him, and they pulled another bag over the two of them, and the squad leader just hugs him and massages him and slaps him, rolls around with him, yelling and screaming, fighting off hypothermia. The rest of 'em were rubbing and massaging him through the bags, getting his blood moving. Well, they revived him. This is a Recon team, so they have just what they can carry for the mission. They didn't have parkas—parkas are dead weight—they're for sentries, not someone who's mobile. But they managed to get enough gear together for this man who was seconds away from death. Once he's revived, they gave him a hot-wet, packed up their gear, including his frozen-stiff pieces of clothing (which are useless now, they're just like big boards), and continued the mission installing the radio relay. We couldn't possibly have carried out our mission without this radio relay. They got it up there. We're out there 16 days, then we're back aboard ship, steaming home. I'm the battalion commander, and we're steaming home before I find out about it! I only found out about it when I forced my subordinate commanders to submit award recommendations (I had eight independent units plus attachments, over 1,200 Marines). I told them that I wanted deserving Marines to get recognized with Navy Achievement Medals. I used my first sergeants and sergeants major as my awards board. They bitched and moaned, "Ahh, we're not giving any awards. Goddamnit, everyone was doing their job!" That bunch of crusty old bastards, they weren't going to give anybody anything! I said, "Goddamnit, you go and make sure that if a Marine did something, he gets an award!" That's exactly how we found out about it! The Recon men didn't say beans about it! The communicator found out that they weren't going to turn in the squad leader for an award, so he did. I never would have found out about it!

Tell me that Marines aren't extraordinary! They continued the mission, a vital mission; they had every reason in the world to come back, but they didn't come back, even though they didn't have enough kit. God-almighty! That was not combat, but there was a bigger threat out there than the enemy; that was the cold! Just phenomenal. I don't know what it is, but it makes people perform things that couldn't be done any other way. I think it's expectation. You would never, ever not do what is expected of you if you're a Marine. You'd literally die rather than having said of you, "Gee whiz, we thought he was going to do this," or "Where were you, pal? We were running out of ammunition." You'd do anything; you'd run through fire rather than have another Marine think that you didn't do enough.

I constantly get asked about this Dong Ha thing, and it's impossible to make people—civilians—understand this. They just don't understand that not to have done that would have been horrendously dishonorable. For one, I was trained to do it. There were only three factors there: The enemy was there, the bridge was there, and I was there, and that's all that was necessary for me to take action. Now it worked, but it was jolly difficult to bring off. There were problems the whole damned time. Everything went wrong, but it worked, and I'm happy it worked. And when it did, my judgment was justified, even a partial success would have been better than nothing. But I got 100 percent success. What I set out to do, I did. I wasn't so overtly confident that I thought it was a done deal, but it did work. Had I not done that, I would have spent a lifetime wondering what would have happened. I maintain, in a humble way, that all Marines think that way. You could take a garden-variety Marine off the street today, put him in that same situation, and he would come to that same conclusion. He would think the same thing, "I have got to do something, because the ghosts of 3 million Marines out there, all of whom made the Corps what it is today, are looking at me and asking the same question, "What are you gonna do, pal? You'd better do something, because we're watching you" To do nothing is dishonorable. That's the way Marines think. I'm convinced of it; I've thought that way my whole life. Not completing the mission is so dishonorable, it's something people don't even want to talk about or think about. It's hard to verbalize to people who are not "of the cloth," such as us. They'll never understand this calling that permeates our whole psyche. We feel so strongly about it. "Do what you came here to do." "Find a way to do it." You never have enough men, you never have the right equipment or enough equipment. Generally, conditions are ghastly.

Do what the hell you came here to do. You find a way to do it.

If you think like that, you will find a way to do it. Never take your first "no," never take your second "no . . . . " You find a way to do it.

People call us fanatics, I guess for a good reason, but it works, and the examples are legendary.

The following wisdom is from the outline that Col Ripley uses for his frequent, and now famous, talk on combat leadership to the young Marine second lieutenants at The Basic School on our base at Quantico, Virginia.

What do you need to know? Everything.

What is important here? Everything.

No one can be sure where the next war will be, but I can tell you exactly where it will end . . . in the mud. And then it will be fought by people like you doing the same things that Marine combat leaders have done for years, in countless battles.

General Lee's great formula for leadership (as expressed by author and historian Douglas Southall Freeman): Know yourself, know your men, be a man.

- Know yourself: self-awareness, self-confidence, self-control, self-discipline, knowing your strengths and faults, having the ability to totally control yourself.

- Know your men: Know all their needs, know what motivates them, know and do every possible way to serve them and help them so that they can better perform the mission. Know each of their individual breaking points and know their weaknesses.

- Personal example: Be a role model. Show perseverance, "stick-to-it-ive-ness," the ability to hang in there, to keep coming back over and over after a series of defeats.

Combat:

Combat is not a state of being, it is an act. Most people see it as a noun; we see it as a verb, an active verb. A verb whose nature is overwhelmingly physical and violent. Combat is not simply being in a "risk environment," if it were, driving your car on the highway would qualify as combat. The cardinal principles are violence and destruction.

Endurance:

We confuse this with fitness, but I'm not talking about fitness or physical strength. I'm talking about mental attitude . . . the attitude that your mind imposes over your physical limitations, the attitude that you will hang on, that you will never admit defeat for any reason, that you will perform your mission and overcome all adversity using every conceivable means. This obviously requires physical endurance, pushing your body when it's screaming for rest, and just as importantly, pushing your men.

The relationship between physical and mental endurance is obvious, but when strength gives out and fatigue overwhelms you, mental endurance is like having an extra bandolier . . . You lock-and-load and keep going.

Risk Tolerance:

Risk-taking is what battlefield commanders are paid for.

The ability to take chances, to weigh what you stand to lose, or gain, against the cost to yourself and your unit. This is the essence of combat command.

The lieutenant's "Golden Rule" that I learned at TBS is the perfect guide: "Do something lieutenant." It may be wrong, but for God's sake, do something! Don't wait for perfect circumstances.

Action Dispels Panic; Inaction Breeds It:

Show me the careful, cautious commander, one who has all of the critical factors weighed before attacking, and I'll show you a mediocre lightweight, if not a total failure, in combat. (Remember Lee and Jackson at Chancellorsville.)

Decisiveness:

Indecision in a commander, or in a small-unit leader, is a fatal flaw. It leads directly to failure. It is defeatist. It demonstrates a leader's lack of moral and mental toughness.

> *"The power to decide on an action and the strength to see it through are probably the most fundamental qualities of a great soldier."*
>
> —Martin Blumenson

If it looks right and smells right, then by damn, do it.

Indecision is a form of cowardice. Your men see this as your inability to make tough decisions, a lack of mental toughness. Men become demoralized when their leaders flounder with hard decisions, won't face the issue squarely or relegate it to a committee. Far better to make that tough decision and stick to it than to constantly search for the perfect, or "safe," course of action.

You must develop a manner of aggressiveness, a "Spirit of Attack." Just how aggressive you are will determine everything you do as a Marine leader, particularly in the infantry. This aggressive mind-set is more than just a competitive spirit, it is a thrill of engaging others in competition, any competition. It's the attitude that linebackers have; you just hope the runner is going to come toward you so that you can get him. It is an offensive attitude, that taking the battle to the enemy is almost always the best course of action.

What does this mean to me? What does it mean to any Marine? It means that success in battle comes only from the offense, from the attack. It means that excessive caution is inherently defeatist.

The three great principles of war: Attack, attack, attack.

I see this as the greatness of Stonewall Jackson: He was always in the attack.

> *"Never take council of your fears. The enemy is more worried than you are. Numerical superiority, while useful, is not vital to offensive action. The fact that you are attacking induces the enemy to believe you are stronger than he is."*
>
> — Stonewall Jackson

> *"Keep going all the time and always forward."*
>
> — MajGen John A. Lejeune, USMC

> *"Hit hard. Hit fast. Hit often."*
>
> —Adm Halsey, USN

A key to this, as you have heard me say, is not just a willingness to attack, but an eagerness to attack. "Leaning forward in a foxhole" expresses it well . . . just waiting to get in there.

You can see it in the faces of your men and simply sense it when they know that contact is imminent, the enemy is close, and they are going to engage. You can watch their animal-like movement, like a pride of lions surrounding and stalking its quarry, ready to kill. There is excitement, there is an "inner-fire" of knowing that in the next few moments, you are going to reach a level of violence, personal commitment, and physical and emotional awareness, as well as a drain on those two essential commodities, as intense as you have ever experienced in your life.

This attitude of aggressiveness, this willingness, this eagerness to engage the enemy, is for the Marine a reservoir of potential energy, like an enormous battery. He calls on when he needs to go into action, despite his physical fatigue, fatigue brought about by days of marching and flogging through the jungle and living without sleep. When he knows he is going to engage, his battery kicks in and he reaches deep into that reservoir, and the spirit transforms into a source of energy which propels him into the fight . . . and fight he does.

He expends that energy willingly and in a magnificent way, until he has dealt the enemy a fatal blow. It's wonderful to see; it's a magnificent realization of what your Marines can do, being led and inspired by you, their leader.

Your actions must be decisive, aggressive, immediate and overwhelmingly violent.

Your success can he measured by enemy casualties, craters on the objective and smoke on your machine-gun barrel.

Training to fight:

The value of boxing, wrestling, martial arts and close-combat training is that it draws out the natural aggressiveness in each of you. This natural aggressive spirit—this eagerness to fight—is found in the male of our species and is your greatest advantage. You must culture and nurture this in yourself and in your Marines. Teach them to fight, to be good at it, and to enjoy it! It is a great confidence builder. Aggressive, violent behavior is naturally imbedded in the male. Today's sociologists would have you believe that this is unnatural, even shameful! Now, criminal outbursts of this natural aggression must be avoided and discouraged, but the natural tendency for this behavior is neither shameful nor unnatural. More to my point, this aggressive behavior in a Marine may be more useful than any other weapon we arm him with.

This natural, aggressive spirit is the ultimate "combat multiplier."

There is no substitute for aggressive fighting spirit:

Take the fight to the enemy.

Resolve that you and your Marines will be standing when no one else is.

Notes From Vietnam

by David Hackworth, Col USA

Colonel David Hackworth, USA (Ret)

Col Hackworth was one of the most successful American infantry leaders of the Vietnam War and is today the most highly decorated living American veteran. After his second tour in Vietnam, Col Hackworth organized and wrote down his thoughts on what needed to be done to improve the effectiveness of Army infantry units. In 1994, he found a copy of his memo and was kind enough to send it to the *Marine Corps Gazette* (October '94), saying, "Since low-intensity conflict is the name of the game for the next couple of decades, you may want to run it for your Marines." It is a timeless review of the basics.

With the battlefield fresh in mind, and with Conant's sage observation, "Behold the turtle: He makes progress only when he sticks his neck out" to spur me on, I offer the following comments regarding infantry in Vietnam. I am not attempting to demean the individual soldier, denounce those responsible for our training system where I recently served, or embarrass senior leaders. It is my only purpose to report my observations based on my two tours as a battalion commander in Vietnam with the hope that lessons may be drawn from my experience.

Infantry Replacements

Contrary to common belief, reinforced by comments from senior infantry commanders in Vietnam, I did not find that the average Advanced Infantry Training (AIT) graduate was "the best trained infantry soldier we have ever sent to battle." Although I found the average infantry replacement technically proficient from an academic standpoint, he did not know how to put his knowledge into practice. In other words, he knew the theory of blocking and tackling cold, but he could not throw a decent block or ground his opponent with a smashing tackle without a lot of "in country" practice, which

Source: *From the Horse's Mouth, Selected Thoughts on Small-Unit Leadership. 121-127*. Reprinted with permission.

unfortunately was expensive in terms of unnecessary casualties. My assessment is that basic and AIT training has failed to stress on a repetitive basis the gut fundamentals that would cause the new infantry replacement in Vietnam to react instinctively to a given combat situation. The product of our individual training system may well be the finest infantry individual replacement we have ever produced for war, but in a conflict such as Vietnam, he still is not adequately trained.

The new replacements who joined my battalion were sadly inept concerning the fundamentals and grossly relaxed when it came to that all-important subject of security and alertness. They simply were not completely trained, not mentally alert, not careful enough and too prone to stumble along staring at the ground and trying trying to figure out a unique way to compute the number of days they had left.

Following that "All American" litterbug habit, the average replacement paid little attention to the scads of debris that he scattered across the battlefield. Hence, he unknowingly provided his frugal opponent with many of the necessities of survival and with the raw material that could easily be converted into weapons that could be used against him.

Individually, the average replacement was poorly disciplined and had to be closely watched and literally forced to do basic tasks like keeping his weapon cleaned and oiled, using correct light and noise discipline, employing effective cover and concealment, and maintaining sufficient interval during movement.

The latter, proper interval, takes on great importance in Vietnam because of the enemy's large-scale employment of mines and boobytraps. Over 50 percent of my battalion's casualties (233 wounded and 2 killed) came from these insidious devices. (This percentage, incidentally, tracks exactly with French casualties from 1946 to 1954.) Here again, my soldiers were insufficiently trained when first arriving in country to deal with mines and boobytraps. After proper battlefield training, my men knew how to handle themselves. However, the old "bugaboo"—poor discipline—was always there causing my men to bunch up, move too fast, move along the quickest and easiest route which was also the "boulevard of mines," and to generally be careless.

Another critical weakness was the soldier's lack of preparation to deal with the Vietnamese people, which is probably a common U.S. worldwide malady. He was not sufficiently oriented concerning the customs of Vietnam, the purpose of the war, and the fact that he was a guest in Vietnam, and how to conduct himself as an invited guest and not an "occupational trooper." Too frequently, because of his inadequate orientation, he played the role of "ugly American" and through some thoughtless act negated all the good that had been done by his fellow soldiers' sacrifices.

On the plus side, the average infantry replacement was a hardcharger and well motivated, unusually brave, and physically tough. When led by strong, demanding infantry sergeants and lieutenants, the average replacement developed into a first-class infantry soldier. We strongly need to revise our infantry AIT program.

The Infantry Junior Combat Leader

The biggest shortcomings of the young infantry leaders (including both noncommissioned officers (NCOs) and junior officers) are the failure to be demanding and their reluctance to ensure that their men do the basic things that will keep them alive on the battlefield.

I believe one of the reasons for this deficiency is that many of the social values acquired as a civilian conflict diametrically with what is expected of a leader. Our training system must recognize this conflict and alter those values. As a case in point, great emphasis is placed in American society on being a popular fellow. The formal part of this training starts in kindergarten when the importance of socializing is first introduced and is thereafter never-ending. The informal training begins at mother's hand almost at first breath. Hence, the young man when first entering the army has about 20 years indoctrination of "being a nice guy." After 4 years of college and ROTC training or 46 weeks of basic combat training, AIT, and officer candidate school, he is supposed to be the well-prepared leader who always places the welfare of the troops just below the accomplishment of the mission. But in actual fact, the average leader has a Pavlovian instinct toward being popular. He must be a good guy! Thus, he becomes a "joiner" instead of an "enforcer."

In Vietnam, good guys let their people smoke at night and take portable radios to the field; allow night ambushes to set up in the abandoned hootch, so they can have protection from the rain and will only need one guard by the door so that everyone else can get a good night's rest. Good guys let their men leave their boots on for several days, resulting in inordinately severe immersion foot. Good guys don't check to ensure that their men protect themselves against mosquitoes or take the required malaria pills and salt tablets. Good guys end up killing their men with kindness!

The average young leader in my battalion generally knew what was required, but did not have the moral courage to enforce the rules. He preferred to turn his head and look the other way rather than make vigorous, on-the-spot corrections. Common deficiencies such as dirty ammunition and weapons, improperly safed weapons and grenades, incorrect camouflage techniques, and the improper use of terrain (using natural cover to provide protection from small-arms fire) went uncorrected. The end result of this was that the soldiers' habits became sloppier and carelessness ran amuck and unchecked. This resulted in casualties that could have been prevented had the leader demanded it.

My experience has been that soldiers in combat will only do what is required of them, and if under weak, permissive leaders, they will try to get away with everything they can. This results in the violation of every basic rule in the book. As an aside, I believe that all the while that they are placing their lives in jeopardy they know they are wrong and will respond to the requirements of a positive, demanding leader. Results: fewer casualties and greater respect for the leader who cares enough for his men to make them "play the game" correctly.

I believe that another serious shortcoming in our small-unit training program is the failure to teach leaders the importance and the techniques of supervising. The average small-unit leader today seems to take it for granted that what he wills will be done, and hence, there is no requirement for him to check.

The nature of combat in Vietnam greatly extends this problem, because small units normally operate on a widely decentralized basis in rugged terrain that greatly restricts inspection visits from higher headquarters. These conditions generally prohibit the more experienced senior NCOs (E8 and E9) and officers (field grade) from checking the platoon and passing on "tips of the trade." Hence, without an experienced, demanding leader, a carelessly led platoon is headed for a violent collision that normally ends in disaster. The infrequency of combat (as compared to World War II or Korea) and seeming security of many areas has a tendency to lull soldiers and leaders into a false sense of security. Consequently, alertness and security become relaxed and the likelihood of enemy attack increases proportionately.

Our training system must inculcate leaders with the burning need to keep their people alert every moment they are in Vietnam and to never let down their guard. The leader must be instilled with the need to supervise his people 24 hours a day. He must check to ensure that fighting positions are adequate; soldiers know the mission, situation, and where listening posts (LPs) are located; proper field sanitation is being practiced; all battlefield debris is destroyed to deny the enemy a source of supply; soldiers are sleeping under cover and protected from "first round bursts"; subordinate leaders are "heads up" and supervising as they should be. A never-ending list of little things must be checked.

For example, are magazines clean, weapons test-fired, LPs out, sectors of fire known, medics looking at health conditions and preventive measures, and stand-to being conducted? But it is the leaders that matter. They have to check constantly. The saying: "The best fertilizer in the world is the bosses' footsteps . . . they make things grow" is the absolute trust. Our school system must teach the leader the importance and the mechanics of checking.

Our training system must get our small-unit leaders out of the classroom and into the bush. Here, they must be taught the gut fundamentals of infantry combat by the finest, most experienced combat leaders we have. We must ruthlessly prune the chaff from the curriculum and drill the basics into the trainees, employing the same instructional techniques as those used in airborne training to teach the five points of performance. Every block of instruction should be reduced to the salient "points of performance," and each student should be required to demonstrate his knowledge by ruthless examination. Student leaders who show ineptitude should be eliminated and not "recycled" in order to show a "low attrition rate."

Small-Unit Infantry Operations

In Vietnam, today's most successful infantry tactics and techniques were yesterday's heresy and madness. When these "overly reckless" ideas were first introduced by farseeing innovators in 1965 and 1966, few commanders took them seriously. Most, because of parochial conventional orientation, looked upon these new concepts with contempt not unlike many reactionary English lords' attitude toward the longbow—before Crecy. But today in Vietnam, these once "wild schemes" have become standard drill. These bold techniques have changed the thrust of the war from uneconomical multibrigade operations to fights that are fought almost exclusively by the squad and platoon.

These operational changes did not occur by the wave of a magic wand. No, indeed; hard work, boldness with attendant risk, imagination, and then through the process of evolution, concepts that worked were polished, expanded, and developed.

I believe our infantry leader training program—to include the complete spectrum of training infantry leaders—has not kept pace with the tactical innovation developed on the battlefield, nor with what type of leadership/tactical training is required to develop first-class small-unit leaders. Hence, I believe our system for training infantry leaders is not in step with the demands or the realities of the counterinsurgent battlefield. The changes that are required do not call for violent revision of our infantry doctrine, but they do call . . . no, demand . . . no, scream . . . for a revolutionary change in our system for training infantry leaders. Following are a few items that should be considered as part of a study designed to produce a better infantry combat leader:

- Emphasize practical work.
- Get the students out of the classroom and into the bush.
- Reduce the curriculum to the barest essentials.

And forget about all the nice-to-have material that has no tangible value on the battlefield, but is taught only because the student may need it someday in garrison. The curriculum must be looked at from the standpoint of "What does an infantry lieutenant/sergeant need to know to fight his element?" The questions, "What is essential?" and "What is nice to have?" must be repeatedly asked as each subject is examined. Only those gut items that are critical to combat must stay. All else must be winnowed out. We must accept the risk that our young combat leaders, fresh out of Fort Benning, may not be too "red hot" concerning garrison activities, or might initially stumble badly as staff officers. The overriding criteria must be that the training objective produces deadly competent, highly motivated and skilled leaders. Benning must realize and accept that it is a school for mechanics—mechanics in the infantry trade.

I believe that Benning has gotten so wrapped around the axle on techniques of instruction, in attempts for optimum sophistication, that it has lost perspective in training "rough, ready, and determined" combat leaders. Teaching techniques that produce business managers at the Harvard Business School have little application in the development of infantry combat leaders.

- Concentrate all instruction on combat leadership.

Teach the leader to be forceful, to strongly exercise authority by "kicking ass," and to develop confidence in himself by making him mentally and physically hard; instill in the leader that he can do the job without much help,

- Stress fire, maneuver, and control.

Quit stressing the necessity of closing with a dug-in guerrilla opponent, because to close normally costs excessively in casualties, regardless of the infantry's skill. If the guerrilla is fighting out of well-prepared positions, he probably did not get trapped, but planned it that way. The basic idea of fighting a guerrilla who is in phase II or III of insurgency, such as Vietnam, should be the destruction of his formations at the smallest cost, and this simply cannot be achieved by attacking him during his occupation of defensive positions. Drive home the following points:

- How to employ scouts.
- The importance of security (constant, never-ending, all-around).

- How to use cover and how never to get an element into a situation where cover does not exist.
- Teach the leader that deception should be basic to his modus operandi (his "way of doing things").
- Teach the value of stay-behinds, decoys, and phony positions.
- Stress not to develop patterns—to analyze everything from the standpoint of "Am I forming an operational pattern, and will the enemy zap me because of my rut?"
- Stress doing the unexpected and unconventional.
- Make the combat leader an expert concerning:

(1) Mines and boobytraps (teach him that casualties increase because of fatigue and get proportionately higher later in the day).
(2) Small-unit patrolling (stress the importance of patrol rehearsals. As a minimum, cover actions to be taken in known danger areas).
(3) Night and day land navigation.
(4) Night and day ambushes.
(5) Rifle platoon in the defense in a jungle environment.

Stress here the absolute requirement for LPs because of the enemy's now frequent use of rocket-propelled grenades and the absolute necessity of firing in defensive concentrations prior to darkness. Emphasize fire discipline, use of claymores, M79s, and frags.

(6) Employment of gunships.

Emphasize here that gunships are not the magic panacea (cure-all) to all problems when a friendly unit is in trouble. My experience has shown that the young leader is quick to call for gunships when, in fact, artillery is the only heavyweight in helping out the endangered unit.

(7) Adjustment of artillery fire.

Stress platoon formations and immediate action drills. In this regard, teach the leader, by actual experience, how to adjust his formations to the terrain and enemy situation. Stress the need to always have a defensive position picked out in his mind, to always have his unit near cover, to always have a fire support element (M60) (crew-served machine gun) set up to provide covering fire.

- Stress not using platoon objectives.

Give the platoon an area of responsibility, a mission, and let them go. Also forget about time. Don't attach a time-frame to a piece of ground. Once you do, an element will get into trouble racing to take the objective on time. Stress the use of the five-paragraph field order and keeping troops informed.

- Drill in the importance of radio communications by:

(1) Ensuring the radio operator is one of the best, most responsible men in the platoon and that maximum cross training be conducted to provide depth in operators.
(2) Stressing the need for radio and battery maintenance.
(3) Teaching the importance of the location of the radio for good communications (I have moved a PRC radio 2 feet and gone from no communications to excellent communications).

And finally, but most important,

- Burn into the small-unit leader's mind that to defeat the guerrilla, he must think and act like a guerrilla. He must adopt the guerrilla's tactics, stealth, cunningness, drive, motivation, and operational techniques. As a leader, he must be more ruthless in his demands upon his people than the guerrilla is with his subordinates. He must understand that the guerrilla can only be defeated by rugged, "gung-ho," superbly led soldiers who can, because of outstanding training, "out guerrilla the guerrilla."

Uniting Hearts and Minds

by Rick Atkinson

Heat whooshed through the rear doors of the C-141, rudely cuffing the hundred soldiers in the cabin. As the pilot cut the four engines, George Crocker peered out at Bien Hoa Air Base through the tiny porthole. We've landed in a furnace, he thought. The temperature had been a brittle 19 degrees when they left Fort Riley, Kansas, the day before and subzero in Alaska during refueling at Elmendorf Air Force Base. At Yokota, where the plane again stopped to refuel, snowplows had been scraping the runways.

There were no snowplows here. The jet exhaust and tropical heat made everything shimmer and blur, as though the world had lost its firm edges. But through the haze, George saw that Bien Hoa was bustling. Cargo planes, troop transports, and Chinooks crisscrossed the tarmac in an elaborate dance. Every few seconds another jet landed or took off with a deep roar. The stink of JP4 fuel and burning human waste—which was incinerated beyond the runway in fifty-five-gallon drums—drifted into the cabin, along with the *thacka-thacka-thacka* sound of helicopter blades that was the mantra of Vietnam.

George hoisted his duffel bag and followed the column across the tarmac into a briefing room. The torpor of the long flight fell away like a cloak from his shoulders. At last I'm finally here, he said to himself. He felt an electric sense of high adventure, of being called to arms. He had read about the excitement that soldiers often felt as they prepared for war—the volunteers mustering before Bull Run, for instance, or the American doughboys striding into France in 1917. Now, on this day in late January of 1967, his turn had come.

At West Point, the war had remained an abstraction. George had listened intently to the lectures delivered by officers returning from Southeast Asia; one of his tactical officers had been an advisor in Laos before the American build-up in Vietnam began in earnest. Yet he rarely felt emotionally engaged by those stories. They seemed remote,

Source: *The Long Gray Line: The American Journey of West Point's Class of '66.* (1989) 200-227. Reprinted by permission of Houghton-Mifflin Company.

almost as distant as the military art lectures on the Napoleonic campaigns. Nearly every great captain, the cadets were told, had been tested in combat early in his career: Lee and Grant in Mexico, Pershing and Marshall in the Philippines, Patton and MacArthur in World War I. The clear implication, of course, was that the men of '66 should be grateful for the chance to be annealed in combat and prove themselves as young warriors. But those had been textbook wars and textbook heroes. A cadet could not smell JP4 and burning feces in the classroom. This was real. After years of preparing for this moment, George felt ready. More than ready, in fact: he felt invincible.

Ranger school and the months of training at Fort Riley had invested him with strong self-confidence. He knew the importance of stealth, of fire control, of using artillery and air support prudently, of avoiding ambushes by steering clear of well-traveled trails. He had a sketchy understanding of the past twenty years of fighting in Indochina: the catastrophic French defeat at Dienbienphu; the Gulf of Tonkin incident in 1964; the First Cavalry's big battle in the Ia Drang Valley in 1965. He felt certain that what he now knew about soldiering could keep him alive.

But there was also a great deal that he and his classmates did not know. They did not understand that for nearly two thousand years the Vietnamese had fought valiantly against foreign invaders and occupiers, Chinese, French, and now American. They were unaware that this protracted resistance had shaped a culture that was martially competent and infinitely patient, one that placed a premium on superhuman courage and sacrifice. They did not know that Ho Chi Minh was a nationalist first and a communist second, and that his relatively recent alliance with Moscow and Peking was a marriage of convenience rather than the manifestation of a cohesive international Marxist plan. They did not comprehend that the Americans had allied themselves with a clique of corrupt and discredited Vietnamese mandarins. Nor did they realize that to many, if not most, Vietnamese the Americans were as emblematic of colonialism and social injustice as the French, whose ill-fated effort to reassert France's glory in Indochina after World War II had been heartily supported by Washington.

In a young lieutenant such ignorance was forgivable, perhaps even necessary. Twenty-three-year-old junior officers who spent their time pondering geopolitical nuances would probably make poor platoon leaders. West Point had taught history that, understandably, was skewed to the prevailing American view of the world, imbued with the unique native blend of blind optimism, self-righteousness, and genuine beneficence. The lieutenants were hardly more benighted than the most senior echelons of the United States government and the American Army. What Lieutenant George Crocker did not know on arriving at Bien Hoa he could not have been expected to know; what the president, the secretary of defense, the Joint Chiefs, and the Army's top generals did not know would cost 58,000 American lives and lose the war.

In the airport briefing room, a young officer recited a welcoming monologue already heard by tens of thousands of American soldiers:

> Gentlemen, welcome to Vietnam. Gentlemen, here you will complete your in-country processing. Gentlemen, it is very hot today and I know that you will all want to complete your in-country processing as soon as possible, and therefore you will pay attention at all times.

Gentlemen, you will refrain from talking. There is a snack bar and ice cream shop next to the finance building. Gentlemen, these facilities are off limits to you until you have completed your processing.

Gentlemen, when you have finished processing, you may write a letter to your families and tell them you have arrived safely in Vietnam. You can tell them that you are twenty-two miles northeast of Saigon. And, of course, you can tell them that you are having a wonderful time.

Now, gentlemen, you are in a combat zone. If a siren goes off, you can assume we are under attack—either incoming rockets or a mortar attack. In the event of such an attack, do not attempt to help. You will only hinder. Are there any questions?

Three hours later, George sat in the back of a truck heading northeast up Route 1 to Cu Chi. This was not exactly what he had expected. He was eager, but the abrupt departure for the combat zone surprised him. Back in the States, he had heard repeated assurances that new lieutenants would have at least a few days to get "acclimatized" by undergoing in-country training at the Army's replacement stations, known as repo depots. None of those guarantees now seemed to hold true.

At Fort Riley, it was conventional wisdom and a point of pride that the 9th Infantry Division had been assembled and packed off to combat faster than any American division since the Spanish-American War. Some soldiers had arrived at Riley before completing basic training; a few units lacked recoilless rifles or starlight scopes and had been forced to borrow M-60 machine guns from the Kansas National Guard. Some battalions had only five captains, though the authorized complement was fifteen.

Even so, the three brigades of the 9th were ready for war. By training and deploying together, the division initially avoided the peculiar chemistry of most in-country units, where green and eager newcomers were mixed together with cautious, war-weary short-timers. In the 9th, nearly everyone was eager and green; morale was very high. While still in Kansas, George's brigade, commanded by Colonel William B. Fulton, had been given two weeks of Christmas leave, and not a single man went AWOL. Everyone came back for the fight. The enlisted troops, who had been pulled from ten different reception stations around the country, included a fair number of Cat Is and Cat IIs—the Army's highest mental categories—as well as a few NCOs who were pulling their second combat tour.

To season his young officers and noncoms, Fulton had decided to fly them to Vietnam ahead of the troops, who would arrive by ship in two weeks for eventual operations in the Mekong Delta. The colonel had been authorized to bring an advance party of 18; instead, he had showed up at Bien Hoa this morning with 385.

George and several classmates were headed for the 25th Division, where they would shadow experienced platoon leaders for a fortnight's apprenticeship. More than two dozen of the 9th's lieutenants had graduated from West Point the previous June, including many of the division's platoon leaders. William Westmoreland, who had complained in 1966 that Vietnam was bogging down in "a protracted war of attrition," now reported that he had enough troops to "go over to the offensive on a broad and sustained basis in 1967."

This first wave of West Pointers from the class of '66 was part of that critical mass. Like George, most remained full of *pro patria* exuberance and tactical department enthusiasm for "tracks in two." But already they could see that the sword cut both ways: word was spreading of the class's first battle death. Billy W. Flynn had been killed on January 23, two days after his twenty-fourth birthday. There would be no tracks in two for Billy Flynn.

The convoy slowed to a crawl and finally stopped in Cu Chi. George grabbed his duffel bag again and hopped out of the truck. The countryside for their twenty-mile trip had displayed an exotic blend of twentieth-century war technology—jeeps and tanks and helicopters—and sixteenth-century Asian peasantry—bullocks and carts and crude huts. The base camp at Cu Chi had been built the year before on an old peanut farm, near the Fil Hol rubber plantation. The camp sprawled across fifteen hundred acres, with a six-mile perimeter. The Army had wasted no time turning the place into a little corner of America, with ice plants, walk-in refrigerators, sports fields, chapels, clubs, swimming pools, and even a miniature golf course.

George still wore his starched uniform from Riley. The first order of business, he figured, would be to find some jungle fatigues and draw his ammunition. Then perhaps he would have time to look around.

A young officer with a clipboard bustled over. "Lieutenant Crocker? See that chopper over there? The one that's landing? Go get on it."

George's eyes widened with surprise. "Me?"

"Now," the officer replied.

The sun was setting when the Huey dropped him off in a jungle clearing. As he ran out from beneath the whirring rotors, he could hear small-arms fire, distant at first and then suddenly much closer. He felt confused, lost. Where the hell was he? Somewhere near the Saigon River in War Zone C, but other than that he wasn't sure. He had been in-country for about six hours and already he was on the fringe of a firefight. As a cadet, he had been told repeatedly to go to the sound of the guns, but he never expected to be asked to do so quite this quickly.

Someone directed him to a tent ringed with sandbags near the landing zone. Inside, the company commander, a plain-spoken young captain named McCarthy, returned George's salute.

"It's a little late to send you down to your platoon on the perimeter," the captain said. "I don't want to get you shot or anything on your first night."

"Thank you, sir."

McCarthy pointed to an extra cot in the tent. "My first sergeant's away. You can have his bunk tonight and we'll link you up with the platoon in the morning."

That night, George lay on the cot, listening to the chatter of automatic weapons. Things were clearer now. He was with a company in the 27th Infantry, which called itself the Wolfhounds. A distinguished outfit with a long history, the 27th's motto was *Nec Aspera Terrant*—Frightened by No Difficulties. During the Korean War, the 27th had been perhaps the finest regiment in the Eighth Army. It was commanded for a time by John H. (Mike) Michaelis, a West Point classmate of Westmoreland's who had been the academy commandant in the early 1950s and later rose to four-star rank.

George had blundered into preparations for one of the largest operations of the war, a massive sweep codenamed Junction City, after the town in Kansas adjacent to Fort Riley. Currently, the Wolfhounds formed part of a blocking force. They were supposed to snare the Viet Cong as other American units drove the enemy from their sanctuaries. The principle was that of an ancient hunting technique, in which beaters pushed the game toward the hungers, but, as usual, the quarry here refused to cooperate.

Pap! Pap! Pap-pap-pap! As George lay on the cot, several rounds punched through the tent, ventilating the canvas with holes the size of a quarter. They sounded like fat raindrops. The sandbags outside had been piled two feet high, but the cots stood about two feet six inches off the ground. George stifled the urge to dive for cover, not wanting to move before the captain did. He watched McCarthy from the corner of his eye. Damn, he thought, why don't we all jut get on the floor?

The captain rolled over casually, as though waking from a nap on the beach. He took the handset from his radio telephone operator, who lay prudently on the ground. "Tell B Company," McCarthy said slowly, "that we're taking some rounds up here."

Crack! At that instant, with a fearful splintering, a bullet shattered the crosspiece of George's cot, two inches from his skull. The canvas collapsed and his head flopped down as though guillotined.

He lurched onto the floor, flattening out next to the radio operator. While he lay there, a few more rounds whizzed through the tent. More stunned than frightened, George suddenly thought of his ordnance professor at West Point, an affable colonel named Morris J. Herbert. This sudden immersion in combat reminded him of a story that Colonel Herbert liked to tell his students. Herbert had graduated from the academy as an artilleryman on June 6, 1950. Two weeks later, the Korean War erupted. He joined the 2nd Division at Fort Lewis, Washington, just in time to board ship. "Don't worry about a thing," his battery commander had said in mid Pacific. "We're going to Japan to train for a couple months because we haven't done anything at Fort Lewis except paint rocks for the past year and a half."

The battery commander was right about the rocks and dead wrong about Japan. Herbert was shocked when the ship pulled into Pusan harbor in southeast Korea. The North Koreans had pushed American and South Korean forces all the way down the peninsula and were within fifty miles of forcing another Dunkirk at Pusan. Just hours after walking down the gangplank. Herbert found himself directing artillery fire as a forward observer. "It was an unreal feeling," he had told his ordnance class. "I couldn't believe these guys were shooting at me. I was a nice guy and they were trying to kill me."

Colonel Herbert's tale seemed less amusing now. Thirty-four members of the 670 men in the class of '50 had been killed in Korea, most of them as green as grass when they died. Dying in combat was something that George Crocker had considered statistically improbable, like getting hit by a bus. But how many of those thirty-four dead officers had assumed that they too were immortal?

I was a nice guy, Colonel Herbert had said, *and they were trying to kill me.* Beyond the obvious instinct for self-preservation, George now had additional reason to stay alive. Twelve days before he left Riley, Vonda had given birth to the Crockers' first child, a daughter whom they named Cheryl. Leaving his wife and baby had been hard, but the separation was made bearable by his unshakable conviction that he was going to see them again in one year. Vonda had begun writing daily letters, which she numbered consecutively. George planned to read number 365; he hugged the ground a little tighter.

On his left hand he wore his West Point ring. Shortly before graduation, an officer had given a brief speech to Company F-2: "A lot of you will go to Vietnam. One of the questions that will come up is 'Should I wear my ring?' I think you should. It will be a constant reminder to do your duty, a constant reminder of duty, honor, country. Don't ever not wear it because of concern that you might lose it or because it will get dirty or because the stone might get knocked out in combat. That's the time when you most need to wear it, because the ideals that it stands for must step forward in combat."

Like Colonel Herbert's reminiscence of life and death at Pusan, that fragment of advice suddenly seemed especially relevant. George had not yet fired a shot at the enemy, but already he better understood what the officer had been talking about. The ring represented a mystical link to the past. It was a talisman, offering strength and courage drawn from the thousands of brave officers who had gone into battle before him. Even men who thought themselves invincible could use that kind of magic.

In McCarthy's bullet-riddled tent, George listened to the fading gunfire. The firefight seemed to be ending but he decided to forgo the comfort of the cot for the safety of the floor; for the remainder of the night, he lay on the ground, dozing fitfully.

The next few days were among the strangest—and very nearly the last—of George's life.

In the morning, the Wolfhounds worked their way along the Saigon River, searching for Viet Cong. When the sweep failed to flush any enemy, Captain McCarthy organized a skeet-shooting contest. While one of his sergeants stood by with a handful of paper plates, the captain strolled down to the water with a shotgun, looking every bit like a quail-hunting squire.

"Pull!" he yelled.

A white plate glided out over the river before disintegrating in a swarm of buckshot. "Pull!"

When he grew weary of skeet, McCarthy took an M-79 grenade launcher and began popping at coconuts high in the trees across the river. The troops, meanwhile, amused themselves by firing at flotsam coming down the Saigon on the premise that it could be a Viet Cong frogman. George watched with a mixture of chagrin and amusement. Nobody, he reflected, ever mentioned *this* in military art.

Later in the afternoon of his first full day in-country, he climbed onto a tank that was bulling its way through the jungle toward a suspected enemy position. Every few minutes it stopped long enough to fire the main gun. When a second tank came clanking up on his right, George shifted over to the left side of the turret. As he did so, the other tank's main gun roared.

Almost simultaneously came a second blast. A mine had detonated between the two tanks, apparently triggered by the concussion of the gun. The explosion flung George from the hull, and the spray of shrapnel spattered against the turret, precisely where he had been a moment before. A soldier standing near him was badly wounded, his side shredded with hot metal.

That night, George went on patrol with the platoon leader he was shadowing. Soon mortar rounds began raining around them. The other lieutenant caught a piece of shrapnel in the arm, and a medic knocked him out with a shot of morphine.

"Well, Lieutenant Crocker," the platoon sergeant said cheerfully, "I guess you're taking over now." They sat motionless in the jungle for the rest of the night. No one slept.

The following day, his third in Vietnam, the company was preparing to board a flock of Hueys for an airborne assault when George had another close call. Three helicopters back, perhaps fifty yards away, there was a gold flash from a soldier accidentally triggering his M-79. A split second later, the grenade landed at George's feet, close enough to spear with a first baseman's mitt. Nothing happened. The grenade was a dud.

George still had enough stateside in him to want to mark the dud for ordnance disposal. But an officer standing at his side moved first: enraged, he scooped up the smoking round in a rag, sprinted to the soldier, and, shrieking like a madman, thrust the grenade into his stomach.

George had experienced the near-fatal consequences of bad luck; now he witnessed the price of poor judgment. Late one afternoon McCarthy called his platoon leaders together for a briefing. While the lieutenants spooned up their C-rations on the perimeter of one of the tank companies, the captain discussed an ambush patrol that would be deployed that evening. The young officer assigned to lead the patrol was an ungainly lieutenant who incessantly pushed his glasses up on the bridge of his nose. George had few regrets at being left behind on the operation; the other lieutenant struck him as the type who, rather than following his instincts, would always pursue the "school solution" that the Ranger cadre had so often warned against.

At dusk, the lieutenant led his men outside the company perimeter to reconnoiter the terrain and select the ambush site; several hours later, he followed the same route back into the jungle. The patrol had been gone for only a few minutes when a volley of gunfire tore through the night. The enemy, apparently having watched the platoon scouts pick their site at dusk, had patiently waited to ambush the ambushers. Four Wolfhounds came running back to the camp, carrying their dead lieutenant on a rubber poncho; his body, not yet stiff with death, flopped about grotesquely. George watched as the four puffing soldiers collapsed on the ground inside the barbed wire. One of them tapped out a cigarette and lit it with his Zippo. His hands trembled and, as he took a deep drag, the orange glow illuminated a face twisted with fear. Every time the soldier inhaled he glanced at the dead man, then abruptly averted his eyes, as though he had seen something immodest.

George felt a churning of emotions. The initial shock of seeing this pitiful platoon leader flopping ingloriously on the poncho quickly gave way to scorn and seething anger, not at the enemy, but at the dead officer. He had made a fundamental mistake and had paid for it with his life. Here was terrible proof that the kinds of errors Charlie Beckwith had cautioned against could indeed be fatal. Needing someplace to ground the sudden rage that surged through him, George discharged it at the dead officer. You idiot, he murmured to the lieutenant, you dumb idiot. You couldn't have given the enemy a clearer picture of your plans if you had handed them a map. *Don't ever do that*, he thought, simultaneously rebuking the dead man and cautioning himself.

But the following night, Lieutenant Crocker came within inches of the same fate. His platoon set up another ambush next to a trail. Before long, two groups of Viet

Cong blundered into the kill sack. In a furious burst of machine-gun fire and clay-more-mine detonations, the Wolfhounds killed several soldiers and sent the rest flee-ing through the jungle.

"Let's drag the bodies back before they come collect their dead," George whispered to the other lieutenant.

"Yeah," the lieutenant agreed, "good idea."

Across the trail stood a patch of chest-high grass. He wasn't certain—it was very dark—but George thought he had seen some of the enemy flee in that direction. Listening for moans, he plunged into the grass. Back and forth he shuffled, feeling with his boots for bodies.

After a few minutes of futile searching, he returned to the trail and grabbed one of the dead Viet Cong by the hair. He expected blood, but not the mask of ants that already shrouded the dead man's head. George jerked his hand away as though he had touched a hot skillet. Everything happened quickly in Vietnam; even the scavengers moved with astonishing speed.

In the morning, the Americans returned to inspect the ambush site. Plainly visible in the swatch of tall grass stood the vertical bamboo triggers of a half-dozen antitank mines. Equally apparent were George's tracks from the previous night, meandering through the minefield as if they belonged to a picnicker out gathering daisies. In several spots the matter grass showed that he had come appallingly close to blowing himself to Cambodia. He had made a mistake almost as foolish as the one that had killed the lieutenant two nights before.

A few days later, in early February, his eventual apprenticeship with the Wolfhounds came to an end. George and the other officers in the advance party traveled by truck to Bearcat, a base south of Saigon, where they rendezvoused with the rest of the 9th Division. At Bearcat, Crocker and several other lieutenants were awarded the Combat Infantryman's Badge. The rectangular patch with a Kentucky long rifle on it carried a certain cachet among the arriving troops, who had just dropped anchor at Vung Tau. The CIB symbolized a kind of blooding, marking the final passage from cadet to warrior.

For George Crocker, the badge also represented a profound transformation in his attitude toward the war. He felt as though his two weeks with the Wolfhounds had aged him ten years. Gone was the eagerness he had felt on the tarmac at Bien Hoa. The four or five brushes with death, the sight and sound of the wounded, the sight and smell of the dead, had swept away the naïve belief in his own invulnerability. He was still confident of surviving the war; after so many close calls he even wondered whether he might be charmed. But the blithe sense of adventure had vanished, just as it had vanished from the soldiers who survived Bull Run or the first wretched weeks in the trenches of France. The name on his fatigue blouse still read CROCKER; but as he mustered his platoon for the move into the delta, he knew with absolute certainty that a different man now wore the uniform.

The deployment of the 9th division into the Mekong Delta in early 1967 marked the resumption of a kind of warfare—riverine combat—that the U.S. Army had last experi-enced more than a century earlier. American soldiers had once had considerable expert-ise in fighting a river war. During the Revolution, one of the principal strategic struggles was over control of the Hudson–Lake Champlain–St. Lawrence axis; West Point itself had first been fortified as part of the thrust-and-parry of that riverine conflict. In the War of 1812, the Americans mounted a river force, and in the grim Seminole War a mosquito fleet of 150 schooners, bateaux, and canoes had hunted Indians in the Florida sloughs, where a fourth of the U.S. Army's regulars subsequently died. With the exception of a foray up the Yangtze during the Boxer Rebellion, however, the Army had not fought extensively on rivers since Grant bisected the Confederacy by taking control of the Mississippi.

Now, more than a century later, riverine fighting was about to come back into fashion. The 9th Division was determined to control the Mekong, one of the world's greatest rivers. Flowing for twenty-five hundred miles from the Tibetan plateau, the Mekong split into four main fingers south of Saigon before emptying into the South China Sea. Command of the river and its myriad tributaries and canals was essential to wresting the delta away from the Viet Cong. But the French riverine experience was not heartening; in 1954 alone, at the end of their Indochina war, the French had lost more than a dozen boats to the Viet Minh. Some of those carcasses still sat in the Mekong mud as a reminder of things gone wrong.

In early 1964, the U.S. ambassador to Vietnam, Henry Cabot Lodge, had remarked, "I would not be surprised to see the Mekong Delta totally cleared of communist forces by the end of 1965." Instead, by the time the 9th Division arrived, the Viet Cong had more than eighty thousand troops in the region. The guerrillas were well supported by the local population—swimming like fish in the sea, in Mao's phrase—and they moved with elusive ease by sampan throughout the delta.

The American strategy aimed to clean out the Viet Cong infrastructure, freeing Route 4—the main road to Saigon—and the rest of the rice bowl from communist domination. If the delta, which had a population density comparable with that of Massachusetts, could be stabilized to produce enough food to feed South Vietnam, other parts of the nation could begin to industrialize. As a base for his riverine force, William Westmoreland picked a site on the northernmost of the four Mekong fingers, west of the town of My Tho. The camp was originally called Base Whiskey, but Westmoreland gave it a loftier name to fit his aspirations: Dong Tam. It meant "united hearts and minds."

George Crocker's first view of Dong Tam was disheartening. He had not expected Windsor Palace, but the camp was little more than a barren mudflat on the north bank of the river. The site was even less appealing than Beckwith's Field Seven had been; at least that had showed some semblance of human habitation. The only sign of life at Dong Tam, besides one pathetic mechanized company camped in the muck, was a large dredge, named the *New Jersey*. It sat in the middle of the river spewing fresh layers of mud on top of the old mud in an effort to build up the riverbank before the monsoon season. Now, with typical American vigor, the Army set out to transform Dong Tam into a thriving fortress. Shortly after he and his platoon arrived, George ordered the men to pitch their tents and begin building hootches from prefabrication kits, which came complete with blueprints, lumber, nails, and even hammers.

The thirty-five men in his platoon, which was part of the 3rd Battalion of the 47th Infantry Regiment, quickly discovered that soldiering in the delta was beset with problems. The mud and brackish water quickly ruined weapons that were not routinely disassembled, cleaned, and oiled. Every morning, George had his men remove the rounds in their rifle chambers, since they would often get damp overnight and cause the weapons to jam. Every three days, each magazine was emptied, and the dirty ammunition replaced with clean bullets. Once the river operations began, the platoon periodically rotated onto one of several World War II ships that had been converted into floating barracks. Offering clean sheets, hot showers, and air conditioning, the ships gave the men a chance to dry out and escape the fungi that thrived inside wet boots. Better still, the Navy returned their laundry clean and fragrant, unlike the *mama sans* at Dong Tam, who rinsed the fatigues in river water and left them smelling, oddly, like oatmeal.

On the day before a search-and-destroy sweep, the men cleaned their weapons and fueled the boats. In the evening, boat captains got briefings on the mission, steaming formations, radio codes, tidal currents, and the latest G2, or intelligence. Before dawn, George and his troops would stand on a pontoon pier, rummaging around in different-colored barrels for claymores, grenades, and smoke canisters. Then, with other platoons from the company, they climbed into eight or ten shallow-draught troop carriers. The boats, each sixty feet long, were protected with armor and a trellis of iron bars to deflect rocket-propelled grenades. Canvas awnings shielded the soldiers form the sun.

In the early morning light, the delta presented a lush palette of blues and greens. Water buffalo, ridden by scrawny peasant boys in conical straw hats, pulled crude plows across the paddies to prepare them for the green rice shoots that would be planted as the monsoon season neared. Like armoured geese, the American boats puttered past in a V formation, often led by a minesweeper. Helicopters scouted ahead for enemy ambushes. Sometimes the river tributaries were only fifty to a hundred feet wide, clogged with fish traps or Viet Cong barricades. Banana and coconut groves lined the banks.

As they approached the landing site, the Americans would open up with "reconnaissance by fire," bombarding suspected Viet Cong positions on both sides of the water with a Monitor—a seventy-five-ton floating fortress—or artillery, which was towed on barges and anchored in the mud with sharp cleats. Later in the war, large flame-throwing boats called Zippos sometimes scorched the banks with thick tongues of fire. The infantrymen then splashed ashore and fanned out, always eyeing the dikes and tree lines across the rice paddies for signs of the enemy. Frequently, another U.S. force would be inserted by helicopter to block the Viet Cong escape routes. Sometimes the enemy stood fast to fight, but more typically the sweeps encountered only sporadic sniper fire or came up empty altogether.

Even so, there were constant reminders of death's ubiquity. The winnowing of the West Point class of '66, which began on the first day of Beast Barracks, had abated temporarily at graduation, only to resume in Vietnam in an infinitely more sinister form. As the war intensified, as ever more lieutenants were shuttled into combat, the manifest of KIAs grew steadily longer.

One of George's classmates who also served in the delta was a native of the Panama Canal Zone named Frank Rybicki, Jr. a man of irrepressible good cheer, Rybicki seemed perpetually happy, whether strumming his guitar, practicing his jitterbug, or simply talking to his friends. At West Point, as president of the Glee Club, he would write to the Miss America candidates from each state where the club was touring, soliciting dates. He adored John Kennedy and had studied on a desk blotter inscribed with the "ask not what your country can do for you" quotation. Rybicki's sister married his academy roommate, Terry Stull, who also joined the 9th as a platoon leader.

One day in late spring, two View Cong companies badly decimated Stull's platoon in a six-hour firefight. Rybicki's platoon was among those ordered to reinforce. "We're coming down to help you out," he told Stull on the phone. "About time we worked together again."

The platoon waded into the Rung Sat Special Zone, near the main shipping channel to Saigon. Also known as the Forest of Assassins, the Rung Sat was an ancient pirate haven, a 350-square-mile nightmare of mangrove trees and nipa palms. Shortly after arriving, Rybicki bogged down in the mud. Without flipping the safety on, he thrust the stock of his rifle to one of his men to pull him out. The soldier accidentally grabbed the trigger, and Rybicki fell dead in a burst of his own gunfire.

By chance, George happened to get word of the accident before Terry Stull did, and it fell to him to inform Stull that his brother-in-law had been killed. *Newsweek* magazine devoted an entire page to Rybicki's funeral at West Point, calling him "an integer in the unending statistics in an unending war," and noting that "he was the second to die in West Point's class of '66, the 101st academy graduate, one of 10,000 Americans lost in what has now become the fifth costliest war in U.S. history." Twenty years later, some of Frank Rybicki's classmates would recall his death with particular anguish; to them it seemed the ultimate metaphor of self-destruction in Vietnam.

In addition to conducting search-and-destroy sweeps on the Mekong, units from the 9th occasionally walked patrol duty near Dong Tam in an effort to thwart the Viet Cong mortar crews who frequently harassed the compound. One night, around the time of Rybicki's death, George had been out with his platoon for several hours on just such a defensive patrol when he heard a harsh whisper. "Sssst! Sir!"

One of his soldiers, flattened against the side of the dike, pointed across the rice paddy. George crawled to the crest of the levee and peered into the darkness. The perimeter of Dong Tam lay only a kilometer behind him to the east. Ahead, a hundred yards to the west, the next dike rose like a dark wall above the field. He saw nothing out of the ordinary and heard only the usual buzzing of countless insects.

He inched along the dike toward the soldier who had whispered. Taking the GI's sniper rifle, George hoisted the starlight scope to his right eye. The night instantly gave way to an eerie twilight. The scope sucked in all available moon- and starlight and painted the landscape with a pale green illumination, as if the world were covered with penicillin mold.

George saw him instantly. A solitary Viet Cong wearing his *ao baba*—the customary black pajamas—stood on the adjacent dike. George couldn't quite make out what the enemy soldier was doing. Sometimes, he knew, the VC liked to reverse the American claymores so that the blast would be directed back at the unwitting U.S. soldiers.

George watched for a while through the scope, the hunter stalking his prey. This was a rare opportunity to watch the enemy at work. But he didn't want the soldier to slip away in the paddy. Easy does it, he told himself. He steadied his breathing, drew a bead on the soldier's heart, and gently squeezed the trigger.

BAM! A single red tracer streaked across the paddy and struck the VC in the chest, knocking him over with a small *splat* sound that carried to the Americans.

Got you! George thought. Got you, you little son of a bitch! Adrenaline surged through him, again quickening his pulse and his breathing. The platoon crouched expectantly behind the dike, but no one returned the fire. The western front of Dong Tam remained quiet.

Back at the base, George exulted, replaying in his mind the red streak of the tracer and the dull noise as the round found its mark. As many of his classmates were also discovering, nothing in the world compared to the exhilaration of combat. Some soldiers never overcame their fear or their revulsion at the killing, but he could understand how others became adrenaline freaks. The world outside the combat zone—the peaceful world at home—seemed oddly tame by contrast, almost boring. Men, Homer had observed, grow tired of sleep, love, singing, and dancing sooner than of war. The enemy here was faceless and nameless—except for gook, dink, slope, or Charlie—and while George did not exactly hate him, killing him was not difficult. It was not difficult at all.

After but a few weeks in Vietnam, he was beginning to realize that war boiled down to a few irreducible truths. No longer did he see it as an adventure; war was brutal, often harrowing. No longer did he imagine that he was invincible; he knew death could claim him at any moment. And it was also true that the killing of the enemy was no longer cloaked in ideology or patriotism. George had heard little discussion in the war zone of the domino theory or just causes or checking the spread of godless communism. Killing was much more elemental, an accession of animal instincts and soldierly axioms: survival against a foe who was trying to kill you; revenge for comrades who had died; loyalty unto death to those who shared the fight; and a fierce determination to be better than the enemy. West Point did not—could not—teach these things; what the academy could teach, implicitly, was how to keep the killing within the warrior's code so that combat did not degenerate into blood lust, nor decent men warp into butchers.

In 1943, George Patton had written in his diary: "War is very simple, direct, and ruthless. It takes a simple, direct, and ruthless man to wage war." Combat required a certain implacability of the best. George Meade had been too much the genteel Philadelphian to crush the Confederates; it took U. S. Grant, that indifferent cadet and one-time Galena shopkeeper, to annihilate the rebellion, simply, directly, ruthlessly.

That requirement held true on Sicily and true at Spotsylvania Court House; now it was true in Vietnam. And Patton's dictum held true even for a young lieutenant in a place named United Hearts and Minds.

In early May, the brigade left Dong Tam and moved inland on a search-and-destroy operation. For three days the Americans tramped through the countryside looking for a fight without finding one. The troops discovered elaborate bunkers and even some new equipment. But the enemy always seemed to stay one step ahead.

On the afternoon of May 3, George was summoned by his company and battalion commanders. "We're going to pull the brigade out but leave a stray-behind ambush," the battalion commander told him. "You're it. Why don't you go up in the chopper now with the S3 and take a look around?"

Sitting in the Huey next to the battalion operations officer fifteen hundred feet above the ground, George saw many Americans but no Victor Charlie. He had few doubts, however, that the enemy was down there in force. Not far away was the hamlet of Ap Bac, now deserted, where in January 1963 the Army of the Republic of Vietnam (ARVN) and the Viet Cong had fought their first major battle. Three hundred and fifty lightly armed VC had humiliated an ARVN force four times its size and had shot down five U.S.-piloted helicopters. The senior American adviser on the scene, a legendary lieutenant colonel named John Paul Vann, had offered a candid assessment of ARVN combat prowess—"a miserable damn performance"—which made front-page headlines across the United States.

Now, four years later, the VC still maintained control. Long since abandoned to the war, the rice fields, dikes, and small banana plantations near Ap Bac had begun reverting to jungle. George, scanning the countryside, saw that an enemy division could hide down there without being detected. This is going to be interesting, he told himself.

Shortly after he returned to the camp, the brigade began to pull out. It took a long time to ferry more than two thousand troops back to Dong Tam in helicopters, and shadows had begun to stretch across the desolate paddies as the last Huey lifted into the sky. George and his platoon crouched in the elephant grass, straining to catch the fading beat of the rotors until even their imaginations could no longer pretend to hear it. They were alone—three dozen scared infantrymen left behind as bait.

George gestured to the platoon. "Okay," he whispered, "let's move out."

Holding their rifles high, they waded waist-deep into a swamp. Their objective was a small canal, perhaps thirty feet wide, about a mile away; from the air it had looked like a twisting black snake. The commander had suggested that they cut through an open area to reach the canal quickly, but George preferred the back door through the swamp. It was an old Ranger tactic: use the least expected route. By moving this way, the platoon would also be able to hear anyone who tried to follow.

As always in the tropics, night fell with the abruptness of a dropped curtain. After reaching a copse of small trees and grass near the canal, the men fanned out in a circle thirty yards in diameter. They couldn't dig in—the water table was only six or eight inches below the surface—so the soldiers scratched small battlements for cover. George helped site the two M-60 machine guns and camouflage the claymore mines along the canal bank. The claymores could be devastatingly effective at close range: weighing three pounds, each mine contained seven hundred steel peas packed into a paste of C-4 explosive. When triggered with a hand-held detonater, a "clacker," the C-4 spat the pellets for about fifty yards with the force of a shotgun blast.

As a final precaution, George raised the artillery firebase on the radio. A battery of 105mm howitzers, mounted on triangular platforms, had been flown into the middle of a rice paddy six miles away. Before the brigade flew back to Dong Tam, George had been assigned an artillery forward observer—a nervous young lieutenant—and one of his sergeants. Using the grids on his map, the FO now called in several rounds, which soon exploded nearby. By registering the proper deflection and elevation, the battery would be able to respond instantly with fire on potential approach routes to the platoon's perimeter.

There was always a chance, George knew, that the rounds would alert the enemy to the platoon's presence. But random explosions were common in Vietnam; something was always blowing up somewhere in the middle of the night. In Beast Barracks, new cadets had been required to memorize a saw that seemed particularly apt now: "A calculated risk is a known risk for the sake of a real gain. A risk for the sake of a risk is a fool's choice." Registering the artillery was a calculated risk.

Once in place, the platoon remained utterly quiet. That was good, George thought, very good. In four months these men had been transformed into a fine combat team. Lieutenant Crocker had been insistent—at times even harshly demanding—that they religiously follow the precepts of Ranger training. He was convinced that all of Beckwith's tricks picked up from the British in Malaya—minimizing noise and light, avoiding smelly insect repellent, stressing guile and subterfuge—saved lives. Several soldiers in the platoon had been wounded, but no one had been killed yet. That was something to be proud of.

George's own flirtation with death, however, had not abated. The near misses he began having during his first week with the Wolfhounds had continued with the 9th. On one occasion, a sniper had wounded two American soldiers in the head and George moved up the perimeter. He assigned each remaining man five trees to watch. See if you can spot any movement, he ordered, and we'll call in some artillery. Suddenly, another shot rang out and the branch a few inches above his helmet fell to the ground as neatly as if snipped with hedge shears.

Not long after that the platoon was deployed on Thoi San Island near Dong Tam. George's platoon sergeant was a savvy career NCO named Diaz, who had been an outstanding instructor at the Army's jungle school in Panama. As they were patrolling across the island, Diaz grabbed George's arm. "Nobody move!" he yelled. "Don't step!" He pointed at the ground. "Look, sir. The banana leaf, but no banana tree." Carefully lifting the leaf, Diaz revealed an undetonated Air Force cluster bomb that had been converted into a booby trap.

When, soon after, the platoon again drew night patrol duty outside Dong Tam, George set out in his usual spot, fourth in the column. But when the men began to slow down and bunch too closely, he moved up front to see why. As he climbed onto a dike next to the point man, a Chinese antipersonnel mine exploded. Shrapnel and barbed wire blew back between his legs, severely wounding the soldier who had taken his place in the file. The fireball flung George into the air and knocked the rifle from his hands. Dazed and temporarily deaf, he called for a helicopter to evacuate the wounded. Then he ordered the platoon back a thousand meters while he and Diaz crouched in the weeds for an hour, vainly hoping to ambush whoever had placed the mine.

Each close call took its toll. The stress, the rush of adrenaline, the inevitable reliving of the episode at night as he tried to sleep, all wore him down. He felt fatigued, as though he had been treading water for a long time. His exuberance ebbed a little with each incident. Always calm, at times he now found himself jumpy and distracted when the platoon prepared for yet another air assault or river sweep.

The drone of a plane interrupted his thoughts. An old C-47 Gooney Bird on a psyops—psychological operation—mission flew past. A steady stream of Vietnamese blared from loudspeakers on the plane's belly, urging the VC to surrender. *You must give up, soldiers. Death will be your only reward if you continue this futile struggle.*

Suddenly, on every side of the platoon, the jungle erupted in a roar of gunfire. Hundreds of enemy soldiers fired their rifles furiously at the plane. Then the .50-calibers opened up, hosing the night sky with tracer rounds.

Still lying quietly in their hiding place, the men in the platoon gaped in disbelief. Tracers stitched green threads through the air. The Gooney Bird, apparently untouched, continued to babble for another minute before lumbering off to proselytize elsewhere. After a few final bursts, the night fell silent again.

George gestured to the men to remain motionless. He found the .50-calibers particularly disturbing. Division intelligence had estimated that only battalion-size VC units or larger were outfitted with the heavy machine guns. At least two or three .50s had been firing; perhaps more. Two or three battalions? Is that possible? he wondered. It would not take long for two or three battalions to overrun three dozen Americans.

Someone shook his arm and pointed at the canal. The black silhouettes of two sampans silently glided by. A moment later, in a crimson burst, several claymores on the canal bank detonated, raking the sampans with steel. A piece of hot plastic from a claymore casing struck George in the back of the neck; he flicked it away with his hand. The boats burned for a few moments before sinking; once again the silence returned.

Not a single soldier in the platoon had fired his rifle yet. George had stressed over and over the importance of not signaling their position at night with rifle fire. Explosions were anonymous, but the popping of an M-16 told the enemy that an American soldier was squeezing the trigger. So far, the men had been admirably disciplined, and that's what would keep them alive: discipline held an infantry unit together, allowing every man to draw strength from every other man. Good infantrymen had once been likened to dangerous vermin that were hard to brush from the seams of the soil.

The VC began to probe. Soon George heard them rooting off to the left. As the enemy moved closer, Diaz lay sprawled on the ground nearby, clutching a pair of grenades. It sounded as though six or eight of them had closed to within a few yards of the platoon.

Out of the darkness, two enemy soldiers cam running toward the perimeter, spraying the brush with their AK-47s. Diaz popped the handles from the grenades, let them "cook" in his hands for two seconds, and flipped them at the charging VC. Both grenades detonated in midair, brilliantly illuminating the scene as the soldiers jackknifed and fell dead. George ordered each man to pull the pin on a grenade. On his command, thirty grenades bounced in front of the perimeter and exploded in a spray of dirt and shrapnel.

Things began happening very quickly now. Two hundred yards away, a large enemy force, still uncertain of the platoon's precise location, rushed at what they mistakenly believed to be the American position. George crawled over to the artillery FO. "Let's get some fire on that bunch over there," he ordered.

There was no response. Petrified, the artillery lieutenant stared blankly. George grabbed him and jerked him upright.

"You get hold of yourself," he growled, his face inches from the FO's. "You get to it or get your sergeant over here to do it."

The FO nodded and raised the firebase on the radio. A minute later, 105mm rounds began raining on the enemy position with the familiar express train sound of incoming artillery. The Americans heard shrieks and moans as the VC retreated, leaving behind the dying.

Half an hour later, the enemy tried again. Once again they missed the platoon by several hundred yards; once again a curtain of artillery fell on the attack. By dawn, it appeared that the enemy had melted back into the jungle. George called the battalion on the radio. Howard Kirk, a classmate from '66, listened on the network back at camp. He thought George's voice sounded cool, controlled, yet frightened: "The sun's up. We killed a few last night. We're searching the dead now and we'll be ready for extraction shortly."

George crawled over the canal to look at the sampans. A dead VC floated in the water. The force of the claymore had wrapped his leg bizarrely around his neck, like twine around a finger. Several other soldiers came over to tug on the edge of a sunken boat in a search for booty.

Diaz snapped his fingers twice and without uttering a word, jabbed his finger at the air. George turned his head. In a woodline 250 yards away, stretching as far as he could see in either direction, were the unmistakable signs of an impending attack. He caught glimpses of black and the glint of metal in the morning light. The Viet Cong made no effort to conceal themselves. George heard whoops and yells followed by the trill of whistles.

He turned back to Diaz. "I guess they found us."

The battalion commander was already in the air aboard his helicopter when George reached him on the radio.

"Sir, I've got a big ground attack about to start and I need some gunships. Right away."

Small-arms fire began slicing into the foliage above the platoon, sporadically at first and then in a heavy fusillade that shredded the leaves and branches. For the first time, the platoon returned fire with them M-16s and M-60s. The artillery lieutenant, having composed himself after George's tongue lashing the night before, called in coordinates to the artillery battery; within seconds the treeline erupted in fire and smoke.

That stalled the first charge. The Americans heard shouted commands as the VC tried to reorganize in the midst of the artillery barrage. For a few minutes, the enemy firing faltered, then resumed even more intensely. Hugging the ground as closely as he could, George spread a red panel to mark his position for the gunships. The gunships, he wondered; where are the gunships?

Thacka-thacka-thacka. As if on cue, a Huey swooped overhead.

"Hey, we're taking some fire," the pilot complained over the radio. "We see you, we see them."

George pressed the radio key. "You want me to throw some smoke?"

"No, don't do that. We've got you. I'm going to make a pass at them."

The gunship veered toward the woodline, raking the trees with machine guns and rockets before circling back.

"We make four or five of them hiding in a ditch right down beside you," the pilot radioed. "You want to go kill them, or do you want us to get them?"

George pressed the key. "Hell, let's not fool around. You get them."

Another ship came on station, followed by two others. A cacophony of gunfire, explosions, and rotor noise washed over the platoon. Enemy bullets had stripped the thicket in which they were hiding as clean as if it had been mowed with a scythe; leaves and small branches covered the ground. Between M-16 bursts, the men pressed their cheeks into the dirt in an effort to lower the crowns of their heads an extra inch.

The battalion commander came back on the radio. "We're getting you out of there. Be ready to extract back about three hundred meters in that open area we talked about."

"Yes, sir. We're ready."

George shouted above the din to Diaz and the squad leaders. "Get ready to go. That clearing over there, about three hundred meters. Ready—GO!"

Like sprinters coming out of their blocks, three dozen men exploded from the brake while the four gunships sprayed the treeline. Running as fast as he could, George passed a beautifully preserved old American M-1 rifle lying on the ground. He suppressed the urge to snatch it and kept sprinting. Several Hueys glided in just as the platoon reached the clearing; the men leaped inside and collapsed panting on the floor.

Once again, George felt the exhilaration of survival. What an immense sense of power there was in pressing a little microphone key and seeing the woods erupt in fire. As the ground fell away beneath the helicopter he saw several more dead Viet Cong spread-eagled below, each body marking the green earth with a dark X.

After landing at Dong Tam, he counted heads and found everyone present and accounted for; the platoon had escaped without a single casualty. The brigade commander, Colonel Fulton, ordered the men into formation. Filthy and exhausted, they stood at attention as the colonel strolled down the line, awarding each a Bronze Star.

"How many did you kill, soldier?"

"I think I got two, sir."

"Good, good. How about you, soldier?"

"At least one, sir, maybe more."

"Good. Very good."

After the ceremony, George walked back to his tent on the southeast corner of the base. Fulton had given him a Bronze Star and also recommended that he receive a Silver Star for "conspicuous gallantry and intrepidity in action."

This small, anonymous firefight, George thought, offered further insights into men at war. However insignificant the battle had been within the larger conflict, it demonstrated, in microcosm, certain verities. The American military historian S. L. A. Marshall had written that most men in combat "are unwilling to take extraordinary risks and do not aspire to a hero's role, but they are equally unwilling they should be considered the least worthy among those present." What soldiers most desire, Marshall wrote, is the esteem of their comrades.

That seemed on target, but another of Marshall's conclusions from his study of American infantrymen in World War II did not track. He had estimated that only one soldier in four fired his weapon when closely engaged with the enemy; the majority, Marshall concluded, were paralyzed with fright or preoccupied with survival. George could not see that. It seemed to him that when told to fire, these men—all of them—had done so with exceptional discipline.

Something about courage was also clearer now. At West Point, the cadets—Cadet Crocker among them—had been full of bravado. They had joked about which hand they would prefer to lose in combat, blustering about how many enemy soldiers they planned to kill. But bravado was grounded in ignorance; true courage was possible only after one gained the visceral comprehension that death was the potential price of valor. The men in the platoon—Lieutenant Crocker among them—had been truly brave.

"Sir?"

Two of his squad leaders and two PFCs stood at the entrance to the tent. It was unusual to see them here. George had made a conscious effort to remain distant from the other soldiers. Any platoon leader could be a great friend to his men, but George believed that getting too close eroded the unit's effectiveness. The biggest temptation to overcome in combat, he had discovered, was the impulse to abandon everything and tend the wounded rather than continuing to fight with the platoon. In February, he had even summoned the squad leaders to make the point explicit. "Maybe it's best that we not get too friendly," he told them. "It might affect how we do business if I know I have to put you guys in body bags."

Now, he waved the four men in.

"Sir," one of the sergeants said, "we're a delegation from the platoon and we don't really know how to say it, but we want to just say thanks for being hard on us and making sure we didn't talk or smoke or whatever. We really appreciated that last night. We know that all the things you were trying to do are worth it."

George shook their hands. When they left, he sat on his bunk and smiled. These guys have learned, he thought; they're true soldiers. And that thirty-second speech was worth more than all the Silver Stars in the United States Army.

George did not write to Vonda about the close calls. Nor did he mention the Silver Star. She tried to read between the lines to learn what was really going on in that place with the strange name. Dong Tam—it was melodious, really, almost like the sound of a bell. *Dong-tam, dong-tam.* But hard information about the war was difficult to come by. George was naturally modest and self-effacing, but sometimes she wished that he were a little more forthcoming about what he was going through.

Vonda and the baby stayed in Kansas until May so that she could finish her graduate classes. A night owl, she often watched the late news while exercising, hoping for a glimpse of her husband in the footage from Vietnam. Her affection for Army life had not diminished after the men all thundered off to war. In part, it was enhanced by the wife of George's battalion commander, Mrs. Lucien E. Bolduc. Unlike some senior officers' wives, she was a free spirit, who hauled her many children about in a van, read French for fun, and didn't seem to care a whit about Old Army protocol. If the Army has other Mrs. Bolducs, Vonda thought, I'm going to like it just fine.

At the end of the college semester, she moved back to Arkansas. Adele Crocker had taken a job as a house mother at Arkansas Tech, so Vonda and Cheryl moved into the empty Crocker house. But Vonda and Adele still saw each other frequently, and at times their visits were difficult, tense. There existed an almost chemical instability between a widow whose only child was in the war zone and a bride left alone with a newborn baby. Vonda's mother counseled forbearance. "Now you just remember all the wonderful things she's done for you," Mrs. Jones urged.

Okay, Vonda agreed, she would try to remember. She knew that it was probably beyond her ability to understand fully the stresses involved when your only son was in combat twelve thousand miles away. Someday, no doubt, she and her mother-in-law were going to be good friends. But until George was out of harm's way, they remained a constant reminder to each other of his absence. Occasionally Vonda would slip a little dig into her daily letter to Vietnam: "I invited Mother Crocker to dinner and prepared this wonderful meal, but I guess she forgot about it because she didn't come."

Unfortunately, George was not going to be out of harm's way any time soon. The struggle for the delta had become intense and bloody, although from a platoon leader's vantage point—usually about six inches off the ground—the Americans seemed to be winning. The 9th Division had secured portions of the countryside where only a few months before ambushes were a near certainty.

Dong Tam had mushroomed almost overnight from a mudflat to a large village, complete with basketball hoops and a club with a patio where officers could buy frozen hamburger patties and charbroil them on the grill. The men in the battalion domesticated the local fauna, including a snake named Python 6, which was fed a live chicken once a week amid a crowd of hooting spectators. The soldiers also kept a pet monkey named Sam, which was taught to leap onto the executive officer's shoulder and masturbate while the enraged major whirled in circles, threatening to shoot the "goddamn thing" with his pistol.

The growing delta war inevitably led to greater numbers of American casualties, and the men of '66 were not spared. One of the more popular platoon leaders was an Army brat of Norwegian descent named Denny Loftheim. Loftheim had been King of Beast in the summer of '65. He liked to reminisce about how he and his brother Jon, also in the class of '66, were once forced to hold hands and skip across Central Area during their own Beast ordeal. Assigned to a reconnaissance platoon in the 47th Infantry, Denny Loftheim sometimes bunked near George Crocker on the barracks ship; some of the other officers—not West Pointers—teased him affectionately about his alma mater by calling him Duty Honor Country.

Loftheim was unusually superstitious, particularly about a photograph that had been taken on the way to Vietnam after the 9th Division left Kansas. Among the young lieutenants in the picture, Loftheim was the only one who had not been killed or badly wounded. He was also disillusioned about the war. Sometimes it seemed so endless, so mindless, that his frustrations spilled out in letters to Jon. "Take the advice of your younger brother," he had written that spring. "Don't come."

On patrol one day, his platoon was crossing a stream when a booby trap detonated, wounding the point man. When Loftheim moved forward to help, a sniper triggered a second blast. The powerful 155mm artillery round blew the young lieutenant to pieces. Several GIs later traced the detonation cord to a blind in the jungle, which was littered with the sniper's cigarette butts. Dinny Loftheim was buried at West Point, a few feet from Frank Rybicki.

Six months into his tour, George's command stint expired and he moved to a staff position as the S3-air, the officer in charge of air operations for the 3rd Battalion. The job offered a different view of the war, either above small-arms range at fifteen hundred feet or "flying contour" at treetop level. Typically, the artillery spotter sat on his right in the Huey and the battalion commander on his left as they directed the troops below.

In mid June, the riverine force boarded a flotilla of nearly seventy boats for an operation codenamed Great Bend. In miserable monsoon heat, the armada steamed from

Dong Tam down the Mekong and into the South China Sea to Nha Be, southeast of Saigon. For four days, the troops plunged through the Rung Sat, where Frank Rybicki had been killed, in an effort to secure the Long Tau shipping channel, which led to the South Vietnamese capital. Failing to find the enemy, the soldiers reboarded the boats on June 18 and moved eight miles to the juncture of two small rivers for another sweep.

Shortly before noon on June 19, George was flying in a Huey above Long An Province, not far from where he and his platoon had been left behind six weeks earlier. Because the battalion commander, Lieutenant Colonel Bolduc, was on R and R, the executive officer had taken his seat in the helicopter. George happened to tune in to one of the other battalion networks when a desperate cry came over the radio.

"Oh God, oh God! Everybody's dead! We're all shot!"

He clapped the earphones closer to his head. The shrieking intensified. "I need help immediately! Please, somebody help us! We're all dying!"

George reached to his left and tapped the executive officer. "Listen to this, sir," he shouted above the rotor noise. "You can't really make out what the situation is, but it's serious stuff."

The major listened for a moment, his features tightening.

"Who is it?"

"I don't know yet, sir. I was just listening to the other battalion net."

Fifteen hundred feet below, explosions blossomed in red and white puffs, and the delicate green stitchery of Viet Cong tracers spread across the rice paddies. "Let's take a closer look," the XO shouted. The Huey pilot looked skeptical but nodded. He and the co-pilot had each wedged a pistol into his crotch for protection against stray bullets from below. The Huey canted onto its side and dropped several hundred feet.

Ping! Ping! Small-arms rounds began punching through the aluminum cabin and ricocheting off the armored doors in front. The artillery observer grabbed his radio and sat on it to avoid taking a round in the buttocks. Scrambling into his seat, the crew chief in back cinched his straps with a sharp tug. George felt the familiar rush of adrenaline as a bullet severed one of the fuel lines. Within seconds, a fine, malodorous mist filled the Huey. He watched the pilot's hands frantically turning the radio knobs to the emergency channel.

"Mayday. Mayday. Mayday."

An ominous succession of warning lights began winking on the control panel. As the RPM limiter flashed red, the engine wheezed and died. The pilot immediately pushed the collective control stick down with his left hand to neutralize the pitch angle. To autorotate the helicopter into an emergency landing, he had to keep the rotors spinning, or glide would turn to plummet. Dropping at thirty feet per second, the pilot peered through the Plexiglas, looking for a place to crash. "Hang on!" he yelled.

George figured that if he held on any tighter, blood would squeeze from his fingers. Thank God it's the delta, he thought. At least the terrain offered plenty of open rice paddies. Farther north, in triple-canopy jungle, autorotating choppers sometimes impaled themselves on teak and mahogany trees.

Fifty feet from the ground, the pilot yanked back on the big cyclic stick with his right hand. The nose of the Huey flared up, further slowing its descent. But as the skids smacked into the earth with a jarring thump, the tail boom nicked the ground and cracked. George and the others flipped their safety harnesses off, grabbed the radios, and raced across the wet ground to a spot forty yards in front of the Huey's nose. They waited for the helicopter to explode, but it just sat there, a pathetic hulk, its fractured tail boom canted at an angle. Feeling as vulnerable as sheep among wolves, the half-dozen men fanned out in a tight perimeter and called for help on the radio. A few minutes later, another Huey swooped in, plucked them from the ground, and carried them to the firebase. They immediately boarded a replacement command helicopter and returned to the battlefield.

The predicament of the ground troops had not improved. Six U.S. infantry companies from the 3rd and 4th battalions of the 47th Infantry had swept across the canals and paddies below while a South Vietnamese battalion tried to block the enemy near Ap Bac. Alpha Company of the 4th Battalion had moved across an open paddy, only to be ambushed by enemy soldiers hidden in an L-shaped bunker complex on the company's front and right flank. Pinned down without cover, some of the Americans lay so close to the enemy that the use of artillery and helicopter gunships was all but impossible. Furthermore, the stout enemy bunkers remained impervious to everything except direct hits with 90mm recoilless rifles or gunship rockets.

As the other five rifle companies maneuvered below, George again tuned in to the 4th Battalion's radio frequency. He heard Alpha Company's commander describing the scene.

"I can't see very far, but I can see four people who aren't wounded and four who are wounded but can still move. Everybody else is either dead or wounded so bad they can't move."

The 4th Battalion commander cut in.

"Everybody?"

"Everybody."

Then George heard another voice from below. This one was familiar.

"Yeah, I'm okay but I've got a lot of wounded. We need to get somebody in here, get this thing stabilized so we can get some dustoffs."

The voice belonged to Fred Bertolino, a classmate who was one of Alpha's platoon leaders. Even in this jam, and in spite of his apparent wounds, Bertolino was soft-spoken.

George flipped back and forth between the battalion networks; his old platoon was down there with the 3rd Battalion. Once again the executive officer ordered the Huey to descend, this time to drop some smoke canisters requested by one of the companies. At one hundred knots the helicopter swooped in almost low enough to pluck at the rice stalks. As the case of smoke was pushed out the door, George heard the familiar crack of bullets puncturing the fuselage, and soon the red warning lights began blinking furiously again. Once again the pilot made an emergency landing; once again they scrambled from the crippled chopper; and once again a rescue Huey hauled them back to the firebase for a replacement.

As the afternoon wore on, Alpha Company's predicament slid from desperate to doomed. Most of those still alive remained trapped in eight inches of paddy water within easy range of the enemy. Every effort to send help was violently repulsed. Both George and Howard Kirk, whose platoon had been moved from the ships to about a quarter of a mile from Alpha, listened to Fred Bertolino's frantic cries for help.

"We're all gonna bleed to death," he pleaded. "We're all finished, including me, if you don't get some help in here." His voice grew weaker and less coherent.

The shooting ebbed with the sunlight. Once more that afternoon, the helicopter in which George was riding was shot down. By the third time, it almost seemed routine. After eight o'clock, the battlefield fell silent. At midnight, when they finally stopped flying to wait for dawn, George saw that both the corps commander and General Westmoreland had arrived. On his right sleeve when he came to the delta, Westmoreland always wore the 9th Division combat patch he had earned during World War II in Europe. That was good politics, but this clearly was not the usual morale-building official visit from Saigon. Like praying monks, the generals knelt in the dirt, poking at a map and wondering what to do.

During the night, the Viet Cong slipped out of their bunkers. They moved west across a stream called the Rach Nui before turning south. After sunrise on the morning of the twentieth, the Americans caught one VC platoon in the open and destroyed it. The rest of the enemy escaped.

Howard Kirk's platoon crossed the Rach Nui to police the battlefield. The dead from Alpha Company lay scattered through the paddy in sodden clumps. Kirk found Bertolino face down in the brown water, where he evidently had lost consciousness and drowned. Kirk helped lift him into a body bag. If Fred Bertolino's family wanted a West Point burial, a spot was waiting for him in the academy cemetery. Dry ground there was never hard to come by.

The firefight was over. Forty-six Americans had been killed and 140 wounded. The 9th Division claimed 250 enemy dead. George Crocker had again narrowly escaped with his life. Once more the thought flashed through his mind that perhaps he was charmed. He wasn't sure how else to explain why so many of his classmates died and he was spared.

George rarely dwelt on the dead. Like getting too close to the troops, that was fraught with danger. By temperament, he was not given to philosophical ruminations on cruel fate. But the death of friends like Loftheim and Bertolino hit him hard, further sapping the boyish excitement he had once felt about the great adventure of combat. Occasionally, as when he heard that Loftheim had been killed, he sat on his bunk at Dong Tam, brooding. It seemed so unfair that such men should die. Why, he wondered, did war seem to single out the best? Why couldn't at least the very best of the best survive? When such fine soldiers died, he thought, their loss was a waste, a pointless, tragic waste.

Robert E. Lee had once mused that it was fortunate war was such a terrible thing because otherwise men would grow too fond of it. The deaths of men like Frank Rybicki and Denny Loftheim and Fred Bertolino served to guarantee that men like George Crocker would never grow too fond of war.

Desert Storm: The Ground War

24 February through 8 March 1991
24 February 1991 (G-Day)

by Alex Vernon with Neal Creighton Jr., Greg Downey,
Rob Holmes, and Dave Trybula

By the final Desert Storm plan, H-Hour had been set for 0400 hours. While off-coast marines feint an amphibious landing, another marine unit and part of the Arab Joint Force attack into Kuwait up the coast in conjunction with the Arab Joint Force's major inland attack into Kuwait. The light component of the Eighteenth Airborne Corps, farthest west, also launches its attack at G-Day, H-Hour. Twenty-six hours later, on G+1 at 0600, Seventh Corps begins the main attack into Iraq and then hooks east into Kuwait to strike the Iraqi's rear defenses from the flank, with the Eighteenth's 24th Infantry and the 3d ACR attacking at the same time on its western flank with the mission of bypassing Kuwait entirely and blocking the Iraq routes into and out of Kuwait from the north. The division's operational plan characterized corps operations of having "a rapid operational tempo that employs complementary heavy and light corps forces supported by massed fires. We accept risk in the depth of Corps operations to surprise the enemy and gain positioning advantage and feasibility for our forces."

The three maneuver brigades of the 24th Infantry Division were to cross the Saudi-Iraqi border abreast. About thirty-five kilometers into the attack, at Phase Line Colt, the division would collapse into two columns: our 2d Brigade leading on the right as the division's main effort, with 1st Brigade following us; and the 197th on the left.

The brigade's three battalions would maneuver in an inverse triangle. Task force 3-69, at the triangle's point, trailed the other two in the reserve position. Task Force 3-15 Infantry led on the right, with Neal Creighton as its lead platoon leader and myself leading a company-team to Neal's rear right in our task force diamond. And Task Force 1-64 Armor led on the left, with Greg Downey as the scout platoon leader out front, Rob Holmes as the lead platoon leader in their "Rogue Diamond" formation, and Dave Trybula leading the battalion's reserve tank company at the opposite point on the diamond.

With Rob at the head of 1-64, Greg scouting to the front of 1-64, and Neal at the head of 3-15, I could not have chosen three more able lieutenants to lead the brigade into battle.

Source: *The Eyes of Orion: Five Tank Lieutenants in the Persian Gulf* (1999) 176-221.
Reprinted by permission of The Kent State University Press.

ALEX VERNON (Delta Mech, Task Force 3-15 Infantry)

That day Captain Baillergeon gave to each platoon leader in Delta Mech a message from Major General McCaffrey to read to our soldiers. Elsewhere the ground war had already commenced, at 0400 in the morning, though our division was not scheduled to attack until 0600 on the twenty-fifth. I read the letter at Sfc. Freight's tank. Title "General Order to Attack," and dated 15 February, it read;

Soldiers of the Victory Division, we now begin a great battle to destroy an aggressor Army and free two million Kuwaiti people. We will fight under the American flag and with the authority of the United Nations. By force-of-arms we will make the Iraqi war machine surrender the country they hold prisoner.

The 26,000 soldiers of the reinforced 24th Infantry Division will be the First to Fight. Our mission is to attack 300 kilometers deep into Iraq to block the Euphrates River Valley. Our objective is to close the escape route for 500,000 enemy soldiers in Kuwait.

On D-Day, 24th ID (M) will be the point of the spear for a general offensive by 700,000 Coalition Allied soldiers. The victory Division attack has the central purpose to smash into the enemy rear and destroy their will to fight. The shock action and violence of the 24th Infantry Division assault will save thousand of American lives from the bloody work of fighting through the fire trenches of Kuwait.

There will be no turning back when we attack into battle. One hundred thousand American and French soldiers of the XVIII Airborne Corps will fight on our flanks. We have the weapons and the military training equal to the task. We pray that our courage and our skill will bring this war to a speedy close.

In WWII, in Korea, in Saudi Arabia...the soldiers of the Victory Division have never failed America. We shall do our duty.

I can't remember what else I may have said. I do remember, while walking from tank to tank checking on morale and equipment readiness, seeing Freight on the top of his tank battling the wind trying to put his maps together. He had the only set the platoon. He had not marked the necessary graphics on any of them. What had taken me several days over the course of a couple of weeks, he tried to do the afternoon before the attack. Perhaps I should have supervised him more closely, to ensure those maps were assembled; but he'd never be able to read the maps anyway. It was like the load plan. We were supposed to load our tanks so that no gear strapped on the side of the turret jutted above the top of the turret. This would ensure that, if we had to button-up during combat, our fields of view through the vision blocks at the base of the commander's hatch would not be obscured by a duffel bag or MRE box. Some platoons required all four tanks to have identical load plans in case crew members had to switch tanks. I only required my tanks to keep the vision blocks clear. Three of my four tanks complied with my order the day I issued it – the tank commanders were grateful they could organize their gear to suit them, as long as they met the basic requirement. But Sfc. Freight, the platoon sergeant, the example NCO, did not. Nor did he the next day. Nor the next. I repeated the order every day. Perhaps I should have stood there while he put his tank in order. I did not. I had given up on Freight

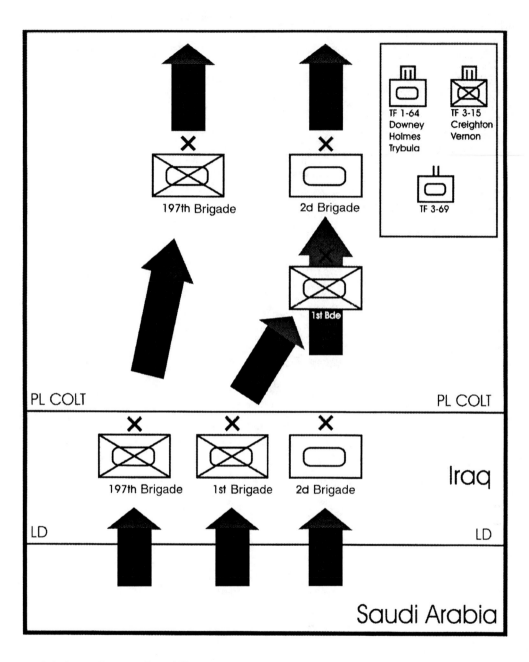

24th Infantry Division Initial Formations

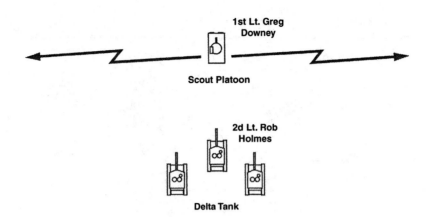

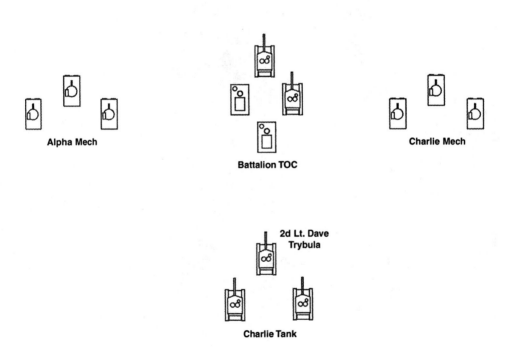

Task Force I-64 in "Rogue Diamond" Formation
Note: vehicle icons in company formations represent platoons.

long ago. His tank would roll across the border looking like the Beverly Hillbillies' family wagon.

Early in the afternoon Captain Baillergeon called us to REDCON 2 – ready to move with fifteen minutes notice. We were going to take advantage of the daylight to cross the berm that marked the border and reassemble in task force formation on the other side. We were also instructed to begin taking the pyridostigmine bromide pills we had been issued a few weeks before. The PB pills were a preventive measure against certain chemical agents, and we were to take them on a schedule, I think every eight hours. My crew hesitated before popping the first pill; we looked at one another, swallowed, and checked our watches. The company led the task force column through the berm – the battalion command sergeant major had positioned his Humvee on the Saudi side of the berm, where he flew both the battalion colors and the American flag. On the other side the task force linked with Alpha Tank, which had spent the night securing the far side of the berm. Fuel HET's drove through each company, to each vehicle, topping us off.

Crossing the berm early also meant moving the LD. The LD, or line of departure, is a graphic control measure used on maps to coordinate the attack of different units. The LD had been the berm; now Phase Line Opus, about ten kilometers farther south and where our forward units had spent the night, became the LD.

Just before 1500 hours, Baillergeon called again to put us in REDCON 1. The D-Day H-Hour fixing attack into Kuwait by the marine and coalition forces in the eastern part of the theater was progressing more rapidly than anticipated. And in our Eighteenth Airborne Corp's western zone, the lead elements of the 6th French Light, and the American 82d and 101st Airborne Divisions, were meeting effectively no resistance. We were fifteen hours ahead of schedule. It was time.

GREG DOWNEY (Scouts, Task Force 1-64 Armor)
February twenty-fourth started as a clear day, with a slight wind and blue skies. About 1000 hours, the remainder of the task force moved north to join us at Phase Line Opus. The desert wind began to pick up, and visibility was getting worse. I has Specialist Lowther monitor the radio while I walked around checking vehicle maintenance.

"Hey, sir, Rogue Six wants to talk to you," Lowther said, out of breath from running to get me. Rogue Six did not like to wait for you on the radio. I jogged back to my track, Lowther behind me, my gas mask bouncing off my hip, my arms swinging wide around my flak cest.

"Rogue Six, Scout Six, over."

"Scout, the Rogue, go to REDCON 4, acknowledge, over."

REDCON4: ready to move in two hours. I didn't have to ask why. The clock was ticking. The task force bumbled a little as all the units scrambled to get into their formation positions.

"Rogue Six, this is Darklord Six, over." That was Captain Hubner, Delta Tank's company commander. Delta would lead the task force's Rogue diamond formation.

"Rogue Six, Darklord needs Class III now, over." I sensed the urgency in Hubner's voice. Delta Team had to be low on fuel after last night's mission. They had come with me across the border last night and had not taken on fuel since. Not good. Hope they get it quick.

"Scout Six, go to REDCON 1 minus, over," ordered Lieutenant Colonel Gordon. Often he didn't bother with his own call sign. He didn't need to. We all knew when the Prince of Darkness was speaking.

"This is Scout Six, wilco," I responded. The call meant I had to be ready to move immediately. It had not even been an hour since the REDCON 4 order.

Well, here we go. This is it. I felt very detached from what was happening. I heard and saw what was going on around, but it didn't feel like I was a part of it, like I was there. Except for the changing weather, that is. The sand was starting to sting a little harder, decreasing our visibility by the minute.

"Scout Six, LD time now," came the call from Rogue Six.

LD time now. The most destructive force I had ever witnessed had just been put into action.

ROB HOLMES (Delta Tank, Task Force 1-64 Armor)

My report broke radio silence. "Lima Delta, continuing mission." I had called the LD to Captain Hubner countless times in training. That night, it has new meaning.

Hubner's M1 followed directly behind mine, about two hundred meters behind my platoon's wedge. First Platoon was behind me to my left and Third Platoon behind me to my right. I headed north at fifteen degrees for eight kilometers toward checkpoint Romeo 54, our first stop on the long march to Basra. I looked over my shoulder as the task force spread out in the diamond formation across the desert. I noticed that another tank has pulled behind me next to Captain Hubner. This would normally be the company executive officer, or second in command, who maneuvered as Hubner's wingman. But experience leading the task force told me the tank beside Hubner wasn't our company XO.

"White One, the is Black Six," Hubner radioed. "Rogue Six says your wingman is too close."

Rogue Six was Flash, the battalion commander. Hubner didn't need him as an excuse to give me an order. It was his way of apologizing for micromanaging my platoon, because Lieutenant Colonel Gordon was micromanaging his company. Hubner and I had learned to deal with Flash. Tactically, we both knew that Flash probably knew best anyway.

The task force traveled in a diamond formation due to the 360-degree nature of the desert battlefield. Delta Tank led, putting the firepower of our fourteen tanks up front. The two mechanized infantry companies held the flank positions. This gave the task force the flexibility to dismount grunts and provide fire support from either direction. As the task force reserve, Charlie Tank held the rear point of the diamond, to serve as a counterattack or maneuver element in any direction, once one of the other companies had engaged the enemy. The symmetrical shape gave us security on all sides, and the ability to react in any direction with either tanks or infantry, as the threat demanded. To use a boxing metaphor, Delta Tank jabbed, then Charlie Tank would swing around from the flank, like a hook. The two mech infantry companies could hold the enemy from each side like a bear hug.

There wasn't supposed to be anything at Romeo 54; it was just a spot on the map Major Diehl thought would make a good rally point for a refuel. The contact was possible, but most likely we would use this stop simply to refuel. The M1's turbine engine really guzzled fuel. As we marched north into Iraq, we would have to replenish out tanks about every one hundred kilometers. Another problem with the turbine engine" As it "breathed" air in, it also sucked in sand. In order to keep our filters clean so that the engine wouldn't suffocate, we had to periodically blow its filters clean with an air hose attached to another tank's turbine. During Desert Shield we had practiced refueling and blowing out our air filters to ensure that in battle we didn't sit still too long.

We hit Romeo 54 at about 2030 and stopped with the three platoons in columns abreast, and Hubner, The XO, and Flash in a fourth column. The fuel trucks moved through us, refueling two tanks at a time. Each tank crew went to action, as synchronized as a stock car pit crew: One soldier prepared the tank to take on fuel; one checked the tracks for loose connectors, broken shoes, and bad tension; the third, in conjunction with a soldier from a neighbor tank, blew out the filters. Meanwhile the tank commanders met me on the ground, a routine we do so I could learn any concerns of theirs and update them on any new information or orders. This time I also wanted to check everybody's nerves and settle them down. We spoke briefly. I joked about the sand being nicer in Iraq, and we broke after the tank commanders gave logistics reports to Sfc. Sikes.

No news from Black Six, Captain Hubner.

We returned to our platoons. The company mounted us, and my platoon led the battalion north. Our next destination was Objective Gray.

NEAL CREIGHTON (Alpha Tank, Task Force 3-15 Infantry)

At 1500 hours on February 24, 1991, Task Force 3-15 was ordered to attack. We were in the midst of receiving fuel when a sandstorm hit. I couldn't see more than two hundred meters in any direction. Captain Schwartz tightened our company formation as we moved forward.

I had marked every leg of the attack on my map with distance and azimuth and written them on index cards. My driver Forbes had a duplicate set of cards and his mission was, once again, to keep track of the distance and tell me when to change azimuth. Our technique worked despite the sandstorm. To verify our location, every ten kilometers I would get a GPS reading over the radio from 2d Lt. Jimmy Kim, the company's fire support officer.

We sped unmolested for over 150 kilometers into Iraq that night. All the task force maneuver training was paying off. We halted short of our first march objective, Objective Gray, in the early morning hours. After stopping, I looked up at Orion. He seemed to shine brighter than ever.

DAVE TRYBULA (Charlie Tank, Task Force 1-64 Armor)

The main body of Task Force 1-64 had just crossed the Iraqi border in the neutral

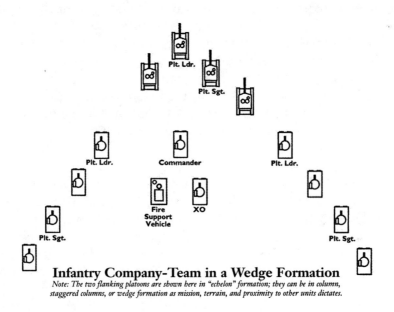

Infantry Company-Team in a Wedge Formation
Note: The two flanking platoons are shown here in "echelon" formation; they can be in column, staggered columns, or wedge formation as mission, terrain, and proximity to other units dictates.

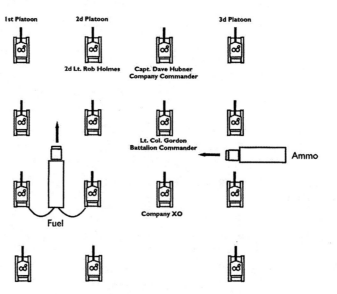

Delta Tank Hasty Resupply

zone as a sandstorm was beginning to build. The storm was easily the worst I had seen in my six months of desert life. Visibility was a quarter mile at best, and this was reduced even more by the large number of vehicles moving in the same area. While the weather hid our attack, it also hid the enemy. I worried that the Iraqis had picked up out movement and were repositioning one of their available divisions. I feared they would attack our flanks as we attacked toward their rear.

About twelve hours into Iraq, my XO called down that the brigade was bypassing any enemy light infantry regiment. The enemy had to know we had attacked into their homeland, yet they showed no sign. My concern grew as the storm worsened and as we progressed deeper into Iraq. Every major American newspaper and news magazine had published a frightfully close version of the attack plan – could the Iraqis really not know where we were? To ensure my platoon would be ready for an Iraqi ambush or counterattack, I put my crews on a rotational sleep plan, drivers with loaders and tank commanders with gunners, ensuring that each tank had two soldiers alert and ready to fight.

We continued to move deeper into Iraq. At about 0200, roughly 260 miles into Iraq, Captain Hadjis spoke over the radio. "Just got intelligence update from higher. The State Department announced a short while ago that the attack into Kuwait is going ahead of schedule with minimal loss of life, and that the United States would not violate the territorial integrity of Iraq." If we weren't violating Iraqi territory, I wondered exactly what we were doing.

My crew let out a cheer. A huge weight had been lifted off out shoulders. No longer was I concerned about Iraqis counterattacking into our flank. I was sure that they had no idea where we were. We were about to close the door on their retreat from Kuwait. The synergy of the raised morale made crews more alert, calmed fears, and focused everyone's attention on the battle ahead.

We pushed through the blinding sandstorm.

GREG DOWNEY (Scouts, Task Force 1-64 Armor)

The terrain was unforgiving as the scout platoon moved deeper into Iraq. The rocky desert ground was extremely rough, and sheer cliffs were everywhere. Drivers had to feel their way through the terrain. Their passive night sights only amplified existing illumination. They were almost totally ineffective due to the blinding sandstorm.

"Sir, I can't see," was West's refrain, all night long.

"That makes two of us, West," I would reply before climbing down off my CFV to check the black hole of terrain in front of us. Incredible. As if what we were doing wasn't hard enough, without the extra crap of the sandstorm. My gunner was having an equally hard time seeing through his thermal sight.

"How far can you see, Lowther?" I asked him.

"About five hundred meters, if I'm lucky," he responded. If we made contact with the Iraqi army, it would be a close-range engagement.

The divisional cavalry moved ahead of us initially, but we passed through it the night of the twenty-fourth. Now everything forward of my scout platoon was enemy.

That made my job much easier. We received orders over the radio to continue to Attack Position Dallas, about one hundred kilometers into Iraq. My scout platoon conducted a recon of the area at Dallas to be occupied by Task Force 1-64, clearing it at 0400 hours on 25 February. For the next few hours we screened forward of the task force. Aside from updating some map graphics and getting some intelligence summaries from the task force intelligence officer, all was quiet.

ALEX VERNON (Delta Mech, Task Force 3-15 Infantry)

The sun did not linger. My impressionistic account of that first night consists of rain and sand and cold, of sounds of radio chatter and track movement and the hum and clanging echoes from inside my turret. With a low ceiling of clouds blocking light from the moon, with falling rain and blowing sand, and still more sand kicked up by the tracks of dozens of armored vehicles, we were blind. Once Baillergeon and I disagreed about the company-team's position in the battalion formation. I knew he could not see as well as I could, since he had his driver literally follow in my tracks, my dust in his face. But Baillergeon would not give; he ordered me to take a sharp left and gun it. A minute later the dust and rain cleared enough for me to see the right skirts of a tank, presumable one of Alpha Tank's, not five meters to my front. I screamed into the intercom for my driver to make a hard right. We missed colliding with that other tank by inches.

Occasionally one of my tanks would slowly drop behind, and I'd call that tank commander over the radio to wake him to wake his drover. My own driver fell asleep fairly often as well. To keep the soldiers rested, all my tank crews had their loaders take turns driving. Some gunners and tank commanders also switched, though I did not, since I led the company.

Sometime during the blur of the night a loud *snap*! Cracked over my left shoulder and the tank jerked left. It continued to pull left while slowing to a stop. I clambered down – the snap and pulling were familiar. As I had figured, the tank had broken track. I would have to jump track, to switch to Sergeant Rivera's tank, and he would take over my broken tank. The company-team meanwhile had stopped behind their crippled lead vehicle, though the task force was driving ahead. Jumping track was always a scramble because I had to grab my maps and battleboards and disconnect and take with me both my ten-channel radio and the auxiliary speaker to swap with Rivera's single-channel in order to monitor both platoon and company nets. If it took too long, we'd lose the rest of the battalion. I thrust the radio and aux to McBryde, the wing tank's loader, and climbed up over the back deck and to the turret. I hollered at McBryde to tell the driver to move as I was lowering myself into the hatch. McBryde and I would have to mount the radio on the move while I tried to relocate the battalion. We accelerated past my broke-dick tank; Rivera and my crew already had the tract jacks out and were going to work. It didn't take long to catch the battalion. Maybe twenty minutes later Sergeant Rivera called me on the radio: "Gold Six, Gold Two, I got you, over." I turned around in the hatch and lifted my RVS-7s from around my neck to my eyes. In the green light of my night vision device, I saw my tank passing the lead Bradley in the platoon following me on the left and moving into place as my wingman in the platoon wedge. Rivera, Dock, and Brunner had fixed the track in the dark, with the wind and sand and rain, with other vehicles flying past them, and found us in amazing time. At the soonest opportunity Rivera and I returned to our proper tanks.

I was glad Rivera had convinced me to keep him as my wingman. A few days before the ground war, I had considered balancing the platoon by swapping him with Sfc. Freight's wingman, putting more experienced wing tank commander with the less-able section leader. Rivera advised me against it. The platoon leader's wingman ran twice the risk of being left behind to fend for himself, since if wither his tank or my tank went down, he would stay with the broken tank. And Rivera was the best man for the job. If he hadn't been able to fix the tank, he would have sat stranded, to be policed up by whatever support unit happened to stumble upon him, or to fight whatever enemy stumbled upon him and his disabled tank.

Once we passed a cluster of stationary M113s. I saw a number of figures and small light sources. Somehow I have the idea that this was 2-4 Cav's TOC. I also remember passing a stationary self-propelled 155 artillery battery. I'll never forget the eerie vision of those boxy tracked howitzers stopped in a semicircle, seen through the green filter of my handheld night vision device and the blowing sand. I did not understand how the unit had gotten ahead of us, as our 2d Brigade was supposed to be leading the way. We refueled once: Alpha Tank set a hasty defensive position to the north of the fuel trucks while the task force rolled through, two tanks per fuel truck. When Bravo and Delta Mech had finished and has assumed defensive positions, Alpha withdrew to refuel.

Despite our blindness that night, in our seventy-ton Abrams tanks and thirty-ton Bradleys we flew. Those soldiers stuffed deep inside the vehicles, the tank gunners and the infantrymen and scouts in the back of the Bradleys, who were more blind than those of us with our heads poked out of the turrets straining to see, must have felt like human cannonballs jettisoned headlong and powerless.

We hit rough terrain in the first hours of the twenty-fifth, about Phase line Yaz. The task force came to a stop until someone found a route through, and we proceeded single file. The natural obstacle turned out to be an extremely deep wadi with nearly vertical walls. As I approached the passage point, trailing Alpha's last tank, I watched the vehicle enter the wadi. I had never seen anything like it. One moment the green glow of the night vision device was filled with the tank's taillights and its hot exhaust, then the bottom of its tread, and then nothing but green darkness until after a few moments more the turret top appeared perpendicular to the ground as the tank climbed the far side; then, again, the taillights and hot exhaust. When we started down, my body told my head that my tank was going to flip over, head first. Had I not witnessed the tank in front of me clear the chasm, I would never have dared it.

On the other side of the wadi the task force clustered together, more or less companies in staggered columns. Vehicles were so close you could in some cases take a long step from the top of one onto another. It was about 0400; we would move again at 0600. the battalion commander must have had complete confidence in the lack of an enemy threat to allow his task force to sit so vulnerable. One artillery round or air bomb could have destroyed several vehicles, and one infantryman's automatic weapon could have sprayed at least a platoon's worth of men.

The storm had stopped.

I had my platoon pull 50 percent security, two men per tank at the ready, the other two asleep. This gave each soldier and hour. I slept on the first shift, as I was the only one in the platoon who had not been able to catch any shut-eye during the night. I also wanted to be awake during daylight, and during wake-up, to ensure everyone woke and was ready to roll. After my nap I ate an MRE, brushed my teeth, and ran an electric razor over my face (you need to be cleaned-shaven for your gas mask to seal properly). The fuel trucks came by about 0530. the soldiers who slept the second shift were shorted; if the fuel truck didn't wake them at 0530, I woke them at 0545.

25 FEBRUARY 1991 (G+1)

ALEX VERNON (Delta Mech, Task Force 3-15 Infantry)

We moved again at 0600. Again we fell into a task force column, as the day's journey began with the climbing of a steep escarpment to our front by a serpentine trail up the side to gain the plateau above.

The task force paused on its way to our first objective during the artillery preparation. Just as my tank pulled to a stop, we felt the familiar snap of the tank track. While my crew set to work, I had the rest of the platoon pull a quick maintenance check on their tanks. Staff Sergeant Rivera discovered several missing end-connectors, center guides, and track shoes on his tread – he would have to break one track side to properly fix it. If he didn't, he risked throwing track and being left behind, or worse, throwing track and becoming a sitting duck during the fight.

Before G-Day I had preset one of my main radio's ten frequencies to the one assigned to Bravo Tank in case I ever needed immediate communication with my tank company. I flipped the switch and called Greg Jackson. After fixing my track the first night, and two tracks now, my platoon was starting to run low on track elements. Greg jumped in the company's maintenance M113 PC and ran to me what parts he could spare. Sometimes I suspect I did not need those parts, but I took the opportunity to hear Greg's voice on the radio and possibly see him in person.

When the task force moved again, my track was up, but Rivera's was still a few minutes away. Since he was my wingman, I decided to stay with him. The task force's XO drove up in his Humvee and screamed at me to leave Rivera. We were closing in on the objective. I took off and rejoined Delta Mech. Rivera us six minutes later.

GREG DOWNEY (Scouts, Task Force 1-64 Armor)

At 0845 hours, we continued the attack. It was the fastest zone recon ever done. Division headquarters was pushing us hard, and we stepped up the tempo. The visibility was improving, observation now about two kilometers. The brigade was headed to Objective Gray, an area that was supposed to have been cleared by the 24th ID's

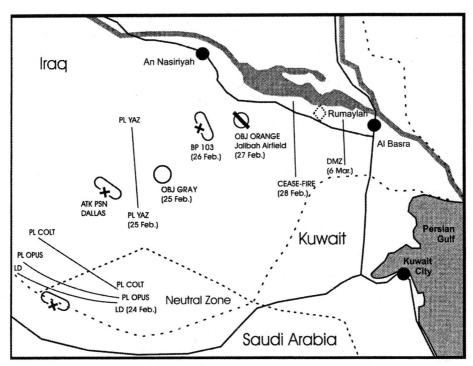

Desert Storm Select Operational Graphics

Long Range Surveillance Detachment. The LSRD ("lurs-dee") is usually inserted prior to an operation in order to provide accurate enemy situation reports of particular areas. Negative contact was reported up to Phase Line Meadow, about ten kilometers short of Objective Gray. As the task force stopped for a resupply on the move, the scout platoon pushed forward.

"Contact! Contact!" It was Staff Sergeant Deem, over the radio. A few seconds later he reported seeing tents and antennas, an early warning radar site. No soldiers or vehicles were observed, but brigade wanted to drop indirect fire on it. It was time to see if our artillery units were as good as they boasted.

The self-dubbed "King of Battle," artillery batteries usually travel five to ten kilometers behind the armor and infantry units, coordinating their movements to ensure they can support the most forward unit, normally the scout platoon. The pace of this attack would not allow for any delay in their movement. The artillery units could receive a fire mission when on the move and perform a "hip shoot" by conducting a short halt, quickly lining up the guns, getting the target data, and firing its first volley.

There were three different sites across my front, so we requested 155-mm howitzer rounds on one site, eight-inch howitzer rounds on the center, and MLRS rockets at the remaining targets. The destruction from the howitzers was immediate – I did not have to call in an adjustment for a second volley. But the MLRS rockets impacted one kilometer over and one kilometer to the left of the target. Initially, I thought I had sent bad target data, but after checking my coordinates, I concluded that the rockets should have hit the radar site dead on. After determining nothing was at the site anyway, we pressed on.

Twenty kilometers later, we met the enemy. My gunner reported targets. We moved closer, discovering the Iraqi soldiers to be young boys and old men. They were a sad sight, with absolutely no fight left in them. Their leaders had cut their Achilles' tendons so they couldn't run away and then left them. What weapons they had were in bad repair and little ammunition was on hand. They were hungry, cold, and scared. The hate I had for any Iraqi dissipated. These people had no business being on the battlefield. The humanity and restraint of my scouts was commendable, above professional standards. We gave rations to them from our own supplies, and my medic administered first aid. We passed the forty-five Iraqi prisoners of war off to Alpha Mech.

As we moved forward to screen Engagement Area V20, we continued encountering Iraqi soldiers, only these were better equipped and in better shape. I told my scout platoon to shoot warning rounds over their heads and give them a chance to surrender. This worked well until we occupied our screen line that night.

Setting a screen line in total darkness was difficult. This was compounded further by the still-ranging sandstorm. At 2030 hours, all three scout sections reported they were set. At 2035, I observed green tracer rounds and a rocket-propelled grenade impact near Red Section.

"Black One, this is Red Two – Contact! Contact!" It was Staff Sergeant Deem again, followed seconds later by the thump-thump-thump of his 25-mm chain gun answering the enemy's fire. During times like this, I had learned to let my leaders fight their battle and not bother them with unnecessary radio traffic. Deem had his hands full enough without my bothering him. I reported to battalion that we were in contact. They wanted to know details I could not give them at the time.

As the fight continued in Red Section's sector, my gunner reported targets moving across my front. I had him fire warning shots over their heads first to see what they would do. After ten rounds of 25 mm, the Iraqis hit the ground. One by one, they stood up, arms extended as high as they could reach. Major Diehl called for a situation report. I told him Red Section has its fight under control. No friendly losses.

Staff Sergeant Deem updated me on what had happened. As far as he could tell, Red Section had killed six to eight Iraqis – the 25-mm high explosive rounds did not leave much left of whatever they hit. I didn't think a body count was really necessary, but battalion was pushing me for one. We counted feet and boots that had feet in them. The platoon took a total of sixty-five Iraqis prisoner that night. Throughout the night, whenever we received sporadic enemy fire, we responded by firing our chain guns in the general direction of the enemy.

ROB HOLMES (Delta Tank, Task Force 1-64 Armor)

The sun was rising as the battalion rolled on. I could now look around and see over fifty armored vehicles in our diamond formation. Captain Hubner and Lieutenant

Colonel Gordon were still right behind me. Hubner was in his hatch reading his map and eating an MRE. I don't think the colonel needed a map. He'd been studying the route for months. Hubner and I, on the other hand, each had navigation devices called Lorans. They were designed for boating and fixed your position by triangulating off ground-based transmitting stations positioned around the world. Dave Hubner was really good using his. I think he wanted to master it for his shrimping trips off Savannah.

I got my Loran only a week before attacking. It came with two AA Batteries, and Hubner told me that I was on my own for replacements. I quickly sent a letter home to my mother and requested two hundred batteries. Believe it or not, she was usually faster than the army. In the interim, Sfc. Sikes confiscated every AA battery in our platoon. Soldiers lost the use of their Walkman radios, flashlights, Nintendo Gameboys, and anything else that used them. My platoon sergeant said he didn't have time to wait on my mother. Underberg meanwhile had rigged a metal clip from an ammo box to hang the Loran inside the tank next to my seat. Then re ran a wire into the light inside the turret so that the Loran ran off the M1's main battery. Now it didn't need AA batteries unless we dismounted. For his services, Underberg negotiated to get his Walkman back from Sikes. The Beach Boys were back.

I looked down at my map. We were close to where the scout choppers had spotted infantry.

The sun was fully visible to my right now. Sergeant Downing was scanning the horizon for contact.

"Sir, I thing I see a building and a water trailer."

M1 gunners can usually see about three thousand meters and clearly identify targets as far as twenty-five hundred. I could see something on the horizon from my hatch without my binoculars, which I never used much when we were moving. I didn't like anything draped around me that I didn't absolutely need, so the binos stayed in their box.

I sent a spot report to Captain Hubner. "Black Six, this is White One; one building, direct front, twenty-five hundred meters, continuing mission, over."

"Fire!" Hubner immediately called back.

"Fire!" he yelled again across the radio.

"Sir, I'm not sure what's out there!" Downing protested to me through his intercom. He was so well trained in peacetime that he instinctively hesitated to fire at an unidentified target.

I dropped down to my seat in the turret and looked through the .50-caliber machine gun sight. The weapon had been in the army inventory for decades and was still loved by soldiers. Back at Fort Stewart, I trained with the .50 cal in the computer simulators. It was about the most fun I had back then, better than any arcade game. I had gotten to the point where I could hit anything, moving or stationary.

The .50 was designed to operate in the defense while stationary. We were approaching at fifteen miles per hour what was in fact a small building and a water trailer about fifteen hundred meters away. I figured why not-this is combat-and pulled down on the red elevation handle, which was connected by wire to the weapon's butterfly trigger, sending a burst of bullets flying high over the targets. I spun the handle to adjust my elevation and fired a second burst, also wildly missing as my driver Bell bounced our tank across the desert. Later, I took much grief from Captain Hubner for even using the weapon while moving, let alone missing way high. Nonetheless, I figured that it was time to quit screwing around.

"Downing, pump a sabot through that building," I ordered through the intercom.

We had battle-carried sabot—had loaded a sabot main gun round in the breach based on the anticipated threat, the Iraqi tanks. An M1A1's sabot round is a 120-mm depleted uranium kinetic energy antitank round that explodes from the tank's main gun at about eighteen hundred meters per second, so fast the main gun doesn't need rifling to keep the round flying straight. Nothing stops it. As a sabot round penetrates a tank turret it fragments the inside turret wall, and these pieces—called *spalling*—join the sabot's high-speed ricocheting inside, shredding the crew and sometimes exploding any rounds waiting to be fired. (Tanker lore also claims that a sabot can enter one side of a crew area and exit the other, the resultant vacuum sucking the occupants out the small exit hole.) A building really called for firing a high explosive HEAT round instead of wasting a tank-killing sabot, but we were closing fast and I was too impatient to order Underberg to reload.

"On the way!" Downing yelled as he squeezed the trigger.

The explosive shook the tank as the turret filled with that distinctive smell of cordite and gunpowder. The sabot round rocketed from the gun tube like a thunderbolt and flew through the building, caving in the wall. Immediately dozens of Iraqi infantry appeared and scattered about six hundred meters in front of us like honeybees from a knocked-over hive.

This time, without even having to think about it, I gave the fire command to my whole platoon. "Dismounts! Direct front! Fire!"

We cut loose with machine guns from all of our tanks at the Iraqi infantry in front of us. The platoon's drivers accelerated to close in on the enemy as the gunners fired several quick bursts. One of the least appreciated aspects of the tank is its shock effect. The weapon systems and optical sights are so sophisticated that we tend to focus on the tank as a long-distance killer and forget the tank's awesome capability in taking ground and crushing obstacles and enemy in its path.

The enemy dismounts threw up their hands as we barreled toward them. My platoon ceased firing, rolled past them and over a dune on the far side of the building.

"Underberg, fire up that building," I ordered. I wanted to ensure we roused anything left after Downing's sabot.

Underberg loved firing his loader's machine gun. He jumped up in his hatch, swung it around, and put one hundred rounds through the target in a few seconds. The building caught fire. A few Iraqis ran out a door. Underberg cut them down, riddling them with machine gun bullets.

As the platoon rounded the far side of the building, we found another fifty dismounts just sitting on the sand in a big group. Arabs never ceased to amaze me. In the last two minutes, about twenty-five .50 cal rounds, a sabot round, and hundreds of machine gun bullets had flown all around these guys, torching their building and killing or wounding who knows how many. It hadn't seemed to bother these folks at all.

At least they mustered the energy to raise their hands to surrender. Had Underberg not been reloading, he probably would have already wasted the whole lot. my platoon rolled a couple of hundred meters past the building and set up in over-watch as the other two platoons encircled the enemy dismounts. We dispersed each tank about 150 meters apart and scanned the horizon.

Our new prisoners barely qualified as soldiers. They were poorly clothed and hardly equipped. They looked gaunt and undisciplined. They were very old and very young. They looked pathetic. Quite a contrast with us. Sure, we looked pretty beat up after seven months of living in the desert, but still, every American had a complete uniform, including a bullet protective vest and Kevlar helmet, a functioning weapon, and plenty of food and water.

Tanks are great for closing with and destroying the enemy, but they aren't worth much in capturing and processing prisoners. I hated sitting still. Let tankers roll across the open battlefield shooting and crushing stuff in our past, and we are happy as clams.

Captain Hubner radioed Flash to request grunts from one of the infantry companies from 3-15 attached to Task Force 1-64. Soon after, a platoon of four Bradleys appeared. Out jumped their dismounts, led by 2d Lt. Mark Jennings. Mark had been my class's first captain our senior year at West Point, the highest ranking cadet in the corps. His predecessors have names like Lee and MacArthur. Mark loved being an infantryman He looked the part: tall, lean, strapping, handsome. And after six months under the Saudi sun, tan.

I kept one eye on our horizon and the other on Mark's platoon as the processed the captured Iraqis using their five Ss checklist: seize the prisoner, secure their weapon, silence them, separate the officers from enlisted men, and search them for maps or other information.

Have fun, Mark. The rest of us needed to get moving again.

Hubner gave us the word, and we headed north. We rolled on, firing up dismounts, herding prisoners, and always moving. We encountered similar skirmished more frequently as we penetrated into Iraq. As we approached the Euphrates River, however, the quality of enemy solider improved. Better equipped and considerably more tenacious – at least these guys shot back at us in a somewhat organized manner. We had yet to face a credible threat to a tank battalion, but the danger was noticeably increasing.

The desert changed as well as we traveled north toward the Euphrates: more vegetation, flatter terrain, and even running water. Underberg kept feeding me mapsheets as we left one and moved to the next. We were both surprised at how quickly we were advancing.

A little later that day, during a refuel on the move (ROM) in the middle of a pretty bad sandstorm, the company first sergeant was trying to bring the fuel trucks to us and got lost. No one knew what to do. We didn't have a clue where he was, and he didn't have a Loran or GPS or anything. I was listening on the company net. Hubner was almost in pain – I could hear it in his voice – trying to talk First Sergeant Walker back to the company. Somehow Sfc. Sikes figured out where Top was. It was amazing. Sikes took off in his tank into the sandstorm, found Top, and brought him and the fuelers to the company. Previously there had been a lot of bad blood between Sikes and Top, due in no small measure to the fact that Sikes had seniority over Walker but the latter was the company's first sergeant. The company listened to Sikes and Top over the radio, very much aware of the animosity between them. But none of that mattered. They had risen above their old feeling and got along fine after that night. The more I think about it, the more I think Sikes damn near saved Walker's hide, or at least kept him in the game, at the risk of getting himself lost or killed. His actions were comparable to diving into the water to rescue a man overboard.

DAVE TRYBULA (Charlie Tank, Task Force 1-64 Armor)

Later on the twenty-fifth, Captain Hidjis spoke over the radio, "Execute desert laager, REDCON 2, leaders in my fix in ten." During the resupply, the commander wanted me in his tank.

I relayed the order to my platoon. Desert laager, REDCON 2, I'll be at the CO's tank. Take a good look at your vehicles while we have the chance and clean the air filters.

My platoon came to a halt in a column with approximately fifty feet between tanks. I had climbed out of my hatch and was putting on my gear when my loader yelled, "One-Two's on fire!" I looked up and saw flames shooting fifty feet skyward from the back of my wingman's tank. I yelled at my gunner, "Sergeant Godfrey get me the fire extinguisher!" It seemed to take him an eternity. Blood rushed through my head and my mind raced. There had been no explosion so I was pretty sure the fire had not been caused by the incoming Iraqi fire. But the flames and smoke were a sure sign of our presence to anyone within twenty or thirty miles. Godfrey finally unfastened the fire extinguisher and threw it out of the hatch to me. I caught it and began to run, forgetting I was still on top of my turret. Somehow I vaulted the nine feet to the ground in stride and continued to run toward the burning tank, arriving at the front of C12 as the driver pulled his lever to activate the tank's halon fire extinguisher system. I moved to the tank's rear, shouting for everyone to move back as well.

The tank's commander, S.Sgt. Bill Brackett, had gotten his handheld fire extinguisher from his gunner, and the two of us stood side by side, discharging our fire extinguishers at the increasingly dangerous flame. The fire was close to igniting the five hundred gallons of jet fuel and the tank's entire basic load of ammunition. I was sure our two five-pound fire extinguishers were futile against the raging inferno.

By the grace of God, we somehow extinguished the flame. I didn't know how. I gave Sergeant Brackett several more fire extinguishers in case the fire reignited, then checked on the rest of my platoon.

When I returned, I spoke to Sergeant Brackett. "Okay, I think we've got this under control. Let's keep a couple of people on it with fire extinguishers just in case, and call maintenance to check out your tank."

Sergeant Godfrey came running up, interrupted, and blurted, "Sir, Black Six want you on the radio now! He said to grab you and get you talking to him ASAP!"

Not knowing what the CO wanted and concerned that the fire had indeed been seen by an Iraqi unit, I instructed Brackett to check our the vehicle and determine how much damage was done. I ran back to my tank and spoke with the commander. He told me a movement order would be issued soon.

My heart was still pounding. The fire reinforced in me the need to check equipment for serviceability. We would have lost one tank, and possible several soldiers to injury, if the fire extinguishers had been empty or not accessible. The whole incident made me extremely proud of my platoon and more confident that we had prepared sufficiently to react to emergencies.

The maintenance team arrived, assessed the vehicle, and fixed it within minutes. Almost as soon as it was ready, we began moving again.

NEAL CREIGHTON (Alpha Tank, Task Force 3-15 Infantry)

We had stopped for a short while. First Sergeant Foote came over to my tank and got out of his Humvee to say something to me. I got out of my hatch and was standing on top of the turret. I don't remember what he told me. When he left I turned back around and stepped into the open loader's hatch. My loader Carroll caught me as I fell on top of him, grabbed my feet, and shoved me back toward the hatch, which was in its upright, open position. My glassed fell off, and I hit the hatch right beneath my eye. I was out, laying on top of the turret.

For a good thirty seconds I didn't know where I was. I got off the tank and headed for the medic; my gunner asked me where I was going, and all I said was "Bank Aid." As soon as I got back Captain Schwartz was on the radio telling me to move out "now." I started navigating again, although I still didn't quite know where I was. For the first two or three minutes leading the task force, I was out of it.

ALEX VERNON (Delta Mech, Task Force 3-15 Infantry)

We hit Objective Gray about 1600; it was an empty sand bowl. The battalion's combat companies formed a circle around the bowl. We refueled and pushed on.

I don't remember much else of this day. At some point we passed another artillery group traveling three or four columns abreast, which held up in a wadi to our south to let us pass to their front. The task force halted again when, driving by a dry creek with greenery, someone spied Iraqi soldiers in the creek. Either the task force scouts or a platoon from Delta Mech were sent to clear the creek. We sat and watched from a distance, Sergeant Dock looking through his sights to give the crew a blow-by-blow account. We recovered a number of weapons and captured several Iraqis. My brief letter of the twenty-eighth, the first I have a chance to write, gives the entire day only two sentences. The second records that on the way to our objective, which we hit about 1600 hours, "our scouts captured about ten POW's." I don't now know if these are the same soldiers as those captured at the creek.

As were watched the infantry investigate the dry creek, the weather turned, dark blue clouds encroaching. By the time we stopped for the night the cold and dark had returned.

When we stopped, Captain Baillergeon called the platoon leaders to his track. An Iraqi Republican Guard division was headed toward us. I believe the unit was retreating through our area, not knowing we were there, instead of counterattacking us. Baillergeon sketched in the sand the different company positions and the engagement area, where all the battalion's fires would be concentrated. He assigned each platoon a portion of the company's part of the engagement area and ordered our platoon into defensive positions covering assigned areas.

The terrain, however, did not accommodate the plan. We sat in an unwaveringly flat piece of desert. No cover or concealment of any sort. The engagement area also had no identifiable features by which we could distinguish it, much less sectors of responsibility to assign each of my tanks within it. So I set my platoon as I had my first night in the desert with 2-4 Cav: I spaced them far enough apart so that no two tanks could be ranged by a single incoming indirect fire round, and far enough apart so that an enemy vehicle could not acquire two tanks in his sights at once, but near enough that we could communicated orally. I did not bother trying to hide us behind any military horizon because the terrain was simply too flat. I arranged the platoon so that if each tank scanned from fender to fender, we would ensure overlapping sectors of fire within the platoon and also with the flanking infantry platoons. Two soldiers awake per tank, and two tanks scanning the engagement area throughout the night.

Early in the evening several Bradleys, Humvees, and medic M113 PCs flew by from the task force combat supply trains behind us toward Alpha Tank's position to our right front. I would later learn from Baillergeon what happened, what Neal Creighton was about to discover.

When my tank wasn't scanning I slept on the back deck. It drizzled all night. I pulled my poncho liner over me and got two or three hours of sleep.

No Iraqi units appeared.

NEAL CREIGHTON (Alpha Tank, Task Force 3-15 Infantry)

Around noon on the twenty-fifth, we attacked Objective Gray. Captain Schwartz gave the word to hit the gas, and we went full throttle. First Platoon moved up on the line with my platoon and the Bradley platoons swung in behind us, covering the gaps in the formation.

Looking to the west, I saw a group of Iraqi soldiers sitting huddled together. They waved a white cloth as we stormed past. We continued to push forward while the gunners scanned for enemy combat vehicles. The company came to a halt on Gray and then moved quickly into hasty defensive positions. Sergeant Davis spotted more enemy soldiers to the north through his gunner's sights, and I reported their location to Captain Schwartz. He ordered a section from my platoon forward with a section from on of the Bradley platoons.

I took my tank north and sent Sergeant Jones northeast. Jones immediately spotted a group of Iraqis and moved toward them with his tank and a Bradley. I saw nothing in my sector and radioed the supporting Bradley to move back to the company. As our drive turned the tank around, we almost ran over twenty Iraqis hiding in a shallow wadi.

"Stop!" I yelled into the mike.

"I got'em, sir." Sergeant Davis had trained the coaxial machine gun on them.

I stared for about half a minute at these fierce soldiers whom we had heard so much about. They were in mixed, dirty uniforms. They looked helpless and desperate. My trance was broken by Pfc. Carrol as he screamed at them in Arabic to lay down. Fear spread across their faces.

"Sergeant Davis, I'm jumping down, so don't shoot or move the turret. Carrol, cover me." Carrol manned the loader's 7.62. I jumped down and walked toward the group. "Carrol, yell out 'friend' in Arabic," I said. Carrol did, and several of the Iraqis rushed up and bear-hugged me.

The nerves on both sides faded. Carrol jumped down to help me frisk the prisoners. Some of the Iraqis began to frisk one another, as if they thought this was some type of American greeting.

We ran over their weapons with our tank and loaded the prisoners on top of our vehicle. As I hopped back on the tank, I heard an explosion and saw a dust cloud rising over the company location. We headed slowly back to the company with the Iraqis clinging on the top of the turret and hull of our tank.

As we neared the commander's tank, I saw my first dead soldiers. Unfortunately, they were Americans. Two fine young men lay in the sand. They were from the Bradley that had supported my move forward only ten minutes earlier. The soldiers were the victims of a terrible mistake. Their platoon leader had instructed them to wear grenades on their LBEs for the several-hundred-kilometer ride in the back of their Bradleys. The vibrations and limited space of the Bradley caused the safety clip to fall off the pin from one of the soldier's grenades. When the Bradley stopped on Objective Gray, the infantrymen exited from the cramped rear door instead of exiting by the dropped Bradley ramp. As the soldier's equipment rubbed the side of the steel doorway, the pin was yanked from the grenade. The explosion killed the soldier and the man behind him. A third soldier was wounded.

The soldiers did not need to wear their grenades for the duration of the movement. They would have had more than enough time to uncrate the grenades when needed. I attributed the mistake to our lack of combat experience. A lesson was learned from the sacrifice of two Americans.

First Sergeant Foote covered the bodies and removed the unexploded grenades from the dead soldiers' belts. He tied strings to the safety pins, placed the grenades outside of our perimeter and detonated them remotely by yanking on the string. My tank was the closest to the grenades, and I didn't know he was doing this until after the explosion startled me.

I moved our tank into a hasty defensive position and put out a net call to my platoon. "All white elements, we will remain here tonight and resume movement tomorrow. Begin preparing hasty defensive positions and start priority of work, out." I looked out over the desert and began to wonder if death would find more of us tomorrow.

26 FEBRUARY 1991 (G+2)

NEAL CREIGHTON (Alpha Tank, Task Force 3-15 Infantry)

We moved out again early in the morning. The fog was so thick I couldn't see fifty meters in any direction. The company tightened the formation and took the lead as the task force advance guard.

As we moved, intelligence reports came over the command net about the enemy on our next objective, Objective Orange. This time we would fight a Republican Guard unit on Jalibah Airfield. We had briefly planned the attack on the airfield though we had not updated the order given the most current information on enemy locations and dispositions. I really never thought we would make it so far so quickly. I relayed the intelligence reports to the platoon over our internal radio net.

Late that night we stopped just short of Jalibah. As darkness fell, the artillery lit up the sky with a constant barrage on the airfield. We would attack very soon. I fell asleep.

ALEX VERNON (Delta Mech, Task Force 3-15 Infantry)

We moved at 0300 hours. The weather was worse than the first night: rain and zero illumination. With my PVS-7s, I could only see the taillights on other vehicles that were yards away. Distinguishing tanks from Bradleys, then one unit from the next, was nearly impossible. The "bud lights" we strapped to our taillights – small, infrared light – emitting diodes visible through our night vision devices, and powered by common rectangular twelve-volt batteries – were invisible. Over the radio we directed each other to flash brake lights, wave flashlights or chem. Lights, spin a turret, or move a gun tube up and down, to identify one another. The task force took over an hour to form, a task that in good conditions takes minutes.

The day eventually cleared, and again as we traveled we encountered surrendering Iraqis. There were too many this time for the scouts to handle, so Lieutenant Colonel Barrett tasked my company to police one group. Initially my tanks sat in overwatch while the infantry searched the POWs, removing weapons and papers, and binding their hands. I joined First Platoon leader, Lt. Brian Luke, on the ground to survey the situation. The Iraqis were in rows, most on their knees, some supine. They were dirty and ragged, and a number did not have shoes. Some had light wounds. Across the road, on the other side of a low mound of sand, Brian and I saw three or four wild dogs, their heads bent, busy, bobbing on the ground; when we approached, we realized they were feeding on Iraqi corpses. Brian chased the dogs off. They hung on the periphery, knowing we'd have to leave eventually, when they could resume their meal.

Brian and I had to move the POWs several kilometers to the task force's collection point. From there, either battalion trucks would transport them to some collection site further back, or they would wait under guard for a collection unit coming forward to gather them. My platoon started walking the POWs, the group sandwiched between my two tank sections; Sergeant Freight's section was leading, their turrets swung to the rear, machine guns ready, my section trailing. Several grunts from Brian's platoon walked on the outside of the Iraqis. Not two hundred meters into this march, we knew it would take too long to walk them to the collection point. I decided to load the Iraqis on the tanks and drive them. Freight's section would carry them, my section would follow, our machine guns locked and loaded.

Because the POWs hands were bound behind them, Sergeants Boss and Dock hauled them onto the back decks of Freight's two tanks. From the ground Dock would get a POW halfway up, the POW's foot on the tank track and Dock underneath him, and from the back deck Boss pulled the man the rest of the way, often by the man's belt. We squeezed about fifteen Iraqis on the back of each tank – those without shoes hung their feet off the sides, away from the blazing hot engine. I ordered the crews of both those tanks to unload the turret-mounted machine guns and button-up inside the turret, hatches closed and locked. This got them out of harm's way, either from an Iraqi or from the machine guns from my section's two tanks, trailing the two tanks carrying the prisoners and now free to shoot without risk to our own.

We delivered the POWs without incident a short time later. The battalion captured roughly one hundred POWs that day.

Later in the afternoon the terrain changed. The dusty, rocky flats gave way to a maze of wadis, berms, and dunes. The dunes particularly were precarious because the sand slid under the vehicles. Twice my tank drove over the tapering end of a dune and slid down the side several meters. A vehicle that crossed too high on a dune could have easily flipped. After passing over the edge of one dune, I looked back to watch my wingman go over, and saw a Bedouin family clustered against it, the parents and two children, hidden from the view of oncoming vehicles. They had been smart to pick a dune, since we couldn't cross straight overtop. Still, they weren't entirely out of danger. I warned my platoon and then the company to stay clear.

The company alternately traveled in staggered-column and single-column formation through the mess of wadis. For much of this leg of the day's attack I could not see Alpha Tank, the battalion's lead company, on which I guided my movement. I caught glimpses, guessed, and sometimes asked Captain Baillergeon to guess for me. Each fork in the wadi, each berm or dune, we had to dodge, presented a choice that could separate us from the task force. Each fork we took, each berm or dune we dodged, also contorted my sense of direction. I did not have a GPS, I did not know to what GIRS we were headed or where we were in relation to that GIRS. The map gave no details of the terrain that Baillergeon and I might have been able to use to steer the company. He and I navigated by glimpses and hunches, and somehow we came out the other side in formation.

GREG DOWNEY (Scouts, Task Force 1-64 Armor)

At 0430 hours my scout platoon continued the zone recon. It had been a sleepless night for my scouts. The pace exacted a toll on us. I could tell by the voices on my platoon radio frequency that we were getting tired. During the last five days, I had slept a total of no more than ten hours. Easy mental tasks were becoming increasingly difficult. My drivers were getting some rest, but the gunners were probably in the worst shape. Lowther had a permanent bruise across his brow from the padded headrest over his gunner's sight. His eyes were fried, shot through with red, from the constant peering through the sight. Yet he never complained. Once in a while I'd nudge him when I thought he'd drifted asleep, when the turret stopped tracking the horizon. He would resume scanning.

We were moving toward Objective Orange, Jalibah Airfield, deep inside Iraqi, almost directly north of Kuwait. I had seen satellite imagery a few weeks before that showed Iraqi tanks and BMPs – the Iraqi version of the Bradley – dug-in around Jalibah. A fight was waiting for us.

En route to Battle Position 103, a position west of Objective Orange, two OH-58D helicopters and an AH-1 Cobra from the divisional air cavalry flew over my section. They landed before I could look up their radio frequency and talk to them on the radio. I dismounted to speak with them. The pilot was pretty shaken up. They had just been engaged by direct fire east of our location. He didn't have much else to tell me. Something was up ahead.

I called back to report to the battalion TOC and pushed to the east. We recon'd through BP 103 and cleared the task force's area. Lieutenant Colonel Gordon had been keeping my scout platoon anywhere from ten to eight kilometers forward of the task force. We pushed east of 103 to screen the zone. First Brigade was passing through our zone behind my screen.

ROB HOLMES (Delta Tank, Task Force 1-64 Armor)

Sometime during the sandstorm, we knew there were targets in front of us. We didn't know what they were at first. No one could really see what was going on, but we knew there was something out there. They turned our to be Iraqi scout trucks. I gave my gunner the order to fire. Sergeant Dowing hesitated.

I started to drop down in my seat to grab the override and do it myself when he fired the gun. He shot way over. And he did it on purpose. I know he did. This was the man who claimed to be the best gunner in the army, and who might very well have been. After Downing missed, my wingman blasted the Iraqi truck from my right flank, igniting a huge explosion.

When things settled down, Downing and I got off the tank and proceeded to yell and scream at one another. He was in tears. I didn't know what to do. We're in the middle of Iraq, and I've got a gunner who hesitated pulling the trigger. To be honest I don't remember how I dealt with him. We mounted back up and kept going. Needless to say the incident stuck in my mind the rest of the time we were in Iraq.

Sergeant Downing was very devout, very evangelical, and during Desert Shield had been really opposed to our attacking. He we never vocal about it, and he maintained his professionalism, but he made it very clear that he did not want to go to war. Hell, none of us did, but we all sure wanted to go home alive. Here's an NCO who have been in the army eleven years, and it wasn't like any of us wanted to go to war, yet his attitude seemed to be, "I can't believe you're asking me to do this."

I'd like to think that I never had any bloodlust. When I gave an order to fire it was with as much prudence as I could have. For the rest of the war I couldn't shake it: He had missed on purpose. I almost looked forward to our next engagement with the enemy, so Downing could destroy a target and restore my confidence.

GREG DOWNEY (Scouts, Task Force 1-64 Armor)

"Jesus Christ, what was that!" screamed Lowther, as dust bellowed in the turret from the concussion.

"West, get us moving!" I yelled over the intercom.

"Blue Six, get you're vehicle moving!" I ordered over the radio to S. Sergeant Hightower, my wingman.

The sound of incoming artillery broke up the hum of my vehicle. Hightower and his crew had exscaped death by inches. An Iraqi forward observer had eyes on us as we occupied the screen. The artillery was not very heavy but pretty accurate. My section was the only one under fire, so I tried to reposition just myself and Blue Six. We received artillery each time we moved. The impacts produced severe concussions inside my vehicle, and the scouts in the crew compartment in back were feeling every round.

"Blue Six, this is Black One, over," I called again.

"Goddamn-it, West, keep us moving, try to find some cover," I said. It was an impossible task in the incredibly flat piece of desert.

I kept waiting for Hightower to move his vehicle or to answer my call on the radio. Neither was happening. The artillery continued to fall around his vehicle, rocking the twenty-six-ton Bradley from side to side. Incoming artillery plays with you. You never know where the next round will fall. I had terrible feelings of paranoia, like somebody was looking at me through a pair of binoculars, carefully plotting my location, and calling for the next barrage. Which is exactly what was happening.

"Answer the goddamned radio, Hightower!" I yelled inside my own turret.

"West, come in from behind Blue Six's vehicle; it looks like there's some low ground. I can't reach him on the radio, so get me close enough that I can run over to talk to him."

West positioned our Bradley behind Hightower's. As I was dismounting, and artillery round impacted off to my right, blowing me off the front slope of my vehicle. Sergeant Hightower was only fifteen meters from my vehicle, but in that short gap rounds were sporadically falling. I could not see him looking out his hatch. The vehicle did not look as if it had been hit. I climbed up on his vehicle and looked down at him through the hatch. He was frantically trying to call me on the radio, not knowing I was only a short distance away. His radio was working fine' he was talking to Sergeants Deem and Smith. Looking back on my vehicle, I noticed one of my radio antennas was missing.

I made it to his vehicle with no problem, so I figured the chances of making it back to mine were good. I had been a sprinter in college. I always liked the one hundred-meter dash – mad and short and over in ten seconds, barely enough running to made me breathe hard. Even though the distance I had to cover back to my vehicle was less than fifty meters, it looked much farther. And now my competition was artillery rounds.

Racing back in a dead sprint, I heard it coming at the last second, like a superfast lawn sprinkler, the type that rotates, spraying a stream of water, rattling. I remember seeing sky, ground, sky, then ground, then my face shoved into the sand. I landed on my head, dazed and startled. I didn't feel any pain at first. Then my right side started to throb. Everything was still attached, but my chemical suit was torn on the right side and I couldn't hear out of my right ear.

Still in shock, I pushed my body up with my arms and got up. I saw something on the ground, something silver. A chain. A medal. My Saint Christopher's medal. Ironic – the last time I had lost it I almost lost my life. I grabbed it, put it in my pocket, and kept running. I didn't bother to check for any blood until I made it back to my vehicle. My hip was numb, but otherwise I felt all right. I replaced the damaged antenna with a new one, regained communications with the platoon, and moved out of the impact area.

I could soon tell from where the enemy was firing the artillery. I was now looking down on its defensive position. I called the battalion fire support officer for some artillery support, but before I could finish the transmission, division artillery was already firing on the Iraqi artillery. Division radar can detect artillery immediately after it is launched and determine its origin within seconds. Then it targets the firing enemy unit for a counterbattery strike. American artillerymen brag that they can get rounds in the air before the initial enemy rounds hit their target.

Once the Iraqi guns were silenced, I went to work on the defenses below me.

The FSO relayed to me that the artillery units were ready to fire. I had already made polar plots on the target. A polar plot is the most accurate means of calling for indirect fire. You use your own known location and a distance and a direction to the target. The Trimpack GPS provided to my ten-digit grid location, the lensatic compass gave the direction to target, and my GVS-5 handheld laser range finder gave me the distance to the target within five meters.

Before high technology made its appearance on the battlefield, survey crews would have to come out to point on the ground where the polar plot would be called in from. They would survey the site, recording the grid location for the artillery observer. The compass has been around for decades, always providing direction for the observer. Distance was determined with a graduated scale superimposed in the lens of the binoculars. Place your target in the scale, do a little battlefield arithmetic, and cross your fingers. As the first rounds hit, you called back adjustments. This method was very time consuming and required firing many more artillery rounds to hit the target.

The first artillery rounds fired were from the eight-inch howitzer. A battalion's worth of artillery impacting all at once is a terrifying sight. I could observe Iraqi infantry moving to the west side of their defensive positions. I was a safe two kilometers away and could easily observe them. Rockets from MLRS came next. I gave different firing data to the FSO because of my previous experience with MLRS rounds landing one kilometer over and one kilometer to the left. This time the rounds were on the mark. We pounded the target area for forty-five minutes, Darkness had fallen and the firing eventually stopped.

My scout platoon continued to screen Task Force 1-64's portion of BP 103 until the task force arrived into position. Iraqi soldiers started moving toward my section at about 2000 hours. As we watched them come to us, some of them fell down, too injured to walk farther, or dying. I dispatched a dismounted patrol, along with my medic, to gather them up and guide them to my location. The medic, Specialist Burton, administered first aid to those who had a chance. Some were not going to last another hour. An Iraqi captain was one of the survivors. To my amazement, he spoke fluent English. I spoke to him for a few minutes to see what he knew while Burton put on tourniquet on a solider missing his hand.

The Iraqi captain told me he was in the Republican Guard 26th Commando Brigade and that there had been 650 men in the brigade. When I asked him how many more men were alive, he said, "This is all…this is all." He started weeping. Only forty-nine Iraqi soldiers remained, all standing before me with horrified looks on their faces. They had just glimpsed hell.

I had called the artillery that erased the lives of over six hundred human beings. In forty-five minutes, I had killed more people than whet lived in my hometown of Merna, Nebraska. Combat is a series of contradictions. One moment you're trying your best to kill the enemy, the next moment you're doing your best to save him. I looked at the shock in the Iraqis' eyes. For the first time during the ground attack, I felt guilt and sorrow.

We handed the POWs off to an infantry platoon from Charlie Mech. I told the platoon leader not to let any others die. There had been enough dying for the night.

The scout platoon moved back to the task force's location to be resupplied. We were low on fuel, food, and water. We have plenty of ammunition, but the medic had used up all of the morphine and most of his first aid supplies on the Iraqis. This was the first time I had seen the battalion in two days. Despite out lack of sleep, we would feel the momentum racing throughout the battalion.

My vehicle radiator had developed a leak, probably from the artillery, so we us some silicone to patch it up. It worked a little, but most of the thirty-five gallons of water we carried for drinking was drained into the radiator. It would be a constant battle to keep the vehicle engine cooling properly.

ROB HOLMES (Delta Tank, Task Force 1-64 Armor)

Late in the afternoon my loader Underberg handed me a special mapsheet. This one had my notes all over it and had been subject to much discussion back at Graceland. I had spent many nights wondering what would happen to us when we arrived at Objective Orange.

Flash had briefed us all about it back in Saudi. The Iraqi Republican Guard used Jalibah Airfield as a key logistical site for fuel, ammunition, and supplies. They defended it accordingly: two tank companies, artillery and mortars, and about one thousand infantry. Jalibah was critical. It sat in the past between Baghdad and Basra. Once we captured it, we closed the door on the Republican Guard's escape from Kuwait. If we could meet the Republican Guard in the flat, open Euphrates River Valley with the main allied force pushing the enemy from behind and the air force ravaging them from above, we would obliterate the enemy.

The sun was setting with Jalibah only about thirty kilometers away when Captain Hubner radioed that we would attack at midnight.

I was not thrilled. The conventional wisdom was that we always want to fight at night because we have better vision. Our thermal sights see three thousand meters while Soviet-made tanks see only about fifteen hundred meters. That's fine if you're getting twenty-five hundred meter shots and the enemy can't touch you, but who cares if you are caught up in an airfield complex and are engaging at three hundred meters? Furthermore, we were still very inexperienced combat soldiers. Regardless of the night sights, command and control suffers at night. Leaders have to spend much more time on navigation, coordination, and most importantly, distributing firepower. I was specifically worried about friendly fire.

My platoon led the task force to an attack position eight kilometers southwest of Jalibah. We parked, lined up, and did our pit crew drill as the fuelers replenished our tanks. Gunners updated their sights; loaders checked their ammo racks; drivers inspected their tracks. Everyone knew the test waiting for us ahead. They were all busy refueling and blowing air filters, so I was brief with a handshake or quip. They were all good men. In peacetime I could easily rank my soldiers based on discipline, competence, and intelligence. Some were terrific; some were a nightmare. At this point though, all I could think about was what good men these guys were. They knew the significance of Jalibah and its heavy defenses, but they all went about their jobs and returned my smile and handshake as I walked by.

Crazy as this sounds, I wasn't nervous. I wasn't even scared. I have always been someone who tries to visualize the future and pray for it. I didn't know what was planned for my future, but I never once thought that I would leave Iraq with even a scratch. Now was no different. The thought of one of my guys getting wounded or killed, however, was absolutely intolerable. I was directly responsible for the men in my platoon. I had seen all the old movies about the officer writing the letter home to the family of a soldier who had been killed. I thought of my parents and brother and my soldiers' families. I couldn't bear even to consider not bringing one home.

As I walked around while we refueled, I had on my game face like never before. I didn't jumped around like at a pep rally, didn't want to go "kick their ass" or anything like that. I just felt intense and focused. My world was very simple. We were about to attack a heavily defended objective that threatened the lives of my men. Get in my way, and I will kill you.

Before we could pull any triggers that night, however, Hubner radioed after having just talked to Flash. Evidently, someone higher had decided to wait until dawn and attack Jalibah with the whole brigade instead of just Task Force 1-64. In addition, two artillery battalions would move up to pound the airfield prior to our assault. I love artillery.

I mounted my tank and realized that we had a couple hours of waiting before we attacked: Sleep! The cliché about combat being a continuous series of emotional swings is really true. I went from being loaded, cocked, lethal weapon to a sleeping baby in a matter of minutes. Sergeant Downing set a schedule for my crew so that three could sleep while one listened to the radio. In four hours we would attack a heavily defended objective, but right now I could crash and make up for the last forty-eight hours of fighting and moving three hundred kilometers through Iraq. I grabbed a blanket, jumped onto the back deck of the M1, and I was out like a light.

ALEX VERNON (Delta Mech, Task Force 3-15 Infantry)

We stopped about 2200 in our assault position for the next morning's attack on Objective Orange. Captain Baillergeon disappeared to the battalion TOC for his orders. On his return trip, he radioed ahead so that the platoon leaders would be waiting at his Bradley. This was about midnight. He briefed us; we returned and briefed our platoons. Fifty percent security again for the remaining hours of the night. I remember lying awake, watching the lights of aircraft overhead, and hearing the distant rumble of bombs.

The plan I remember: The task force would travel to the airfield to our direct east in a box formation: Bravo and Alpha Tanks the front left and right corners. As we neared the airfield my company would move forward, on line with and on the right of Alpha Tank to prepare to assault the runway, while the left side of the box would peel off to the northern edge of the compound to occupy a hasty defense guarding our flank. Meanwhile Task Force 1-64 Armor, to our south, would also hit the airfield with two companies, and leave two companies watching its flank on the southern edge of the compound. As 3-15's rightmost unit, my company team was to link with 1-64's leftmost unit at the west side of the airfield for our synchronized run across it, four companies with all platoons abreast. I remember Delta Tank, Rob Holmes's company, as 1-64's leftmost unit in the assault plan, the unit with which I was to ride side by side down the center runway.

Splitting the assault force between the two task forces did not make much sense to me. I regretted already that the only way I could talk with the company beside me was by calling up the chain from company to battalion to the brigade net, where the task forces talked, and then back down Rob's chain to his company. Not the sort of immediate communication you need with the fellow beside you in a battle. It did not occur to me at the time to set one of my programmable frequency switch settings to Delta Tank's net so I could talk to Rob during the assault, much less call his unit to attempt some sore of preattack coordination. I was tired, I guess, and not used to thinking beyond my express orders. Battle drills don't leave much room for creative initiative – for much of the war I felt very much just along for the ride. I did look forward to seeing Rob, my Fort Stewart roommate and one of my closest friends, on my right flank. One of our cadet company mates, a man from small-town Mississippi, had once described Rob as having been born with a horseshoe up his butt. Short of my being in Delta Tank or being in Delta Mech, I could not have been any closer to that horseshoe.

DAVE TRYBULA (Charlie Tank, Task Force 1-64 Armor)

Just prior to dusk on 26 February, the company commander returned from a quick orders brief at the tactical operations center and called all the platoon leaders and the company's fire support officer over to his tank. He spoke in a quiet voice: "We're going to stay in our hasty defense tonight until around 0300. Then we will move as a task force reserve in the rear of the diamond while the brigade conducts a deliberate attack to seize Jalibah Airfield. Task Force 3-15 will attack in the north. Okay, lets look at the map. An on-order boundary had been established between us and 3-69 along this road south of Jalibah," he said, pointing to the road on his map. "We anticipate setting a base of fire with the mechanized infantry companies along this position and conducting a western envelopment with Delta Tank and us. The runway is our on-order boundary with 3-15 for the assault. We will use company Vee formation, which means that Dave, you'll lead the company's envelopment. Remember to make a bold movement to the flank prior to turning back toward the assault position. Rogue Six said he would work a smoke mission to mark your turn. Any questions? Good, go back to your platoons, make sure they know what is going on. We will pull out of the hasty defense and form up not later than 0300. Anticipate receiving an intelligence update from battalion prior to movement. Keep your sleep plan going. Your people need to be fresh in the morning.

27 FEBRUARY 1991 (G+3)
The Assault on Jalibah Airfield

GREG DOWNEY (Scouts, Task Force 1-64 Armor)

After the resupply, the scout platoon moved out at 0200 hours. The task force was right behind us. Lieutenant Colonel Gordon was gambling that we would not hit any resistance as we approached BP Bed, our attack position for Objective Orange. It was very secure feeling. An armored task force that could defeat anything the enemy had to offer surrounded me. I was accustomed to having only my wingman, with my other two sections two and a half kilometers away on each flank. I realized it wasn't me against the whole Iraqi army, though at time it had certainly felt that way.

We closed on BP Bed at 0300 hours. Rogue Six's voice came up on the net. Flash Gordon sounded like an old man, the weariness of battle having begun to take its toll on the tough warrior. The words were drawn from the bottom of his exhausted lungs. Despite his fatigue, he knew exactly how the battle would be fought. He had visualized this fight in his mind for several weeks, analyzing the enemy's actions and reactions, developing counteractions for the task force to respond with, and picturing himself and his armored task force destroying the enemy in a very detailed manner. In Gordon's mind, the battle had already been fought and won.

The scout platoon was to run coordination points between the flanks. Red Section would tie into Task Force 3-15 Infantry, the battalion on our left. Blue Section would tie into Task Force 3-69 Armor, the battalion on our right. My section would go forward of the task force, providing a security blanket for Delta Tank. Blue Section was successful with their link-up with the left flank company of Task Force 3-69, but Red Section could not establish link-up with 3-15. I had my Red Section return to my location after receiving approval from Lieutenant Colonel Gordon.

We moved east to observe the objective. We had not traveled far when I could see the huge hangars through my thermal sight, the heat of the concrete-constructed hangars illuminated through my optics. At 0500, the artillery preparation started. Once again, the devastation was unbelievable. I watched Iraqi soldiers running across the airfield to the west side. The enemy knew our approach direction because of

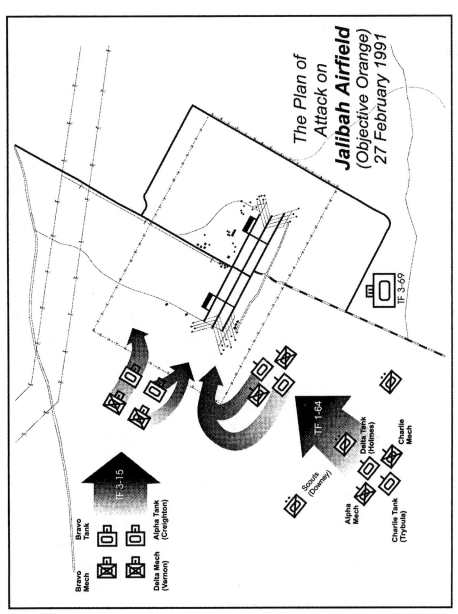

The labels within the figure:

The Plan of Attack on **Jalibah Airfield** (Objective Orange) 27 February 1991

TF 3-69

TF 1-64

TF 3-15

Bravo Mech

Bravo Tank

Alpha Tank (Creighton)

Delta Mech (Vernon)

Scouts (Downey)

Delta Tank (Holmes)

Charlie Mech

Alpha Mech

Charlie Tank (Trybula)

The Plan of Attack on Jalibah Airfield (Objective Orange), 27 February 1991.

where the artillery was coming from. What the did not know was that an armored brigade of 116 M1A1 tanks and over sixty M2A1 Bradley Fighting Vehicles would descend upon them within the hour.

"Lowther, what do you think is going through their minds right now?" I asked, squinting my eye against my thermal sight, observing the chaos on the airfield.

"I don't know, sir, but in about an hour, their asses will be going through it," said Lowther, laughing as he traversed the turret to another part of the airfield.

At 0600 hours, the brigade started its move. Red Section was driving along the left boundary of the task force, and I pulled my own section over to its location. I wanted to get out of the way before the task force rolled up to the airfield.

"Black One, this is Red Two," S.Sergeant Deem called over the radio, "I've got a missle coming." Deem's report immediately sent my eyes into a frantic search. Deem had observed a white puff of smoke rising from the corner of the airfield, the signature of an antitank missile. I focused my eyes on the area and could see the wire-guided missile flying our way. The missile moved more slowly than I thought it would, giving us time to react. Before the war I had skeptically received training, and skeptically trained my platoons, on the sagger dance battle drill, named after the popular Soviet-manufactured version of this infantry weapon, the cousin of our own TOW. I thought we'd never have time to dodge an incoming missile, but they didn't travel nearly as fast as the tank's sabot rounds, and we watched this one coming. It was tracking Deem's vehicle.

"This is Red Two, I'm popping smoke, then doin'a hard left." Deem was telling his wingman what signal would be to start his evasive maneuver. The smoke would also help throw the missile off course, as it would cloud the view of the Iraqi soldier tracking Deem's Bradley in his sights to guide his missile, through the wire, to its target.

"This is Red Two, take a hard right, and do it fast!" Deem yelled.

He launched his on-board smoke grenades to provide a smokescreen and did a hard left turn. The missile hit right where he turned from, throwing debris back into his wingman's vehicle. A near miss, but enough to let up know they had some fight left in them.

A white phosphorous artillery round hit directly on top of the position where the enemy missile had been fired from. No more missiles were launched from that location.

"Contact, contact...choppers! Engaging one HIND!" came S.Sergeant Deem's voice again, mixed with the distinctive thump-thump-thump of his chain gun. Deem was quickly becoming an enemy magnet, engaging an MI-24 HIND-D helicopter on the north side of the airfield. The blades were moving, and the crew was desperately trying to get it off the ground.

"Black One, this is Red Two...I've lost my turret, no power...I can't fire!" he screamed over the net an instant later, his fury transmitting over the radio. He had squeezed off twenty rounds at the helicopter before his turret lost all power, shutting down his weapon systems. The helicopter exploded, the fuel and ammunition igniting from the 25-mm rounds. Deem was finally rattled, the first time I had ever seen him lost control of his emotions. Within one minute, he had dodged a near miss from an antitank missile, destroyed an attack helicopter, and lost his weapon system.

"Black One, this is Red Three, target...target destroyed!" Sergeant Wiggins announced over the radio, finishing the job that Red Two had started.

"This is Black One, roger, get Red Section over here behind this hill," I said, trying to get them under control. I brought them back to my location, where we were pulled up behind a small hill. I looked at Deem's face as he pulled his vehicle over to my location. It was the face of combat; dirty, greasy, dark circles under tired eyes, stress line chiseled in his forehead. He gave me a look that said he's had enough.

" Lowther, go over to Red Two and see if you can get his turret running again," I said, sending my gunner to work his magic with his self-taught mechanical skills. "And don't come back until it's fixed.

"Back in two, sir," Lowther bragged, smiling as he slid through the small hatch on top of the turret.

I looked out across my front. The dust clouds rose from the battlefield. Task Forces 1-64 Armor and 3-15 Infantry were beginning the main attack on the airfield. For once it time for my scouts to sit back and watch.

NEIL CREIGHTON (Alpha Tank, Task Force 3-15 Infantry)

The radio broke my half-conscious daze. "White Six, report to my tank, over." I had slept for only an hour the past day and the commander's voice seemed as if out of a dream. The MLRS battery had pummeled the airfield all night long, and the spectacle and my nerves kept me awake.

"Lieutenant Creighton, did you hear the CO call?" asked Sergeant Davis from the gunner's position.

"Yeah." I keyed the radio, "Black Six, this is White Six, I'm en route to your position." I turned to Davis, "Tell the platoon to get ready to move and that I went to the commander's tank to receive the attack order." I crawled out of my tank commander's position, grabbed my map and compass, and jumped off the tank.

As I arrived at Captain Schwartz's tank, he took roll call of all four platoon leaders, the XO, the fire support officer, and the first sergeant. "We don't have much time and the attack is going to be simple," the captain said as he pointed to his sand-covered map. "Neal, the airfield is that way about five kilometers at a ninety-degree azimuth. Due east. You get us there and to the right hasty defensive position. When Neal's Second Platoon busts onto the airfield, First Platoon will bring its tanks on line with Neal's, and the Bradley platoons will fall behind the tanks, on line, covering the gaps. We still think that a battalion of T-55 tanks is protecting the airfield." Before the captain could start another sentence, the battalion commander broke over the command net.

"Wild Bunch Six, move now."

Without even looking at the commander, I raced toward my tank and mounted the side. I was in the hatch within twenty seconds. This was not how I had pictured combat. Our first major objective and I had not thoroughly updated my platoon. Now that we were past Objective Gray, we were just reacting to fragmentary orders. The brigade staff probably had time to update his attack order, but by the time the plan was finalized and had gone through the battalion, the company had no time to change anything.

For anything unexpected we now had to rely on all the training and battle drills developed during Operation Desert Shield. Any last minute update was a formality and only a confidence builder. It was better that the platoon had received some rest instead of doing rehearsals all night. Desert Shield had been our rehearsal.

I put on my helmet and keyed the mike. "All white elements, enemy airfield five kilometers at ninety degrees. Possible T-55 battalion in defense. Follow my move in wedge and at the airfield come on line, out."

Without further communication, my platoon moved forward at fifteen miles per hour. I looked behind to see fifty-four other combat vehicles behind us in the task force formation. My position was the tip of the task force spear. Eventually, the entire force would move into a box formation with the two tank company-teams on line and the two mechanized company-teams following, on line and in reserve. All this would happen when my tank hit the airfield.

In the distance, I saw a great plume of smoke rising over the airfield, probably caused by a fire started during the night's artillery strike. Then I spotted a Bedouin family squatting in a wadi to our to our direct front. "All white elements, Bedouins direct front. Don't run them over, out." The family had camped right on the task force route and now clearly feared for their lives. The women and children were lying down headfirst while an older male stood erect waving a white flag to protect them from us. I could not help but admire the courage of this Bedouin who was facing such a strange and terrible sight. He stood firm. The task force stormed past his family without injuring them.

The perimeter of the airfield came into view. We closed quickly on a chain-link fence that was supported by large cinder-block posts. I saw Task Force 1-64 Armor moving across the southern sector of the field as we approached.

"Sir, should I run over the fence?" asked Forbes.

He thinks this is training. "Center on a cinder block, and Sergeant Davis, move the gun tube over the side so it won't get smashed." We exploded through the fence. The First Platoon moved on line with mine, and the Bradleys moved into our gaps. Bravo Tank maneuvered up on line with our company, and the attack speed dropped to around eight miles and hour. I heard a loud boom and ducked down in my hatch as the enemy fired their mortars.

ROB HOLMES (Delta Tank, Task Force 1-64 Armor)

I must have jumped three feet, drawn my .45, and landed inside the turret all in one motion. I woke to what sounded like the end of the world. Ten kilometers south of us, two artillery battalions had begun the most awesome display of firepower that I had ever seen. The sky was ablaze as rockets flew over us headed toward Jalibah. I was eight kilometers away from the airfield, asleep on a seventy-ton tank, and I felt the concussion like I was in an earthquake. My nap was over.

All of us woke and watched the sky and horizon on fire. As far as I was concerned, the artillery could do this for days. I knew, however, as always, it would soon be our turn to actually take the objective.

At dawn my platoon moved forward in a wedge formation with Delta Tank and the rest of the task force behind us. We rolled north at fifteen miles per hour headed to Jalibah. I didn't need a map. We were only eight clicks away, traveling almost straight north, and besides, I could navigate based on the explosions of the artillery barrage that I could see and hear. Bell wasn't accelerating, but as we got closer to Jalibah I felt we were moving faster, as if we were being drawn to it. The sand was rolling and firm with sparse vegetation. Tank country. To the east the sky was a brilliant blue and orange' to the west a silent darkness lingered.

Artillery was flying over us and raining down on Jalibah. I looked right and left as First and Third Platoon came abreast of mine in attack formation. We were now only about four kilometers away from the objective. Charlie's tanks did the same on our right. The task force's two mechanized infantry companies followed behind our tanks with their Bradleys on line.

We crested a dune and rolled gently into a huge basin. There it was.

Don't picture LaGuardia. There were two paved runways with several hangars on both the north and south sides. A chain-link wire fence surrounded the complex. We accelerated to twenty miles per hour and led the battalion into the valley. Artillery was landing all over the objective as Task Force 1-64 rolled into the basin. I saw Flash over my shoulder, bandanna blowing and sunglasses on, as he barked orders into his radio demanding more artillery.

"I got something hot!" Sergeant Downing screamed into the intercom.

"Fire and adjust!" I answered.

My command gave the gunner control over the fire system so he could engage without approval from me. This allowed him to acquire and engage targets at will while I maneuvered the platoon. There were no friendlies on Jalibah, so anything that came up hot Downing was free to blast. I had matured a lot since my first skirmish with dismounts only forty-eight hours earlier. I wasn't screwing around anymore with my .50-caliber machine gun.

Downing didn't waste time. The turret exploded as he fired the main gun. Underberg reloaded the breech, and my gunner engaged another target in a bunker adjacent to a hangar – my confidence in Sergeant Downing was back.

I had told my platoon to fire first and fast the night before, and they listened. As we rolled onward toward the airfield, my gunners were blasting main gun rounds as fast as the loaders could heave them into the breech. I scanned the airfield for targets and talked Downing onto those he didn't see.

Task Force 1-64 was an awesome display, thirty M1s shooting on the move as we assaulted the objective. We rolled into the valley closer to the airfield as artillery continued to pour down.

Then I felt like I was hit by a freight train.

Next thing I knew I was crumpled in a heap inside the turret. My head was spinning and my helmet was on crooked. I tried to pick myself up, not really sure what had just happened. I was dizzy but could stand. I looked around inside the turret:

Everybody seemed okay. Bell was driving. Underberg was loading, and Downing kept engaging targets. What the hell just hit me?

I stood back up in my hatch and looked around as we rolled toward the airfield. Violent clouds of sand and smoke were exploding all around us. The Iraqis were mounting a defense, launching mortars at us as our tanks rolled closer. One must have splashed next to us, barely missing my tank and knocking me over with its concussion.

My platoon crashed through the chain-link fence around the complex and led Delta Tank into the hangar complex. Iraqi infantry immediately surrounded us. Arabs have a weird way of appearing out of nowhere. This was not good. Tanks hate urban terrain that restricts maneuver. We were boxed in because of the fence and hangars, and these guys weren't surrendering. Iraqi grunts were everywhere. I couldn't believe anyone was still alive after our arty barrage. My platoon's gunners switched from their main guns to machine guns, and our tank turrets spun around spraying bullets in every direction and rumbling in a constant purr.

DAVE TRYBULA (Charlie Tank, Task Force 1-64 Armor)

At 0245 I began pulling my platoon out of its hasty defensive fighting positions and headed back toward the company commander's tank to take the lead in the company's formation. The foggy darkness made our night vision devices range to only fifty feet. The only means of seeing was through the gunner's thermals. To see in a particular direction, we had to point the main gun that way. I didn't like pointing my gun at things we didn't intended to shoot. By 0300 hours, my platoon was in formation and we waited for the word.

While we waited like thoroughbreds before the Kentucky Derby, the battalion gave an intelligence update with the exact location of two enemy light infantry battalions and two tank companies in the vicinity of Jalibah Airfield. I plotted these locations on the map, and I ensured all my tank commanders had the same information. I also told them to switch to sabot after firing their first HEAT round.

The attack began with my company trailing as the task force reserve, and it stayed that way until the lead company was in range to set up a support-by-fire position near the airfield. As Delta Tank, the lead company, set the base and oriented north-northeast, Alpha Mech and Charlie Mech moved to reinforce them. A platoon and the executive officer from Alpha Mech broke west to provide flank security. The task force was to leave a kilometer gap for my company to move through in order to assault the enemy's flank.

As Delta set the base, the task force commander ordered my company to "punch left." We began a bold movement to the west to gain an assault position on the enemy's flank. The two mechanized infantry companies relieved Delta Tank, which joined us in the assault position. This created and L-shaped brigade formation as Task Force 3-15 stampeded the enemy directly to the north.

When the commander ordered the envelopment, I quickly turned west to push through the gap that Alpha Mech was supposed to create on our flank. The company was racing behind me. As I approached Alpha Mech, I could clearly see them firing toward the airfield. Knowing the gap was to the west, I angled more to the left and rapidly found the point of penetration. Instead of being one kilometer wide, the gap was closer to five hundred meters, and our forces were firing directly across it. Realizing the danger of crossing there, I started moving west and reported the situation to my commander. "Black Six, the flank platoon of Alpha Mech is split only a little but is oriented back toward the airfield and is firing at this time. I am executing movement to the west of the entire unit and will not shoot the gap."

Roger, Red One, execute. Rogue Six has called in a smoke mission where you are to execute your turn."

As I closed on Alpha Mech's flank platoon, I made sure that they saw me and understood my company's intention not to pass through the gap but to move around it. Maneuvering past them, I was now in the lead. There was no one in front of me to guide off and no visible security. There was just open desert and the sounds of firing tanks. Bradleys, and artillery thundering across the battlefield. The white phosphorus round hit just in the distance, showing me where to turn east. When my platoon started to receive mortar fire, we closed our loaders' hatches, leaving only the tank commander exposed so we could better maintain command and control and prevent fratricide. As we neared the smoking remains of the white phosphorus shell, we turned and headed for the main runway. The remainder of the company moved on line and continued rolling toward the assault position. I could now see the fence around the outer edge of the airfield. The fence was made of simple chain-link, seven or eight feet in height, attached to cinder-block pillars. Each pillar was four inches by four inches. As we approached, I told my drive to center on one of the pillars in order to concentrate the whole force of the tank at a single impact point. We crushed the pillar like papier-mâché.

The fence clung to the mine plow mounted on my tank's front slope and was dragging alongside my vehicle. There was a real possibility of the fence becoming entangled in the track and disabling my tank. Before I had time to figure our a solution, my wingman accelerated his tank forward on my right side and stopped on the fence. As my tank moved forward, his halted tank created enough tension to snap the fence. He repeated the same procedure on my left side. With the fence now gone, we reached the main runway and stopped to establish an assault position. We waited for Delta to arrive on our right. I saw Task Force 3-15 continuing the attack in the north.

ALEX VERNON (Delta Mech, Task Force 3-15 Infantry)

The shaking tank, shaken by the ground reverberating from the artillery barrage against the airfield several kilometers away, woke me. It was still dark. Behind me, to the west, the horizon flashed white when our artillery fired – the white streaks from the MLRS missiles like laser beams streaming overhead, so close they seemed that I felt an urge to reach up and touch them – then before me, to the east, the horizon flashed orange when the rounds impacted. I remember retreating behind the tank against the morning chill with my gunner, talking with Sergeant Dock about the devastating amount of ordnance falling on the enemy while we basked comfortably in the warmth of the tank's turbine exhaust. The next thing I remember, the task force is in formation rolling toward the objective. Ahead of us the ground peaked into a military horizon; once we rolled over that rise, we would be able to see the airfield.

A tank main gun fired. It has come from Bravo Tank, my armor company, on the battalion box's upper left front. Captain Baillergion reported that an Iraqi truck had been spotted and fired upon. Later I learned that the firing tank did not have time to call for permission, as the truck almost crossed the military horizon and gone out of sight. It had been destroyed before it could get word to the airfield's defenders of our attack. We peaked shortly thereafter and saw the airfield several kilometers below us.

About halfway to the airfield I made my move, breaking right and increasing speed to come on line on Alpha Tank's right. I was the task force's rightmost unit; once we hit the airfield I was to link with Task Force 1-64's leftmost unit and assault down the runways. As we approached the fence I saw the leftmost 1-64 unit, which I presumed to be Delta Tank – I may have seen the identifying sideways triangle markings on their track skirts – to my right. Our two companies were angled toward one another, toward the same space. Behind my platoon and Delta's lead platoon the companies were already cramming together with no room to pull up into a line formation and much more vulnerable to indirect fires. I veered left to make room

Just before we struck the fence, Private Brunner, my loader, pointed to the gun, and I yanked back the commander's override joystick control for the main gun, putting the gun tube in the air so it would clear the top of the fence – otherwise the gun would have struck the fence before the tank, which at the very least would have thrown the MRS boresight. On the tip of the gun, the muzzle reference system is set during boresighting so that if combat throws off a gun's boresight, a gunner can quickly do an MRS update to restore some measure of accuracy by "reminding" the gun where to point. Like any memory system, this one wasn't perfect, but we didn't need to worsen matters by ramming it headfirst into a fence post.

Past the fence a lone concrete building and a few underground bunkers, only their sandbag tops visible, lay between by platoon and the airfield. Sergeant Dock asked to fire on the building; I issued the command: "Fire and adjust." In a billow of smoke the front wall disappeared. We rolled past. I didn't see the sandbag-covered bunker directly in the tank's path until we were too close to fire it up with a HEAT round, and the coax machine gun would have been ineffective against such a deep and fortified position. I could try to dodge it, potentially screwing the formation behind us and allowing Iraqi infantry to pop out of the bunker after we passed, with easy shots at our rear, I could attempt to straddle the bunker, exposing the tank's thin underbelly to whoever inhabited the bunker; or I could order my driver to aim one tread at the bunker and squash it. "Hit the bunker, Reynolds, Crush it." We hardly noticed the bump.

NEAL CREIGHTON (Alpha Tank, Task Force 3-15 Infantry)

We weren't firing and there were targets everywhere. "Sergeant Davis, we have MIGs and choppers. Fire the sabot in the tube at that bunker. Carrol, load HEAT until I tell you different."

Sergeant Davis fired the main gun, and a 120-mm armor-piercing sabot round sped across the field and slammed into a bunker and out the other side, the concussion probably killing anyone inside. Carrol loaded HEAT as my platoon erupted in a volley of fire. "Sir, I got a chopper," Davis screamed.

"Let me see." I moved down and checked through the sight. "Okay, it's a HIND, fire!" the round hit squarely on the chopper, and it disintegrated into a ball of flame.

I moved back up to look out. "All white elements, this is White Six, I want all tank commanders up unless you're clearing fires – otherwise we will shoot each other, our formation is too tight!" Fear had caused a number of vehicle commanders to stay down within the protection of their turret armor. In that position, they were unable to see adjacent vehicles and were hitting each other with their coaxial machine guns and near missing each other with main gun rounds. My tank commanders followed instructions and popped back out of their hatches.

My wingman, Sergeant Jones, was deadly. He shot two helicopters and a MIG before my own tank could get a round off at them. The company hit the center of the field and bypassed a T-55 hidden in a berm complex. The enemy tank opened fire at our rear. Within two hundred meters of the enemy tank, Sergeant Harris traversed his main gun over the rear and fired. The T-55 exploded and we moved on. At that range it had probably filled his entire sight picture. No need to lase for distance.

Enemy infantry tried to hide in shallow bunkers and some tried to surrender. Most that moved were quickly cut down under a swath of machine gun fire. The burning helicopters, jets, and dead soldiers seemed almost unreal. Task force 3-15 rammed through the fence on the northeastern side and left the airfield perimeter. To our rear we left behind the burning wreck of Jalibah Airfield. My soldiers were alive. It was the happiest moment of my life.

ROB HOLMES (Delta Tank, Task Force 1-64 Armor)

This was wild. Iraqis were everywhere. While Sergeant Downing sprayed rounds at the enemy dismounts, I searched for heavy targets like tanks that could do real damage.

I shouldn't have dismissed the immediate threat. Underberg jumped into the turret and pulled me down inside after him. He screamed and pointed out the hatch. I looked up and heard bullets flying overhead. Some enemy dismounts had gotten behind our tank. Not good. Antitank weapons work best when fired at the tank's rear, where the armor is thinner. A tank's design is a balance of three variables: firepower, maneuverability, and survivability. The more armor, the more survivable, but the less maneuverable. The armor is thinnest at the least likely target areas: the bottom of the hull, top of the turret, and the rear. Dismounted enemy, therefore, try to get in behind a tank to fire missiles at its rear.

Underberg jumped up into the whistling bullets, swung his machine gun to the rear, and let loose a burst of his own. Underberg wasn't even thinking; he was just fighting. To this day I marvel at the bravery of my men. When he ran out of ammo, he dropped back down into the turret. Another batch of enemy bullets flew over out hatches.

Sergeant Downing meanwhile was engaging targets to our front and searching for Iraqi tanks that could have wrecked our day with one shot. I still needed to deal with this punk rag to my rear. Captain Hubner had bailed me out of varying degrees of trouble ever since he'd taken command of Delta Tank, and I needed another favor.

"Black Six, this is White One; I got dismount behind me. Can you get him?"

Hubner replied from behind us by opening up with his coax machine gun. It was only a quick burst. After a pause, I heard his main gun fire.

"I got him." Hubner radioed calmly. I later learned his gunner's coax had jammed, so he had switched to his main gun and pumped a 120-mm sabot round through the Iraqi grunt. Vaporized is Dave Hubner's word for what he saw – one instant there was a man in front of his tank, and the next instant nothing.

Flash ordered the battalion to sweep to the left around the hangars and charge down the runways. This was classic Gordon: bold maneuver and attack, attack, attack. No one hated being caught up in the hangars with enemy grunts crawling all over us more than Flash. I led my tanks around the hangar complex. One hundred meters to my left, my platoon sergeant was crushing bunkers and antitank weapons beneath his tread. His turret was traversing smoothly right and left, discharging main gun rounds about every ten seconds.

He looked over at me and smiled. Sfc. Randy Sikes was one cool customer. All hell was breaking loose around him, but he could still find a way to give a nod of comfort to his young lieutenant. While I took half a second to remember how lucky I was to have him in my platoon, he pulled out a camera and took a picture of me! After that, I wouldn't have been surprised if he got out a thermos of coffee and taken a little break while his gunner took out more targets.

"Choppers!" My wingman, Sergeant Garback, shouted across the radio. He had rounded a corner and found four helicopters lined up on the runway. Garback was from Lexington, Kentucky, and usually had a wad of tobacco in his mouth. Now was no different. As I looked over, his tank fired at the nearest chopper, and the target exploded. From his commander's hatch, Garback discharged a stream of spit. Then Third Platoon, like a shark feeding frenzy, unloaded on the remaining three. Jeff White in his Alabama Drawl calmly sent his report to Captain Hubner: "Black Six, this is Blue One; three choppers destroyed, 0730, continuing mission, over."

"Save some for us, Bambi!" my loader radioed anonymously to Jeff. Anonymously, yet unmistakably Underberg.

Sergeant Downing continued engaging targets at will. Underberg had reloaded his 7.62 mm, and when he wasn't slamming the next round in the tube for Downing, he was at his weapon spraying dismounts. Bell just kept driving. Before any maneuver, I always would go over the mission with my driver and let him get a good look at the map. Bell had a high IQ and was a very quick study. He always knew what we were trying to do and could generally be counted one to drive without a whole lot of super-vision.

My platoon rolled down the runways. I looked over, and parallel to us was my roommate, Al Vernon, and his four M1s. I had seen him only twice since August. We made eye contact, and he gave me a little wave. We kept rolling and firing. Seven months ago, out lives had revolved around beer and girls, and wondering if we would ever get any field time. Well that had certainly changed.

My platoon reached the end of the runway, having blasted everything in our path. Flash ordered Delta Tank to set up a defensive positions and let the infantry root through all that we had shot up. I love grunts. They are great to have around for stuff like this. I saw my classmate, Mark Jennings, dashing around with his platoon, herding prisoners and clearing bunkers.

After a wild-as-hell forty-five minutes, a calm settled over the battlefield. I pulled myself up out of my hatch, sat on my turret, and drank a canteen of water. Underberg popped open a Mountain Dew. Bell jumped out of his hatch to take a leak and quickly check the track on his tank. Downing was already asleep inside the turret. The last hour had been pretty crazy. I looked over at my other tanks. The crews were stretching, walking around, and shaking off the fury. Some were shaking their heads; others were reenacting the battle with hand gestures; Howard was yelling at someone. Thank God. Everyone seemed to be okay.

DAVE TRYBULA (Charlie Tank, Task Force 1-64 Armor)

I set my tank on the center runway and began to scan for targets. We rapidly spotted several enemy aircraft sitting on the tarmac. My platoon sergeant called me and requested permission to fire. I told him to open fire, then reported to the commander that we were in contact with the enemy. An enemy HIND-D attack helicopter was hit with a HEAT round and vanished in flames. My gunner next identified a MIG-23 aircraft and was ready to engage. I dropped down and looked through my sight. As I told him to fire, I saw and sabot round go through it. We were too late – someone else had hit the bull's eye. My platoon erupted in a volley of fire, hitting enemy targets at will. Then we were told to move forward. The entire airfield was on fire. The action so far had seemed to take fewer than fifteen minutes.

As Task Force 3-15 finished its violent charge in the north, my commander issued another order. "Execute assault, keep it slow and deliberate, make sure you are on line with the guy on your left and right." As we started rolling forward, someone started humming. "The Battle Hymn of the Republic" over the radio. The music gave me chills as we finished off the enemy at close range.

I made sure I could see all of my tank commanders out of their hatches as we started to engage Iraqi tanks to our front. The tanks were so well dug into the ground it was almost impossible to identify them until we were right on top of them. Fortunately, their positions were pointed south, and we were assaulting from the west. I saw an enemy tank emerging from the ground: "Enemy tank direct front." I grabbed the override and slewed the gun onto the tank. "Do you see it?"

My gunner responded, "Identified, I got it sir!" Letting go of the override, I yelled "Fire!" Sergeant Godfrey pulled the trigger. I watched our sabot round hit the enemy vehicle. The tank exploded. The sabot round had caused a catastrophic kill.

We were straddling the runway and devastating the enemy. Within minutes my platoon had shot fifteen tanks, two MIGs, and one helicopter. This was significant work for my four tanks. Most important, all my soldiers were alive.

As we continued to push forward, my platoon was on line with Task Force 3-15 to the north and Third Platoon from my company and Delta Tank to the south.

Second Platoon and the headquarters tanks from my company were behind us because there just was not enough space on the airfield to fit them on line with us. This was extremely dangerous because the trailing tanks were shooting between the tanks in front of them. Mostly the tank commanders stayed up, out of their hatches, so they could maintain awareness, but in at least one case the tank commander sat in his seat inside his turret to look through his sights with his gunner when he gave the command to fire, without having ensured they were clear of friendly personnel. I know this because that Sabot round whistled by so close to me that its wake picked me up off of the tank commander's seat that I was standing on. I had to catch myself on the vision blocks around the hatch to stop from falling to the turret floor on my way back down. I called that tank commander on the radio and told him to get control of his tank.

As the battle finished, I updated my commander on what had happened. We were sitting on the east side of the airfield. Out of the blue, a master sergeant came over to my tank carrying a tape recorder and a notepad. He told me that he was an army historian. I thought he had lost his marbles. There was no way a historian would be here so soon. I made a radio call in order to verify the historian's identity and then we sat down on top of my tank and talked. The brigade was waiting while 1st Brigade moved north across our front heading for the Tallil Airfield. During this time we called the support platoon forward to top us off with fuel and ammunition. We expected the worst was yet to come and wanted every bullet possible when the big fight with the Republican Guard Divisions came.

ALEX VERNON (Delta Mech, Task Force 3-15 Infantry)

Rounds of some sort ricocheted off the right side of my turret. I felt fairly safe. I had ordered my tank commanders to ride open-protected for the attack, though I think that most other tank commanders assaulting the airfield rode with their hatch fully open. The tank commander's hatch had three positions: open, open-protected, and closed (buttoned-up). In the open position, the hatch is swung open and locked vertically behind the commander, covering his back and allowing him to stand on his seat and out of the hatch from the waist up. With the hatch closed, the commander must sit in his seat and use periscopes that peer out at the base of the cupola to see. The open-protected position is the compromise between the vision of the open position and the safety of the closed. That hatch locks horizontally several inches above the commander's head. He stands on the bottom of the commander's platform, with overhead cover and about six inches between the top of the cupola and the bottom of the hatch by which he can see the battlefield. Given the speed of our attack, a bullet or piece of shrapnel had only a very slight window of opportunity on any of my commanders. From the time we crashed through fence, my platoon's loaders had been down in the turret, doing their jobs, heaving rounds into the breech, and unexposed to rounds and shrapnel. Occasionally one of them might pop out of his hatch to help the tank commander scan for targets and threats wherever the gunner wasn't looking, wherever the main gun wasn't pointed.

I also saw rounds striking the ground beside my tank, "walking" in direction of the attack. I called Baillergeon and told him to call off any Bradleys firing – they were at this point still behind my tanks and had no business shooting through my platoon. I don't know it what I saw striking the ground had come from friendly Bradleys, and I have a hard time imagining them shooting the ground fifty meters to front. It could have been shrapnel from Iraqi mortar rounds (which I didn't know were fired at us until reading these other accounts while writing this book), though once I called Baillergeon, the problem stopped. After the battle, Staff Sergeant Rivera bragged about his "window shot," which at first I didn't understand. He apparently had not only shot out of his sector but also between my and Sfc. Freight's tanks. From his place in the platoon wedge to my left rear, Rivera's round had flown behind me and in front of Freight, who trailed me on my right. What I saw divoting the desert to my right could have been the shoes from his sabot round. A sabot round is a dart of depleted uranium with a diameter much smaller than the 120-mm gun that shoots it. It has a pair of "shoes" that fit around either side of the dart, giving it the proper 120-mm diameter while the projectile shoots down the tube. Once the round leaves the gun the shoes fall away, like the space shuttle's booster rockets. I told Rivera to never do that again.

When I had veered left at the fence, to make room for the converging companies, I must have veered too far. My platoon, with my company behind me, never linked up with Task Force 1-64, and never found the runway. We crept slowly along what must have been the north side of the complex. A series of buildings stood to our immediate right, and between these I saw open space with some Abrams in the distance, what could have been the airfield proper, where I was supposed to be. The Bradleys of Bravo Mech – or maybe the Bravo Mech Bradleys attached to Alpha Tank, the unit that was supposed to be on my immediate left – fired their 25-mm chain guns on anything and everything that wasn't a good guy, once on a rust-red cylindrical storage tank on stilts not twenty meters from me. The storage tank smoked but did not explode; it had probably stored water instead of fuel – not that the trigger-happy Bradley gunner could have known it. We drive beyond the buildings and into an open space – this too may have been the airfield, though again I never saw any tarmac. We rolled east, Task Force 1-64 somewhere in the south to my right, and Bravo mech (as I recall thinking) on my immediate left (though if we all managed to maneuver according to the plan, Alpha Tank – with a platoon from Bravo Mech – was the unit on my left). You could still see the fence marking the northern edge of the airfield several kilometers away. The tops of antiaircraft guns poked out of the ground. Dug-in positions, protected by sandbags, also pitted the area. Sergeant Dock fired his second main gun round at one of the antiaircraft guns and joined the rest of the platoon in spraying the dug-in positions with coax machine gun rounds. Brunner may have fired some 7.62 from his loader's position as well. I never bothered to fire my M2.50 caliber; it was too unwieldy for such close quarters, there were no valid targets for it which the tank's two 7.62 machine guns couldn't handle, and I have a formation to control and a company to lead.

I don't remember the two Bradley platoons of my company-team ever coming fully on line for the course of the battle. We kept more or less in our company wedge formation, the battle was over by 1000 hours, according to a letter I wrote several days later. I did not see a single enemy soldier.

On the eastern side of the airfield we halted in formation. Fuel trucks came forward. Sergeant Freight gathered ammunition expenditure information over the platoon net. My crew heard what he reported and knew he had added wrong. I radioed Freight on the platoon net and told him to try again. Again, he reported a bad total count to Top. "Jesus Christ, sir," muttered Dock. At my tank was Venderwerker, my old driver, who busted a gut laughing at Freight. Said Freight needed to enroll in a remedial math class. I didn't respond to Vanderwerker. With the eyes of the crew on me, I called Freight on the platoon net and told him the correct numbers to give to the first sergeant. My four tanks had fired a total of eight main gun rounds. If we had fired more rounds than Freight had fingers to count them, I might have felt more forgiving.

We listened to some small arms fire from the airfield behind us; a number of Iraqis had hid in their bunkers and hangars and emerged after we had swept by. Friendly infantry – either some of ours sent back or from a following unit – were clearing the objective while we ate lunch, cleaned our weapons, and took on ammunition.

GREG DOWNEY (Scouts, Task Force 1-64 Armor)

I watched as Task Forces 1-64 and 3-15 rumbled across the far side of the airfield. I felt like I was sitting on the bench at a basketball game. I wanted to be up there with them – until a radio transmission brought me back to reality.

"Rogue Six, this is Hammer Six," came a distress call over the task force radio frequency. This was the Charlie Mech commander, Capt. Bob Hamowitz. He sounded pretty shaken up. "Rogue Six, Rogue Six, this is Hammer Six, I'm taking casualties! Receiving fire! Receiving fire!"

"This is Rogue Six, settle down or you're going to lose more soldiers." Gordon was trying to bring Captain Hamowitz to his senses. Three M2 Bradleys had taken direct hits from behind.

ROB HOLMES (Delta Tank, Task Force 1-64 Armor)

I didn't have a scratch, but I was exhausted. The fuelers and ammo trucks quickly arrived and replenished the tanks. I jumped off my M1 and walked over to Sfc. Sikes. He was sitting on the turret with his coffee thermos. He looked like he had just finished a run at a gunnery range for the thousandth time. Sikes made a pretty weird sight, sitting on his tank drinking coffee while the airfield burned behind him and choppers flew above. He told me he would get me a copy of the picture he had taken when we got home. He also added that he would get the logistics reports from the platoon after he finished his coffee.

I walked over to Captain Hubner's tank. He was devouring and MRE while still in his hatch. He needed a shave, a new uniform, and about a month of sleep. He looked like the rest of us.

"How are you, Robert?" Hubner had been under a lot of stress from the weight of command and the expectations from Flash. Now, however, he was smiling and eating as we rehashed the battle.

In a cloud of dust, Rogue Six rode onto the scene. Hubner looked at me as he stuffed an entire chocolate bar into his mouth. "Back to work," he mumbled.

Flash jumped out of his hatch and stood on top of the turret, surveying the destruction. He then dismounted and walked over to us, cracking a smile at me and nodding with a gruff. "Lieutenant Holmes" as he looked up at Hubner.

"It's over, Dave." Flash proclaimed. Perhaps he forgot we were still deep inside Iraq. He looked at me and announced, "We beat' em to the river. We can turn east and crush them head on."

He was right. The 24th Infantry Division had won the race to the Euphrates and could now meet and destroy the Republican Guard as they fled Kuwait. Saddam's forces couldn't hide in the desert, and now they couldn't run either.

I left Hubner and Flash and walked back over to my tank. Along the way I saw a West Point classmate, John Ford, being escorted to one of the medic choppers. He had taken an AK-47 round while we were mired in the hangars. He was walking fine and his arm was already bandaged up, though he had a pretty bad grimace on his face. We made eye contact, and he managed a slight nod as he climbed aboard the chopper. His father has won a Purple Heart in Vietnam; now John has one, too.

A calmness settled over the battlefield. Buildings were burning, choppers were buzzing above us and grunts hustling around us, but it was better than the past hour. Regrettably, the calm didn't last.

"Cease fire! Cease fire! Cease fire!" Captain Hubner screamed into the radio.

No one in Delta Tank was shooting. No one was even moving. First and Third Platoons were relaxing outside their tanks just as we were. It was very unusual for Hubner to sound this frantic on the radio. Dave could certainly get excited, but we have all grown used to his calmness and politeness. He ordered his platoon leaders to switch to the battalion frequency immediately.

A sickening feeling settled in on the task force. As 1-64 and 3-15 assaulted the airfield, the brigade commander had held Task Force 3-69 Armor in reserve, in a support-by-fire position south of the airfield. After our tanks had raced down the runways, a platoon of our infantry Bradleys pulled into the hangar complex to kill or capture anything we had missed. Tanks from 3-69, from about twenty-five hundred meters south of Jalibah, misidentified the Brads as enemy vehicles still in action. In about ten seconds, friendly sabot rounds obliterated three of the four Bradleys. American had been killed by Americans.

Fratricide is an awful subject. Better communications, coordination, and rehersals can reduce it, but the fact remains: Warriors have suffered from friendly fire accidents since the days of bows and arrows. Later, I heard many versions of what happened, but I really don't think any of us even cared who did it. We all hated that it happened.

I watched from atop my turret as the choppers flew in to evacuate the wounded. I saw the horrible side of full body bags for the first time. About a dozen men were wounded and six were killed. It was an awful feeling. Until now, we had always moved on before anyone had time to process the casualties, who had always been dead Iraqis anyway.

As if this wasn't enough, Delta Tank's first sergeant, Randy Walker, walked up with a horrible look of disgust. Having just processed a group of prisoners, he was shaking his head as he told me these Iraqis had been captured barefoot with bloody feet, some with cut Achilles' tendons. They had no choice but to fight; they could hardly walk.

I looked over at a pathetic assembly of prisoners crying out as our medics tended to them. The Middle East is another world. I just wanted to finish this job and get back to Georgia.

GREG DOWNEY (Scouts, Task Force 1-64 Armor)

Our first fratricide incident had just occurred. As we discovered later, a company from Task Force 3-69 Armor had engaged what they thought were enemy vehicles; instead, they were friendly ones from my task force. Two soldiers died, several were injured. A terrible waste of lives at the hands of our own people.

Objective Orange was secured at 0730 hours. Isolated pockets of resistance were still present on the airfield, but every enemy tank or BMP was destroyed. My scout platoon moved forward to screen east of the task force.

ALEX VERNON (Delta Mech, Task Force 3-15 Infantry)

According to the division's postwar Victory Book, some two thousand Iraqi soldiers, eighty antiaircraft guns, twenty aircraft, several helicopters, and a tank battalion were "knocked out of action" during the fight for Jalibah. Another source cited Colonel Kern, our brigade commander, in its claim that about one thousand Iraqis defended Jalibah: Approximately 150 killed, the rest captured, and twenty-four T-55 tanks were destroyed.

While Delta Mech refitted, Captain Baillergeon vanished to the task force TOC for orders, and when he returned he called his platoon leaders to his track. We were going to continue east on a movement to contact mission; our objective was not a piece of ground, in other words, but any Iraqi units we happened across. Division expected us to encounter a Republican Guard Division. The RG were touted as Iraqi's best. Furthermore, battalion only carried with it one full replacement set of M-1 main guns rounds, and that was now substantially diminished without guarantee that the battalion sores would be able to restock from the division's support battalions before our next fight. When I briefed the order to the platoon's tank commanders, I instructed them that all fires had to receive my permission, except in the case of immediate danger. I wanted tight control over my ammunition. I did not want to waste rounds and then run out in the middle of a tank battle.

By noon or so Task Force 3-15 continued mission. South of us, to our right Task Force 1-64 paralleled our move.

27 FEBRUARY 1991 (G+3): AFTER JALIBAH

ALEX VERNON (Delta Mech, Task Force 3-15 Infantry)

Just east of Jalibah sat a large storage site surrounded by a fence. Partially underground storage areas were visible as rows of humps. As we approached the site, Captain Baillergeon ordered me to pull alongside the company to my front left –

Bravo Mech, I think, or maybe Alpha Tank. I refused. A number of Bradley turrets of the platoon I was to pull beside were pointed ninety degrees off their right side, where Baillergeon wanted me to go. I was remembering the Bradley's wild shooting at nothing at Jalibah and refused to move until those turrets spun forward. It took several minutes, and several repetitions of my request, before all the Bradley guns faced forward and I moved up.

A main gun blast from my right surprised me. I looked over to see the smoke dissipating around Sfc. Freight's gun tube. Out of the blue, he had fired at a truck clearly out of range. I chastised him over the platoon net for engaging without my permission. I reminded the platoon of the ammunition shortage. We were expecting to hit the Republican Guard units, armed with T-72's, the best tanks in the Iraqi inventory. My gunner also spotted two trucks on the horizon, in the storage area, retreating from our advance. Dock wanted to shoot. But the range demanded a main gun round over machine gun, the trucks were in fact on the edge of the main gun's range, we needed to conserve our main gun rounds, and the trucks presented no threat to us. They were fleeing the battle. I did not let him shoot.

We passed on the north side of the storage site and pushed east following an unbelievably high powerline strung along gigantic steel beam towers. The terrain was a flat as any we had seen in the Middle East. We stopped once, when the scouts identified several occupied enemy bunkers. Lieutenant Colonel Barrett chose to deploy the battalion mortars against them, even though the scouts were danger-close. I am thinking now that some of the mortar rounds did indeed fall dangerously close to the scouts. I believe the bunkers were eventually taken out by TOW missiles from either the scouts or one of the infantry companies' Bradleys.

GREG DOWNEY (Scouts, Task Force 1-64 Armor)

Operational graphics were now issued over the radio. We had very few graphic control measures beyond Objective Orange. The GIRS points we plotted on our maps before the ground attack became critical. We drew lines from one point to the next, much like a connect-the-dots- puzzle. As the lines were drawn on the map, I could see we were headed toward Basra, Iraq, located at the tip of the Persian Gulf.

Maj. Ken Boyd, the task force executive officer, issued a fragmentary order to me. Objective Storage was an unplanned mission. We would conduct an area recon of it and report back to battalion. We arrived at Objective Storage at 1300 hours. I could see enemy soldiers running around the area. Objective Storage was an ammunition depot that covered a square kilometer. A huge powder keg.

"Sir, I've got infantry running for cover," Lowther reported over the intercom. My gunner was not as nervous and jittery as he was when the ground attack first started.

"West, slow down, I don't want to get too close. Pull around to the right of that high ground. Stay low, slow down!" I said to my driver, trying to keep some terrain between my vehicle and the Iraqi soldiers who had already spotted me.

"Blue Five, follow me," I called to Staff Sergeant Hightower, my wingman, who was covering my movement from a few hundred meters away.

I ordered the platoon sergeant's Blue Section to get a closer look while I maneuvered my section around the south side. As I worked my way around the area, I started receiving direct fire from an S-60 antiaircraft gun.

"Damn, sir, that's awful close," West offered from the driver's seat.

"West, get us moving! Go, go, go!" I hollered back, trying to steer the vehicle over the intercom.

Sand was flying into the vehicle as the incoming rounds impacted nearby. I moved to the first piece of low ground I could find. The gunner on the S-60 lost sight of my section, but I had backed myself into a corner. We had no way out without being seen. I radioed Sfc. Smith, the platoon sergeant, and instructed him to get some artillery firing on the target. I received no response. He had not been very dependable prior to the ground attack, and I knew he was not going to help me out now.

"Lowther, watch the radios. Tell Rogue Six what's going on up here. I'll be right back." I climbed out the hatch.

"Where the hell you going, sir?" Lowther asked, trying to figure out what had just happened.

I dismounted my vehicle, low-crawled up to higher ground with a pair of binoculars and compass, and tried to observe the target. The S-60 was only about four hundred meters away. The enemy had heard us coming and waited for me to come around the berm before engaging. Luckily for us, the S-60 is an antiaircraft weapon, not designed for ground battles. It is slow, and the gunner does not have much protection.

I radioed my polar plot to the task force FSO. It took about three or four minutes for the eight-inch rounds to land on the target. I made sure the FSO knew my section was danger-close, and he relayed the message to the artillery battalion. The first volley destroyed everything. Secondary explosions went off inside the ammunition depot. I contacted the FSO for more artillery and made adjustments that would destroy the entire area.

I watched as Iraqi soldiers ran from bunker to bunker, wagering their lives on where they thought the next artillery barrage would land. Looking through my binoculars, I could see their faces and sense their fear. It was strange being within shouting distance of these guys but experiencing nothing close to what they were going through. I felt like I was watching a movie, totally detached from the agony and suffering.

Lieutenant Colonel Gordon wanted the battalion mortar platoon to fire some missions for me. I called a polar plot to the mortar platoon leader, and the mortars fired a few missions. They had just pulled out of their firing points when artillery impacted right on top of them. I saw and heard the rounds impact behind my position, not knowing the mortar platoon was the target. The FSO found out that our division artillery counterbattery radar had picked up the mortar rounds' trajectory signature, assumed they were Iraqi, and called a mission on them. Fortunately, we did not sustain any losses, but our artillery units learned a valuable lesson. I later discovered that during Desert Shield a memorandum had been passed down to artillery and mortar units, cautioning them about friendly mortars being identified as enemy artillery.

ROB HOLMES (Delta Tank, Task Force 1-64 Armor)

Division Intelligence detected an enemy position to our front. Flash ordered Delta Tank to stop and await fuel while he moved the battalion's mortar platoon out in front of the diamond formation. He ordered them to launch a volley at the objective to soften them up before we hit them with the tanks. Fine with me. We needed fuel, and I needed sleep. It would take the mortars probably thirty minutes to execute the movement and fire, so I has some time. I sank down into my hatch, leaned against my .50-cal sight, and was asleep immediately.

I woke to an exploding horizon and rounds landing one hundred meters in front of my platoon. I was beginning to wonder if I would ever sleep again. Waking up was hell. I jumped up and saw flame, smoke, and sand, and the mortar platoon racing past us to the rear.

Bell already had the engine started, but before moving he asked excitedly, "Sir, can I back up?" Tank-drivers never reverse without permission because they can't see anything to their rear. In this case, however, Bell's courtesy was really annoying.

"Get us out of here, Bell!" I ordered my platoon back and radioed Black Six.

Captain Hubner responded nonchalantly, "Rogue Six says not to worry – that's friendly artillery."

I didn't give a hoot in hell about the origin of the artillery. Its destination on the other hand, was damn revelant. My platoon stopped about five hundred meters back and watched the rounds fall smack dab where the mortars had been and just in front of where I had taken my little siesta. Thank God our arty was slow because they were definitely accurate. Had the counterbattery strike come just a couple minutes earlier, they would have been successful.

DAVE TRYBULA (Charlie Tank, Task Force 1-64 Armor)

Leaving Jalibah on our way east toward Basra, the task force identified an enormous ammunition stockpile, something like twenty-two acres of ammunition, and called artillery fire upon it. Unfortunately, the artillery round would not start the ammunition on fire, so the mortar platoon was called to the flank of the task force to do a quick hip shoot with white phosphorus rounds to ignite the ammo. The mortars rapidly positioned themselves, hung two rounds each, and departed the area. No sooner had the mortars cleared the area then an incredible mass of artillery rounds cam crashing down on the area. The mortars were out of the area just in time to avoid injury from our division's counterbattery fire.

GREG DOWNEY (Scouts, Task Force 1-64 Armor)

My scout platoon moved around Objective Storage, now ablaze from secondary explosions within the ammo dump. The task force had closed in on us, closer than I preferred. We were encountering numerous bunker complexes, therefore slowing my movement as we recon'd the zone.

"What was that?" West mumbled.

"Goddamnit, somebody is shooting at us!" I said, knowing it wasn't enemy.

The tracer of a tank round caught my eye as it blazed across the front of my vehicle, just under the barrel of my 25-mm chaine gun. Glowing bright red as it flew away, it impacted down range from me.

I yelled over the battalion radio frequency to cease fire. Lieutenant Colonel Gordon asked who fired the round. Captain Hubner, Delta Tank's commander, admitted it had been one of his tankers. One of his gunners had caught a glimpse of my turret as we worked our way through the bunkers and fired before correctly identifying the target. I wiped the sweat off my forehead. The incident was much too close for me. We had survived too much and too long to die from friendly fire. Rogue Six slowed the battalion so I could get the scouts farther forward of the task force.

We continued our zone recon up to BP 1-64. Encountering light resistance, we avoided bogging ourselves down with POWs and kept moving east. By 1800 hours, the task force intelligence officer reported that twenty-one Iraqi divisions had already been significantly destroyed. I seemed the war would be ending soon.

The scout platoon screened five kilometers forward of BP 1-64. We were overlooking a highway that initially did not have traffic on it. As the night passed, I started observing vehicles moving north on the road. Red Section was reporting artillery fire on its location, so I pulled them back. Gordon sent Charlie Mech forward to give me more direct firepower.

As the columns of vehicles approached, I gave my polar plots to the FSO over the radio. Calling for fire at night made determining the direction a little more challenging. I had devised a technique to determine target azimuth by placing a strip of luminous tape on the end of my vehicle's 25-mm gun barrel. My gunner would aim the main gun at the target, and from the top of my vehicle I would shoot an azimuth in the direction that the gun barrel pointed. I lines up my compass parallel to the glowing tape. My azimuth was always accurate. All I had to do them was estimate the distance to the target by using the reticle in the Bradley's thermal sight.

We waited to make sure that the targets were the enemy before we engaged them. The columns consisted of wheeled and tracked vehicles. As soon as my gunner identified a BMP, we requested artillery. The M2 Bradleys from Charlie opened up and dished havoc on the column. After about thirty minutes of direct and indirect fires, the enemy quit using the route. We had caught part of the Iraqi army by surprise during its withdrawal north.

The operational graphics were passed out over the radio net for our next mission. Staff Sergeant Deem came over to my vehicle to chat. We looked at the map graphics and the reports of heavy enemy armor in our zone. The Republican Guard was somewhere ahead.

"Deem, if we survive this battle tomorrow it will be a miracle," I soberly remarked. It probably was not the most professional thing to say to one of your soldiers, but we both knew it to be true. After being fired on by both enemy and friendly units, I felt our luck was going to run out. Deed evidently agreed.

"Shit, sir, this is longer that I thought we would live." He said in matter-of-factly, then rubbed his tired eyes with his dirty hands.

I stood there, trying to focus on the map, my eyes and my mind long past the threshold of effectiveness, totally fatigued by the last few days of nonstop activity. I was too exhausted, mentally and physically, to be afraid. Fear takes energy, and I simply didn't have any to spare. The darkness of the desert night hid the destruction going on around us. You could hear it though, artillery rounds landing in the distance, tanks firing, and fighter aircraft flying above.

ALEX VERNON (Delta Mech, Task Force 3-15 Infantry)

Our direction of attack took us through Iraqi farmland. MLRS missiles continued to streak overhead. Large berms and ditches, segregating the land into squares for irrigation purposes, made the area difficult to maneuver through. The battalion moved through these in two columns, both steering through the fields as best they could, occasionally colliding, occasionally almost losing sight of one another. We could not go around the farmland because we did not know its extent – it was not on any maps – and we did not want to deviate from our assigned axis, and risk moving into another unit's sector, or creating a detour that would take too much time to recover. We did our best to avoid mangling the farmland, steering around the perimeter of each square from one break in a berm to the next. Iraqi farmers – fellaheen – waved and clapped as we rolled through. One bearded, turbaned man with bright eyes and a huge smile tossed tomatoes up to us, which my loader Brunner and my gunner Dock ate like apples. Was he thanking us for so obviously sparing his farmland? For ending the war? For taking on Hussein? Maybe he was simply reaching out to us, tired man to tired man. I can't claim to really remember what those tomatoes looked like, but in my mind's eye they were large, plump, red, vine ripe, and blemish free. Their juice and seeds oozed down Brunner's face, which he wiped with the sleeve of his MOPP suit.

We stopped for the night at what must have been the eastern edge of the farmland. In the dark the battalion formed into a horseshoe-shaped defense around a common engagement area. Captain Baillergeon sent a Bradley to drive the engagement area, a common procedure in preparing a defense, if one has the time. The vehicle driving around in the engagement area helps the rest of the company judge ranges, keys them to rises and dips in the terrain that the enemy might use for cover, allows platoons and sections to coordinate who can see and engage what areas of the battlefield, and reveals to the commander where he needs to preplot indirect fire (wherever his direct fire weapons can't target). It also identifies sectors of responsibility, and some vehicle commanders use it to practice crew gunning drills. We could also boresight our guns on the vehicle if it stood stationary long enough. That night this preparation drill was cut short when a Bradley in its defensive position reported two Iraqi BMP fighting vehicles in the engagement area. The Bradley driving the area saw nothing but sped back to its position. The company never acquired a clear fix on either BMP other than a few Loch Ness glimpses of what might have been something.

We were to move again at 0600 hours the next morning, maybe earlier, for an attack to our final objectives. On the way we expected to meet and do battle with the Hammurabi Armored division, the only Republican Guard unit still combat-effective, estimated at 60-percent strength, and equipped with Iraqi's best tanks, the T72.

I once again hit the back deck for my allotted sleep time. I was not there long when the ground shook with falling artillery, much closer than anything I had yet felt. It had to be Iraqi. I moved toward my hatch to listen to the radio. The next explosions rocked my tank – I jumped into my tank commander's position, bringing down the hatch and locking it behind me, faster than I ever had before. While Brunner closed his loader's hatch, I called "incoming" across the platoon net and heard myself echoed on the company net. Artillery terrifies tanks. Not only does it carry the threat of chemical and biological agents, it also comes from above, and the turret top has some of our thinnest armor. A few moments later the shelling lulled; I donned Kevlar and flak vest, ordered my crew to stay buttoned-up inside, and headed on foot to the commander's and the XO's Bradleys. We weren't using our radios unless we absolutely had to, so as not to give our position away, and I wanted to know what was going on. During my fast walk the shelling picked up again, though a little farther away. At the headquarters' section. I found the artillery officer assigned to the company, 2d Lt. Bill Lockard, on the radio and in a huff. I learned that the second round of shelling, the close call that had rocked my tank, had been friendly response to the shelling begun by the Iraqis. Bill had heard an officer on the battalion's artillery fire support team call the mission to the artillery unit, and as the artillery fell on our position he realized that the coordinates he heard that officer or NCO give were the coordinates Bill had earlier reported to the battalion fire support team as our Delta Mech company-team's position. It took him several minutes to have the mission aborted. I still remember his fuming: "That idiot should lose his job over this, He ought to be relieved right now. Fucking moron. He ought to be court-martialed."

DAVE TRYBULA (Charlie Tank, Task Force 1-64 Armor)

As we closed on the city of Basra we halted short and moved all of the artillery forward in preparation of the attack toward the city. We reduced security to 50 percent so we could get some sleep before we started rolling again at 0500 the following morning. But all night long artillery and rockets shot from all directions around us toward Basra. We had a hard time sleeping. The time to depart came and went and we did not move; I was not sure what was going on, but the artillery had finally stopped shooting. As I looked to the sound of an MLRS launcher shooting its rockets, I noticed that the rockets did not have their normal trajectory. They looked like an Apollo moon shot and were actually ATACMs missiles being fired at great distances.

ROB HOLMES (Delta Tank, Task Force 1-64 Armor)

The sun was setting as we pulled into a hasty battle position and waited on more fuel and ammo. Captain Hubner summoned his three platoon leaders to his tank and told us that Saddam was trapped. Allied forces had pushed the Iraqis out of Kuwait and forced them smack into us. He also reported that a Republican Guard regiment was bottled up to our front, bounded by the Euphrates to the north and the allies to the south. He figured that his would be the final battle, but it could get pretty bloody.

Planes filled the sky and artillery shook the ground that night. Saddam's forces were getting pummeled. I settled in my hatch and waited for Hubner's call to attack. We had been baptized at Jalibah, but I could tell people were stressed about this next trial. We all sensed that things had gone well so far. My dad always jokes about how closer you got to a war, the less you knew what was going on. Nevertheless, we all knew where we were on the map and what it meant. It really was almost over. I just hoped no one started getting too cautious.

"All elements, this is Black Six," Hubner's voice broke the radio's silence. "As of 0600, fire only it fired upon. Repeat – fire only if fired upon."

What? I jumped off my tank and ran over to Hubner's. This was quite a change in the rules of engagement, and I didn't like it. I worried we were getting timid after the fratricide at Jalibah. I hated the friendly fire, but three hundred kilometers inside Iraq was no time to start tying our hands.

"What's up, sir?" I asked. Hubner was slouched on his turret eating an MRE.

"I think it's over. President Bush is speaking on midnight," he announced with a smile.

I yelled over to Underberg to get my beat-up old radio from my bags. Hubner and I trotted back over to my tank, arriving just in time to hear the distinctive bing preceding the commentator's classic opening, "2400 hours Greenwich Mean Time, this is the BBC World News." My tank commanders gathered around. The president's address was short and sweet: total surrender by the Iraqi forces in theater.

I couldn't believe it. I thought Desert Storm would last a month, two weeks at least. I never figured we could do it in four days! In one hundred hours, we had dismantled the fourth-largest army in the world. The 24th Infantry Division had traveled farther and faster than any division in military history, and Task Force 1-64 had led the way. Happy as we were, congratulations could wait. I was ready to get the hell out of Dodge and catch the first plane back to Georgia.

ALEX VERNON (Delta Mech, Task Force 3-15 Infantry)

At 0400 on 28 February, the task force began to assemble, fully expecting to hit an Iraqi division head-on that day. The artillery preparation for the morning attack had already begun. By 0430. Baillergeon relayed to the company that as of 0500, we were to cease fire on order of President Bush. The war was over. I felt some relief. But I had heard enough stories of the skirmishes still going on across the DMZ in Korea to stay wary. We were still deep in Iraq, between retreating Iraqi units and Baghdad. We were not yet home. My weapons remained locked and loaded.

The Cease-Fire: 28 February-8 March 1991

Before this had come the news of the battle of Cambrai. There for the first time the Tanks had fought as we had always wished, across good ground, without a preliminary bombardment, and in large number – over 400. With their help General Byng had won what up to that time was the greatest victory of the war, the greatest in the territory gain and prisoners captured, and the greatest in its economy both of lives and ammunition.

ALEX VERNON (Delta Mech, Task Force 3-15 Infantry)

Our artillery barrage continued until exactly 0500; later in the morning, rumors of approaching enemy armor started the shelling again. We spent the morning in the same location we had spent the night. Delta Mech's infantry patrolled the immediate area and discovered a bunker complex, where they captured nine soldiers, including two colonels and one general. Some soldiers had not wanted to surrender because they had heard we would torture them before executing them – I remember talk of an Iraqi soldier either committing or threatening to commit suicide rather than be caught by us. Some of the Iraqi privates; identification cards revealed that they were all of fourteen years old. The complex proved a souvenir cornucopia: Our infantry found brand new AK-47s, folding AK-47s, money (the one bill with Hussein's picture), television monitors, typewriters, VCRs and the general's oak desk. This apparently was a Republican Guard light infantry division command post. Captain Baillergeon made off with the general's rank insignia. After the war, I learned of an Iraqi officer found dead in a bunker, having been shot in the head at close range. The American officer who found him surmised that he'd been killed by an Iraqi soldier in his command.

My tankers pleaded to accompany the infantry on their next excursion to the bunker. I passed their request to Baillergeon, who summarily rejected it. Brian Luke, the First Platoon leader, kept us in mind and after his next trip brought some loot for us. Our first spoils. Brian gave me an Iraqi magazine and a Koran. He knew I liked books.

Baillergeon reported that in Bush's address to the nation on the cease-fire, the president described Hussein's confusion. Hussein didn't know the location or strength of his own units, and when learned about the 24th sitting inside Iraq, he assumed we must be an airborne division. Other rumors I remember hearing around this time: The Iraqis at Jalibah thought our artillery preparation another air strike, some actually firing antiaircraft guns into the sky at nothing, and the rest leaving the safety of their bunkers when the arty prep stopped, thinking the air strike over, just in time to see us crash through the fence; and some Iraqi soldiers dubbed us the "Ghost Division" because we had materialized from the nowhere of the empty desert.

GREG DOWNEY (Scouts, Task Force 1-64 Armor)

For the first time since the start of the ground war, I reduced platoon security below 100 percent. I told my drivers, gunners, and track commanders to go to sleep. The rest of the crews manned the turrets and radios. Despite the excitement over the cease-fire, I immediately fell into a deep sleep.

Specialist Burton was standing over me when I woke. All I could understand was the order to move. I called the battalion TOC for details and was told to continue to recon east toward Basra. The cease-fire was in effect, but the scattered enemy may not have known that. I issued the rules of engagement that allowed us to engage any enemy that displayed hostile actions. Pretty broad criterion for ROE. We started out at about 1200 hours.

DAVE TRYBULA (Charlie Tank, Task Force 1-64 Armor)

Almost simultaneously with the order to cease offensive operations, we received the order to push east to occupy the outskirts of Basra. Cease offensive operations and move forward through enemy territory? I verified with Captain Hadjis that this did not restrict my ability to engage targets encountered. The company's traveling formation spread out on line to cover the maximum width possible – we couldn't afford to bypass any pockets of resistance, equipment, or danger areas and leave them to surprise more vulnerable support units following us. We moved through abandoned bunker complexes and were heading east when Sgt. Steve Godfrey, my gunner, screamed for us to stop. He pointed out the half uncovered mine directly to our front. I directed the platoon to drop its mine plows and clear lanes through the minefield. Before entering the minefield any farther, I backed up my tank to give our plow enough room to dig into the ground. I also reported the situation to the commander.

"Black Six, this is Red Six, encountered minefield, dropped plows, making three lanes. Recommend White, Blue, and Black" – the other two tank platoons and the company headquarters' vehicles – "consolidate at my rear and follow through."

"Roger, Red. White and Blue, execute. Black Six out." With these two simple transmission we were able to get the entire company through the minefield unharmed and continue toward Basra.

As I caught my breath and calmed from this brief excitement, I became irate at myself. I had known that the Iraqis emplaced minefields in from of their defensive positions, yet as I was coming through their positions from the backside, I had failed to apply this and had come close to injuring soldiers and damaging our tanks. I vowed to be more vigilant.

1 MARCH 1991

ALEX VERNON (Delta Mech, Task Force 3-15 Infantry)

We pushed east toward Basra. About twelve kilometers later, in the early afternoon, the company stopped at what we soon discovered was an abandoned medical complex. After the infantry platoon cleared it, Captain Baillergeon let my tankers explore the site. We found three modified American M113s and one 557 medic truck. We also found a type 59 or type 63 Chinese command track, also modified into a medical vehicle. These were plush medical vehicles, with padded sides, padded seats and benches, and built-in supply cupboards. All were dug-in deeply, and all had Republican Guard markings. We also saw a dug-in black Chevy Beretta automobile in the center of the complex – one of those too-strange-not-to-be-true discoveries. Bob McCann, Bravo Tank's First Platoon leader, owned a black Beretta, and I regret not thinking to filch a hubcap from it to replace his missing one back home. (It has been speculated that the Iraqis placed junk in dug-in positions as decoys, that we might waste missiles, bombs, and artillery on them instead of on tanks and other combat track.)

At first we were very careful about our search, as we feared the Iraqis might have rigged booby traps for us. It became quickly apparent, however, that the occupants had left in a hurry, and recently. Food was left on plated, pencils in notebooks on cots, clothes on the sand floor. They lived in bunkers, some dug deep with sand stairs and roofs; some not so deep, with draped canvas for walls and ceiling. The former were smaller and housed fewer people, probably officers. Most of the living spaces were not tall enough for any of us to stand upright. I scored a protective mask and a wood-handled bayonet for myself.

A Republican Guard division had occupied the entire area. Piles of ammunition littered the landscape – tank, artillery, and small arms rounds. This day, and for the next several days, we were accompanied in our traveling by the earth-jarring explosions of division engineers destroying these ammo heaps behind us.

Not long after the bunker, Sergeant Dock reported movement around a cluster of buildings a kilometer to our front. The company on our left noticed them as well. I plopped down in my seat and through the sight watched a handful of armed Iraqi soldiers dashing between buildings. A pair of vehicles in the area, not moving. Lieutenant Colonel Barrett gave the other company permission to attack. With a burst of Bradley 25-mm and Abrams main gun rounds, they closed on the area and secured it.

My company then ran into a truck sitting in the middle of the road we straddled. A running automobile sat stopped in front of it. Several Iraqis were leaning and reaching into the cab, doing something. Trying to start it? Recovering weapons? Booby trapping it? Baillergeon had a Bradley shoot warning rounds over the truck. The Iraqis scurried into the running car and sped away. Wanting to take no chances, Baillergeon chose to destroy it at a distance with a high explosive tank round. I asked my platoon if anyone had a HEAT battle-carry; Sergeant Miller assented. Baillergeon had his thinner-skinned Bradleys back off. I told Miller to lock on the truck, and for him and his gunner to speak their fire commands over the platoon net. I echoed every command over the company net.

"Ready."

"Ready."

"Fire."

"Fire."

"On the way."

"On the Way."

I had expected a more dramatic explosion, as had the watching infantry. A small flash and puff of smoke, the sound of crunching metal and glass, and the truck jerked, then rocket back to stillness. Very anticlimactic, especially as it was the last round of any sort, large or small, Second Platoon, Bravo Company, 1-64 Armor, would fire.

Some minds might make something representative of the event, of the protracted, nervy anticipation, the lack of any backlash, the quick, almost anticlimactic end. The battle for Jalibah too feels slightly representative: the preparation by bombing; the overwhelming size of the attacking force, almost too big; the lack of fight in the defenders; and the greatest damage inflicted on ourselves we inflicted on ourselves.

We moved on.

NEAL CREIGHTON (Alpha Tank, Task Force 3-15 Infantry)

It was now two day after the battle of Jalibah. As I reached into my tank's bustle rack, I found an almost empty case of bottled water. Ever since eating the contaminated lettuce during Desert shield, I was extremely careful about what I consumed. The thought of drinking the army's "purified" water did not sit well with me. Looking up, I saw Lieutenant Seal, one of the infantry platoon leaders attached to the company, walking toward my tank. "Hey Wayne, do you have any bottled water to spare?" I yelled.

"No, we're almost out, but I hear there's an enemy conex about two kilometers north of here loaded with bottled water. It's a Republican Guard supply point that my guys saw while on patrol last night. Let's hit it. You ask the captain – he'll let us out if you ask. You're his pet."

I grinned, "No, I think you're his pet. He keeps saying how he wants to put you on a leash." Placing my CVC on my head and pressing the transmit key, I began to think about what I was going to say to the commander. "Black Six, this is White Six, over."

"This is Black Six," He responded.

"This is White Six. We would like to replenish some Class 1. Can we talk at your position, over?" I waited for his response wondering if he knew what the hell I was talking about.

"This is Black Six, is this the mission Wayne wanted?"

Turning to Wayne I grinned again. "You already asked him, you bastard."

"Yeah, but eh said 'no' to me," Wayne replied.

I hesitated and then grabbed the transmit key, "Roger, same mission, over."

"This is Black Six. Okay. I know where you are going, but be back in two hours, out."

"You son of a bitch," Wayne yelled. "I told you you're his favorite!"

"Yeah, and I told you he wanted to keep you on a leash. I guess I'm taking you for a walk." We discussed the mission briefly. Wayne decided to take his wingman and his dismounts. I decided to take my wingman, Staff Sergeant Davis. After briefing the involved crews, we mounted up and headed north, Wayne's track in the lead.

As we moved through enemy territory, I was amazed. Everywhere lay abandoned vehicles, uniforms, weapons, and ammunition. It seemed most of the Iraqi army had deserted wholesale. We halted temporarily as Wayne checked his map. I dismounted with an M16 rifle and entered a bunker to the right of my tank. Uniforms were scattered about the floor and food sat on an unlit butane stove. Clearly, the last meal in this bunker had been interrupted. The most likely explanation was that the U.S. Air Force had ruined these soldiers' dinner. Hard to believe this was the same Republican Guard we were taught to fear. I moved out of the bunker and remounted my tank.

We continued north. Eventually Wayne broke the radio silence. "White Six, this Gray Six, I have the target in sight. Bring up the big guns, over."

"This is White Six, roger out." My two tanks moved forward until we had a good view of the supply point. There were seven conexes – metal transportable walk-in storage bins – surrounded by a bunker complex. No enemy movement. After observing the area for several minutes, I radioed Wayne. "Gray Six, this is White Six, negative movement. Let's move in."

Wayne's Bradleys moved in as my tanks covered them. "White Six, this is Gray Six, we are in and it's a mother of all supply points, over."

"This is White six, roger out." I brought my section forward to join Wayne. Once we had entered the supply point, I dismounted. "Damn, this place is stocked," I yelled to Staff Sergeant Davis. Most of the conexes were open, and bottled water was everywhere. I was again astonished at how quickly the Iraqis had abandoned things. I would have destroyed the water with main gun or machine gun rounds instead of allowing it to fall into enemy hands.

In one conex we found water with pictures of Saddam on the label and packets of Kraft cheese. I wondered if Kraft knew they were proving nourishment to the Republican Guard. Davis's crew began to load the turrets of both tanks with Iraqi water. Before we departed, Wayne took a picture of my watered-down tanks. We headed south, back toward the company area, with enough water to service the Alpha Tank Wild Bunch for at least three days.

2 MARCH 1991

ALEX VERNON (Delta Mech, Task Force 3-15 Infantry)

We followed a powerline east. In the late morning we stopped; tanks from Task Force 1-64, which had been moving parallel to us on our right, crossed in front of us barreling north. We were then about thirty miles north of Kuwait and about as far to the west of Basra, Iraq. I didn't understand. Why send the farther unit? Why have one unit cross in front of another? Captain Baillergeon ordered the company-team into a hasty defense in sector and called the task force for a situation report. The battalion gave him a nonanswer, which he relayed to me: "Never mind, just do your job."

I have since asked Dave Trybula what happened. He remembers that 1-64 "had just gone into a hasty defense and pushed our Mech companies forward when we got word of an Iraqi armor battalion in the 2nd Brigade, before we closed to do battle." Colonel Gordon recalls thinks somewhat differently: "Following 1st Brigade's engagement at Rumaylah Oil Fields, 1-64 was ordered into the complex and small town to secure it and block the road going east into Basra. To do that, we crossed in front of 3-15 at about 1500-1600 and occupied the positions. Your Task Force 3-15 remained to our south for the day."

As far as I knew, the cease-fire was nonexistent. I continued to hear rumors of Iraqi armored movement, and I continued to hear artillery and direct fire. I would later learn – much later, years later – that the other brigade's battle at Rumaylah resulted in the destruction of nearly one thousand Iraqi vehicles and unknown numbers of Iraqis trying to escape the area, some of whom were purportedly civilians (including women and children) fleeing Kuwait in this military convoy.

That day we found a group of abandoned artillery pieces, and with them some American equipment. Two M1A1 gunner's quadrants without serial numbers. A Texas Instrument calculator.

GREG DOWNEY (Scouts, Task Force 1-64 Armor)

Our zone went right through the Rumaylah Oil Field area, a congested, build-up area on the map. I anticipated a very slow rate of movement with us having to go block by block through urban areas.

As we worked our way through the oil refineries, we observed the devastating effect of our coalition air power. There was a large amount of unexploded cluster bomblets on the ground and numerous burnt-out hulks of former armored vehicles. My scout platoon moved very deliberately, bounding within sections, leap-frogging out way through the maze of building and huge oil storage tanks. There were so many places an Iraqi tank could be hidden. After moving across a wide-open desert for the last six months, I was becoming claustrophobic among the tight confines of this area.

I saw movement to my front left as we moved farther east. Looking through my binoculars, I could see the gun tube of a tank. After taking cover behind a berm, my gunner raised the TOW missile launcher. The tank had acquired us – we could see the end of his gun tube staring at us. The fire support office reported to me that all our artillery was out of range, so I requested permission to engage with the TOW. Although the enemy tank had not fired at me, he was tracking me and my wingman everywhere we moved. I could not maneuver any farther east with the tank there so I launched a TOW missile. My gunner tracked our missile to the target and destroyed the tank. We continued our movement east.

Red and Blue sections were not encountering any resistance. Abandoned tanks and BMPs cluttered the area, making it hard to move quickly. It was getting hard to determine which enemy vehicles were manned and which ones abandoned. As I moved over a berm, I came face-to-face with a BMP-1. It fired one 73-mm round at me, which hit in front of my vehicle. My gunner responded with a burst of 25-mm that hit the side of the BMP. My wingman was firing also.

Neither of us saw the red truck. Before we could stop firing, it had driven between us and the enemy. The BMP exploded first, then the truck burst into flames. I can't described how it felt. Shock maybe. Panic. Seized. Overcome. We had inadvertently shot innocent victims.

I raced my section to the truck's location. What I saw sickened me. An old man, two women, and six children were jumping out of the burning truck. My soldiers poured out of our Bradleys, ran to them, and tried to administer first aid. They were in awful shape, especially the old man. He had taken a 25-mm armor piercing round through his chest. The majority of the children were injured from the high explosive rounds. One woman had lost her leg below the knee. I felt angry and helpless.

Why did they have to be in the wrong place at the wrong time? How could this have been avoided? I called for additional medical support. We were losing the old man. Specialists Burton was doing his best to keep him alive. The woman who had lost her leg was stabilized after Burton applied a tourniquet and gave her a shot of morphine. The kids were scared, but we patched them up. They would survive.

The battalion medical aid station arrived with the battalion surgeon. Lieutenant Colonel Gordon arrived with them. I felt horrible and expected Gordon to Chew my ass our after he saw what had happened. Instead, he asked if everything was okay, then told me to continue with the recon. My wingman's gunner, Corporal Saylor, was pretty shaken up. Along with my gunner, he had pulled the trigger.

"Saylor, you okay?" I asked, knowing he wasn't.

He couldn't answer; tears were coming our instead of words.

"Saylor, you have got to pull yourself together. Things like this are bound to happen, even when you don't want them to." I didn't know what else to say.

"Sir, let's give Saylor a break," Hightower offered.

"All right. A couple hours out of the gunner's seat, then you're going back to it," I said, remembering years before how my dad had forced me not to let my fears make decisions for me, and made me crawl back into the ditches after I had nearly died in one.

"Let's get going, We have work to do." I walked back to my Bradley, looking at the old Iraqi man lying on the ground, breathing his last breaths.

I couldn't take my eyes off him. His face was blue from his lungs giving up. I tried to block it out, but the mental imprint it left would stay with me. He had been caught up in something out of his control, and it cost him his life as he tried to protect the lives of his family. This was the lowest, darkest side of combat. I wish that I had not experienced it. This incident continues to haunt me.

"West, get us out of here," I voiced over the intercom.

"Hey sir, the old man going to make it?" West asked.

"I don't think so, West…I don't think so," I replied, taking one last glance at him as the medics pulled out a body bag.

DAVE TRYBULA (Charlie Tank, Task Force 1-64 Armor)

We soon encountered the Rumaylah Oil Fields, or at least the main pipelines leading from the fields. Though not impossible to cross, the oil pipelines – about three feet in diameter and stretching aboveground – made for slow and difficult going. Next to each pipeline was a trench about six feet deep and eight feet across; evidently the Iraqis were preparing to bury the entire pipeline system under ground. Since we were heading perpendicular to the series of pipes, we had to drive the tanks gently over each pipe, which amazingly did not damage them, and then over the trench on the other side. We slowed to less than ten miles per hour.

When it seemed the series of pipelines would never end, we were through them and setting up a defensive perimeter at a power station just shy of Basra. After a quiet night we moved forward into the warehouse district of Basra and set up a perimeter inside a recently abandoned Republican Guard base camp. As the company cleared the camp, we opened an arms room and discovered brand new AK-47s and pistols still in cosmoline. We took these outside to provide Soviet weapons familiarization training on a life-sized picture of Hussein that was also in the cam. My gunner brought me the map that had been hanging on the brigadier general's wall. It was hand-drawn and showed his unit's entire defensive position, just west of the camp.

NEAL CREIGHTON (Alpha Tank, Task Force 3-15 Infantry)

In the morning I gazed through my commander's sight and saw fifteen Iraqi troops carriers moving through a four-lane intersection. I keyed the mike. "Balck Six, this is

White Six, observing fifteen trucks with troops moving northwest through an intersection two kilometers at ninety degrees, over."

"This is Black Six, roger, go forward and seal the intersection, out."

My platoon crept forward, bypassing numerous bunker complexes that seemed to cover almost every square kilometer of the Euphrates River Valley. The company followed one kilometer behind us. The other platoons stopped to drop thermite grenades down the hatches of Abandoned T-72 tanks to destroy them. When we reached the intersection, the platoon formed a coil with each tank squarely facing down one of the approaching road sections. My tank pointed south, Sfc. Wilson's east, Sergeant Harris's north, and Staff Sergeant Jone's west.

"White Six, this is White Three, I have the enemy truck approaching," Harris shortly reported. I looked over and saw him peering through his binos.

"White Six, this is White Five, enemy truck my direction, radioed Sergeant Wilson as a transport approached him as well.

"All white elements, the is White Six. Do not shoot unless necessary. We are supposed to be at cease-fire. Observe and report, out."

Harris waved at the enemy truck as it approached. The enemy driver hit the gas in an effort to run our roadblock. Now it was necessary to fire, since our mission was to prevent movement through the intersection. Sergeant Harris jumped down into the tank commander's position and let out a warning burst from his coaxial machine gun., the shots flying well over the truck. Iraqi soldiers jumped from the truck, searching for cover as they fired AK-47s at our position. Harris traversed his main gun and opened up with his machine gun, sending Iraqi vehicle crashing into a ditch.

"White Six, this is White Five, I still have one approaching. Do you want me to hold fire, over?" I knew Wilson's gunner was adjusting his coax on the target.

"If he tries to challenge, open fire. If he stops, let him go, over." Then I spotted a truck coming down the road in my sector toward my tank. Damn. I didn't want to shoot any more of these guys. Why on earth were they challenging M1A1 tanks with AK-47 assault rifles" It was plain stupid. And didn't they know there was a cease-fire? I was angry at them for putting me in the position of potentially having to fire on them for no good purpose. The truck on my road looked like it was going to try to bull its way through our four, too. I instructed my gunner to fire a warning burst at the truck.

"Stoppage!" His gun had jammed. He was yanking the charging handle on the machine gun, wedged in the turret between himself and the main gun.

"Sir, can I fire from my position?" asked Pfc. Carrol in a low voice. He had never fired his loader's machine gun before, and this was a hell of a time to break it in.

"Okay, Carrol, but warning shots only."

"Yes, sire." He pointed and fired. The bullets sprayed wildly in the direction of the truck. The first burst hit the front grill. The truck flipped on its side and rolled into an embankment. "I didn't mean it, sir. It's just hard to fire!"

"One heck of a warning shot, Carrol. Good thing you didn't mean business."

Enemy soldiers scrambled from the back of the damaged vehicle.

"Sir, we got troops coming out of the back with weapons, and I fixed the jam in the coax.

"All right, take them out."

I watched through the commander's sight extension as Davis place the coax reticle on the lower part of the enemy soldiers' bodies and let go a one hundred round burst, cutting most of the Iraqis down at the legs.

To my left rear, Sfc. Wilson was having similar engagement with Iraqi dismounts, and Sergeant Harris had chased numerous enemies into bunkers with his fire.

"White Six, this is Black Six, continue to push northeast. The medic tracks are coming up to pick up the wounded. What's your status, over?" Captain Schwartz radioed.

"We have about twenty-five injured Iraqis up here and all other enemy movement has stopped. We need to be careful going by the bunker complexes. Some enemy took cover in them, over," I replied.

"This is Black Six, roger. Move now, out."

The medics arrived and began loading the injured Iraqis into their tracks. My platoon turned east in a wedge formation. To my right, one Iraqi lay dead and another lay dying. He looked up at me as we passed, raised his arms, and, looking straight into my eyes, made his last communication on this earth: a peace sign.

We headed toward Basra, not knowing we had fired our last shots of the war.

After the engagement at the crossroads, we sat twenty kilometers south of Basra for several days. The engineers began to blow up everything the Iraqi army had left behind. Every few minutes an explosion would send smoke clouds way into the air. At first I was startled by the force and concussion of each explosion. But, as time went on, I stopped noticing the blasts and even fell asleep to them. What amazed me was how the body became conditioned to the noise. Most sane people would be terrified after hearing one Iraqi ammunition dump explode. We no longer noticed.

3-8 MARCH 1991

ALEX VERNON (Delta Mech, Task Force 3-15 Infantry)

We stopped moving east on 3 March. In the evening, Raynolds and McBryde played catch with our football, Dock and Vanderwerker smoked orange spice tea bags, and I took a bitch bath, while two Iraqi artillery pieces burned about four hundred meters away. Around us the upward drifting black smoke of destroyed Iraqi equipment and munitions smeared the horizon. After my bath, my first in nearly two weeks, I burned my nasty undergarments.

About 2230 the following evening, Captain Baillergeon called me on the radio. "Have Reynolds prepare his gear; he leaves at 0530 with Bravo Tank's advance party to go back."

"How far back?" I asked.

"All the way over," The Baillergeon called Lt. Brian Luke.

"Say again, Home Station, over?" asked an incredulous Brian.

"Roger."

"Wilco, out." Wilco is radio lingo for will comply.

What elation. People starting home. I jumped up and down on my seat in my hatch, banging the upright hatch behind me back and forth. I could hardly sleep that night.

The next day my platoon left Delta Mech and returned to Bravo Tank. Bob McCann, Bravo's First Platoon leader, had already departed with Brian, Reynolds, and the others in the advance party. I also learned that as the senior platoon leader I was originally to have gone home instead of Bob, but that would have left Sfc. Freight in command of my platoon – something Captain Swisher was not willing to do. Freight was good enough to take a platoon to war but not good enough to take it home. The day was cold, miserable, and wet. We spent most of the morning huddled in our vehicles out of the weather. We were to leave the next morning, 6 March, to pass through Kuwait and our Seventh Corps on our way to the port.

It didn't happen. I was told that Iraq had not released POWs on the fifth, as it was supposed to have done; also, our route out had not yet been established. We would instead establish positions on the Demilitarized Zone. He told us the division would likely move on Monday the eleventh, straight through Kuwait, down the coast, to Dhahran.

After the brigade commander's Huey lifted away, the company moved down Highway 8 to its new position. Two platoons occupied forward positions along east-west roads at the edge of the DMZ to stop all military traffic – ours from wandering east, Iraqis from going west. The First Platoon, less Bob McCann, stayed at the company command post in reserve. Matt Hoagland's Third Platoon guarded a piece of the highway. They spent some of their time posing for pictures with a dead Iraqi soldier under an overpass and chasing off wild dogs with AK-47s. My platoon was assigned a dirt road parallel to and several kilometers south of the highway. I positioned Freight's section forward of mine about one hundred meters, facing east. My section sat back in reserve, and also to halt east-bound American traffic.

Iraqis came our way all day long from both directions. For those headed west that saw my platoon and tried to skirt around us to the south, I radioed the company, and the platoon in reserve was dispatched to run them down. The first group to pass through my position came on foot. Sixteen soldiers. We put them face down on the ground to search them. Sergeant Boss's rough handling surprised one man, who started to resist. Boss shoved him back to the ground. While Boss and several others frisked the Iraqis. Freight watched them from behind his .50 cal, and I covered them on the ground with an M-16. I remember how strange that felt, my standing over these men, my finger on the trigger, the safety off, ready. To kill. How unreal it all was. I felt very suddenly like a boy, a child out of place. Not like an officer in command. Not like a man prepared to kill. While the CVC worn in the tank fits snugly around the ears, the Kevlar helmet's sided jut away from the head, creating a hollow that catches air around the ears, an effect which at that moment amplified my self-conscious disjointedness.

After satisfying ourselves that the Iraqis had no weapons, we let them pass. I didn't know it, but while we had the Iraqis on the ground, Sergeant Miller had placed several dirty magazines open in the middle to the road. I saw them when the Iraqis saw them, as we walked toward the tanks. Most of the Iraqis laughed; others held their stern visage.

Captain Swisher had ordered that we give no food to the Iraqis. Despite my sympathy for these ragged scrapes of men, I had enforced the orders for the first several groups that had asked. But we had boxes of MREs to spare, and I finally stopped objecting to my soldiers giving MREs to any Iraqi who asked.

One group hung around us to hitch a ride from Iraqis who came through with vehicles. Once, when two Iraqis pickup trucks with room to spare refused to take on any others, the two groups cursed at one another before the trucks zoomed away. One of the Iraqis left behind turned to me and muttered, in perfect English, "Look – Arab dung."

When one crowded truck drove through, a passenger shouted "Chicago!" Another moment too strange not to be true.

The last group came from the direction of Basra. One spoke English and told us that Hussein had a unit of T-72 tanks assaulting the city. "Home, brother, sister, no more." He asked which towns now had American, which Iraqis. I indicated the general location of the DMZ. He shook his head. "Saddam…Finished…," he said, crossing his arms at the wrists in from of his chest to express capture (I supposed) and drawing his finger across his neck. I didn't know just how close to Basra we were – I didn't have the 1:50,000 mapsheet with Al Basra on it, and didn't know that it was on the next mapsheet to the east of the one I had. We were on the outskirts; the main city was less than thirty kilometers away.

The civil war being waged in Basra gave credence to many of the rumors and reports I had heard throughout Desert Shield and the air war of Hussein's adversarial leadership style: Some Iraqi soldiers occupying Kuwait, we had heard, provided weapons to the Kuwaiti resistance; others shot themselves (the Kuwaiti resistance managed to kill up to thirty Iraqi soldiers a day). By November there had been fifty-four attempts on Hussein's life. One of Hussein's maltreated divisions had attacked one of his elite, well-fed, and well-equipped Republican Guard units. At a rally in Baghdad, Iraqi citizens chanted "we don't need Kuwait." Hussein executed his wife and some children. The starving Iraqi army occupying Kuwait resorted to eating animal from the Kuwait City zoo.

Part of my tasking that day on the DMZ involved occasionally sending out a section to patrol the general area. On one of its patrols, my section found an Iraqi military trailer. We pawed through it. The maps and plotting instruments led me to the conclusion that it had belonged to an artillery unit. I snatched a number of the maps for myself. I noticed one of them depicted the port of Dhahran, Saudi Arabia, where we had first stayed and where the ships transporting our equipment had berthed. Using the latitude and longitude of that map, I checked the others and verified that some of them were also maps of Saudi Arabia. At the time the discovery reinforced my belief that Hussein had had plans to move against us into Saudi those first weeks of Desert Shield.

We returned to the company for the evening. Another platoon relieved us.

That night a blast of light turned the sky orange. It woke me. The boom followed a minute later, shaking the tank. Smaller flashed and booms continued for several minutes. Wild dogs yelped.

One of the other Bravo Tank platoons reported stopping a truck with a box strapped atop the cab roof. When they asked the Iraqi soldier driving what was in the box, he answered, "My brother." Later the platoon stopped a bus of Kuwaitis returning home from wherever they had been held prisoner in Iraq. Some of their hands had been smashed flat with sledgehammers.

A number of us spent the next morning crawling all over a T-72 tank that first Platoon had recovered from the DMZ the evening before. Later, my platoon and the XO, Greg Jackson, recovered a T-55 with a mine plow from the DMZ. We hoped that the mine plow would make it compelling enough for the division to take home. It was not.

Both tanks were small, uncomfortable, poorly made, and dangerous. No comparison to our own. Our mechanics had tried to start the T-55, failed, and so towed it back to the company. I looked through its periscopes and sites. Terrible visibility. The tank had no radio or antennas indicating that it had once had a radio. The joint welding was crude. The turret interior was cramped and uncomfortable. These Soviet-made vehicles have a crew of three: the commander, the gunner, and the driver. An auto-loader replaced the human loader crew position. The rounds are thus stored in racks inside the crew compartment. The crew members surely bumped against the rounds as they worked, and any penetration of the turret becomes catastrophic. Crawling on these tanks, I understood why I had seen so many with their turrets popped of, and also why the Iraqis could never have conceived the distance of our attack, especially through the extreme terrain – the ravines, escarpments, dunes, wadi mazes, and soggy septkas – that they knew better that we did. And, as it happened, through that atrocious weather, and at that speed – "double the rate we had anticipated," reflected Major General McCaffrey, "and we had anticipated a rate of battle that was unheard of." Those machines, and the Iraqi soldiers riding in those machines, could never have done what we had done. It would have been too much for them, Indeed Iraq's entire defenses were oriented south, toward Kuwait and the Saudi eastern provinces, and we had rolled in from the west.

Greg Jackson's gunner found a roll of film in the T-72. Once home, he had it developed. A group of Iraqi soldiers, five or so, posing on the tank. Big smiles. A moment exactly like many of our own.

Captain Baillergeon, a few days into the cease-fire, had told his lieutenants that division staff was planning an on-order attack against Basra. Basra? Sir? The city was experiencing a civil war already. Our war was over. What was McCaffrey thinking? His trademark aggressiveness was about to go too far. So my self-preservation instinct protested, anyway. I didn't know that Basra had been a contingency objective all along. I didn't consider that McCaffey was doing what good leaders do, what he had done at the port in August when an offensive was the last thing on everybody else's mind: Planning for the most likely battle so the he and his unit would be ready in case the call came.

One hundred hours into Iraq, we stopped exactly when we should have. All other challenges of maintaining the coalition and continuing our attack aside – challenges of increasing the burden on a logistics system just beginning to really feel the strain, of diplomacy, more restrictive terrain, additional casualties, collateral damage to the civilian population, the threat by the civilian population and a nation defending its home, a possible extended occupation force, and morale (both ours in the thick of it and the American public's) – the larger issues of mission and morality necessitated our ceasing violent operations. Once Hussein surrendered, we had lost our mandate. What could our mission have been? Removing Hussein either by force or as a condition of surrender would have only repeated Iraq's moral crime, the impingement on an independent nation's sovereignty (the latter solution of doubtful efficacy). It had been estimated that as much as one-third of the Iraqi army's armored force escaped our encirclement of the Kuwaiti theater back into Iraq. But to prosecute the further destruction of the Iraqi army, of the disorganized, battered, retreating troops, would have been the moral equivalent (on a much larger scale) of shooting a mugger in the back after he's dropped his knife, turned, and fled. When you can no longer claim self-defense, the act becomes murder.

"Thank God we stopped when we did," Jeannie Novak, the lieutenant who had seen us off at Hunter Army Airfield and who had traveled with a support battalion attached to the division, had reflected to me. "We were too full of success. There had been too much winning."

We had succeeded in our purpose, the liberation of Kuwait and the restoration of its legitimate government, and it was time to go home. As my brother Eric wrote in a letter just prior to the ground war, "True heroes do what has to be done and no more."

Combat Advice for New Infantry Lieutenants

From the United States Military Academy Class of 1950

Your responsibility is tell us what you want the platoon to do. My responsibility as your Platoon Sergeant is to get it done.

Leadership means that most of the time our Lieutenant goes last, but there are those times when the Lieutenant just has to go first

To lead soldiers, you first must be one

I am the Infantry . . . Follow Me!

Source: Combat Advice for New Infantry Lieutenants (1999). Reprinted by permission of TROG Press.

Introduction

In times far past, new officers joined their units and learned on the job. Then the vast expansion of our Army for World War II produced a broad range of branch specific training programs for newly commissioned officers as well as branch specific Officer Candidate Schools. For a variety of reasons beyond the scope of this document, the decision was made in 1949 to send the West Point class of 1950 directly to their units without attending their Branch Basic Course. In the spring of 1950, after having made their branch choices, the graduating class received their initial "first assignment" orders to units on occupation duty in Europe, units in the United States, Panama, Alaska, Hawaii and Far East Command (FECOM).

Graduating 6 June, these new lieutenants departed West Point on their long awaited Graduation Leave. On 25 June 1950, the North Korean Army invaded South Korea, rapidly overwhelming the South Koreans. Military history courses and texts can inform you in great detail of the series of developments by which the United States and United Nations decided to resist Communist aggression, sending first air support then ground troops to aid South Korea. By mid-July a very tenuous perimeter was established to protect the port of Pusan, in the extreme south east corner of the Korean peninsula. US divisions (1st Cavalry, 24th Infantry and 25th Infantry) had been taken from occupation duty in Japan, 2nd Infantry Division brought from Fort Lewis, Washington, 29th Infantry Regimental Combat Team from Okinawa, 5th Regimental Combat Team from Hawaii and 5th Marine Brigade from the US, all to stem the tide; only 7th Infantry Division remained in Japan as FECOM reserve. After Inchon landings on 15 September by newly reactivated X Corps (consisting of 1st Marine Division and 7th Infantry Division), the US 3rd Infantry Division joined X Corps in October. UN forces crossed the 38th parallel in early October in pursuit of the retreating and shattered North Korean Army. Chinese Communists entered the war in November, concurrent with extremely bitter winter weather for which US forces were not well equipped. The combined winter's severity and massive Chinese attacks were devastating to United Nations units.

Lieutenants on orders to Hawaii or Fort Lewis were recalled from Graduation Leave to ship out with their units in July. Those on orders to FECOM arrived in August. Due to extreme officer shortages and immediate threats to the Pusan perimeter, new lieutenants joined their companies to assume platoon command just before— or in some cases during—attacks. Many of them became company commanders; some immediately, as their very first assignment in Korea. One briefly commanded a battalion (all other officers in that battalion were killed, captured or missing in action, separated from their unit).

Compilation of this collection of combat advice had its origins in an *Assembly* article about one member of this class, Dave Hughes, describing advice he had received from his first Company Commander, John Flynn, USMA '44 who passed on to Hughes what he had learned in World War II. The article described Hughes combat tour in Korea, to include eventually becoming Company Commander himself. (Excerpts of this article are included.) A very logical connection presented itself: many other members of that class would have similar experiences to relate, concerning what they learned about combat and how they learned it. A request was sent to those members of the class of 1950 who were commissioned Infantry, remained on active duty as career Infantry officers and went directly to Korea after graduation—as opposed to a year or two of troop duty and attending Infantry Officers Basic Course at Fort Benning before their combat duty tour in Korea. (Almost all of them served also in Vietnam, commanding battalions and brigades in that war. Some went on to become generals, commanding at higher levels before retirement.)

They were asked to respond with "new lieutenant in Korea" experiences, focusing on conventional war against a capable and determined enemy force which was willing to suffer substantial casualties in its tactical operations—as opposed to a very different type of combat experience gained since Korea from pursuit of an always elusive guerrilla force in Vietnam, or fighting assorted poorly trained enemy units in Panama, Grenada, Somalia or Haiti, and surrender prone Iraqis of Desert Storm. They considered such topics as advice received from Company Commanders or other experienced officers, information they *wished* some combat experienced officer had told them so they would not have had to learn it the hard way, problems they experienced which would be largely resolved by current equipment, useful items to take along and suggestions for professional reading.

Compiled here are the collective recommendations as combat advice for new Infantry lieutenants from 33 members of that class. The wisdom they offer was hard won at great personal effort, courage and sacrifice—they sincerely hope it will help you, a new Infantry lieutenant, as they "grip hands 'though it be from the shadows."

Officers Providing Combat Advice

Colonel John R. Flynn, USMA '44
Colonel George L. Ball
Lieutenant Colonel John L. Begley
Lieutenant Colonel Malcolm W. Chandler
Colonel Herschel E. Chapman
Colonel William D. Davis
Colonel William B. DeGraf
Lieutenant Colonel Charles F. Dickerson
Colonel August J. Dielens
Lieutenant Colonel Ray M. Dowe
Colonel Albert J. Fern
Lieutenant Colonel John E. Fox
Colonel J. Ross Franklin
Lieutenant Colonel Louis V. Genaurio

Colonel Joseph T. Griffin
Lieutenant Colonel Phillip H. Harper
Colonel Charles W. Hayward
Colonel John D. Howard
Colonel David R. Hughes
Lieutenant General James M. Lee
Colonel John M. Murphy
Lieutenant Colonel Charles W. Newcomb
Lieutenant Colonel Howard N. Parks
Colonel Clifton A. Prichett
Lieutenant Colonel Robert D. Reed
Lieutenant Colonel Mark C. Rhoads
Lieutenant Colonel John R. Shaffer
Colonel Charles R. Smith
Colonel Samuel W. Smithers
Major General Jere W. Sharp
Colonel Walter C. Stanton
Colonel William A. Steinberg
Lieutenant Colonel Francois X. Therrien
General Volney F. Warner

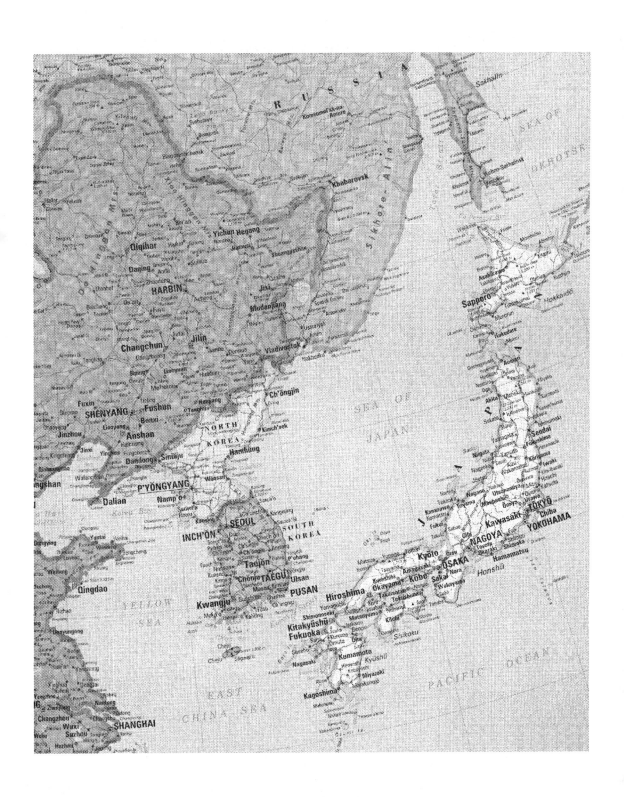

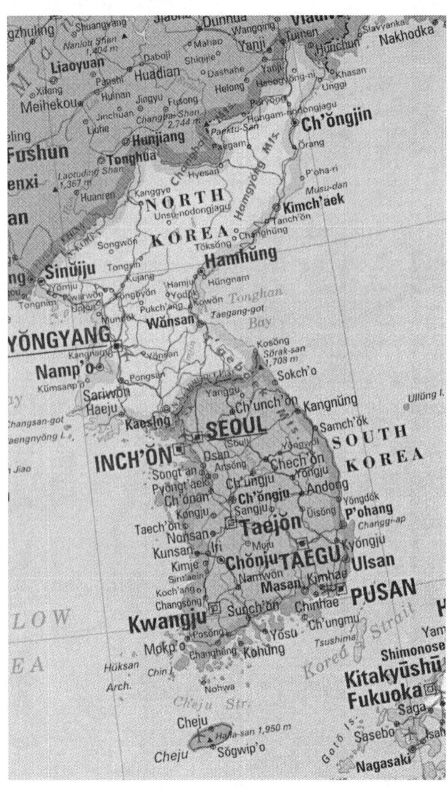

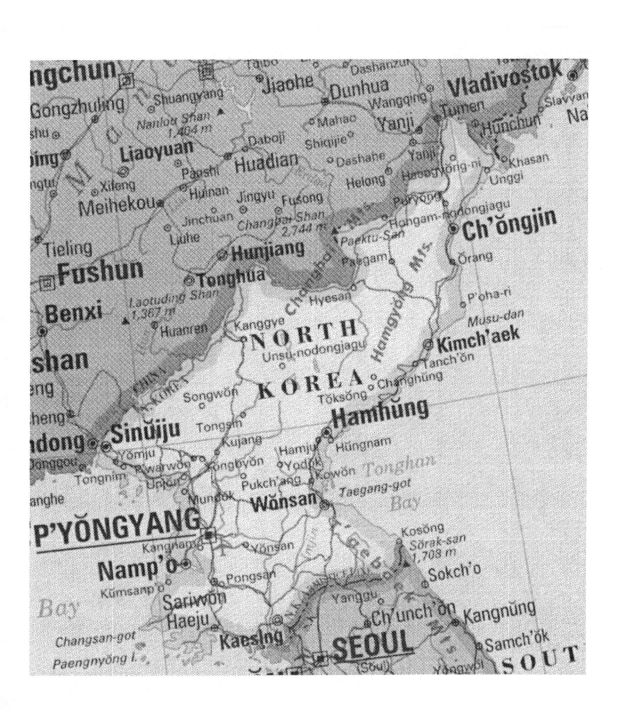

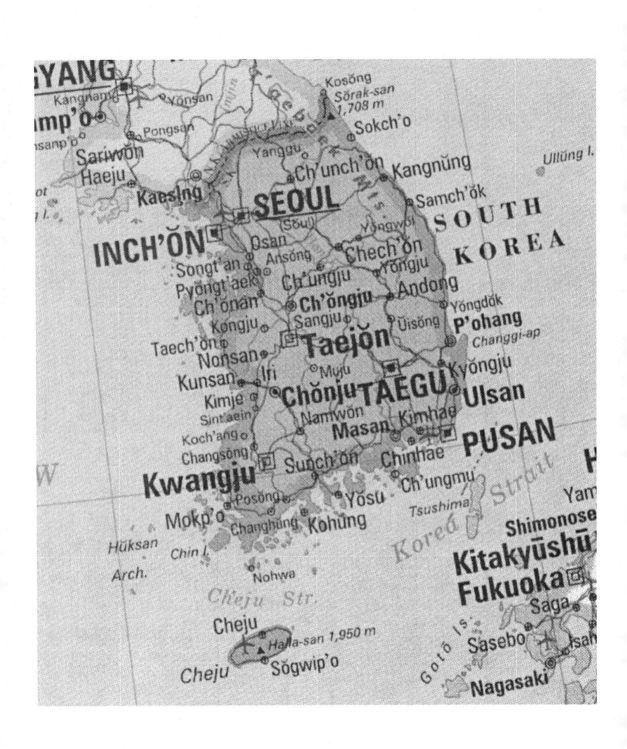

Colonel John R. Flynn (then Captain), Commanding Company K, 7th Cavalry Regiment, 1st Cavalry Division

As background, I served as an Infantry lieutenant in combat in Europe in World War II after graduation 6 June 1944. At first I was a Rifle Platoon Leader and then for four months the Platoon Leader of Special Combat Patrol Platoon (the only one in the regiment), in the 264th Infantry Regiment, 66th Division. Just before the Korean War, I was in G-3 Section of 3rd Infantry Division at Fort Benning from the time of its reactivation in 1949 until I took over a rifle company in the 1st Battalion, 30th Infantry under "Cider" Joe Stillwell, son of "Vinegar" Joe Stillwell of World War II China-Burma-India Theater fame.

The company I commanded in 1st Battalion, 30th Infantry had a homosexual as Commanding Officer who left a big footprint of debris upon his relief and dismissal— Section 8's, AWOL's, low morale, a sick outfit. Before I was called to the now provisional battalion destined for Korea, I tore up and destroyed Section 8 (Unsuitability) paperwork and Section 9 (Undesirable), retrieved all the AWOL's, initiated special field training for all the NCO's and soldiers, and in general kicked ass with vigor, sometimes in conflict with the Battalion Commander. With regard to the AWOL's, I established communications with relatives and friends of the AWOL's, wrote letters to them, and strongly advised them to get their miscreants back to Benning quickly before they ended up in Leavenworth. In about only two months all the AWOL's were back, the undesirables were on the road to soldiering, and the outfit was shaking the residue of the homosexual captain whose main entertainment (other than sexual) was playing pool in the rec [recreation] room with the troops. Soon after the North Koreans invaded South Korea, I got orders to join the newly activated provisional battalion as a Rifle Company Commander.

[Occupation units in Japan were "reduced to two-thirds strength" by the deactivation of one battalion. Various divisions in the US were then tasked to organize a battalion for immediate shipment to Japan, to fill the occupation divisions. Thus the "provisional" battalion of this narrative.]

As I arrived at the Company, the troops were arriving from all parts of Fort Benning. Upon my arrival, I made the decision to interview *all* new soldiers instead of delegating this to the First Sergeant or to some other officer. As each new soldier arrived, I interviewed him to determine his skill, special training etc. and then with the Company Chart in the hands of the First Sergeant, notified the soldier of his squad and platoon assignment. *I learned a great deal of detail about the quality of the men, which reinforced my confidence in the unit.* I was very pleased with the overall talent pool, and as time went on, fell back on the information and knowledge that I had accumulated during this process. Whenever possible, we were able to assign/fit the soldier into a slot with which he felt comfortable.

I was especially attentive to using highly skilled soldiers (weapons platoon, recoilless rifles, mortars etc.) in their specialty areas. Some of these soldiers knew or had served with each other in the past and again, whenever possible we put them in the same squad or platoon. You must remember that the anxiety level was high—within weeks they would be on a very hectic, unstable battlefield with no squad, platoon or company training behind them. 200 soldiers were literally dumped into a hodge-podge with new officers, NCO's and companions/comrades. I got to know each soldier and he got to see and talk with his company commander. In some cases, personal affairs were addressed at a correctable level; this reduced the soldier's uncertainty about the situation.

Two incidents during this period are interesting. Michael Contaldi and a Greek kid named Pannapoulus (spelling?), both about 17 or 18 years old, got into trouble in Columbus while "under the influence" of adult beverages and broke into a jewelry store window resulting in jail detention. During the interview and assignment sessions, I was informed by the First Sergeant that they had been released by the judge with the understanding that if their unit took them to Korea, they were "free" men. My First Sergeant knew a little about them and advised me not to take them back. I interviewed each one and decided that their youthful indiscretion did not bar them from soldiering. Contaldi was a private, served as company headquarters runner, was decorated, went up the ladder and became a Platoon Sergeant, even *with bad feet*. He had an outstanding combat record. A few years ago I talked to him on the phone, he is doing well and is healthy. Pannapoulus became a Squad Leader and was wounded and evacuated on the Hill 314 Battle (fight in which the Battalion received the Presidential Unit Citation). He is alive and well also. I am happy that I took a chance with them.

Special trust and confidence. The early days of activation and organization at Benning were spent setting an example, communicating with precision, and explaining how critical top flight performance and reliance on their follow soldiers would be to their success and survival. Again, we never once did any tactical training, either individual or unit training of any kind in preparation for Korea which was a battlefield controlled by the enemy. I was always inclined to use mission-type instructions/orders in situations which were fluid, unstable or unpredictable. The battlefield provided sufficient stimulus to the soldier, NCO or officer with an average brain to react properly in the interest of himself or the unit. Overly detailed orientation, instructions or orders tend to confuse many people when they cannot reconcile the contradictions. George Bush understood that at the high level: he said "kill Iraqis in Kuwait and eject them from Kuwait." How could anyone not understand the mission?

When Lieutenant Dave Hughes joined "K" Company late one night in November 1950 (after the Chinese entered the war), I spent considerable time in describing the situation, history of events, the key people in the company, cautionary behavior etc. I took him personally to his deployed platoon, introducing him to key NCO's and others. For many reasons, he became permanently identified with "K" Company. He was grabbed by the Assistant Division Commander for Aide de Camp duty. He could have cushioned it out with a warm cot, good food and no risk till the end of his tour. But he fought to get back to "K" Company, and was assigned to command the company. I had departed in January for special assignment (building a six plus three division evacuation line) near the Pusan/Naktong river area.

[Initial success of Chinese Communists in driving UN forces out of North Korea and then in their advance down into South Korea, led to concerns that the Pusan perimeter might have to be reoccupied. The plan was for a six division perimeter along the Naktong, then over to the coast at Pohang, with a smaller three division perimeter around Pusan itself. Should the Chinese success continue, the three division "inner perimeter" could cover the withdrawal of units from the outer perimeter. Naval gunfire would then cover the withdrawal of units from the inner perimeter if necessary. Each regiment sent a combat experienced captain back to lay out their unit's portion of the fortified line, which was then actually built by Construction Engineer units.]

Such negative thinking was changed after a new Commanding General took over Eighth Army (General Ridgeway), and turned our efforts toward attacking north and pushing the Chinese out, rather than being focused on further withdrawals south, or possibly getting pushed out of Korea entirely. Then I became S-3 of 2nd Battalion, 7th Cavalry and later S-3 of the Regiment until wounded 24 June 1951 and evacuated home. Hughes still thinks that commanding "K" Company was the pinnacle of his life/service.

******

Only half of what you encounter with the combat unit you join will be standard US Army—organization, equipment, personnel. The other half will be unique to the time, place, and war. You have to take it as it is, and make as much as you can out of it.

A lot of Army unit operations—tactics, techniques—are formulaic; sound doctrine which has been distilled from the hard won experience in the field. (The basics, such as always putting out LP's and OP'S, requiring range cards and firing stakes in the defense, checking the line all night long even in "quiet situations," cleaning weapons, changing socks and many others must be followed to the letter, all the time.) But that doctrine we think of as "tactics" was designed to apply to the "average," interchangeable combat unit in any war at any time, for an Army superior in mass to its enemies, not numerically inferior.

[In World War II even though the Germans had huge numbers across the entire front, we crushed them with overwhelming mass at the point of attack. Not only troops, but firepower. A single division on a critical river crossing, for example, was supported by vast reinforcing fires from Corps artillery and higher level units—27 artillery battalions firing to support the normal four artillery battalions of that division's own artillery! That is an awesome amount of massive firepower.]

This is a production line approach to war—at which America is magnificent. But to get superior results, or overcome the disadvantage of inferior numbers, weapons, terrain, you have to be willing to think outside of the box; to apply principles of war to the immediate tactical situation; to come up with a solution unheard of in field manual doctrine that will get your job done better, with fewer casualties. Learn to think and innovate tactically, not always just follow rules without thinking. Don't ever get caught by the watchful enemy in always operating by the same pattern.

When you can, let all the men of your unit about to go into action understand, not only what your mission is, what you expect of them, and what orders they are to follow, but the reasons for your tactical decisions. Let them in on your thinking process. The reason for this is that things never will go exactly according to plan. But American soldiers are great at getting the job done, when they understand what that job is, and in the absence of appropriate orders, will take the initiative and surprise you by their success.

If you are rifle-in-the-hand Infantry, learn to listen to the sounds of battle. Ask old hands what every sound means—whose weapons or equipment, doing what. Listen intently at times during combat operations to derive a mental picture, from sounds alone, of what is going on.

Don't be afraid to ask your men how they would carry out a tactical mission, before you decide on your own course of action. You never can tell who will have a new, or better idea. Just make sure they all know what your decision is; there is no uncertainty in your mind once it is made up.

The darker it is and the more spread out your men, the more important it is to keep the unit intact and worried men's spirits up by communicating frequently with them. Make them know you are always there and will support them.

Higher headquarters will bug you to make reports to them. And never think to keep you informed except when a new order is issued. Make sure you pry as much information out of higher headquarters as you can; when you get reports from your subordinates, you give them information also.

Control of fear can be a conscious matter. It is based on the fact that very few people can think about more than one thing at a time. To control fear among your men, keep them busy. If you see a soldier frozen with fear, find something, anything, for him to do that requires him to think about what he is doing. While thus engaged, he can not think about being afraid. To control your own fear, find something for YOU to do. Actually, officers, with their additional duties and responsibilities, their additional training and realization of how many things really need to be done soon (before the attack, or before we get hit, or while on the move), actually have a great advantage in combat. Your training makes you see so very many things that need to be done, that you can stay mentally busy virtually all the time and have no time for fear. When fear grips you, find something to do. Anything will suffice, but it is, of course, better to analyze your tactical situation and find the most critical leader tasks in relation to combat preparations for your unit in those particular circumstances.

Communicating Clearly Always have a notebook and pen or pencil. When receiving orders or instructions, take notes. When giving orders or instructions, insist that your subordinates take notes. Remember that a short pencil is always better than a long memory. Give instructions or orders from notes. On instructions given or corrections made, use your notes to insure that you positively follow-up on everything. Gain a reputation among your subordinates as a leader who always follows up on everything you tell them to do. Make it so that in your unit there is one more item to add to the certainty of death and taxes, and that is your follow-up on instructions issued. Also take notes and follow up when any of your soldiers or NCO's ask you to help them in some way or to get information they need. Make certain they all understand that your tenacity in following up also works to help them solve their problems just as much as it does to check up on them.

Get positive feedback on your instructions by asking direct questions. Do not end by asking "Are there any questions" or "do you all understand" or something similar. That type question leads to disaster, because human nature makes us not want to expose ourselves as the one who didn't get it or the one who does not understand. Or if there was a part you did *not* make clear, your subordinates may be reluctant to point out your mistake by asking a question. The proper way to insure complete and correct understanding is to ask direct questions: "Sergeant Jones, what time do we cross the LD?" "Sergeant Smith, what unit will be on our right flank?" and so on until you have spot checked each subordinate on several items.

Clearing trench lines or fortified positions This creates the danger of leaving some enemy bypassed and then coming up out of a hole to fire on your unit from the rear. Insist that each squad leader assign two riflemen as "tail gunners" who move at the rear of the squad, staying close together with one man watching and covering to the rear, and the other covering the area between the squad and the two tail gunners. These two must communicate constantly, and move in a leapfrog manner, alternating the direction of their observation and coverage as they leapfrog, and stay close enough to the rest of the squad, say 10 or 15 yards, to not get left behind.

Ambush your back trail and reenter friendly lines from patrols Rear security on night combat patrols must be alert for infiltrators trying to tag-along with the patrol back into friendly lines. Stop the patrol about 100 to 150 yards short of the reentry point, and establish security to both flanks and the rear. The Patrol Leader must then personally and positively identify every man, starting from the point man and working back to last man in rear security. (Patrol leader must be prepared to shoot any infiltrator discovered.) Then the Security Team Leader, at least one automatic weapon and two or three riflemen set up a hasty ambush covering the patrol's back trail, during the patrol's reentry to friendly lines. When the rest of the patrol is back inside friendly lines, all patrol personnel set up in firing positions to support, if necessary, recovery of rear security element. Then use a flare gun signal, radio call or unique and prearranged sequence of rifle shots to notify Security Team Leader to carefully leapfrog his element the remaining distance back into friendly lines, under protection of already established support positions of the rest of the patrol.

50% sleeping bags on position This is the only way you can keep soldiers alert and on watch at night. They are all dog tired; the night cold is unpleasant at best in the summer and brutal in the winter. Use two man fighting positions, with only one sleeping bag between them. When it is time to change the guard, you can be assured that the cold one coming off watch will apply positive peer pressure to get his buddy up and out of the sleeping bag, so he can get warm and get some sleep. You and your Platoon Sergeant also pull 50% alert, with one of you always out checking the line. Not only does this provide direct and close supervision, but it lets the troops know that their leaders are sharing their hardships rather than sleeping while they pull watch.

Sleep with a weapon and sleep in tennis shoes Many nights you will only cat-nap sitting up with your full uniform and web gear on, your boots on and your rifle across your lap. Even on those nights when you *can* take off your web gear and boots for a couple hours of actual sleep, be ready to be up at an instant's notice, with your rifle where you can secure it without hesitation or wondering "where did I put it this time?" A pair of tennis shoes are lightweight to carry, will let you rest your feet out of your boots, let your boots air out some, but will still allow you to be fully mobile immediately on getting out of your sleeping bag when you don't have time to put on boots and tie them to keep from tripping on the laces.

Learn weapons employment and read the preface to SLA Marshall's *Pork Chop Hill* Too often in Korea junior leaders, both officers and NCO's did not adequately apply their training concerning proper employment and emplacement of weapons, with regard to using the military crest of high ground, rather than the topographical crest, proper fields of observation and fire from positions and areas of dead space in front of their defenses which could have been easily covered by more attention to weapons employment in laying out the defensive position with regard to the nature of the terrain. Learn weapons employment as it relates to terrain, and emplace positions which provide interlocking bands of grazing fire across the entire platoon front.

Get to know your men and do something special for them Learn their strengths and their capabilities, so you can lean on those. Learn where they need to improve or to learn more or to pay more attention to detail in what they already know; then insist that they work on correcting these performance areas. Learn where they are from and take an interest in them as individuals. Get your Platoon Sergeant to get you a roster of birthdays, and on a man's birthday, give him an "In Platoon R & R" of no ambush patrol or OP/LP duty. Have him bring his sleeping gear back to the platoon CP and get a full night's sleep without being on 50% alert (awake half the night in one or two hour intervals). Of course you still have to insist that he dig his own individual shelter/fighting position, so you won't be taking the chance of getting him killed on his birthday during a fight that starts while he is sleeping in an exposed position. His squad can get along without him for one night, and the troops will all eat this up. Keep your own birthday a secret and do not take such an R & R yourself. This is for the troops only.

Officer/NCO duty differences, leader and assistant Always have an assistant squad leader assigned, even if your squads are down to two veteran PFC's and the rest are all new replacements. Learn and understand the division of labor among leader tasks. The Squad Leader directs the squad tactically while the Assistant Squad Leader takes care of logistics—such tasks as redistributing ammunition after or during a fight, requesting resupply, evacuating and reporting casualties, filling out casualty tags, organizing and supervising supply carrying parties, weapons cleaning and weapons maintenance, changing socks, caring for feet, taking malaria pills etc. The Squad Leader must be free to concentrate on fighting and employing the squad tactically without being burdened down by housekeeping chores.

Likewise, as Platoon Leader, you must stay focused on tactics! To establish and maintain security is always your first priority. In the defense, that means OP's or LP's out and manned; on the move or in the attack it means selection of proper formations for the terrain and visibility, with front, flank and rear security elements moving at such a distance to keep your whole unit from being surprised by an enemy move. You concentrate on proper placement of machine guns and anti-tank weapons, and on moving them as often as necessary as situations change; squad sectors and boundaries and areas of responsibility and coordination with adjacent units; fields of fire for all weapons; planning or controlling the use of supporting fires; and replacing casualties by repositioning or reassigning remaining available soldiers, NCO's and weapons to insure proper coverage of assigned sectors. Your Platoon Sergeant, no matter what his rank, handles the logistics and administrative duties in your platoon. He is the beans and bullets guy who supervises the Assistant Squad Leaders in their support function of taking that load off of the Squad Leaders.

Your Platoon Sergeant will also supervise the platoon in the execution of the many, many tasks which must be accomplished in the "running of the platoon." For example, you will lay in the defensive position by first putting out security (OP's and LP's), emplacing crew served weapons for proper sector coverage and adequate fields of fire, and designating squad boundaries and coordinating points. Then your Platoon

Sergeant takes over and supervises "how" the platoon digs in, and prepares the defense—how and when soldiers rotate between and among the duties of some being on OP or LP duty, some staying deployed ready to defend from hasty positions, some digging their own fighting positions or helping dig in the crew served weapons, laying commo wire out to the OP, carrying supplies or sandbags, eating, using a dig-it-yourself field latrine, changing socks and cleaning weapons etc. In other words, you tell your platoon sergeant what to do (a mission type order) and stay out of his way while he and the other NCO's get it done.

While the platoon digs in under NCO supervision, you continue to focus on tactics. You need to plan additional supporting fires, plan ambush or security patrols, analyze your sector and adjacent sectors to plan locations for alternate and for supplementary fighting positions for possible enemy approaches not covered by the primary positions you have designated, or from the flank or even the rear should they penetrate an adjacent unit and come at you from a different direction. Finally you will use some of this time to dig your own foxhole at the location you designated for the platoon CP.

As the work progresses, you must also find time to observe and inspect to insure that proper standards are being attained. You should check early on the digging in of the crew served weapons to insure that they are going in at the proper location and will have the fields of fire you intended. Do not wait until the position is completed until you check fields of fire, so you won't have to direct that it be moved after all the hard work is done. Spot check a few other positions, to insure that your "trace" of the platoon position worked out within squad sectors to provide proper coverage across your front. Again, adjustments must be made before the digging is finished.

Check observation and fields of fire from inside the fighting positions, quiz soldiers about who is on their right and their left flanks, what and where are their sector limits, inspect their range cards and their aiming stakes and their ammo supplies, ask them to tell you where the OP is located out to their front, who is out on OP duty now, have they changed their socks, have they eaten yet, and have they written home lately? If time and the immediate tactical situation permit (and your unit has received the Stars and Stripes recently), ask how their favorite team is doing.

While you check, always manage to find something that is being done right or something that is being done well for which to praise each soldier and his NCO leader, who is with you as you check his area. Ask each NCO leader before you leave his sector, "is there anything more I can do to help you or is there anything you need that I can help you get?" Let them all know that you are there to support them in every way you can.

Make corrections as necessary, to the NCO, in terms of *what* is wrong and needs to be corrected. Don't make your corrections in terms of *who* is wrong, which only causes a defensive reaction. For example, say "the fixing aperture in this position isn't lined up right—it won't cover the assigned sector, and must be adjusted to permit coverage to the mouth of that gully." That's much better than "Sgt. Jones, you let Pvt. Smith dig in the wrong place and now he can't cover his assigned sector." Notice that in both cases you are pointing out the same mistake, but in the "what" is wrong example, you are not making it a personal attack on anyone. The proper correction gets much quicker results. If the problem needs more serious attention, call the NCO away, out of hearing of his men. Be firm, be specific, but stay focused on what rather than who is wrong.

Over time, you must demonstrate to your soldiers and your NCO's that you know your job, that you set high standards and insist that they all meet those standards, and that your efforts are directed at improving their capabilities to accomplish the platoon's mission and to survive. Before very long, you will discover that by the time you find the opportunity to start digging your own foxhole, it will already have been dug, while you were busy taking care of your responsibilities and your men.

****

What can my contribution be? One of the best bits of advice came from my dad, Class of '15. When you get to your unit, he said, the regimental commander and battalion commander will talk to you. Listen to them just a little. Pay a bit more attention to your company commander, but when you get a chance, get off to one side and talk to the First Sergeant and really listen to him.

In my case, I joined the 21st Infantry, 1st Battalion. B Company, which had been Task Force Smith. It was good to talk to LTC Smith. He said that they had been in some pretty tough situations but COL Stephens, Regimental CO, never left them.

I would want to tell you new Infantry Lieutenants to try not to worry about scare stories from the veterans. Then get with your Platoon Sergeant and listen hard to him and stick with him like glue for the first days. Watch, listen, learn. You may be fuzzy on patrolling, putting the platoon in a defensive position, sectors of fire with range cards and aiming stakes, attack formations, etc. Keep your eyes and ears open and pretty soon you will be able to do it all.

Don't be sensitive to taking a second place to that Platoon Sergeant. It would be stupid to charge in with a braggadocio attitude. Set an example and your men will respect you and know that you are the platoon leader.

Be with your men most of the time. Don't go back to the company CP all the time when you are in defense. Stay with your guys. Be wet and cold with them. Share willingly in their hardships and their discomforts.

Be out there in front and lead. Take patrols out, even if they are squad size. Lead them from the front. Your eyes and ears may be better than anyone else's. When you are coming back from a patrol, be back in the rear of the column and sort of mother them back into friendly lines.

Keep telling your men what a great job they are doing. There isn't much joy and fun in combat, so a pat on the back goes a long way.

Learn fire adjustment, communications, compass work, map reading (always know where you are on the map), but realize there may be times when you don't have a map.

Personal items to have. Some things come to mind such as a small notebook, a few sheets of stationary (encourage your men to write home, and you follow your own advice), a miniature toilet kit, flannel long johns if it's cold, a good pocket knife such as Swiss Army. There could be more but don't get bogged down. Have a pocket size Book of Common Prayer.

This is what I believe new Infantry lieutenants need. I am aware that response time is of importance, so in keeping with Patton's dictum "A poor plan executed violently now is better than a perfect plan next week, because next week may be too late," here is my poor plan.

May God bless this attempt to help at least one lieutenant in his baptism of fire. We often speak of baptism and I believe baptism of fire is an apt phrase. One is truly born again and never quite the same after his first experience of someone emptying an AK in his direction or dropping several mortar rounds in close proximity.

Map reading   My first advice to the young lieutenant, and this is all based on my own personal experience, is to really learn map reading. The way the Army has got it set up now with these compass courses and pacing yourself off, you could pass the test but you don't really learn to read a map. This caused me inordinate problems in Korea, particularly with the high mountainous country there and difficulty in distinguishing between different pieces of terrain. In an attack one time, in a raid, I had to have the Battalion Commander from the Battalion OP actually physically point the hill out to me, because from the map (I had it on my map but from an overlay) I wasn't sure which one it was and I just wanted to make sure. So learn your map reading and that will help you not only as a lieutenant but also for the rest of your career.

Weapons   The other thing to do is really learn your weapons, the functioning of them and the employment of them. We were surrounded one time by Chinese and in the midst of a real fire fight—they were in our trenches—and an automatic rifleman, a BAR man, handed me his weapon and he wanted me to fix it because it was malfunctioning and he wanted me to adjust the gas port and I started screwing around with that for about 30 seconds until I realized how stupid this was. I had other things to do and I gave him my carbine. Know your weapons, the mechanics of them so you can strip them down and clean them and take care of them.

You know, at West Point we never learned to take a trigger [housing] group apart on an M-1 [Garand Rifle, caliber .30-06] or I never learned it and that caused me some problems one time. On the employment of weapons, this I can recall as a battalion commander [in Viet-Nam] spending time with a rifle company commanded by a lieutenant out of West Point. I joined them in late afternoon to spend the night with them, and I was astounded when I went around. They had no idea how to put their Claymores [Antipersonnel Weapon M-18] out, how to employ their machine guns, how to register in fires, and so I taught them. It wasn't a question of chewing them out, and I noticed a lot of the soldiers just followed me around. They all wanted to learn this. It was like they'd never heard it before. So learn to read a map and learn your weapons.

Fire and maneuver. Now that is something that everybody knows the words to, but we don't know how to do it. I noticed it in a rifle platoon that when we used fire and maneuver, the soldiers firing were afraid to fire too close to the maneuvering element. They lacked confidence in themselves, I suppose, or maybe it was something else. But when we were back in reserve, I trained them in fire and maneuver. I had an AR man fire about five feet off to one side of me from about twenty yards away to show them how close the supporting fires should be to the maneuver element. This is kind of a war story, but as I was seeing those muzzle flashes I suddenly remembered that this AR man was a soldier to whom I had previously given an Article 15! 1 did this to demonstrate to the soldiers that you have got to fire close to the attacking element or it is not going to do any good. When you are fighting an enemy like the Chinese or the North Koreans and they are dug in, unless that direct rifle or machine gun fire is going right into their bunkers and close to the maneuvering element you are not going to do any good.

Extra ammunition: You can't ever have too much ammunition or too many frag grenades in the face of a massive Infantry attack or counterattack.

For a relief in place, every man in the unit, from the Company Commander and all the other officers, the First Sergeant and all the way on down, all carry a can of machine gun ammo (30 cal, 200 rounds), plus extra small arms ammunition and extra frag grenades. Yes, you will of course coordinate with the unit you are relieving to leave most of their ammunition on position, but you still take all the ammunition onto the position that you can possibly carry.

In the attack, you will almost always leave your packs behind in the assembly area. Make field expedient ammo packs out of sandbags and tent ropes or commo wire or extra web belts. Carry extra machine gun ammunition still in the 200 round cans, plus extra small arms and extra frag grenades—all in that same sandbag pack. Wrap several extra sandbags around the ammo can, both to cushion the load against your back and to keep the can's corners from wearing a hole in the sandbag pack too quickly. You can always use a few extra sandbags on the objective. Run an extra tent rope around the pack and tie it with a quick-release around your chest to keep the load snug to your body (that way it will not restrict your movement or affect your balance), but be ready to untie it and drop it quickly if you get snagged up on brush or barbed wire. Again, everyone in the company carries this extra load of ammo, from the Company Commander on down. This way, all your ammunition resupply arrives on the hill at the same time you do, and you are much more ready to repulse a counterattack. Platoon sergeants still redistribute ammunition, but there is no waiting for resupply.

In the defense, make everyone except the machine gunners keep all their extra ammunition [extra being that amount which is not in their cartridge belt—now ammunition pouches] and all their grenades in a sandbag with a field expedient shoulder strap and carrying handle of rope or commo wire. When you need to move people to plug a gap or reinforce a more threatened sector, there is no time for them to gather up all the extra ammo they have in their foxholes, and it can't be left behind— it must all be ready to move with them right now.

Sandbags are a must for ammunition. Talk to the Ammunition Sergeant in the S-4 section and get ammunition resupply sent forward in sandbags tied closed at the top with rope or commo wire. Wooden cases may be fine for ammo in trucks or stockpiled under a tarp at S-4, but on the line, cases are impossible. The only way to move a full case of ammunition is for a healthy soldier to carry it walking upright, Ammunition in sandbags can be carried by a soldier wounded in one arm; it can be dragged in the low-crawl, or dragged by a soldier with a leg wound. It can be identified by "feel" in the dark, to determine if that sandbag contains frag grenades or smoke grenades or machine gun ammunition or small arms. If you can't get S-4 to cooperate, break it down into "sandbag drag loads" as soon as it arrives on position. (You might try this for persuasion: Challenge whoever won't approve the sandbag system to show you how fast he can drag a full case of ammunition across rough terrain while moving in a low crawl.)

Make the field expedient packs or carry bags by tying a small rock (1" diameter) in the corners of the sandbag and using that as an anchor for tying on the carrying handle or shoulder straps. Sandbags are not very sturdy material and a rope or commo wire punched through the sandbag material will soon rip out under the stress of the ammunition weight. But when tied around a rock in the bag corner, the stresses are distributed in such a way that the sandbag will not tear.

Additional responsibilities   The second point is that West Pointers, when they get over there will probably get captain's jobs very quickly. In Korea, the World War II captains did not want to command, they had done their war and we had a lot of lieutenants commanding companies even though it was their first time in combat.

Commanding lieutenants when you are a lieutenant is kind of hard. I had a rifle company as a lieutenant and I had a bunch of lieutenants I had known as lieutenants,

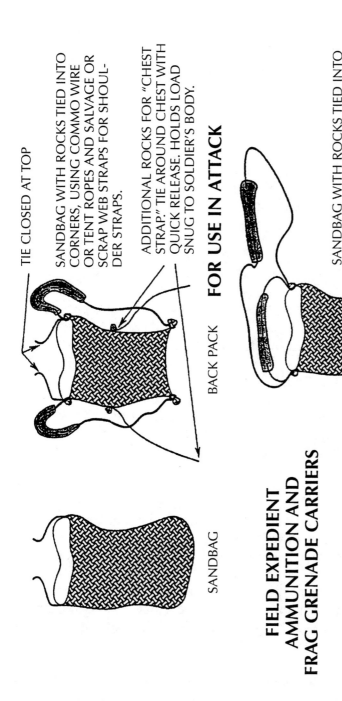

TIE CLOSED AT TOP

SANDBAG WITH ROCKS TIED INTO CORNERS, USING COMMO WIRE OR TENT ROPES AND SALVAGE OR SCRAP WEB STRAPS FOR SHOULDER STRAPS.

ADDITIONAL ROCKS FOR "CHEST STRAP." TIE AROUND CHEST WITH QUICK RELEASE. HOLDS LOAD SNUG TO SOLDIER'S BODY.

BACK PACK

FOR USE IN ATTACK

SANDBAG

SANDBAG WITH ROCKS TIED INTO CORNERS, USING COMMO WIRE OR TENT ROPES AND SALVAGE OR SCRAP WEB STRAPS FOR CARRYING HANDLE AND OVER SHOULDER CARRYING STRAP.

CARRY PACK

FOR USE IN DEFENSE

FIELD EXPEDIENT AMMUNITION AND FRAG GRENADE CARRIERS

Even in this "pack", keep all machine gun ammunition in original issue waterproof cans, 200 rounds each.

and I had a hard time commanding them or leading them or whatever. I was sort of intimidated by them. When they would do things that I knew were wrong, or fail to do those things they ought to do, it was very awkward for me and difficult. So I generally did nothing. I did a very bad job in leading these other lieutenants. I'm not so sure how you learn that but at least be aware of it, that if you are the company commander but you are only a lieutenant, you are still the company commander and you have responsibilities towards the other officers, whether it's comfortable or not.

I was also intimidated by my First Sergeant, a World War II veteran who drank a lot and I never did anything about that. It was wrong and frankly, I still correspond with this guy and I'll probably be seeing him here in a month or two. I did not exercise command authority and/or leadership because I was intimidated.

Listen to your NCO's I know that is an old saw, but in my rifle company in Korea I had three World War II sergeants and they made us. We weren't really platoons and squads, we were sort of three blobs, each blob under one of those sergeants and that's how we operated. The key to that is making sure that the sergeant knows what he is doing, that his experience matches the task you assign. The sergeant in a combat situation might have the gained the rank but not the experience. In one unit, I had a platoon leader who was a Master Sergeant. But in one situation when the unit was back off the line in reserve, when I told him to move his platoon from point A to point B I discovered that he did not know how to form up the platoon, fall them in and march them. He had risen from private to Master Sergeant in combat, but he did not know about [close order] drill and command in this type situation. As a young lieutenant, learn to rely on your NCO's in those situations where they have the necessary experience, because their knowledge will save your life.

Being liked Don't make the mistake of wanting to be liked. In our culture, we want to be liked. Don't go out of your way to make yourself disliked, but don't let wanting to be liked get in the way of doing what you know needs to be done. I had a sister company, commanded by a classmate named . . . well it doesn't make any difference what his name is, but when our battalion pulled back in reserve, my classmate wanted to be a good guy and he had them playing sports all the time and I had my company training all the time. I even traded my company's allocation of sports equipment for ammunition, for mortar ammunition. His company didn't train at all while we were in reserve, and when we went back on line, my classmate's company was on a very strategic position and they were overrun leaving only eight survivors. My company had to make a diversionary raid to get that hill back. I took about twelve casualties, including myself. I was in the hospital about six months and my company was without any officers for a month or two because all the other officers were hit either in that operation or in previous ones. I'm not saying that if he had not tried to be the nice guy that this hill would not have been overrun, but the consequences were tremendous.

Continuing along this vein of being a nice guy, and not doing your job, we didn't dig in over there. The ground was awfully hard and rocky, and it was easier to just scrape out a little hole and then bring in timber and build bunkers. The Chinese of course had to dig. You could never see where they were because they would never survive if we could see them because of our air and artillery. I had an experience on a hill one time where we had a perimeter with a machine gun bunker in the middle. They (the Chinese) got into our perimeter and the first thing they went for was that machine gun bunker and blew it up with a satchel charge because they were able to see it and know where it was. I should have had it dug in and camouflaged, and had it in a different position where it could get some decent [fields of] fire which it didn't have from the pinnacle of this little knob that I was on. That was sort of covered in the first part of this thing, the part about weapons employment and knowledge of weapons employment and how to use them.

You have to make soldiers do what they don't want to do and in a combat situation your inclination sometimes is to feel sorry for them but you are not being good to them at all. Again, this is a theoretical thing and we all know it, but when it comes to the execution, we are all human and we get tired and we get feeling certain ways too, and we let our emotions take charge and we fail to make soldiers do things which are for their own good. For example being very tired after a long day and they want to just rest and lay around—forcing them to dig in and put in their claymores and put in the machine guns properly and register [defensive] fires and all those kinds of things that are so necessary in the sense of military discipline but that our culture, and the way we live, does not lead us to want to do [enforce strict discipline and more hard physical labor on soldiers who are already very tired and want to rest]. I guess you could sum it all up by saying that the military culture is diametrically opposed to the civilian culture from which we come.

Religious faith Religion, and belief in a faith can carry one through the most difficult of times. My faith was pretty much formed at West Point and Cadet Chapel. [Note: Chapel attendance was mandatory for Cadets from earliest times under Colonel Thayer's tenure up until January 1973.] 1 know that when back in reserve one time, I had a chaplain come down and the whole company kneeled down and we asked for God's blessing on us and I really didn't know why I did this, and I still don't now why I did this, but we were very blessed. I did a similar thing as a battalion commander in combat, and we were very blessed, but as a brigade commander in the Cambodian operation I didn't have time for God and apparently He didn't have time for me and things didn't work out too well.

One does not force his religious opinion [on others], one is not a screaming zealot, but it is my feeling that ultimately to get yourself through combat, one needs a strong faith of some sort, and I would strongly recommend God if somebody doesn't have that faith already. I think troops sense it, and it has a subconscious effect if not a conscious effect on soldiers to know that their lieutenant is not only a Godly, but hopefully a virtuous individual.

I can recall being an Assistant Platoon Leader in a Ranger Platoon in Korea. [Airborne Ranger Companies were formed and assigned on a basis of one company per Infantry Division, with the method of employment frequently being allocation of one Ranger Platoon to each Infantry Regiment.] The Platoon Leader was a very immoral guy and I think he was a coward. In fact I know he was a coward. We got special additional R & R's in the Rangers, and he went on R & R to Japan and when he came back he would recount his sexual exploits with the platoon, and the platoon reflected this. When I joined the platoon we were back at Regimental Headquarters and the platoon would lay around a lot and drank a lot. The lack of virtue on the part of the platoon leader led to a lack of respect, and although the troops seemed to laugh and like it, in their hearts they didn't. His lack of character, in my opinion was directly reflected in the platoon.

When he was away on R & R one time I told the platoon that I had been honored to be assigned to a Ranger unit but that I thought they were a disgrace, and I told them that I was going to run them until I couldn't breathe anymore and that I was going to keep running them and I did run them until they all dropped, and I took them out on patrol every night for a week. Later when the Ranger units were disbanded, they all came down to my company to get into it and they didn't come to the Platoon Leader's unit, where he was, they didn't want to serve with him. The point of all this is not about me, but it is about the troops. They want their leader, their Lieutenant to be different, they want him to stand for something.

Take care of your troops Now along that line, the lieutenant has to take care of the troops and they have to know it. You do that in a variety of ways, you care about them, you learn about them, and who they are and where they come from and what they think. One of the ways you care for them in a lasting way is of course knowing your job and being willing to do and to make them do what needs to be done to bring them back alive. Also you take care of your men in the matter of awards. In a platoon, you don't have any administrative capability and it's hard when a guy does something deserving of an award to write it up and follow it through, and make certain the award recommendation doesn't get lost. This will affect these guys for the rest of their lives, that Bronze Star for Valor or maybe a Silver Star means so very much to them. The lieutenant has to go that extra mile and be concerned enough about his soldiers that when they merit awards, to push it through and fight for them to get what they deserve.

You also fight for them to get the equipment and supplies they need, when there are not enough grenades or guys don't have radio batteries or socks or cold weather gear or hot weather gear, they have to know that you go to bat for them and get what they need, and sometimes you gotta stick your neck out, and get yourself in trouble with superiors but the soldiers know it and it lets them know that their Lieutenant will do what has to be done. I guess the bottom line of this is that to do what is good for the soldiers is not what the culture says is good for them, but to do what will train them and enable them to do the job they are supposed to be doing.

Another vital part of taking care of your men concerns how you treat a new replacement or replacements coming into your platoon. If they come to you just before you jump off in an attack or a relief in place, and you have no time to get them settled into your platoon, then send them back to company headquarters until the dust settles and the smoke clears on this pending action. Unless they are well fit into your outfit, they are only a danger to themselves and to the rest of your unit. In the defense or in an assembly area in reserve, pair them up with a good solid soldier for a few days to learn the ropes with someone whom they can ask all their questions. When you get an NCO replacement, pair him up for a day or two with a solid NCO who has a similar position so he can scrape the edge off of his newness and gain a better perspective on how the unit operates.

The rest of this you will seldom have time to do yourself, but you should if time permits. Even if you turn over the bulk of this process to your NCO's, if at all possible, shake his hand, learn his name, and give him at least a quick oral outline of how he will be settled in to your platoon. Let him know that you are glad to have him in your platoon, that he has joined a good unit, a fighting unit and that his leaders are concerned about him. Under your Platoon Sergeant's supervision (and he must know what you expect this process to include just as well as if you were doing it yourself) a solid NCO must then check the replacement's gear and his weapon, and his basic issue of what he needs to fight a war—ammunition, grenades, water purification tablets, and rain gear or cold weather gear.

In the defense or in an assembly area, always try to keep a five gallon can of drinking water near the platoon CP, and insure that he fills or tops off his canteen(s). A replacement should come to you having been issued rations, but never take that for granted. You and all your NCO's should always carry one or two extra C-ration meals in your pack; ask the replacement if he has eaten and if not, get him a C-ration out of that stockpile of extras. In the defense, keep an extra half case of C-rations at the platoon CP for this purpose. Build up and maintain an ammunition supply point in your platoon area and issue him some extra ammunition or grenades—even if he already has a basic load. This clearly informs him that his platoon is here to fight.

In these first few minutes, this introduction sets the tone that the Chain of Command in this platoon looks after the troops and that this is a fighting outfit. Tell him that he will be shown how to sharpen his bayonet and be expected to keep it sharp. Total time spent in this quick check and orientation is only three or four minutes but this will have a big impact. Make certain that your, Platoon Sergeant makes it a standard drill to the extent that every NCO will cover the same topics and just as completely as if you or your Platoon Sergeant were doing this personally.

In the defense or assembly area, when the replacement is put into his position, he must know his sector of fire, left and right limits shown on the range card and defined by the aiming stakes, challenge and password, names of soldiers or NCO's on his left and right, location of any LP or OP to his front, the names of soldiers on duty out there now, and what is the signal for their withdrawal. He must be told whether or not there are any patrols out to his front, what are your platoon signals to fire the FPL or signals to tell everyone to get under cover for protection against incoming friendly air-burst artillery, plus where the aid station and platoon ammo supply point are located.

Motivation Finally, I will talk a little about motivation. I got to West Point about two weeks late after Beast Barracks started and I had just turned 18. Fifty percent of my classmates were World War II veterans, so I was considerably younger and far less experienced. I started off behind the eight ball and for four years I was still behind the eight ball. When you get to Beast Barracks two weeks late it is tough to catch up. It is tough enough starting on 1 July! I wanted to quit the first day, but the thought of disgracing my father and letting him down kept me going really for the four years.

My father was a Russian emigrant who came to this country at 14, with a little sack of gold coins around his neck but somebody stole that. He taught himself English, put himself through Medical School and when World War II came along he joined the Army and I think he was one of the youngest captains in the United States Army. Just before we graduated in June of 1950 General Eisenhower came to West Point and he introduced me to his wife as "Dan's boy," which I have never forgotten as an indication of what a truly great country we have, when the son of an emigrant can be introduced by the future President of the United States as Dan's boy.

I was not really a good Cadet. I was borderline in aptitude, I was busted as a Sergeant and I got my one stripe back before graduation because the Com had served with my father in North Africa. I had very little confidence in myself, and I had never really done anything very good in my life, high school or West Point. West Point was really not a very happy place for me. I loved the Academy but the officers were "the enemy" and I was never sure if I was going to graduate. When I did finally graduate, I found that God had given me a certain ability with soldiers, and I got three accelerated promotions and I found what I really like to do and that was to be a soldier. As far as the motivational, whether it was in jump school—I was always afraid to jump—or in combat, my West Point heritage really played a strong role. It was no longer my father but although I sort of had negative views about living at West Point, as an ideal, as an institution I really loved it.

At West Point where a lot of my classmates were rather cynical about it, I really believed everything they said about Duty, Honor, Country, and I really believed all they said about being prepared to give your life for your country. This may sound a little bit melodramatic, but to me, it was far better to die than to disgrace West Point. I have always had a tremendous underlying pride in being a West Pointer although I've never wanted to go back there. Even going back there as a Major one time I was sort of depressed. I just felt nervous, that I was in a hostile area. But as I get older, and I am 70 now, I find that increasingly West Point as an ideal is meaningful to me. I would have to say that graduating from West Point and my conversion to the Roman Catholic faith are the only two really good things I've ever done in my life. The motivation was that you're a West Pointer; people expect big things out of you; you've got to do them.

When I was the Assistant Ranger Platoon Leader, a Sergeant Miller came to me back at Regiment and he said "You know Lieutenant, you're a West Pointer in this platoon." This platoon that I was in, the discipline was terrible and it was a rag-tag outfit, for Airborne Rangers they had become very bad, because of the faulty leadership they had, and the Sergeant's point to me was that I had better get out before something really bad happened, and he mentioned that with being a West Pointer, people would expect more of me and of course I had very little control over this platoon since I was the Assistant Platoon Leader and so I took his advice.

I went down as a Platoon Leader to a rifle company and within two weeks, I don't remember exactly what happened whether the Ranger Platoon mugged some farmer or something, but they were disbanded and the whole platoon came down to the rifle company where I had become a rifle platoon leader and they all wanted to join my unit and I told them I can't take all you guys but I think I took maybe five of them. The point of all this is that West Pointers are expected to be different, they are expected to give more. I think that has always sort of carried me through. It's a paradox. I was a poor Cadet. I really wasn't happy there, but on the other hand, the pride of going there, and of being a West Pointer—maybe even more today than before, because I am getting old, West Point as an ideal and what it stands for is extremely meaningful in my life. I would say again, although it is said so often, that one has a special affinity for West Point. Our classmates are starting to drop now, and go to a better world. There is a great love there, it is sort of an academic love, I can't quite explain it. It is not the personal love, so much as one feels for special friends, but I guess it is love for an ideal.

I see my old classmates now, bald headed and fat and sort of old and crotchety, and I think back on when we were young and vigorous, and I'll finish on this one war story. In May of 1950 in International Relations or History or something, I made a presentation to a pretty good segment of my class. I ran out of time, and as God is my witness, I said "I've run out of time, I don't have time to cover Korea, but it's not important, it doesn't make much difference anyway." That was in May of '50, the North Koreans came across the 38th Parallel in June, and I think my first classmates were dead in August, one of whom was Jim Michaels whom I never knew very well. But I can remember so clearly, sitting around with him after intramurals one time, and Jim said to me: "If anyone can ever prove there's not a God, I hope he never tells me." And Jim, as I said, I think was killed in August of 1950.

******

It is asking a lot for a gray haired old soldier to pull out things that happened almost 50 years ago. My experience tells me that advice from "old farts" is seldom read and if so, not given much credibility.

My initial assignment in August 1950 was as a Machine Gun Platoon Leader, Co H, 2nd Battalion 19th Infantry, 24th Division. That lasted until Christmas, then I became a rifle platoon leader in G Company with a three week break in a hospital in Kobe Japan as a result of a grenade wound. In July '51 I became AdC to 2nd Div CG and rotated back to Campbell with him in Oct '51 when he assumed command of 11th Airborne Div.

You should read *The Forgotten War, America in Korea 1950–1953* by Clay Blair. Published NY Times Books 1987 and Anchor Books 1989. It is the only book that I am aware of except unit histories or histories of a single fight, that depicts events, times and places as I remember them. It also coincided with stories I have shared with contemporaries.

Although Beast Barracks and Camp Buckner provided basic Infantry training, the detailed training an Infantry officer needs in combat was just not there—especially more than two years later. The map reading instruction we received as Yearlings from MT&G [ancestor of today's Earth, Space and Graphic Sciences] was a godsend which I'll mention later . . . That we survived at all is probably that we were bright enough to pay attention and listen to our experienced NCO's and follow their advice in the handling of a small unit.

My initial experiences were with a Company Commander that lacked the leadership young shavetails should expect. My later experiences were with competent, solid Commanding Officers but by then I had learned what I should have known when I arrived. Fortunately we had a few World War II sergeants that knew their business and went out of their way to help.

A couple of things that were done for us early on that were greatly appreciated. First, All lieutenants in my battalion were pulled together and given formal instruction in how to call for and adjust artillery and mortar fires. This was done during a lull, by the Battalion Artillery Liaison Officer and we got to practice shoot more fire missions as individuals than we would have at Benning. Second, one of our Battalion CO's made each rifle company do live fire exercises while in reserve. This was not popular but I have to admit very educational.

The following are "Combat Tips" that might be useful. They are in no particular order or priority. Interspersed are some observations.

Knowledge of Infantry weapons, how to employ them and maintain them is basic but so important.

The ability to request properly and direct fire support from mortars, artillery, tanks and aircraft is a must skill for the Infantry leader.

Although onerous and unpleasant, soldiers must dig in when not moving if you are within enemy artillery or mortar range.

Soldiers have a natural tendency to bunch up. Keep 10 yards interval on approach marches, going through chow lines etc. This must be enforced over and over.

The American Army has a tendency to become road bound. Combat in Korea was and will be a fight for high ground. The hills are steep and the overall terrain rugged. Infantry will have to get used to movement on foot and as I remember it, it's all uphill.

Unsophisticated armies use the hours of darkness to their advantage. Either the platoon sergeant or the platoon leader must be awake at all times and out checking every position on line, frequently. Double [two man] foxholes with one man awake in each was the norm. In winter, only 50% of sleeping bags were brought forward. Sleep is difficult when one is uncomfortable, so you are assured of one man being awake.

Learn to cat nap. Sleep when you get a break during daylight hours. Your judgment is much better when you're not fatigued.

Keep an extra pair of dry socks around your waist. When you change, put the damp pair there to be dried by body heat.

Stay off the skyline (not as easy as it sounds).

Always carry a pocket notebook with pencil or pen. Take notes when receiving orders or instructions from your Commander. Insist that your subordinate NCO's do likewise, and that they take notes when you give them instructions or orders.

I was surprised how thirsty we got in winter. Make adequate liquids available to troops year around. Seems very basic, but you and all your troops know how often and how much it is "normal" to urinate. Drink enough fluids to maintain that normal rate. If you are urinating less frequently, then the urine will be darker in color, with an unusually strong odor. That simply means you are losing too much body liquids to sweat, with not enough left over to flush waste from your digestive system. So tell your troops to drink till their urine is clear and in "normal" amounts/frequency.

Pistols were carried by some platoon leaders in addition to the carbine. I never saw anyone use one in anger. The M-16 seems to me to be a good weapon for platoon leaders.

As a take along item the new multiple use pocket tools with pliers and knives etc. would have been useful. Zip-lock bags for use as a map case would be useful also.

40 mm grenade launcher [M203] would have solved many of our close-in problems. When you are too close [to the enemy] to use artillery and mortars and yet out of hand grenade range, the inaccurate rifle grenade just didn't do the job. When a 57 mm RR was available, it worked well for bunker busting. Your LAW would do a great

job on that. Several LAW's fired in a volley at one single bunker would be the best way to be sure that it gets knocked out on the first try.

New items now available such as GPS (great for night patrols), night vision devices, <u>reliable</u> small radios and lightweight binoculars all appear to be a must for junior leaders. I always carried binoculars on my chest without the case (shorten the strap). Horizontal and vertical scales on the military binocs are useful if one learns how to use them. Lasers [range finders] may also be a must at platoon level.

I mentioned map reading as a skill I learned as a Cadet. I was surprised in Korea and throughout my career that a number of officers are limited in that skill. The instruction we received as Yearlings where we actually made maps from our own surveys and by using stereo pairs gave us a solid foundation needed to read terrain by observation and to use a map accurately. It is an essential skill that I do not believe will be superseded by modern equipment.

The North Koreans and Chinese were usually well dug in. "The North Koreans were stubborn in defense and usually had to be killed. Chinese on the other hand could be forced to withdraw.

Light discipline will be easier to enforce now that there are fewer smokers. It is still extremely important. If you don't smoke, don't start. If you do smoke, Quit!

Know where your unit boundaries are. One day in North Korea I came very close to ambushing a friendly patrol that had strayed into my zone. (Again the importance of knowing where you are on the map.) On the same patrol, friendly artillery began registering near my position. Turned out to be the adjacent Division.

When friendly patrols are operating forward of your position <u>every</u> man in the platoon must know this. When friendlies return also put out the word.

Rumors fly all over the place. Keep everyone informed of the situation with as much information as you have. Put bad rumors to bed quickly. "We'll be home by Christmas" is one [General] MacArthur should have never let get started.

Present day communications coupled with more accurate fire support, be it artillery, armor or air, should overcome many of the difficulties we experienced.

The terrain in most of Korea generally limits a company in the attack to the width of one platoon or less because you're going up one ridge line. Well controlled, accurate and timely fire support works a lot better than cold steel.

Only once did my unit encounter enemy air and this was "washing machine Charlie" dropping 120 mm mortar rounds on our bivouac area one bright night just north of Pyongyang in North Korea. Scared the hell out of everyone but did zero damage. We really have not had to contend with enemy air since World War II. Consequently, our concealment has not been a top priority in training. We should be prepared for "what if?"

The GI's of the 1950 Army (many that I had served with came from occupation duty in Japan) had little regard or feelings for the people and soldiers of Korea. This bad attitude may still exist and it may come as a shock to find tough, capable and well disciplined soldiers on the other side. KATUSA's [Korean Augmentation to US Army] who proved they were good soldiers helped our GI's reduce their disdain for the Korean Army units which frequently bugged out. I believe some US units in Korea still have KATUSA's assigned and your unit might also. They are good soldiers, extremely tough with exceptional endurance.

A surprising number of soldiers are killed in traffic accidents. Officers and NCO's must demand that vehicles are operated safely, especially at night when under black out conditions.

I would hope that by now we have an effective counter mortar radar system useful to companies and battalions. The Russian 120 mm mortar was and probably still is an effective weapon that deserves all the counter battery fire we can muster.

When in the attack, all platoons except the lead platoon carried extra ammunition both for small arms and direct and indirect fire support weapons. When engaged, this extra weight was usually discarded but normally it was more than halfway up the hill, to be recovered as soon as possible. Most units had a contingent of Korean civilian laborers to haul supplies up the hills. Helicopters would help here but landing areas are non-existent on the hills and stuff would have to be dumped from a hover.

A sense of humor goes a long way when conditions are extreme. Trust the GI to provide it most of the time.

Important! Never forget that the average American GI is the greatest soldier in the world. He thinks for himself and will get the job done given the slightest chance. It has always been a privilege to lead him.

One final item I'll address with some reluctance. After 30 years service with two wars under my belt and almost 20 more years to reflect on that service, I still have not reached a solid opinion about controlling physical fear—either my own or someone else's. I do know that because of their individual make-up and training some handle it better than others. Duty Honor Country helps and it helped me. The moral fear of disgrace helps and it helped me. Leaders who set the example have units that overcome fear better than those whose leaders do not. You can not tell ahead of time those who will be under control and who won't be. Most of us learn to manage fear but each of us has to learn to face that monster in his own way. Almost everyone somehow manages. I always assumed that the soldiers I lead were braver than I was and I couldn't let them discern that weakness.

Incidentally I commanded an Infantry Battalion in Korea 1969–70. 1 had a chance to observe the Korean Army. There's a world of difference between the Korean Army of 1950 and the Army I saw in 1970. The North Korean Army could be in for a nasty shock if they try something.

******

I got no advice from my CO in Korea. I just was told where the platoon headquarters was and sent on my way. That was during the Battle of the Naktong River. There was not even an orientation on what was happening, partly because no one really knew what was going on.

As you lead your platoon into combat for the first time, whether you have just joined an experienced unit or are leading a platoon you have trained, there are several important things you should remember.

First, your most important consideration is the accomplishment of your mission. You and your unit are expected to carry out certain roles or do certain things as part of a larger plan. For the plan to succeed, each element needs to play its part by fulfilling its mission.

Close behind the mission is care for your troops. You stand between them and the rest of the world. You must do all that you can to ensure their health and well being. The most important thing you can do, of course, is see that they stay alive and well. At times you may do things they do not like but that are needed to keep them secure and healthy, such as digging in and checking the alert level all night, even when there seems to be no immediate threat. You must see that they are fed and supplied, that mail is distributed, that weapons are clean and functioning and many other things.

You must be loyal to your troops and to your superiors. Admit when you are wrong. Praise whenever you can. Give credit that is due to others.

Ensure discipline at all times. Troops need time to rest and, if possible, to play, but not at the expense of proper discipline. Demand respect for yourself and for your NCO's. Don't get familiar. You are not their buddy but their boss. Reward when you can. Punish when you must, but be reasonable, fair, and consistent.

Set the example. Be the leader. Always have your men look up to you. Be sure you are proficient in your job and keep learning. Shave every day, if possible (and it usually is). Keep your uniforms as clean as possible. Dig your own hole. Look at every emplacement. Plan for contingencies and practice them if appropriate. Eat after all your men are served, so that if anyone goes hungry, it is you.

Develop cohesion in your platoon. Men fight for the men beside them. The closer they feel to those men, the greater the sacrifices that will be made to keep the unit safe and the mission done. Give the men pride in the platoon and in themselves. Make them feel special.

Train whenever the chance occurs. You can always find things that need work: fire distribution, cover and concealment, communications, first aid, etc. Training improves their proficiency, emphasizes chain of command, aids in cohesion, increases discipline, and occupies idle time. You must recognize that every day in combat is a training day and that every minute when the enemy is not shooting at you is an opportunity for training. Every leader ought to aim at finishing each day with his troops smarter, better, more proficient than they were at that day's dawning. Be certain to praise and encourage your soldiers and NCO's for what they are doing right, not just correct them for what is wrong. Include yourself on the roster of personnel to be trained—think about your day and what you have learned. Pat yourself on the back when you deserve it, and figure out what went wrong on the other situations—then learn from it all, so that you also become more proficient at your duties each day.

******

I flew to Haneda AFB in Japan . . . then took a train to Sasebo where shortly we boarded a "coaler" ship to the port of Pusan arriving September 1st, 1950 . . . on board that ship were several classmates . . . some of whom would never make it back to the U.S., but rather would be killed in action. . . . At Pusan I boarded a train for the 24th REPL Depot, located in an apple orchard near Taegu . . . subsequently, a vehicle arrived to take me to the Battalion OP of the 3rd Battalion, 19th Infantry, part of the 24th Division . . . the OP was on a hill . . . it was there I met the Battalion CO who briefed me on the situation . . . the 24th Division, I learned, was in 8th Army Reserve . . . subsequently a runner from my company (K Co), arrived to take me to the Company CP . . . there I met the CO and XO who were at the time playing cribbage . . . both of those officers had had WWII experience and had been on duty in Japan when the Korean War broke out...they briefed me on the situation and shortly thereafter a platoon runner arrived to take me to my platoon where I met Master Sergeant Barnes, who was to be my Platoon Sergeant.

Barnes was a veteran of WWII in Europe and looked like one of the two GIs in Bill Mauldin's Stars and Stripes cartoons . . . Barnes was a good man and stayed close with me, teaching me all the ropes of what to expect . . . shortly thereafter, after the 7th Division landed at Inchon, the 19th Infantry headed north toward the Naktong River behind the 24th Division's 21st Infantry Regiment . . . the going was fast as the invasion at Inchon caused the enemy to withdraw rapidly north through Seoul to Pyongyang and north toward the Yalu River . . . we followed in pursuit only to be stopped by the massive invasion of the Chinese who caused us to withdraw south to a place named Ichon . . . there we reorganized . . . and from then on the war began to act like a yo-yo with advances and withdrawals by both sides . . . some hot action in our area involved an attack on Hill 584 in south west Korea. My company lost its commander and two platoon leaders . . . although I survived, I was subsequently transferred to the First Battalion as a platoon leader and company exec . . .

In those days units of the 19th Infantry were about half Korean and half American with a common practice of sharing foxholes . . . the winter of 1950–51 was bitter cold and there was a problem of frostbite . . . the way to beat that is to frequently change socks, keep them dry and change the pads in your snow boots often . . . but frankly we spent a lot of time just staying warm . . . the Chinese and North Koreans were in worse shape because their footwear was so flimsy . . . I saw many a case of really bad frostbite in their troops.

I would say a lesson I learned was to never rest on your laurels once you have secured an objective, but be ready to repulse a counterattack immediately . . . another lesson is to make sure you keep track of where your troops are . . . at one point when my platoon was on the Out Post Line of Resistance (OPLR), my platoon was split by enemy attack on New Year's Eve 1950 . . . and it was almost a week before we got together again . . . even then I had lost some and never knew their whereabouts until after the conflict when I saw their names on a TV screen at home after they had been repatriated . . .

I spent 15 months in Korea the latter part of which was at Regimental Headquarters . . . I would say I was really "green" and "young" . . . my formal training came at Fort Benning after I returned from Korea as a student officer in the Associate Company Officers' Course . . . USMA should have given us tougher field training . . . our experiences during Yearling Summer were helpful but no where near hard enough . . . the combined arms training Cow Year just barely gave us a hint of combat coordination . . . too much time spent on social outings, dress up events . . . and finally the leadership experience had when those of us who as First Classmen were merely cadet sergeants was minimal . . . I know that personally I was ranked right in the middle of my company militarily as a cadet . . . I longed to be in charge but never got the chance . . . I believe a lot of these deficiencies in cadet training have been corrected . . . if not, I recommend not only tough academic training but even tougher military training . . . I revere my experience at West Point . . . I love the place, and I hope it will continue to learn and give its cadets the toughest challenges possible. Korea 1 Sep 50 to 1 Nov 51

******

As a man who chose Infantry over every other Branch in the Army, I have nothing but the greatest respect for the honor and the traditions upheld by Infantrymen through the ages.

Permit me to offer a few thoughts, with the understanding that they are the reminiscences of an old man whose very short experience as a Rifle Platoon Leader in Korea hardly qualifies him as an expert.

• The class of 1950 had one distinct advantage over any class that might have to go directly to combat in the future. We joined units with senior noncommissioned officers and many commissioned officers in the grades of Captain and above who were veterans of WWII, and who understood the demands of the conventional war we were called upon to fight in Korea. It is my perception that not since that time has the Army had a truly experienced cadre to meet the contingencies that have arisen. In all likelihood, we will never again have the luxury of fighting a war even remotely similar to our last one.

• There are few lessons from Grenada, Sudan, Haiti, Desert Storm, Bosnia, Kosovo that can be applied to the next situation to arise. Even in Korea, any future conflict is likely to be much less conventional (or more unconventional) than our contingency plans envision, but still significantly different from any of the "peacekeeping" actions of recent times. So, the lieutenants of tomorrow are not likely to have the base of applicable experience in their units that we had in the summer of 1950. Even so, my first piece of advice has to be:

Earn the respect and trust of your Noncoms by respecting and trusting them. Listen, really listen to them. Consider their opinions, then use your own best judgment to make your decisions. Likewise, respect and trust your superiors; let them know that they can count on you to be totally trustworthy and to give your very best effort at all times.

• It is almost inevitable that young men thrust into combat directly from the Military Academy would have feelings of self-doubt. I presume that Tactics Instruction still progresses through the years so that by First Class year Division/Corps/Army maneuvers are more familiar than Platoon and Company tactics. I remember with considerable clarity the insecurity I felt because we did not have the opportunity to attend the Basic Course before going into combat. But the fact is most of us survived, and I do not know of a single case where the Basic Course would have made a life or death difference (but it sure would have made things easier!) Therefore, gem of wisdom number two is:

Regardless of the training you may have missed, trust yourself, your judgment, your West Point experience. You will be amazed at how much you know that you didn't know you knew. Not only that, but you'll learn faster than you would ever have thought possible. The threat of someone shooting at you has a way of speeding up thought processes.

• One of the first challenges to a young person going into combat is to come to grips with the reality of his mortality. There is a very real chance that the conflict will result in death. It is essential to rationalize this possibility—to ask the question of oneself "Am I willing to give my life for these soldiers who depend on me to lead them into (and out of) combat?" The answer for any small unit leader/commander simply must be "Yes!" Any other answer would be unthinkable. But not every combat death is heroic; however, every one is tragic. Great moral support and comfort can be derived from a faith in the Almighty, a sense of "not my will but Thy will be done." So:

Believe in something greater than yourself. Don't be ashamed. There really is a fate worse than death—a death without the faith that something better lies ahead.

******

I will try to be brief. The first lesson I learned in combat turned out to be the most important and it stood me in good stead throughout my military career. When we arrived in Korea, straight from graduation leave, I was assigned to the 19th Infantry Regiment, 24th Division, and given command of a rifle company.

When a couple of days later the North Korean forces broke through the Naktong Perimeter at Pohang on the coast, we were rushed in to restore the line. After receiving my op order for the attack at dawn plus 30, I followed the book and took my NCO's forward on a recon of our axis of attack. I selected what looked like an appropriate route considering all the "by the book" factors. We jumped off following the selected route, when a quarter mile into our approach we came to a deep ravine with a very high cliff on the other side. Not wanting to fail in my first action as a leader, and in spite of knowing how vulnerable we would be to someone simply dropping a bunch of grenades and/or just picking us off as we tried to climb the cliff, we went straight on up.

We reached the top with great difficulty and carefully peered over the top only to see a multi-platoon enemy force deployed in a half moon around the hill below us, anchored on each side to the cliff. Obviously they believed no one would take such a difficult and risky approach. We destroyed the entire enemy force without the loss of a single man. Then lo and behold, looking down the other side of the mountain we had captured, there was a whole CP group, lined up in a chow line and laying around.

The FO who had clambered up the hill with us called in artillery fire followed by an air strike using F-51's—it was amazing. The rest of the battalion had been held up along the "logical approach" and we were able to take some of the pressure off of them from our vantage point. All because that draw was so narrow it didn't show on the map.

The lesson learned—always seek the route that offers the best likelihood of surprise—stood me in great stead, both in combat and peacetime maneuvers. Later, as an armored infantry company commander, we were commended by the corps commander for a similar surprise maneuver in which we got behind the "enemy" (aggressor) lines and captured their command group and got out (an embarrassment to the 14th Armored Cav who were playing the aggressor in that maneuver) and were named the outstanding AIB [Armored Infantry Battalion] Company in the Seventh Army Field Tests one year for similar sorts of things.

The lesson I learned is that the easiest way is probably not the best, especially if you can achieve surprise by another way, would be my first answer to what new Infantry lieutenants really need to know in combat.

******

No doubt you are aware that recalling events some 49 years in the past lends itself to providing inaccurate data—or at least the potential of doing so. For my part, where ever I feel the comments made are "iffy" I will insert a (?) at the end of the comments.

I need to provide some background information in order to put my comments in some form of context that will be meaningful. Upon graduation, I was assigned to the 5th Regimental Combat Team (5th RCT) stationed at Schofield Barracks, Hawaii. While on graduation leave, those orders were rescinded and instead I was ordered to Camp Stoneman, California, for further assignment to 8th Army . . . translation, to Korea! I, along with a number of classmates, arrived at Camp Drake, Japan (home of the First Cavalry Division) in late August 1950.

Our first night there, we went to the Officer's Club for supper. A 1st Lieutenant, AG type, was at the club and singled us out during the evening. He informed us that the 1950 West Point graduates would all be assigned to the 7th Infantry Division, located in Hokaido (?) where we would receive 30 to 60 days training before heading to Korea. That news provided a modicum of relief to me, and I returned to my BOQ that evening with improved morale. A bulletin board in the BOQ entryway had a section delineated for "orders," so I checked it out to see if I knew anyone on it. Sure enough! There was someone I knew on orders to Korea the next day . . . me!! As well as most of my classmates who had arrived that same day. LESSONS LEARNED NUMBER ONE, Never believe volunteered information, especially if it seems to be happy news, until it comes to pass.

My orders were for assignment to the 21st Infantry Regiment, 24 Division. We were told to be ready the next day, after drawing some equipment (helmets, carbine, protective masks, sleeping bags, etc.) for shipment to Sasebo, Japan where we would take an overnight inter-island ferry to Pusan, Korea. In addition to my group, our travel mates included returnees (previously wounded) as well as other replacements from the States and even some "homesteaders" from Japan. During the evening "cruise," I observed some veterans standing at the railing, throwing helmets and protective (gas) masks over the side! When asked why they were doing so, the reply was "you won't need them in Korea." I directed them to cease doing so, and instead turn the equipment in when they reached their units. I'm sure such instructions fell on deaf ears. I guess the point of this story is to advise (warn) young officers not to be swayed by information of this nature from "veterans" . . . a la Lessons Learned #1.

After landing in Pusan, we boarded a train for Taegu. At Taegu we switched trains. Those of us going to the 21st Infantry boarded one headed for Pohang—near the east coast of Korea. (I could not help but notice that as we left our initial train car, wounded were being loaded through the car's windows to take our place, headed for hospitals. Not a great "morale builder" for anxious, green replacements, to say the least!) Five of us new graduates headed for Pohang, with instructions to report to the 21st Infantry Replacement Detachment. From here, we were loaded on trucks the next day(?) with assignments to the 3rd Battalion, 21st Infantry Regiment. Upon arrival at 3rd Battalion, we were taken to the CP where the CO, LTC "Mac" McConnell and S-3 welcomed us and we were given our assignments. I was assigned to I Company, with the other four to Companies K, L and M. We were told to leave all of our heavy gear (sleeping bags, other luggage) at the Battalion CP and to write any letters we wanted to send back home, before meeting our company guides. We were further told that the battalion was jumping off in the attack within the hour . . . so get going to our units!

I remember riding across a rice paddy in a jeep, and being told to stay low, as a sniper was being flushed out. From the company rear, at the base of a hill (mountain!) I proceeded by foot up to the forward company CP, where I was introduced to the Company Commander, the XO and Lieutenant Maihafer. Also present was SFC (?) Sumpsky, the Weapons Platoon Sergeant. The Company Commander was giving out the attack orders, and had little to say in the way of a greeting or advice. Lieutenant Maihafer told me that he had just been reassigned from the Weapons Platoon to command the 3rd Platoon, as the former Platoon Leader was killed the day before. I was to take over the Weapons Platoon. Lieutenant Maihafer informed me that SFC Sumpsky was "a good man" and could be relied upon. I remember telling Lieutenant Maihafer that I didn't know much about weapons support, and he advised me to rely on SFC Sumpsky's "advice." (SFC Sumpsky was a World War II veteran, field artillery, overweight and I guess, pushing 40, with a very good attitude, considering.)

So, here I was, a brand new 2nd Lieutenant, about to stand before his first platoon of enlisted men, a few minutes before moving into an attack of a hill defended by North Koreans. It was at this point that I made my first big decision in combat! I pulled SFC Sumpsky aside and told him that I would like him to tell me what orders to give as we made the attack. I asked him to do so as inconspicuously as possible, while assuring him I would get up to speed on how to employ the platoon as quickly as possible. I was conscious at the time that what I was doing was not out of the Leadership Manual, was potentially very dangerous as regarded my future relations with the platoon, as well as with SFC Sumpsky. Had I not had some reassurances earlier from Lieutenant Maihafer that SFC Sumpsky could be relied upon, I am not sure if I would have taken such a risk! As it turned out, I made the right decision, and we took our objective and dug in for the night.

I shared a foxhole with SFC Sumpsky and set up a schedule for taking turns for staying awake. SFC Sumpsky said he would take the first watch. I settled down but naturally could not get to sleep—knowing, I felt, that the North Koreans would counterattack in the next few minutes. About 15 minutes later, I heard SFC Sumpsky snoring! Needless to say, I stayed awake that whole night, while SFC Sumpsky got a good night's rest. (We received no counterattack that night.)

I guess the import of the above is to stress LESSONS LEARNED NUMBER TWO, namely, get to know your men as quickly as possible, especially your next in command. I was able to make big gains in this regard by engaging the squad leaders as well as the soldiers in conversation at every opportunity. Not just military subjects, but personal ones as well, e.g. where they came from in the States, whether they were married, had previous military experience, etc. I tried to eat some C-rations with different squads during the day; to ask about their weapons (60 mm mortars, 57 recoilless rifles), while trying not to show too much ignorance about such! It worked well for me, and by the time we pulled back into reserve for the first time since the war broke out (25 June), I felt like I had a good rapport with my men.

While in reserve for those few days, I set up my CP in the vicinity of all my squads, rather than congregate with the other company officers. Not only did this approach help me to gain the confidence of my men, but it gave me insights into their capabilities, attitudes and reliability. Once that knowledge was gained, it helped me to make decisions, both during the heat of combat, as well as setting up defensive positions and making other preparations. For example, if I had what I felt was a critical piece of terrain in my sector, knowing my men helped me to decide which squad or section should be assigned that area.

Which leads me to a LESSONS LEARNED NUMBER THREE, learn to listen to and go with your instincts. Field manuals give you the basic ground work for making decisions, but all too often I was confronted with situations where there were not any clear cut answers, gleaned from the theory contained in the FM's. At such times, your initial instincts will usually serve you well. Again, having a good working knowledge of your men's abilities and personalities, coupled with adequate information (intelligence) will serve you well in most instances.

Only a few months later, Lt. Maihafer was wounded and evacuated, and I was ordered to command the 3rd Platoon. Once again, I was the "new kid on the block" as far as my platoon was concerned. What I encountered in this situation was a World War II experienced Infantry platoon sergeant, Master Sergeant Robinette, who early on showed a resentment of my authority. In retrospect, it was not so much a resentment as his inability to keep up, physically. As he became less able to do so, I began to rely more heavily on the Assistant Platoon Sergeant, SFC Sullivan for support.

SFC Sullivan hit it off personality wise immediately, whereas MSGT Robinette was more of an introvert and was hard to draw out. I suspect Robinette suspected this early on. Eventually, because of his lack of physical stamina, he was moved to company headquarters and then to medical evacuation (?). SFC Sullivan became the platoon sergeant and remained so until wounded and evacuated in the early spring of 1951 (?). The point here is to reinforce how important it is to get to know your men early on.

Other than Lt Maihafer's advice upon my joining the company, I have no recollection of receiving any advice from the company commander or any of the other combat experienced officers. The company commander did reflect an important example to me early on of how important it is to maintain a sense of humor. His sense of humor, although dark at times, was a tension reliever to some degree. It was when he stopped displaying such that we knew something was wrong. (Shortly after the Naktong River crossing, this company commander had a nervous breakdown (?) or battle fatigue (?), was relieved of command and then medically evacuated.)

In May 1951, I contracted hepatitis A and was medically evacuated to Kyoto, Japan for two months. I then returned to the 21st Infantry, and was subsequently assigned as a platoon leader of the Regimental Heavy Mortar Company (4.2" mortars). Once again I was the new inexperienced leader as far as 4.2" mortar employment was concerned. My past experiences helped me to assimilate the knowledge necessary for my new command. I involved myself to the full extent in learning everything I could about 4.2" mortars and their proper employment. A lot of it I learned by asking the old hands, NCO and enlisted men, questions and seeking their counsel. LESSON LEARNED NUMBER FOUR. As a newly commissioned or newly assigned officer, learn your unit's mission and capabilities to the best of your ability, as quickly as you can. Not only will it provide you with increased self-confidence, but it will have the same effect for your subordinates carrying out your orders.

The last thing I would offer in the way of advice to an inexperienced young officer is to give your subordinates as much information about what is going on as you can. In retrospect, I wish my seniors had been more forthcoming with "the situation" as they knew it rather than taking such a strict "need to know" approach on several occasions. One such instance is when we were about 15 miles from the Yalu River, preparing to pass through our 2nd Battalion the next morning to close on the Yalu. The Chinese entered the battle that evening and our battalion was told to saddle up that evening and start marching south. The 2nd Battalion in front of us was loaded on all available 2 1/2 ton trucks and moved south past us that same evening. When we asked for information on why the sudden reversal of plans, we were given no answers. This only caused the tension and anxiousness to increase. The point again, give the troops whatever information you have. Don't withhold it, and don't be averse to saying you don't know, if you really don't.

Most of the equipment problems I experienced centered mainly around a *lack of*, opposed to having equipment that was *not able to do the job*. The 21st Infantry, as you know, made up Task Force Smith 1st Battalion, that is. However, because the Truman Administration had let the services deteriorate, i.e,. cutback, at the outbreak of hostilities instead of having three fully equipped heavy weapons companies per regiment, there was only one set of equipment. [In the Regimental system D, H and M companies were the heavy weapons companies for the three battalions.] The heavy weapons were rotated among the three companies for training purposes. When one company had the weapons (81 mm mortars, 57 mm recoilless rifles and heavy machine guns—30 caliber water cooled), the other two companies were weaponless. On 25 June 1950, M Company had the weapons, so they were shipped out with 1st Battalion, even though they had not trained with the rifle companies of 1st Battalion.

One exception to my above statement about "not being able to do the job" was in the case of having the 2.36 inch rocket launcher (Bazooka) as opposed to the 3.5 inch that we received later. Survivors of Task Force Smith, some of whom were reassigned to the 3rd Battalion after TF Smith was decimated, told many a war story of how the 2.36 inch rockets bounced off of T-34 tanks. They also related how our M-24 tanks were no match for the T-34. Another example of "not having" was that until late January-early February 1951 my unit received no winter gear—shoe pacs, parkas etc. We survived most of the winter of '50-'51 mainly with field jackets, ponchos and what gear we could get Sears & Roebuck to send us from the States.

With regard to recommendations for a reading list, *This Kind of War* (Fehrenbach) I found to be pretty accurate as it described 21st Infantry Regiment actions in which I was involved. (He even mentions my name—misspelled—in one incident involving sleeping bags.) I have read SLA Marshall's *The River and the Gauntlet*, as well as *Men Against Fire*. In those passages involving actions in which my unit participated, I have found him to be highly inaccurate in some cases. In my opinion, SLA Marshall was a good novelist writer. Lots of what he wrote could never be verified (unless some Korean/Chinese veterans could be queried). Yet he was revered by some of the senior brass in his hey day so perhaps his work would be beneficial to newly commissioned Infantry officers.

I hope this will be of some help. I would reiterate once more that regardless of the equipment, the interface with your men, and continued concern for their welfare and well being will serve you best in combat or training.

******

1. Recon patrols MUST be carried out to the letter . . . no hiding out . . . and reports on what was found must be truthful and accurate ... don't let anyone fake it!
2. Dig In !!! As soon as possible after reaching objective
3. Watch use of sleeping bags at night . . . have at least half of unit fully alert

4. Take care of health . . . brush teeth daily . . . wash whenever you can . . . don't take a chance on drinking water . . . use water purification tablets

5. Field sanitation is vital!!

6. Take malaria pills on schedule!!

7. Take extra care with your FEET!!!

8. Lay off alcohol, despite temptations

9. Insist on regular maintenance of weapons, commo equipment and vehicles. Hold inspections, particularly in reserve areas

10. Make inspections tough, even in the field

11. Be HARD BUT FAIR with your troops

12. Learn to read your maps!! . . . know where you are, where your troops are and where your units are . . . including adjacent units

13. Stay as DRY as you possibly can

14. Stay alert when in helicopters and other aircraft

15. Make sure you know who's in charge

16. REPORT accurately and promptly any thing out of the ordinary or unexpected

******

I joined the Third Platoon, "I" Company, 17th Infantry Regiment, 7th Division at Camp Fuji, Japan. The morning I arrived, they were just recovering from a typhoon—all the tents had been flattened (purposely to prevent being blown away). There were six foot deep crevasses in the pumice. You can imagine that tent pegs would not have held ten minutes in the kind of wind they experienced. No trees to break the wind, or come to think of it, to fall on anyone. Obviously they did not have time to mess with a green 2nd Lieutenant, so they sent me off immediately as part of the Advance Party to prepare our transport ship to receive the troops, en route to Pusan. None of us had any idea of the plans for Inchon.

My Company Commander was Captain Morrisey, who really did not offer much advice—even less from our Exec, 1st Lieutenant Thuse. I remember him primarily for the 10" barrel 357 Magnum revolver he carried around like a cowboy. We kidded him that if we could not raise the artillery by radio we could always call on him for some indirect fire support. The advice and assistance during my OJT came primarily from the NCO's, most with lots of WWII combat experience. Shortly after arrival in Pusan Harbor as "Floating Reserve," we took aboard the other half of our very under-manned platoons—Korean boys, probably rounded up off the streets. They had no Army experience, even the one who spoke a little English, assigned as my runner/interpreter. They had no idea how to use the latrines on board ship or how to eat with knives and forks, and generally disliked the food which never had enough rice and was far too bland for their kimchi-jaded palates. I have to say, however, that their morale was generally good. They looked forward to fighting the North Koreans—and I think, would far rather be with us than with a South Korean unit.

Some of the advice received from the veteran NCO's, on retrospect, was pretty foolish. In short order I was prepared, on landing, to remove my collar brass (the North Koreans were reported to have excellent sharpshooters), strap my carbine bayonet to my boot and go ashore as light as possible. We left backpacks aboard ship with the promise that they would catch up with us at our first respite (they never did). We went ashore with necessities (toilet articles) in spare grenade pouches, belt hanging from the pack's shoulder harness rather than tight around our waist. We felt really "combat ready," but would have been woefully short of ammo and grenades had we encountered some stiff fighting. We came ashore at Inchon in lighters almost with a brass band welcome. We could not even hear any artillery, as it had displaced inland with the Marines and other elements of the Army for the battle for Seoul.

My unit was ordered southeast to cut off the surrounded North Koreans in the south. One of my first assignments was to guard a couple of disabled tanks, and to stay with them even when they were towed to an Ordnance Depot, until my company sent vehicles to pick us up. One of my most embarrassing moments came when I went into breakfast at the Depot's Officers Mess. With no shower or clean clothes in over a week, and no collar brass—was I grungy. A General was sitting at the head of the table, yards away, as I had chosen to sit at the other end with lots of empty seats between myself and the Depot officers, feeling very out of place but very hungry. The General hollered to me, asking who I was—if I was an enlisted man, shove off to the EM Mess, if not where was my brass and why did not I come up and join the other officers where I belonged.

They were all very friendly and helpful when I filled them in on who I was and how I got there (without brass) and I ate like a king! Needless to say I located some brass and added it to one of the grenade pouches, and then found a laundry and shower unit for my unit and myself. I noticed that immediately after these amenities of civilization the men began to treat each other with a lot more respect. There are lots of stories about men becoming like animals when the minimal creature comforts are long denied. Our ability to function as a team was clearly affected.

Point of this incident is realize that you will have to take with your unit what you might need during an initial debarkation rather than count on equipment left on board ship ever catching up with you—and do not ever "go light" on ammunition and grenades, regardless of "advice from veterans." Then also to try and provide your unit with minimal standards of sanitation/hygiene whenever possible. (With the current style of camouflaged or subdued collar insignia, at least today's officers don't have to carry their collar brass in a grenade pouch.)

Our next assignmnent was to establish a roadblock to prevent escaping North Koreans from raiding villages in our area. It was only later, when I took a two squad reconnaissance patrol eastward that I realized how close we were to what seemed to be a major escape route running south to north. There was evidence that huge numbers had passed by only nights before. My men kept asking me why we were not setting up ambush sites. Of course, my answer was that we were following orders—to see and not be seen. We could only hope that our reports were resulting in more action somewhere along that route. In retrospect, I could have at least have taken the initiative to volunteer such action as well as report the information. I believe that I allowed my sense of newness and low rank to overcome what might have been important to my men and to overrule what should have been my instinct to recommend ambushes be established or even done it on my own and merely reported that fact, instead of "asking for permission" or waiting to be told.

Not too long afterward we were moved to Taegu for training in anticipation of the landing in the Wonsan area of North Korea. An interesting lesson was learned by the American soldiers. An infiltration site was chosen and the GI's were to demonstrate to our Koreans how to take advantage of cover and concealment in moving up the hill where the Korean men were observing. The Koreans noticed many butts sticking up and flashes of sunlight on weapons, and when the whistle blew for the GI's to all stand up they were all about 100 yard out and most had been spotted—no surprise to the Koreans. Then they asked to try it, and proceeded to crawl in about the same amount of time to within about 20 yards of where the American GI's were observing with only one or two being seen or heard. The South Korean soldiers in my unit gained lots of respect from our guys on that one.

The landing in North Korea was a duplicate of Inchon for my unit. I don't know who established the initial beachhead, but the beach masters were much in evidence with their bull horns directing our "combat" landing. Our subsequent trek to the Yalu River was marked by several actions outstanding in my mind.

The first was a patrol I conducted rather deep into unoccupied territory. (I really did not know the situation.) Our mission was to reconnoiter a route for the Regiment to cross the Ungi River, and my patrol route was along a ridge line. To get onto the ridge we had to go up a steep hillside on several switchbacks. I sent one jeep up to the top while covering their path from the bottom with .50 caliber and .30 caliber machine guns. Although we lost sight of their fluorescent panels in the scrub brush, the sergeant in charge reported that the way was clear and so we followed, meeting him not at the top, but about twothirds of the way up. The sergeant claimed he had returned to meet us.

However, further along we discovered a dead North Korean officer with his 9 mm pistol still prominently in its holster. Knowing that if the jeep had really gone that far, the prized souvenir would have been in some GI's possession, I pried out the admission that they had not really gone to the top, but had waited for us where we met them. I made it clear to everyone the danger such false reports had put our mission in, and had the Sergeant back to Private forthwith. Unfortunately, a similar action on the part of a commissioned officer occurred on the same mission. Another patrol had been sent out on a route in the valley below our ridge line, and I heard the officer reporting his position over the radio about a mile beyond his actual location. I could clearly see his panels and confirmed our location and his with several of my NCO's. (Of course I did not mention his incorrect report to them, but did report it to the Commanding Officer, because the safety of the entire Regiment depended on the accuracy of our reports.)

Accuracy of patrol reports can not be overemphasized. It is unfortunate that many others in our society—then and now—do not place the same value on honesty and accuracy as we do. You must make it clear to your subordinates from the very first that you expect and demand truthfulness from them and enforce those standards of accuracy in reporting.

As it turned out, neither of those two routes was used and we were ordered to attempt a crossing of the Ungi at another point. We were ordered to cross on foot, at a supposedly shallow location. The North Koreans were no where in sight on the other side, but the water was running so swiftly that there was no ice, in spite of the fact that the temperature had been below zero for several days. There were no assault bridges or assault boats available to us so that was it! The first men into the water moved knee-deep about 20 yards out and then fell into the water because of the numbness in their legs. We had to crack the ice off of them when they were retrieved. Fortunately we were able to thaw them out with fires and put them into trucks in their mummy sleeping bags. We did not lose any one then, but we easily could have had the North Koreans been defending on the other side.

That night we were told "no fires," although the temperature had dropped to 38 degrees below zero. I lost my Platoon Sergeant that night to frostbite, because he had suffered previous frostbite in the Battle of the Bulge in 1944. Stupid orders like that from senior officers who would be spending the night in heated hooches did not help morale much. Nor did the orders the next day that we would be crossing the Ungi on a bridge which had been captured intact by another unit, several miles up river. Our "crossing" turned out to have been just a feint, although no North Koreans had been seen within miles by anyone.

I honestly do not have any "advice for new lieutenants" about such situations. "No fires" is an order which can have obvious tactical merit for counterintelligence purposes, but when no enemy were in the area, there was no enemy air reconnaissance or air attack threat, and the temperature was so brutally cold, the order was simply impossible to comprehend, much less explain to the unit's soldiers. Likewise, the orders to attempt a river crossing by wading across a ford in weather that severe, were hard enough to follow, much less attempt to explain to subordinates.

Today, on the no fires situation I would put three soldiers sitting on their back packs together in a tight "shoulder-to-shoulder" circle facing outward, then light a single ration heating tablet (trioxane I think they are called) on a bed of rocks placed inside a .30 caliber ammo can with the lid left open just a crack, to serve as a field expedient stove in the middle of that small circle. By keeping the small of their backs warm (the kidney region), they could survive the night fairly well and still let me comply with the "no fires" order. Since all our blood circulates through our kidneys, if one can keep that area warm, that heat will warm the entire body. (Heating tablets give off very little light and it certainly would not be visible from inside the ammo can inside the three man circle. The heat tablet would heat up the rocks and let them radiate heat to the mens' kidneys for 15 or 20 minutes without burning anyone, then throw in another single heat tablet.)

Part of our travel north was in trucks, leapfrogging other units. With the beastly cold weather, one of the problems was sweaty feet inside thermal boots which would then freeze during the truck rides. The soldiers would often compound the sweating problem by getting their boots and feet very hot next to the fire at breaks or extended halts. The men were very tired and I often had to resort to threats of punishment if they did not make the effort to take off their boots, dry their feet and the inside of their boots, and change to dry felt liners and dry socks (from their underarm automatic sock dryers).

During our pursuit of the retreating North Koreans we were under constant pressure from our higher headquarters to make maximum speed. On one occasion, we had taken a prisoner, and I personally heard the order given to a Sergeant by a Captain (neither members of my unit), to take the prisoner to the POW camp and be back in ten minutes. We all knew that the nearest POW camp was at least 30 miles to our rear. The Sergeant specifically asked if the time factor was a direct order, and was told that if he was not back in ten minutes he would lose his stripes. The Sergeant carried out the obvious intent of the order, by shooting the prisoner out of sight of the men and returned, obviously greatly upset. This action was observed by many men and officers, and I was somewhat heartened to learn that the Captain would be tried. I am not sure of what charge, nor do I know the outcome, as I was never called as a witness. The obvious lesson here is that we must never become "like the enemy" or we will have lost all that is worth fighting for (even though we may win the battle).

Upon reaching Hyesanjin, my company ("I" of the 17th Infantry) was augmented by a platoon of tanks and a battery of 105 mm howitzers into a task force called Task Force Cooper after the Major commanding (*Time* Magazine, December 1950). We were to move south along the Yalu river to contact the 32nd Infantry Regiment or the 1st Marine Division which was reported to be moving to the river through the Chosen Reservoir area. There was a fairly high mountain range between our Regiment and the other units (through which, we later learned, the ChiComs were coming *en masse* to outflank us). Fortunately for us, as it turned out, the going was very slow. The road along the cliff side had been blown out in numerous places and we had only moved a few miles before we found out the Chinese were across the Yalu river to our south and threatened to cut us off.

For two days and nights we remained in a perimeter defense waiting for Headquarters to provide instructions as to our revised mission in light of the rapidly changing enemy situation. Two days and two nights of higher headquarters ordered 100% alert status took its toll and by the second night we could have been overrun easily. Another of those not-too-well-thought-out orders. When we were finally given orders, we sent the vehicles on one route with orders to torch any vehicle which broke down, while we undertook a 35 mile forced march north to a railhead. We were on the last train into Hamhung, and there set up a perimeter to receive men from the 32nd Infantry and the 1st Marine Division who were fortunate enough to escape from the Chosen trap.

Our company was assigned to an OPL [Outpost Line of Resistance] several miles outside the city. The OPL was located on a string of low hills commanding a wide valley through which the Marines and 32nd Infantry would be coming. My platoon was spread out over a mile and a half in squad sized positions. The gaps were covered by fire and observation, which was good during the day, and had to be patrolled at night. We set up all kinds of warning devices, but could not use demolitions on trip wire devices because of the expected passage of friendly troops.

One night there was heavy firing from an adjacent platoon's position and shortly thereafter the whole platoon came trooping into my position along the ridgeline. Our phone line which followed the ridgeline was knocked out and our radios were not working. The other platoon leader gathered his troops and set up a defensive position with my weapons squad on our flank. He soon discovered that three of his men were missing and about the same time we heard another burst of firing from back on his vacated position. Everything grew quiet for about an hour and then my Weapons Squad Leader asked to take four of his men back along the ridge to see if he could fix the break in our phone line. Although daylight was still several hours away, I let go with his promise to move very slowly and avoid contact with the enemy.

About an hour later, my phone rang. My Sergeant had found and fixed the phone line break, and reported that he was in the other platoon's position having found the three missing soldiers alive and occupying the original position. They had a captured antique enemy machine gun, incapable of firing, and about 20 dead North Koreans were on the position. The story from the three men was that their position had been attacked by a group of about 50 North Koreans who were shouting their heads off but not firing. Their unit had initially defended by fire but had then withdrawn, leaving them in the confusion. The North Koreans had dragged the old machine gun up onto the position after they occupied it. The three soldiers had backed off the hill together, and from hiding, had realized the North Koreans were gathering up US equipment which had been left behind, and appeared to be preparing to go back the way they had come. The three soldiers were pretty mad and counterattacked, killing those North Koreans found on the hill and reoccupying their platoon's position, where they were found by my Sergeant and his small patrol.

The lesson we drew from this was that the more noise an enemy unit makes in a very fluid situation, the less likely they are a serious threat to our forces. I recommended the three men for medals, and I think they received them. I do not know what happened to the Lieutenant who got forced off of his position. I am sure that his superiors had words, if not more, with him. My Weapons Squad Leader, whom I also recommended for a medal, was not given anything more than a "well done" from the Company Commander, but he was happy with that and the reputation for bravery that he and the other men gained and carried. The rest of this lesson is that even with high tech tools in today's Army, men with guts and determination will always be needed.

The final matter I would offer to new Infantry lieutenants before combat is on the subject of personal faith. I have tried hard to think of how to say this without sounding too "religious," but can not seem to find any way better to express this than to excerpt from a brief talk I prepared for a nearby church at their monthly Men's Prayer Breakfast. I notice on the TV that both the former Chairman of the Joint Chiefs and the current Army Chief of Staff were both in attendance at a recent national event of this nature so these observations can not be too far out of line. Beyond the usefulness of any other combat tips or lessons learned of which you may be made aware, I believe with all my heart that this is the most important preparation a young Infantry lieutenant can have. It will not make you fearless, bu tit goes a long way toward keeping you focused on your mission and concern foryour men, when everything around you is "going to hell."

During my first year as a cadet I found a group of men who were not just confident in their faith because of the way they were raised by their families or because of regular attendance at their church, but because of their calm assurance that while their bodies might belong to Uncle Sam, their souls were truly God's. I learned from them the same assurance of faith and belonging to God. That assurance carried me through many dark hours, in Korea and also later in Vietnam. Traveling in a supposedly secured area, my jeep hit a mine, blew up, the gas tank ruptured and ignited, threw the vehicle on its side engulfed in flames, with my driver and myself inside.

My FIRST thought—and I submit to you that this was a truly supernatural occurrence—was "Well, Lord, if this is my time to go, I am ready." Of course, my SECOND and completely natural thought was "But I am going to try and get out of this jeep." I got out, although the gasoline burns were so severe that I was evacuated to Walter Reed. I am convinced that as a soldier, as a husband and father, then later as a businessman after retirement, and even now as a grandfather, my life has been of far greater INTEGRITY because of the confidence which God has given me that I am truly His. This is the most important preparation a young officer can have.

******

It has been 48 years since I have been in combat of any note. Vietnam doesn't count for me. I spent nearly all of it in Saigon.

I arrived in Korea in mid-August 1950. 1 was assigned to the remnants of Task Force Smith. Initially I had the 4th Platoon (Mortars) until September 19th when we crossed the Naktong River and lost a whole bunch of new lieutenants. From that time until the middle of June I had 2nd Platoon, B Company, 21st Infantry Regiment.

Despite the long interim time frame, it was, of course, a period I will never forget. Without going into a long thoughtful diatribe, here are a few small clues I remember.

Save the cardboard from cases of C-rations and K rations. Put it under your sleeping bags. It is great protection against the elements and cold ground beneath you.

Don't eat local fruit without thoroughly washing it.

Never walk in ravines in the attack. If you must travel in a valley, keep troops on ridges alongside your progress. Always, always travel just below the ridge lines.

On a reconnaissance patrol, don't pick a fight, even to unload excess ammunition (like ammunition for the recoilless rifle). Get the information and get out.

Always orient yourself on a map and know where you are.

Soldiers will all sleep at night if you and your Platoon Sergeant don't take turns to patrol the perimeter.

If you take reasonable precautions with air-ground recognition panels, attacks from the air are not too dangerous.

Don't expect your troops to be heroes. If you put them on outpost or to act as rear guard, they will run away when the enemy attacks.

Always meticulously check culverts and other hiding places when in the attack.

Most fighting is a matter of maneuver. Both sides will avoid direct conflict if possible.

Helicopter evacuation is not simple when you have enemy contact. Helicopter pilots are extremely reluctant to land nearby when there is a possibility of enemy fire.

Hand to hand combat is a very remote possibility.

Tanks always attract enemy fire. Immediately when the shooting starts, dismount and take cover.

On patrols, establish contact with your spotter/radio relay aircraft immediately.

Keep a diary. You may want to write a book later. Send home a copy of unit rosters and battalion officers rosters—great for getting in touch with someone years later.

Helmets are a pain and generally not useful except to boil water.

Bayonets are generally useless except for digging. Carry a durable switchblade or pocket knife on a chain. You'll probably lose it, but it will be handy on occasion.

An entrenching tool works best when is is shaped like an ax (blade 90 degrees to handle).

Troops are not motivated by politics. They are motivated by survival.
Mines are the scariest enemy (and friendly) weapon.

Pistols and carbines are for show only.

The average soldier cannot hit a target more than 100 yards away.

******

What I consider most important in the education of new 2nd Lieutenants *en route* to combat would be proficiency in map reading, familiarity with weapons and their proper employment, necessity of sharing the privations and hardships of your troops, reliance on your NCO's and leading from the front. Being in superb physical condition is a must. Very few 30-year-old company commanders could keep up with their units, much less lead from the front. More experience on all the foregoing would have made me a much better platoon leader in those early days in Korea. Matters on which I would like to expand, however—and my input is not necessarily limited to only lessons learned in Korea—are as follows.

Take Objectives with Fire Power, Not Soldier Courage   The ability to accomplish the foregoing requires a full understanding of how to adjust fires of organic mortars, supporting artillery, Naval offshore support and close support aircraft. Always ensure that you personally "have their push" [know their radio frequency] and have the ability to get on it with your own communications gear. Even though you have attached artillery and mortar forward observers, Air Force forward air controllers and Anglico teams (if they still exist) who have that specific task—the ultimate responsibility for putting steel on target remains yours. When you outrun your organics [go beyond the range of unit organic mortars] and move out from under the range fan of your supporting artillery, it is very comforting to have a brace of fighter aircraft, or better yet, a flight of four doing lazy eights in the grid square behind you as you attack over a major hill mass without opportunity to observe what is on the other side—and it is not always greener grass! Of course, now we have UAV and satellite systems to assist, but I suspect more often than not those reconnaissance assets will be unavailable to platoon leaders.

Hold Objectives with Fire Power, Not Soldier Courage Once the Chinese entered the Korean War and we had been overrun several times, we understood that a perfectly aimed shot at 1,000 meters did not mean much when you were faced with 300 or 400 Chinese troops appearing 200 meters in front of your position at first light. The bayonet has too short a range, and the side arm, as others have commented, is only useful "inside an elevator." So eventually we added an A4 or an A6 machine gun to each squad in the platoon, recruited indigenous civilians to A-frame ammunition to support those guns, plus carry mermite cans full of fragmentation grenades when we could get them. Then we taped double banana magazines on every M2 carbine we had and confiscated some old Thompson sub-machine guns from Chinese prisoners. The result was that we could fire an FPL of hard bullets reminiscent of Fort Benning's "mad minute." This FPL was part of complete fire plan, carefully laid out with sectors assigned to cover the entire front, range cards and aiming stakes on each position. Practice firing of the FPL from time to time is also great for morale.

[.30 caliber Browning machine gun M1919A4 was the air cooled light machine gun on a tripod, controlled with a Traversing and Elevating (T&E) Mechanism; .30 caliber Browning machine gun M1919A6 was the same gun with a bipod and shoulder stock. Both required at least a two man crew, just as does the 7.62 mm light machine gun M60. Koreans are truly remarkable for the prodigious amounts of weight they can carry on an A frame. A "mermite can" was an insulated food container for bringing hot meals from a rear field kitchen to feed on the front line. Fragmentation grenade capacity would be approximately 50 to 55 grenades, which would certainly be an A frame load. The banana magazine was a 30 round magazine for the .30 caliber carbine M2, which was the selective fire semi- or full-automatic version of that weapon. Thompson refers to the .45 caliber sub-machine gun which the US had provided as military assistance to Chinese Nationalist forces in the 1945–1948 Chinese Civil War, which had been captured by the Chinese Communists and then issued to many of their troops in Korea. Firing the same ammunition as the .45 caliber M1911A1 Colt pistol and the M3 submachine gun then issued to tank crewmen, ammunition for Thompsons was readily available through normal supply channels. FPL or Final Protective Line is the equivalent term to Final Protective Fires.]

Digging in is always important, but sometimes there are reasons that it just simply is not going to occur. But you must always fire in your Night Defensive Fires. In fact, you should also "shoot a box" prior to darkness for any distant outpost in front of your position. If you have poor maps or if you are not exactly sure where you are on the ground (in either defense or attack), have your supporting artillery fire one round of smoke or a flare to mark "center of sector," then reorient. (Artillery batteries always know where they are.)

The Cav Commander in *Apocalypse Now* is not the only one who loves the smell of Napalm, be it morning, noon or night! Using Napalm in front of a defensive position is a marvelous way to stop a major assault. I am sure it is written up in some engineer handbook somewhere [see *Flame Field Expedients*, Field Manual 5-34, Engineer Field Data] , but you can jury-rig 55 gallon drums by first filling them with Napalm, placing a white phosphorus grenade in the bung, then putting 1 1/2 pounds of TNT underneath the barrels prior to digging them one-third of the way into the ground. Wrap det cord around the middle, hook up a blasting cap to the result and then run two telephone wires back to the platoon position for each dram. Rig the ends to a "naily board" terminal so that when the circuit is complete, the system can be detonated either individually in a threatened sector, or all at once if the attack is across your entire front. 300 to 400 attacking enemy troops will certainly cover your entire platoon position. This Napalm system takes a little time, but it works. Do not take hills with soldier courage. Do not hold hills with soldier courage either.

Consequences of Your Decisions Maintain some emotional (not physical) distance from your men. In the final analysis, soldiers will live or die based on your decisions. You cannot escape this responsibility and must deal with the results for the rest of your life. Soldiers do not need your friendship. They need your leadership and your competence if they are to survive and to accomplish their assigned missions. Remember, if you put your best man on point continuously, he will eventually get killed. But if you put your worst man on point, you may all get killed. If you always take the point yourself, you will get killed. Deciding whose life is to be placed at the most risk, and when, is the most critical decision you will ever make.

You must make dispassionate decisions. Friendships make all of this more difficult. Favoritism is devastating to morale. You must conquer your own fear daily and willingly share the risks of your soldiers. Dead heroes can not lead. Standing tall during incoming is stupid. Groveling instead of returning fire is worse. In a way, it is not so much the fear of getting killed, but how you have to live before it happens—living underground like an animal, constantly hungry, cold, apprehensive and hitting the ground at every unidentified noise.

Killing is reprehensible and much easier to do at long range without the observation of results. Infantry does not have that option, as you "close with and destroy the enemy force." Engaging the enemy at greatest range is a far better option. When the fear of getting killed becomes less than the revulsion at how you have to live before it happens, it is time to leave the unit and put at least one hill mass between you and the fight.

Believe me, I would have been a much better Infantry platoon leader had I known the foregoing before the fact rather than after. The bottom line is, Lieutenant, to lead soldiers you must first be one.

******

Wish this information had been around 50 years ago when I needed it.

I spent the months of June and July 1950 in Europe as a tourist on graduation leave. It was interrupted on 25 June by the invasion of South Korea. I was in Paris at the time and met a number of my classmates whose leaves had been canceled, and they were returning to the states to report for duty to units to which they had been assigned. I was on orders to report to FECOM [Far East Command, but not to any specific unit] in August and decided to stay in Europe unless recalled which I was not. I figured that it might be the last opportunity to see that part of the world, and I wanted to make the most of it.

As well as I can remember, I reported to Camp Stoneman, California in mid-August and began preparations for shipping out to Japan. That took place the last week of August. I was in Japan for a few days, just long enough to continue processing and found myself docking in Pusan harbor on or about 1 September. That same day we were transported by rail to Miryang, one of the few towns still held by our forces in the Pusan Perimeter. The next day or two was a blur of movements through Division, regimental, and battalion headquarters.

I was delayed from joining my unit—Fox Company, of the 9th Infantry Regiment, 2nd Division—because it was cut off by North Korean Forces who had broken through the Pusan Perimeter. The only briefing of significance that I can remember, which I and six of my classmates attended who were all assigned to the 9th Infantry included a greeting from the Assistant Division Commander, Brigadier General Bradley: "Gentlemen, welcome to the El Alamein of Korea." His words, though disturbing at the moment, were prophetic. The perimeter was restored. I joined my company and served as a platoon leader for ten days until I was wounded on 14 September during a preliminary attack prior to the breakout on 15 September. I was evacuated to Japan and then on to CONUS. The point of this narrative is to show you that although my own combat experience was limited in time, the lesson to be learned is that we never know when the bullet or frag with our name on it will be incoming.

After being released from the Naval Hospital in Charleston, South Carolina in late February 1951 (all US Army facilities were full or still closed by the time of my arrival), I reported to Fort Benning, Georgia, where I served on the map reading committee at the Infantry School until spring of 1953. Then I received orders to attend an Associate Company Officers Course and completed Airborne training. I volunteered to return to Korea in July, where I was assigned to command the Heavy Mortar Company, 14th Infantry Regiment, 25 Infantry Division. This time I was properly briefed and much better trained to perform my duties.

I wish I could offer some gems for the graduating Infantry lieutenants. In my case it was a no-brainer that going from an academic environment to a combat zone was not the best course of action to ensure success or survival. I don't mean to trivialize this compilation of advice for new Infantry lieutenants, but attendance at branch schools after graduation prepares one for service in the real Army, certainly if that service includes duty in a combat zone.

One of our classmates (who went on to wear four stars) served his first assignment in the 82nd Airborne Division and then went to Infantry Basic Course before coming to Korea. He said that on an hour-for-hour basis he learned more at the Infantry Basic Course than any other school he attended in his career, obviously including Command and General Staff College and Army War College. New Infantry lieutenants who are fortunate enough to attend Basic Course should count their blessings and study much harder than they ever did for mere academic courses. Final exams after Basic Course will be combat and life or death.

******

In brief background, my assignments included Pioneer and Ammunition Platoon Leader, Headquarters Company, 3rd Battalion, 15th Infantry Regiment, 3rd Infantry Division, 17 August 1950; 75 mm Recoilless Rifle Platoon Leader, Company "M," also in 3rd/15th; then Reconnaissance Officer, Company "M" from 14 November 1951 until 9 January 1952. The Regiment departed 31 August for Korea, but was shifted to Japan as Theater Reserve for a period of about two months. We landed at Wonsan, North Korea on 10 November, and participated in X Corps operations on east side of the Korean Peninsula with 1st Marine Division and 7th Infantry Division.

The Class of 1950 was delighted to expect a tour of troop duty after graduation before attending the branch basic course. We, and the Department of the Army thought some troop duty would make us more attentive students. We would quickly regret that change of program. You will all thank God for every opportunity you are provided to learn Infantry skills before entering combat.

The most important advice I can give to a new platoon leader is to listen to and work closely with your Platoon Sergeant. You should find him to be a seasoned NCO with a wealth of knowledge to share with you. Weigh his advice carefully and do not be afraid to follow that advice. He can be a key to your success.

Pay close attention, not just to tactics, but to learning all skill areas. Signal communications, indirect fire control techniques, range cards and firing stakes when assigning sectors of fire, how to lay mine fields and install tactical barbed wire, and how to tie these obstacles into perimeter defense were critical tasks starting from Day One. Mine removal and first aid were also needed skills. I was fortunate to have some very fine NCO teachers.

I found my platoon well trained and their conduct and performance in very dangerous situations was exemplary. Adding to the leadership and training problems we faced in Japan was the filling of about 30 to 40 percent of our authorized strength with south Korean civilian males pulled out of the battle area. These men were totally untrained and spoke no English. In the few weeks we had in Japan, they were integrated into our team fairly well and developed into valuable and loyal soldiers. Later, when I took over the 75 mm Recoilless Rifle Platoon, Chong Gu Nan would carry the rifle itself and Yu Hin Gue the tripod—normally a task for five soldiers.

Know your equipment, particularly weapons. You never know when that knowledge will be critical. The first time I fired a recoilless rifle, a rifle grenade or .50 caliber machine gun was in combat. Training time is golden—take full advantage of it to improve skills, expand familiarization and cross-training of many men for any task normally assigned to just a few.

Because you are a Military Academy graduate, many officers expect you to be more knowledgeable than you really are. This is a compliment, but also creates challenges. You must resolve to try just that much harder to live up to that expectation. Do not expect much counsel from your superiors when in combat operations.

Combat duty is physically demanding. Keep yourself and your troops in good shape.

Before you ever consider your day done ensure that your men are secure, essential combat needs attended to and all unit equipment is cleaned, inspected for functioning and serviceability, and ready for tomorrow—or for the middle of the night. During unit movement, pay close attention to items being accidentally (or intentionally) dropped or discarded. For example, warm clothing needed at night becomes too hot to wear and too heavy to carry during the day.

There are times in preparation of a defensive position when leading and supervising requires you to pitch in and help string barbed wire or employ the shovel. If your other tactical duties are taken care of—security out, supporting fires planned, communications established plus fields of fire, range cards and aiming stakes checked—then not only pitch in but lead the way.

Communicate with all your personnel, listen to their concerns and level with them about the tactical situation to the maximum extent feasible. This works both ways, as they may reveal information of which you are not aware but need to know.

On patrol planning, always include emergency medical evacuation and indirect fire support details.

Congratulations on your graduation, on your choice of Infantry as your branch, and best wishes for a long and successful military career.

******

I arrived in Korea in October 1950, when the unit I was assigned to, the 5th Regimental Combat Team, was just below the Yalu River. I was assigned to the Third Battalion, "M" Company, that is, the Heavy Weapons Company. My first duty assignment was as Platoon Leader of the 75 min Recoilless Rifle Platoon; I was then assigned as the Platoon Leader of the Machine Gun Platoon, and later I was assigned as the Platoon Leader of the third Platoon of "L" Company, that is, Love Company. I was in that assignment in the spring offensive of 1951 when I was wounded and went to the hospital in Japan, and when I came back the battalion gave me command of "K" Company, which I held for only two weeks, but then "L" Company came open and I was switched back over to my old outfit and I commanded "L" Company for several months. I remained in the combat assignments, the rifle company assignments until the Regiment was transferred down to Koje-do to guard prisoners and I was made the Assistant Regimental S-3 and remained there until June 1952 when I returned to Fort Benning, to attend the Officers Basic Class, by the way.

First off, a new lieutenant going into combat should keep two things in mind. He must accomplish his mission and he must take care of his men. Those are paramount. All other things flow from them.

Under mission, things that I learned and practiced in Korea, from experience, and from others, are as follows.
The basic Infantry play in the attack playbook is in three parts. An assault element, a base of fire, and a flanking or maneuvering element. Old Field Manuals referred to these teams as the ABC teams. I practiced that in training my people in Korea and it seemed a novelty to some, but it did please my superiors that I knew the proper terms. To tell one story about learning from someone who had been there for a while, we

were attacking one day, going up a long ridge line, and to our right flank was a company of another battalion. There was a low mountainous prominence ahead of that company. It all of a sudden sort of exploded. Smoke went every place. The artillery was coming in, mortars were coming in, machine guns were firing into the clouds of dust and smoke on the hill. After a while I could see the Infantry move up the hill and go into the assault under cover of the machine guns and the artillery and the rifle base of fire. Up until that time I had seen my companies not do that well. They would make contact and then go right straight forward. I later learned that this adjacent company commander was a Military Academy graduate, Class of 1945, and he was doing things by the book, and it worked. When I became a company commander, I always did it that way myself.

Always take and hold the high ground. I am sure that I learned that from the people who had been there, since the 5th RCT had come into the Pusan Perimeter in August and spearheaded the Eighth Army attack up the western side of the Korean peninsula. They were hardened, very successful combat veterans, under a great commander, Colonel John Throckmorton. This pertains to mountain warfare, which we would certainly face in Korea again, or in Kosovo. Attack up fingers, on the high ground, not in the gullies, valleys or gorges. Attack up the fingers, attacking each fortified position singly as you advance.

In defense, make the enemy always attack a broad front. In setting defense, avoid inviting enfilade fire. Set warning devices, such as booby traps and trip flares, as far out as possible. Then register your organic mortars in on those areas covered by your early warning devices, and register your artillery on beyond that. At night, leaders at all levels must check the line. Soldiers will go to sleep. Even though the danger is obvious, they will go to sleep. Even more important is for leaders to check the line when danger is <u>not</u> obvious. All night and every night, whether enemy action is likely or unlikely, leaders must prowl their turf, to keep their alert status up. The keys to night defense are alertness and light; that is, illumination when the enemy attack is detected. In my command of a brigade in Viet-Nam I continued to employ those two principles to great advantage.

With regard to using alertness and light, when you detect something, you hit it with everything but the kitchen sink. I recall the Platoon Sergeant of my 2nd Platoon in "L" Company, SGT Sally, developed what he called the "grenade barrage." He would put a huge pile of grenades in front of his bunker and the men would do the same thing, When the Chinese start their grenade attack, he came back and hit them with his grenade barrage from every position in his platoon. Just a small anecdote to illustrate a bigger point: When you go, go all the way. Hit them with everything you've got, very massive, sudden, violent. [Korean War era term "barrage" meant the same as today's "final protective fires" from your supporting artillery—massive and continuous fires. Sgt. Sally's choice of words was not coincidental—he meant that his platoon would provide its own "barrage" very close in, with all the firepower at their disposal.]

Now on to the category of taking care of your men. It gets into a lot of things, such as, you are an Infantryman, right there in a platoon of men. You are all human beings, but you are the officer, you are the leader. You must make sure that the men know that and respect that, but at the same time, you have to get down with them, laugh with them, talk with them, fight with them, to gain their respect.

But you also have to make them do things to take care of themselves, that they would not otherwise do. A good example of that was the care of the feet. Up in North Korea it was extremely cold, during our fight there and during the long retreat, sometimes reaching 30 degrees below zero. The men were very ill equipped, I repeat, ill equipped, in the way of winter clothing, and measures had to be taken to take care of their feet, to prevent cold weather injuries.

The best way to do it, and I learned this over there, from my leaders, people who had been there before, was to always keep a spare pair of socks under your field jacket, under your underwear, up next to your skin, keeping them warm and dry. At night, take off the boots, take off the wet socks, wring them out, put on the dry socks and put the wet ones back in your bosom. Men won't do that in 20 to 30 degrees below zero weather unless you make them. So my platoon would just sit down on the bank, aside of the road, after a long march, take off the boots, take off and wring out the wet socks, put on the dry ones and put the wet ones back in their bosom. We had no cases of trench foot or cold injury.

I also learned, that under these very trying conditions—constant danger and constant discomfort to put it mildly—the men do appreciate things that you do for them. They develop a strong loyalty to leaders who take care of them. I learned it from my leaders over there. I tried to practice it myself. One good example was when we had come back into reserve after a very tough campaign in which we had been weeks on the front line. We came down the hill—it took hours to get down off the front line hill and into the reserve area—and when we got there all the companies were laid out, side by side. In my company, "L" Company, the First Sergeant had found some huge pots and had filled them with water and had them boiling hot, waiting on us. This was for the men shaving, or washing up or bathing or what ever they wanted to use it for.

The other company First Sergeants had not done that. I can remember our men looking from side to side at the other companies and hearing them saying, "Lord I'm glad I'm in "L" Company." That was said by a black soldier, one who had come from an all black segregated unit [when units were integrated in 1951), to our unit, into my unit, and was the first one that I know of. We had hung a BAR [Browning Automatic Rifle] on him because he was so big. We took care of him, and welcomed him into our unit, and he became a part of the platoon. It meant a lot to me because he was the one who said, "Lord I'm glad I'm in "L" Company."

Another example of other people doing good things was when we had been on the hill an awfully long time. It was a very high hill and it took hours to get up there. We were reached only by what they called the Cho-gi Trains (cho-gi: Korean for "go"] of Korean civilians who brought up our ammunition and supplies on A frames, and who on occasion brought up hot food in mermite cans but most of the time it was just C rations. But one particularly cold morning, we looked and the Cho-gi train was coming up and the Koreans had unusual loads on their A frames. And what it turned out to be was that the Battalion Commander had sent the battalion mess up there, and they had taken those huge aluminum stoves that stood about four feet high, broken them down and put them on the back of the Cho-gi train. They came up on the mountain, on our position, set up and fired up those stoves, and served us a hot breakfast, with eggs to order. That does not sound like much, but to us it was the most wonderful thing that had ever happened.

Another example was when I first got to the 75 mm Recoilless Rifle Platoon, there were two ROK [Republic of Korea] soldiers in there, and everybody liked them and they were good fighters. But they were given rice for their food and we were given C-rations. The C-rations of course had candy and cigarettes in them, and the ROK soldiers got none of that. I saw that and the first time I got a C-ration meal and noticed they did not have any, I gave mine to them. Later on the Platoon Sergeant said to me, "Lieutenant, the men really appreciated that." I did not think it was anything at all, but after those words, I knew it was a big thing. Just a little something, a way of taking care of your men, no matter who they are.

The last thing I learned over in Korea has to do with morale, which I've already discussed to some extent, but pride in unit, *esprit de corps*, was extremely important. It is something that motivated men to do something that they did not want to do, and that is to go up a hill in a hail of enemy bullets. That pride in unit, desire to protect and be a part of with their fellow soldiers—to protect their fellow soldiers and be a part of something bigger than themselves, grew out of loyalty to and trust in and of their leaders. I saw units there that were poor units, and they had very, very poor leaders. There was no pride in unit, there was no trust in the leaders. That all goes back to my opening salvo, accomplishing the mission and taking care of the men.

One thing that I did in Love Company, that just came on a whim—we came across a fuel tank, a wing drop tank from one of the aircraft that had been supporting us. It was in good shape. I had somebody, and I don't even remember who, paint on the side of it in good block letters. "L" Company—Lee's Miserables, taken from the old and well known *les miserables* of Victor Hugo. (It was said with an English pronunciation, Lee's Miserables, as a plural noun, rather than the French pronunciation "ley miserab.")

We carried that thing around with us. When we were in the reserve, or when my company rear was set up, they would put that thing out front, put it up on some rocks, and let people know that was "L" Company. When we moved, we would put it on the top of a truck, heaping full of supplies with canvas over the load, but old "Lee's Miserables" would be up on top. It mean a lot to the men, and created a lot of pride, in my opinion. Nearly 50 years later I am still getting letters from the men of "L" Company, and they never fail to mention "Lee's Miserables" and that old wing drop tank.

With regard to items of equipment that it would have been nice to have had, that we now have, I would have to include the grenade launcher, which will be very helpful, especially going up those hills, those fingers and taking out those bunkers, one by one. Grenade launchers would have been great; as we tried to do it by hand, throwing grenades up hill at a very small target of the bunker firing port, and of course some of our own grenades rolled back downhill on us and wounded our own people.

For night defense, the modern night vision devices would have rendered the Chinese almost useless in their favorite attacks because they always attacked at night. They would crawl up the hill close to our positions with sacks of their grenades with which they would begin their attack. To have spotted them much earlier than we did would have been a great help.

Obviously the attack helicopter will be extremely valuable in Korea in fire support. This is because, unlike artillery, they can support you while you are moving to the objective, whereas you need to get a cease fire from the artillery pretty soon as you get close to the objective.

******

To ensure accuracy, I must make clear that I went to Korea in October 1950 as a Cavalry Lieutenant and was assigned to Tank Company, 9th Infantry Regiment, 2nd Infantry Division. [Each Infantry Regiment in the Infantry Division had an organic tank company in this time frame.] My 13 months combat experience as a Platoon Leader and Company Commander led me to transfer to the Infantry.

My experience was totally different from that of Dave Hughes. I joined my company in mid-October at Pyongyang where the 9th Infantry Regiment was securing the airfield. I found myself in a group of Reserve Officers, who, to a man, did not want to be there. Although only one of them had any significant World War II combat, they felt they had had their war and it was time for the younger generation to have its war. All the conversation concerned rumors that the Division was going home soon and would be back at Fort Lewis before Christmas. In addition, I was not assigned a platoon and did not receive a single word of counsel or advice.

When the 8th Cavalry Regiment was rendered combat ineffective by the Chinese in late October near Unsan, the 9th Infantry was attached to the 1st Cavalry Division. In the move north, I was still not assigned a platoon. However, when we were tasked to attach a platoon of tanks to the 2nd Battalion for a blocking assignment east of Kunuri, I was told by a senior platoon leader that I would be going with it. We rode out in a jeep with the tanks following. On arrival at our designated location he pointed up at a hill 400 yards away as the location of G Company, whereupon he got back in the jeep and departed.

At this point I got seriously to work at the business of being a combat leader although I really did not know a lot about it. At Fort Hood in August I received several days of familiarization along with the other new lieutenants. This was an asset; but I still did not know much about leading a platoon in combat.

The one most important asset I brought with me from West Point was an ingrained belief that a leader has to always set the example and from that first moment as a Platoon Leader in Korea until my last moment as a Brigade Commander in Viet-Nam I never violated it. Even in those moments when I was personally scared shitless I never violated the poker face that is essential to maintaining the troops' confidence in their leaders. Without knowing the consequences at the time, I instinctively took several actions that first day that made a lasting impression on my men. I remained with my platoon that night and every other night, whereas my predecessor had always jeeped off to the Battalion CP to spend the night. Further, I always stood watch as a crew member on my tank. 47 years later when I searched for and found members of that platoon, most spoke of how West Point lieutenants were different.

The words "West Point" were certainly an asset. The word travels fast that there is a new lieutenant from West Point and although it is not always so, the troops are prepared to accept him as top notch unless he prove them wrong. On the personal side, I was always aware that failure on my part would, in the minds of many, be reflected as a failure by West Point.

******

I reported to Camp Stoneman, California with orders to Korea, by way of Camp Drake, Japan, arriving in Korea for assignment in early September. This was during the very fierce fighting on the Pusan perimeter, with enemy breakthrough attempts all along the line. The Battalion S3 told me that the Battalion Commander, Lieutenant Colonel John T. Corley had been up at the Combat Outpost Line (COPL) for the past 16 days, and that there was no way of knowing when he would be back. A short time later the battalion headquarters was notified that Lieutenant Colonel Corley had just been reassigned to command of the Regiment.

Lieutenant Colonel Corley had been my Company Tactical Officer at the Military Academy. Anyone who has ever known or served under him knows that he was one of the most highly dedicated and most highly decorated, aggressive, hard-core, no-nonsense combat commanders in the Army. To this day, he is a legend in the First Infantry Division as a result of his unsurpassed combat record in that famous division in World War II. (Commanding Third Battalion, 26th Infantry Regiment, Lieutenant Colonel Corley was awarded the Distinguished Service Cross, Five Silver Stars, Four Bronze Stars and the Purple Heart. Battlefield promoted to Colonel in Korea, Colonel Corley received his second Distinguished Service Cross and three more Silver Stars.)

Upon his return to the Battalion CP, Lieutenant Colonel Corley told me I would be going to command the 1st Platoon in "K" Company, which was up on the COPL. He told me that I would be replacing Lieutenant Tittel, and that I was to inform that officer he was to remain on the "King One" outpost position with me for 24 hours, during which time he was to brief me on the enemy situation, terrain, organization of the platoon's defensive perimeter and on security matters, etc.

Following my interview with Lieutenant Colonel Corley, I was given my first assignment, even before going to "K" Company, to organize and emplace a 65 man "platoon" of South Korean recruits into defensive positions for the northern approach to the Regimental CP near Haman. Having no interpreter, I grabbed the first two recruits, pointed to their entrenching tools, pointed in the direction from which the enemy attack would likely come, and made digging motions at the location I had selected for the first position. With the rest of the recruits tagging along behind me, I moved to the next position I had selected about five yards down the line, and repeated the "digging motions instruction" to the next two men. This process was repeated until the entire 65 man unit was in position along the defensive line.

As I moved back and forth along the line, checking their progress, one of those recruits asked me in badly broken English "You show me how to load carbine?" Combat circumstances at that time were such that the only training US troops were able to give these South Korean "citizen soldiers" prior to their being committed to action was "on the job" training in a live combat environment. Despite the tragic conditions under which they were, by necessity, placed in harm's way, without exception they displayed an exceptional love of country, devotion to duty, discipline, self-sacrifice and courage. That night, during the enemy's unsuccessful attempt to overrun the Regimental CP, a number of these nameless young South Korean soldiers died in their foxholes I had showed them how and where to dig, but not one man withdrew to the rear.

Upon my arrival at the "King One" position on the COPL, at the extreme left flank of the Regiment's sector, Lieutenant Tittel welcomed me to the platoon, introduced me to the Platoon Sergeant, and took me on a "cook's tour" of the position. He briefed me on all aspects of the operation, to include the platoon mission, enemy situation, terrain, organization of the perimeter defense and security. At the end of the 24 hour period, he said good-bye to me and the men in the platoon, wished me good luck and departed with the carrying party.

Following a meeting with the Platoon Sergeant and Squad Leaders, together with the Squad Leaders of the attached 60 mm mortar squad and the .50 caliber heavy machine gun squad, I made a thorough ground reconnaissance of my area of responsibility and confirmed what Lieutenant Tittel had pointed out in the terrain portion of his briefing. That portion of the COPL for which I was responsible was characterized by a saddle which consisted of two hilltops approximately 75 yards apart. The area between the two hilltops consisted of open terrain. After making my first estimate of the situation, I developed the following defensive plan. I retained the major portion of my 57 man reinforced rifle platoon in a perimeter defense around the higher of the two hilltops, and deployed a 23 man force consisting of two rifle squads, reinforced by one of the platoon's two light machine guns.

I instructed the Sergeant I placed in command of this force to organize a perimeter defense around the smaller hilltop, which was located to the right of the main position. I ordered a telephone line run from my command post to that of the other hilltop, and provided him with an EE-8 field telephone. (My platoon was very short of NCO's with not even all squad leaders being Sergeants.) I instructed the NCOIC of that position to call me 1.) if and when his position came under enemy attack, and 2.) if and when he and his men began to run low on ammunition, under which circumstances he was to be prepared to withdraw his troops back to the main platoon perimeter on my order. I issued orders to the chain of command within the main platoon position that priority of fires of all organic and attached weapons would be given the withdrawing force.

At approximately 2230 hours the NCOIC of the detached element called and reported that his position was under attack in what appeared to be a probing action. The main platoon position came under attack at the same time. Shortly after the fire fight began, the NCOIC of the detached elements abandoned his position and withdrew back into the main platoon position. I immediately relieved the Sergeant, called the detached elements on the land line and told the soldier manning the phone to get PFC Boyd on the line. PFC Boyd was one of a number of the members of the unit who were in confinement in the Eighth Army stockade in Gifu, Japan at the time the war broke out. He and a number of his fellow stockade inmates were given the option of completing their sentences or of volunteering to fight in Korea. In the short time that I had been able to observe the men in my platoon, PFC Boyd had impressed me as being a highly self-confident, levelheaded and forceful young soldier. I ordered him to "hold what you've got," to call me when he and his men started to run low on ammunition, and to be prepared to withdraw on my order.

A thick blanket of fog clung close to the ground, which made visual detection of the enemy virtually impossible. This eerie and nerve-wracking condition was evidenced by a PVT Betts, a rifleman manning the detached elements' perimeter. He was standing on top of a cliff located just below the topographical crest of the hill when a North Korean soldier with his burp gun [Russian sub machine gun PPSH, so called because of the high rate of fire which sounded like a burp] slung across his back climbed over the top of the cliff just a few feet from where PVT Betts was standing up, trying to see through the fog. Betts was holding his M-1 rifle in a horizontal position at about waist level with his finger on the trigger when he sensed, rather than saw, someone moving toward him. The enemy soldier was moving slowly towards him in a crouched position when PVT Betts squeezed the trigger, hitting the North Korean just below the eye.

At approximately 0400 hours, after an all night fight, PFC Boyd called on the field phone to report that he and his men were out of machine gun ammunition and grenades, and down to between two and three clips of M-1 ammunition per rifleman. I ordered PFC Boyd to "bring the troops home," and issued orders for all available firepower within the main position to support the withdrawal. The enemy continued to press the attack until I yelled to the .50 caliber machine gunner to "play me a tune on that big bad fifty!" Several well aimed bursts from the fifty and like magic, the enemy on that smaller hilltop broke contact and withdrew over the northern edge of the ridge line, leaving a number of their dead in the approaches to our two positions. PFC Boyd led his men back into the main platoon perimeter without losing a man.

At first light, I led a patrol of two squads back onto the other hilltop without encountering any resistance. I had been required to make a hasty decision about combat replacements to reestablish the chain of command, and had to rely on my judgment of the men formed in just over 24 hours. I was confident that PFC Boyd had the forceful strength of character to assume command under difficult circumstances. Look for the potential leaders among your men whom you may have to appoint to leadership positions as combat replacements.

At approximately 1600 hours that afternoon, I received orders to withdraw my platoon from King One position, and rejoin the rest of "K" Company which was on the Battalion's right flank. King One was taken over by a platoon from "L" Company commanded by a Lieutenant Elliot. We were relieved of our attachments, and moved by truck some 9,000 yards to rejoin our company where I first met my Company Commander, Captain Swartz.

That same evening, Lieutenant Elliot's unit, Second Platoon of "L" Company was overrun and COPL position King One was lost to the enemy. In the course of that attack, Lieutenant Elliot's men withdrew, leaving him alone at the outpost, wounded and unable to move, having been shot in the stomach. Captain Swartz asked me how long it would take me to get back up to King One, and I replied that it would take a couple of hours after moving the 9,000 yards back to the battalion's left flank. He then asked me how many men did I want, and I said, "Sir, give me my Platoon." My platoon and I arrived at the rear of a small knoll just below the top of the ridge line of the King One position at approximately 2230 hours.

I took my Platoon Sergeant and my radio-telephone operator with me up to where we could see over the top of the knoll, leaving the rest of the platoon concealed behind the knoll. The distance from the top of the knoll to the top of the ridge was approximately 25 to 30 yards. From my position on top of the knoll, I observed silhouetted against the skyline on King One what appeared to be a force of 100 to 150 enemy. When the enemy detected myself and my two men, they began motioning for us to come up on the ridge, waving their arms, yelling what sounded like "Ah-no-nay, ee-dee-wah, ee-dee-wah." (I later learned it meant in Korean "Hello, come here, come here.") I am convinced the only reason the enemy chose not to attack or try to capture us then is that they had no way of knowing what size force I might have had concealed behind and below the knoll.

I reported my situation to the Battalion Commander and was directed to stand fast and dig in where I was. During this exchange, my Platoon Sergeant told me that the men were pulling back. I told him that no one was going anywhere until I received the order to go and ordered them to go, and we were still not going anywhere until all of our men were accounted for and we had all our equipment. I recommended to the Battalion Commander that my unit withdraw to more defensible terrain prior to digging in, so that I would at least have enough distance between my unit and the enemy to register mortar fires. I was told to use my own discretion, and we pulled back to dig in with all men and equipment accounted for.

The next day my platoon was ordered to return to King One position with the mission of obtaining the names from the dog tags of the soldiers who had been killed with Lieutenant Elliot. At this time, a dozen or so South Korean soldiers were attached to my platoon. While moving back up to King One, I passed out, overcome by heat stroke. When I regained consciousness, I was surprised to learn that instead of having been evacuated to the aid station for treatment, two of my South Korean soldiers had carried me up onto the objective with the rest of my platoon.

At this time, the unit to Third Battalion's left flank was attacking but was helped up by an enemy machine gun position. The adjacent company commander had requested 81mm mortar fire support but the initial rounds of white phosphorus landed on the company CP and set the Company Commander's field jacket on fire. I had been monitoring that fight over the radio, and after the mortar "cease fire" was arranged I called the Company Commander and announced that my unit was standing by to assist if needed. He first asked if we could observe the enemy machine gun position to his right front from where we were.

I quickly began scanning the area with binoculars and soon detected the North Korean machine gun squad on the side of the hill, clearly silhouetted against the skyline as viewed from our position, at a range from my platoon of approximately 800 to 1,000 yards. The enemy machine gun was located in the impact area of a Willie Peter [Korean War era phonetic alphabet designation for Whiskey Papa or White Phosphorus] mortar round which had burned the grass on that part of the hillside a dark brown color. The enemy's brown uniforms blended in perfectly with the burned grass area as a background. I immediately informed the adjacent Company Commander, who asked if I could knock the gun out. I answered "Wilco, out." I had in my platoon at this time a total of five BAR's [Browning Automatic Rifle, caliber .30], which was two more than the authorized one per rifle squad. The most proficient and experienced automatic rifleman in the platoon was a man who had won the Silver Star during an enemy night attack, killing 55 North Koreans stacked up in front of his position next morning.

I ordered him to take up a sitting position and, at the same time, ordered the loading and stacking by his side of every BAR magazine in the platoon, filled with a mixture of one round tracer with four rounds ball. I stood directly behind the gunner and while looking through my binoculars, instructed him to fire a burst and then to adjust his next burst in response to my fire commands. With the tracer ammunition, it was possible for me to see the strike of the bullets in the impact area with every burst of fire. Once I had made the necessary corrections in deflection and got the gunner delivering his fire along the gun-target line, it was merely a matter of making adjustments in range with fire commands such as "short . . . . add 200."

The instant the gunner delivered one burst at the correct range along the gun-target line, I yelled, "target . . . fire for effect!" With that, the gunner delivered a heavy volume of accurate, sustained fire onto the target. Looking through my binoculars, I saw the enemy machine gunner and other squad members literally shot off the side of the hill. The next thing I saw were the lead elements of the adjacent company moving up onto the high ground in their attack. Within minutes after my BAR gunner knocked out the enemy machine gun, my platoon which was located in open terrain right at the base of Sobuk-san, came under a heavy volume of enemy mortar fire. The enemy fire was ineffective, however, as my men and I were well dug in.

By paying attention to actions of nearby units, even though my platoon was not directly involved, I was able to sense an opportunity to be of assistance on my own initiative without being directed to support that unit, which was even from a different Regiment. By using the skills of my most capable BAR gunner and my own improvised modifications of artillery fire adjustment commands, I could place accurate fire on an enemy at what would have to be considered extremely long range.

I continued in "K" Company for about six weeks, and was then reassigned to "I" Company to command the Weapons Platoon in about mid-October. Both Company "I" and Company "L" had lost most of their officers during September in the break-out from the Pusan perimeter. Company "I" was commanded by First Lieutenant Teague, who had previously been the Regimental I and R Platoon Leader [Intelligence and Reconnaissance]. The Regimental Commander had allowed Lieutenant Teague to choose any lieutenant from "K" Company and I did not know why he had chosen me, since I did not know him. I later learned from Lieutenant Teague that the reason I was selected was during World War II, Teague had been a Sergeant in a rifle company commanded by my older brother, USMA Class of '44, and now was Teague's chance to get even!

Sometime between the first and middle of November, while Lieutenant Teague was the Company Commander, I was involved in a patrol action which was extreme-ly "minor" in the grand scheme of things, but which speaks volumes about the nature of the conflict between the free democracies and the communist or other tyrannical system of government. At about 1600 hours, Lieutenant Teague had gone to Battalion Headquarters and while he was gone I received orders to lead a patrol to rescue a US Navy fighter pilot who had been shot down behind enemy lines. The situation, as it was explained to me was as follows: Just prior to this time, a friendly patrol had returned to US lines and reported that a Navy pilot off an aircraft carrier had been shot down and was lying wounded in a Korean farmhouse about six miles behind the North Korean lines. I called Battalion to request a litter jeep and was told there were none available. I improvised one by strapping a litter on my jeep, and taking a First Aid kit.

One of my men volunteered to be my driver and one of my NCO's volunteered to go along and "ride shotgun" in the back seat with a BAR. At about 1620 hours, with my two men and our interpreter, we set out driving cross country through the dry rice paddies and along the paddy dikes, as there were absolutely no roads in this area. Just after dark we arrived at what seemed as if it must be our objective, as it was the only farmhouse for miles around. Inside, much to my surprise, instead of finding a downed Navy fighter pilot, I found a wounded North Korean Infantry officer. He had been shot in the knee during a battle a few days before and had received no medical treat-ment of any kind. It was obvious that he was suffering great pain and that serious gan-grene had set in to his badly swollen, greenish-yellow colored knee. We placed the prisoner on the litter and headed back towards friendly lines.

An Eighth Army standing order at that time directed that all vehicles would travel with their lights on at night, and that any vehicles moving at night without headlights would be considered to be enemy vehicles and were to be engaged as such. As. a result, while driving around behind enemy lines we drove with just the jeep's "cat's eyes" on, and then just as we arrived at where I estimated our front lines would be, we turned the headlights full on. On the return trip, the prisoner had begun yelling and screaming in a very loud voice. I asked my interpreter what he was saying, and was told that he was yelling because of the extreme pain he was in. I told my interpreter to make it very clear to him that if he did not stop yelling, I would put him out of his misery once and for all. He chose to suffer in silence during the remainder of the patrol.

My impromptu patrol returned to friendly lines about 2000 hours without any serious mishaps, and transported the prisoner directly to Battalion Headquarters. While the Battalion Surgeon injected the prisoner with morphine and then began to treat his wound, I held his head in my lap, lit a cigarette and put it in the prisoner's mouth. Through my interpreter, I obtained not only tactical information from the prisoner but also this "non-tactical" information which is so very telling, about the nature of our conflict in Korea and also throughout the entire Cold War.

Question: How old are you?
Answer: 19 years old.

Question: What is your rank and branch of service in the North Korean Army?
Answer. I am a First Lieutenant, Infantry.

Question: How long have you been in the North Korean Army?
Answer: Six weeks.

Question: Have you ever heard of "Democracy?"
Answer: No.
Question: Have you ever heard of "Jesus Christ?"
Answer: No.

By the time the interrogation was completed, the morphine had reduced the pain he was feeling to the point that he was beginning to feel relaxed and was able to enjoy his cigarette. Within a short time, however, I noticed that he had tears in his eyes. I asked the interpreter to find out what he was crying about. The prisoner answered that he was told by his superiors that if he were captured by the Americans, he would be first tortured, then killed. Instead of either of those things happening to him, he said "the Americans gave me something to relieve my pain, treated my wound and gave me an American cigarette." I have often wondered when POW's from both sides were released and prisoners we held were given the choice of returning to life under Communism or choosing freedom by remaining in South Korea—which way of life did this young man choose?

After several replacement Captains arrived, one of them, a Captain Pirowski took command of "I" Company and Lieutenant Teague became the XO. Captain Pirowski had also been a Sergeant in World War II. While my first Company Commander, Captain Swartz, was a no-nonsense, demanding commander, Captain Pirowski was more inclined to accept lesser performance and was not prone to making any waves.

One night, at about 0200 hours, Captain Pirowski called me to his CP to inform me that a PVT Wiggins, a member of my Weapons Platoon had refused to perform Guard Duty, and that he had broken the stock of his carbine over the head of the Sergeant of the Guard, thus fracturing his skull. Briefly, the circumstances were that the Sergeant of the Guard had posted members of his relief, including PVT Wiggins. When the Sergeant of the Guard went back to check his guard posts, PVT Wiggins was no where to be found, on or around his post. The Sergeant of the Guard then found PVT Wiggins asleep in his foxhole, back in the Weapons Platoon area. When the Sergeant tried to make Wiggins get up and return to his guard post, Wiggins fractured his skull with the carbine stock.

Captain Pirowski asked me what I thought he should do about PVT Wiggins. I said, "Court-martial him, Sir." The captain then asked, "On what charge?" I responded, "Sir, just for openers—quitting his post without being properly relieved, disobeying the lawful order of his superior, striking a superior while in the performance of his official duty, destruction of government property, plus assault with a deadly weapon." Captain Pirowski then told me "I haven't had a Court-martial in my company in seven years and I'm not going to start now." Quite concerned over his unwillingness to take action I was convinced to be essential to maintain good order and discipline, I replied "Sir, in that case you had better have a good answer ready when the CID [Criminal Investigation Division of the Military Police] officer comes up here and wants to know how the Sergeant's skull got fractured." There was not any CID investigation. I have wondered about this incident for a long time. I could have possibly gone to the Battalion of Regimental Commander over this matter, but did not feel I should violate the Chain of Command, nor be disloyal to my Company Commander. Nor do I have any sage, infallible advice for any young lieutenant who encounters a similar situation in the future.

We soon had problems much more severe than this, however. As we moved north in pursuit of the retreating North Koreans, winter came before the victory we thought was so certain. As of Thanksgiving time, in fact up until I was wounded and evacuated on 30 November 1950, my men did not have any "winter gear." Their heaviest outer garment was their field jackets. In the absence of winter gloves or mittens, my men wore OD Army wool socks on their hands to keep them from freezing. Several of my men cut arm and leg holes at the top and bottom of the lightweight summer sleeping bags and were wearing them as outer garments. Almost simultaneous with the arrival of severe winter weather was the entry of the Chinese Communists into the war.

In early November, my battalion had relieved part of a Regiment of the 1st Cavalry Division near Kunu-ri. We then crossed the Chongchon River on a footbridge, and by the day after Thanksgiving we were attacking with all three battalions abreast against light North Korean resistance. Then the rifle companies of my battalion received word to halt their advance and remain in place. Sometime later, I think it was by means of an airdropped message, word came to pull back generally over the same route we had used to advance. Our withdrawal was orderly and unopposed. Morale was generally high and when we were stopped for the night I remember hearing the sounds of what seemed to be a fairly major fight off to our northeast, which would have been in the sector of the 2nd Infantry Division.

The next morning, our battalion's withdrawal continued, and for the rest of the day. We crossed to the south side of the Chongchon River, which was then defended by tanks with machine gun mounting reconnaissance jeeps interspersed between the tanks. After dark we went into what was essentially an assembly area posture northwest of Kunu-ri to await orders. We were not ordered to establish a defensive position and no tactical barbed wire was emplaced. We were simply told to "stand fast" and that orders would be forthcoming. I can't remember if the rifle companies tied in with any other battalion on our flanks. Some companies might have sent out patrols, but I don't know for certain. The consensus was that the rifle companies would be moving out the next morning.

Throughout the night, units of the 2nd Division moved south along the road on foot and in vehicles. Sometime after midnight, Kunu-ri, which was to our right rear (to the southeast) came under attack and my platoon's 60 mm mortar section fired some illumination rounds in their support but the ammunition was defective and made only very brief "fire trails" in the sky.

At first light, "I" Company had no orders to either move out or to defend in place. There was a definite lull in the actions around us, evidenced by absence of close-by battle sounds. By early afternoon, we suddenly were hard pressed by Chinese Communist forces, the attacks coming from our rear (southwest) as well as our front. By then word had come from a spotter plane acting as a radio relay, to move out southwest.

When we were told to move out, just prior to the final Chinese assault which overran us at Kunu-ri, I was in a ditch with my Platoon Sergeant and Sergeant Cross, my 60 mm mortar Section Sergeant. I told my Platoon Sergeant to move out and that Sergeant Cross and I would cover him. When I turned to tell Sergeant Cross to go next, he was already gone. Shortly thereafter I was wounded by what I now think was a concussion grenade, which resulted in my becoming confused, disoriented and in a state of near shock. About 30 yards to my front I saw one of my men standing up with his hands raised above his head. When he saw me he yelled "it's too late, Lieutenant."

I looked over my shoulder to see what he was looking at and saw approximately 40 to 50 Chinese soldiers completely covered from head to foot with pieces of green foliage, running in a crouched position toward us. They were armed with .45 caliber Thompson submachine guns, and were chanting in a loud "sing-song" sounding chant. I yelled to the soldier to move out and then slowly staggered toward the rear.

At that point a sergeant, whose name I regret to this day that I do not know, was in a dry irrigation ditch and saw that I was wounded and about to be captured. By that time, the Chinese had taken the soldier to my front captive, and were dragging him off to their rear. The lead elements of enemy assault forces were only about 20 yards from me when the sergeant, who had neither a helmet nor a weapon, grabbed me by the arm and yelled over the noise of battle "Come on, Lieutenant, you can make it!" The sergeant and I locked an arm around each other's waist and, as though running a three-legged race, made a mad 50 yard dash to a larger irrigation ditch to our rear. With the adrenaline pumping harder and faster with the sound of each enemy bullet whistling past our heads, and without either of us saying a word to the other, at a point about 10 feet from the ditch, we both did a flying somersault through the air and rolled into the bottom of the ditch.

In the ditch we found Lieutenant Teague and about 14 of our troops. By this time the Chinese were within only minutes of overrunning the ditch. With the exception of Lieutenant Teague and the 14 of our men in the ditch, the rest of the men in the three rifle companies of Third Battalion had made a mass exodus to the rear. Lieutenant Teague was senior officer present; everyone waited for his orders. He was, unfortunately, apparently paralyzed with fear as evidenced by his constantly staring at the oncoming enemy as though suffering from "target fixation."

Realizing that Lieutenant Teague was not going to issue any orders, I tried to encourage others in the ditch to leave. The sergeant who had brought me into the ditch and two other of our men and I all crawled about five yards along the bottom of the ditch and then headed out of the ditch toward the rear. A Platoon Sergeant from "L" Company, who was later evacuated with me, had been in the ditch with Lieutenant Teague and our 14 men. When I asked him how he got out of there he said, "When I saw that Lieutenant Teague was not going to issue any orders, I took the last chance there was to get out of there alive."

I am not at all certain of the sequence of events during the rest of our narrow escape. I remember a B-26 bomber passing over me with its bomb bay doors open and dropping bombs on the advancing Chinese. I also saw an AT-6 spotter plane crash land close to our route of escape. Both the pilot and the spotter survived the crash and joined my little group in our march south. By then there was a heavy fog which mixed with the smoke all around us. As we moved toward the rear, there was a railroad embankment which provided some cover from enemy fire coming from the southeast. There was a road running parallel to that embankment. Suddenly, out of the fog a single American tank appeared. It was from the Regimental Tank Company of the 5th Regimental Combat Team.

On the tank was a Company Commander from the 5th RCT, Hank Emerson, whom the Regimental Commander, Colonel Throckmorton, had sent out to rescue the spotter aircraft crew. I told Hank that the spotter crew was safe with me and my group, and so Hank turned his tank around and began pulling back to our lines with myself and other wounded riding on his tank. Hank took us to an aid station and then I went by ambulance in a convoy headed further south, until I was finally evacuated from an airstrip at P'yongyang.

As far as Combat Advice to new Infantry Lieutenants to be derived from this tragic incident, where do I start? Although there are many "lessons learned" to be drawn here, I will focus on what you should realize, and what you must be prepared to do, rather than on what I perhaps should have done. Situations such as Korea in general, and November 1950 in particular actually happened. Looking back and studying history, it might have been the fault of the US Secretary of State, who, in a "major foreign policy address" specifically named American security interests in Asia as including Japan, Taiwan and the Philippine Islands; since he did not mention Korea, the Communists concluded they could attack without American opposition. War came with our forces drastically reduced after World War II, and not ready for another war. We did not have adequate equipment or training. The sudden advent of severe winter weather was an incredible blow to our units, totally lacking winter field gear.

As UN forces swept north after Inchon and our breakout from the Pusan perimeter, the Chinese publicly warned that they would intervene if we entered North Korea, but that statement of Chinese national purpose was ignored or overlooked. The extended frontages on which we operated across the northern portions of the Korean Peninsula (which is much wider than the southern or central area) meant that there would be gaps between units through which the Chinese could attack. Even if every UN unit had performed a perfect defensive operation in their own small sector, when entire Chinese divisions swarmed through the gaps and attacked our supporting artillery, overran supply units in our rear and cut our lines of communication, the option to "defend in place" quickly evaporated into thin air. We could repulse only so many massed attacks until we ran out of ammunition; there could have been no resupply. Isolated unit situations were inevitable. What should you learn from this?

First, if your unit mission is suddenly changed from attack to withdrawal, even if you do not receive a thorough briefing on the change in situation—we were told nothing about the massive Chinese attacks going on all around us—you must quickly realize that the situation must be pretty grim and it is now time for you "to circle your own wagons," no matter what the other nearby units are doing. Prepare your unit and yourself for what may well be a long fight with a short stick. Give your men all the information you have, and explain why you are suddenly requiring much more vigilant security measures and a higher readiness state. Even if other units take no extra precautions and thus increase their risk of being caught totally unaware and unprepared, make certain that *your* unit is ready to go to an instant full stand-to, on only a few seconds notice. Until the crisis fully develops, make as many preparations as you can, but also try to rest as many of your troops as you can for a coming ordeal which will likely be extremely strenuous and harrowing.

Second, prepare your platoon to abandon and destroy whatever equipment you could not carry with you when you have to move out light and fast on foot. Remember that I was a Weapons Platoon Leader; mortars and recoilless rifles are strictly support weapons, not much use for close combat and certainly too heavy and much too cumbersome to be carried in a fighting withdrawal. When it is time to pull out—which you may be told, or you may have to conclude for yourself based on observing other units pulling out or a rout developing—have your platoon ready to move and fight, to escape and evade, to SURVIVE AS A PLATOON! Study maps and recall terrain through which you have recently passed; determine where to go and what route to take. You prepare your platoon, just as for an ordinary patrol assignment, with a route and an organization and a mission and a plan, to allow your platoon to survive and fight another day.

If there is still a coherently organized plan for withdrawal of your company or battalion, then of course you must assume full responsibility for executing any mission you are assigned, even if you are to be the rear guard of the rear guard. That comes with the responsibilities you willingly, knowingly undertake when you accept your Infantry commission and aspire to lead American troops in combat. However, if there is no coherent plan, and you can see that others around you—peers or superiors—are frozen with fear or crippled by indecision, then realize that it is up to you to make the best decision you possibly can with the information available to you, to save the greatest number of American soldiers you can convince to move with your platoon.

Although one certainly must hope that our Army will never get caught in such a tactical disaster again, recognize that virtually any war can have situations which degenerate to the point where you and your platoon may be on your own. So plan every action you take, every single day and night in training or in combat, to strengthen internal cohesiveness and develop close teamwork in your platoon. Every action and every opportunity must engender greater bonds of trust between and among your troops, their leaders and their Lieutenant, the unit esprit and the confidence which all must have in themselves, their capabilities and in their fellow soldiers and immediate leaders. Everything you have learned about leadership and setting the example, practiced on a daily and hourly basis, must be faithfully applied to making everything your platoon does an investment in becoming a stronger, more tightly knit band of brothers who know for a fact their leaders, their buddies and themselves are all ready for the worst that fate or war can throw at them, and that they can and will prevail, no matter what may come their way.

Third, know in advance what I learned on that November day nearly fifty years ago now, that you can make your own version of that mad 50 yard dash with enemy bullets whistling past your head, that you can keep going and keep fighting and keep trying and pull others along with you and survive terrible odds and frightfully incredible ordeals, by the simple procedure of being determined to never give up, never quit trying and never quit believing you can and will succeed. I hope that you or any other American Infantryman never has to endure what we did at Kunu-ri when the Chinese entered the Korean War. But no matter what comes, you must believe you can succeed, and simply never give up. Good luck, Infantry Lieutenant!

******

News accounts of current conditions in Korea suggest a scenario which is realistically frightening. Too many elements of the jigsaw puzzle have fallen and are falling into place. The Chinese may see a tantalizing opportunity to finish a move that was denied them almost 50 years ago.

As part of the force screening the withdrawal from North Korea, my platoon of the 15th Infantry, Third Infantry Division, was one of the last to board ship just before Christmas of 1950. Two lessons stand out from that approximately two months of what was, in our sector, essentially guerrilla warfare (against North Korean remnants that were either bypassed in our march north, or left as deliberate stay behind forces), occasionally reinforced by Chinese main forces.

The Third Division, having arrived somewhat later than most of the other US elements had their complete issue of cold weather gear. It was a godsend—except that one of our neighboring companies lost over a platoon, slaughtered still in their sleeping bags. It was the only instance that I remember of a large scale night assault in our sector by almost certainly Chinese instead of North Korean troops. Lesson: Security! Even on mountainous defensive positions, don't let that warm sack be your grave. It makes no difference whether your sector is "quiet" " or if there have been constant enemy probing attacks every night for many weeks, **security is your first and foremost responsibility**—you and your Platoon Sergeant must check the line **all night, every night** to insure that your platoon is on proper alert.

On the final stage of the withdrawal, which we secured for elements being pushed back from further north on the eastern side of the Korean peninsula, the route of our troops was littered with discarded equipment. I personally picked up three fully serviceable M1 rifles. Lesson: What you leave behind can be used against you.

The North Korean/Chinese used their own version of Shakespeare's Birnam

Wood. To guard against air and long range ground observation, each individual enemy soldier would cut and carry with him an evergreen sapling just large enough to shield him, particularly from air observers. I saw an artillery observer catch what appeared to be a unit of somewhere around company size on what appeared to be a wooded hill until the artillery rounds started falling. Those trees started darting in all directions. I suspect that method of camouflage is still in their Field Manuals (Operation Killer, late January 1951).

Later, in our push to recover ground lost when the Chinese entered the war (Operation Killer, this on 3 February 1951), I was wounded by what was most likely one of our M2 carbines. This was essentially a problem of locating enemy positions from where fire was coming. Initially the enemy gunner fired a burst of five or six rounds. I moved with four or five of my soldiers behind what we thought was a masking knoll. I was hit by a single shot from apparently the same enemy soldier. Lesson: There may be technical devices available now, but back then, old soldiers taught us the "crack and thump" method to locate from where fire was coming; this method may still be useful today.

The "Crack and Thump" method as I knew it in Korea was from my platoon NCO's who were Infantry vets from WWII. Later on, when I returned to the states and taught basic training, the Army issued a POI [Program of Instruction] titled Small Arms Fire Course which standardized the method during the advanced part of basic training. The guts of the method was/is to count quickly—one Airborne Ranger, two Airborne Ranger, three Airborne Ranger—as soon as you hear the "crack" (which is the sound of the several times supersonic bullet passing near you) and the "thump" which is the sound of the enemy rifle (traveling at only the speed of sound). You try to determine the direction or location from whence the "thump" came; the distance in 100's of yards is the highest number you count. The method still works at longer ranges even after the bullet slows down to a whir or whisper. Obviously, this is an approximate method, but with practice, one can get quite good at it. If the shooter is real close, one can't distinguish crack from thump. It's even difficult at 100 meters. Also, the crack appears much louder than the thump, if you're the target. The thump may be mistaken for an echo.

In the middle '50s as a company commander in Germany, I taught the method to my company on one of Hohenfels' live fire ranges. [Most units in Germany were stationed in a camp, or *Kaserne*, which had only a small local training area. Major field training and weapons firing was all done at one of four major training areas—Hohenfels, Wildfleken, Grafenwohr and Baumholder—usually a rail movement for unit tracked vehicles and road convoy for wheels and troops to spend three to four weeks of intensive training, two or three times each year.) The company was seated in the stands. A very reliable shooter, located about 200 meters behind and slightly to the side of a line from the stands to the impact area, fired rounds on signal so that the trajectory passed to the right side and about 10 or 15 meters above the stands.

This was in the days of the draft. My company had a real cross-section of young men — a superb, eager bunch of gung-ho types. Their reaction to the first round was split between "from the front," and "right side." After coaching, they were quickly able to recognize the "thump" and distinguish it from echoes and the "crack" and also to adjust their directional hearing. It's quickly learned, because of the realism and sensation one gets from imagining himself as the target.

I doubt if the method is still taught and, by now, there should be a pocket size gadget doing a better job anyway. It's a nightmare to teach within the safety rules. For realism, it should be framed as a squad or platoon tactical exercise, such as a patrol. The range must be of ideal terrain, the weapons must be "blocked" in, as for an infiltration course, and each weapons site must be guarded by a safety officer and so on. But, the crack of a bullet gets one's attention, for it says that you're in the target area. Where the fire is coming from is an imperative question which you must learn to quickly and accurately be able to answer! With the above procedure, you can teach yourself and your men this vital skill.

A word on the subject of field sanitation. That late January–early February time period was very bitterly cold, even as far south as we were. The hills were covered with ice and snow. To relieve yourself was a real challenge. I had developed a bad case of hemorrhoids for which, in a war, I quite logically refrained from seeking treatment. As my gun shot wound was not deemed sufficiently serious to warrant shipment home, I was treated in an Army Hospital in Yokohama. Lieutenants were scarce, and needed back at the front. They patched up my leg wound, and attempted to solve my other problem by performing a hemorrhoidectomy, then sent me back to my battalion. The latter medical situation gave me much more long term trouble than the leg wound. It was a particular problem under combat conditions of providing for one's own field sanitation requirements. Lesson: One must figure out a way to take care of oneself, even in the most demanding circumstances.

Lastly, the most helpful advice I got from a senior officer, was from a member of the Class of '45. He advised me to find a copy of FM 7-10, *Rifle Company Operations* and keep it in my pocket where it was readily available and to study it at every opportunity. I did. It was the most important and useful of all. Lesson: Not certain if the numbers are still the same, but obtain a copy of *Rifle Platoon Operations* and study the covers off.

The same member of the Class of '45 also advised me that when taking over a new outfit (he had a platoon in mind, but I found it sound advice in other cases) to take the unit at face value—start fresh, let the word get around that you have accepted all of your men as competent soldiers unless and until they prove otherwise. Especially in view of scarce resources, such advice proved extremely valuable for me, as some of the unit's previous "problem soldiers" decide to clean up their act when offered such a clean slate "free" fresh start with their new commander.

******

My experience in combat in Korea is limited to late August and the first three weeks of September, 1950 since I was wounded and evacuated on 21 September after our breakout from the Pusan perimeter on 15 September. However, I do have some thoughts on combat and also on my almost two years in the hospital recovering from those wounds.

"What a young Infantry lieutenant really needs to know as he faces combat for the first time."

The very first thing he must know is the composition and organization of an Infantry platoon, as to its sub-units, personnel and equipment—in other words, he must know the platoon TO&E [Table of Organization and Equipment]. This must sound trite and almost shameful to admit but absolutely essential. We had been taught this during our second summer at West Point but we were also taught the TO&E of many other units to which we might be assigned when we made our branch choices and went to units almost three years later. Since we were not going to attend branch basic schools—I'm certain many others have mentioned this situation—I have always since wondered why someone in all those high staff positions from Department of the Army, to Far East Command, to Eighth Army Headquarters in Korea or various Division Replacement units to Regimental and Battalion Headquarters through which we passed did not consider at least providing us with a simple one sheet of paper summary of who and what we would find—and by reasoning to a logical conclusion—what we would not find, in our new commands.

By the time we got to our companies it was way too late and we could only struggle along and learn it the hard way. Those of us who joined units on the Pusan perimeter usually got to our Company CP when it was under attack or conducting an attack. "Glad to meet you Lieutenant . . . What was your Name . . . see those men going up that hill over there . . . hurry and catch up with them because that is your platoon." As one classmate recounted at a recent reunion: "My Company Commander told me to reposition my machine gun and I did not even know I was supposed to have a machine gun, much less where the damn thing was."

Then the young Infantry lieutenant needs to know how to employ his unit, both offensively and defensively. He needs to know and understand the capabilities and the limitations of an Infantry platoon. He needs to know how to move his unit tactically in situations he is likely to encounter. In short, he needs to know all that is taught in the Basic School at Fort Benning. For any Infantry lieutenants who ever have to go into combat without Basic School under their belts, get a copy of the Field Manuals on Infantry Platoons and Infantry Companies—read and study them in every spare moment of your trip through the replacement pipeline. If you are lucky enough to go to the Basic School, then sit up, pay attention, take notes, study hard and learn all you can in every class.

He needs to know his men—the NCO's and the privates. He needs to know their capabilities, their backgrounds, their personalities. But he should not become so intimately involved with them that he cannot handle (emotionally) their being wounded or killed.

He needs to know why they are "here" (wherever "here" is), so that he can answer the question his soldiers will ask: "What are we doing here?" Somehow or other, he must learn to transmit to his men an image of confidence—not fearlessness—but just plain confidence, despite his own fears. He must somehow (I hope some of these letters will do a better job of explaining "how" to do this than I can) be able to conquer his own fears.

When engaged in actual combat, in a fire fight, he must be able to determine when the situation requires that "the lieutenant goes first." One of my experiences in such a situation occurred on 12 September during our attack on Hill 409 within the Pusan perimeter. It was a pretty bad situation; we had several casualties and were pinned down by an enemy machine gun within only 50 yards of the crest of the hill. All of a sudden my machine gunner, whose gun had been destroyed by enemy fire, came charging up behind me with a rifle that he had picked up, hollering and screaming like a mad man.

When I looked behind me to see what was happening, I recall the fleeting thought that I should be leading this charge. His action energized me to get up and get my platoon moving up that hill. With my carbine and some grenades, I first ran and then crawled alone to where I could knock out the machine gun and get my platoon to the top of that hill. I don't see this as heroism. There are occasions when "leadership" means that this time the lieutenant goes first. This was one of those times. I suspect that many of our classmates who were killed may have made that choice once too often.

A young Infantry lieutenant needs to know what to do if he himself becomes wounded. While he should not be consumed with this possibility, it is a very practical subject which I know from discussions with my classmates occupied some of their thoughts. It was probably even more so for those who were platoon leaders for most of their year or more in Korea. In fact, I still may have a letter I received from a good friend in the Spring of 1951 when I was in the hospital. He was convinced he had it made now; "They made me a Company Executive Officer so now I have a 50 yard head start on the bastards."

In the case of my being wounded, it was an attack on a lightly held hill when the North Koreans were in retreat after the breakout. It was a typical open slope with no cover anywhere on a nice sunny afternoon. I recall giving the arm and hand signals to move one squad forward and as I turned around I felt like a sledge hammer had hit my right foot. Two rounds from a burp gun had hit me but this did not put me out of action or even in need of a medic's attention. But as I continued moving to my right, I was hit at the back part of my leg and felt a sudden burning sensation in my abdomen. I pulled my shirt tail out and could feel that the round was protruding from my stomach but had not broken the skin for an exit wound. I was unable to walk. I learned later that the round had shattered my left hip and then went through the intestines, causing considerable internal damage. I was still conscious, however, and not in much pain.

My Assistant Platoon Sergeant and my platoon medic dragged me back down the hill and across a rice paddy about some 60 or 70 yards where we were able to gain some protective cover behind a dike. Other soldiers would provide covering fire while another wounded soldier and I were dragged from dike to dike. Each time they dragged me over a paddy dike it caused considerable pain in my leg and hip, until we finally reached a collection point out of range of the enemy's fire. My platoon went on to take the hill; my days of recovering had just begun.

I was taken by litter jeep to a Regimental collection point during which time I was in and out of consciousness but in those lucid moments I was aware of what had happened. In this area helicopter evacuations were available and I was told I would be on the next flight out to a MASH unit. Each time a chopper would come in I was told I was next until it got dark. I was then put in an ambulance for what was a several hour trip to the 8076th MASH unit in Miryang. The hours at the collection point was an example of medical triage in action. To this day I do not know which side of the triage I was on. I was operated on for obvious abdominal wounds. By a strange coincidence a high school soccer teammate who had been two years ahead of me in school assisted at the operation and saw to it that I wrote a note to my wife as evidence that I was OK and probably would make it back home. My shattered hip had not yet been noticed. It was not until I arrived at Saint Albans Naval Hospital, Long Island, two weeks later, the hip damage was discovered.

What does all this have to do with what a young Infantry lieutenant needs to know as he faces combat for the first time? I think that once wounded, there are now several different levels of fear and concern which must be handled. Will I make it? How bad are my wounds? Won't I make it? Should I have told my Assistant Platoon Sergeant to move on toward taking the hill and leave me for some rear elements to find and treat? I do not know all the answers but the subject gave me much thought and is worthy of consideration by those going into battle for the first time, and each time. How do I pass my command to my subordinates should I become a casualty?

Finally, how does this young Infantry lieutenant face the prospect of prolonged hospitalization with all the physical and emotional problems of pain and immobility? He must be able to handle continuous pain and the emotional aspects of being immobilized in a body cast for an indeterminate period of time. While this may not compare with the hardships of continued combat or the unimaginable deprivations suffered by POW's, this situation does have a unique life of its own and requires similar strengths of character.

Ultimately, the time will come when recovery is assured even though accompanied by some permanent disabling feature. By that time, he needs a real sense of humor to deal with the realities of physical limitations. For example, Saint Albans specialized in orthopedic and neurological injuries. When we all became ambulatory we would go out for an afternoon to have a few beers at a local bar and then go bowling. On the first such occasion, we wondered how to choose up sides? We finally decided on the "legs" *vs.* the "arms." Those of us with leg impairments could only hobble up to the foul line, but we could really zing the ball down the alley. Those with nerve or arm injuries could run up to the foul line but could only drop the ball and let it find its own way down the alley.

In another situation, while some of us were still in body casts, we attended the wedding of one of our comrades who was marrying a Navy Nurse. The men with bad arms but good legs put those of us with full body casts on gurneys and pushed us over to the Officers Club for the Wedding Reception. There we were parked (literally) in a corner and fed martinis which we would balance on our body casts at chest level with our plates of food and have a great time. Even though we did not have to worry about anyone driving home under the influence, we did have to be concerned about our ambulatory but arm wounded and inebriated gurney pushers as to whether they would get us back to our wards safely. They did.

And finally, finally—the one absolutely essential element with which that young Infantry lieutenant facing combat for the first time must be armed, is a profound and abiding faith in God. Without that, no matter how he expresses it, feels it, lives it, I do not see how he can survive any of the hardships we are now talking about in combat, or in the challenges of life in general.

******

After 48 plus years with almost 26 of those in retirement, I have difficulty in transposing the experiences of that era to today's scenario. Of course there are some basic rules, but my experiences came as a result of the exigencies of the time, many of which were strictly personal and pertained uniquely to our situation at that time. I usually attend the annual reunion of the 3/34th-2/21st [2nd Battalion, 21st Infantry was organized out of the remnants of 3rd Battalion, 34th Infantry which was deactivated], where nostalgia and reminiscences are the order of the day. Many of the stories vary with subsequent tellings. I would say it is good comradeship but poor history.

Personally, I have not felt that going straight into combat was a disfavor to our class, even though it was not a particularly pleasant experience at that time. A person could probably almost always figure out a more favorable time for him to enter combat than right now, but it is a fact of life that when people are shooting at each other, someone will probably be hurt.

Always concentrate on learning your assigned job as well and as fast as you can, but don't make the mistake of thinking you will stay in that position for a long time. On two occasions I had to take over a new position on an immediate basis due to other officers becoming casualties. When I retained from the hospital (after being wounded when I had only been in the unit three days), I was assigned to a different company. I moved from my initial rifle platoon assignment to command of a weapons platoon and had to learn mortars on the job and fast. Good thing that I had that mortar platoon experience because then I was assigned to command of my company while still just a lieutenant. As an officer, recognize that you are the one who is responsible, not your NCO's.

Most of the time you are safer in a line company than in a headquarters, because the farther back toward the rear one goes, the more lax the security. I had a very good friend who was seriously wounded while in the aid station back at Regimental Headquarters, with just a bad cold. A group of Chinese that had been bypassed attacked the Regimental CP that night and he was seriously hurt by a grenade.

I was involved in one incident which, oddly enough, has been written up a couple of times, by *Look Magazine* and by the old *New York Herald Tribune*, in each case with a mixture of truth and inaccuracy. In early September 24th Division was the Eighth Army Reserve, having been relieved on line by the newly arrived 2nd Division in late August. When the North Koreans struck the north east portion of the Pusan perimeter, capturing the port of Pohang and cutting off one South Korean Division, 24th Division was ordered north to reinforce that threatened sector. My unit, 2nd Battalion, 21st Infantry, was punched into the line between two South Korean units, and fought a series of defensive and delaying actions. My company had some attached tanks, and were holding a roadblock when we were hit with a very strong and sudden, violent night attack.

At the time of the incident, I had been assigned as weapons platoon leader for three days. The company was at about 50 percent strength and had four brand new 2nd Lieutenant platoon leaders. Except for us new lieutenants, morale in the company was on empty. I guess we did not know any better. When the main attack came shortly after midnight, the platoon on our right disappeared, along with my 60 mm mortar section. When I went to look for them I ran into the North Koreans and drew fire, which I reported to my Company Commander. At that time, the company CP came under attack also, and we took to some ditches along the road. Note: Learn to crawl very quickly while someone is throwing hand grenades at your position.

The company pulled back to consolidate our position but we were still missing one rifle platoon and my mortar section. I asked the Company Commander if I could try to find the missing men and he said OK. My search took me to our rear platoon, and the platoon leader said that he had seen some men moving to the rear of their position. The sun was just coming up and in the predawn grey I could see some men walking along a railroad overpass which crossed the road we were on, just to our rear. As I got close enough to see them a little bit more clearly, some of them waved and so I waved back and moved toward them.

Three of them jumped down off of the overpass onto the road where I was, and one put out his hand, as if to shake hands. Then I noticed the red star on his hat, and realized that he was reaching to take my carbine, and that the other two definitely had me covered with their weapons. He handed me a document which I could just barely read in the growing light; the headline was enough for me . . . . it said "Welcome POW." The three North Koreans took my carbine and my watch, standing there in the road as dawn came. At this point I was rapidly beginning to realize that my tour of duty would be disrupted in addition to other things more unpleasant. Note: Be careful of approaching any unidentified person during periods of marginal visibility.

I knew that the company was intent on withdrawing further toward Kyonju on this road, and that they would be coming this way fairly soon. There were rice paddies on both sides of the road so tanks would have to be on the road. The North Koreans were preparing to lead me away when the tanks came south. The lead tank was firing right dead ahead down the road, and the other tanks firing to the flanks. As the lead tank approached the underpass, firing, two of my captors took cover in the ditch while the remaining captor and the other North Koreans up on the railroad overpass were all concentrating on the oncoming tank. Noting that everyone was focused on something other than guarding me, I decided to remove myself from the area.

I jumped the North Korean who still had my carbine. (When he took my weapon, he also took my bayonet from its sheath, and had obligingly fixed the bayonet on my carbine.) I grabbed my carbine back from him and bayoneted him through the throat. He started to make noises, so I clubbed him in the head with the carbine stock, hitting him so hard that I broke the stock completely into two pieces. (This is embarrassing, but I knew the carbine would not fire since I had not yet cleaned the cosmoline from the barrel.) I ran to join my own troops on the other side of the underpass. My old friend Sgt J. Leyba from Trinidad, Colorado, to this day claims he saved my life that morning by not shooting me as I came around the corner of the overpass berm. I concede the fact. Note: It is not a great feeling to have to use such extreme measures to preserve one's well-being, but consequences of any alternative would have been much worse.

The company managed to clear the roadblock and we then rejoined the battalion. As we were relaxing for a few minutes later that morning, I noticed a bit of blood on the cuff of my field jacket. A brief inspection revealed a hole in the front and back of the upper right sleeve, and through my arm as well. When the battalion's situation stabilized, this wound led to my medical evacuation back to Japan for about three weeks. On my return from the hospital, my battalion was in North Korea. Note: The results of one night's work, after only three days in the unit—a Combat Infantryman's Badge, a Purple Heart, three weeks in the hospital in Japan (with a five day pass to Tokyo) and a much better appreciation of what happens in ground combat situations.

Lessons Learned:
- Not everything goes according to the plan.
- Sometimes there is no plan. Think of Something!
- You are not in an airplane or on on a ship shooting at something miles away. Ground combat will be up close and personal.
- Don't concede anything. Don't ever give up!
- Escape at the earliest possible opportunity, when your return to US lines will be the shortest, quickest and easiest. Hope for the best, but expect and prepare for the worst.

******

I was a platoon leader in the 1st Battalion, 9th Infantry Regiment, 2nd Infantry Division from 30 August 1950 until February 1951, then Assistant S-2 for the 9th Infantry Regiment until March 1951, and until April 1951, S-2 of lst Battalion, 9th Infantry Regiment. To put these comments in the proper context, my service entailed a rapid deployment through the replacement stream, entering Korea through the port of Pusan and joining the 2nd Infantry Division which had been in combat since July of 1950, fighting along the Naktong River in the Pusan perimeter. When I joined them they had just been repulsed from their defensive positions along the Naktong River and were being pushed back towards Pusan, and it was an extremely fluid situation.

Subsequently, we crossed over the Naktong River and broke out of the Pusan perimeter and attacked north in the latter part of September, following of course, General MacArthur's famous invasion at Inchon with X Corps—First Marine Division and 7th Infantry Division—where we got behind the North Korean divisions and from then on for us it was a rapid movement, and advance to contact, crossing the 38th Parallel and moving into North Korea. Until, of course, the Chinese Communists entered the war in our particular sector with a very large contingent of several divisions on or around Thanksgiving 1950. From then it was a withdrawal, or in more realistic terms, a retreat through a six to eight mile roadblock ambush south of Kunu-ri, and back towards Pyongyang, the capital of North Korea. That was followed by a reconstitution period of about two or three weeks near Seoul and Inchon City, then by mid-January moving back into the lines in the central sector, south of Wonju.

My comments fall in the category of useful items of advice or guidance that I *wish some combat experienced officer had told me before I had to learn them for myself*, and learn the hard way. To best understand the nature of the central focus of that portion of the Korean War, our withdrawal—a kinder word than retreat—of the 2nd Infantry Division after the Chinese intervention on or about 29 November 1950, one should read *The River and the Gauntlet*, by SLA Marshall or at least those portions dealing with the gauntlet—that six to eight mile roadblock between Kunu-ri and Sunchon. I will not try to describe in detail my experiences in that withdrawal because they are mostly a combination of everything which is contained in that book. [Early chapters set the stage with the advance to and crossing of the Chongchon River; middle chapters describe the Chinese onslaught against forward units; and the later chapters depict the carnage in the roadblock area itself as both line units and support units attempted to extricate themselves and their equipment.]

The Replacement Pipeline On passing through the seemingly endless "processing" periods and locations prior to arrival at your combat platoon leader assignment—you may not spend too much time on this if you are with one of the ready force units. You will be flown right to or very close to the combat theater and very shortly, maybe even with helicopters, be in the combat environment within a day or two. However in my case, we all went through the pipeline, with four or five days at Camp Stoneman in mid August 1950. Some of us had our new wives with us and spent as much time as possible with them at hotels off post. Then by train to McCord Air Force Base, on to Japan at Camp Drake, outside of Tokyo and Yokahoma. On our arrival at Camp Drake, there were some veterans en route back to Korea after medical treatment.

Exercise a reasonable amount of caution and common sense in listening to war stories from "veterans" and taking them as gospel, because combat stories tend to get embellished. Case in point about weapons. One of our group was told by one of these veterans that he would want to carry an M-1 rifle. So he turned in his carbine and obtained an M-1 and spent a bunch of time relearning how to assemble and disassemble the M-1. Then he listened to another viewpoint which insisted that he would have to have a carbine for full automatic firepower when the enemy comes at him in waves. Back to turn in his M-1 and draw a carbine again. As I recall, he went back and forth two or three times, so be careful how much emphasis you place on war stories from veterans in the replacement pipeline.

In the processing period, at each location, use the time professionally and work on increasing your physical conditioning. Marching and getting used to your boots, and hopefully you brought an older, well broken pair of boots. I can't imagine anything worse than having a brand new shiny pair of boots to be broken in. Use all the time you have available in road marching, working out the legs. I am not talking about going to a gym and doing weight lifting to strengthen the legs, but duration and endurance for the legs, and that means marching, marching, marching. Get off the pavement or sidewalk, even if there is just a ditch, but march on rough terrain if you can find it. If there are no hills to go up, then go up stairs again and again, or find a picnic bench or other object to step up on and back down, lifting your weight with first one leg then the other. Work up in increasing increments over time until you can "go up hill" for 30 minutes without being winded or having your legs too tired to go another step.

Try to get a feel for moving around at night, and I am not talking about downtown with the bright lights. If you can find an unlighted area where you are located, try to become accustomed to moving at night, even just walking around at night, trying to observe at night and learning to deal with your night vision. Think about locating and estimating distances in front of you as you move in the dark, and practice using off-center viewing by looking alternately to first one side of the trail or path and then the other. Remember that at night, the area in the direct center of your field of vision will be less visible than just off to either side, and you will see objects much more clearly and distinctly by looking off to one side or the other.

One of the most difficult things for a new platoon leader is to feel comfortable at night, moving at night. Of course, if you get the opportunity to experience troop duty in a training situation before you ship out, then work hard on getting as much night training as possible in patrol type night movement, or in just moving around a defensive position in the dark. Learn to get along without a flashlight. Keep items always in the same place in your pack, and put them back in their place so you can find anything and everything at night, without a light.

In my own case, a mistake I made is that I was married on 24 June and the North Korean invasion came on 25 June. What a great sense of timing! I did not have to report to Camp Stoneman until about the middle of August. I had time, if I had been smart and had known what I was getting into, even while on leave, instead of lazing around, I could have gotten in shape and could have done all these things I am telling you about, and I would have been ready to go, a lot better than I was. But once you are in the pipeline, use that time to get in shape instead of laying around the BOQ or the barracks or going out at night to party instead of improving your night movement skills.

We left Camp Drake by train to Sasebo, then by coal barge across to Pusan and again by train up to Division Rear at Miryang, about 20 miles or so. On the way, our train was attacked by the South African Air Force, with two fighter planes I suppose getting a little mixed up as to where the lines were and which way was south or north, but they strafed us with .50 caliber machine guns and put a rocket in the engine, killing the engineer and fireman, who were then carried back down the length of the train. It was the first time most of us had ever seen a dead man.

Once at Regimental Headquarters, the briefing was on the side of a road for about 15 minutes, then down in a jeep to the Battalion CP. The Battalion Commander told us, "Look, I don't have time to talk to you now, we are trying to collect the rest of the battalion coming back from the Naktong, some of them are behind enemy lines, but we know they are trying to work their way out, so just stay out of the way. You, _____, you are going to "A" Company and I think Lieutenant _____ is still alive with about 16 men somewhere and you'll be joining him so find him when he gets in and report to him. Good bye."

That night, the Battalion CP got attacked and if was of course our first time. We did not know what to do, what position to be in, or where to go, or where to fire. We were in a couple of slit trenches, and some Sergeant came by and saw these two guys in this slit trench and it looked like we were asleep which we certainly were not. So he yelled and screamed and kicked us and told us to get up on the line and start firing. We did. We sure enough did, and in a hurry.

Taking over your first platoon Now of course your new platoon will be sizing you up immediately, trying to figure out who you are and what you are and are you going to be able to cut the mustard. Your first requirement is to let them know you are in charge. If the situation permits, start to get into some training. Size up your NCO's quickly. We all know you are supposed to take advice from your Platoon Sergeant. But you may not have a very good Platoon Sergeant, and he may not be of the type that you are going to be getting very good advice from and you may have to do it on your own, or you may have to work with one or more squad leaders who seem to be more articulate, or a lot sharper.

Start talking to each individual in your platoon as soon as time permits. This is not sitting down and getting buddy-buddy with them, but finding out about where they are from and start finding out their strengths and skills. Keep a roster in your pocket notebook with enough data that you can let each soldier know you are interested in him. Check on his individual equipment and his weapon. Memorize the names as soon as you can, and treat all your new replacements the same way. For all of them, replacements and soldiers already in the platoon when you take charge, find out as soon as you can how good they are with their weapons—can they hit anything with it?

Get to a rifle range or create a makeshift firing range in your platoon sector with the impact area out towards enemy lines, and get to firing those weapons. You should participate in firing those weapons, and have other soldiers (and yourself) fire the BAR and the machine gun. Emphasize cross training and having as many men as possible capable of taking over that firepower and keeping it going in a fight as casualty replacements. Be certain that you learn at the absolute minimum, how to reduce stoppages on all weapons in your platoon. If time permits, learn or improve your skills at complete assembly and disassembly, until you can literally do it blindfolded, for those situations which arise in the dark. Rather than letting your "Platoon Leader Ego" be threatened by seeking this instruction, your NCO's will gain respect for you on the basis of your being willing to seek this additional professional competence.

Another thing you can do is have them start sharpening their bayonets. Let each squad leader borrow your sharpening gear, and then give each squad leader one of the little key chain Fiskars or CrockStick knife sharpeners you brought with you for his squad. [See "Equipment to take along with you" section.] Get into some hand to hand training, with some simple throws and counters, and you get into the pit for some of this. Let them see that you are not afraid to get tossed on your ass and can still get up and come back charging hard after a fall. Be certain you pick a partner/opponent who is much bigger than you are, and you may even get lucky enough (or be good enough) to knock him on his ass once or twice.

To let them know you are in charge and gain that initial respect, if there is a patrol requirement—even just a squad patrol—you take that patrol out as the patrol leader at the first opportunity. Get up close to the front—not on the absolute point, and not to imply that way up close is always the best place to control the formation—so that your soldiers can see (and the word will spread instantaneously throughout your platoon) that you are not afraid to get up front and share the risks and dangers with your men. On later patrols or larger patrols you may find there are better places from which to control, such as behind the lead squad, or with the assault element, but on this first patrol, you get your butt up front Lieutenant. And no matter what the tactical situation degenerates into, never, never, never, never show them that you are just as scared as they are. Suck it up, keep cool and just muck it out.

Concentrate on the care of feet. I know that with Desert Storm it seemed like everyone is going to ride into battle. That may not be the case if you go to a place like Korea. You are going to walk, and you are going to walk, and you are going to walk. Get as many blister pads as you can from the medics, and have them teach (or refresh) the men how to treat a blister, and the NCO's how to check for blisters, and have each man carry his own blister pad treatment and know to take care of it just as soon as it starts. Extra socks coming up through the supply system can be just as important as rations and water, when the marches are long or the weather turns bitterly cold. A pair of good cushion boot insoles will help you a lot (see Take Along Items section).

One problem which we did not have in Korea that you will have in your war, is what to do about the American addiction to every young person having their own favorite style of music always and immediately available by radio, boom box, tape or CD player or Walkman or Discman. There may be an Armed Forces Radio station established somewhere in the rear, and the Morale Meisters will be convinced they are doing just the right thing for the troops. That may be fine for the rear echelon units, but in a front line situation it will be a fatal disaster if you do not get way out in front on this matter. Do not allow, and absolutely prohibit, any of your soldiers having a radio, tape or CD player or any other electronic entertainment device in your platoon, whether you are on the offensive, or in a defensive position or any other time. The reasons are simple, straightforward and beyond argument.

Your soldiers will be carrying such a heavy load of ammunition, grenades, extra machine gun ammunition, spare batteries for your tactical radios, Claymores, LAW's, rations, water and who knows what else, that you simply can not allow the extra weight of excess personal entertainment gear to sneak into their burden. If any of them claim they don't mind the extra weight, and that they are strong enough to carry it anyway, just keep giving that particular soldier another 200 round can of machine gun ammunition or another half dozen frag grenades to carry until he finally gets the point.

The main problem, however, is not weight but the potential that they will become too intent on listening to some favorite album at the wrong time, and not be 100 per cent focused, alert for the sound of approaching enemy into the position or will not hear the launch report of an enemy mortar attack. Listening to music over an external speaker is a no-brainer, in terms of risks that the music represents for disclosing your position or giving an enemy unit something on which to guide while moving to their final attack positions in the dark. Even worse would be the soldier whose hearing is totally divorced from the task of combat alertness because he has the music coming in over a set of earphones. This can get you all killed!

No matter how clearly and logically and emphatically you explain this to your soldiers and emphasize it through your chain of command, you will probably still have someone write home to whine and complain; you might even have someone write their Congressman, but stick to your guns. Keeping them alive and the platoon intact must take the highest priority in this matter. Do not concern yourself with what other leaders allow in their units, you are only responsible for your platoon. Back in the rear, soldiers may have huge elaborate stereo sets—but in your platoon, soldier ears are for detecting a lone infiltrator or a major attack. (Company and battalion headquarters should be as vigilant—recall my first fire fight was in defense of the battalion CP—but they probably will not restrict radios etc. You just do in your platoon what you know is tactically correct, Lieutenant.)

This next part will seem to be in direct contradiction to the comments above on prohibiting radios and tape players, etc. in your platoon, but a "modern day" electronic device which will be very helpful—and the use of which can be controlled so as not to be tactically dangerous—will be a small pocket micro-cassette recorder, suitable for "voice only" recording and playback. It does not produce any where close to decent quality of sound to make it useful to play music. This type recorder is about the size of a bar of soap, with the cassette about the size of a box of matches. This will allow you to "take notes" when on the move and the situation will not allow you to stop and write something down, and yet you can later play back the tape to review the notes you made. This will also be very effective to record "eye witness" statements after an action, to assist in promptly completing recommendations for valor awards to your soldiers who are deserving of such important recognition.

Another valuable use of this small recorder is for sending "letters" home, and receiving similar "letters from home." Allow your soldiers to have and use this type recorder if they want, and just supervise through your chain of command to preclude the practice of recording or listening to such "letters" to become a dangerous distraction from combat alertness. Take an ample supply of blank micro-cassettes with you, as well as some small envelopes padded with bubble wrap, in which to send the tapes home. Your parents, wife or girl friend(s) can mail some more blank tapes and padded envelopes when you need them.

Detection and location of enemy fire At the first possible chance, whether this is with a couple of your buddies in the pipeline, or in a reserve mission with your platoon, or even while you are up on line, make an opportunity to learn for yourself, and teach your men, how to locate an enemy firing position and to get a feel for what bullets sound like cracking over or past your head. Find a place where you can put two or three good marksmen in locations where they can fire safely over your head or off to one side or the other. Then practice figuring out where each shot came from, as each one fires from a different location. After you have it worked out with you as "the trainee," then take your squad leaders, and then have them take their squads. You have to train yourself and your entire platoon to look up, to get your heads up after that first initial volley when you hit the ground, and look for and detect that enemy location. (Some will hit the ground and "stay" hitting the ground longer than necessary, but that is a different problem for you to deal with.)

Formation for attack I think your Field Manuals today must still be teaching about platoon formations. In my days as a Lieutenant, we had the platoon diamond and platoon wedge, and echelon right or left. Now it may be different names, but you are going to be trying to figure out "what type of formation do I use to get these guys squared away and what are the signals I am supposed to give and when?" While there are different formations for movement to contact, and for moving up towards the objective, and you will have part of your platoon providing a base of fire, but the bottom line is that at some point, you and part or all of your platoon will be in the final assault.

In my situation where on our short trip after graduation we did not have any Fort Benning Infantry Basic Course, I was trying to figure out which formation to use and when. As I mentioned, Lieutenant _____, my classmate, had come over with the 2nd Division and by virtue of survival had become the Company Commander before I joined the company. As the only other officer, I was sort of the 1st, 2nd, 3rd and Weapons Platoon Leader, but our company was so small we only had about one decent sized platoon. _____ told me to forget about all that formation business, and when going into the final assault, just form that damn skirmish line, and kick butt and get them all firing as they go up that hill. Of course we spread out as we crossed open ground such as a rice paddy, but we did not get involved in worrying about a particular formation. I kept the machine guns close to me so I could get their NCO's to get them into action quickly as a base of fire; then I took the rest and started to fire and maneuver against our objective or the enemy force firing on us.

When I first got "a platoon" it was about five or six US soldiers with one NCO and 36 South Korean high school kids who had been given fatigues and boots and steel pots and marched around the school yard for a week and sent up to us as replacements. The uniforms and steel pots were too big for them and the combat boots hurt their feet, and they had only fired the M-1 rifle a few times. Needless to say, we were an elite fighting outfit as you can well imagine. To get them up in a skirmish line was about the most one could expect of them, with the amount of training and experience they had NOT received. It would probably have been the same situation if all our replacements had been US enlisted men right out of basic training. There was no other choice but to get whatever troops up on the line that we could, to preclude being pushed back into the Sea of Japan and out of South Korea entirely.

Make maximum use of supporting fires This basically revolves around your knowledge, or your quick learning if you are not sure, on how to call in the organic mortars which will be more available to you than will artillery fires. You may have had some classes on this but very few opportunities to call in and adjust live fires. You have simply got to learn how to do it, and do it fast and well and confidently. Not only you, but you have to teach your NCO's if they do not know how, and then about two or three soldiers in each squad so that the unit has adequate back up to keep the supporting fires coming in case of casualties. Try to do it at every chance, using white phosphorus founds as spotting rounds. Even if you are in a quiet sector get some fire missions going, and do not feel that you are wasting ammunition because the mortar crews need the additional practice also. To assure your unit's capability to call for supporting fires, try to obtain additional radios if you can.

Maybe your radios work better than ours did, if I am to believe all the industrial advertising claims in *Army* magazine about how wonderfully all the present day communications gear performs under all sorts of adverse conditions. But for us, it was a matter of the radios not working much of the time and so we tried to get extra radio sets as back up. Even if yours work great, they can be damaged by incoming and you can seldom afford to wait on a replacement through the supply system when you need that fire support right now. So get some extra radios if you can, but try not to talk about them around the supply types because they do not like to hear about it and they have a very different point of view than yours, even when it is a matter of life and death in your platoon.

Whenever you have a mortar or artillery forward observer with you on position or getting ready for a patrol, talk to them to learn more about fire adjustment. Always have their call signs and radio frequencies so you can link into their fire direction center on their nets if you have to. All of this, taken together, means that you must understand how important it is for you and your unit to be able to always bring in all the available fire support when it is necessary, and this skill will save many lives.

We had rather limited air support compared to what is available today and will be available to your units in combat. There is one caution, however, with regard to your responsibility as a leader to select and request the most appropriate form of supporting fires, whether artillery or air (either Army helicopters or fixed wing aircraft). Keep in mind during a developing engagement that the air support has a limited time on station and must eventually depart to refuel, even if they might still have bombs, rockets or machine gun and cannon ammunition. In some cases, they might argue for you to use the air support first, before they have to refuel. Keep in mind though that you have to brief the air support on your location, the tactical situation and enemy locations before they can be of any help. When this group of aircraft departs, you have to start over with briefing the next flight. If you are under extremely heavy enemy attack, this delay between flights can be crucial, even deadly.

Artillery, on the other hand, "has a memory," and once they have registered on your defensive fires, they can come back to that fire mission very quickly. I strongly recommend that if you have both types of support available in the early stages of a developing fight, always get your artillery support registered first, then have them suspend firing while you bring in any available air support. Then should the enemy attack become critical, you can always release the air support and return to artillery to get the continuou support you might require when you are extremely hard pressed. If you need to use air and artillery both at the same time, that will be possible only if the air support can avoid having to fly through the artillery shell trajectories. The best way to accomplish this is to request that the aircraft make their support runs in a direction perpendicular to the artillery gun-target line. If the enemy air defense capabilities are such that this flight route is possible, then bring in both air and artillery at once.

Establishing defensive positions and fire plans This relates back somewhat to the previous topic on supporting fires, but in South Korea, you are dealing with pretty steep hills, and as you get into North Korea the hills get higher and steeper until the mountains are literally up in the clouds. The challenge here is to determine how and when to use the military crest as opposed to defending behind the actual top or the ridge line, or the topographic crest as the subject is laid out in the Field Manuals.

Case in point, a unit of the 5th Marine Regiment pushed through us at one point, down on the Naktong River to retake some high ground. We later followed along behind them and were going to take over their positions as they were pulled back to ship out for the Inchon landings. As we pulled in behind their positions, they were all dug in, by the book, on the military crest of the hill—which put them under direct observation and fire from North Koreans on a facing hill of about the same height, at about 500 to 800 yards range. The Marine unit could not move, because they were literally pinned down while in their own foxholes, taking casualties whenever any one tried to move about, and even while in their foxholes from North Korean .50 caliber machine gun and recoilless rifle fire. (These were weapons they had earlier captured from US or South Korean units.) When we took over that hill, we put our positions right on the back side of the ridge line, so we had some solid ground between our foxholes and the North Korean observation and fire.

When you get your position established, sectors of fire assigned and start digging in, plan to add "crawl trenches" within the position as soon as you can after the primary fighting positions are completed. In most cases you will not be in a position long enough (we were not until well into the spring of 1951) to be able to entrench the entire platoon position, that is, with connecting trenches between positions and throughout the position. But you will have both the opportunity and the need for shallow, one foot deep crawl trenches within your defensive position, located and oriented so that they can still be covered by fire from the positions they connect. These will allow you and your men to have limited movement within your position while being protected from enemy direct fire weapons, but they will not be useful to an enemy force which gets inside your position because anyone in those trenches can still be seen (and shot if it is an enemy soldier) from your own fighting positions.

Another problem in the area of defensive positions is the matter of plunging fire or grazing fire. We all know that we are supposed to lay out our positions to have grazing fire across the entire platoon front, and we should seek to attain that ideal solution. But on very precipitous and mountainous terrain, where there is no gradual slope, let alone even terrain, it simply is not always possible to have grazing fire. Clearly defined sectors of fire, covering the entire front are still very important, even though you may not have enough of an even slope for grazing fire. After assigning sectors of fire, check to see that the soldiers have understood their sectors by checking range cards. If there is no immediate threat of incoming fire, get two adjacent soldiers together and have each one describe his sector of fire, using his range card, and then check the next man to insure that there is no gap uncovered between them, and that each man knows how his fires interlock with those of the men on his flanks.

Many times in very mountainous terrain, you are faced with the dilemma of being only able to fully occupy and "defend" on part of your mountain, and the challenge is to determine whether to focus on the highest terrain, or the mountain top (where you can neither detect nor engage enemy forces moving through the valley floor), or to set up on a lower finger of the ridge where you can control and observe the valley floor (but run the risk of having the enemy get to the high ground above you). If the situation involves the enemy trying to move large troop formations past you to create havoc in the Regimental of Division rear area, you have to be down where you can engage and disrupt that major troop movement on the valley floor, on roads, in stream beds and so forth. Recognize in advance that there will never be "enough troops to go around" so that you can focus in one area and have an entirely different unit take care of the other one. Our unit's solution was to outpost whichever location we felt least threatened or least able to contribute to the major mission's accomplishment and put the main body in the best position for the mission assigned.

Whether your solution is high, low or somewhere in between, you have a vital task to be certain your platoon's position can be identified from the air. Air ground panels (believe we called them VS 17, with bright pink on one side and blaze orange on the other) are excellent for this purpose, much less weight than smoke grenades, and can be used over and over again. To avoid adding the entire burden to one man, obtain as many additional panels as you possibly can, and cut them up so that every soldier and leader (you included) can carry a two square foot segment. Even though the entire panel might be easier to spot from the air, since you will have the equivalent of several such panels, the combined total of the smaller segments will not only exceed the single panel for visibility, but will allow you to identify the trace of your entire position.

The use of trip flares was not done well enough in my platoon in Korea. I say trip flares because they are much more advantageous than rigging grenades on a trip wire as an early warning device. The grenade is difficult to rig without having some explode, and someone is going to forget where all the trip wires are and set one off by accident. All you really need is early warning of enemy movement, and that will be mainly at night. As for rigging trip flares, you will of course analyze the terrain to decide where the trip wires are to be strung so the enemy will hit the wire and set off your early warning. But always position the flare itself on the forward, or enemy side, of a rock, stump, mound of earth, or a vertical bank that you cut back into the side of the hill, so that the burning flare's light is blocked from coming back to illuminate your positions and blind your troops. You want the enemy to be both illuminated and blinded while your troops are hidden in the dark and can see the illuminated area without looking directly into the burning flare which is extremely bright.

As a corollary to this point of flares *vs.* grenades, frag grenades are much too valuable, and too expensive in terms of weight to carry, for them to be expended as mere trip wire devices. You will have to exercise close supervision, at first, to ensure that your soldiers neither discard nor "accidentally drop" the grenades they have been issued, as they are heavy. But for defense against massed attacks, the grenade is an excellent, reliable weapon. Especially in very steep and rugged terrain such as Korea.

Connected with this discussion of defensive positions, is consideration of the psy-war noise makers of the Chinese and Koreans. Seems like something out of ancient history and in a way, it is, since the Chinese have been using this tactic since at least 500 BC and it is found in the writings of Sun Tzu. They used cymbals, trumpets or bugles, drums and even whistles, as signal devices and to unnerve our troops if they could. No one would tend to think that American troops would laugh this off, but when they are all extremely worn out after five or six weeks of continuous combat, with very little sleep night after night, and the last several times they heard these signals meant a Chinese attack, each additional time the signals are heard, an attack is anticipated, even if it does not come.

As as a sidelight to these signal procedures, keep in mind that we had to rely on some radios which were often ineffective, and many times we had to send a runner between platoon and company for communication. Consider using distinctive whistle signals of your own in a defensive situation with certain simple prearranged codes to designate immediate action drills such as "shift to occupy alternate positions," or if you have been on the position long enough to add overhead cover to your fighting positions or build bunkers, "everyone get under overhead cover because VT fused artillery will be sweeping our position in ____ minutes." [See "Equipment to take along with you" section.)

Field sanitation and personal hygiene Living in the dirt and mud of a combat zone, after having taken "clean laundry and daily showers" for granted all your life, means that you have to strongly emphasize personal hygiene. We used our steel helmets as a wash basin, but your newer one piece helmet cannot be so used. You will probably carry an extra canteen cup as your wash basin. A common household (kitchen or bathroom) sponge weighs next to nothing and takes up very little room in your pack, but it can be used as wash cloth, and also, when rinsed and squeezed dry, can serve as a makeshift towel. Another important consideration in this matter is that although humans have a rather limited capability to use our noses to inform us of the world around us, after you have been on the line for several weeks, you will notice that any one coming from the rear, such as replacements, is easily identified by even our limited sense of smell.

Deodorant soaps, shaving cream additives and after shave lotion can easily be detected (smelled) by anyone who is or has become unaccustomed to those particular scents. For a night patrol or anyone out on an LP or OP, this will be extremely dangerous since the enemy will be even more unaccustomed to those smells than you have become in a few weeks. Consider getting your platoon medic to order "surgical soap" and rubbing alcohol through medical supply channels. This soap has no smell at all, and the smell of rubbing alcohol dissipates in only a few minutes at most. (Rinse out a plastic bug repellent bottle to carry the alcohol.) For shaving, surgical soap will not be as effective as your favorite brand of shaving cream, but it can be made to suffice for shaving. It has no scent to disclose your LP's location or your patrol's ambush position either.

One more item on field sanitation. War does not take time out for anything. Place your field latrines as carefully as any other position in your perimeter, and of course put them on the back side of any hill you are defending, out of enemy observation and direct fire. Be careful when and where you answer the call of nature. Squatting down over a hasty slit trench with your pack and web gear off, your rifle leaning up against your pack and your trousers down around your ankles is a hell of a situation in which to find yourself when an enemy attack begins, but that can and will happen. Just be certain when you are away from your CP for anything for any length of time, even just to take a crap, that your Platoon Sergeant knows where you are and when you will be back and that he is in charge until you return—so that he can take care of fighting the platoon while you are low crawling back from the latrine.

Sleep management, cold weather and fires In the ungodly cold of North Korea in November of 1950, 25 degrees below zero at night in some cases, there was a great temptation to start fires. You must understand that prior to the Chinese contact around Thanksgiving, we were engaged in a movement to contact against a beaten and retreating North Korean Army. They attempted to protect their main body with a very light reconnaissance screen opposing us, and that element could usually be forced to withdraw with a few rounds of artillery or mortar fire and some small arms fire, once they were detected. The danger of a North Korean attack, even a spoiling attack, was extremely remote. Amongst many of the support and combat service support units to our rear, there was a strong tendency to allow fires to keep warm. Of course it gave any position away, and as some of you know who are experienced in northern climes, once you have come to a fire to warm up, you suffer much more—at least it seems colder—when you have to move away from that fire.

On the night of the 25th of November, my platoon was on some high ground with Baker Company to our left front (northwest) some 1500 to 2000 meters away, and during the day we could hear them slightly engaged but no one was very concerned because we thought they were just dealing with another North Korean recon screen. We were told nothing different about our tactical situation, we had been moving very long distances every day and were thoroughly fatigued, and in the absence of any information telling us to modify our alert procedures, after we had our defensive plan and sectors of fire all squared away, I allowed half of the platoon to use sleeping bags that night. For some dumb reason or another, I allowed the Platoon Sergeant to start a small fire in a small draw behind our platoon position. As for myself, this was the first time in about three weeks that I was considering taking off my shoe-pacs and crawling into the sleeping bag, which I did.

Of course it was Murphy's Law, and the Chinese hit us that night and overran our position. After we put up what I thought was a fairly good fight, I had to run down a mountain in my stocking feet, without my field jacket, pile cap or steel pot, but I did have my rifle. Luckily, the next day I was able to find another pair of shoe pacs in a half fallen down Korean hooch which had apparently been used by some unit as some type of a supply point before they also were obliged to withdraw in a hurry.

Sleep management is a very necessary and very important system to establish in your unit. It means getting your people and your subordinate leaders to sleep some during the day. If you are on the move, then make every effort to stop and get set up in your defensive position in time to allow your troops to get an hour or two of sleep before it gets completely dark or in the early part of the night. That way you have a chance of maintaining the necessary 50 per cent alert during the rest of the night when the North Koreans or Chinese will most likely attack. With our air superiority, they had to use the cover of darkness to protect themselves from our air observation for artillery fires or air strikes. When you are in a defensive position, it is equally important to get sleep during the day and get everybody rested before the next night.

One thought about the extremely cold weather we encountered after Thanksgiving in North Korea. We had not received our issue of cold weather gear which created an extreme hardship on us all. Since that time, the Army has developed very effective cold weather gear, and since we have kept troops in Korea since 1953, the cold weather gear has been upgraded and modernized since then. You should not have to be very concerned about keeping your troops and yourself warm but there are a few areas where a little extra would be very helpful. (See "Equipment to take along with you" section.) However, you must keep in mind that as a leader, you share the hardships with your soldiers, whatever those might be, and it would be inappropriate for you to take extensive and elaborate "extra warm gear" over and above what is available for issue to your men.

Magazine Discipline Most of my soldiers were riflemen armed with that greatest and most durable, most effective of all rifles, the M-1 Garand. Their ammunition came in bandoleers of eight round clips, ready to load and fire and never worry about what happened to the empty clip. As a leader, I had a very different problem concerning my soldiers armed with magazine fed weapons such as the M-1 or M-2 carbine, the BAR and US Army Thompson . 45 caliber submachine guns which we quite often were able to "liberate" from the ChiComs.

The magazine gave us a very valuable high rate of sustained fire against massed Communist attacks but created its own problems. When it became necessary to reload in the heat of battle, the soldier was naturally concentrating on reloading the "next" (full) magazine, and quite understandably had other things on his mind rather more important than worrying too much about what to do with the now empty magazine. Since each such weapon only had so many magazines—and ammo resupply for those weapons came as loose rounds in 20 or 50 round boxes—magazine recovery for subsequent reloading and reuse was a leadership challenge.

The necessity for a rapid reload and return to firing (or being ready to fire) meant that there was certainly not enough time to neatly and carefully replace the empty magazine in its web gear carrying pouch, but neither could it be just dropped to the ground. In a defensive situation, that meant it would at the least get dirty and probably malfunction, or at the worst get stepped on and dented or bent. In either case it was rendered useless on a temporary or permanent basis. In an attack, during a withdrawal, or on a patrol, any dropped magazine was essentially lost and gone forever.

My unit's approach to solving this problem was greatly assisted by GI innovation and ingenuity. Field packs of that era consisted of a back pack and a separate smaller pack. Designated a "musette bag," although I don't remember what the term actually meant, this other pack had a combination of straps and buckles which allowed it to be fastened onto the bottom of the regular back pack. It did not work very well for its original purpose, but when fastened to the soldier's web belt on the left hip or left side, it became a moderately satisfactory solution to the empty magazine recovery problem.

Since virtually all your soldiers today have M-16's with magazines, you will face the same problem of recovering their magazines to be later reloaded—but there will certainly not be any "musette bags" still in the supply tent back at S4 or even in the supply system. With the ammo limitations which derive from funding constraints, today's units don't do enough live fire training with amounts of ammunition which would be realistic in terms of the massed attacks we confronted in Korea in 1950–1951, so neither your soldiers nor your NCO's have been "tuned in" to the magazine recovery problem from their present training experiences. You will have to come up with your own solution, and you can be certain that just taking a hard-nosed "I'll make them do it right or else" position will not solve your problem.

The Viet-Nam era "butt-pack" might be a candidate solution but it doesn't fasten closed easily and is not deep enough to retain magazines if the soldier has to move about quickly when the pack is not closed. A better approach will be cut up some salvage fatigue trousers, making the legs into two pouches from each leg (four pouches per pair of trousers being sacrificed to this worthwhile cause). Sew the "half leg" closed across the bottom, thus giving you a pouch about 12-14" deep. (Soldiers still have small sewing kits for minor field uniform repairs, don't they?)

Rig some straps to fasten the pouch to the left side of the web gear, and bend a piece of wire from a C-ration case into an oblong loop about 6" by 3". This loop, sewn into the top edge, will keep the bag "open enough" that your soldiers can easily drop their empty magazines into the pouch in minimum time, and yet it will be "closed enough" that the contents won't bounce out and get lost as the soldier moves around. Since the magazines are all loose to rattle around and bang against each other, this will obviously not work for a patrol continuing their clandestine night movement after a fire fight, but once contact is broken, the magazines can be put back into an ammo pouch at a more deliberate pace than is possible during the fire fight.

Movement to Contact This is essentially a series of long marches, and is what we were doing in the month of November before the Chinese attack. The problem here is that on these long foot marches, you find a complacency settling in, as soldiers mechanically and robot-like stay on the move, putting one foot in front of the other one, but their minds are a million miles away. The symptoms are hands in pockets, heads down, weapons at sling arms and just "barely awake" as they move down the MSR Main Supply Route) or the trail or the path. I would counter this by requiring a certain number of men per squad, on a rotating basis, to be on "duty alert" maintaining good observation to the front, flanks and rear, weapons at the ready and concentrating on the fact that we were still in a war. At the same time, you as the Platoon Leader have to be on the alert, always analyzing the terrain in front of and around you, war-gaming likely locations for enemy positions, and developing, modifying and updating your plan of action for what the platoon will do in the event of enemy contact—where do you put the base of fire, what will be the maneuver element, over what route to each possible enemy position you identify. This mental drill keeps you alert and still in the war. (This same drill, constant war-gaming should be your habitual procedure on patrol.)

As the day's march ends, regardless of how tired the men are, you must make them dig in, if it is at all possible. Even when the ground is frozen solid at 20 degrees below zero, in much of that country it is possible to construct expedient concealment and frontal protection by piling rocks and using small depressions you will find in the terrain.

Return to front fine duty Usually this would pertain a return from a hospital stay after being wounded, which is a case that happened to me along the Naktong River in the Pusan perimeter. A relatively minor wound of mortar shell fragments in my elbow became infected in the routine dirty environment of combat. The wound was not bad enough to keep me from duty, but the infection got completely out of hand. The medics had to send me back to Japan for surgery and recovery. Unfortunately, as a young Lieutenant (did not know I had been promoted to 1st Lieutenant, by the way), I did not realize the extent to which I would lose my physical conditioning during three to four weeks in the hospital.

Going from the muddy foxhole to the clean and dry of a hospital with sheets on the beds and showers and real food is a wonderful boost to the recovery process.

However, you must start into your physical workout routine for all major muscle groups not impaired by your wounds while you are still in good shape. It is always easier to stay in shape than it is to *get back* in shape. You will get out of shape rapidly, if you do not set a rigid goal of maintaining your conditioning level.

You may find, if you are not careful, that your good, broken in combat boots get lost in the process of the hospital personnel getting you out of your dirty (and in many cases bloody) field uniform. Avoid letting those valuable boots get away if at all possible. If you find they are gone, then make it your highest priority to get issued new boots at the earliest possible moment, and begin to get them broken in just as soon as you can. Your workout and boot/foot conditioning plans should include as much endurance work as possible, and as much vertical exertion (stairs, a bench step location or actual hills) as you can. In my case, I left the hilly, but lower terrain of the Naktong, and rejoined my unit in North Korea where as I said, some of the mountains were in the clouds. As I climbed that mountain to return to my platoon, it took me three times as long as it should have, if I had only realized the necessity to keep in shape in the hospital.

Keep yourself informed of the tactical situation at all times Take it as your personal responsibility to stay informed, and do not let the Company Commander or the Company Headquarters ignore you or leave you uninformed about what is going on outside the little world of your platoon and company. As an example of this, I referred earlier to the situation where an adjacent company was more heavily engaged than we realized, on 25 November. Had I been told, or had I made it a habit to aggressively seek out additional information and learned for myself the extent of the Baker Company fight (to which Marshall devotes an entire chapter—number two—of *The River and the Gauntlet*), I certainly would never have even thought about letting my Platoon Sergeant start a "small fire" nor would I have allowed anyone into sleeping bags or out of their shoe pacs that night, most of all myself! Report any combat actions you can see or hear and if you can not get through by radio, send a runner to ask for or report information. The runner can go back to Company Headquarters or to an adjacent platoon to use their radio or field telephone, but stay in communications.

As another example of this requirement, about a week after that incident, I found myself as the only officer commanding about 180 men on a hilltop who were the remnants of all three rifle companies of 1st Battalion of the 9th Infantry. I had no radios, but I did have a field telephone EE-8 and a wire running back down to my own Battalion CP which was behind me, at the bottom of that hill. I was grabbed up out of my platoon in the afternoon, and told by the Battalion Commander (or the Exec or the S-3, I can not exactly remember who) to take command of those elements and to hold that hill until they got back to me with further orders the next day. The first problem was that they did not give me any map, and I was not experienced enough to ask for one because a map, even a sketch map, would have helped out considerably for my future.

During the night, we received rather extensive enemy artillery shelling, and I was calling down to my battalion to request counter battery fire, and all of a sudden the phone line rang open. I sent a runner down to learn what was happening at the Battalion CP and to request the counter battery fires, and the runner came back up about an hour later saying that there was nobody there. I had been sent up there on such short notice that I had not had time to organize the force as well as I should have.

I did get the men from the three companies, "A," "B," and "C" into company groups together with the most senior NCO I could locate placed in charge of his group, in essence each of those NCO's being the Company Commander. So I felt I did have the bare bones necessity of a chain of command, with runners from each company to carry any orders I might have to issue during the night. Luckily, we were not attacked that night and the next day a jeep came from my battalion with orders to withdraw to a new position about three or four miles south, where the Regiment had located two or three Lieutenants from that battalion and elements of their battalion staff, who took over and reorganized as well as they could—much better than I had been able to on short notice, and we prepared for the movement south through Kunu-ri.

Withdrawal or retreat operations We have, of course, all learned that we never retreat, but we use the term withdrawal instead. But there will be times, when the enemy force is so strong, or that enemy forces have gotten around behind you or on your flanks, that you must break contact and escape to live to fight another day. A perfect example of this is the withdrawal of the 2nd Division from Kunu-ri. As one who survived this ordeal, there are certain key points which I would like to bring to your attention. You must do everything you can to maintain unity of command and unit integrity, and at the platoon level that is just as important as it is at the division level. In this operation, unit integrity was first weakened, and then became almost non-existent at the division level, and partially all the way down to the lower levels, which resulted in small fragments of units and individuals trying to get on any vehicle that was going south.

At the platoon level, you must do whatever you can to keep however many men you have left, together as a unit. This will vastly increase chances for success and survival for the entire unit, rather than allowing your platoon to become fragmented into groups of one, two or three soldiers. Your wounded have to be cared for, and taken along with you during the withdrawal.

If you have to load onto a vehicle or vehicles, maintain unit integrity by a squad or a fire team on each vehicle, and on sequential vehicles so that you can still keep your platoon together to the maximum extent possible. Have a simple plan to be prepared to dismount and fight when it is required. At the earliest opportunity, make it completely clear, get it across, that you are going to have to fight, and fight as a unit, to get out of there—that individuals trying to crawl along the ditches without fighting, without returning fire, are not going to make it. If you have to dismount from the vehicles, you do it as a unit.

In a multi-division sized ambush such as this, there are going to be vehicles destroyed or wrecked along the way, and even more at critical choke points such as bridges, passes or defiles. You must realize that as an officer, you can not just sit there waiting for somebody else to make a decision—you take whatever action is necessary to clear the blockage and dislodge the vehicle or vehicles blocking the route. You take your men, set out whatever security screen or base of fire element the situation requires, and then take command of whoever else is available or whatever equipment you might find useful and at hand, and simply make it happen to get that route cleared of whatever is blocking you. While you are dismounted, insure that some of your soldiers keep a very short leash on the drivers of the vehicles on which you are riding, to make certain those vehicles are still available for your unit when the obstacle is cleared and the convoy resumes movement.

A rather interesting sidelight to this ordeal. When we finally cleared the ambush zone and closed on the American lines, I reported in to the Regimental Commander of the unit we had reached, and found him to be Colonel John T. Corley, who had been a Tactical Officer when I was a cadet. After I had briefly outlined my situation, Colonel Corley, with his most stern "tactical officer" look on his face and tone of voice said to me: "Mister, you did not shave this morning." I could only start to answer "no sir," as a reflex action, when I noticed the smile in his eyes and the grin starting on his usually expressionless face. He then handed me his own shaving kit, and directed someone to get me some hot water. Colonel Corley assured me that after I had a chance to clean up and get some chow for my men, he would arrange transportation for my platoon on to where he was aware that my battalion was in an assembly area to regroup.

******

This worked for me during the winter of 1950–51. I was a weapons platoon leader for a short time, then a rifle platoon leader. I joined the 7th Cavalry Regiment in late November, just before the Chinese intervention. I was wounded for the second time in March 1951 during Operation Killer; then evacuated to Japan and on to the States. Hope this bit of information is useful, and sure wish I had been able to draw on such a collection of combat advice back then. I knew so little of the essential details of tactics and practically nothing about 60 mm mortars and 57 mm recoilless rifles when I became a weapons platoon leader.

When I was a rifle platoon leader I found that it was very difficult for the men on watch in their foxholes to stay awake at night. We always had two men to a hole, which meant that each man would be awake and alert for two hours, then off duty to sleep for two hours, and so on. Squad Leaders shared a hole with their Assistant Squad

Leaders. My Platoon Sergeant and I also took turns every two hours. When I went to check my men I found that there were almost always some who were asleep when they were supposed to be on duty. We solved this problem without having to resort to punishment by having each Squad Leader (or Assistant Squad Leader, whichever one was on watch) move from foxhole to foxhole during his entire time on duty.

I knew that the guys were lonely and often scared, but also that they all loved to have someone to talk to. When they knew that someone was coming to visit them in a little while, they would be busy thinking of things they wanted to discuss with their leader. The leaders took this opportunity to get to know their men better, plus provide one-on-one training—to go over and emphasize various subjects about our situation and operations and soldier skills on an individual basis. (The talking was in a very low voice and would not give away our position; also the rest of the squad was still on the alert and listening for any sounds of an enemy's approach.) To assure myself that leaders could spend some time with all their men, troops rotated on even hours, squad leaders on odd hours, and my Platoon Sergeant and I on the half hour. As a consequence of all this, I was confident that the men were awake and alert, and both my Platoon Sergeant and I confirmed that all night long when we made our nightly rounds. My soldiers were also happy to have their leaders come see them and share their lonely nighttime vigil.

******

Graduation and my 22nd birthday occurred on 6 June 1950. A whole new life was beginning with our long anticipated 60 day Graduation Leave. Then North Korea invaded on 25 June. George Foster, a Company B-2 classmate called and asked if we could share a ride cross-country. He was back home in Washington DC and his new Pontiac was sitting in San Antonio. I swung down from New England and we headed for San Antonio. We drove two cars to El Paso where I sold my Ford for $1500—a modest profit since I had paid $1465 for its purchase. George picked me up and we continued to San Francisco where he sold his Pontiac. Then on to Camp Stoneman.

After a few days we boarded aircraft and were split up, George went commercial to Hawaii and then to Japan; I went by Air Force transport to Japan by way of Alaska. I never saw George Foster again. After a short period of time, he was killed in action way up in North Korea. [1st Lieutenant George E. Foster, Platoon Leader, 32nd Infantry Regiment, 7th Infantry Division, KIA 2 December 1950.] This brings up a second incident. Before graduation, the graduates to be gathered by branch (Infantry, in our case) to select their desired postings, world-wide. When my name was called, one of the five slots for Hawaii was still available. As I stood up to announce my choice, Bill Otis, another company B-2 classmate and World War II veteran said: "Give me a break. I want to take my new wife to Hawaii." I replied that it would cost him a fifth of Canadian Club. Bill was killed almost before I reached Korea, [2nd Lieutenant William E. Otis, Jr. Platoon Leader, 5th Regimental Combat Team, KIA

11 September 1950, the day after his 25th birthday; awarded the Silver Star, posthumously.]

"C" Company About the end of August I reached Korea and proceeded to the 24th Infantry Division Replacement Company. From there it was a short hop to the 21st Infantry Regiment, and to the 1st Battalion (Lieutenant Charles B. Smith, Commanding). This 1st Battalion was the famed "Task Force Smith" now brought up to strength by adding its companies "A" and "D." Five members of the class of 1950 were assigned to 1st Battalion, 21st Infantry. Lieutenant Colonel Smith asked if anyone had a preference for assignment. I remember raising my hand and when queried, I replied that under the circumstances a Rifle Platoon was the unit for which I was best qualified. I was assigned to "C" Company.

I was offered transportation to "C" Company and accepted. Typically, as we approached, mortar fire was hitting the company CP. I jumped from the jeep, dismissed the driver and dove behind a rock to ask a soldier there where the Company Commander was. The soldier pointed him out and I made a short hop to and dove behind his cover. My words were something like: "Captain, I am Lieutenant _____, reporting in." Captain Wyrick's reply was: "Good. See those people trying to take that hill? They are yours. Go get 'em." And I left.

My platoon took that hill mainly because of the NCO's. Good fortune was with me. My Platoon Sergeant, Master Sergeant Frank Kaplan, had been an NCO who received a commission during World War II but then reverted to his enlisted rank after the war. He had been captured in the Philippines and had survived the Bataan Death March. The Assistant Platoon Sergeant was Sergeant First Class Lewis Reid. He had enlisted in the Army two years before I was born and had served with Merrill's Marauders during World War II. Master Sergeant Kaplan recommended setting up a defensive position as soon as possible, since the North Koreans would almost certainly counterattack very soon. I introduced myself to the men and told them that for the time being I would be reliant upon Master Sergeant Kaplan and the other platoon NCO's because they had more experience than I had. However, I also told them that they would see it and feel it as I took over the decision process. Then the men were released to their squad leaders and I continued my first lesson with Master Sergeant Kaplan, as he set up a platoon perimeter, assigned squad sectors and emplaced weapons. Then it started raining.

Everything darkened with the growing intensity of the rain. Hearing small noises was impossible. I stood up to shake some of the water off and I saw the little man standing in front of me at a distance of maybe four or five feet. I yelled: "They're in the perimeter!" The North Korean hit the trigger but nothing happened. He panicked trying to get a second round into the chamber, then the burp gun went off—straight into the ground, but it started climbing. His weapon quit firing when I hit him. I knew that my being on the Military Academy boxing team would someday prove useful. As he got back up I hit him in the face with a butt stroke from his own weapon and he went down for good. I was well inside the perimeter, our squads were around the perimeter, and North Koreans were both inside and outside.

After some anxious moments the firing ended, the rain ended, and the daylight grew in intensity. Our casualties were three wounded and we had 13 North Koreans dead in and around our perimeter. With full daylight, Captain Wyrick and First Sergeant Godbey arrived on our position. The First Sergeant pointed out that I had some 19 bullet holes in my trousers and shirt, at about two or three inch intervals, from my trousers cuff, ending at my right armpit—probably because my arm and fist were raised and delivering a right cross. He stated: "Lieutenant, we broke you in right!" Captain Wyrick also noted that someone else had apparently shot my canteen off. I had now been the Platoon Leader of 2nd Platoon, "C" Company, 21st Infantry Regiment for less than one day.

2nd Platoon 2nd Platoon was comprised of approximately 30 men rather than the normal 40 plus. Each rifle squad had two BAR's while the TO&E called for only one. We had two light machine guns, the A-6 [M1919A-6 with a shoulder stock and bipod which could be carried by one man] and the A-4 [M1919A-4 with a tripod and a two man load]. The A-4 was only effective then at about 20 to 30 yards range, since the assistant machine gunner had been killed in a withdrawal and the tripod was then lost, plus the barrel had been "shot out" and worn nearly smooth of rifling. Spare parts were unavailable. We mounted the A-4's pintle in an open end up steel helmet and would not give it up because whether the attacker was hit by a bullet coming head on or coming sideways tumbling out of control was completely irrelevant. At close range, a .30 caliber bullet was deadly at any attitude. Eventually replacement parts became available, but I never asked where the extra weapons came from. The platoon was heavy on NCO's. They had been assigned from other divisions in Japan, and had gone with Task Force Smith in early July, 1950.

The North Koreans would attack head on, then flank one or both sides and/or attempt to encircle the unit. During the defense of the Pusan perimeter, we did not have enough strength to man a continuous line. Instead, we mounted strong points, and defended between the strong points by fire. In a perimeter defense, the platoon was on its own, and plans of action were developed at the platoon level. For example, in a withdrawal, I would leave one squad in place, and withdraw with the wounded and the platoon (-). I would then set up those elements in a defensive position and cover by fire the withdrawal of the last squad out. My personal position was flexible. This method proved quite effective.

At a 24th Division reunion in about 1995 1 ran into Command Sergeant Major Bob Niarhos at the 21st Infantry Hospitality Room. He had been my best squad leader the 2nd Platoon. After over 40 years, the meeting was rather emotional, so we drifted off to quietly toast our reunion. Then, he stated that he wanted to go back into the hospitality room so he could tell everyone in there a story. "There were three platoon perimeters on line, and we held the center one. All night long, all three units were under mortar fire and massed enemy Infantry attacks. Come daylight, we looked right and left and we were all alone. Then the Lieutenant says to me: 'Sergeant, you must give me 15 minutes to get the wounded out and get set up to cover your withdrawal. I looked around and could see about 250 North Koreans getting ready to attack from the front, maybe 100 more on the left and another 100 on the right. Then I looked at my squad with five men—and that included the wounded—and I replied: 'Lieutenant, not one damn second more."

In retrospect, Command Sergeant Major Niarhos was probably the best soldier I ever encountered. He served three combat tours in Korea and four in Viet-Nam. His last duty assignment was as Command Sergeant Major of the 24th Infantry Division. I went to his funeral in Georgia in 1998 to find that Fort Bragg had assigned a Command Sergeant Major with a detail of 36 Rangers to his funeral.

Mr. Lee and the KATUSA's Lee Sang Yun ended World War II in Manchuria with the Japanese Army, into which service he had been press-ganged early in the war. He lead a group of other Koreans south toward freedom following the war's end. His group evaded Russians, North Koreans and South Korean Border Police to finally reach Pohang years later. He asked to assist the Americans and was assigned to my platoon as an interpreter in September 1950.

This was about the same time that the first KATUSA's (Korean Augmentation to the US Army) reached us. They arrived late one afternoon, and I told Mr. Lee to see that they were integrated into our squads. That he did, as he interviewed them. Fortunately we were not attacked that night for the KATUSA's did not even know how to load their rifles. The squads began intensive training and with that, the KATUSA's developed into good troops.

Crossing the Naktong River Just as I received word that we would be making a river crossing and that 2nd Platoon would lead the assault, Master Sergeant Kaplan was pulled off the line, because of his age. He was sorely missed by myself and by the men. We were trucked to the Naktong, near Waegwan, where we waited for our pontoon boats. I would guess that by then, everyone knew what was going to occur. Boat crews were assigned and we began our trek to the water, carrying our boats about 100 to 200 yards. As we reached the near bank, North Korean mortar fire began to range in on us. We began to paddle, but some men had to use their rifle buts since we received insufficient paddles for each man. The mortar fires were now falling on both banks and in the water, plus machine gun fire in the water and on the far bank.

I was in the front of my boat, and one KATUSA kept moving up in front of me. I would push him aside, but he would soon be back. Then I was not fast enough and he caught a fatal burst of machine gun fire. His death probably averted my own. We hit the beach with no place to go. We held only a few yards of beach, with everyone crouched behind a low bank. As I moved along the line, I remember one soldier was very visibly frightened and shaking. He was sure that a machine gun sweeping the bank would get him. I took one of his grenades, stood up and threw it, then told him I had destroyed that particular gun position (actually came no where close with my throw). He calmed down and was ready to soldier.

Captain Wyrick said as he pointed to my gold bar, "You, do something." I grabbed every available NCO I could, and stated that in five minutes I would jump the bank and that they were to follow with the men at fixed bayonets. I will never forget one of the NCO's asking, "What if they don't have one?" I remember two machine gun emplacements in our way, and I remember my tongue hanging out from the run until my second wind kicked in. We reached the top and I tried to set up a defense before the expected counter-attack began. Our company strength was down considerably.

A radio message announced that a flight of USMC Corsairs were coming in. They came in low first with a dry run, I would guess to verify our positions and identity, and yet their approach scattered the counterattacking North Koreans. As soon as they realized the aircraft were not firing, they regrouped and started at us again. This time the North Koreans were met by the Corsairs with all guns blazing. They came in so low that the few of us on the hilltop were hit by falling machine gun links. Then the remainder of the company arrived and we were told to get to the end of the line.

The Route North Following the Naktong crossing, everyone was headed north except for 2nd Platoon. All troops were being loaded on trucks and the vehicles ran out just before us. I was given about two days of rations and told to head north to join the unit as soon as possible. We walked and we hitched rides. We acquired additional rations and confiscated chickens and eggs and rice. When we finally rejoined the company, we were much better fed and quite well rested.

Once with the company, we began extensive patrolling. 2nd Platoon did both reconnaissance and combat patrols—specifically the long range patrols of many days duration. Reconnaissance patrols were for a specific purpose and combat was to be avoided, while combat patrols allowed us to look for trouble. On these patrols, I liked having along both a 60 mm mortar and a 57 mm recoilless rifle. Most of our movement was at night.

At a reunion, Mr. Lee and my radio operator, Bill Anderson were talking about the evening when we ran into a North Korean Regimental CP. My patrol, with attachments, numbered about 50 men. We had wiped out our objective when Mr. Lee reported the KATUSA's had found an airplane hidden by covering it with rice straw.

This was "bed-check Charlie," a biplane that had put-putted over our lines after dark on the Pusan perimeter. If anyone fired at him, he dropped hand grenades, so the ground troops soon left him alone. My approach was not quite so benevolent. Armed with only my cigarette lighter I scored my first aircraft kill. Only four more and I could claim to be an "Ace." Until the reunion I had never related the story about "Charlie" as it would have seemed but a fairy tale. Later that evening I related Mr. Lee's story to Captain (now Colonel) Wyrick. He confirmed "I remember when you radioed that in."

2nd Platoon as Point Platoon As we advanced north there was a continuing need for a lead (point) platoon. At first, the 2nd Platoon performed its share of point missions, and then more than its share. I queried Captain Wyrick and his reply was that the 2nd Platoon succeeded.

Our plan when confronted with a North Korean rear guard type defense was comparatively simple. The lead or point squad would immediately pick up the fire and the A-4 machine gun moved up to join that squad. (We had finally obtained a replacement tripod and new barrel for this gun.) With the base of fire in action, I would flank (right or left) with the remaining two rifle squads. The order was simple. As an example, I would call: "Flank left, 1st Squad left, 3rd Squad right, machine gun with 3rd Squad, Move!" This machine gun was the A-6 with shoulder stock and bi-pod; quite easily carried along with the maneuver element.

Automatically the squads sent a flanker left or right, depending an their positions. In the above example, the maneuver is to our left as we faced in the original direction of travel. Within the maneuver element, 1st Squad will be on the left, and 3rd Squad on the right of that formation. Both squads sent out a point man. I would be the maneuver element leader, while my Platoon Sergeant moved to control the base of fire from wherever he had been in the formation. If, by chance, I were to be with the lead squad at the time of the encounter, it was more logical for me to control the base of fire and my Platoon Sergeant would assume command of the maneuver element.

Our rapid response in returning fire with an entire squad and a machine gun pinned the defensive force down and the quick maneuver prevented their receiving any reinforcements before we were already on top of them. Best of all, the entire platoon knew exactly what was to happen and we were able to deploy from the march into the attack quite rapidly. There occurred one exception. The defensive fires hit our platoon from the flank. I notified Captain Wyrick and he dispatched another platoon to assume point duties while we took on the defensive unit.

While some may think that the Principles of War are for Generals and grand strategy, analysis of our operations in this movement to contact will confirm that I applied these same Principles, in microcosm, at the level of 2nd Platoon. *Mass* was provided by the almost immediate, heavy volume of fire. I *maneuvered* a pardon of my platoon. Our rapid response was adequate to gain us at least momentary *surprise*. Our *objective* was to clear the North Korean delaying force and continue our movement north. The *offensive* was paramount in these actions. Each squad put out a flanker and since we were acting as the company's advance guard, those both gave us *security*. *Unity of command* was observed because whether I took the maneuver element or my Platoon Sergeant did, we both followed the same plan of action. My plans, well understood and frequently rehearsed, were always an excellent example of *simplicity*. Again, the mass of firepower and rapidity of our response allowed us to attain results quite out of proportion to the size of my unit, which clearly demonstrates *economy of force*. In this brief synopsis one can identify all of the nine Principles of War, defining and guiding the tactics of this new Infantry lieutenant.

The 38th Parallel   With 2nd Platoon frequently on point, we continued advancing north. One day soon, after a march of 20 plus miles, word came down that we were approaching the 38th Parallel and that we were to stop south of it and not cross. On arrival, and with the troops quite worn out, Master Sergeant Reid and I went up the prominent hill to our front for a reconnaissance. As we mentally positioned our squads and weapons, a North Korean soldier moved out from behind a tree. He stood there momentarily with his rifle to his shoulder. He had his bayonet fixed. All I could see or think of was that bayonet, and I went in under it with my own. He went down and Master Sergeant Reid asked "Lieutenant, why didn't you just shoot him?" My reply: "I forgot I had a trigger on this thing."

I located one squad and the reserve squad on this hill, and the remaining squad on a lesser hill across the main route we had been following. As often happened in our move north, we had a section of tanks attached, and I located these to provide coverage on this main route. The only event of that evening was the approach of an enemy truck moving fairly rapidly south toward our position. Our Section Leader's tank fired and the vehicle exploded in a huge ball of flame. It had apparently been transporting drums of gasoline as its cargo.

The next morning, following a C ration breakfast, we were cleared to cross the 38th Parallel. 2nd Platoon was on point, followed by the section of tanks and then the company minus. The company vehicles carried our platoon bedrolls. There were many meeting engagement incidents, but our fast response and rapid movement to hit them fast proved extremely successful. A second point in our favor was that the North Koreans all up and down their chain of command, did not realize that we had crossed the 38th Parallel.

By late afternoon, the troops were all tired so I formed a new point team. Master Sergeant Reid and I both had automatic carbines, each with a 30 round magazine; I took two BAR men forward with us, who each had a 20 round magazine. Our total up front was 100 rounds for instant firing without anyone reloading. Our regular packs went on the decks of one of the tanks. Master Sergeant Reid and I covered the center of the road and the BAR men covered the shoulders as we proceeded north. As we rounded a bend, coming straight at us were four North Korean soldiers at sling arms, leading an ox loaded with a 120mm Soviet mortar. We cut loose and blazed away with all our one hundred rounds. When the dust cleared, the ox was dead and the four North Koreans were headed north. I yelled "left to right," as we reloaded and we then ended that situation.

The main incident of our first day in North Korea involved a motor pool we located on our left flank just after Sergeant Niarhos' squad had taken the point. As I moved forward to join the point, a sentry challenged us and Sergeant Niarhos replied in the Korean language. The sentry relaxed and lit a cigarette just as Sergeant Niarhos reached him. It was his last cigarette. The squads came forward and I gave my orders to move in a skirmish line. Small arms engaged all their personnel as grenades went into vehicle cabs. Then we swung to the right and moved back to our route of advance north. No one in our unit had been hurt. As coordinated and planned before hand, the section of tanks then moved in to mop up. We continued a short distance then went into defensive positions for the night.

To the Yalu As the 24th Division continued north, "C" Company basked in the luxury of being battalion reserve. In late October, as we approached Sinanju, "C" Company moved to the battalion point and 2nd Platoon was detailed to take Sinanju. A walled city, Sinanju was a road and rail junction on the Anju River and the Yellow Sea. Fortunately, resistance was minimum. 1st Battalion went into defensive positions in and around Sinanju, and 2nd Platoon was stationed on the ancient city's wall itself. With the distance to cover and the number of troops available, no attempt was made to set up a continuing defense line. Small strong points were established at key positions and one squad was held in reserve. One section of tanks filled in a gap in the northern face of the wall. In the meantime, the rest of 24th Division as part of a larger force, advanced to within 20 miles of Sinuiju, border supply base of the Chinese, laid waste by US bombers.

About 10 November, a force of some 80,000 Chinese and North Koreans attacked and the 24th Division fell back some 50 miles to defensive positions south of Sinanju. The see-saw back and forth began and would continue through Thanksgiving until the end of the month, when we headed south back across the 38th Parallel. During the fluid situation, Sinanju was taken a second time, with 2nd Platoon being on the point again because "they had done it before." This second time, the entire 1st Battalion, 21st Infantry occupied the town. The gap in the northern wall face became the boundary and coordinating point between "A" Company to the west and "C" Company to the east, with 2nd platoon on the company left flank.

Late one evening, noises began to the front of the city wall's northern face, and in the early morning hours, a charge was made by mounted Chinese cavalry and accompanying Infantry. I recall that the supporting artillery at first did not believe that the targets identified in our fire requests were for real. As the fight continued, the artillery supported us with all they had. Flares illuminated the growing carnage. Come morning, hundreds of bodies (soldiers and Mongolian ponies) were scattered across the north wall of Sinanju. 1st Battalion maintained this defensive position as the rear guard, while 24th Division withdrew to the south.

Rear Guard to Defensive Positions Finally 1st Battalion pulled out from Sinanju with "C" Company in the trail and 2nd Platoon as the absolute rear guard. After a few days, the Chinese advance elements were spotted by 2nd Platoon. We set up a strong point which included a 57 mm recoilless rifle and a 60 rum mortar. As soon as the Chinese were within range, the platoon opened up with all weapons; they scattered and we double timed out to the rear. This was repeated over the next several days. We were lucky that the Chinese in our area were only a supporting attack and never came at us in the overwhelming numbers or rapid flanking envelopments which so many other units encountered.

The main problem we faced then was overwhelming fatigue as we continued without ever stopping to regain our strength. One evening, a sergeant called me over and I found a soldier prone in the snow. I bent over to check for wounds and discovered that he was actually sound asleep, having fallen from a standing (marching) position and he was so tired the fall did not awaken him. Never have I seen soldiers so utterly exhausted. When we finally closed on the rest of our company, the battalion was placed in a defensive position north of Seoul.

2nd Platoon was sent out an a long, sweeping reconnaissance patrol to gather information concerning the enemy dispositions to our front. As we were headed back

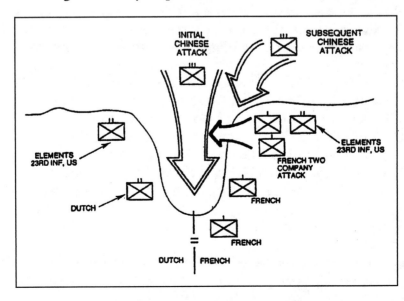

to US lines after accomplishing our recon mission, we reached a frozen lake which had to be crossed to return to the American positions. Since it was totally devoid of any cover or concealment, I gave orders that stressed maintaining our dispersion as the highest priority, not to mention my concerns that the take's ice might have been weakened by mortar and artillery shelling.

We dispersed with no man near any other, which was a tactic I had stressed over and over when crossing open terrain. Approximately half way across, enemy mortar fire began. Only one man was hit, and the nearest soldier ran to pick him up and we all double timed across the rest of the lake while maintaining our wide open dispersal. We reached the friendly side and welcome cover with no one else having been hit. As a result of repeated training in immediate action drills and sound discipline, 2nd Platoon made it through one more challenge.

Le Bataillon Francais (ONU)   Toward the end of March 1951, I received orders to report to the UN Reception Center in Pusan for duty as US Liaison Officer to the French forces. *En route*, I passed through the headquarters of the 2nd Infantry Division and its 23rd Infantry Regiment to which the French Battalion (ONU) was attached. ONU, in English would be translated as United Nations Organization. This battalion was organized as a reinforced infantry battalion with four rifle companies instead of the normal three; its heavy weapons company had four 81 mm mortars and four 75 mm recoilless rifles rather than the usual complement of only three of each type. Outside of organic vehicles, the French were dependent on the US forces for all other support.

The battalion had a dual staff structure, with one representing the French government in dealings with higher headquarters, and the other element for operational matters. I saw little conflict within this system. The Commanding Officer was Lieutenant Colonel Montclar, who had requested a reduction in rank from General in order to obtain this command. During World War II, he had commanded Free French Forces fighting alongside of US Army units in Italy. I particularly liked Lieutenant Colonel Krockbourne, the Deputy Commander. He had served 25 years in the Foreign Legion, was a very knowledgeable Infantry officer and a skillful, patient teacher.

I was welcomed into the battalion, quite probably because of my fluency in French. (I had grown up in pre World War II New England, where there were then 252 schools giving instruction all in French and over 100 French language newspapers. In fact, with the Military Academy being my first English speaking school experience, one of my biggest academic challenges at West Point, as an American citizen, was learning English!)

By now, the full force of the Chinese spring offensive was being felt all along the UN lines. The Dutch battalion was also attached to the 23rd Infantry Regiment.

During a major Chinese attack, a supporting artillery fire mission mistakenly landed on the Dutch Battalion Headquarters. In the confusion which followed, the French Battalion was moved from a division reserve position to fill the gap. Two French companies joined with the Dutch line units to blunt the penetration, while the two remaining French companies launched an attack against the flanks of the Chinese forces, to encircle and entrap Chinese forces in the penetration.

As the maneuvering French companies penetrated the Chinese columns to their front, the French were hit on their northern flank by a second, equally large Chinese force. It was by then determined that the two French companies were being pinched in between two Chinese Regiments. The two attacking French companies simply continued their attack, eventually closing on 23rd Infantry elements holding the western shoulder of the Chinese penetration, on the opposite side of the gap. As I recall the enemy order of battle figures, four Chinese divisions in column, with their regiments also in column, poured through that gap and pushed the UN forces back over 20 miles. When the lines stabilized (and prior to the subsequent UN counter offensive which eliminated the penetration), the combined US 23rd Infantry Regiment, Dutch Battalion and French Battalion casualties were in the high two thousands.

At one point during this extremely fluid situation an American three quarter-ton truck stopped and a young US corporal informed me that he was from the 23rd Infantry's 4.2 inch mortars. Now he and his crew were lost and alone and he did not know what to do. He had a mortar and ammunition in his truck. I told him the best thing for him to do was to look at the hills to our front and engage the Chinese he could see from right there. I ordered him to mount his mortar behind the truck where the ammunition would be easily available and commence firing. I acted as both FO and FDC although he could see the target as clearly as I could. After he ran out of ammunition, I told him to load up his mortar and crew, and pointed him south to where he could link up with other American units. I thanked him for his assistance.

Later, as I watched with Lieutenant Colonel Krockbourne as this battle ebbed and flowed, a Chinese sniper fired at us and the shot ricocheted off a Sherman tank behind us. He pointed out the sniper in a tree and I took the few steps to the tank. With the tank's exterior phone, I directed the tank commander's attention to the tree with the sniper's position therein. The turret rotated, the tube elevated slightly and the tree disappeared. Both the ability to direct supporting fires and confidence in that ability is very valuable in a rapidly developing combat situation.

Shortly thereafter, I was told by the French Battalion Commander that one of his rifle companies (which had occupied a blocking position in the initial fight), had been cut off and was now some 20 miles behind the enemy lines. He asked me if I would go rescue his company. What can one say, other than "Oui, mon Colonel." The battalion's officers, and I include myself in this statement (as I had been completely accepted into the unit and "awarded" one of their regimental crests which I wore on my uniform) as often as not would answer "Oui, mon General."

With a 1/4 ton jeep and driver, I crossed the lines and raced north. We hit a mine, the driver was killed and the jeep destroyed. Armed with the driver's rifle, I continued on foot, alone. When I could hear the sound of firing, well behind the Chinese lines, I knew I must be getting close. When I was near enough for them to hear me, I began to yell to them and they recognized me, then provided covering fire for the last portion of my journey to their position. Total strength of that rifle company, counting wounded, was 28 men. All the officer's were KIA and the only surviving NCO's were corporals.

I explained to the remaining NCO's that we must break out after dark, with all men carrying rifles only. Crew served weapons were to be field stripped and all their parts widely dispersed in the snow. Available ammunition was divided evenly, although we could not afford the risks of firing unless mandatory to survive. We would travel only at night, hide during the day and rely primarily on our bayonets as weapons. These NCO's proceeded very professionally with their tasks of preparing the men, destroying the crew served weapons, and redistributing all the ammunition, all the while they maintained the integrity of our defensive position and concealed breakout preparations from enemy observation.

When dark came, we feinted in one direction, broke out in another and even with some of our wounded on field expedient litters, we disappeared into the night. We were able to evade any contact with Chinese forces, travel clandestinely by night, and three days later we reached American lines with our small force intact. On one other occasion I was obliged to temporarily assume command of a French rifle company in combat due to the demise of all other officers. I was always impressed with the professionalism of the French NCO's. While I also have the greatest respect for my 2nd Platoon NCO's, I very much admire the manner in which the French Infantry units manage to grow their own NCO replacements from within, by means of the daily NCO school.

Perhaps this reflected the Foreign Legion influence of Lieutenant Colonel Krockbourne, since the NCO school is a strong tradition in the Foreign Legion. Every day, even in combat, those privates who have demonstrated the discipline, aptitude for Infantry service and potential to become NCO's were gathered for a lesson taught by a unit NCO "expert." Map reading, camouflage, automatic weapons employment, mortar gunnery, radio use and repair, demolitions, field sanitation and small unit tactics were among the subjects; the "students" practiced hands-on with all the equipment or weapons, and captured all the details in their small pocket notebooks because they knew they would be frequently questioned by the senior NCO's on the subject matter they had been taught. When, eventually, there was a unit NCO vacancy, that promotion went to their most qualified internal replacement.

In September 1951, I was asked by the battalion to go to the French consulate in Pusan to discuss some battalion problems, which I did. Prior to returning, however, I visited the Eighth Army Personnel Center, also in Pusan. Having been directed to the desk of a Lieutenant Colonel who dealt with officer assignments, I asked if he could give me any idea when I could be rotated home. His answer to my question was a question in return: "Who the hell are you?" I explained to him where I was assigned and how I got there, and was rather amazed to discover that apparently no one there was aware that US Liaison Officers were serving with most of the Allied Nation units. I was directed to return to my duty with the French battalion, and that I would be notified of any further developments. I found that when dealing with the Army Personnel System, a direct and determined approach will achieve the most successful results.

By the time I reached the battalion, a TWX was awaiting me with orders to return to Eighth Army Personnel Center for out processing and shipment home. While awaiting passage back to the United States, I was assigned to help train an Infantry company from Thailand. While I was involved in this training, a small "delegation" of three French officers came from the battalion and presented me with the Croix de Guerre (Cross of War] with palm. This is equal to our Distinguished Service Cross. I felt both proud and thankful—to have been able to serve and be recognized for my service to two Armies, to have survived this war, and to be going home. On my return to the United States, I was assigned to Fort Benning, Georgia—to attend the Infantry Officer's Basic Course.

******

I was assigned to "G" Company, 9th Infantry Regiment, 2nd Division on 29 August 1950. The 2nd Division bad been ordered to Korea from Fort Lewis, Washington, the post and unit I had selected in May as my first assignment.

The last major North Korean assault on the Pusan perimeter started on or about 26 August 1950. The 2nd Division was overrun. The 9th Infantry Regiment was particularly hard hit, with two battalions on line. The regiment's third battalion was securing a critical airfield and thus was not involved with this action. A Marine Brigade which had been withdrawn to prepare for the coming Inchon landings was hastily committed to restore this portion of the Pusan perimeter. Eighth Army had no other reserve; in 2nd Division, the only remaining reserve was the Division Band.

I met the Regimental Exec at the Regimental CP, and he simply assigned me to 2nd Battalion. A jeep took me to a Battalion outpost where the Battalion S-3 was running the battle, trying to retake certain key terrain. He pointed to a small group of houses almost totally destroyed by shell fire and told me "Take two cases of M-1 ball [ammunition] and join "G" Company there." The jeep was under direct fire on the way to the Company CP, where the First Sergeant thanked me for the ammunition and pointed to a hillside where he said I could find the Company Commander, First Lieutenant Muñoz On the hillside, I joined Lieutenant Muñoz who pointed to a group of soldiers and said "You have 2nd Platoon, go find Sergeant Kaufman." We were under North Korean artillery, mortar, automatic weapons and small arms fire all this time.

Now, six years earlier, I had turned 18 in August and enlisted in the US Army for Infantry duty. I did well enough in Basic Training to be promoted to Corporal upon completion. I had graduated from LaSalle Military Academy, an ROTC Honor Military School, and on the basis of this training I was sent directly to Fort Benning to attend Infantry Officer Candidate School, starting a class in October 1944. My classmates in OCS were almost all combat veteran NCO's from the Pacific Island campaigns, who had demonstrated such a high level of ability and potential that their unit commanders were willing to give up a valuable asset—a veteran, combat proven NCO small unit leader—so that the Army would gain an Officer leader. (Soldiers in Europe who demonstrated such capability and potential were sent to OCS at Fontainbleu, France.)

In about the 11th week of OCS I was injured (wounded?) by a grenade fragment during a village assault live fire combat exercise and that set me back about six weeks. Because of this setback, I graduated in early May 1945 and went to Camp Croft, South Carolina as a platoon leader, training officer *et.al.* The mission at Camp Croft was that of an IRTC [Infantry Replacement Training Center] receiving civilians and training combat ready replacements ready to board troop transport ships 16 weeks later. The Battalion Commanders and Company Commanders at Camp Croft were all combat veterans from all theaters of the war and were superb officers. We had twelve sergeants in my company, all combat veterans. It was here that I developed and confirmed an overriding respect for the ability and professionalism of Army Non-Commissioned Officers, further reinforcing the respect for NCO's that I had gained by training with and learning from those combat veterans who were my OCS classmates.

Through May, June, July and early August I taught and led a company through a complete IRTC cycle and in August was assigned as company commander to take the next cycle. Of course none of us knew anything at all about the Manhattan Project, and we all <u>knew</u> (not just expected) that we would soon join these Infantry replacements and all those veteran divisions coming back from Europe to stage for the ground invasion of Japan, and so there was a distinct sense of urgency and clear focus to the manner in which we approached our training duties. Then came the atomic bomb and Japan's surrender. We ran one more cycle and closed Camp Croft. In January, I went to Amherst College in preparation for my reporting to the Military

Academy on 4 July 1946. So as we return to the Pusan perimeter and my taking over 2nd Platoon of "G" Company, 9th Infantry, I was not a new shavetail 2nd Lieutenant, but I was a <u>replacement</u> officer.

Sergeant First Class Kaufman was running the battle in 2nd Platoon when I joined the unit. He was a World War II combat Infantry Platoon Sergeant, highly decorated. We got along famously. As noted, I had learned to rely on NCO's who, as my classmates, helped me through a very tough and competitive OCS program. I further had the experienced cadre at Camp Croft on whom I had relied for guidance and advice, so I deferred to Sergeant First Class Kaufman that day and the next several days and nights. In the combat which followed, 16 days and nights, we were constantly fighting. So in the formative days of first combat, I was fortunate to have Sergeant First Class Loren Kaufman and Sergeant Joe Barger with me.

Within about a week, most of the lost territory had been retaken and "G" Company was in fairly solid defensive positions. Because of our heavy casualties, our units were at that time assigned KATUSA's [Korean Augmentation to the US Army] as replacements. Our platoons were usually only eight or ten GI's including two sergeants and about 30 to 35 Koreans who had received little if any training and in many cases came to us not even knowing how to load their American rifles. Because of their limited training, many lacked the confidence to fully keep up with the platoon in difficult combat actions.

On the night of 5-6 September, 2nd Platoon was on a small hill about 3,000 yards from the main company position when that was overrun and we were directed to retake it. Moving through the darkness, Sergeant First Class Kaufman and I heard someone in a ravine below our route. My Platoon Sergeant moved toward them to determine who they were and discovered they were North Koreans. About ten of them came towards us and I bayoneted the first two. Behind me, the platoon scattered in the sudden confusion. I picked up a machine gun which had been dropped and fired down into the ravine. The next morning there were 22 dead enemy in that ravine.

As we pressed forward with our counterattack, I determined that a flanking movement would be our best chance. Sergeant First Class Kaufman, two squad leaders and I started our assault, but the platoon did not follow. We four charged that hill. We encountered a machine gun nest with five North Koreans—Sergeant First Class Kaufman shot two and bayoneted the remaining three. Moving up, I killed several— six or seven—in that area. By late morning, there were 122 dead North Koreans on that hill and the rest of the enemy fled the field. For his actions in this fight, Sergeant First Class Kaufman was recommended for the Medal of Honor. However, the actual award of his Medal of Honor was posthumous, as he was killed in action about six months later.

Due to casualties, I was reassigned to "F" Company which had lost all of its officers except for its company commander. When he was seriously wounded two days later, I became the Company Commander as we moved to cross the Naktong River on about 20 September, to take advantage of the Inchon Landing. We then pushed north rapidly, and were involved in extensive combat patrols of company size in pursuit of the fleeing North Korean units. This type of operation provided us with the opportunity to train our units and the Korean soldiers came along very quickly. By the time we went into North Korea, past Pyongyang and met the Chinese along the Chongchon River and fought at Kunu-ri, most of them gave a much better account of themselves in combat than had been the case along the Naktong and the Pusan perimeter.

In March 1951, after I was assigned as the Regimental S-2, I made it a point to intercept and interview all Koreans returning to our Regiment from the hospital after having been wounded. Under my staff supervision I had the standard Regimental Intelligence and Reconnaissance Platoon, made up of Americans of course. However, my confidence in the Koreans was such that I created a "special" additional I & R Platoon, made up of all Koreans selected from those whom I interviewed on their return to our unit from hospitalization. Staffed with Korean NCO's and led by two fine Korean officers, this special Korean I & R platoon built up to about 60 men and their combat performance was superb.

What about "words of wisdom?" I had, fortunately, been through the Fort Benning OCS which was intensely focused on leadership in Infantry combat in wartime. The same focus continued at the Military Academy as our Tactical Officers and instructors were all proven combat leaders and it rubbed off on the Corps of Cadets. I was as ready as one could get for the assignment and circumstances of the battlefield.

I had a strong moral and religious base from my family—a strong mother and father, and two tough brothers who were combat Infantrymen. With regard to words of guidance from my Company Commander, the first words I received from Lieutenant Muñoz after joining 2nd Platoon were "Take your platoon and take that hill." Which I did—with the utilization of all that I had learned in ROTC, OCS, at Camp Croft teaching IRTC and at the Military Academy. It was all there in the Field Manuals and in the lesson plans.

My tactical instructions to an new Infantry lieutenants are thus quite simple. **Do not ever "throw away the book."** Always stick to the basics, as taught by the Infantry School at Fort Benning. All of that information is built on a solid foundation of a historical data base created through blood and courage of countless battles. There is (or was when I was there) a sign at Fort Benning which stated something to this effect: "Campaigns and Battles are made up of hundreds and thousands of small unit actions and the Army which wins most of the small unit actions wins the war."

Learn what is in the basics and stick by the book. Stick to the nuts and bolts of how to organize and conduct a patrol, how to care for soldiers' feet, follow rules of field sanitation, use a map and compass, call for supporting fires, and how to lay out a defensive position with sectors of fire and FPL's [Final Protective Line, now termed Final Protective Fires, or FPF's], with range cards in the day time and aiming stakes to clearly identify at night each soldier's sector of fire and his part of the FPL. In the fighting in the central sector, after 2nd Division moved back onto the UN defensive lines around Wonju in 1951, we laid out our defensive positions exactly by the book. My soldiers knew how and why to use aiming stakes, and knew that I would check those aspects of our defensive preparations. Each soldier knew that he must use his aiming stakes to identify his portion of the FPL and kept firing that FPL even though he often could not see any enemy in between illuminating flares—and the Chinese stacked up literally hundreds of dead in front of one single machine gun whose gunner used his aiming stakes exactly as called for by the basics of Infantry combat.

I have always held the opinion—and expressed it often in many forums—that a West Point graduate is ready for any assignment and can meet circumstances and difficulties that might overwhelm others. The West Point graduate is part of the United States Army—an institution older than the Nation itself—an institution with a history of success unmatched by any other US institution. The Army's history is ample proof. The development and progress of the Army is probably not understood by others who have not lived with it. West Point is a very big part of the Army and of its record of success. I am certain the Military Academy will continue to provide graduates who are fully prepared for service as combat ready, innovative, competent officers who are technically and tactically proficient.

******

I was commissioned into the Infantry after dreaming of becoming a USAF fighter pilot. The Air Force Academy did not exist then. In my dreaming I could not visualize that cancer as a First Classman would negate passing a pilot's physical. So I did not pay attention during ground (Army) training as a cadet. This was immature on my part but true, and could be a lesson to others who might not get branch training before combat.

Had Ranger or similar training been available for our class it would have been most helpful in Korea. I was in "A" Company, 1st Battalion, 35th Infantry, 25th Division. We did not often say the "1st Battalion" part, since everyone knew which letter companies were in which battalion. I was there from August 1950 until January 1951. My Company Commander the entire time was Captain Sidney B. Berry. [Later as Brigadier General Berry he was Assistant Commandant of the Infantry School at Fort Benning; as Lieutenant General Berry he was Superintendent of the Military Academy.] He was an officer of extraordinary ability and unbounded courage. He was wounded 2 September, and in the hospital for about three weeks.

Reporting In Lieutenant King, the Acting Commander met me at the Battalion CP and drove back towards "A" Company in a jeep. The positions were located on the smallest, most constricted perimeter around Pusan. Eighth Army Commander, General Walker had decreed that there would be no retreat from these positions, that we must all hold no matter what. Before we reached the hill where my new unit was, Lieutenant King decided to stop so we could take a quick bath in a nearby creek. While in the creek, the North Koreans started shelling our unit and from where we were we could see one explosion throw what looked like thousands of pieces of OD green material into the air. Lieutenant King decided that there must have been a company formation to cause such a scene.

We rushed up the hill as two litter jeeps come down with wounded. Luckily there were only about four wounded; the "company formation" scenario turned out to be only a stack of summer weight sleeping bags which had just been received. We had two tanks on our position which often drew fire from the North Koreans who were using captured US 57 mm recoilless rifles. Did no damage to the tanks but made life miserable for the Infantry. Stay away from tanks or any other attractive target which will draw fire.

First Patrol After about a week on the hill, I was ordered to lead a night patrol to the enemy ridge to our front, about 1000 yards. The mission was to determine if the North Koreans were using a rail line to resupply their units. I was scared to death as I had never even been on a patrol, much less lead one. The rail line ran from the foot of our hill through the enemy ridge. In the matter of route planning, I decided that we would tip-toe on the railroad ties, because moving silently through the brush covered terrain was impossible. I can remember thinking that this was hardly the Fort Benning solution, but I also thought the North Koreans would think nobody was stupid enough to patrol along the tracks so they would not have any ambush there.

En route we heard movement about 30 yards to our left flank. Certainly it was a large enemy patrol, from the amount of noise. Everyone froze as I had instructed them and luckily, fire discipline prevailed, for we could see nothing. After what seemed an eternity—probably two to three minutes—the noise approached our position and turned out to be a loose, abandoned cow. Without further incident, but with our hearts pounding we reached the enemy ridge line. I stopped the patrol, went about 50 yards farther and was down on my hands and knees to put my ear to the tracks to listen for handcarts. Then all hell broke loose as our own artillery came whistling into our location. Luckily no one was hit and we returned to our lines at about daylight. The Battalion S-2, who had requested the patrol mission, did not bother to debrief us. I hope he was too busy getting chewed out for not notifying the artillery of our mission and route. Thanks to the US Air Force, I do not think the North Koreans were using the railroad.

Do not rely on others to coordinate anything for you—notify the artillery yourself of any patrol or detached element you have out. I should have talked to the artillery to arrange for supporting fires, which would have solved the problem.

The BAR Man We broke out of the Pusan perimeter in mid-September. Our first objective was the enemy ridge at which we had been staring for 20 plus days. In the approach, while attempting to talk on my radio, I could see bullets kicking up the dirt in a pattern rapidly approaching me. Seeing no enemy, I fatalistcally thought, "this is it." Then suddenly the bullets stopped about three yards from me as a BAR man to my left opened up on the enemy firing. He had seen the North Korean and literally stretched him out with a full 20 round magazine. I never learned that soldier's name, but he certainly saved my life that day.

Recognize that as "a leader" you are a prime target. When you have to use your radio or make a map check, try to seek concealment at least; cover would be better.

On military appearances Our company had a very unmilitary looking platoon leader who had a banjo butt and wore wire rimmed glasses. The first night on our objective beyond the Pusan perimeter, his platoon received the brunt of the North Korean counterattack. He inspired his men by moving from one position to the next, directing fire where it was most needed, even after being severely wounded. He and his platoon repulsed the counterattack with the loss of only one man while killing at least five enemy.

Personal, physical appearances have little to do with combat success. No one can see inside a man's heart.

North Korean Army breakup For three days we were against quite stiff resistance. Even their support troops, such as artillery units, stood their ground and slugged it out with our forces. We overran one direct fire artillery piece whose crew fought us just as if they had been Infantry. No retreat, no surrender, but fought till we killed them all. Then we had no more contact at all, as the enemy units seemed to have dissolved. We pursued but could not regain contact; we were part of a tank Infantry task force to push ahead to a link-up with 7th Division which had landed at Inchon. In our mad dash north, we cut loose from logistical support, and made the serious mistake of drinking local water—from rice paddies no less. We all suffered from severe diarrhea for at least the next three months. When winter came (and after we finally got our winter uniform issue), having to contend with diarrhea while wearing long-johns, OD wool trousers and field pants was a challenge.

Carry treated water any time you can. But always use the purification tablets if you are forced to rely on local water sources. Make certain every one of your soldiers has a bottle and a spare bottle of whatever tablets you are now issued for this purpose. There is seldom, if ever, time enough to boil your water for purification.

NCO support and professional knowledge After the link up with 7th Division, we were tasked to seek out North Korean units which had been bypassed and cut off south of the 4th Parallel. During this series of missions, we were based out of Taejon. Since I had received no Infantry training except for (what was now some two years past) familiarization demonstrations during West Point summer training, my lack of professional knowledge was obvious to all. First Sergeant McFarland, a fierce-looking Scotsman from Georgia took me under his wing and taught me basic Infantry tactics and weapons when we were not on patrol during this period.

It is your responsibility to know your craft. Do not try to bluff on any items of which you are not certain. Rather, seek and accept the assistance and instruction of your unit NCO's. They will go to great lengths in their efforts to help you learn, and will respect your honesty is seeking to learn.

Movement to Contact in North Korea As we crossed the 4th Parallel, the North Koreans kept withdrawing north just ahead of us. My platoon made no significant contact during this period. Unusual for a platoon leader, I do not remember being required to read a map in North Korea. We moved as a company and Captain Berry and his radio operator were always at the front. We did not have enough maps to go around, and I can remember looking at Captain Berry's outdated, inaccurate, Japanese surveyed, hachured map and wondering how anyone could navigate with such a poor map.

What I recall of significance in this period may seem minor. In South Korea, we were prohibited from killing any farm animals we might encounter as it was hoped the displaced farmers would come back onto their land soon. In North Korea, that restriction was removed and pigs or chickens were fair game. They were killed, butchered, cooked and eaten immediately, for a diet of only C-rations over several months made us crave fresh food. Corporal Blevins, a farm boy from West Virginia, usually did the butchering and cooking. He always presented me with the *piece de resistance*—the pig's testicles—for it was known that I had lost one of my own from cancer while a cadet. On one occasion while moving through an abandoned hamlet, a formation of five or six chickens, in column, were marching along parallel to our route of march. On a whim, I threw my trench knife at the lead bird from a range of about ten yards and speared it clean through the breast. We had a good meal that afternoon and all who observed this thought I must be a fantastic knife-thrower.

I could have conjured up no end of resentment over the pig nuts by taking it as disrespectful or, in today's buzz word, as "insensitive" to my medical condition. Instead, I took it good naturedly. I appreciated my troops looking after their lieutenant.

Chinese intervention The easy pace of limited contact and pleasant fall weather ended together when the Chinese and winter hit us full force a few days after

Thanksgiving. After a first fight in which one of our platoons was forced off their position and Captain Berry had to reform them as the counter attack force, our contact dwindled down to little or none. As other units around us were being hit extremely hard and being forced off their positions, and as Chinese units exploited gaps between units (we were spread rather thinly) and moved rapidly to our rear to attack artillery and supply positions, we were ordered to withdraw as part of the overall pullback of Eighth Army.

We had instances of units being separated in the dark and by use of multiple routes of withdrawal, including one time when I was concerned that one of my mortar squads could not be located overnight. (We were withdrawing cross country in a snow storm in the dark.) It had been with a rifle platoon which ended up on a different route than the company main body, but it was found the next morning on our next delay position.

In any fluid situation, it is difficult to keep track of detached elements. I searched for my mortar squad up until the last minute when I had to withdraw with the rest of my platoon and the company. I could only trust in the ability of my fellow platoon leader and my squad leader, as my major responsibility was to the remainder of my platoon.

As we continued south in good order, we were aware of other units in a less orderly condition. There were supporting units which abandoned their equipment in flight. In our situation, as we pulled back through a series of successive delay positions, we had almost unbelievable instances of several Chinese soldiers who surrendered to us as we were withdrawing. They were evidently dissatisfied with conditions in their army and had no fear of walking up to our positions with their hands up. We had no way of transporting them to POW collection points, so they joined us in our march south and willingly carried some of our equipment and supplies. Throughout the withdrawal, refugees were a serious problem. Fearing the Chinese and returning North Korean Army, and anxious to escape communism, thousands of civilians were moving south, blocking roads, and providing a means for civilian-clothed NKA troops to get to our rear.

Regimental Outpost Line Finally we reached the far bank of the Im Jin River, about 30 miles south of Seoul. "A" Company manned a three mile long regimental outpost line in front of our main defenses. We were right on the river, and our operations were severely hampered by the flood of refugees. At first they came over a railroad bridge which was still standing. After it was demolished by explosives, the refugees still came across the river on the ice. Because of our earlier experience with communist soldiers in civilian clothes mingling with refugees and attacking in our rear, we were ordered not to let refugees pass through our lines; they stacked up by hundreds in front of our outpost line.

Most refugees were women and children and old men. As their crying, protesting and pleading grew louder, the condition of the refugees became a terrible morale problem for us. We hated to see human beings suffer as they did. Some attempted to sneak through our lines at night, so great was their fear of the communists and great their desire to reach safety in the south. Some tripped our anti-personnel mines and were killed or injured. The sight of wounded women and children was demoralizing to us as we attempted their rescue and evacuation by field ambulance.

One day a US Brigadier General visited the demolished bridge site. He was the only General Officer I saw in Korea. I explained to him the refugee situation and the resulting morale problem among our soldiers. I recommended to him that we should allow the refugees to pass through our lines and let someone else screen them in our rear. I believe it was the next day that we received word to let the refugees pass through our lines. It was a great relief to all of us.

Do not be reluctant to approach senior officers to inform them of matters which have an adverse impact on your soldiers. When you inform them of a problem, be prepared to provide a recommendation also.

Evacuation to Walter Reed Sometime after Christmas, I went to the battalion aid station to have an opening in my cancer operation incision cleaned and dressed. The incision had never closed since the operation at Walter Reed in February 1950, about four months before graduation. The company aid men had been cleaning and dressing it heretofore, but the smell and amount of putrid discharge were increasing due to our continual living in the dirt. The medics immediately air-evacuated me to Tokyo General Hospital, where I was told I would be sent on to Walter Reed. There I was operated on for infections throughout my stomach, but luckily there was no recurrence of cancer.

Final observations Having led a relatively privileged and sheltered life as an Army Brat and cadet, I was impressed with the loyalty and the dedication of the underprivileged enlisted men in "A" Company. Most were from the south, from Appalachia and Hawaii. I do not remember a single act of cowardice or desertion. Much of this can be attributed to the training in Japan and the leadership of Company Commanders both in Japan and Korea. I witnessed this same dedication of enlisted men in Vietnam, despite many news stories and TV coverage of "bad discipline." In research for a paper I was writing at the Army War College, I discovered that the "bad" statistics from Vietnam, at the height of that war's unpopularity, just equaled those same type of statistical indicators from World War II.

I believe that our politicians and other leaders—such as the presidents of top universities—grossly underestimate and do not really appreciate the dedication of our enlisted soldiers, especially the Infantrymen. If this dedication was accurately and appropriately recognized, combat pay for the Infantryman would be greater than that of other non-Infantry soldiers and all the Ivy League universities would offer ROTC largely dedicated to the Infantry. This would put us more in line with the priority which the British and Germans give their Infantry, in recognition of their greater responsibilities and sacrifices in combat.

******

In trying to capture any such first experience in combat, one is reminded of many references to the randomness of war. First there is which unit will you join? Then, over the geographic sweep of the battlefield and based on strategy of US higher commanders, where will that unit be sent? Finally, if your unit is attacking, where will enemy commanders place their emphasis for a determined last ditch defense, or only on trading space for time in a planned withdrawal? If your unit is in the defense, where will the enemy make their main attack, or where will it be only a supporting attack or even just a feint? Virtually any one of the accounts provided from the Class of 1950, from the Naktong to the Yalu or the Chongchon could have easily happened to any one of the other units and thus to one of the other officers providing their version of "lessons learned." The fact is that each and every Infantry lieutenant who is *en route* to an active combat theater has, at the onset, the same mathematical chance as any other lieutenant of being in those biggest battles which will someday fill the history books.

In Korea, Chinese divisions were "only" 10,000 soldiers, compared against 13,000 to 15,000 for a US division. The difference was mainly in logistical units, which translates primarily into long term staying power. But at the front line, and for the duration of a given attack, the Chinese battalion had three rifle companies of 120 to 150 soldiers plus a heavy weapons company with mortars, recoilless rifles and extra machine guns. Three regiments of three battalions each—all with combat experience in the early stages of the war—even though they were in that "smaller" division, they were tactically our equal in any particular battle. And in that first year, there were some big ones.

You do the math. Two Chinese divisions against the 8th Cav in that first attack at Unsan. Multiple Chinese divisions on a six mile ambush zone that chewed up 2nd Division at Kunu-ri. Three enemy divisions in one attack against that part of the 7th Division with the Marines at Chosen Reservoir. Other attacks made by entire divisions or multiple divisions against one unit, or along the boundary between two adjacent units. Any one of the lieutenants in another unit that was not hit too hard, could just as easily have been in the thick of any one of the biggest battles against such massive numbers of Chinese troops. Those massive numbers are why Korea's first year was so difficult for US units.

In any one of these big fights it soon became a matter of six or seven battalions against one battalion, as recorded on some higher headquarters Enemy Situation

Map. But at the front, far removed from the grease pencil notations on any map, it was ten or twelve companies crashing against one company, with four or five of those companies focused against only one platoon, first overwhelming that one small element—then moving on to concentrate similar massive force against the next position, now exposed to attack from its flanks and rear.

In reality, the Cav battalions at Unsan, the Marines and 7th Division at Chosen, or 2nd Division at Kunu-ri presented a target little or no different from what the French and Indians found with General Braddock's long column strung out through the woods, the Zulu impis at Rourke's Drift or Isandhlwana, the Sioux and Northern Cheyenne at the Little Big Horn, Santa Ana's regulars at the Alamo, or the Germans attacking the British 1st Airborne Division at Arnheim. Unless defenders are trained, organized, deployed and supplied for long-term sustained mutual support, the continuous crush of massive attacking forces against one small defending unit at a time will eventually prevail.

Positions must be sited to provide mutually supporting fires, with your soldiers organized, trained and adequately supplied for long-term sustained fires—across the width of your defensive sector, in depth within your sector and over the duration of the battle. Duration means in the sense of always having the majority of your unit firing or ready to fire while only one segment reloads (something on the order of two thirds firing with just one third reloading at any given time).

Extra ammunition and grenades must be in possession of the soldiers in the foxholes doing the fighting, with all the protective packaging removed so the ammo is ready for immediate use. Ammunition in some rear supply point—even if it is just back at the company CP, much less at battalion S-4, or even ammunition in the front line positions but still sealed up tightly against the weather—is essentially useless to troops under massive attack on the firing line. Soldiers must be both skilled and practiced at fire discipline, and be alert to your signals as to whether they should be providing suppressive fires against any likely enemy locations, or firing only at enemy soldiers clearly visible as targets, or firing their assigned portion of the unit's FPL [now final protective fires]. They must have teamwork developed and honed from extensive practice that allows them to stagger their periods of firing and reloading for a continuous, effective curtain of defensive fires, giving your enemy no possible respite during which to fire or to advance unopposed.

Your platoon's main firepower, the machine guns, must be sited to cover your sector and protect your platoon—but some of your riflemen's positions must be sited to protect your machine gun positions. Other rifle positions must be layered in depth, higher on the hill and a little to the rear, to cover those forwardmost positions protecting your machine guns—always the enemy's primary target. You must keep the enemy well out of hand grenade range of your machine guns. Those machine gun positions must be dug into the folds of the earth—whether natural or man-made with berms—to protect them against longer range direct fires from enemy recoilless rifles (or now closer in attacks by the enemy's small anti-tank rocket grenades and rocket launchers, just as you would plan to use our LAW as your own bunker-busting weapon of choice).

Few defensive sectors will have such ideal terrain that you can cover your assigned front from only the primary positions. Most sectors will also require selection and construction of supplementary positions for more complete coverage. Then you must plan for and construct alternate positions to defend against an enemy approach from other than the expected direction. These are the positions which will allow you to refuse a flank against an enemy penetration through an adjacent unit.

Additional alternate positions in your rear allow you to convert your linear defense into a perimeter, if the enemy threatens to surround your platoon—but you will have to plan and rehearse the sequence and the signals for withdrawing your outer flanking positions. Their withdrawal will have to be covered by fire from soldiers closer to your center, whom you have already pulled off line to provide covering fire in this new direction from positions for that purpose. Your plans, signals and rehearsals must include thinning your lines to occupy and fight from those flank and rear positions for an all-around defense.

Your supporting mortar and artillery fires must be carefully planned and then all pre-registered with pin-point precision accuracy—ready not only to protect a threatened sector, but also ready to be shifted and moved to a different sector as required, in an absolute minimum of time and with an equal minimum of communication needed. Consider code words for multiple fires to block enemy access from a specific direction. [For an example of one version of rapidly shifting artillery support, read "The Incredible Patrol" in the second portion of SLA Marshall's *Pork Chop Hill*, which he devotes to analysis of six separate combat patrol actions. Develop such a plan for your unit with your FO.]

Look at the "normal" or "usual" amount of ammunition and grenades your soldiers are issued, and work it out with the stubby pencil drill; determine just how long that amount of ammunition will provide sustained fires, and how many times each squad leader could launch a volley of grenades against a sudden onslaught of the enemy. How many magazines are your men issued, and how long will those last in a serious fight? How long before that defensive well runs dry?

How much more will be needed for an all-out attack that starts at oh-dark thirty and keeps on without slackening for the rest of the night? Increase your platoon's stockpile of munitions and grenades accordingly, even though the Ammunition Sergeant and the Battalion S-4 would rather keep that ammunition on trucks in easily-accounted-for, still depot sealed weather-tight cases. They may well complain to the Battalion Exec when they have to come pick up that "excess" ammo from your platoon position because the mission has changed to an attack—and you can't possibly carry it all on your backs. Stick to your guns. Insist that the supply system must support your defensive mission, rather than letting "staff convenience" drive the tactical train.

But all of this will not happen simply because you may have read about it here—or thought about it at Fort Benning or during some approach march or preparation for a relief-in-place. It will only come to pass if <u>you will make it happen</u>, Lieutenant, by careful planning and skillful terrain analysis; by explaining to your NCO's what your tactical deployments will accomplish, and by them explaining it to their soldiers; by your platoon rehearsing the signals for type of fires and sequence reloading and the shift to alternate positions; by cross-training other soldiers to take over from a machine gunner or an automatic rifleman killed or wounded, and by cross-training of all your NCO's to call for supporting fires should you or your Forward Observer be knocked out, or your radios destroyed by incoming.

It is up to <u>you</u> to put this all together, each time and every time (even in an assembly area when you are in reserve) with persistence and tenacity—because the enemy's big attack may not come right away or even against the first many positions you occupy, or first many nights or weeks you prepare such a strong defense. The temptation to complacency will be quite powerfully seductive when your troops are dead tired, the weather is on the far side of miserable, and you have insisted on such elaborate defensive preparations many times before—but the enemy attack you prepared your platoon to face has not yet come as you expected. Everyone knows the story about the little boy who cried wolf, but you must still provide your platoon with that quality of dedicated, determined and decisive leadership which results in a cohesive, well-knit defensive capability—on each and every hill, each and every position, each and every night.

******

As a Platoon Leader in the 15th Infantry I had six Americans and 66 KATUSA's. They had been rounded up off of the street and came to us with essentially no military training. With no interpreter and none of us who spoke the other's language, it was a matter of hand and arm signals. I would point to an object and then point to them to get them to pick it up. I don't know where SLA Marshall came up with his conclusion that soldiers will not fire their weapons in combat. Both my American and KATUSA soldiers would willingly fire when we were attacked. In fact, they were almost too willing to engage. If there was movement or noise to their front, they would fire—but so would others on their flanks. I would have to try and listen to determine if we were taking any incoming fire. If not, I had to get my soldiers to cease fire, so I could conserve ammunition.

About SLA Marshall. His writings could only be as accurate as the information he was given by the soldiers, and the American GI is certainly not above telling a war story or two. After I was wounded and hospitalized, I had been released to return to my unit from the hospital at ASCOM City. I was given the detail of rounding up a bunch of soldiers from another division whom Marshall wanted to interview about a particular battle involving their division. So I rounded up a bunch of veterans from among the more lightly wounded of that unit's personnel in the hospital and assembled them in a large room to talk to BG Marshall. They blew a bunch of smoke and told him some wild war stories; he swallowed it all—hook, line and sinker.

On the subject of "lessons learned" one obvious fact presents itself. In order to learn the lesson, one must first survive the incident in order to transform what happened into a lesson to be learned. For example: 'drop to the ground when you hear incoming' is a lesson survivors of incoming learn in one lesson. I certainly hope this effort by our classmates will help our new Infantry lieutenants to learn our lessons before they face such a survival learning situation themselves.

Do Not Skyline Yourself My platoon and the 3rd platoon of Able Company of the 15th Infantry under my command were ordered to move down a ridge line and clean out the enemy on the right flank of the Third Battalion of the 15th Infantry in February 1951. As we got close to the Third Battalion, we could see Chinese troops running down the hill on the north side of the Third Battalion objective about 300+ yards away. To speed them up I got all the sharp shooters in our two platoons to start firing at the Chinese from the prone position for the greater accuracy required at that range. My runner and I stood behind them directing fire. It was like shooting at fish in the bottom of a barrel. We tried to make the enemy think that a whole battalion was moving in on them—not just two platoons.

The enemy soon located us and returned fire with a vengeance. I am sure they spotted me and my runner since they zeroed in on the two of us right away and wounded my runner with a burst of machine gun fire. Luckily, my runner's wounds were superficial and he returned to the Company in a few weeks. What I failed to consider is that no one will sit still while being fired at. As a minimum they will shoot back or worse, they will bring in artillery fire on top of you. The lesson here is do not let the enemy know where you are by sky lining yourself on a ridge.

Avoiding an ambush In North Korea in 1950, my company was caught in an ambush which should never have happened. Other units in our Battalion had been ambushed in the same location where we were hit. But we were too anxious to keep moving so we took a short cut and got into the middle of the previously known ambush site before sending two platoons up the two hills which overlooked the ambush site. As the two platoons moved up the hills overlooking the site, the Company Commander assembled the weapons platoon leader and the reserve platoon leader (me). Just as we arrived at the Company Commanders' position, the ambush was sprung!

The results were disastrous. The weapons platoon leader could not get to his mortars nor could I get to my platoon to influence the action. The other two platoons rushed down the two hills is disarray and were basically ineffective as units. They did return fire as did everyone else. Casualties were high and the operation was not a success. After dark we were able to disengage and return to our Battalion perimeter. The lesson to be learned is to never try and clear an ambush site the way it is described above. Secure the site by securing the hills around it first; then and only then go into the ambush site itself.

******

First, keep in mind that about 35% of the Class of 1950 went to Korea in the summer of that year [1950]. The majority of the class went to Europe or stateside assignments which later provided the opportunity for branch basic courses before going to Korea, if they went at all. However, the most important factor was that all of us who were rushed into the fray (July and August of '50) had never attended a basic branch course. Earlier, post-war classes ('46 through '49) had done so—we did not. Clearly we had been instructed in battlefield tactics while Cadets but we were sorely deficient in the more mundane technical matters (maintenance of crew-served weapons, communications, logistics, etc.). In short, our on-the-job-training was a real problem, at first.

Also, many of us led platoons that were decidedly more Korean than American. My first rifle platoon consisted of six Yankees and 66 (!) South Koreans! (The highest ranking NCO was a buck sergeant.) In fact, from July through November of 1950, my regiment truly amounted to an Asian regiment. Fortunately, four of my soldiers spoke Japanese which, as you know, the ROK's understood as well. [Japanese was learned by the American soldiers while on occupation duty; and was learned by Koreans while their country was occupied as a protectorate by the Japanese in 1905 and formally annexed by Japan in 1910; Korea only regained its independence from Japan at the end of World War II.]

We suffered one other problem: the leadership of many senior officers was purely abysmal. Our first regimental commander was relieved from command the same day we '50-types arrived and joined the regiment. My battalion commander was a cowardly drunk, a liar and totally incompetent. He also was relieved from command, but only after causing considerable carnage. Looking back, I am convinced the Army failed us in that respect. We youngsters expected—indeed demanded—much better leadership than we got in those early weeks and months of the Korean War.

Now to us useful points:

Integrity As a leadership factor, nothing is more important to a troop leader or small unit commander. Almost without exception, units of my regiment eventually performed well in combat because the platoon and company officers were honest, reliable, committed professionals, dedicated to their jobs. They believed in themselves and in each other; and, most importantly, were able to convey, to inculcate that confidence into their subordinates. Especially from January '51, our platoons and companies excelled in all our operations. (One must note, though, that senior commanders of poor quality were gone from the scene by that time.)

As for '50, 1 have always felt that integrity was West Point's greatest "gift" to us all. We succeeded under the most stressful conditions because we trusted one another. To me, it is a point of pride that I never worked with a classmate who was other than honest and honorable in those early months of combat. We learned quickly and did our job with confidence because, to otherwise—to slough off or slack off—was unthinkable and dishonorable, resulting in failure and undue loss of lives.

Troop Leadership Any leader/commander must realize that "you fight the war with the troops at hand." Preparedness is vital. Slogans, stylized uniforms and morale-building programs are fine, perhaps necessary; but nothing beats well trained troops. That means drilling, training and conditioning at a constant pace. Soldiers must be ready, able and willing to fight. (Garrison duty in the Occupation forces—especially in Japan—had clearly neglected combat readiness, reflected in the "SNAFUed" days in that first summer in Korea.) [In his very thorough reference work on these early days of the Korean War entitled *Fighting on the Brink: Defense of the Pusan Perimeter*, Brigadier General Uzal W. Ent describes in detail the difficult conditions of service for the occupation forces stationed in Japan and Okinawa, including understrength units, garrison duties such as interior guard, plus the required focus on assigned duties of governing and rebuilding—not significantly different from today's "nation building" and peace keeping missions—which left little time for tactical training in the years immediately prior to 1950. General Ent also confirms and documents the relief of numerous field grade commanders in the summer/fall 1950.]

To a fair degree, intense training also serves to keep troops overworked, a factor which, in itself, builds morale and self-confidence. Troop units which are overworked—even in the dullest days of combat—simply have no time to get out of shape, to become bored, or to feel sorry for themselves.

Therefore, a leader/commander must be <u>demanding</u> but fair. In the "old" days we used to say: "You can always start off as an SOB, and become a nice guy later; but you can't do it in reverse." In World War II, Patton understood that better than anyone.

Troop welfare other than training is important, though. Leaders must fight <u>for</u> their men. Soldiers, by definition, are individuals with all the normal human frailties, needs and desires. In my time that meant getting to know all my men personally, their names, their backgrounds, their strengths and weaknesses. Again as per Patton: "You're not here to die for your country; you're here to make the other poor SOB die for <u>his</u> country."

Courage This point may seem superfluous to a West Pointer. However, no one really knows his breaking point until he meets the ultimate test. Two things always served me well under fire: the realization that fear is normal; and, my obligation(s) to my men.

The points are interwoven, in that planning for an attack always found me preoccupied with the possibility of overlooking some detail which could result in the deaths of my men. Naturally, being human included concern about my own demise as well. But, this all boiled down to ensuring <u>success</u> at the <u>lowest risk</u>. In other words, get the job done, but plan it well. Don't leave things to chance, and don't "play it by ear," or "wing it."

A final observation: Field Marshall Sir William Slim (China, Burma, India Theater, World War II) commented: "I have known men who were very brave, yet had no integrity; but I have never met a man of integrity who was not very brave, as well." Therein lies another "vote" for Integrity, West Point's gift to us all.

******

Looking through odds and ends of my files I came across a photo, not very sharp and clear because I took it with a miniature camera. Taken just as our troop transport pulled into Pusan Harbor on 1 September 1950, it shows five of our classmates, and vividly illustrates the impact of the war on the class of '50, particularly on those of us in the first wave of infantry graduates to arrive in the front lines. Over the next several months all six of us were wounded—the five in the photo and myself— one of them mortally so, who died in a hospital in Japan, plus one KIA in an action for which he won the Distinguished Service Cross. Another in the photo also won a Distinguished Service Cross, and one was captured at Kunu-ri when the Chinese Communist ambush destroyed almost a third of 2nd Division in November of that first year. He spent almost three years as a POW.

Another classmate in the Division was wounded but did not ever receive the Purple Heart. His Company Commander told him he was lucky to have gotten a "million dollar wound," the kind that meant evacuation to the United States and safety. But it was too dangerous to leave his platoon position and leave his platoon without a Platoon Leader to even go to the battalion aid station for treatment (and to get the paperwork started for the Purple Heart). So he just stayed on position, and stayed in the fight. He let his platoon medic treat the wound and change the bandages periodically and finished his full tour.

Pusan was a disappointment, low and squalid. Docking was slow, with no apparent sense of urgency aboard ship or ashore. Signs on archways greeted us as "Righteous UN Soldiers." The train which awaited us was only an ancient steam engine, five empty flat cars and two passenger cars which were little more than boxcars with windows. Rows of wooden seats and nothing else. No latrines, but in one corner of each car had been cut a hole in the wooden floor, which obviously sufficed, based on stains, debris and smell. The trip forward to 2nd Division at Miryang was at a speed which never seemed to exceed that of a brisk walk, except for the frequent halts and other delays. We heard firing, and saw Navy Corsairs zoom low overhead. After one series of halts and delays, a shot up steam engine, still smoking, was towed back in direction of Pusan, with its engineer's dead body dangling half out of the cab window. The Navy Corsairs had mistakenly shot up one of our own trains, which could have just as easily been the one on which we were riding towards the front, having never yet even heard the sounds of enemy gunfire. War includes much random chance.

The journey to our eventual first units of assignment was agonizingly slow, with delays of enemy roadblocks to be cleared between each headquarters and the next. These kept us overnight on occasions, two or three new lieutenants in a foxhole on the perimeter of that unit, but I was involved in no combat. Between battalion headquarters and my company there were no roads, so our jeep driver followed a ridge line which had been outposted and successfully defended the night before. On one high point there were the bodies of four or five enemy soldiers, but on another a squad outpost had been hit by at least a reinforced platoon of the enemy. They had not only held their ground, but had inflicted terrible damage on their attackers. There were the bodies of at least 25 enemy soldiers around the American squad's position and littering the slope below. The entire squad had obviously fought bravely but most of the enemy's casualties were apparently inflicted by a single sergeant with a jeep-mounted .50 caliber machine gun. The combination had been deadly. We continued on to the company position where I joined my first combat unit, Fox Company of the 38th Infantry.

At full strength, an Infantry company of that era had six officers and a little over 200 enlisted men. When my company arrived in Korea it had its full complement of men and equipment. As a result of its first week in combat, it had lost all of its officers and had its enlisted strength reduced to 89. All the others were either killed, wounded badly enough to require evacuation, or missing in action. The company had also lost its three 60mm mortars, three 75mm recoilless rifles, and two of its three machine guns.

When I joined the company with another lieutenant replacement, we were met by the new company commander Captain Nicholas Gombos who had been a battalion staff officer but had been transferred in only the day before, along with a First Lieutenant from Easy Company who had been sent over to Fox Company. The morning of our arrival Captain Gombos had led the company's successful attack to recapture Hill 115 from which the company had been forced the previous day. The men were still cleaning up the debris from the action and strengthening their positions. They all seemed to be in good spirits, something which, I think, had to be credited in large part to Captain Gombos. He always seemed to be bursting with enthusiasm and a lot of this rubbed off on the men. None of us can control what happens to us and around us; but as a leader, Lieutenent, you can and must control how you respond to those events—with enthusiasm and an infectious positive make-the-most-of-things attitude.

The first order of the day was reorganization. Since casualties from the first week in combat had decimated the original organization, the remaining men were consolidated into two rifle platoons and a headquarters section. Since both the other lieutenants were First Lieutenants with several years service, they were assigned a platoon. Although I was the junior lieutenant by far, I became the Company Executive Officer. This worked out well for all concerned. It put the more experienced lieutenants in direct charge of the troops and put me in a position to be of considerable assistance to Captain Gombos while gaining needed experience.

Our position was atop a broad, relatively flat topped hill and seemed almost perfectly sized for our understrength company. About 35 two-man foxholes made a circle about fifty yards in diameter, with the perimeter on the military crest of the hill. About ten yards inside the circle was the company CP but nothing else, which proved to be very fortunate. There was no shade on the hill, only bare ground, a few spare tufts of grass and two or three small bushes. Over the next couple of days we were under constant but ineffective enemy mortar fire. We could hear the distant "thunk" of the incoming mortar long enough in advance to get in our foxholes before impact. The enemy's point of vantage for adjusting their mortar fires let them observe that they were hitting inside our perimeter, on top of the hill, but they could not determine that the firing was totally ineffective on our empty hilltop.

My first night on the line, I volunteered to take the first watch in our CP foxhole with Captain Gombos and the artillery FO. Both men had been on their feet for the last 36 hours, and appreciated my offer. I resolved to stretch that first watch as far into the wee hours of the morning as I possibly could. Looking down the valley at night towards the Naktong was eerie. It was like looking into a vast amphitheater for which I had a box seat to see the fires of eleven burning hamlets, tracer fires for an action in Easy Company's sector off to our left and an occasional artillery flare. I caught myself starting to doze off around 0200 and awakened the FO to take over the watch. Better to admit that I was tired, than take a chance on falling asleep by pushing beyond my limit. Both Captain Gombos and the FO got all but two hours of an entire night's sleep, and I could make do on only four hours.

Over the next days, the absence of trees on our hilltop exposed us to getting baked for a while by the sun, in between the rain storms. But the barren hill protected us from tree bursts on the incoming mortar fire which would have been very deadly. I learned to take the long way around the perimeter rather than trying to shortcut across the hilltop in between enemy mortar salvos, since I was told by Captain Gombos that discretion is the better part of valor.

I also learned another valuable lesson during one of those frequent rains. Our ponchos were not much help, since they would keep the rain off, but in the high humidity, they were like a steam bath inside. More trouble than they were worth, it was easier to just get soaked, which everybody did. Captain Gombos taught me that "A good officer is never cold, wet or hungry." We were both soaked and shivering at the time, but he spoke the words sincerely. He was saying that a good officer knows how to contend with the elements and provide for his men and for himself, but even if conditions keep him from adequately doing this, he still does not let that personal discomfort affect the manner in which he carries out his duties. I have always remembered that profound bit of advice which so succinctly, yet completely captures the nature of duty first, no matter what the conditions or personal discomfort.

Our artillery FO procured a BC (battery commander's) scope and was finally able to locate the enemy mortar positions, and after what seemed an interminably long time of enemy mortar fire without pause, and the FO ad adjusting our own guns, he put a first adjusting salvo directly on the enemy positions. We could hear the distant screams, and after a second salvo, and a third, we were no longer bothered by the mortars. I got to look through the BC scope on the last salvo and as it hit I thought I could see arms and legs flying through the air. I resolved to learn as much about adjusting artillery fire as I could, and would certainly recommend that same approach to any new Infantry lieutenant.

To improve our position, we were issued concertina barbed wire and I was tasked to install it. Although I had limited training in constructing double-apron barbed wire fences, I had no experience with concertina although the task seemed simple enough. But bouncing the rolls open into the characteristic concertina as dark approached on a wet hillside in combat proved to be a little more complex. With the rolls spread out and staked down it appeared we were making good progress when one of the end section anchor stakes pulled out of the water soaked ground and that section began to roll downhill. That put additional stress on stakes securing the next section, which pulled out and allowed that section to roll, putting too much stress on the stakes of the next, and so on. We watched in helpless dismay and, for myself, embarrassment. Fortunate for us, the slope was not too steep, and there were some bushes a short ways downhill that stopped the runaway. I decided to stake it more securely where it had stopped, and just leave it there. I also learned a valuable lesson about the limited holding power of fencing stakes in saturated soil.

When we were relieved on that position for a night withdrawal, Captain Gombos put me in charge of the movement. After the incoming unit's commander had been fully briefed on our position and situation, our organization for the departure was simple. One rifle platoon led out, followed by the headquarters section then the other platoon. It started to rain as we pulled off the hill. We initially followed the same ridge line over which I had joined Fox Company. The rain, mud and darkness made for difficult going. We all carried heavy individual loads, making it difficult to maintain our footing and balance, but the biggest problem was the vehicles. They actually had to be man-handled, by four men on each side of the two jeeps and six men on each side of the three-quarter ton. When the ridge line trail finally became a primitive road, footing was easier for the men, but the march was more dangerous for those trying to keep vehicles out of the ditches on either side of the one lane ox cart track. The exertion of pushing vehicles out of the ditch, as well as the danger of getting injured required that I rotate all the men in our company through the assignment to vehicle escort duty.

As we finally moved about two miles on the cart track and then onto the MSR [main supply route] which was a relatively good gravel road, the travel became easier and we could move out at a brisker pace. Far enough from the enemy lines to turn on black-out lights, I sent the vehicles on ahead to our assembly area. Although we had no maps at all, I frequently checked with Captain Gombos to verify our direction of march and for any additional instructions he might have. For the first months of the war, maps were always in very short supply; even those we did have were old black and white Japanese maps, sometimes with a limited purple overprint in English. But map or no, Captain Gombos knew where we were going and kept us pressing ahead. By the time I arrived with the foot troops at our assembly area, it had been all laid out and we bedded down for what was left of the night.

Daylight and breakfast were followed by our new mission on a blocking position which was tactically rather quiet. One platoon position was sited to control a small strewn bed through which the enemy continually attempted to infiltrate, with the results that two or three of them were killed every night for the week we were there. The other platoon and the CP position had no enemy activity after we moved into position. On the approach march however, I was marching with the machine gun crew when the sergeant ahead of me suddenly threw down his load of machine gun ammunition and started rapidly firing his M-1 into the bushes. The action was over before the rest of us knew what was happening. The sergeant had not seen the enemy—he had smelled them. Their distinctive diet gave them a very strong odor. Sure enough, a search of the bushes turned up two dead North Korean soldiers, waiting in ambush along that path. When one has been away from civilization in the field for a few weeks, any sort of different smell is quite easily detected.

The rains continued and filled our foxholes. I learned how to sleep high and dry in all but the most heavy rains by the use of a drain sump in my foxhole and by piling up a thick layer of reeds which I gathered from a nearby stream bed and placed on the floor of my position. When I rolled over or moved about they were very noisy which was of no consequence during the day but an embarrassment at night. But I was dry. My other experience in field fortifications was somewhat more involved. Captain Gombos decided to upgrade the CP foxhole into a first class bunker, complete with overhead cover.

I gathered a few men from the rifle platoon which shared our knoll position and with the men from headquarters section began the task. One of the things I had *not* been taught at the Military Academy was how to construct a bunker. I had been schooled in how to construct a rather demanding plate girder bridge from scratch, but not a simple bunker. There was the further problem of tools. We had a couple of shovels and an axe from the company vehicles. The men had their entrenching tools. These were of little help in the slate outcroppings which lay just beneath the topsoil.

Some men filled our few available sandbags from the sandbars alongside the stream, and others tried to find suitable beams from among the burned out houses nearby. The rest struggled to enlarge and deepen the existing CP foxhole. Dug into the reverse slope of our knoll, the back, or inner wall was actually the remaining bank of the hill as we progressed with our digging. The front, or outer wall, we had to construct with rocks, dirt and a varied assortment of partially burned planks which the timber party was able to locate. We even incorporated a rather tall and very sturdy chest of drawers which had somehow escaped being burned in an otherwise destroyed house. Properly reinforced and laterally supported by available short beams, the chest of drawers was sited to open into the bunker and make the drawers available for storage in the CP. We eventually located enough beams for our overhead cover, and although it was no text book bunker example, it proved to be quite satisfactory. I would recommend that a new Infantry lieutenant learn the fundamentals of constructing field fortifications at the earliest possible opportunity but still be prepared to improvise with materials at hand.

The time on this position was a great learning experience for me; an opportunity to gain an understanding of the techniques and procedures that make a military unit more proficient. Being my first unit I had never been exposed to many of them. Of course I did have an awareness of some from tactics classes at the Military Academy, but those classes had covered a wide variety of topics and many types of units and there was not often any opportunity for hands-on practical application. Besides, at the time there was no sense of urgency and often I had not been very interested. Now there was a strong sense of urgency and I was very interested. Whether the subject was daily events in the rifle platoons, how to adjust artillery fire, organization of the the Division and its units or field communications, I soaked up ideas and information like a sponge from other officers or from our NCO's. My best source was Captain Gombos. Better than anyone else, he seemed to realize how unprepared I was. Even though he was a captain and my company commander, he was never condescending in his teachings.

As the middle of September approached, we knew we would be attacking out of the Naktong perimeter. On the afternoon when we were given our attack order, we also received our first replacements, young Koreans who had a 2nd Division shoulder patch sewn on their too big fatigues and only about three days of any type of military training before they joined us (speaking no English at all). Due to their smaller stature, they had all been issued the smaller semi-automatic carbine rather than the M-1 Garand rifles which our soldiers carried. Captain Gombos acted quickly and by taking six GI's from each of the two platoons he formed a third rifle platoon with me as the platoon leader. Then he spread all the Koreans equally among our three platoons and we were ready to move our to launch our attack. We were to seize the northernmost portion of Hill 209 and then attack along the ridgecrest to secure the rest of that position.

The objective was about three miles from our knoll position. We made our night approach march in the rain, and were in attack positions at the base of the hill by the next morning, right on schedule. Our promised air support did not materialize until much later in the day and the artillery preparation seemed skimpy. Nevertheless, Fox Company crossed the LD on time and began our attack. The other two platoons were to secure the initial objective with my platoon in reserve. Since I had no radio, I kept my platoon close enough that I could observe the action and be responsive to any orders from Captain Gombos. I had paired up my 12 Koreans one-for-one with my 12 GI's and had them organized in two squads with myself in the middle of the formation. By about 0900, the two leading platoons had secured the initial objective at the north end of the ridge and were beginning to attack south along its crest.

The attack along the ridge crest had scarcely gotten started before it bogged down. The two leading platoons had somehow allowed themselves to be "pinned down." Captain Gombos was determined to get them unpinned. There was an intermediated high point of ground about two hundred yards further up the ridge. He instructed me to take my platoon and seize it. I moved my platoon forward parallel to the ridge line but sufficiently downslope to be out of the enemy's sight and fire. When we were just beyond the positions of the "pinned down" platoons, I moved my platoon up and over the crest and formed a skirmish line which straddled the ridge. I was in the middle with half of my men on either side. We began our attack.

All of the fighting took place along the relatively broad crest of the ridge where there were a great number of enemy foxholes, many of which were occupied by enemy soldiers. But the enemy positions were situated to repel an attack up from the east side of the mountain, not along its crest. Attacking along the crest we just took out their positions, one at a time. I learned to always attack, if possible, from an unexpected direction, and of course, resolved to always prepare a defensive position for an attack from any direction! Only about five or six of us were directly involved in the fighting and I was right in the middle of it. I learned very quickly about the value of fire superiority and of fire discipline. We kept firing as we moved, firing at a slow but relatively constant rate as we moved forward at a waking pace. Our use of marching fire kept the enemy's heads down.

As we neared each foxhole, we would concentrate our fire on its lip until we could move up and look down into the hole and shoot the enemy who was usually huddled at the bottom. This marching fire was extremely effective and should be used whenever the amount of enemy fire allows our troops to advance. It would be criminal to stand up and walk your troops into an enemy position from which the enemy is still able to deliver fire on your unit. But if you can gain even an initial degree of fire superiority, marching fire will allow you to retain that critical advantage.

On one occasion, while I was changing magazines, an enemy poked his head up about ten yards away. I pointed at him and the south Korean who was closest to me fired at him until he ducked down out of view. I got the new magazine in place, moved to the hole and shot the North Korean cowering in the bottom. In those few minutes of action I personally killed three or four of the enemy and my men had killed a similar number of others, all in the same fashion. I decided to capture the next enemy, or at least give him a chance to surrender.

By this time we were on the platoon's objective, but there were still several enemy occupied foxholes. I approached the nearest one, firing my carbine. On reaching it I looked down and saw what seemed to be no more than a boy cringing in the bottom. His rifle was leaning harmlessly against the side of the hole. I stooped down and seized it and threw it aside. Next, I knelt on one knee, reached down and, grabbing him by the collar, hauled him bodily out of the hole. I was amazed at my physical strength, but the adrenaline was obviously pumping strongly. Once I got him out of the hole, I saw he had a hand grenade hooked on his belt. I was in the process of taking it away from him when one of my men yelled, "Look out, Lieutenant." Quickly I glanced at other nearby holes but could see no enemy. Suddenly my eyes fit on the problem. While I was capturing my prisoner, another enemy soldier in a nearby hole had thrown a hand grenade and it had landed about a yard away from my left foot. Just as I saw the grenade it exploded, jarring me up and spraying me with shrapnel. I was hit all over.

My legs, especially my left leg, got the larger pieces, but my left hand was hit by a mass of smaller pieces and immediately welled up in blood. Another hand grenade came at me but it missed and exploded harmlessly a few yards down slope. I did not know which hole it had come from but I knew we were on top of our objective. Using my prisoner as a makeshift crutch, I hobbled around and with my Platoon Sergeant's assistance, made certain our objective was secured. Then I sat down. My wounds were not life threatening, but they were hurtful and they were hurting. My war, for a time, would perhaps not be over, but would be delayed by a hospital stay.

My newly organized platoon did not have an assigned medic, but since our attack had "unpinned" the other two platoons, they resumed their attack along the ridge. As they passed through our position, a medic from another platoon bandaged my hand (the most obvious wound), and gave me a shot of morphine since there was no available manpower to carry wounded off the hill during our company's continuing attack. Someone found a litter for me to lie on, and covered me with a blanket as a precaution against shock. The promised air support arrived and as I drifted in and out of consciousness, I can remember that the Navy Corsairs were coming in so low over our hilltop on their attack runs that I could clearly see the pilots' faces.

The mopping up our objective continued under direction of my Platoon Sergeant. One unusual incident of which I was not aware at the time was explained to me later, after my return from the hospital. When my men discovered the foxhole occupied by the North Korean who had thrown the grenade at me, they found he was a diehard who refused to surrender. Someone pulled the pin on a grenade and flipped it into the hole. To everyone's surprise, it was flipped right back and there was a wild scramble as those present tried to take cover before it exploded. A second grenade brought the same results. Then two men threw grenades in at the same time. Both grenades came flying right back. Finally one of the men pulled the pin on a grenade and held it until the last possible moment before flipping it into the hole. This time it exploded before it could be hurled back. The men crept forward and found the body of a North Korean sergeant. They also discovered the secret of how he could flip the hand grenades back so quickly.

It was a two-man foxhole with a short tunnel cut into one of the walls. The Sergeant had firmly pegged two corners of a triangular piece of sturdy cloth to the side of the hole opposite the tunnel. He was in the tunnel with the third corner. Whenever a grenade landed on the cloth, he just gave his corner a sharp tug and the grenade was sent flying back out of the hole. He had further protected himself by propping a dead comrade at the mouth of the tunnel. It was rather ingenious, but it failed him in the end.

******

After graduation I was assigned to the 82nd Airbonne Division at Fort Bragg but volunteered for Korea the week I reported in. It took me three separate trips to the Pentagon until I finally got orders to Korea, arriving there four months after many of my classmates. I was assigned to the 5th Cavalry Regiment of the 1st Cav Division, and joined them at Chipyong-ni. Our Regimental Commander, Colonel Marcel Crombez personally made all platoon leader assignments, and he told me I would be given a different assignment in four or five months, if I survived. [Colonel Crombez and the entire regiment had been the relief force which fought through to relieve the 23rd Infantry Regiment at Chipyong-ni when it was cut off and surrounded there in February of 1951. That action, and Colonel Crombez' actions in relieving the 23rd Infantry is described in Russell Gugeler's *Combat Actions in Korea*.]

I remember climbing up the hill in several feet of snow to assume command of the Second Platoon of C Company. Although the Marines on our right flank to the east were under heavy Chinese attack, the 5th Cav positions were not hit very hard. After a few days, we moved several times, first to Hongchon and then near Chunchon. After about six weeks we were pulled back into reserve (and our first showers in all that time) but we did not stay in the rear for long. The retreat of the Sixth South ROK Division required that we occupy a blocking position in their rear. Our mission was to tie in with the Australian Battalion on our flank, but as my platoon moved into position along a creek bed it was almost nightfall and we discovered that the Australians had not been notified of our movement. Their supporting artillery battery of New Zealand 25 pounders began to shell us but I was able to get that fire turned off without any casualties in my platoon. I learned the importance of immediate coordination with units on my flank, and also of having the means to quickly communicate with those units by having their radio call signs and frequencies before moving into position.

Then the Chinese attack came. Their soldiers were infiltrating among the retreating South Koreans from the Sixth ROK. The difficult task of distinguishing between allied ROK soldiers retreating and enemy Chinese soldiers attacking was made considerably easier by the fact that over half of my platoon strength was made up of KATUSA's. After about two days of this type action, we were hurriedly moved into blocking positions just north of Seoul which was under attack and in danger of being captured again.

Unfortunately, the Commander of our battalion emplaced our units on the wrong ridge with the result that there was a huge gap between those elements of the 5th Cav and the regiment to our west. Seeing that gap, I took a squad patrol from my platoon and set out to try and make contact. When we reached the top of the hill (the one we were supposed to be defending), it was a weird situation to find all the prepared positions with signs indicating which position was to be occupied by a light machine gun. To my north, I could see a Chinese Communist battalion only about 400 yards away and moving up that hill in the attack. I immediately radioed for assistance. Our B Company was dispatched to join my squad by coming up the south side of the hill. We managed to hold off that attack until our reinforcements arrived and Seoul was saved. Our Battalion Commander was relieved.

In mid May, Colonel Crombez kept his promise about a different duty assignment, and I was sent to the Fifth Air Force. Close air support was then a mixture of newer jet aircraft and World War II vintage propeller driven fighter bombers. For controlling that close air support, dual seater T-6 trainer planes were fitted with wing stations for white phosphorus marking rockets and an extra fuel tank for an operating capability of four hour flights. The Air Force pilot would communicate with the fighter bombers and mark targets with his Willie Peter [now Whiskey Papa] rockets, while the aerial observer in the other seat maintained radio contact with the units we were supporting. The only major drawback, from my point of view, was that the extra fuel tank was directly under my seat in the aircraft! The squadron to which I was assigned flew out of Pyongtek. The T-6 was a very durable and rugged aircraft and although we flew so low that we took lots of hits from ground fire, few were shot down. I flew as an observer on 60 missions then was replaced by another observer and went back to the 5th Cav.

Upon my return, the Battalion Commander called me in and informed me that I would not be going back to C Company. While I was gone to Fifth Air Force, B Company had discovered a serious proble. The Third Platoon Leader was a homosexual and had hit on and tried to seduce several of his men, but had of course been turned down. Word of his actions had spread in the platoon but before it reached B Company, he had been assigned to take a combat patrol across the Imjin River. His platoon became engaged by the Chinese on the far side, and he ran off, leaving his platoon and four of them had been captured. I was to be assigned to replace him and rebuild the unit's damaged morale and esprit.

With the help of some excellent NCO's I was making good progress in restoration of the unit's capabilities, but realized they needed some combat success to bolster their confidence. From flying over the area as an observer, I felt I knew the terrain quite well, and so planned a patrol back across the Imjin to the area in which they had been abandoned by their previous lieutenant. As we were working our way up onto some high ground north of the river, I was informed by a spotter plane that a Chinese patrol was approaching that same hill from a different direction but was still much lower down the slopes. The tactical situation was almost tailor-made for a low risk high return confidence building opportunity.

I moved the platoon up onto the crest and got them all deployed before the Chinese patrol walked right into our sights and almost down our gun barrels. In the battle, I was slightly wounded by a grenade and had to resort to bayonet work when my carbine jammed, but we routed the Chinese patrol and even captured several. As a confidence building exercise it worked just as I had planned, although I had no way of knowing it would be as successful as it was. This action took place on 26 September and the platoon was well on the way to recovery as a fighting unit.

On the first of October, the battalion jumped off in the attack for a major UN offensive against the well dug in Chinese positions. Again, the area of our attack was one which I had overflown frequently, and knew quite well. (I would of course recommend to new Infantry lieutenants that they truly master map reading skills on the ground, but also suggest that if there is an opportunity for any aerial reconnaissance flights, that is an excellent opportunity to really get to know the terrain over which you will be operating.)

Over the next two weeks B Company along with the rest of our battalion pushed hard against the fortified Chinese positions. Their extensive dugout and tunnel complexes were very little affected by US artillery and air strikes. As a result, our progress was slow and our casualties were extensive. The Chinese mortars and artillery were particularly hard on us. My company lost all six of its officers killed or wounded, and our artillery FO, my classmate, who was also killed. I was wounded and evacuated on 17 October, and on 18 October the Company First Sergeant led the final assault with only 25 remaining B Company troopers to take our objective.

I was wounded in the right temple by mortar fragments from a Chinese 82mm round, which severed the optic nerve in my right eye, and was so deeply lodged in my head that the evacuation and intermediate medical facilities left it in place until I reached Walter Reed. Two months later, in December it was finally removed without further complications. Field hospital doctors had feared for damage to my other eye if they tried to remove it and so their efforts were mainly to stabilize me for the trip back to Japan and then on home. After those four months in the 82nd Airborne I was in really great physical condition from the daily Airborne PT and rigorous field training. Just before I departed for Korea, I had weighed 195 pounds—in October when I reached the field hospital, from the generally debilitating conditions of our continuous combat, from malaria and from a case of intestinal worms I had picked up, my weight was down to only 126 pounds.

While in Japan, one of my classmates who had done his time on the front lines and was then in a less exposed assignment came to visit me in the hospital. He had heard I was wounded but had no details of my injuries. Knowing that I was a sports fan, he took the effort to locate and obtain a bunch of sports magazines. He was very embarrassed to learn that I had lost one eye and the other was bandaged shut, and felt terrible about his "gift." His initial thoughts were that it would be perceived as extremely thoughtless, and that I would be even more depressed by the reminder that my eyesight was at risk. I was glad to reassure him that I appreciated his visit and his making the effort to dredge up the magazines. Other guys in the ward were glad to read them and even read them to me.

After having had to fight to get my orders to Korea in the first place, I then had to fight to stay in the Infantry, with only one good eye, one plastic eye and an extra hole in my head. We lost 41 of our classmates killed and had another 84 wounded during our baptism of fire, defending Korea against Communist aggression and preventing their enslavement. The price was high but we did not shirk our responsibilities.

The Korean Veterans Association invited a group of our classmates to the dedication ceremony for a monument we erected at the Korean Military Academy to our classmates who gave their lives in that war. On the memorial are two quotations, one from the poet A. E. Housman, and one from the 1950 *Howitzer*, written by the yearbook editor, who was himself killed in Korea. From Housman:

> Here dead we lie because we did not choose
> To live and shame the land from which we sprung.
> Life, to be sure, is nothing much to lose;
> But young men think it is, and we were young.

From our classmate, a noble statement of dedication, hauntingly prophetic:

> We pledge our hopes, our faith, our lives,
> That Freedom shall not die—
> We pray thy guidance, strength, and grace,
> Almighty God on High.

******

Summary

One cannot, without an intimidating risk of leaving out something critical, determine which items from all the previous comments should be considered "most important" for inclusion in a summary or conclusion. In Infantry combat, proper attention to many little details make up the elements of success and victory, while any one of those details—if ignored or neglected—can spell death and defeat. All are equally important. However, to summarize and to reinforce your understanding, below noted are combat essentials of particular significance to your future, repeated here again for emphasis.

. . . a new lieutenant going into combat should keep two things in mind . . . accomplish his mission and . . . take care of his men. Those are paramount. All other things flow from them.

Don't get familiar. You are not their buddy but their boss. Don't make the mistake of wanting to be liked. Reward when you can. Punish when you must . . . reasonable, fair, and consistent.

Be with your men most of the time. Don't go back to the company CP all the time when you are in defense. Stay with your guys. Be wet and cold with them. Share willingly in their hardships and their discomforts.

Set the example. Be the leader . . . Be sure you are proficient in your job and keep learning. Shave every day, if possible (and it usually is) . . . Dig your own hole. Look at every emplacement. Plan for contingencies and practice them if appropriate. Eat after all your men are served, so that if anyone goes hungry, it is you.

"A good officer is never cold, wet or hungry." We were both soaked and shivering at the time, but he spoke the words sincerely. He was saying that a good officer knows how to contend with the elements and provide for his men and for himself, but even if conditions keep him from adequately doing this, he still does not let that personal discomfort affect the manner in which he carries out his duties. I have always remembered that profound bit of advice which so succinctly, yet completely captures the nature of duty first, no matter what the conditions or personal discomfort.

Develop cohesion in your platoon. Men fight for the men beside them; the closer they feel to those men, the greater the sacrifices . . . made to keep the unit safe and the mission done. Give your men pride in their platoon and in themselves. Make them feel special . . . A sense of humor goes a long way when conditions are extreme. Trust the GI to provide it most of the time.

. . . every day in combat is a training day and every minute when the enemy is not shooting at you is an opportunity for training. Every leader ought to aim at finishing each day with his troops smarter, better, more proficient than they were at that day's dawning. Be certain to praise and encourage your soldiers and NCO's for what they are <u>doing right</u>, not just correct them for what is wrong. Include yourself on the roster of personnel to be trained—think about your day and what you have learned. Pat yourself on the back when you deserve it, and figure out what went wrong on the other situations—then learn from it all, so that you also become more proficient at your duties each day.

Before you ever consider your day done, ensure that your men are secure, essential combat needs attended to and all unit equipment is cleaned, inspected for functioning and serviceability, and ready for tomorrow—or for the middle of the night.

On the subject of "lessons learned" one obvious fact presents itself. In order to learn the lesson, one must first survive the incident in order to transform what happened into a lesson to be learned. For example: 'drop to the ground when you hear incoming' is a lesson survivors of incoming learn in one lesson. I certainly hope this effort by our classmates will help our new Infantry lieutenants to learn our lessons before they face such a survival learning situation themselves.

When you can, let all the men of your unit about to go into action understand, not only what your mission is, what you expect of them, and what orders they are to follow, but the reasons for your tactical decisions. Let them in on your thinking process. The reason for this is that things never will go exactly according to plan. American soldiers are great at getting the job done, when they understand what that job is; in the absence of orders, they will take initiative and surprise you by their success.

Know map reading, weapons employment and control of supporting fires. Earn the respect of your soldiers and your NCO's . . . Trust in and depend on your NCO's . . . . take out that first patrol mission assigned your platoon, with you as Patrol Leader, and get your butt up front, Lieutenant . . . Combat duty is physically demanding. Keep yourself and your troops in good shape.

I would of course recommend to new Infantry lieutenants that they truly master map reading skills on the ground, but also suggest that if there is an opportunity for any aerial reconnaissance flights, that is an excellent opportunity to really get to know the terrain over which you will be operating.

Ask each NCO leader before you leave his sector, "is there anything more I can do to help you or is there anything you need that I can help you get?" Let them all know that you are there to support them in every way you can . . . Important! Never forget that the average American GI is the greatest soldier in the world. He thinks for himself and will get the job done given the slightest chance. It has always been a privilege to lead him.

I would recommend that a new Infantry lieutenant learn the fundamentals of constructing field fortifications at the earliest possible opportunity but still be prepared to improvise with materials at hand.

Security! Even on mountainous defensive positions, don't let that warm sack be your grave. It makes no difference whether your sector is "quiet" or if there have been constant enemy probing attacks every night for many weeks, **security is your first and foremost responsibility**—you and your Platoon Sergeant must check the line **all night, every night** to insure that your platoon is on proper alert.

. . . For example: being very tired after a long day and they want to just rest and lay around—forcing them to dig in and put in their claymores and put in the machine guns properly and register [defensive] fires and all those kinds of things that are so necessary in the sense of military discipline but that our culture, and the way we live, does not lead us to want to do [enforce strict discipline and more hard physical labor on soldiers who are already very tired and want to rest]. . . . and

Although onerous and unpleasant, soldiers must dig in when not moving if . . . within enemy artillery or mortar range . . . and

Dig In !!! As soon as possible after reaching objective . . . and

Digging in is always important, but sometimes there are reasons that it just simply is not going to occur. [Position is solid rock, or ground is frozen rock solid.] But you must always fire in your Night Defensive Fires . . . . you should also "shoot a box" prior to darkness for any distant outpost in front of your position.

We really have not had to contend with enemy air since World War II. Consequently, our concealment has not been a top priority in training. We should be prepared for "what if?"

Accuracy of patrol reports can not be overemphasized. It is unfortunate that many others in our society—then and now—do not place the same value on honesty and accuracy as we do. You must make it clear to your subordinates from the very first that you expect and demand truthfulness from them, and enforce those standards of accuracy in reporting. Communicate with all your men, listen to their concerns and level with them about the tactical situation . . . . This works both ways, as they may reveal information of which you are not aware but need to know.

Integrity As a leadership factor, nothing is more important to a troop leader or small unit commander. Almost without exception, units of my regiment eventually performed well in combat because the platoon and company officers were honest, reliable, committed professionals, dedicated to their jobs . . . . As for '50, 1 have always felt that integrity was West Point's greatest "gift" to us all. We succeeded under the most stressful conditions because we trusted one another.

There is a very real chance that . . . conflict will result in death. It is essential to rationalize this possibility—to ask the question of oneself "Am I willing to give my life for these soldiers who depend on me to lead them into . . . combat?" The answer for any small unit leader . . . simply must be "Yes!" Any other answer would be unthinkable. But not every combat death is heroic; however, every one is tragic. Great moral support and comfort can be derived from a faith in the Almighty, a sense of "not my will but Thy will be done." So, this heartfelt bit of advice:

Believe in something greater than yourself. Don't be ashamed. There really is a fate worse than death—a death without the faith that something better lies ahead.

. . . I notice on . . . TV that both the former Chairman of the Joint Chiefs and . . . current Army Chief of Staff were both in attendance at a recent national event of this nature so these observations can not be too far out of line. Beyond the usefulness of any other combat lessons learned of which you may be made aware, I believe with all my heart this is the most important preparation a young Infantry lieutenant can have. It will not make you fearless, but it goes a long way toward keeping you focused on your mission and concern for your men, when everything around you is "going to hell."

. . . I am convinced that as a soldier, as a husband and father, then later as a businessman after retirement, and even now as a grandfather, my life has been of far greater INTEGRITY because of the confidence which God has given me that I am truly His. This is the most important preparation a young officer can have.

. . . And finally, finally—the one absolutely essential element with which that young Infantry lieutenant facing combat for the first time must be armed, is a profound and abiding faith in God. Without that, no matter how he expresses it, feels it, lives it, I do not see how he can survive any of the hardships . . . in combat, or in the challenges of life in general.

. . . plan every action you take, every single day and night in training or in combat, to strengthen the internal cohesiveness and . . . close teamwork in your platoon. Every action and opportunity must engender greater bonds of trust . . . among your troops and their leaders and their Lieutenant; the unit esprit and . . . confidence which all must have in themselves, their own capabilities and in their fellow soldiers and . . . leaders . . . You can keep going and keep fighting and keep trying and pull others along with you and survive terrible odds and frightfully incredible ordeals, by . . . being determined to never give up, to never quit trying and never quit believing you can and will succeed . . . no matter what comes, you must believe you can succeed, and simply never give up.

. . . when engaged in actual combat, in a fire fight, you must be able to determine when the situation requires that "the lieutenant goes first."

Remember, if you put your best man on point continuously, he will eventually get killed. If you always take the point yourself, you will get killed. But if you put your worst man on point, you may all get killed. Deciding whose life is to be placed at the most risk, and when, is the most critical decision you will ever make. You must make dispassionate decisions. Friendships make . . . this more difficult. Favoritism is devastating to morale.

You must conquer your own fear daily and willingly share the risks of your soldiers. Dead heroes can not lead.

Control of fear can be a conscious matter. It is based on the fact that very few people can think about more than one thing at a time. To control fear among your men, keep them busy. If you see a soldier frozen with fear, find something, anything, for him to do that requires him to think about what he is doing. While thus engaged, he can not think about being afraid. To control your own fear, find something for YOU to do . . . . Your training makes you see . . . many things that need to be done . . . you can stay mentally busy . . . all the time and have no time for fear. When fear grips you, find something to do. Anything will suffice, but it is . . . better to analyze your . . . situation; find the most critical leader tasks in relation to combat preparations for your unit . . .

Courage No one really knows his breaking point until he meets the ultimate test. Two things always served me well under fire: the realization that fear is normal; and, my obligation(s) to my own men.

The points are interwoven, in that planning for an attack always found me preoccupied with the possibility of overlooking some detail which could result in the deaths of my men. Naturally, being human included concern about my own demise as well. But, this all boiled down to ensuring <u>success</u> at the <u>lowest risk</u>. In other words, get the job done, but plan it well. Don't leave things to chance, and don't "play it by ear," or "wing it."

Summary

The readings in this final chapter of the text provided examples of officer's fighting their nations wars. These passages assisted your understanding of:

- what superiors, subordinates, and the Nation expect of officers as Warfighters
- the Principles of War as the foundation of tactical decision-making.
- the advantages of using mission-type orders and the critical importance of commander's intent.
- the application of Troop Leading Procedures when carrying out missions

In the first passage of this chapter you read of the 82d Airborne Division's exploits in Normandy, achieving victory overcoming insurmountable odds. You learned about LTG James M. Gavin's role as a commander on the ground and the challenges and hazards of Airborne operations in forced-entry situations.

The next selection took you with B Company, 2nd Battalion, 16th Regiment of the 1st Infantry Division on April 10th, 1966 in the Republic of Viet Nam during "Operation Abilene". A mission that is considered a success, despite incurring over 80 percent casualties during the firefight, accomplished through the ceaseless efforts of leaders at all levels.

The next two readings by Colonels Ripley and Hackworth related the lessons learned from their experience in Viet Nam. In these writings we learned of the importance of Officers being technically and tactically competent on all aspects of employing their units to the utmost effect.

Then we moved on to a passage from Rick Atkinson's The Long Grey Line and looked at a recent United States Military Academy graduates experience as a young infantry officer in Viet Nam. In this passage we learned how then Lieutenant Crocker underwent his final transformation from West Point cadet to a Warfighter.

Then we jumped forward in Desert Storm and followed lieutenants Vernon, Holmes, Creighton, Downey, and Trybula through the breach and into the maelstrom of the largest armored battle ever witnessed on the face of the planet. This reading enhanced your understanding of the importance of all the branches in the

Army as well as providing practical examples of the need to use Troop Leading Procedures in order to accomplish the mission at hand.

Finally, as our last selection we studied the combat lessons from the frozen, rugged, and sometimes forgotten battlefields of Korea. These young men graduated from West Point on June 6, 1950 and were sent immediately to their units without the benefit of any branch schooling. This perspective of combat is far different when contrasted with our more recent experiences. Unlike our Iraqi foes who more often than not capitulated upon the outset of a firefight, they fought a tough, determined, and entrenched adversary who would resist to the bitter end no matter what sacrifices needed to be made.

In closing, the duty of every officer in the United States Military is to fight and win our nation's wars. U.S. Army officers accomplish this mission through their diverse specialties which all contribute to achieving decisive victory on the modern battlefield. It is not only the Armor and Infantry officers who engage and destroy the enemy with direct fire, but it is also the Military Intelligence officer providing real-time situational analysis to the Chemical officer protecting the force with concealing smoke hazes. The Ordnance and Transportation officers moving and fixing equipment ensuring that the maximum amount of combat power is available at the decisive point on the battlefield. The lessons these readings have taught were often paid for in blood. As you enter the brotherhood of arms, take what others have bought you and use it. Your country and your soldiers deserve it.

Bibliography

"The Professional Officer." United States Military Academy Strategic Vision – 2010. July 2000. p. 8

CHAPTER I: THE OFFICER AS A SERVANT OF SOCIETY

Snider, Don, "What is Now Worth Dying For?" Veteran's Day Speech, November 1999

"American Ideals." The Armed Forces Officer, Armed Forces Information Service, Department of Defense, U.S. Government Printing Office 1998, p. 66-68.

Ladd, Everett C. (ed), "American Society: Where are we Headed?" The Public Perspective, The Roper Center: Hall & Bill Printing Company, Feb / Mar 1997, p. 1-30.

Toner, James, H. "The US Military: Sovereign or Subordinate," True Faith and Allegiance: The Burden of Military Ethics Chapter 2. Lexington: University of Kentucky Press, 1995, p. 22-38.

Maslowski, Peter, "Army Values and American Values" Military Review, April 1990, p. 10-23.

Nye, Roger. "The Commander's Concept of Duty," The Challenge of Command, New Jersey: Avery Publishing Group, Inc, 1986, p. 115-130.

Snider, Don. USMA Class of 2000 100th Night Banquet Remarks, February1999.

CHAPTER II: THE OFFICER AS A MEMBER OF A TIME-HONORED PROFESSION

Huntington, Samuel. "Officership as a Profession," The Soldier & the State, Chapter 1, Vintage Books, 1957, p. 7-18.

Huntington, Samuel . "The Military Mind: Conservative Realism of the Professional Military Ethic, The Soldier & the State, Chapter 3, Vintage Books, 1957 p. 59-79.

Bloomenson, Martin. "On Entering the Military Profession," Army, September 1996.

Lloyd J. Matthews, "Is the Military Profession Legitimate?" Army, January 1994.

Snider, Don and Watkins Gayle. "The Future of Army Professionalism: How Should We Think About It?" March 2000.

CHAPTER III: THE OFFICER AS A LEADER OF CHARACTER

Wakin, Malham. "The Way to Do is to Be." War Morality and the Military Profession p. 196-197.

Wakin, Malham. "The Ethics of Leadership" War Morality and the Military Profession. p. 200-216

Puryear, Edgar F. Jr. 19 Stars. Presidio Press. Novato, CA, 1994. p. 287-289 and 336-349.

Pyle, Ernie. "Captain Waskow" retrieved online, August, 2000 from: http://www.ghgcorp.com/burtond/36th/36infpyle.html

Garcia, Daniel P and McCaffrey, Barry R. GEN, (Ret). Garcia, Gen Barry R. McCaffrey. "Vietnam Letters." Army Magazine. Nov 1997 p. 24-37.

"Doing What's Right: Shaping the Army's Professional Environment." Paramters. U.S. Army War College Quarterly Volume XIX, U.S. Army War College: p. 11-15.

Nye, Roger. "The Commander as Moral Arbiter," The Challenge of Command, New Jersey: Avery Publishing Group, Inc, 1986: p. 99-113.

Leadership in Combat: An Historical Appraisal by the USMA History Department.

Stockdale, ADM James B. (Ret). Address To the Class of 1983, United States Military Academy, West Point, July 1979.

Cornum, Rhonda and Copeland, Peter. She Went to War, The Rhonda Cornum Story, California: Chapter 1 and Chapter 3, Presidio Press, 1992 p. 1-18, 43-59.

CHAPTER IV: THE OFFICER AS A WARFIGHTER

Booth, T. Michael and Spencer, Duncan. "The Airborne's Watery Triumph," No End Save Victory, New York: G.P. Putnam's Sons, 2001 p. 421-441.

Wilson, George C. "Legacy", Mud Soldiers, New York: Chapter 1, Charles Scribner's Sons, 1989 p. 7-42.

Ripley, COL John, USMC (Ret). Thoughts on Small Unit Leadership from McKeldin, Ted (ed.) From the Horse's Mouth, Selected Thoughts on Small-Unit Leadership.

Hackworth, COL David , USA, (Ret) "Notes From Vietnam." from McKeldin, Ted (ed.) From the Horse's Mouth, Selected Thoughts on Small-Unit Leadership p. 121-127.

Atkinson, Rick. "Uniting Hearts and Minds." The Long Gray Line; The American Journey of West Point's Class of '66. Houghton Mifflin Company, Boston, 1989. p. 200-227.

Vernon, Alex; with Creighton, N., Downey, G., Holmes, R., and Trybula, D. "Desert Storm: The Ground War.", The Eyes of Orion; Five Tank Lieutenants in the Persian Gulf War. Ohio: Chapter 4, Kent State University Press, 1999 p. 176-251.

Combat Advice for New Infantry Lieutenants. TROG Press, West Point NY, 1999.